George Rawlinson

The Five Great Monarchies of the Ancient Eastern World Or

The History, Geography and Antiquities of Chaldea, Assyria, Babylon, Media and

Persia

George Rawlinson

The Five Great Monarchies of the Ancient Eastern World Or
The History, Geography and Antiquities of Chaldea, Assyria, Babylon, Media and Persia

ISBN/EAN: 9783741180613

Manufactured in Europe, USA, Canada, Australia, Japa

Cover: Foto ©Andreas Hilbeck / pixelio.de

Manufactured and distributed by brebook publishing software (www.brebook.com)

George Rawlinson

The Five Great Monarchies of the Ancient Eastern World Or

THE

FIVE GREAT MONARCHIES

OF THE

ANCIENT EASTERN WORLD;

OR,

THE HISTORY, GEOGRAPHY, AND ANTIQUITIES OF CHALDÆA,
ASSYRIA, BABYLON, MEDIA, AND PERSIA,

COLLECTED AND ILLUSTRATED FROM ANCIENT AND MODERN SOURCES.

By GEORGE RAWLINSON, M.A.,

CAMDEN PROFESSOR OF ANCIENT HISTORY IN THE UNIVERSITY OF OXFORD;
LATE FELLOW AND TUTOR OF EXETER COLLEGE.

IN FOUR VOLUMES.—Vol. III.

LONDON:
JOHN MURRAY, ALBEMARLE STREET.
1865.

LONDON: PRINTED BY W. CLOWES AND SONS, STAMFORD STREET,
AND CHARING CROSS.

CONTENTS OF VOL. III.

THE THIRD MONARCHY.

MEDIA.

CHAPTER I.
Description of the Country 1

CHAPTER II.
Climate and Productions.. 44

CHAPTER III.
Character, Manners and Customs, Art, &c., of the People.. 73

CHAPTER IV.
Religion 93

CHAPTER V.
Language and Writing 137

CHAPTER VI.
Chronology and History 157

APPENDIX.
Note A.—Translation of the First Fargard of the Vendidad 238

THE FOURTH MONARCHY.

BABYLONIA.

CHAPTER I.
EXTENT OF THE EMPIRE 241

CHAPTER II.
CLIMATE AND PRODUCTIONS 298

CHAPTER III.
THE PEOPLE 321

CHAPTER IV.
THE CAPITAL 337

CHAPTER V.
ARTS AND SCIENCES 370

CHAPTER VI.
MANNERS AND CUSTOMS 428

CHAPTER VII.
RELIGION 458

CHAPTER VIII.
HISTORY AND CHRONOLOGY 460

APPENDIX.
NOTE A.—THE STANDARD INSCRIPTION OF NEBUCHADNEZZAR IN PART TRANSLATED 524
NOTE B.—ON THE MEANINGS OF BABYLONIAN NAMES 527

LIST OF ILLUSTRATIONS.

Map of Media .. .. *To face title-page.*

	Page
1. Stone base of a pillar at Hamadan (after *Morier*)	21
2. Plan of the country about Hamadan (after *Flandin*)	22
3. Plan of Takht-i-Suleiman (*Sir H. Rawlinson*)	27
4. View of the great Rock of Behistun (after *Ker Porter*)	31
5. View in Mazanderan—the Caspian Sea in the distance (after *Fraser*) ..	37
6. Pigeon-towers near Isfahan (after *Morier*)	60
7. The destructive Locust (*Acridium peregrinum*)	63
8. The Scorpion (*Scorpio crassicauda*)	65
9. Persepolitan horse, perhaps Nisæan (after *Ker Porter*)	68
10. Head of an Arian, from Persepolis (after *Prichard*)	75
11. Mede, or Persian, carrying a bow in its case, from Persepolis (after *Ker Porter*)	82
12. Bow and quiver, from Persepolis (after *Flandin*)	83
13. Persian or Median spear, from Persepolis (after *Ker Porter*)	84
14. Shield of a warrior, from Persepolis (after *Flandin*)	84
15. Median robe, from Persepolis (after *Ker Porter*)	85
16. Median shoe, from Persepolis (after *Flandin*)	85
17. Median head-dress, from Persepolis (ditto)	86
18. Mede, or Persian, wearing a collar and earrings, from Persepolis (after *Ker Porter*)	87
19. Colossal lion at Hamadan (after *Flandin*)	92
20. Fire-temples, near Nakhsh-i-Rustem (ditto)	123
21. Lydian coins (after *Humphreys*)	206
22. View of the Lebanon range	230
23. View of the Lake of Antioch (after *Ainsworth*)	288
24. Hares, from the cylinders (after *Lajard*)	312
25. Babylonian fish (from the Assyrian sculptures)	315
26. Locusts, from a cylinder	316
27. Susianian mule, Koyunjik (drawn by the author from a slab in the British Museum)	317
28. Susianian horses, Koyunjik (after *Layard*)	317
29. Babylonian dog, from a gem (after *Lajard*)	318
30. Babylonian cows and oxen, from the cylinders (ditto)	319
31. Heads of Babylonian men (drawn by the author from sculptures in the British Museum)	324
32. Head of a Babylonian woman (ditto)	325
33. Heads of Susianians (ditto)	325

LIST OF ILLUSTRATIONS.

	Page
34. Heads of Babylonians, from the cylinders (after *Layard*)	320
35. Head of an Elamite chief, Koyunjik (drawn by the author from a relief in the British Museum)	326
36. Chart of the country round Babylon (reduced from the map of M. *Oppert*)	339
37. View of the Babil mound, from the *Kasr* (after *Oppert*)	353
38. Ground-plan of the *Babil* mound (after *Oppert* and *Selby*)	354
39. Ground-plan of the *Kasr* mound (after *Oppert*)	355
40. Ground-plan of the *Amram* mound (ditto)	357
41. General chart of the ruins of Babylon (reduced from the map of Capt. *Selby*)	359
42. Chart of ancient Babylon	374
43. Birs-i-Nimrud, near Babylon	381
44. Elevation of the Birs, restored	383
45. Part of a stone frieze, from the *Kasr* mound, Babylon (after *Layard*)	390
46. Piers of bridge at Babylon, restored	393
47. Babylonian brick (after *Birch*)	394
48. Lion standing over a prostrate man, Babylon (from a sketch drawn on the spot by *Claude Clark, Esq.*)	398
49. Statuette of a mother and child, found at Babylon (after *Ker Porter*)	399
50. Figure of a Babylonian king (drawn for the present work from an engraved figure in the British Museum)	400
51. Figure of a dog, from a black stone found at Babylon (drawn by the author from the original in the British Museum)	401
52. Figure of a bird, from the same (ditto)	401
53. Animal forms, from the cylinders (after *Layard*)	402
54. Grotesque figures of men and animals, from a cylinder (ditto)	403
55. Men and monsters, from a cylinder (ditto)	404
56. Serio-comic drawing, from a cylinder (ditto)	404
57. Gate and gateway, from a cylinder (ditto)	410
58. Bronze ornament, found at Babylon (after *Ker Porter*)	411
59. Vases and jug, from the cylinders (after *Layard*)	412
60. Vases in a stand, from a cylinder (ditto)	412
61. Vase with handles, found in Babylonia (after *Birch*)	413
62. Babylonian glass bottles (after *Layard*)	413
63. Conical head of an engraved black stone brought from Babylon (drawn for the present work from the original in the British Museum)	418
64. Babylonian Zodiac (ditto)	419
65. Babylonian of the lower ranks, from a cylinder (after *Layard*)	429
66. Babylonian of the upper class, from a cylinder (ditto)	429
67. Babylonian wearing a long under-garment, from a cylinder (ditto)	430
68. Babylonian soldier conducting prisoners, from a cylinder (after *Layard*)	430
69. Patterned tunic, from a cylinder (after *Layard*)	431
70. Babylonian wearing a short open coat, from a cylinder (ditto)	431
71. Costume of a Susianian chief, Koyunjik (drawn by the author from a bas-relief in the British Museum)	432
72. Costumes of the Babylonian priests, from the cylinders (after *Layard*)	434
73. Priest-vizier presenting captives to a king (drawn by Sir H. *Rawlinson* from a rock-tablet near Suri-Zohab)	436
74. Babylonian bow, from a black stone in the British Museum	437
75. Babylonian quiver and dagger	437
76. Lion attacked with spear and axe, from a cylinder (after *Layard*)	438

LIST OF ILLUSTRATIONS.

		Page
77. Axes, Chaldæan and Babylonian, from the monuments	..	434
78. Babylonian four-horse chariot, from a cylinder (after *Layard*)	..	439
79. Men ploughing, from a cylinder (ditto)	..	449
80. Milking the goat, from a cylinder (ditto)	..	449
81. Babylonian harp and harper, from a cylinder (ditto)	..	452
82. Babylonian women making an offering to a goddess, from a cylinder (ditto)	..	454
83. Babylonian women gathering dates in a garden, from a cylinder (ditto)	..	455
84. Babylonian saw and hatchet, from the cylinders	..	460
85. Religious emblems of the Babylonians, from the cylinders	..	467

ERRATA.

In Vol. II.

P. 58, in title of woodcut, *for* "carved" *read* "covered."
P. 367, note 8, line 2, *for* "1940" *read* "3940."
P. 490, line 28, *for* "grandees" *read* "grandsons."
P. 493, *for* "Muini" *read* "Minni."

In Vol. III.

P. 398, note 4, *for* "Mr. Claude Clark" *read* "Mr. Claude Clerk."

THE THIRD MONARCHY.

MEDIA.

CHAPTER I.

DESCRIPTION OF THE COUNTRY.

> Χώρην παντοδαπὴν ἀντέρπεται, οἱ μὲν ἐπ' αὐτῆς
> Πέτρας αἱ φύουσιν ἀφαυγέα παρκεσσίτην,
> Οἱ δ' ἐκὰς ἐν λασίησι νενασμένοι ἐλαμστῆσι,
> Πάντα καλὰ νέμοντες ἄδην βεβριθότα μαλλοῖς.
>
> DIONYS. *Perieg.* 1030-1033.

ALONG the eastern flank of the great Mesopotamian lowland, curving round it on the north, and stretching beyond it to the south and the south-east, lies a vast elevated region, or highland, no portion of which appears to be less than 3000 feet above the sea-level.[1] This region may be divided, broadly, into two tracts, one consisting of lofty mountainous ridges, which form its outskirts on the north and on the west; the other, in the main a high flat table-land, extending from the foot of the mountain-chains, southwards to the Indian Ocean, and eastward to the country of the Affghans. The western mountain-country consists, as has been already observed,[2] of six

---

[1] See the author's *Herodotus*, vol. i. p. 65; *Geographical Journal*, vol. i. p. 440, 2nd edition. Compare iii. p. 112; Fraser, *Khorasan*, p. 152; Chesney, *Euphrates Expedition*, vol. note.   [2] See vol. i. p. 259.

or seven parallel ridges, having a direction nearly from the north-west to the south-east, inclosing between them valleys of great fertility and well-watered by a large number of plentiful and refreshing streams. This district was known to the ancients as 'Zagros,'[3] while in modern geography it bears the names of Kurdistan and Luristan. It has always been inhabited by a multitude of warlike tribes,[4] and has rarely formed for any long period a portion of any settled monarchy. Full of torrents, of deep ravines, of rocky summits, abrupt and almost inaccessible; containing but few passes, and those narrow and easily defensible; secure, moreover, owing to the rigour of its climate, from hostile invasion during more than half the year; it has defied all attempts to effect its permanent subjugation, whether made by Assyrians, Persians, Greeks, Parthians, or Turks, and remains to this day as independent of the great powers in its neighbourhood as it was when the Assyrian armies first penetrated its recesses. Nature seems to have constructed it to be a nursery of hardy and vigorous men, a stumbling-block to conquerors, a thorn in the side of every powerful empire which arises in this part of the great Eastern continent.

The northern mountain country—known to modern

---

[3] Polyb. v. 44, § 0; 54, § 7; 55, § 6; Strab. xi. p. 759; Plin. *H. N.* vi. 27; xii. 12; Ptol. vi. 2; Amm. Marc. xxiii. 0, p. 404; &c. The name Zagros more especially attached to the central portion of the chain from the mountain district south of Lake Van to the latitude of Isfahan. A good general description of the range is given by Q. Curtius:—"Namque Parais ab altero latere perpetuis montium jugis clauditur, quod in longitudinem MDC stadia, in latitudinem CLXX procurrit. Hoc dorsum a Caucaso monte ad Rubrum mare pertinet; quoque deficit mons, aliud munimentum, fretum objectum est." (*Vit. Alex. Mag.* v. 4.) Diodorus Siculus well describes the delightful character of the region (xix. 21).

[4] Xen. *Anab.* iii. 5; Strab. xi. 13, § 3; Arr. *Exp. Al.* iii. 17.

geographers as Elburz—is a tract of far less importance. It is not composed, like Zagros, of a number of parallel chains, but rather consists of a single lofty ridge, furrowed by ravines and valleys,[a] from which spurs are thrown out, running in general at right angles to its axis. Its width is comparatively slight; and, instead of giving birth to numerous large rivers, it forms only a small number of insignificant streams, often dry in summer, which have short courses, being soon absorbed either by the Caspian or the Desert. Its most striking feature is the snowy peak of Demavend,[b] which impends over Teheran, and appears to be the highest summit in the part of Asia west of the Himalayas.

The elevated plateau which stretches from the foot of these two mountain regions to the south and east is, for the most part, a flat sandy desert, incapable of sustaining more than a sparse and scanty population. The northern and western portions are, however, less arid than the east and south, being watered to some distance by the streams that descend from Zagros and Elburz, and deriving fertility also from the spring rains. Some of the rivers which flow from Zagros on this side are large and strong. One, the Kizil-Uzen, reaches the Caspian. Another, the Zenderud, fertilises a large district near Isfahan. A

---

[a] Ker Porter, *Travels*, vol. I. p. 357; Fraser, *Khorasan*, p. 244.

[b] Ker Porter well describes the majestic appearance of Demavend from the neighbourhood of Teheran, the present capital of Persia: "The mountain of Demavend bears N. 65° E. of Teheran, about forty miles distant; and is seen, raising its lofty and pale summit to the north-east of the town; forming a magnificent pyramid that shoots up from the high range of Elburz, which bounds the wide plain in that direction." (*Travels*, l. s. c.) Recent ascents of Demavend have proved it to have an elevation of more than 20,000 feet. (See the author's *Herodotus*, vol. i. p. 412, note [1].) Ararat is only 17,000 feet; and the highest peak in the Caucasus does not exceed 18,000 feet.

third, the Bendamir, flows by Persepolis and terminates in a sheet of water of some size—Lake Bakhtigan. A tract thus intervenes between the mountain regions and the desert which, though it cannot be called fertile, is fairly productive, and can support a large settled population. This forms the chief portion of the region which the ancients called Media, as being the country inhabited by the race on whose history we are about to enter.

Media, however, included, besides this, another tract of considerable size and importance. At the north-western angle of the region above described, in the corner whence the two great chains branch out to the south and to the east, is a tract composed almost entirely of mountains, which the Greeks called Atropatêné,[1] and which is now known as Azerbijan. This district lies further to the north than the rest of Media, being in the same parallels with the lower part of the Caspian Sea. It comprises the entire basin of Lake Urumiyeh, together with the country intervening between that basin and the high mountain chain which curves round the south-western corner of the Caspian. It is a region generally somewhat sterile, but containing a certain quantity of very fertile territory, more particularly in the Urumiyeh basin, and towards the mouth of the river Araxes.

The boundaries of Media are given somewhat differently by different writers,[2] and no doubt they

---

[1] This name was derived from Atropates, the governor of the region at the time of the battle of Arbela, who made terms with Alexander, and was allowed to keep the province, where he shortly made himself independent. (Strab. xi. 13, § 1; Diod. Sic. xviii. 8.)

[2] Strabo makes Media to be bounded on the north by Matiani and the mountain region of the Cadusians (Elburz); on the east by

actually varied at different periods; but the variations were not great, and the natural limits, on three sides at any rate, may be laid down with tolerable precision. Towards the north the boundary was at first the mountain chain closing in on that side the Urumiyeh basin, after which it seems to have been held that the true limit was the Araxes, to its entrance on the low country, and then the mountain chain west and south of the Caspian. Westward, the line of demarcation may be best regarded as, towards the south, running along the centre of the Zagros region; and, above this, as formed by that continuation of the Zagros chain, which separates the Urumiyeh from the Van basin. Eastward, the boundary was marked by the spur from the Elburz, across which lay the pass known as the Pylæ Caspiæ, and below this by the great salt desert, whose western limit is nearly in the same longitude.[1] Towards the south there was no marked line or natural boundary; and it is difficult to say with any exactness how much of the great plateau belonged to Media and how much to Persia. Having regard, however, to the situation of Hamadan, which,

---

[1] Parthia and the Cossæans; on the south by Sittacené, Zagros, and Elymais; on the west by Matiané and Armenia (xi. 13). Pliny says that it has on the east the Parthians and Caspians; on the south Sittacené, Susiana, and Persis; on the west Adiabené; and on the north Armenia (*H. N.* vi. 26). The Armenian Geography makes the northern boundary Armenia and the Caspian, the eastern Aria or Khorasan, the southern Persia, and the western Armenia and Assyria (pp. 357-365). According to the most extensive view, Media begins at the Araxes, includes the whole low region between the mountains and the Caspian as far as Hyrcania, extends southwards to a little below Isfahan, and westward includes the greater part of Zagros. More moderate dimensions are assumed in the text.

[2] The salt desert projects somewhat further to the west, a portion being crowded on the route from Teheran to Isfahan. (See Fraser's *Khorasan*, p. 142; Ouseley, *Travels*, vol. iii. p. 109; Ker Porter, *Travels*, vol. I. p. 372.)

as the capital, should have been tolerably central, and to the general account which historians and geographers give of the size of Media, we may place the southern limit with much probability about the line of the thirty-second parallel, which is nearly the present boundary between Irak and Fars.

The shape of Media has been called a square;[4] but it is rather a long parallelogram, whose two principal sides face respectively the north-east and the south-west, while the ends or shorter sides front to the south-east and to the north-west. Its length in its greater direction is about 600 miles, and its width about 250 miles. It must thus contain nearly 150,000 square miles, an area considerably larger than that of Assyria and Chaldæa put together,[5] and quite sufficient to constitute a state of the first class,[6] even according to the ideas of modern Europe. It is nearly one-fifth more than the area of the British Islands, and half as much again as that of Prussia, or of peninsular Italy. It equals three-fourths of France, or three-fifths of Germany. It has moreover the great advantage of compactness, forming a single solid mass, with no straggling or outlying portions; and it is strongly defended on almost every side by natural barriers offering great difficulties to an invader.

In comparison with the countries which formed the seats of the two monarchies already described, the general character of the Median territory is undoubtedly one of sterility.[7] The high table-land is

---

[4] Amm. Marc. xxiii. 6. "Medi—pugnatrix natio, regiones inhabitans ad speciem quadratæ figuræ formatas." Comp. Strab. xi. 13, § 8.
[5] See vol. i. pp. 6 and 227.

[6] Compare Polybius, x. 27, § 1:— 'Ἔστι τοίνυν ἡ Μηδία κατὰ τὸ μέγεθος τῆς χώρας ἀξιοχρεωτάτη τῶν κατὰ τὴν Ἀσίαν δυναστειῶν.
[7] So Strabo: 'Η πολλὴ μὲν οὖν

CHAP. I.   GENERAL STERILITY OF THE TERRITORY.   7

everywhere intersected by rocky ranges, spurs from
Zagros, which have a general direction from west to
east,[1] and separate the country into a number of
parallel broad valleys, or long plains, opening out
into the desert. The appearance of these ranges is
almost everywhere bare, arid, and forbidding. Above,
they present to the eye huge masses of grey rock
piled one upon another; below, a slope of detritus,
destitute of trees or shrubs, and only occasionally
nourishing a dry and scanty herbage. The appearance of the plains is little superior; they are flat and
without undulations, composed in general of gravel
or hard clay, and rarely enlivened by any show of
water; except for two months in the spring, they
exhibit to the eye a uniform brown expanse, almost
treeless, which impresses the traveller with a feeling
of sadness and weariness. Even in Azerbijan, which
is one of the least arid portions of the territory, vast
tracts consist of open undulating downs,[8] desolate and
sterile, bearing only a coarse withered grass and a
few stunted bushes.

Still there are considerable exceptions to this
general aspect of desolation. In the worst parts of
the region, there is a time after the spring rains
when Nature puts on a holiday dress, and the country
becomes gay and cheerful. The slopes at the base of
the rocky ranges are tinged with an emerald green;[10]
a richer vegetation springs up over the plains,[11] which

ὑψηλή ἐστι καὶ ψυχρά (xi. 13, § 7).
Compare Kinneir, *Persian Empire*,
pp. 108, 144, 149, with Fraser, *Khorasan*, pp. 162-165.

[8] This is more especially the case
in Irak, the most southern portion
of the country. (Kinneir, p. 108.)

[9] Sir H. Rawlinson in *Geograph.
Journ.* vol. x. pp. 43, 44, 55, &c.
Even here a tree is a rarity. (Morier,
Second Journey, p. 237.)

[10] Fraser, p. 163.

[11] Ker Porter, vol. i. pp. 285, 367,
&c.

are covered with a fine herbage or with a variety of crops; the fruit trees which surround the villages burst out into the most luxuriant blossom; the roses come into bloom, and their perfume everywhere fills the air." For the two months of April and May the whole face of the country is changed, and a lovely verdure replaces the ordinary dull sterility.

In a certain number of more favoured spots, beauty and fertility are found during nearly the whole of the year. All round the shores of Lake Urumiyeh,[1] more especially in the rich plain of Miyandab at its southern extremity, along the valleys of the Aras,[2] the Kizil-Uzen,[3] and the Jaghetu,[4] in the great *ballook* of Linjan,[5] fertilized by irrigation from the Zenderud, in the Zagros valleys,[6] and in various other places, there is an excellent soil which produces abundantly with very slight cultivation.

The general sterility of Media arises from the scantiness of the water supply. It has but few rivers, and the streams that it possesses run for the most part in deep and narrow valleys sunk below the general level of the country, so that they cannot be applied at all widely to purposes of irrigation. Moreover, some of them are, unfortunately, impregnated with salt to such an extent, that they are altogether use-

---

[n] Ker Porter, vol. I., pp. 228, 231, &c.; *Geograph. Journ.* vol. x. p. 29.
[1] *Journal of Geographical Society*, vol. x. pp. 2, 5, 10, 13, 39, &c.; Kinneir, *Persian Empire*, pp. 153-156; Morier, *Second Journey*, p. 264; Ker Porter, vol. ii. pp. 592-607.
[2] Ker Porter, *Travels*, vol. i. p. 217; Kinneir, p. 153; Morier, pp. 234-236. The plain of Mogban on the lower Aras is famous for its rich soil and luxuriant pastures. The Persians say that the grass is sufficiently high to hide an army from view when encamped. (Kinneir, l. s. c.)
[3] *Journal of Geograph. Society*, vol. x. p. 59; Ker Porter, vol. i. p. 267.
[4] *Geograph. Journ.* vol. x. pp. 11, 40, &c.
[5] Kinneir, p. 110.
[6] Rich, *Kurdistan*, pp. 80, 130-134, &c.

less for this purpose;[1] and indeed, instead of fertilizing, spread around them desolation and barrenness.

The only Median streams which are of sufficient importance to require description are the Aras, the Kizil-Uzen, the Jaghetu, the Aji-Su, and the Zonderud, or river of Isfahan.

The Aras is only very partially a Median stream.[8] It rises from several sources in the mountain tract between Kars and Erzeroum,[9] and runs with a generally eastern direction through Armenia to the longitude of Mount Ararat, where it crosses the fortieth parallel and begins to trend southward, flowing along the eastern side of Ararat in a south-easterly direction, nearly to the Julfa ferry on the high road from Erivan to Tabriz. From this point it runs only a little south of east to long. 46° 30' E. from Greenwich, when it makes almost a right angle and runs directly north-east to its junction with the Kur at Djavat. Soon after this it curves to the south and enters the Caspian by several mouths in lat. 39° 10' nearly. The Aras is a considerable stream almost from its source. At Hassan-Kaleh, less than twenty miles from Erzeroum, where the river is forded in several branches, the water reaches to the saddle girths.[10] At Keupri-Kieui, not much lower, the stream is crossed by a bridge of seven arches.[11] At the Julfa ferry it is fifty yards wide, and runs with a strong current.[12] At Megree, thirty miles further

---

[1] Ker Porter, vol. I. pp. 220, 370, &c.; Morier, *Second Journey*, pp. 167, 233; *Geograph. Journ.* vol. xxxi. p. 38.

[8] According to Strabo (xi. 13, § 3), the lower Araxes was the boundary between Armenia and Media Atropatênê. Thus even here one bank only was Median; and the upper course of the river was entirely in Armenia.

[9] See Hamilton's *Asia Minor*, vol. I. p. 183.

[10] Ibid. l. s. c.

[11] Ibid. p. 185.

[12] Ker Porter, vol. i. p. 215.

down, its width is eighty yards.[13] In spring and early summer the stream receives enormous accessions from the spring rains and the melting of the snows, which produce floods that often cause great damage to the lands and villages along the valley. Hence the difficulty of maintaining bridges over the Aras, which was noted as early as the time of Augustus,[14] and is attested by the ruins of many such structures remaining along its course.[15] Still, there are at the present day at least three bridges over the stream, one, which has been already mentioned, at Keupri-Kioui, another a little above Nakshivan, and the third at Khudoperinski, a little below Megree.[16] The length of the Aras, including only main windings, is 500 miles.[17]

The Kizil-Uzen, or (as it is called in the lower part of its course) the Sefid-Rud, is a stream of less size than the Aras, but more important to Media, within which lies almost the whole of its basin. It drains a tract 160 miles long by 150 broad before bursting through the Elburz mountain chain, and descending upon the low country which skirts the Caspian. Rising in Persian Kurdistan almost from the foot of Zagros, it runs in a meandering course with a general direction of north-east through that province into the district of Khamseh, where it suddenly sweeps round and flows in a bold curve at the foot of lofty and precipitous rocks,[18] first north-west

---

[13] Kinneir, p. 321.
[14] Virgil, Æn. viii. 728. "Pontem indignatus Araxes."
[15] Ker Porter, vol. II. pp. 610, 641, &c.
[16] Kinneir, l. s. c.
[17] Colonel Chesney estimates the whole course of the Araxes, including all its windings, at 830 miles. (*Euphrates Expedition*, vol. I. p. 12.)
[18] Sir H. Rawlinson estimated the height of these rocks above the stream at 1500 feet. (*Geograph. Journ.* vol. x. p. 50.)

and then north nearly to Miana, when it doubles
back upon itself and turning the flank of the Zenjan
range runs with a course nearly south-east to Menjil,
after which it resumes its original direction of north-
east, and rushing down the pass of Rudbar[19] crosses
Ghilan to the Caspian. Though its source is in direct
distance no more than 220 miles from its mouth, its
entire length, owing to its numerous curves and
meanders, is estimated at 490 miles.[20] It is a considerable stream, forded with difficulty, even in the
dry season, as high up as Karagul,[21] and crossed by
a bridge of three wide arches before its junction with
the Garongu river near Miana.[22] In spring and
early summer it is an impetuous torrent, and can
only be forded within a short distance of its source.

The Jaghetu and the Aji-Su are the two chief
rivers of the Urumiyeh basin. The Jaghetu rises
from the foot of the Zagros chain, at a very little
distance from the source of the Kizil-Uzen. It collects the streams from the range of hills which divides
the Kizil-Uzen basin from that of Lake Urumiyeh,
and flows in a tolerably straight course first north
and then north-west to the south-eastern shore of
the lake. Side by side with it for some distance flows
the smaller stream of the Tatau, formed by torrents
from Zagros; and between them, towards their
mouths, is the rich plain of Miyandab, easily irrigated from the two streams, the level of whose beds
is above that of the plain,[23] and abundantly productive
even under the present system of cultivation. The

---

[19] Ibid. p. 64; Kinneir, p. 124.
[20] Chesney, *Euphrates Expedi-tion*, vol. i. p. 191.
[21] *Geograph. Journ.* vol. x. p. 59.
[22] Ker Porter, vol. l. p. 267; Morier, *First Journey*, p. 267.
[23] *Geograph. Journ.* vol. x. p. 11.

Aji-Su reaches the lake from the north-east. It rises from Mount Sevilan, within sixty miles of the Caspian, and flows with a course which is at first nearly due south, then north-west, and finally south-west, past the city of Tabriz, to the eastern shore of the lake, which it enters in lat. 37° 50'. The waters of the Aji Su are, unfortunately, salt,[M] and it is therefore valueless for purposes of irrigation.

The Zenderud or river of Isfahan rises from the eastern flank of the Kuh-i-Zerd (Yellow Mountain), a portion of the Bakhtiyari chain, and receiving a number of tributaries from the same mountain district, flows with a course which is generally east or somewhat north of east, past the great city of Isfahan—so long the capital of Persia—into the desert country beyond, where it is absorbed in irrigation.[1] Its entire course is perhaps not more than 120 or 130 miles; but running chiefly through a plain region, and being naturally a stream of large size, it is among the most valuable of the Median rivers, its waters being capable of spreading fertility, by means of a proper arrangement of canals, over a vast extent of country,[2] and giving to this part of Iran a sylvan character,[3] scarcely found elsewhere on the plateau.

It will be observed that of these streams there is not one which reaches the ocean. All the rivers of the great Iranic plateau terminate in lakes or inland seas, or else lose themselves in the desert. In general

---

[M] Ker Porter, vol. i. p. 220; Morier, *Second Journey*, p. 233.
[1] Kinneir, p. 109.
[2] According to Kinneir the whole *bullock of Linjan*, a district *seventy miles long and forty wide*, is irrigated by canals cut from the Zenderud, which render it one of the most productive parts of Persia (p. 110). Ker Porter speaks of the "great quantities of water which are drawn off from the Zenderud for the daily use of the rice-fields all around Isfahan" (vol. i. p. 420).
[3] Ker Porter, vol. i. pp. 411 and 431; vol. ii. p. 60.

the thirsty sand absorbs, within a short distance of their source, the various brooks and streams which flow south and east into the desert from the northern and western mountain chains, without allowing them to collect into rivers or to carry fertility far into the plain region. The river of Isfahan forms the only exception to this rule within the limits of the ancient Media. All its other important streams, as has been seen, flow either into the Caspian or into the great lake of Urumiyeh.

That lake itself now requires our attention. It is an oblong basin, stretching in its greater direction from N.N.W. to S.S.E., a distance of above eighty miles, with an average width of about twenty-five miles.[4] On its eastern side a remarkable peninsula, projecting far into its waters, divides it into two portions of very unequal size—a northern and a southern. The southern one, which is the larger of the two, is diversified towards its centre by a group of islands, some of which are of a considerable size. The lake, like others in this part of Asia,[5] is several thousand feet above the sea level. Its waters are heavily impregnated with salt, resembling those of the Dead Sea. No fish can live in them. When a storm sweeps over their surface it only raises the waves a few feet; and no sooner is it passed than they rapidly subside again into a deep, heavy, death-like sleep.[6] The lake is shallow, nowhere exceeding four fathoms, and averaging about two fathoms—a depth which,

---

[4] Kinneir goes considerably beyond the truth when he estimates the circumference at 800 miles. (*Persian Empire*, p. 166.)

[5] Lake Urumiyeh is 4200 feet above the sea level; Lake Van 5400 feet. Lake Sivan is less elevated than either of these; but still its height above the sea is considerable.

[6] See *Geographical Journal*, vol. x. p. 7. Compare vol. iii. p. 56; and see also Kinneir, l. s. c.

however, is rarely attained within two miles of the land. The water is pellucid. To the eye it has the deep blue colour of some of the northern Italian lakes, whence it was called by the Armenians the Kapotan Zow or "Blue Sea."[7]

According to the Armenian Geography, Media contained eleven districts;[8] Ptolemy makes the number eight;[9] but the classical geographers in general are contented with the two-fold division already indicated,[10] and recognise as the constituent parts of Media only Atropatēnē (now Azerbijan) and Media Magna, a tract which nearly corresponds with the two provinces of Irak Ajemi and Ardelan. Of the minor subdivisions there are but two or three which seem to deserve any special notice. One of these is Rhagiana, or the tract skirting the Elburz Mountains from the vicinity of the Kizil-Uzen (or Sefid-Rud) to the Caspian Gates, a long and narrow slip, fairly productive, but excessively hot in summer, which took its name from the important city of Rhages. Another is Nisæa, a name which the Medes seem to have carried with them from their early eastern abodes,[11] and to have applied to some high

---

[7] *Armen. Geogr.* p. 364. It has been ingeniously conjectured that Strabo's Σπαῦτα (xi. 13, § 2) is a corruption of Καπαῦτα, due to some ancient copyist. (See St. Martin's *Recherches sur l'Arménie*, tom. i. p. 59; and compare Ingigi, *Archæolog. Armen.* vol. i. p. 160, and *Geogrph. Journ.* vol. x. p. 9.)

[8] These were Atropatia (or Atropatēnē), Ithea (Rhagiana), Gilanis (Gihilan), Mucania, Dilunia, Amatania (Hamadan), Dambuaria, Rjarastania, Atolia, Chessaia, and Rhorania (pp. 363, 364).

[9] Ptolemy's districts are Margiana, Tropatēnē (i. e. Atropatēnē), Choromithrēnē, Elymais, Sigriana, Rhagiana, Daritis, and Syro-Media (*Geograph.* vi. 2).

[10] *Supra*, p. 4.

[11] The proper Nisæa is the district of Nishapur in Khorasan (Strabo, xi. 7, § 2; laid. Char. p. 7), whence it is probable that the famous breed of horses was originally brought. The Turanian horses of the Atak are still famous throughout Persia. (See the *Geograph. Journ.* vol. ix. p. 101.)

upland plains west of the main chain of Zagros, which were peculiarly favourable to the breeding of horses. As Alexander visited these pastures on his way from Susa to Ecbatana,[12] they must necessarily have lain to the south of the latter city. Most probably they are to be identified with the modern plains of Khawah and Alishtar, between Behistun and Khorramabad, which are even now considered to afford the best summer pasturage in Persia.[13]

It is uncertain whether any of these divisions were known in the time of the great Median Empire. They are not constituted in any case by marked natural lines or features. On the whole it is perhaps most probable that the main division — that into Media Magna and Media Atropaténé — was ancient, Atropaténé being the old home of the Medes,[14] and Media Magna a later conquest; but the early political geography of the country is too obscure to justify us in laying down even this as certain. The minor political divisions are still less distinguishable in the darkness of those ancient times.

From the consideration of the districts which composed the Median territory, we may pass to that of their principal cities, some of which deservedly obtained a very great celebrity. The most important of all were the two Ecbatanas — the northern and the southern — which seem to have stood respectively in the position of metropolis to the northern and the

---

[12] Arrian, *Exp. Alex.* vii. 13. Compare Diod. Sic. xvii. 110, § 6.
[13] *Geographical Journal*, vol. ix. pp. 100, 101. Compare Ker Porter, vol. ii. p. 84.
[14] I suspect that the *Varena* of the Vendidad is Atropaténé, so named from its capital city, which was often called Vara or Vera (infra, p. 24, note ⁽ᵐ⁾); and I believe that the Bikan of the Assyrian inscriptions designates the same district. (See vol. ii. p. 473, note ⁸.)

southern province. Next to these may be named Ithages, which was probably from early times a very considerable place; while in the third rank may be mentioned Bagistan—rather perhaps a palace than a town — Concobar, Adrapan, Aspadan, Charax, Kudrus, Hyspaostes, Urakagabarna, &c.

The southern Ecbatana or Agbatana—which the Medes and Persians themselves knew as Hagmatán[1]—was situated, as we learn from Polybius[2] and Diodorus,[3] on a plain at the foot of Mount Orontes, a little to the east of the Zagros range. The notices of these authors, combined with those of Eratosthenes,[4] Isidore,[5] Pliny,[6] Arrian,[7] and others, render it as nearly certain as possible, that the site was that of the modern town of Hamadan,[8] the name of which is clearly but a slight corruption of the true ancient appellation. Mount Orontes is to be recognised in the modern Elwend or Erwend—a word etymologically identical with *Oront-es*—which is a long and

---

[1] Hagmatana, or Hagmatan, is the form used in the Behistun Inscription, which was set up in Media within a short distance of the city itself. The Achmetha (אחמתא) of Ezra (vi. 2) drops the last consonant (just as 1 Chr. v. 26 drops the same letter from Harran); but otherwise it fairly represents the native word. Of the two Greek forms, Agbatana, which is the more ancient, is to be preferred.
[2] Polyb. x. 27.
[3] Diod. Sic. ii. 13, § 6.
[4] Ap. Strab. ii. p. 79.
[5] *Mans. Parth.* p. 6; ed. Hudson, in his *Geographi Minores*. The "Apobatana" of this passage is beyond a doubt Ecbatana.
[6] *H. N.* vi. 14 and 26.
[7] *Exp. Alex.* iii. 19, 20.

[8] Chardin believed Hamadan to occupy the site of Susa (*Voyages en Perse*, tom. iii. p. 15), and the late Archdeacon Williams argued with much learning and ability that Ecbatana was at or near Ispahan (*Geography of Ancient Asia*, pp. 9-18); but with these exceptions there is an almost unanimous consent among scholars and travellers as to the identity of Hamadan with the great Median capital. (See Ritter's *Erdkunde*, vol. ix. pp. 98-100; and compare Heeren, *As. Nat.* vol. i. p. 250, E. T.; Sainte Croix, *Mém. de l'Académie des Inscriptions*, vol. L. pp. 108-141; Ouseley, *Travels in the East*, vol. iii. p. 411; Morier, *Second Journey*, pp. 264-271; Ker Porter, *Travels*, vol. ii. pp. 90-115, &c.)

lofty mountain standing out like a buttress from the Zagros range,[9] with which it is connected towards the north-west, while on every other side it stands isolated, sweeping boldly down upon the flat country at its base. Copious streams descend from the mountain on every side, more particularly to the north-east, where the plain is covered with a carpet of the most luxuriant verdure, diversified with rills, and ornamented with numerous groves of large and handsome forest trees. It is here, on ground sloping slightly away from the roots of the mountain,[10] that the modern town, which lies directly at its foot, is built. The ancient city, if we may believe Diodorus, did not approach the mountain within a mile or a mile and a half.[11] At any rate, if it began where Hamadan now stands, it most certainly extended very much further into the plain. We need not suppose indeed that it had the circumference, or even half the circumference, which the Sicilian romancer assigns to it; since his two hundred and fifty stades[12] would give a probable area of fifty square miles, more than double that of London! Ecbatana is not likely to have been at its most flourishing period a larger city than Nineveh; and we have already seen that Nineveh covered a space, within the walls, of not more than 1800 English acres.[13]

The character of the city and of its chief edifices

---

[9] Ker Porter estimates the length of Mount Orontes at 30 miles from the point where it leaves the main range (*Travels*, vol. II. p. 130). Kinneir (*Persian Empire*, p. 126) says that "Elwend proper" is "not more than twelve miles" long. The height of Orontes is estimated by Ritter at "10,000 feet at the least." (*Erdkunde*, vol. ix. p. 87.)
[10] Ker Porter, p. 101.
[11] Τῶν γὰρ Ἐκβατάνων ὡς δώδεκα σταδίους ἀπέχων ἐστὶν ὄρος ὃ καλεῖται Ὀρόντης. (Diod. Sic. ii. 13, § 7.) [12] Diod. Sic. xvii. 110, § 7.
[13] See above, vol. i. p. 320.

has, unfortunately, to be gathered almost entirely from unsatisfactory authorities. Hitherto it has been found possible in these volumes to check and correct the statements of ancient writers, which are almost always exaggerated, by an appeal to the incontrovertible evidence of modern surveys and explorations. But the Median capital has never yet attracted a scientific expedition. The travellers by whom it has been visited have reported so unfavourably of its character as a field of antiquarian research, that scarcely a spadeful of soil has been dug, either in the city or in its vicinity, with a view to recover traces of the ancient buildings. Scarcely any remains of antiquity are apparent. As the site has never been deserted, and the town has thus been subjected for nearly twenty-two centuries to the destructive ravages of foreign conquerors, and the still more injurious plunderings of native builders, anxious to obtain materials for new edifices at the least possible cost and trouble, the ancient structures have everywhere disappeared from sight, and are not even indicated by mounds of a sufficient size to attract the attention of common observers. Scientific explorers have consequently been deterred from turning their energies in this direction; more promising sites have offered and still offer themselves; and it is as yet uncertain whether the plan of the old town might not be traced and the position of its chief edifices fixed by the means of careful researches conducted by fully competent persons. In this dearth of modern materials we have to depend entirely upon the classical writers, who are rarely trustworthy in their descriptions or measurements, and who, in this instance, labour under the peculiar disadvantage of being mere reporters of the accounts given by others.

Ecbatana was chiefly celebrated for the magnificence of its palace, a structure ascribed by Diodorus to Semiramis,[14] but most probably constructed originally by Cyaxares, and improved, enlarged, and embellished by the Achæmenian monarchs. According to the judicious and moderate Polybius, who prefaces his account by a protest against exaggeration and over-colouring, the circumference of the building was seven stades,[15] or 1420 yards, somewhat more than four-fifths of an English mile. This size, which a little exceeds that of the palace mound at Susa, while it is in its turn a little exceeded by the palatial platform at Persepolis,[16] may well be accepted as probably close to the truth. Judging, however, from the analogy of the above-mentioned palaces, we must conclude that the area thus assigned to the royal residence was far from being entirely covered with buildings. One-half of the space, perhaps more, would be occupied by large open courts, paved probably with marble, surrounding the various blocks of building and separating them from one another. The buildings themselves may be conjectured to have resembled those of the Achæmenian monarchs at Susa and Persepolis, with the exception, apparently, that the pillars, which

---

[14] Diod. Sic. ii. 13, § 6.
[15] Polyb. x. 27, § 9.
[16] The circumference of the palace mound at Susa is about 4000 feet, or 1333 yards. (Loftus, *Chaldæa and Susiana*, plan, opp. p. 340.) That of the Persepolitan platform is 4578 feet, or 1526 yards. (Ker Porter, vol. i. p. 582.) The Assyrian palace mounds are in some instances still larger. The circuit of the Nimrud mound is nearly 1900, and that of the Koyunjik platform exceeds 2000 yards.

formed their most striking characteristic, were for the most part of wood rather than of stone. Polybius distinguishes the pillars into two classes,[1] those of the main buildings (οἱ ἐν ταῖς στοαῖς), and those which skirted the courts (οἱ ἐν τοῖς περιστύλοις), from which it would appear that at Ecbatana the courts were surrounded by colonnades, as they were commonly in Greek and Roman houses.[2] These wooden pillars, all either of cedar or of cypress,[3] supported beams of a similar material, which crossed each other at right angles, leaving square spaces (φατνώματα) between, which were then filled in with wood-work. Above the whole a roof was placed, sloping at an angle,[4] and composed (as we are told) of silver plates in the shape of tiles. The pillars, beams, and the rest of the wood-work, were likewise coated with thin laminæ of the precious metals, even gold being used for this purpose to a certain extent.[5]

Such seems to have been the character of the true ancient Median palace, which served probably as a model to Darius and Xerxes when they designed their great palatial edifices at the more southern capitals. In the additions which the palace received under the Achæmenian kings, stone pillars may have been introduced; and hence probably the broken shafts and bases, so nearly resembling the Persepolitan, one of which Sir R. Ker Porter[6] saw in

---

[1] Polyb. x. 27, § 10.
[2] The Assyrian courts seem, on the contrary, to have been quite open.
[3] Polyb. l. s. c. Οὔσης γὰρ τῆς ξυλίας ἁπάσης κεδρίνης καὶ κυπαριττίνης, κ.τ.λ.
[4] That the Persians in some cases used sloping roofs, rather than flat ones, we may gather from the "Tomb of Cyrus."
[5] Polyb. l. s. c. τοὺς κίονας, τοὺς μὲν ἀργυραῖς τοὺς δὲ χρυσαῖς λεπίσιν περιειλῆφθαι, τὰς δὲ κεραμίδας ἀργυρᾶς εἶναι πάσας.
[6] See his Travels, vol. ii. p. 115. The shaft and base were also seen by Mr. Morier in 1813, and are figured by him in his work entitled

the immediate neighbourhood of Hamadan on his visit to that place in 1818. But, to judge from the description of Polybius, an older and ruder style of architecture prevailed in the main building, which depended for its effect not on the beauty of architectural forms, but on the richness and costliness of the material. A pillar architecture, so far as appears, began in this part of Asia with the Medes,[1] who, however, were content to use the more readily obtained and more easily worked material of wood; while the Persians afterwards conceived the idea of substituting for these inartificial props the slender and elegant stone shafts which formed the glory of their grand edifices.

Stone base of a pillar. (Hamadan.)

At a short distance from the palace was the "Acra" or citadel, an artificial structure, if we may believe Polybius, and a place of very remarkable strength.[2]

---

[1] a Second Journey through Persia. (See p. 268.) It is from this work that the above illustration is taken.

Sir H. Rawlinson, who visited Hamadan frequently between 1835 and 1839, saw five or six other pillar bases of the same type.

[1] The rare use of pillars by the Assyrians has been noticed in the first volume (p. 380, note [4]). If, as seems probable, they were more largely employed by the later Babylonians, we may ascribe their introduction to Median influence. (See the chapter on the "Arts and Sciences of the Babylonians.") A pillar architecture naturally began in a country where there was abundant wood. The first pillars were mere rough posts, like those which support the houses of the Kurds and Yezidis. (See Layard's Nineveh and Babylon, p. 252.) These were after a time shaped regularly, then carved and ornamented; while finally they were replaced by stone shafts, which may have been first used where wood was scarce, but were soon perceived to be of superior beauty.

[2] Polyb. x. 27, § 6. "Ἄκραν ἐν αὐτῇ χειροποίητον ἔχει, θαυμασίως πρὸς ὀχυρότητα κατεσκευασμένην.

22 THE THIRD MONARCHY. Chap. I.

Here probably was the treasury, from which Darius Codomannus carried off 7000 talents of silver, when he fled towards Bactria for fear of Alexander.[9] And here, too, may have been the Record Office, in which were deposited the royal decrees and other public documents under the earlier Persian kings.[10] Some travellers[11] are of opinion that a portion of the

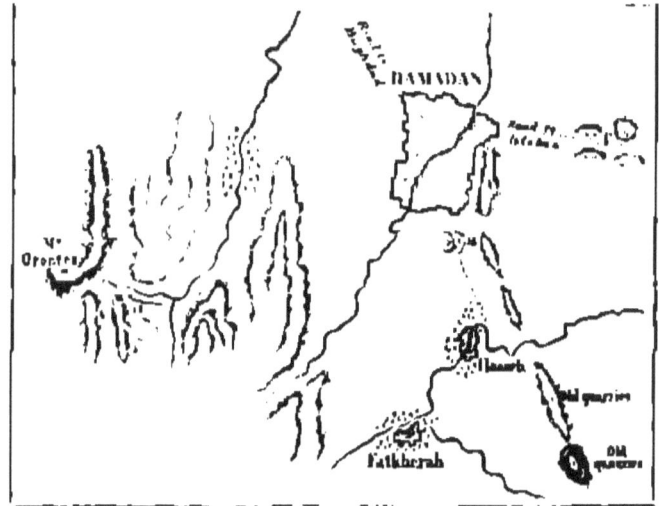

Plan of the country about Hamadan.

A. Ancient citadel.   B. Figure of lion.   C. Remains of buildings.   D. Cuneiform inscriptions.

ancient structure still exists; and there is certainly a ruin on the outskirts of the modern town towards the south, which is known to the natives as "the inner fortress," and which may not improbably occupy some portion of the site whereon the original citadel stood. But the remains of building which

---

[9] Arrian, *Exp. Alex.* lii. 19.   [10] Ezra vi. 2.
[11] As Ker Porter (*Travels*, vol. ii. p. 101).

now exist are certainly not of an earlier date than the era of Parthian supremacy,[12] and they can therefore throw no light on the character of the old Median stronghold. It may be thought perhaps that the description which Herodotus gives of the building called by him "the palace of Deioces" should be here applied, and that by its means we might obtain an exact notion of the original structure. But the account of this author is wholly at variance with the natural features of the neighbourhood, where there is no such conical hill as he describes, but only a plain surrounded by mountains. It seems therefore to be certain that either his description is a pure myth, or that it applies to another city, the Ecbatana of the northern province.

It is doubtful whether the Median capital was at any time surrounded with walls. Polybius expressly declares that it was an unwalled place in his day;[13] and there is some reason to suspect that it had always been in this condition. The Medes and Persians appear to have been in general content to establish in each town a fortified citadel or stronghold, round which the houses were clustered, without superadding the further defence of a town wall.[14] Ecbatana accordingly seems never to have stood a siege.[15] When the nation which held it was defeated in the open field, the city (unlike Babylon and Nineveh) submitted to the conqueror without a struggle.

---

[12] This is the decided opinion of Sir H. Rawlinson, who carefully examined the ruins in 1836.
[13] Polyb. l. s. c.
[14] Herodotus expressly states that the northern Ecbatana was a city of this character (i. 98, 99). Modern researches have discovered no signs of town walls at any of the old Persian or Median sites.
[15] Ecbatana yielded at once to Cyrus, to Alexander (Arrian, *Exp. Alex*. iii. 19), and to Antiochus the Great (Polyb. x. 27).

Thus the marvellous description in the Book of Judith,[16] which is internally very improbable, would appear to be entirely destitute of any the slightest foundation in fact.

The chief city of northern Media, which bore in later times the name of Gaza, Gazaca, or Canzaca,[17] is thought to have been also called Ecbatana, and to have been occasionally mistaken by the Greeks for the southern or real capital.[18] The description of Herodotus, which is irreconcileably at variance with the local features of the Hamadan site, accords sufficiently with the existing remains of a considerable city in the province of Azerbijan; and it seems certainly to have been a city in these parts which was called by Moses of Chorêné, "the *second* Ecbatana, the seven-walled town."[1] The peculiarity of this place was its situation on and about a conical hill, which sloped gently down from its summit to its base, and allowed of the interposition of seven circuits of wall between the plain and the hill's crest. At the top of the hill, within the innermost circle of the defences, were the Royal Palace and the treasuries; the sides of the hill were occupied solely by the fortifications; and at the base, outside the circuit of the outermost wall, were the domestic and other buildings which constituted the town.

---

[16] Judith i. 2-4. According to this account the walls were built of hewn stones nine feet long, and four and a half broad. The height of the walls was 105 feet, the width 75 feet. The gates were of the same altitude as the walls; and the towers over the gates were carried to the height of 150 feet.

[17] See Strab. xi. 13, § 3; Plin.

H. N. vi. 13; Ptol. *Geograph.* vi. 2; Am. Marc. xxiii. 6; Armen. *Geogr.* § 87, p. 304, &c. Another name of the city was Vera. (Strab. l. s. c.)

[18] See the paper of Sir H. Rawlinson "On the Site of the Atropatenian Ecbatana" in the tenth volume of the *Journal of the Geographical Society*, pp. 65-158.

[1] Mos. Chor. *Hist. Armen.* ii. 84.

According to the information received by Herodotus, the battlements which crowned the walls were variously coloured. Those of the outer circle were white, of the next black, of the third scarlet, of the fourth blue, of the fifth orange, of the sixth silver, and of the seventh gold.³ A pleasing, or at any rate a striking effect was thus produced—the citadel, which towered above the town, presenting to the eye seven distinct rows of colour.³

If there was really a northern as well as a southern Ecbatana,⁴ and if the account of Herodotus, which cannot possibly apply to the southern capital, may be regarded as truly describing the great city of the north, we may with much probability fix the site of the northern town at the modern Tukht-i-Suleïman, in the upper valley of the Saruk, a tributary of the Jaghetu. Here alone in northern Media are there important ruins occupying such a position as that which Herodotus describes.⁵ Near the head of a valley in which runs the main branch of the Saruk,

---

³ Herod. I. 98.

³ This whole description has no doubt a somewhat mythical air; and the plating of the battlements with the precious metals seems to the modern reader peculiarly improbable. But the people who roofed their palaces with silver tiles, and coated all the internal wood-work either with plates of silver or of gold, may have been wealthy enough and lavish enough to make even such a display as Herodotus describes. There is reason to believe that in Babylonia at least one temple was ornamented almost exactly as the citadel of Ecbatana is declared to have been by Herodotus. (See the author's *Herodotus*, vol. ii. p. 484, 2nd edition, and compare ch. v. of the "Fourth Monarchy.")

⁴ The view maintained by Sir H. Rawlinson in the paper already referred to (supra, p. 24, note ⁿ), while in England it has been very generally accepted, has been combated on the Continent, more especially in France, where an elaborate reply to his article was published by M. Quatremère in the *Mémoires de l'Académie des Inscriptions et Belles Lettres*, tom. xix. part. I. p. 419 et seqq. It must be admitted that the only ancient writer who distinctly recognises two Median Ecbatanas is the Armenian historian above quoted. (See above, p. 24, note ¹.)

⁵ The ruins at Kileh Zohak, described by Col. Monteith in such glowing terms (*Journal of the Geographical Society*, vol. iii. pp. 4, 6), are in reality quite insignificant.

at the edge of the hills which skirt it to the north, there stands a conical mound projecting into the vale and rising above its surface to the height of 150 feet. The geological formation of the mound is curious in the extreme.⁶ It seems to owe its origin entirely to a small lake, the waters of which are so strongly impregnated with calcareous matter, that wherever they overflow they rapidly form a deposit, which is as hard and firm as natural rock. If the lake was originally on a level with the valley, it would have soon formed incrustations round its edge, which every casual or permanent overflow would have tended to raise; and thus, in the course of ages, the entire hill may have been formed by a mere accumulation of petrifactions.⁷ The formation would progress more or less rapidly according to the tendency of the lake to overflow its bounds; which tendency must have been strong until the water reached its present natural level—the level, probably, of some other sheet of water in the hills, with which it is connected by an underground syphon.⁸ The lake, which is of an irregular shape, is about 300 paces in circumference. Its water, notwithstanding the quantity of mineral matter held in solution, is exquisitely clear, and not unpleasing to the taste.⁹

---

⁶ The best description of the Takht-i-Suleiman ruins will be found in the *Geographical Journal*, vol. x. pp. 46-53. Sir R. K. Porter is both less complete and less exact. (*Travels*, vol. ii. pp. 558-561.)

⁷ This theory was first broached by Ker Porter. Later travellers agree with him.

⁸ One of the peculiarities of the lake is, that whatever the quantity of water drawn off from it for purposes of irrigation by the neighbouring tribes, it always remains at the same level. Sir H. Rawlinson thus explains the phenomenon: "I conclude," he says, "the lake to be connected by an underground syphon with some other great fountain in the interior of the adjacent mountains, which is precisely at the same level as itself, and which has other means of outlet." (*Geographical Journal*, vol. x. p. 48.)

⁹ Ibid. p. 50; Ker Porter, vol. ii. p. 558.

Formerly it was believed by the natives to be unfathomable; but experiments made in 1837 showed the depth to be no more than 156 feet.

Plan of Takht-i-Suleiman (perhaps the Northern Ecbatana).

The ruins which at present occupy this remarkable site consist of a strong wall, guarded by numerous bastions and pierced by four gateways, which runs round the brow of the hill in a slightly irregular ellipse, of some interesting remains of buildings within this walled space, and of a few insignificant traces of inferior edifices on the slope between the plain and the summit. As it is not thought that any of these remains are of a date anterior to the Sassanian kingdom,[10] no description will be given of them here. We are only concerned with the Median city, and that has entirely disappeared. Of the seven walls, one alone is to be traced;[11] and even here the

---

[10] *Geograph. Journal*, vol. x. p. 51.
[11] In its present condition the hill could not receive seven complete circular walls, from the fact that towards the east it abuts upon the edge of the hilly country, and is consequently on that side only a little elevated above the adjacent ground. But as the water has now for some time been drawn off on this side, the hill has probably grown in this direction.

Median structure has perished and been replaced by masonry of a far later age. Excavations may hereafter bring to light some remnants of the original town, but at present research has done no more than recover for us a forgotten site.

The Median city next in importance to the two Ecbatanas was Raga or Rhages, near the Caspian Gates, almost at the extreme eastern limits of the territory possessed by the Medes. The great antiquity of this place is marked by its occurrence in the Zendavesta among the primitive settlements of the Arians.[1] Its celebrity during the time of the Empire is indicated by the position which it occupies in the romances of Tobit[2] and Judith.[3] It maintained its rank under the Persians, and is mentioned by Darius Hystaspis as the scene of the struggle which terminated the great Median revolt.[4] The last Darius seems to have sent thither his heavy baggage and the ladies of his court,[5] when he resolved to quit Ecbatana and fly eastward. It has been already noticed that Rhages gave name to a district;[6] and this district may be certainly identified with the long narrow tract of fertile territory intervening

---

[1] Rhages occurs as *Ragha* in the first Fargard of the Vendidad. It is the twelfth settlement, and one in which the faithful were intermingled with unbelievers. (Haug in Bunsen's *Egypt*, vol. iii. p. 490, E. T.)

[2] Tobit i. 14; iv. 1; ix. 1; &c.

[3] Judith i. 5 and 15.

[4] *Behistun Inscription*, col. ii. par. 13.

[5] Arrian, *Exp. Alex.* iii. 19. Arrian only mentions the Caspian Gates; but there can be little doubt that Rhages was the place where they were to await Darius. Comp. ch. 20.

[6] Rhagiana occurs as a district in Isidore (*Mans. Parth.* p. 6) as well as in Ptolemy. In the former the MSS. have Rhatiana (PATIANH for PAΓIANH), which Hudson perversely transforms into Matiana, a district lying exactly in the opposite direction. Strabo points to Rhagiana in his expression, τὰ περὶ τὰς 'Ράγας καὶ τὰς Κασπίους πύλας (xi. 13, § 7). Diodorus calls it an eparchy—τὴν ἐπαρχίαν τὴν προσαγορευμένην 'Ράγας (xix. 44, § 5).

between the Elburz mountain-range and the desert,¹ from about Kasvin to Khaar, or from long. 50° to 52° 30′. The exact site of the city of Rhages within this territory is somewhat doubtful. All accounts place it near the eastern extremity; and as there are in this direction ruins of a town called Rhei or Rhey, it has been usual to assume that they positively fix the locality.⁸ But similarity, or even identity, of name is an insufficient proof of a site;⁹ and, in the present instance, there are grounds for placing Rhages very much nearer to the Caspian Gates than the position of Rhei. Arrian, whose accuracy is notorious, distinctly states that from the Gates to Rhages was only a single day's march, and that Alexander accomplished the distance in that time.¹⁰ Now from Rhei to the Girduni Sudurrah pass, which undoubtedly represents the Pylæ Caspiæ of Arrian,¹¹

---

⁷ See especially Isidore, L. s. c.; and compare C. Müller's Map to illustrate this author (Tab. in Geographos Minores, No. 10). C. Müller makes the boundary westward the Karaghan hills, thus extending Rhagiana half a degree to the west of Kasvin. He greatly exaggerates the rivers of the region.

⁸ Fraser, Khorassan, p. 286; Morier, Second Journey, p. 365; Ouseley, Travels, vol. iii. p. 174; Ker Porter, Travels, vol. i. p. 357; Heeren, Asiatic Nations, vol. i. p. 233, E. T.; Ritter, Erdkunde, vol. viii. pp. 595-604; Winer, Realwörterbuch, ad voc.; C. Müller, Tabulæ, l. s. c.; Geographical Journ. vol. xxxi. p. 38.

⁹ Names travel. The modern Marathon is more than three miles from the ancient site. New Ilium was still further (six miles) from old Troy. The shores of the Black Sea have witnessed still more violent changes. The ancient Eupatoria was at Inkerman; the modern is 50 miles to the northward. Cherson (or Chersonesus) was at the mouth of the Sebastopol inlet; it is now on the Borysthenes or Dniepr. Odessus was at Varna; Odessa is three degrees to the north-east.

¹⁰ Exp. Alex. iii. 20.

¹¹ This point is well argued by Mr. Fraser (Khorassan, pp. 291-293, note), whose conclusion seems to be now generally adopted. Pliny's Pylæ Caspiæ, on the other hand, (H. N. vi. 14) would appear to be the Girduni Siyaluk, another pass over the same spur, situated three or four miles farther north, at the point where the spur branches out from the main chain. This pass is one of a tremendous character. It is a gap five miles long between precipices 1000 feet high, scarped as though by the hand of man, its width varying from ten to forty feet. (Sir H. Rawlinson, MS. notes.)

is at least fifty miles, a distance which no army could accomplish in less time than two days.[12] Rhages consequently must have been considerably to the east of Rhei, about half-way between it and the celebrated pass which it was considered to guard. Its probable position is the modern Kaleh Erij, near Veramin, about 23 miles from the commencement of the Sudurrah pass, where there are considerable remains of an ancient town.[13]

In the same neighbourhood with Rhages, but closer to the Straits, perhaps on the site now occupied by the ruins known as Uewanukif, or possibly even nearer to the foot of the pass,[14] was the Median city of Charax, a place not to be confounded with the more celebrated city called Charax Spasini, the birthplace of Dionysius the geographer, which was on the Persian Gulf, at the mouth of the Tigris.[15]

The other Median cities whose position can be determined with an approach to certainty, were in the western portion of the country, in the range of Zagros, or in the fertile tract between that range and the desert. The most important of these are Bagistan, Adrapan, Concobar, and Aspadan.

Bagistan is described by Isidore[16] as "a city situated on a hill, where there was a pillar and a

---

[12] Alexander's marches seem to have averaged 100 stades, or about 22 miles. The ordinary Roman march was 20 Roman miles, equivalent to 18½ English miles.
[13] Sir H. Rawlinson, MS. notes. In Erij we have probably a corruption of Rhag-es.
[14] Uewanukif is six or seven miles from the commencement of the pass (Fraser, p. 291). Isidore places Charax directly under the hill. (ὑπὸ τὸ ὄρος ὁ καλεῖται Κάσπιος, ἐφ' οὗ αἱ Κασπίαι πύλαι, p. 6.)
[15] Plin. H. N. iv. 27, ad fin.; Ptol. Geograph. vi. 3; Steph. Byz. ad voc. Χάραξ. Hudson's identification of Charax Spasini with Anthemusias or Charax Sidæ (Isid. Mans. Parth. p. 2) is a strange error.
[16] Mans. Parth. p. 6. Βάγιστανα (leg. Βάγιστανα) πόλις ἐν' ὄρει κειμένη.

statue of Semiramis." Diodorus has an account of the arrival of Semiramis at the place, of her establishing a royal park or paradise in the plain below the mountain, which was watered by an abundant spring, of her smoothing the face of the rock where it descended precipitously upon the low ground, and of her carving on the surface thus obtained her own effigy, with an inscription in Assyrian characters." The position assigned to Bagistan by both writers, and the description of Diodorus," identify the place beyond a doubt with the now famous Behistun, where

View of the Rock of Behistun.

ἔνθα Σεμιράμιδος ἄγαλμα καὶ στήλη. Compare with Βάγιστον the modern Bisutan and Behistun.

[17] Diod. Sic. ii. 13, § 1-2.
[18] Diodorus, as usual, greatly exaggerates the height of the mountain, which he estimates at seventeen stades, or above 10,000 feet, whereas it is really about 1700 feet. (*Journal of Asiatic Society*, vol. x. p. 187.)

the plain, the fountain, the precipitous rock, and the
scarped surface are still to be seen,[19] though the
supposed figure of Semiramis, her pillar, and her
inscription have disappeared.[20] This remarkable
spot, lying on the direct route between Babylon and
Ecbatana, and presenting the unusual combination
of a copious fountain, a rich plain, and a rock suitable
for sculptures, must have early attracted the attention of the great monarchs who marched their armies
through the Zagros range, as a place where they
might conveniently set up memorials of their exploits.
The works of this kind ascribed by the ancient
writers to Semiramis were probably either Assyrian
or Babylonian, and (it is most likely) resembled the
ordinary monuments which the kings of Babylon
and Nineveh delighted to erect in countries newly
conquered.[21] The example set by the Mesopotamians
was followed by their Arian neighbours, when the
supremacy passed into their hands; and the famous
mountain, invested by them with a sacred character,[22]
was made to subserve and perpetuate their glory by
receiving sculptures and inscriptions[1] which showed
them to have become the lords of Asia. The practice
did not even stop here. When the Parthian kingdom
of the Arsacidæ had established itself in these parts at

---

[19] Ker Porter, *Travels*, vol. ii.
pp. 150, 151; Sir H. Rawlinson, in
Journal of the Geographical Society,
vol. ix. pp. 112, 113.

[20] They were perhaps destroyed
by Chosroe Parviz, when he prepared
to build a palace on the site. (Ibid.
p. 114.)

[21] Supra, vol. ii. pp. 96, 354, 501,
&c.

[22] Bagistan is "the hill of Jove"
(Διὸς ὄρος), according to Diodorus
(ii. 13, § 1). It seems to mean really
"the place of God." We may thus
compare the name with the "Bethel"
of the Hebrews.

[1] The tablet and inscriptions of
Darius, which have made Bebistun
famous in modern times, are in a
recess to the right of the scarped
face of rock, and at a considerable
elevation. (Ker Porter, vol. ii. p.
154.)

the expense of the Seleucidæ, the rock was once more called upon to commemorate the warlike triumphs of a new race. Gotarzes, the contemporary of the Emperor Claudius, after defeating his rival Meherdates in the plain between Behistun and Kermanshah, inscribed upon the mountain, which already bore the impress of the great monarchs of Assyria and Persia, a record of his recent victory.[2]

The name of Adrapan occurs only in Isidore,[3] who places it between Bagistan and Ecbatana, at the distance of twelve schœni—36 Roman or 34 British miles—from the latter. It was, he says, the site of an ancient palace belonging to Ecbatana, which Tigranes the Armenian had destroyed. The name and situation sufficiently identify Adrapan with the modern village of Arteman,[4] which lies on the southern face of Elwend near its base, and is well adapted for a royal residence. Here, "during the severest winter, when Hamadan and the surrounding country are buried in snow, a warm and sunny climate is to be found; whilst in the summer a thousand rills descending from Elwend diffuse around fertility and fragrance."[5] Groves of trees grow up in rich luxuriance from the well-irrigated soil, whose thick foliage affords a welcome shelter from the heat of the noonday sun. The climate, the gardens, and

---

[2] The inscription, which is in the Greek character and language, is much mutilated; but the name of Gotarzes (ΓΟΤΑΡΖΗC) appears twice in it. His rival, Meherdates, is perhaps mentioned under the name of Mithrates. (Sir H. Rawlinson, in *Geograph. Journ.* vol. ix. pp. 114-116.)

[3] *Mans. Parth.* p. 6. The true reading seems to be 'Αδραπάναν, as edited by Höschel.

[4] Arteman is one of three villages—Toom, Sirkan, and Arteman—which lie close together, and are generally known under the common title of Toosirkan. (Sir H. Rawlinson, MS. notes.)

[5] Ibid.

the manifold blessings of the place are proverbial throughout Persia; and naturally caused the choice of the site for a retired palace, to which the court of Ecbatana might adjourn, when either the summer heat and dust or the winter cold made residence in the capital irksome.

In the neighbourhood of Adrapan, on the road leading to Bagistan, stood Concobar,⁶ which is undoubtedly the modern Kungawar, and perhaps the Chavon of Diodorus.⁷ Here, according to the Sicilian historian, Semiramis built a palace and laid out a paradise; and here, in the time of Isidore, was a famous temple of Artemis. Colossal ruins crown the summit of the acclivity on which the town of Kungawar stands,⁸ which may be the remains of this building; but no trace has been found that can be regarded as either Median or Assyrian.

The Median town of Aspadan, which is mentioned by no writer but Ptolemy,⁹ would scarcely deserve notice here, if it were not for its modern celebrity. Aspadan, corrupted into Isfahan, became the capital of Persia under the Sefi kings, who rendered it one of the most magnificent cities of Asia. It is uncertain whether it existed at all in the time of the great Median empire. If so, it was, at best, an outlying town of little consequence on the extreme southern confines of the territory, where it abutted upon Persia proper.¹⁰ The district wherein it lay

---

⁶ Isidore, *Mans. Parth.* l. s. c.
⁷ Diod. Sic. ii. 13, § 3.
⁸ Ker Porter, *Travels*, vol. ii. pp. 141, 142; Ollivier, *Voyage dans l'Empire Othoman*, tom. v. pp. 47, 48. ⁹ *Geograph.* vi. 4.

¹⁰ See above, p. 0. It is strange that so acute a writer as the late Archdeacon Williams should not have seen that this position was fatal to his theory, that Isfahan represented Ecbatana.

was inhabited by the Median tribe of the Parætaceni.[11]

Upon the whole it must be allowed that the towns of Media were few and of no great account. The Medes did not love to congregate in large cities, but preferred to scatter themselves in villages over their broad and varied territory. The protection of walls, necessary for the inhabitants of the low Mesopotamian regions, was not required by a people whose country was full of natural fastnesses to which they could readily remove on the approach of danger. Excepting the capital and the two important cities of Gazaca and Rhages, the Median towns were insignificant. Even those cities themselves were probably of moderate dimensions, and had little of the architectural splendour which gives so peculiar an interest to the towns of Mesopotamia. Their principal buildings were in a frail and perishable material,[12] unsuited to bear the ravages of time; they have consequently altogether disappeared; and in the whole of Media modern researches have failed to bring to light a single edifice which can be assigned with any show of probability to the period of the Empire.

The plan adopted in former portions of this work [13] makes it necessary, before concluding this chapter, to glance briefly at the character of the various countries and districts by which Media was bordered —the Caspian district upon the north, Armenia upon the north-west, the Zagros region and Assyria upon the west, Persia proper upon the south, and upon the east Sagartia and Parthia.

---

[11] The Parætaceni had another city, called Parætaca, the site of which is uncertain (Steph. Byz. ad voc.)

[12] See above, p. 20.

[13] See vol. I. pp. 31 and 259.

North and north-east of the mountain range which under different names skirts the southern shores of the Caspian Sea and curves round its south-western corner, lies a narrow but important strip of territory —the modern Ghilan and Mazanderan. This is a most fertile region, well watered and richly wooded, and forms one of the most valuable portions of the modern kingdom of Persia. At first it is a low flat tract of deep alluvial soil, but little raised above the level of the Caspian; gradually however it rises into swelling hills which form the supports of the high mountains that shut in this sheltered region, a region only to be reached by a very few passes over or through them.[14] The mountains are clothed on this side nearly to their summit with dwarf oaks, or with shrubs and brushwood; while, lower down, their flanks are covered with forests of elms, cedars, chesnuts, beeches, and cypress trees. The gardens and orchards of the natives are of the most superb character; the vegetation is luxuriant; lemons, oranges, peaches, pomegranates, besides other fruits, abound; rice, hemp, sugar-canes, mulberries are cultivated with success; vines grow wild; and the valleys are strewn with flowers of rare fragrance, among which may be noted the rose, the honeysuckle, and the sweetbriar.[1] Nature, however, with her usual justice, has balanced these extraordinary advantages with

---

[14] The mountains are pierced by the two streams of the Aras and the Kizil Uzen or Sefid Rud, and the low country may be entered along their courses. There is a pass over the Elburz chain from Firuz-kuh to Pul-i-sefid, 80 or 90 miles to the east of Teheran. This would seem to be the "Pylæ Caspiæ" of Dionysius (*Perieg.* 1035-1038).

[1] The authorities for this description are Kinneir, *Persian Empire*, pp. 159-183; Ouseley, *Travels*, vol. iii. pp. 221-336; Fraser, *Khorasan*, p. lviii; Chesney, *Euphrates Expedition*, vol. I. pp. 216, 217; Todd, in *Journal of Geographical Society*, vol. viii. pp. 102-104.

View in Mazanderan—the Caspian Sea in the distance.

peculiar drawbacks: the tiger, unknown in any other part of Western Asia,[1] here lurks in the thickets, ready to spring at any moment on the unwary traveller; inundations are frequent, and carry desolation far and wide; the waters, which thus escape from the river beds, stagnate in marshes, and during the summer and autumn heats pestilential exhalations arise, which destroy the stranger, and bring even the acclimatised native to the brink of the grave.[2] The Persian monarch chooses the southern rather than the northern side of the mountains for the site of his

---

[1] Tigers sometimes stray from this region into Azerbijan. (See Morier, *Second Journey*, p. 218.)

[2] Kinneir, p. 160; Chesney, vol. i. p. 216; Fraser, *Travels near the Caspian Sea*, p. 11.

capital, preferring the keen winter cold and dry summer heat of the high and almost waterless plateau to the damp and stifling air of the low Caspian region.

The narrow tract of which this is a description can at no time have sheltered a very numerous or powerful people. During the Median period, and for many ages afterwards, it seems to have been inhabited by various petty tribes of predatory habits, —Cadusians, Mardi, Tapyri, etc.—who passed their time in petty quarrels among themselves and in plundering raids upon their great southern neighbour.[4] Of these tribes the Cadusians alone enjoyed any considerable reputation. They were celebrated for their skill with the javelin[5]—a skill probably represented by the modern Persian use of the *djereed*. According to Diodorus, they were engaged in frequent wars with the Median kings, and were able to bring into the field a force of 200,000 men![6] Under the Persians they seem to have been considered good soldiers,[7] and to have sometimes made a struggle for independence.[8] But there is no real reason to believe that they were of such strength as to have formed at any time a danger to the Median kingdom, to which it is more probable that they generally acknowledged a qualified subjection.

The great country of Armenia, which lay north-west and partly north of Media, has been generally described in a previous volume;[9] but a few words

---

[4] Strab. xl. 13, § 3; Diod. Sic. ii. 33, § 4.
[5] Strab. xi. 13, § 4. 'Ακοντισταὶ ἐλαφροί.
[6] Diod. Sic. ii. 33, § 3 and § 6.
[7] After the battle of Arbela Darius hoped to retrieve his fortunes by means of a fresh army of Cadusians and Sacæ. (Arrian, *Exp. Alex.* iii. 19.)
[8] Diod. Sic. xv. 8, § 4; xvii. 6, § 1.
[9] See vol. I. pp. 260, 261.

will be here added with respect to the more eastern portion, which immediately bordered upon the Median territory. This consisted of two outlying districts, separated from the rest of the country, the triangular basin of Lake Van, and the tract between the Kur and Aras rivers—the modern Karabagh and Erivan. The basin of Lake Van, surrounded by high ranges, and forming the very heart of the mountain system of this part of Asia, is an isolated region, a sort of natural citadel, where a strong military power would be likely to establish itself. Accordingly it is here, and here alone in all Armenia, that we find signs of the existence, during the Assyrian and Median periods, of a great organised monarchy. The Van inscriptions indicate to us a line of kings who bore sway in the eastern Armenia,—the true Ararat—and who were both in civilization and in military strength far in advance of any of the other princes who divided among them the Armenian territory. The Van monarchs may have been at times formidable enemies of the Medes. They have left traces of their dominion, not only on the tops of the mountain passes [10] which lead into the basin of Lake Urumiyeh, but even in the comparatively low plain of Miyandab on the southern shore of that inland sea.[11] It is probable from this that they were at one time masters of a large portion of Media Atropatênê; and the very name of Urumiyeh, which still attaches to the lake, may have been given to it from one of their tribes.[12] In the tract between the Kur and Aras,

---

[10] *Journal of the Geographical Society*, vol. x. pp. 21, 22; and compare above, vol. II. pp. 180, 181.
[11] *Geographical Journal*, vol. x. p. 12.
[12] The Urumi are coupled with the Nairi in an inscription of Asshur-idanni-pal; and the Van monarchs always call themselves "kings of the Nairi."

on the other hand, there is no sign of the early existence of any formidable power. Here the mountains are comparatively low, the soil is fertile, and the climate temperate.[13] The character of the region would lead its inhabitants to cultivate the arts of peace rather than those of war, and would thus tend to prevent them from being formidable or troublesome to their neighbours.

The Zagros region, which in the more ancient times separated between Media and Assyria, being inhabited by a number of independent tribes, but which was ultimately absorbed into the more powerful country, requires no notice here, having been sufficiently described among the tracts by which Assyria was bordered.[14] At first a serviceable shield to the weak Arian tribes which were establishing themselves along its eastern base upon the high plateau, it gradually passed into their possession as they increased in strength, and ultimately became a main nursery of their power, furnishing to their armies vast numbers both of men and horses. The great horse pastures, from which the Medes first, and the Persians afterwards, supplied their numerous and excellent cavalry, were in this quarter;[15] and the troops which it furnished—hardy mountaineers accustomed to brave the severity of a most rigorous climate—must have been among the most effective of the Median forces.[16]

On the south Media was bounded by Persia proper —a tract which corresponded nearly with the modern

---

[13] Morier, *Second Journey*, p. 245; Ker Porter, *Travels*, vol. i. pp. 193-194. [14] See vol. i. pp. 259, 260. [15] Supra, p. 15.

[16] On the known superiority of mountain troops in ancient times see Herod. ix. 122, and compare Plat. *Leg.* iii. p. 695, A.

province of Farsistan. The complete description of this territory, the original seat of the Persian nation, belongs to a future volume of this work, which will contain an account of the 'Fifth Monarchy.' For the present it is sufficient to observe that the Persian territory was for the most part a highland, very similar to Media, from which it was divided by no strongly marked line or natural boundary. The Persian mountains are a continuation of the Zagros chain, and Northern Persia is a portion—the southern portion—of the same great plateau, whose western and north-western skirts formed the great mass of the Median territory. Thus upon this side Media was placed in the closest connection with an important country, a country similar in character to her own, where a hardy race was likely to grow up, with which she might expect to have difficult contests.

Finally, towards the east lay the great salt desert, sparsely inhabited by various nomadic races, among which the most important were the Cossæans and the Sagartians. To the latter people Herodotus seems to assign almost the whole of the sandy region, since he unites them with the Sarangians and Thamanæans on the one hand, with the Utians and Mycians upon the other.[1] They were a wild race, probably of Arian origin,[2] who hunted with the *lasso* over the great desert mounted on horses,[3] and could bring

---

[1] Herod. iii. 93. The Sarangians dwelt about the lake in which the Holmend ends; the Thamanæans between that lake and Herat. The Utians (Uxians) inhabited a part of the Zagros range; the Mycians seem to have dwelt on the Persian Gulf, in a part of the modern *Mek*-ran.

[2] See the author's *Herodotus*, vol. iv. p. 172, and compare vol. i. p. 554 (2nd edition).

[3] We can only account for their carrying the *lasso* into battle (Herod. vii. 85) by regarding it as the weapon with which daily use had made them familiar.

into the field a force of eight or ten thousand men.[4] Their country, a waste of sand and gravel, in parts thickly incrusted with salt, was impassable to an army, and formed a barrier which effectively protected Media along the greater portion of her eastern frontier. Towards the extreme north-east the Sagartians were replaced by the Cossæans and the Parthians, the former probably the people of the Siah-Koh mountain,[5] the latter the inhabitants of the tract known now as the *Atak*,[6] or "Skirt," which extends along the southern flank of the Elburz range from the Caspian Gates nearly to Herat, and is capable of sustaining a very considerable population. The Cossæans were plunderers,[7] from whose raids Media suffered constant annoyance; but they were at no time of sufficient strength to cause any serious fear. The Parthians, as we learn from the course of events, had in them the materials of a mighty people; but the hour for their elevation and expansion was not yet come, and the keenest observer of Median times could scarcely have perceived in them the future lords of Western Asia. From Parthia, moreover, Media was divided by the strong rocky spur[8] which runs out from the Elburz into the desert in long. 52° 10' nearly, over which is the narrow pass already mentioned as the Caspian Gates.[9] Thus

---

[4] They furnished 8000 horsemen to the army of Xerxes (Herod. l. a. c.), which was probably not their full force.

[5] Cossæans is explained by some as *Koh-Siam*, inhabitants of the *Koh-Siah*, or *Siah-Koh*, a remarkable isolated mountain in the salt desert, nearly due south of the Caspian Gates.

[6] Fraser, *Khorasan*, p. 245.

[7] Ἀσγυρινοί. Strab. xi. 18, § 6.

[8] A good description of this spur and of the true character of the "Caspian Gates" is given by Mr. Fraser in his *Khorasan*, pp. 291-293, note. The reader may compare the author's article on Rhages in Dr. Smith's *Biblical Dictionary*, vol. ii. p. 990.

[9] Supra, p. 29.

Media on most sides was guarded by the strong natural barriers of seas,[10] mountains, and deserts, lying open only on the south, where she adjoined upon a kindred people. Her neighbours were for the most part weak in numbers, though warlike. Armenia, however, to the north-west, Assyria to the west, and Persia to the south, were all more or less formidable. A prescient eye might have foreseen that the great struggles of Media would be with these powers, and that if she attained imperial proportions it must be by their subjugation or absorption.

[10] The Caspian Sea was a great protection from the barbarians of the North.

Chapter II.

CLIMATE AND PRODUCTIONS.

Ἡ πολλὴ μὲν ὑψηλή ἐστι καὶ ψυχρά· ἡ δ' ἐν ταπεινοῖς ἐδάφεσι καὶ κοίλοις οὖσα εὐδαίμων σφόδρα ἐστὶ καὶ πάμφορος.—STRAB. xi. 13.

MEDIA, like Assyria, is a country of such extent and variety, that, in order to give a correct description of its climate, we must divide it into regions. Azerbijan, or Atropatênê, the most northern portion, has a climate altogether cooler than the rest of Media; while in the more southern division of the country there is a marked difference between the climate of the east and of the west, of the tracts lying on the high plateau and skirting the Great Salt Desert, and of those contained within or closely abutting upon the Zagros mountain-range. The difference here is due to the difference of physical conformation, which is as great as possible, the broad monotonous plains about Kasvin, Koum, and Kashan, divided from each other by low rocky ridges, offering the strongest conceivable contrast to the perpetual alternations of mountain and valley, precipitous height and deep wooded glen, which compose the greater part of the Zagros region.

The climate of Azerbijan is temperate and pleasant, though perhaps somewhat over warm,[1] in sum-

---

[1] Morier complains of the "oppressive heat of the low countries" in Azerbijan during the summer (Second Journey, p. 295). He found the thermometer rise to 99½ degrees at Miana early in June. (Ibid. p. 208.)

mer; while in winter it is bitterly severe, colder than that of almost any other region in the same latitude.² This extreme rigour seems to be mainly owing to elevation, the very valleys and valley plains of the tract being at a height of from 4000 to 5000 feet above the sea level. Frost commonly sets in towards the end of November, or at latest early in December; snow soon covers the ground to the depth of several feet; the thermometer falls below zero; the sun shines brightly, except when from time to time fresh deposits of snow occur; but a keen and strong wind usually prevails, which is represented as "cutting like a sword,"³ and being a very "assassin of life."⁴ Deaths from cold are of daily occurrence;⁵ and it is impossible to travel without the greatest risk. Whole companies or caravans occasionally perish beneath the drift, when the wind is violent, especially if a heavy fall happen to coincide with one of the frequent easterly gales. The severe weather commonly continues till March, when travelling becomes possible, but the snow remains on much of the ground till May, and on the mountains still longer.⁶ The spring, which begins in April, is temperate and delightful; a sudden burst of vegetation succeeds to the long winter lethargy; the air is fresh and balmy,

---

² The latitude of Azerbijan is that of Bœotia, Corfu, Southern Italy, Sardinia, Southern Spain, the Azores, Washington, and San Francisco. It is also that of Balkh, Yarkand, and Diarbekr. These last-named places, and some others in the same latitude in Tartary and China, are perhaps as cold.

³ Ker Porter, *Travels*, vol. i. p. 257.   ⁴ Ibid. p. 260.

⁵ Ibid. p. 247. "Scarcely a day passes," says the writer, "without one or two persons being found frozen to death in the neighbourhood of the town" (Tabriz).

⁶ Fraser speaks of the winter in Azerbijan as lasting six or seven months (*Winter Journey*, p. 332). Birds, he says, are often frozen to death (p. 341). According to Kinneir (*Persian Empire*, p. 158), the snow remains on the mountains for nine months.

the sun pleasantly warm, the sky generally cloudless.
In the month of May the heat increases—thunder
hangs in the air—and the valleys are often close and
sultry.⁷ Frequent showers occur, and the hail-storms
are sometimes so violent as to kill the cattle in the
fields.⁸ As the summer advances the heats increase,
but the thermometer rarely reaches 90° in the shade,
and except in the narrow valleys the air is never oppressive. The autumn is generally very fine. Foggy
mornings are common; but they are succeeded by
bright, pleasant days, without wind or rain.⁹ On the
whole the climate is pronounced healthy,¹⁰ though
somewhat trying to Europeans, who do not readily
adapt themselves to a country where the range of
the thermometer is as much as 90° or 100°.

In the part of Media situated on the great plateau
—the modern Irak Ajemi—in which are the important towns of Teheran, Isfahan, Hamadan,
Kashan, Kasvin, and Koum, the climate is altogether
warmer than in Azerbijan, the summers being hotter,
and the winters shorter and much less cold. Snow
indeed covers the ground for about three months,
from early in December till March; but the thermometer rarely shows more than ten or twelve
degrees of frost, and death from cold is uncommon.¹¹
The spring sets in about the beginning of March,
and is at first somewhat cool, owing to the prevalence
of the *baude Caucasan* or north wind,¹² which blows

---

⁷ Morier, *Second Journey*, p. 303.
⁸ Kinneir, l. s. c. Compare Morier, *Second Journey*, p. 300.
⁹ Morier, pp. 243, 297, &c.
¹⁰ Kinneir, l. s. c.; Chesney, *Euphrates Expedition*, vol. i. p. 221; Morier, p. 230.
¹¹ An instance of death from cold in this region is recorded by Mr. Fraser (*Khorassan*, p. 144).
¹² Kinneir, p. 121; Ker Porter, vol. i. p. 201. According to the latter writer, this wind "continues to blow at intervals till the end of May."

from districts where the snow still lies. But after a little time the weather becomes delicious; the orchards are a mass of blossom; the rose gardens come into bloom; the cultivated lands are covered with springing crops; the desert itself wears a light livery of green. Every sense is gratified: the nightingale bursts out with a full gush of song; the air plays softly upon the cheek, and comes loaded with fragrance. Too soon, however, this charming time passes away, and the summer heats begin, in some places as early as June."² The thermometer at midday rises to 90 or 100 degrees. Hot gusts blow from the desert, sometimes with great violence. The atmosphere is described as choking;¹⁴ and in parts of the plateau it is usual for the inhabitants to quit their towns almost in a body, and retire for several months into the mountains.⁶ This extreme heat is, however, exceptional; in most parts of the plateau the summer warmth is tempered by cool breezes from the surrounding mountains, on which there is always a good deal of snow. At Hamadan, which, though on the plain, is close to the mountains, the thermometer seems scarcely ever to rise above 90°, and that degree of heat is attained only for a few hours in the day. The mornings and evenings are cool and refreshing; and altogether the climate quite justifies the choice of the Persian monarchs, who selected Ecbatana for their place of residence during the hottest portion of the year.¹ Even at Isfahan, which

---

¹³ "The heats of Teheran," says Mr. Morier, "become insupportable by the middle of June." (Second Journey, p. 351.)
¹⁴ Ibid. p. 358.
¹⁵ This is especially the practice at Teheran. (Kinneir, p. 119; Morier, p. 351; Ollivier, Voyage, tom. v. p. 91.)
¹ See Morier, Second Journey, p. 270. Compare Kinneir, Persian Empire, p. 126; Ker Porter, Travels.

is on the edge of the desert, the heat is neither extreme nor prolonged. The hot gusts which blow from the east and from the south raise the temperature at times nearly to a hundred degrees; but these oppressive winds alternate with cooler breezes from the west, often accompanied by rain; and the average highest temperature during the day in the hottest month, which is August, does not exceed 90°.

A peculiarity in the climate of the plateau which deserves to be noticed, is the extreme dryness of the atmosphere.[2] In summer the rains which fall are slight, and they are soon absorbed by the thirsty soil. There is a little dew at nights,[3] especially in the vicinity of the few streams; but it disappears with the first hour of sunshine, and the air is left without a particle of moisture. In winter the dryness is equally great; frost taking the place of heat, with the same effect upon the atmosphere. Unhealthy exhalations are thus avoided, and the salubrity of the climate is increased;[4] but the European will sometimes sigh for the soft, balmy airs of his own land, which have come flying over the sea, and seem to bring their wings to him still dank with the ocean spray.

Another peculiarity of this region, produced by the unequal rarefaction of the air over its different portions, is the occurrence, especially in spring and summer, of sudden gusts, hot or cold,[5] which blow

---

vol. ii. p. 121; Ollivier, *Voyage*, tom. v. p. 53. Ollivier says: "En été le climat est le plus doux, le plus tempéré de la Perse."

[2] Ker Porter, vol. i. p. 441; vol. ii. p. 123; Morier, p. 153; Ollivier, tom. v. pp. 190 and 209. The last-named writer mentions as a proof of the dryness, that during a long stay in the region he never saw a single small ! Morier, however, notes that he saw several (p. 154, note).

[3] Morier, p. 154.

[4] On the salubrity of Isfahan, see Morier, p. 153; Ker Porter, vol. i. p. 407.

[5] See Morier, *Second Journey*, Appendix, pp. 405-408; Ouseley, vol. iii. pp. 110-112; and the passages quoted in the next note.

CHAP. II.   EXTRAORDINARY EFFECTS OF HEAT.   49

with great violence. These gusts are sometimes accompanied ' with whirlwinds,' which sweep the country in different directions, carrying away with them leaves, branches, stubble, sand, and other light substances, and causing great annoyance to the traveller. They occur chiefly in connection with a change of wind, and are no doubt consequent on the meeting of two opposite currents. Their violence, however, is moderate, compared with that of tropical tornados, and it is not often that they do any considerable damage to the crops over which they sweep.

One further characteristic of the flat region may be noticed. The intense heat of the summer sun striking on the dry sand or the saline efflorescence of the desert, throws the air over them into such a state of quivering undulation as produces the most wonderful and varying effects, distorting the forms of objects, and rendering the most familiar strange and hard to be recognised. A mud bank furrowed by the rain will exhibit the appearance of a magnificent city, with columns, domes, minarets, and pyramids; a few stunted bushes will be transformed into a forest of stately trees; a distant mountain will, in the space of a minute, assume first the appearance of a lofty peak, then swell out at the top, and resemble a mighty mushroom, next split into several parts, and finally settle down into a flat table-land.' Occasionally, though not very often, that semblance of water is produced' which Europeans are apt to suppose the usual effect of mirage. The images of objects are re-

---

' Morier, *First Journey*, p. 174; *Second Journey*, p. 202; Ouseley, vol. iii. pp. 73 and 375.

' Fraser, *Khorasan*, p. 165, note.
' Morier, *Second Journey*, p. 292.

VOL. III.   E

flected at their base in an inverted position; the desert seems converted into a vast lake; and the thirsty traveller, advancing towards it, finds himself the victim of an illusion, which is none the less successful because he has been a thousand times forewarned of its deceptive power.

In the mountain range of Zagros and the tracts adjacent to it, the climate, owing to the great differences of elevation, is more varied than in the other parts of the ancient Media. Severe cold[9] prevails in the higher mountain regions for seven months out of the twelve, while during the remaining five the heat is never more than moderate.[10] In the low valleys, on the contrary, and in other favoured situations,[11] the winters are often milder than on the plateau; while in the summers, if the heat is not greater, at any rate it is more oppressive. Owing to the abundance of the streams and the proximity of the melting snows, the air is moist; and the damp heat, which stagnates in the valleys, breeds fever and ague.[12] Between these extremes of climate and elevation every variety is to be found; and, except in winter, a few hours' journey will almost always bring the traveller into a temperate region.

In respect of natural productiveness, Media (as already observed)[13] differs exceedingly in different, and even in adjacent, districts. The rocky ridges

---

[9] Chesney, *Euphrates Expedition*, vol. I. p. 80; Kinneir, p. 144; *Journal of the Geographical Society*, vol. x. pp. 20-22.
[10] Chesney, l. s. c. In Ardelan, which is much lower than many parts of the range, Morier found the air quite "cool" in June (*Second Journey*, p. 272). Kinneir notes that in the same region there was frost in July, 1810 (*Persian Empire*, p. 144).
[11] As at Tomirkan. (Supra, p. 33, note [4].)
[12] See Layard, *Nineveh and its Remains*, vol. i. pp. 159-165.
[13] See above, p. 7.

of the great plateau, destitute of all vegetable mould, are wholly bare and arid, admitting not the slightest degree of cultivation. Many of the mountains of Azerbijan, naked, rigid, and furrowed,[14] may compare even with these desert ranges for sterility. The higher parts of Zagros and Elburz are sometimes of the same character; but more often they are thickly clothed with forests, affording excellent timber and other valuable commodities. In the Elburz, pines are found near the summit,[15] while lower down there occur first the wild almond and the dwarf oak, and then the usual timber-trees of the country, the Oriental plane, the willow, the poplar, and the walnut.[16] The walnut grows to a large size both here and in Azerbijan, but the poplar is the wood most commonly used for building purposes.[17] In Zagros, besides most of these trees, the ash and the terebinth or turpentine-tree are common; the oak bears gall-nuts of a large size; and the gum-tragacanth plant frequently clothes the mountain-sides.[18] The valleys of this region are full of magnificent orchards, as are the low grounds and more sheltered nooks of Azerbijan. The fruit-trees comprise, besides vines and mulberries, the apple, the pear, the quince, the plum, the cherry, the almond, the nut, the chesnut, the olive, the peach, the nectarine, and the apricot.[19]

---

[14] Fraser, *Winter Journey*, p. 353.
[15] Morier, *Second Journey*, p. 362.
[16] Ibid. l. s. c.; and see also p. 354.
[17] Morier, *First Journey*, pp. 274 and 277; *Second Journey*, p. 262. The wood of the plane is preferred for furniture.
[18] Ollivier, tom. v. p. 59; Chesney, vol. I. p. 128.
[19] *Journal of the Geographical Society*, vol. x. p. 3; Ker Porter, vol. L p. 394; Rich, *Kurdistan*, pp. 106, 163, &c. It was probably from some knowledge of this tract that Virgil spoke of Media as "abounding in trees." (Georg. ii. 136. "Medorum silva ditissima terra.")

On the plains of the high plateau there is a great scarcity of vegetation. Trees of a large size grow only in the few places which are well watered, as in the neighbourhood of Hamadan, Isfahan, and in a less degree of Kashan.[20] The principal tree is the Oriental plane, which flourishes together with poplars and willows along the watercourses; cypresses also grow freely; elms and cedars are found,[21] and the orchards and gardens contain not only the fruit-trees mentioned above, but also the jujube, the cornel, the filbert, the medlar, the pistachio nut, the pomegranate, and the fig.[22] Away from the immediate vicinity of the rivers and the towns, not a tree, scarcely a bush, is to be seen. The common thorn is indeed tolerably abundant[23] in a few places; but elsewhere the tamarisk and a few other sapless shrubs[24] are the only natural products of this bare and arid region.

In remarkable contrast with the natural barrenness of this wide tract are certain favoured districts in Zagros and Azerbijan, where the herbage is constant through the summer, and sometimes only too luxuriant. Such are the rich and extensive grazing grounds of Khawah and Alishtar near Kermanshah,[25] the pastures near Ojan[26] and Marand,[27] and the cele-

[20] On the verdure and shade of Isfahan, see Ker Porter, vol. I. p. 411; on that of Hamadan, see Morier, Second Journey, p. 262, and Ker Porter, vol. II. p. 91. On Kashan, see the last-named writer, vol. I. p. 389; and compare Ollivier, tom. v. p. 169.

[21] Ker Porter notes "a species of cedar not unlike that of Lebanon" at Kashan (l. s. c.). Morier notices elms "with very thick and rich foliage," and a peculiarly "formal shape," near Isfahan (First Journey, p. 169; compare Second Journey, p. 263).

[22] Ollivier, tom. v. p. 191.
[23] Morier, Second Journey, p. 271.
[24] As the soap-wort, which is the "most common shrub" in the country between Koum and Teheran. (Morier, First Journey, p. 183.)
[25] Journal of the Geographical Society, vol. ix. p. 100.
[26] Morier, Second Journey, p. 277.
[27] Ibid. p. 302.

brated Chowal Moghan or plain of Moghan, on the lower course of the Araxes river, where the grass is said to grow sufficiently high to cover a man on horseback.²⁰ These, however, are rare exceptions to the general character of the country, which is by nature unproductive, and scarcely deserving even of the qualified encomium of Strabo.²⁹

Still Media, though deficient in natural products, is not ill adapted for cultivation. The Zagros valleys and hill-sides produce under a very rude system of agriculture, besides the fruits already noticed, rice, wheat, barley, millet, sesame, Indian corn, cotton, tobacco, mulberries, cucumbers, melons, pumpkins, and the castor-oil plant.¹ In Azerbijan the soil is almost all cultivable, and if ploughed and sown, will bring good crops of the ordinary kinds of grain.' Even on the side of the desert, where Nature has shown herself most niggardly, and may seem perhaps to deserve the reproach of Cicero, that she behaves as a step-mother to man rather than as a mother,² a certain amount of care and scientific labour may render considerable tracts fairly productive. The only want of this region is water; and if the natural deficiency of this necessary fluid can be any how supplied, all parts of the plateau will bear crops, except those which form the actual Salt Desert. In modern, and still more in ancient times, this fact has been clearly perceived, and an elaborate system of

---

²⁰ Kinneir, *Persian Empire*, p. 153, note.
²⁹ See the passage quoted at the head of this chapter.
¹ Ollivier, *Voyage*, tom. v. p. 14; Chesney, *Euphrates Expedition*, vol. i. p. 123; Rich, *Kurdistan*, pp. 60, 130, 134, &c. Manna is also a product of this region. (See above, vol. i. p. 273.)
¹ Morier, *First Journey*, pp. 261-260; *Second Journey*, p. 257; Kinneir, *Persian Empire*, p. 140.
² "Homo non ut a matre sed ut a noverca natura editus est in vitam."

artificial irrigation, suitable to the peculiar circumstances of the country, has been very widely established. The system of *kanats*, as they are called at the present day, aims at utilising to the uttermost all the small streams and rills which descend towards the desert from the surrounding mountains, and at conveying as far as possible into the plain the spring water, which is the indispensable[4] condition of cultivation in a country where—except for a few days in spring and autumn—rain scarcely ever falls. As the precious element would rapidly evaporate if exposed to the rays of the summer sun, the Iranian husbandman carries his conduit underground, laboriously tunnelling through the stiff argillaceous soil, at a depth of many feet below the surface. The mode in which he proceeds is as follows:—At intervals along the line of his intended conduit he first sinks shafts, which he then connects with one another by galleries, seven or eight feet in height, giving his galleries a slight incline, so that the water may run down them freely, and continuing them till he reaches a point where he wishes to bring the water out upon the surface of the plain.[5] Here and there, at the foot of his shafts, he digs wells, from which the fluid can readily be raised by means of a bucket and a windlass; and he thus brings under cultivation a considerable belt of land along the whole line of the *kanat*, as well as a large tract at its termination. These conduits, on which the cultivation of the plateau depends, were established at so remote a date that they were

---

[4] Ollivier says: "Il faut noter que dans presque toute la Perse il n'y a aucune sorte de culture sans arrosement." (*Voyage*, tom. v. p. 217.)

[5] Ollivier, tom. v. pp. 308, 309; Ker Porter, vol. i. p. 296; Morier, *Second Journey*, pp. 163, 164.

CHAP. II. PRODUCTIONS OF THE HIGH PLATEAU.

popularly ascribed to the mythic Semiramis,* the supposed wife of Ninus. It is thought that in ancient times they were longer and more numerous than at present,⁷ when they occur only occasionally, and seldom extend more than a few miles from the base of the hills.

By help of the irrigation thus contrived, the great plateau of Iran will produce good crops of grain, rice, wheat, barley, Indian corn, *doura*, millet, and sesame.⁸ It will also bear cotton, tobacco, saffron, rhubarb, madder, poppies which give a good opium, senna, and assafetida.⁹ Its garden vegetables are excellent, and include potatoes, cabbages, lentils, kidney-beans, peas, turnips, carrots, spinach, beet-root, and cucumbers.¹⁰ The variety of its fruit-trees has been already noticed.¹¹ The flavour of their produce is in general good, and in some cases surpassingly excellent. No quinces are so fine as those of Isfahan,¹² and no melons have a more delicate flavour.¹³ The grapes of Kasvin are celebrated, and make a remarkably good wine.¹⁴

Among the flowers of the country must be noted, first of all, its roses, which flourish in the most luxuriant abundance, and are of every variety of hue.¹⁵

---

* Strab. xvi. 1, § 2. Compare Diod. Sic. ii. 13, § 7. An excellent description of the *kanat* system is given by Polybius (x. 28, § 2).
⁷ Ollivier, p. 214. This writer also supposes that much more care was taken in ancient times to economise the water arising from the melting of the snows and from the spring rains, by means of embankments across the lower valleys of the mountains, and the formation thereby of large reservoirs (p. 214). These reservoirs would be the *ideia* of Strabo.
⁸ Ollivier, pp. 163, 108, &c.; Kinneir, p. 108.
⁹ Ollivier, p. 108; Kinneir, p. 38.
¹⁰ Chesney, *Euphrates Expedition*, vol. i. p. 80; Ollivier, l. s. c.; Kinneir, p. 38.   ¹¹ Supra, p. 52.
¹² Kinneir, p. 88; Ollivier, p. 191; Morier, *First Journey*, p. 230.
¹³ Ollivier, pp. 101, 102.
¹⁴ Morier, *Second Journey*, p. 203.
¹⁵ Ker Porter, vol. i. p. 410; *Geographical Journal*, vol. x. p. 29; Ollivier, tom. v. p. 40, &c.

The size to which the tree will grow is extraordinary, standards sometimes exceeding the height of fourteen or fifteen feet.[14] Lilacs, jasmines, and many other flowering shrubs are common in the gardens, while among wild flowers may be noticed hollyhocks, lilies, tulips, crocuses, anemones, lilies of the valley, fritillaries, gentians, primroses, convolvuluses, chrysanthemums, heliotropes, pinks, water-lilies, ranunculuses, jonquils, narcissuses, hyacinths, mallows, stocks, violets, a fine campanula (*Michauria levigata*), a mint (*Nepeta longiflora*), several sages, salsolas, and fagonias.[17] In many places the wild flowers during the spring months cover the ground, painting it with a thousand dazzling or delicate hues.[18]

The mineral products of Media are numerous and valuable. Excellent stone of many kinds abounds in almost every part of the country, the most important and valuable being the famous Tabriz marble. This curious substance appears to be a petrifaction formed by natural springs, which deposit carbonate of lime in large quantities. It is found only in one place, on the flanks of the hills, not far from the Urumiyeh lake. The slabs are used for tombstones, for the skirting of rooms, and for the pavements of baths and palaces; when cut thin they often take the place of glass in windows, being semi-transparent.[19] The marble is commonly of a pale yellow colour, but occasionally it is streaked with red, green, or copper-coloured veins.[20]

---

[14] Ollivier, p. 184; Ker Porter, vol. L p. 337.
[17] A correct account of the botany of Persia is still a desideratum. The above particulars are collected chiefly from Ollivier and Chardin.
[18] Morier, *First Journey*, pp. 263 and 300; Rich, *Kurdistan*, p. 360. Hence the abundance of excellent honey. (Rich, p. 142.)
[19] *Geographical Journal*, vol. x. p. 4; Morier, *Second Journey*, p. 285; Ker Porter, vol. ii. p. 527.
[20] Morier, l. s. c.

In metals the country is thought to be rich, but no satisfactory examination of it has been as yet made. Iron, copper, and native steel are derived from mines actually at work; while Europeans have observed indications of lead, arsenic, and antimony in Azerbijan, in Kurdistan, and in the rocky ridges which intersect the desert.[1] Tradition speaks of a time when gold and silver were procured from mountains near Takht-i-Suleïman,[2] and it is not unlikely that they may exist both there and in the Zagros range. Quartz, the well-known matrix of the precious metal, abounds in Kurdistan.[3]

Of all the mineral products none is more abundant than salt.[4] On the side of the desert, and again near Tabriz, at the mouth of the Aji Su, are vast plains, which glisten with the substance, and yield it readily to all who care to gather it up. Saline springs and streams are also numerous,[5] from which salt can be obtained by evaporation. But, besides these sources of supply, rock salt is found in places,[6] and this is largely quarried, and is preferred by the natives.[7]

Other important products of the earth are saltpetre, which is found in the Elburz,[8] and in Azerbijan;[9] sulphur, which abounds in the same regions, and

---

[1] Chardin, *Voyages en Perse*, tom. iii. p. 29; Ker Porter, *Travels*, vol. i. pp. 206 and 380; *Geographical Journal*, vol. x. p. 56; Morier, *First Journey*, pp. 283, 284; Ouseley, *Travels*, vol. iii. p. 406.
[2] *Geographical Journal*, vol. x. p. 55. A mountain in this quarter is called by the natives *Zerreh Shurdn*, or the mountain of the "Goldwashers."
[3] Chesney, *Euphrates Expedition*, p. 72.

[4] Chardin says: "Il n'y a rien de plus commun en Perse quo le sel." (*Voyages*, tom. iii. p. 30.)
[5] Supra, p. 9, note [7].
[6] *Geographical Journal*, vol. x. p. 62; Chardin, l. s. c.; Morier, *Second Journey*, pp. 257 and 288; Rich, *Kurdistan*, p. 123.
[7] Morier, *Second Journey*, p. 288.
[8] Kinnair, p. 40; Chardin, tom. iii. p. 29.
[9] Morier, *First Journey*, p. 284.

likewise on the high plateau;[10] alum,[11] which is quarried near Tabriz; naphtha and gypsum, which are found in Kurdistan;[12] and talc, which exists in the mountains near Koum,[13] in the vicinity of Tabriz,[14] and probably in other places.

The chief wild animals which have been observed within the limits of the ancient Media are the lion, the tiger, the leopard, the bear, the beaver, the jackal, the wolf, the wild ass, the ibex or wild goat, the wild sheep, the stag, the antelope, the wild boar, the fox, the hare, the rabbit, the ferret, the rat, the jerbon, the porcupine, the mole, and the marmot. The lion and tiger are exceedingly rare: they seem to be found only in Azerbijan,[15] and we may perhaps best account for their presence there by considering that a few of these animals occasionally stray out of Mazenderan, which is their only proper locality in this part of Asia. Of all the beasts, the most abundant are the stag and the wild goat, which are numerous in the Elburz, and in parts of Azerbijan,[16] the wild boar, which abounds both in Azerbijan and in the country about Hamadan,[17] and the jackal, which is found everywhere. Bears flourish in Zagros, antelopes in Azerbijan, in the Elburz, and on the plains near Sultaniyeh.[18] The wild ass is found only in

---

[10] Kinneir, l. s. c.; Morier, *First Journey*, p. 284; *Second Journey*, p. 355; Rich, *Kurdistan*, p. 123; Ker Porter, vol. i. p. 374.
[11] *Geographical Journal*, vol. x. p. 62. Alum is also found in the Zagros range. (Rich, l. s. c.)
[12] Ibid. pp. 123 and 231.
[13] Ker Porter, vol. i. p. 380.
[14] Morier, *Second Journey*, p. 289.
[15] Sir W. Ouseley heard of lions near Koum, but he saw no signs of them. (*Travels*, vol. iii. p. 108.) Mr. Morier observed marks of a lion's foot in Mount Sohond, which impends over Tabriz. (*Second Journey*, p. 204.) He heard of tigers in the same region, and saw the skin of one which had been killed. (Ibid. p. 218.)
[16] Morier, *Second Journey*, pp. 241, 359, 364.
[17] Morier, pp. 241, 302; Ollivier, tom. iii. p. 64.
[18] Chesney, *Travels*, vol. iii. pp. 213, 217, and 240; Morier, *Second Journey*, p. 205.

the desert parts of the high plateau;" the beaver only in Lake Zerilar, near Suleimaniyeh."

The Iranian wild ass differs in some respects from the Mesopotamian. His skin is smooth, like that of a deer, and of a reddish colour, the belly and hinder parts partaking of a silvery grey; his head and ears are large and somewhat clumsy; but his neck is fine, and his legs are beautifully slender. His mane is short and black, and he has a black tuft at the end of his tail, but no dark line runs along his back or crosses his shoulders." The Persians call him the *gur-khur*, and chase him with occasional success, regarding his flesh as a great delicacy. He appears to be the *Asinus onager* of naturalists, a distinct species from the *Asinus hemippus* of Mesopotamia, and the *Asinus hemionus* of Thibet and Tartary."

It is doubtful whether some kind of wild cattle does not still inhabit the more remote tracts of Kurdistan. The natives mention among the animals of their country "the mountain ox;" and though it has been suggested that the beast intended is the elk," it is perhaps as likely to be the aurochs, which seems certainly to have been a native of the adjacent country of Mesopotamia in ancient times." At any rate, until Zagros has been thoroughly explored by Europeans, it must remain uncertain what animal is meant.

" Ouseley saw them near Kasvin (vol. iii. p. 381); Ker Porter in the desert below Isfahan (vol. i. pp. 459-461).

" Rich, *Kurdistan*, p. 186.

" See the description of Ker Porter (l. s. c.), who carefully examined a specimen killed by one of his party. Morier and Ollivier differ from him with respect to the existence of a line down the back and a bar across the shoulders (Ollivier, tom. iii. p. 65; Morier, *Second Journey*, p. 201); but they appear to have had less satisfactory means of judging.

" See the *Annals and Magazine of Natural History*, vol. vi. No. 34, p. 243. " Rich, *Kurdistan*, p. 237.
" Supra, vol. I. p. 284; vol. II. pp. 132, 133.

Meanwhile we may be tolerably sure that, besides the species enumerated, Mount Zagros contains within its folds some large and rare ruminant.

Among the birds the most remarkable are the eagle, the bustard, the pelican, the stork, the pheasant, several kinds of partridges, the quail, the woodpecker, the bee-eater, the hoopoe, and the nightingale. Besides these, doves and pigeons, both wild

Pigeon towers near Isfahan.

and tame,[m] are common; as are swallows, goldfinches, sparrows, larks, blackbirds, thrushes, linnets, mag-

---

[m] Tame pigeons are bred on a large scale, mainly for the sake of their dung, which is the favourite manure of the melon-grounds. All travellers remark the numerous pigeon-towers, especially in the neighbourhood of Isfahan, some of which bring in an income of two or three hundred pounds a-year. (See Kinneir, p. 110; Chardin, tom. iii. p. 39; Morier, *First Journey*, p. 155; *Second Journey*, p. 140.)

pies, crows, hawks, falcons, teal, snipe, wild ducks, and many other kinds of waterfowl. The most common partridge is a red-legged species (*Caccabis chukar* of naturalists), which is unable to fly far, and is hunted until it drops.[28] Another kind, common both in Azerbijan and in the Elburz,[29] is the black-breasted partridge (*Perdix nigra*)—a bird not known in many countries. Besides these, there is a small grey partridge in the Zagros range, which the Kurds call *seska*.[30] The bee-eater (*Merops Persicus*) is rare. It is a bird of passage, and only visits Media in the autumn, preparatory to retreating into the warm district of Mazenderan for the winter months.[30] The hoopoe (*Upupa*) is probably still rarer, since very few travellers mention it.[30] The woodpecker is found in Zagros, and is a beautiful bird, red and grey in colour.[31]

Media is, on the whole, but scantily provided with fish. Lake Urumiyeh produces none, as its waters are so salt that they even destroy all the river-fish which enter them.[1] Salt streams, like the Aji Su, are equally non-productive, and the fresh-water rivers of the plateau fall so low in summer that fish cannot become numerous in them. Thus it is only in Zagros, in Azerbijan, and in the Elburz, that the streams furnish any considerable quantity. The

---

[28] Rich says: "Hundreds of partridges are taken by parties of sportsmen stationed on opposite hills, who frighten the covey by shooting as soon as it comes in their direction. The birds at last become alarmed and confused, and drop to the ground, when they are easily taken." (*Kurdistan*, p. 237.) Compare 1 Sam. xxvi. 20.

[29] Morier, *Second Journey*, pp. 234 and 359.

[30] Rich, *Kurdistan*, p. 143.

[30] Ollivier, *Voyages*, tom. v. p. 125.

[30] I have found a mention of the hoopoe only in Morier, who saw it near Kasvin. (*First Journey*, p. 255.)

[31] Rich, *Kurdistan*, p. 164.

[1] *Geographical Journal*, vol. iii. p. 56; vol. x. p. 7; Morier, *Second Journey*, p. 286; Kinneir, p. 155.

kinds most common are barbel, carp, dace, bleak, and gudgeons.² In a comparatively few streams, more especially those of Zagros, trout are found, which are handsome and of excellent quality.³ The river of Isfahan produces a kind of cray-fish, which is taken in the bushes along its banks, and is very delicate eating.⁴

It is remarkable that fish are caught not only in the open streams of Media, but also in the *kanats* or underground conduits, from which the light of day is very nearly excluded. They appear to be of one sort only, viz., barbel, but are abundant, and often grow to a considerable size. Chardin supposed them to be unfit for food;⁵ but a later observer declares that, though of no great delicacy, they are "perfectly sweet and wholesome."⁶

Of reptiles the most common are snakes, lizards, and tortoises. In the long grass of the Moghan district, on the lower course of the Araxes, the snakes are so numerous and venomous, that many parts of the plain are thereby rendered impassable in the summer-time.⁷ A similar abundance of this reptile near the western entrance of the Girduni Siyaluk pass⁸ induces the natives to abstain from using it, except in winter.⁹ Lizards of many forms and hues¹⁰ disport themselves about the rocks and stones, some

---

² Morier, *Second Journey*, p. 253; Chardin, tom. iii. p. 44; Ouseley, vol. iii. p. 50; Rich, *Kurdistan*, p. 60.
³ Rich, p. 67; Fraser, *Travels in Kurdistan*, vol. i. p. 7. Trout occur also in the Elburz. (Ouseley, vol. iii. p. 125.)
⁴ Chardin, tom. iii. p. 44. "Un manger fort délicat." ⁵ Ibid.
⁶ Fraser, *Khorasan*, p. 400.
⁷ Kinneir, p. 153, note; Morier, *Second Journey*, p. 250; Chesney, *Euphrates Expedition*, vol. i. p. 82.
⁸ See above, p. 29, note ⁿ.
⁹ Sir H. Rawlinson, MS. notes. Compare Pliny, *H. N.* vi. 14: "Præterea serpentium multitudo, nisi byeme, transitum non sinit."
¹⁰ Ker Porter, vol. i. pp. 390, 391.

quite small, others two feet or more in length." They are quite harmless, and appear to be in general very tame. Land tortoises are also common in the sandy regions.¹³ In Kurdistan there is a remarkable frog, with a smooth skin and of an apple-green colour, which lives chiefly in trees, roosting in them at night, and during the day employing itself in catching flies and locusts, which it strikes with its fore paw, as a cat strikes a bird or a mouse.¹³

Among insects travellers chiefly notice the mosquito,¹⁴ which is in many places a cruel torment; the centipede, which grows to an unusual size;¹⁵ the locust, of which there is more than one variety; and the scorpion, whose sting is sometimes fatal.

The destructive locust (the *Acridium peregrinum*, probably) comes suddenly into Kurdistan¹⁶ and southern

The destructive Locust (*Acridium peregrinum*).

Media¹⁷ in clouds that obscure the air, moving with a slow and steady flight, and with a sound like that of heavy rain, and settling in myriads on the fields, the gardens, the trees, the terraces of the houses, and even the streets, which they sometimes cover completely. Where they fall, vegetation presently

---

¹² Ker Porter measured one, and found it exceed two feet (l. a. c.). Chardin says that some which he saw were an ell in length. (*Voyages*, tom. iii. p. 38.)
¹³ Ker Porter, l. a. c.
¹⁴ Rich, *Kurdistan*, p. 173.
¹⁵ Ibid. p. 172; Chardin, tom. iii. p. 39; Ouseley, vol. iii. p. 122.
¹⁶ Chardin, l. a. c. This writer adds that its bite is dangerous, and has been known to prove fatal in some cases. But recent travellers do not confirm this statement.
¹⁶ Rich, p. 171.
¹⁷ Kinneir, p. 43; Chardin, l. a. c.

disappears; the leaves, and even the stems of the plants, are devoured; the labours of the husbandman through many a weary month perish in a day; and the curse of famine is brought upon the land which but now enjoyed the prospect of an abundant harvest. It is true that the devourers are themselves devoured to some extent by the poorer sort of people;[18] but the compensation is slight and temporary; in a few days, when all verdure is gone, either the swarms move to fresh pastures, or they perish and cover the fields with their dead bodies, while the desolation which they have created continues.

Another kind of locust, observed by Mr. Rich in Kurdistan, is called by the natives *shira-kulla*, a name evidently identical with the *chargôl* of the Jews,[19] and perhaps the best clue which we possess to the identification of that species. Mr. Rich describes it as "a large insect, about four inches long, with no wings, but with a kind of sword projecting from the tail. It bites," he says, "pretty severely, but does no harm to the cultivation."[20] We may recognise in this description a variety of the great green grasshopper (*Locusta viridissima*), many species of which are destitute of wings, or have wing-covers only, and those of a very small size.[21]

The scorpion of the country (*Scorpio crassicauda*) has been represented as peculiarly venomous,[22] more especially that which abounds in the city and neigh-

---

[18] Chardin, tom. ii. p. 221.
[19] Lev. xi. 22. The resemblance of the word *shira-kulla* to *chargôl* (חרגל) is striking, and can scarcely be a mere accident. *Shira-kulla*, however, is translated "the lion locust," a meaning which cannot possibly be given to *chargôl*.
[20] *Kurdistan*, p. 195.
[21] Cuvier's *Animal Kingdom*, edition of Carpenter and Westwood, p. 561.
[22] Chardin, tom. iii. p. 38.

bourhood of Kashan;[a] but the most judicious observers deny that there is any difference between the Kashan scorpion and that of other parts of the plateau,[24] while at the same time they maintain that,

The Scorpion (*Scorpio crassicauda*).

if the sting be properly treated, no danger need be apprehended from it. The scorpion infests houses, hiding itself under cushions and coverlets, and stings the moment it is pressed upon; some caution is thus requisite in avoiding it; but it hurts no one unless molested, and many Europeans have resided for years in the country without having ever been stung by it.[b]

The domestic animals existing at present within the limits of the ancient Media are the camel, the horse, the mule, the ass, the cow, the goat, the sheep, the dog, the cat, and the buffalo. The camel is the ordinary beast of burden in the flat country, and can carry an enormous weight. Three kinds are em-

---

[a] Ollivier, tom. v. p. 170; Ker Porter, vol. I. p. 390; Ouseley, vol. iii. pp. 87-89.
[24] Ollivier, p. 171; Kinneir, p. 43.
[b] Ker Porter remarks that neither he himself, nor any of his "people," were ever stung during their stay in Persia (l. s. c.). So Ouseley (p. 91).

ployed—the Bactrian or two-humped camel, which is coarse and low; the taller and lighter Arabian breed; and a cross between the two, which is called *ner*, and is valued very highly." The ordinary burden of the Arabian camel is from seven to eight hundred-weight; while the Bactrian variety is said to be capable of bearing a load nearly twice as heavy."

Next to the camel, as a beast of burden, must be placed the mule. The mules of the country are small, but finely proportioned, and carry a considerable weight.¹ They travel thirty miles a day with ease,² and are preferred for journeys on which it is necessary to cross the mountains. The ass is very inferior, and is only used by the poorer classes.³

Two distinct breeds of horses are now found in Media, both of which seem to be foreign—the Turkoman and the Arabian. The Turkoman is a large, powerful, enduring animal, with long legs, a light body, and a big head.⁴ The Arab is much smaller, but perfectly shaped, and sometimes not greatly inferior to the very best produce of Nejd.⁵ A third breed is obtained by an intermixture of these two, which is called the *bid-pai*, or "wind-footed," and is the most prized of all.⁶

The dogs are of various breeds, but the most esteemed is a large kind of greyhound, which some suppose to have been introduced into this part of

---

" Chesney, *Euphrates Expedition*, vol. I. p. 82.
" Ibid. p. 682.
¹ Chesney says that the ordinary burden of a mule in Persia is three hundred weight. (*Euphrates Expedition*, vol. i. p. 81.)
² Ibid. l. s. c.
³ Chardin, *Voyages*, tom. iii. p. 33;

Chesney, l. s. c.
⁴ Kinneir, *Persian Empire*, p. 40; Fraser, *Khorassan*, pp. 268, 270. Fraser observes, that "on the whole the Turcoman horses approach more to the character of the English horse than any other breed in the East."
⁵ Kinneir, l. s. c.
⁶ Chesney, l. s. c.

Asia by the Macedonians, and which is chiefly employed in the chase of the antelope.[7] The animal is about the height of a full-sized English greyhound, but rather stouter; he is deep-chested, has long, smooth hair, and the tail considerably feathered.[8] His pace is inferior to that of our greyhounds, but in strength and sagacity he far surpasses them.[9]

We do not find many of the products of Media celebrated by ancient writers. Of its animals, those which had the highest reputation were its horses, distinguished into two breeds, an ordinary kind, of which Media produced annually many thousands,[10] and a kind of rare size and excellence, known under the name of Nisæan. These last are celebrated by Herodotus,[11] Strabo,[12] Arrian,[13] Ammianus Marcellinus,[14] Suidas,[15] and others. They are said to have been of a peculiar shape;[16] and they were equally famous for size, speed, and stoutness.[17] Strabo remarks that they resembled the horses known in

---

[7] The antelope is commonly chased by the falcon and greyhound in combination. The falcon, when loosed, makes straight at the game, and descending on its head, either strikes it to the ground, or at least greatly checks its course. If shaken off, it will strike again and again, at once so frightening and retarding the animal that the dogs easily reach it. (See Chardin, tom. iii. p. 42, and Kinneir, p. 42. Compare the similar practice of the Mesopotamian Arabs, described in Layard's *Nineveh and Babylon*, p. 482.)

[8] Ollivier, tom. v. p. 104; Chesney, vol. i. p. 587; Layard, p. 482, note.

[9] See the narrative of Ker Porter, *Travels*, vol. i. pp. 444, 445.

[10] Diodorus Siculus says that the great horse pastures near Baginstan nourished at one time 100,000 horses (xvii. 110, § 6). Strabo tells us that Media furnished annually to the Persian king 3000 horses as a part of its fixed tribute (xi. 13, § 8). Polybius speaks of the vast number of horses in Media, which supplied with those animals "almost all Asia." (ὀχεδὸν ἅπασαν χορηγεῖ τὴν Ἀσίαν. Polyb. x. 27. § 2).

[11] Herod. vii. 40. Compare iii. 106 and i. 189.

[12] Strab. xi. 13, § 7.

[13] Arrian, *Exp. Alex.* vii. 13. Arrian gives the form Νυσαῖοι, in place of the Νισαῖοι of Herodotus, and the Νησαῖοι of Strabo.

[14] Amm. Marc. xxiii. 6.

[15] Suidas, ad voc. *Νισαιον*.

[16] Ἰδιόμορφοι. Strab. l. s. c.

[17] Μέγιστοι (Strab.), ἄριστοι (Suid.), ὥριστα (Strab.).

his own time as Parthian;[19] and this observation seems distinctly to connect them with the Turkoman breed mentioned above, which is derived exactly from the old Parthian country. In colour they were often, if not always, white. We have no representation on the monuments which we can regard as certainly intended for a Nisæan horse, but perhaps the subjoined figure from Persepolis may be a Persian sketch of the animal.[19]

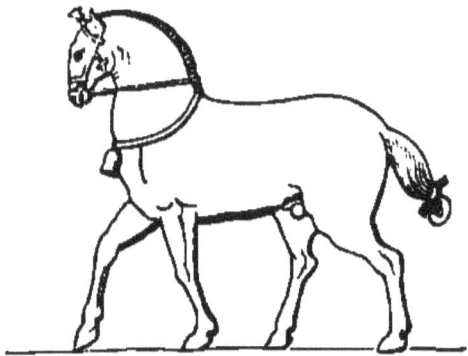

Persepolitan horse, perhaps Nisæan.

The mules and small cattle (sheep and goats) were in sufficient repute to be required, together with horses, in the annual tribute paid to the Persian king.[20]

Of vegetable products assigned to Media by ancient writers the most remarkable is the "Median apple" or citron.[21] Pliny says it was the sole tree for which

---

[19] Loc. cit.
[19] The horns represented, though not large according to English notions, is considerably above the usual standard on the Persian monuments.
[20] Strab. xi. 13, § 8.
[21] It has been questioned whether the "Malum medicum" was the orange or the citron. I decide in favour of the citron, on account of the description in Dioscorides. Τὸ μῆλον ἐπίμηκες (oblong), ἐρρυτιδωμένον (wrinkled), χρυσίζον τῇ χρόᾳ, κ.τ.λ. (De Mat. Med. i. § 166.)

Media was famous,[a] and that it would only grow there and in Persia.[b] Theophrastus,[c] Dioscorides,[d] Virgil,[e] and other writers, celebrate its wonderful qualities, distinctly assigning it to the same region. The citron, however, will not grow in the country which has here been termed Media.[f] It flourishes only in the warm tract between Shiraz and the Persian Gulf, and in the low sheltered region south of the Caspian, the modern Ghilan and Mazenderan. No doubt it was the inclusion of this latter region within the limits of Media by many of the later geographers that gave to this product of the Caspian country an appellation which is really a misnomer.

Another product to which Media gave name, and probably with more reason, was a kind of clover or lucerne, which was said to have been introduced into Greece by the Persians in the reign of Darius,[g] and which was afterwards cultivated largely in Italy.[h] Strabo considers this plant to have been the chief food of the Median horses,[i] while Dioscorides assigns it certain medicinal qualities.[j] Clover is still cultivated in the Elburz region,[k] but horses are now fed almost entirely on straw and barley.

Media was also famous for its silphium, or assafetida, a plant which the country still produces,[l]

---

[a] *H. N.* xii. 8. "Nec alia arbor laudatur in Media."
[b] Ibid. "Nisi apud Medos et in Perside nasci noluit."
[c] *Hist. Plant.* iv. 4.
[d] *De Mat. Med.* l. § 106.
[e] *Georg.* ii. 126-135.

Flos ad primos totax; animum et olentia Medi
Ora fovent illo, et senibus medicantur anhelis."

[f] Ollivier, tom. v. p. 101; Chesney, vol. i. p. 80.
[g] Pliny, *H. N.* xviii. 16.
[h] See Varro, *De Re Rustica*, I. 42; Virg. *Georg.* l. 215; Pliny, l. s. c.
[i] Strab. xl. 13, § 7.
[j] *De Mat. Med.* ii. § 176; iv. § 18.
[k] See Morier, *Second Journey*, p. 361.
[l] Chesney, vol. I. p. 80; Chardin, tom. iii. p. 17.

though not in any large quantity. No drug was in higher repute with the ancients for medicinal purposes; and though the Median variety was a coarse kind, inferior in repute, not only to the Cyrenaic, but also to the Parthian and the Syrian,[34] it seems to have been exported both to Greece and Rome,[35] and to have been largely used by druggists, however little esteemed by physicians.[36]

The other vegetable products which Media furnished, or was believed to furnish, to the ancient world, were bdellium, amomum, cardamomum, gum tragacanth, wild-vine oil, and sagapenum, or the *ferula Persica*.[37] Of these, gum tragacanth is still largely produced, and is an important article of commerce.[38] Wild vines abound in Zagros[39] and Elburz, but no oil is at present made from them. Bdellium, if it is benzoin, amomum, and cardamomum were perhaps rather imported through Media[40] than the actual produce of the country, which is too cold in the winter to grow any good spices.

The mineral products of Media noted by the ancient writers are nitre, salt, and certain gems, as emeralds, lapis lazuli, and the following obscurer kinds, the

---

[34] Pliny, *H. N.* xxii. 23. Compare Strab. xi. 13, § 7.
[35] Diosc. *De Mat. Med.* iii. 84; Plin. *H. N.* xix. 3.
[36] Compare Strab. xi. 13, § 7 ad fin. with Diosc. iii. 84.
[37] Bdellium is called a Median product by Pliny (*H. N.* xii. 9); amomum by Pliny and Dioscorides (*De Mat. Med.* i. § 14); gum tragacanth by Pliny (xiii. 21) and Theophrastus (*De Hist. Plant.* ix. 1); sagapenum by Dioscorides (iii. 85); wild-vine oil (*Œnanthe*) by Pliny (xii. 28); and cardamomum by the same writer (xii. 13). Theophrastus expresses a doubt whether amomum and cardamomum came from Media or from India (viii. 7).
[38] Ollivier, tom. v. p. 343.
[39] Rich, *Kurdistan*, p. 144.
[40] See above, note [37]. Kuhn argues that this was the case also with the Silphium or Assafœtida, which (he thinks) is scarcely to be found in Media Proper. (See his edition of Dioscorides, vol. ii. p. 530.)

zathene, the *yassinades,* and the *narcissitis.* The nitre of Media is noticed by Pliny, who says it was procured in small quantities, and was called "halmyraga."[1] It was found in certain dry-looking glens, where the ground was white with it, and was obtained there purer than in other places. Saltpetre is still derived from the Elburz range, and also from Azerbijan.[2]

The salt of Lake Urumiyeh is mentioned by Strabo, who says that it forms naturally on the surface,[3] which would imply a far more complete saturation of the water than at present exists, even in the driest seasons. The gems above mentioned are assigned to Media chiefly by Pliny. The Median emeralds, according to him, were of the largest size; they varied considerably, sometimes approaching to the character of the sapphire, in which case they were apt to be veiny, and to have flaws in them.[4] They were far less esteemed than the emeralds of many other countries. The Median lapis lazuli,[5] on the other hand, was the best of its kind. It was of three colours—light blue, dark blue, and purple. The golden specks, however, with which it was sprinkled —really spots of yellow pyrites—rendered it useless to the gem-engravers of Pliny's time.[6] The *zathene,*

---

[1] Plin. *H. N.* xxxi. 10.
[2] See above, p. 57, notes [8] and [9].
[3] Strab. xi. 13, § 2. Λίμνη ἔχει τὴν Σπαῦταν, ἐν ᾗ ἅλες ἐπιανθοῦντες πήγνυνται.
[4] *H. N.* xxxvii. 5. Compare Solinus, *Polyhist.* 20.
[5] Pliny's name for this gem is "sapphiros;" but it has been well shown by Mr. King that his "sapphiros" is the lapis lazuli, and his

"hyacinthus" the sapphire. (*Antique Gems,* pp. 44–47.)
[6] *H. N.* xxxvii. 8. Neither the lapis lazuli nor the emerald are now found within the limits of Media. The former abounds in Bactria, near Fyzabad; and the latter is occasionally found in the same region. (Fraser, *Khorasan,* Appendix, pp. 105, 106.)

the *gassinades*, and the *narcissitis*, were gems of inferior value.[7] As they have not yet been identified with any known species, it will be unnecessary to prolong the present chapter by a description of them.

---

[7] See Plin. *H. N.* xxxvii. 10 and 11. The *narcissitis* is mentioned also by Dionysius. (See the passage placed at the head of the first chapter.)

CHAPTER III.

CHARACTER, MANNERS AND CUSTOMS, ART, &c., OF THE PEOPLE.

"Pugnatrix natio et formidanda."—AMM. MARC. XXIII. 6.

THE ethnic character of the Median people is at the present day scarcely a matter of doubt. The close connection which all history, sacred and profane, establishes between them and the Persians,[1] the evidence of their proper names[2] and of their language,[3] so far as it is known to us, together with the express statements of Herodotus[4] and Strabo,[5] combine to prove that they belonged to that branch of the human family known to us as the Arian or Iranic, a leading subdivision of the great Indo-European race.

---

[1] On this connection see Dan. v. 28 ("Thy kingdom is divided and given to the Medes and Persians"), vi. 8, 12, 15 ("the law of the Medes and Persians"), Esther i. 3 ("the power of Persia and Media"), i. 14 ("the princes of Persia and Media"), i. 19 ("the laws of the Persians and the Medes"), x. 2 ("the book of the chronicles of Media and Persia"); and compare Herod. i. 102, 130; Æsch. *Pers.* 781-775; Xen. *Cyrop.* i. 2, § 1, et passim; Beh. *Ins.* col. i. par. 10, § 10; par. 11, § 7; par. 12, § 3; par. 13, § 2; par. 14, § 7. Medes were frequently employed as generals by the Persians. (See Herod. i. 156, 162; vi. 94; Beh. *Ins.* col. ii. par. 14, § 6; col. iii. par. 14, § 3.) The closeness of the connection is perhaps most strikingly shown by the indifferent use in the Greek writers of the expressions τὰ Περσικά and τὰ Μηδικά for the Persian war, ὁ Πέρσης and ὁ Μῆδος for the invader. Compare μηδίζειν, μηδισμός, and the like.

[2] See the analysis of the Median and Persian Proper Names in the author's *Herodotus*, vol. iii. pp. 444-455, 2nd edition.

[3] See the author's *Herodotus*, vol. i. p. 652, note [6].

[4] Herod. vii. 62. Οἱ Μῆδοι ἐκαλέοντο πάλαι πρὸς πάντων Ἄριοι.

[5] Strab. xv. 2, § 8. Ἐπεκτείνεται δὲ τοὔνομα τῆς Ἀριανῆς μέχρι μέρους τινὸς καὶ Περσῶν καὶ Μήδων..... εἰσὶ γάρ πως καὶ ὁμόγλωττοι παρὰ μικρόν.

The tie of a common language, common manners and customs, and to a great extent a common belief, united in ancient times all the dominant tribes of the great plateau, extending even beyond the plateau in one direction to the Jaxartes (Syhun) and in another to the Hyphasis (Sutlej). Persians, Medes, Sagartians, Chorasmians, Bactrians, Sogdians, Hyrcanians, Sarangians, Gandarians, and Sanskritic Indians, belonged all to a single stock, differing from one another probably not much more than now differ the various subdivisions of the Teutonic or the Slavonic race.* Between the tribes at the two extremities of the Arian territory the divergence was no doubt considerable; but between any two neighbouring tribes the difference was probably in most cases exceedingly slight. At any rate this was the case towards the west, where the Medes and Persians, the two principal sections of the Arian body, are scarcely distinguishable from one another in any of the features which constitute ethnic type.

The general physical character of the ancient Arian race is best gathered from the sculptures of the Achæmenian kings,' which exhibit to us a very noble variety of the human species—a form tall, graceful, and stately; a physiognomy handsome and pleasing, often somewhat resembling the Greek;*

---

* See the author's *Herodotus*, vol. i. pp. 550-555, 2nd edition.

† The only certain representations of actual Medes which the sculptures furnish are the prostrate figure and the third standing rebel in the Behistun bas-relief. But the artist in this sculpture makes no pretence of marking ethnic difference by a variety in the physiognomy.

‡ Dr. Prichard observes of the type in question: "The outline of the countenance is here *not strictly* Grecian, for it is peculiar; but it is noble and dignified; and if the expression is not full of life and genius, it is intellectual and indicative of reflection. The shape of the head is entirely Indo-European, and has nothing that recalls the Tartar or Mongolian." (*Natural History of Man*, p. 173.)

the forehead high and straight, the nose nearly in the same line, long and well formed, sometimes markedly aquiline, the upper lip short, commonly shaded by a moustache, the chin rounded and generally covered with a curly beard. The hair evi-

Arian physiognomy (Persepolis).

dently grew in great plenty, and the race was proud of it. On the top of the head it was worn smooth, but it was drawn back from the forehead and twisted into a row or two of crisp curls, while at the same time it was arranged into a large mass of similar small close ringlets at the back of the head and over the ears.

Of the Median women we have no representations upon the sculptures; but we are informed by Xenophon that they were remarkable for their stature and their beauty.[9] The same qualities were observable in the women of Persia, as we learn from Plutarch,[10] Ammianus Marcellinus,[11] and others. The Arian races seem in old times to have treated women with a certain chivalry, which allowed the full development of their physical powers, and rendered them specially attractive alike to their own husbands and to the men of other nations.

The modern Persian is a very degenerate representative of the ancient Arian stock. Slight and supple in person, with quick, glancing eyes, delicate features, and a vivacious manner, he lacks the dignity and strength, the calm repose and simple grace of the race from which he is sprung. Fourteen centuries of subjection to despotic sway have left their stamp upon his countenance and his frame, which, though still retaining some traces of the original type, have been sadly weakened and lowered by so long a term of subservience. Probably the wild Kurd or Lur of the present day more nearly corresponds in physique to the ancient Mede than do the softer inhabitants of the great plateau.

---

[9] Xen. *Anab.* iii. 2, § 25. In accordance with his statement in this place, Xenophon makes the daughter of Cyaxares, whom he marries to Cyrus the Great, an extraordinary beauty. (*Cyrop.* viii. 5, § 28.)

[10] Plut. *Vit. Alexand.* p. 676, D.
[11] Amm. Marc. xxiv. 14. "Ex virginibus, quae speciosae sunt captae, ut in Perside, ubi feminarum pulchritudo excellit." Compare Quint. Curt. iii. 11; Arrian, *Exp. Alex.* iv. 19, &c.

COURAGE.

Among the moral characteristics of the Medes, the one most obvious is their bravery. "Pugnatrix natio et formidanda," says Ammianus Marcellinus in the fourth century of our era, summing up in a few words the general judgment of antiquity.[a] Originally equal, if not superior, to their close kindred, the Persians, they were throughout the whole period of Persian supremacy only second to them in courage and warlike qualities. Mardonius, when allowed to take his choice out of the entire host of Xerxes, selected the Median troops in immediate succession to the Persians.[1] Similarly, when the time for battle came he kept the Medes near himself, giving them their place in the line close to that of the Persian contingent.[2] It was no doubt on account of their valour, as Diodorus suggests,[3] that the Medes were chosen to make the first attack upon the Greek position at Thermopylæ, where though unsuccessful they evidently showed abundant courage.[4] In the earlier times, before riches and luxury had eaten out the strength of the race, their valour and military prowess must have been even more conspicuous. It was then especially that Media deserved to be called, as she is in Scripture, "*the* mighty one of the heathen"[5] —"*the* terrible of the nations."[6]

Her valour, undoubtedly, was of the merciless kind. There was no tenderness, no hesitancy about it. Not only did her armies "dash to pieces" the fighting men of the nations opposed to her, allowing appa-

---

[a] Amm. Marc. xxiii. 6. Compare Nic. Dam. Fr. 9; Diod. Sic. xi. 6; Herod. i. 95; &c.
[1] Herod. viii. 113.
[2] Ibid. ix. 31.
[3] Diod. Sic. xi. 6, § 3. Δι' ἀνδρείαν προκρίνας αὐτούς.
[4] See Herod. vii. 210.
[5] Ezek. xxxi. 11.
[6] Ibid. verse 12.

rently no quarter,' but the women and the children suffered indignities and cruelties at the hands of her savage warriors, which the pen unwillingly records. The Median conquests were accompanied by the worst atrocities which lust and hate combined are wont to commit when they obtain their full swing. Neither the virtue of women nor the innocence of children were a protection to them. The infant was slain before the very eye of the parent. The sanctity of the hearth was invaded, and the matron ravished beneath her own roof-tree.* Spoil, it would seem, was disregarded in comparison with insult and vengeance; and the brutal soldiery cared little for either silver or gold,* provided they could indulge freely in that thirst for blood, which man shares with the hyæna and the tiger.

The habits of the Medes in the early part of their career were undoubtedly simple and manly. It has been observed with justice that the same general features have at all times distinguished the rise and fall of Oriental kingdoms and dynasties. A brave and adventurous prince, at the head of a population at once poor, warlike, and greedy, overruns a vast tract, and acquires extensive dominion, while his successors, abandoning themselves to sensuality and sloth, probably also to oppressive and irascible dispositions, become in process of time victims to those same qualities in another prince and people, which had enabled their own predecessors to establish their power.[10] It was as being braver, simpler, and so

---

[1] Isaiah xiii. 15 and 18.
[2] Ibid. verse 16. "Their children also shall be dashed to pieces before their eyes; their houses shall be spoiled, and their wives ravished."
[3] See verse 17.
[4] Grote, *History of Greece*, vol. iii. p. 157, 2nd ed.

stronger than the Assyrians, that the Medes were able to dispossess them of their sovereignty over Western Asia. But in this, as in most other cases of conquest throughout the East, success was followed almost immediately by degeneracy. As captive Greece captured her fierce conqueror,[11] so the subdued Assyrians began at once to corrupt their subduers. Without condescending to a close imitation of Assyrian manners and customs, the Medes proceeded directly after their conquest to relax the severity of their old habits and to indulge in the delights of soft and luxurious living. The historical romance of Xenophon presents us probably with a true picture, when it describes the strong contrast which existed towards the close of the Median period between the luxury and magnificence which prevailed at Ecbatana, and the primitive simplicity of Persia Proper,[12] where the old Arian habits, which had once been common to the two races, were still maintained in all their original severity. Xenophon's authority in this work is, it must be admitted, weak, and little trust can be placed in the historical accuracy of his details; but his general statement is both in itself probable, and is also borne out to a considerable extent by other authors. Herodotus and Strabo note the luxury of the Median dress,[13] while the latter author goes so far as to derive the whole of the later Persian splendour from an imitation of Median practices.[14] We must hold then that towards the latter part of their empire the Medes became a comparatively luxurious people, not indeed laying aside

---

[11] Horat. *Epist.* II.1,156. "Græcia capta ferum victorem cepit."
[12] Xen. *Cyrop.* i. 3, § 2, et seqq.
[13] Herod. i. 135; Strab. xi. 13, § 9.
[14] Strab. l. s. c.

altogether their manly habits, nor ceasing to be
both brave men and good soldiers, but adopting
an amount of pomp and magnificence to which
they were previously strangers, affecting splendour
in their dress and apparel, grandeur and rich ornament in their buildings,[15] variety in their banquets,[16] and attaining on the whole a degree of
civilisation not very greatly inferior to that of the
Assyrians. In taste and real refinement they seem
indeed to have fallen considerably below their
teachers. A barbaric magnificence predominated in
their ornamentation over artistic effort, richness in
the material being preferred to skill in the manipulation. Literature, and even letters, were very
sparingly cultivated.[17] But little originality was
developed. A stately dress, and a new style of architecture, are almost the only inventions to which the
Medes can lay claim. They were brave, energetic,
enterprising, fond of display, capable of appreciating
to some extent the advantages of civilised life; but
they had little genius, and the world is scarcely indebted to them for a single important addition to the
general stock of its ideas.

Of the Median customs in war we know but little.
Herodotus tells us that in the army of Xerxes the
Medes were armed exactly as the Persians, carrying on
their heads a soft felt cap, on their bodies a sleeved
tunic, and on their legs trowsers. Their offensive

---

[15] See above, p. 20.
[16] Xen. *Cyrop.* l. 3, § 4. Παντοδαπὰ ἐμβάμματα καὶ βρώματα.
[17] The use of writing by the Medes
is indicated in the Book of Daniel
(vi. 9). The existence of a Median
literature seems to be implied by the
mention in Esther of the "book of
the chronicles of the kings of Media
and Persia" (i. 2). The actual work
alluded to may perhaps have been a
Persian compilation; but the Persian
writer would scarcely have ventured
to write the "chronicles of the kings
of Media," unless he had Median
materials to go upon.

arms, he says, were the spear, the bow, and the dagger. They had large wicker shields, and bore their quivers suspended at their backs. Sometimes their tunic was made into a coat of mail by the addition to it on the outside of a number of small iron plates arranged so as to overlap each other, like the scales of a fish.[1] They served both on horseback and on foot, with the same equipment in both cases.[2]

There is no reason to doubt the correctness of this description of the Median military dress under the early Persian kings. The only question is how far the equipment was really the ancient warlike costume of the people. It seems in some respects too elaborate to be the armature of a simple and primitive race. We may reasonably suppose that at least the scale armour and the unwieldy wicker shields (γέρρα), which required to be rested upon the ground,[3] were adopted at a somewhat late date from the Assyrians. At any rate the original character of the Median armies, as set before us in Scripture,[4] and as indicated both by Strabo[5] and Xenophon,[6] is simpler than the Herodotean description. The primitive Medes seem to have been a nation of horse-archers.[7] Trained from their early boyhood to a variety of equestrian exercises,[8] and well practised in the use of the bow, they appear to have proceeded

---

[1] Herod. vii. 61. On the scale armour of the Assyrians, see above, vol. ii. pp. 31–33, and 44–47. On that of the Egyptians, see Wilkinson in the author's *Herodotus*, vol. iv. p. 65, 2nd edit.

[2] Herod. vii. 86.

[3] See above, vol. ii. pp. 48, 49; and compare Herod. ix. 62; Xen. *Anab.* t. 8, § 9, &c.

[4] Compare Isaiah xiii. 18; Jerem.

l. 9, 29; li. 11, &c.

[5] Strab. xi. 13, § 9.

[6] Xen. *Cyrop.* li. 1, § 6.

[7] Of course the Medes had always some footmen, but their strength was in their horse. I do not believe in their using chariots. (Nic. D. Fr. 10.)

[8] Xen. *Cyrop.* l. 4, § 4. Compare Strabo, who says (l. s. c.) that the famous Persian educational system was wholly copied from the Median.

against their enemies with clouds of horse, almost in Scythian fashion, and to have gained their victories chiefly by the skill with which they shot their arrows as they advanced, retreated, or manœuvred about their foe. No doubt they also used the sword and the spear. The employment of these weapons has been almost universal throughout the East from a very remote antiquity, and there is some mention of them in connection with the Medes and their kindred, the Persians, in Scripture;[a] but it is evident that the terror which the Medes inspired arose mainly from their dexterity as archers.[b]

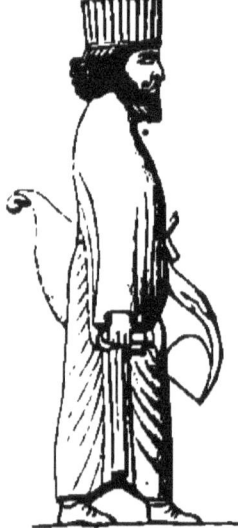

Mede or Persian carrying a bow in its case (Persepolis).

No representation of weapons which can be distinctly recognised as Median has come down to us. The general character of the military dress and of the arms appears, probably, in the Persepolitan sculptures; but as these reliefs are in most cases representations, not of Medes, but of Persians, and as they must be hereafter adduced in illustration of the military customs of the latter people, only a very sparing use of them can be made in the present chap-

---

[a] The sword is mentioned in connection with the Medes and Persians in Jeremiah l. 35-37. "The bow and the spear" are united in vi. 23, and again in l. 42.

[b] The fame of the Medes as archers passed on to the Persians, and even to the Parthians, who with the tastes inherited the name of the earlier people. Hence the "horribilis Medus" (Hor. Od. i. 29, 4) and the "Medi pharetra decori" of Horace (Od. ii. 16, 6).

ter. It would seem that the bow employed was short and very much curved, and that, like the Assyrian,[11] it was usually carried in a bow-case, which might either be slung at the back or hung from the girdle. The arrows, which were borne in a quiver slung

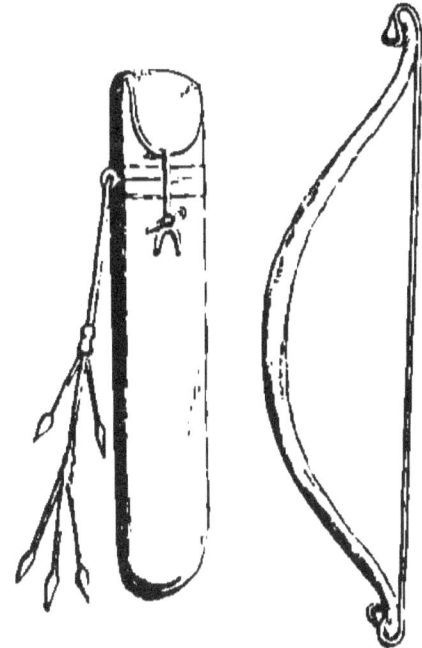

Bow and quiver (Persepolis).

behind the right shoulder, must have been short, certainly not exceeding the length of three feet. The quiver appears to have been round: it was covered at the top and was fastened by means of a flap and strap, which last passed over a button.

[11] Supra, vol. ii. p. 55.

The Median spear or lance was from six to seven feet in length. Its head was lozenge-shaped and flattish, but strengthened by a bar or line down the

Persian or Median spear (Persepolis).

middle.[12] It is uncertain whether the head was inserted into the top of the shaft, or whether it did not rather terminate in a ring or socket into which the upper end of the shaft was itself inserted. The shaft tapered gradually from bottom to top, and terminated below in a knob or ball, which was perhaps sometimes carved into the shape of some natural object.[13]

The sword was short, being in fact little more than a dagger.[14] It depended at the right thigh from a belt which encircled the waist, and was further secured by a strap attached to the bottom of the sheath and passing round the soldier's right leg a little above the knee.

Median shields were probably either round or oval. The oval specimens bore a resemblance to the shield of the Bœotians, having a small oval aperture at either side, apparently for the sake of greater lightness. They were strengthened at the centre by a circular boss or disk, ornamented with knobs or circles. They would seem to have been made either of metal or wood.

Shield of a warrior (Persepolis).

---

[12] Compare the Assyrian spear-heads, vol. ii. p. 62.

[13] The lower end of the Persian spears terminated frequently in an apple or pomegranate (Herod. vii. 41; Athen. Deipn. xii. p. 514, B). According to Clearchus of Soli, this practice was adopted by the Persians from the Medes, and was intended as a reproach to the latter for their unmanly luxury. (Athen. p. 514, D.)

[14] So Xenophon calls the Persian sword ἀκινάκης ἢ κοπίδα. (Cyrop. i. 2, § 13.)

DRESS OF THE MEDES.

The favourite dress of the Medes in peace is well known to us from the sculptures. There can be no reasonable doubt that the long flowing robe so remarkable for its graceful folds, which is the garb of the kings, the chief nobles, and the officers of the court in all the Persian bas-reliefs, and which is seen also upon the darics and the gems, is the famous "Median garment" of Herodotus, Xenophon, and Strabo.¹ This garment fits the chest and shoulders closely, but falls over the arms in two large loose sleeves, open at bottom. At the waist it is confined by a cincture. Below it is remarkably full and ample, drooping in two clusters of perpendicular folds at the two sides, and between

Median robe (Persepolis).

these hanging in festoons like a curtain. It extends down to the ankles, where it is met by a high shoe or low boot, opening in front, and secured by buttons.

These Median robes were of many colours. Sometimes they were purple, sometimes scarlet, occasionally a dark grey, or a deep crimson.² Procopius says that they were made

---

¹ Ἐσθὴς Μηδική. Herod. I. 135; vii. 116; Στολὴ Μηδική. Xen. Cyrop. viii. 8, § 15; Στολὴ Περσική. Strab. xi. 13, § 0. This, Strabo expressly says, was adopted from the Medes.
² Xen. Cyrop. viii. 3, § 3. 'Ἐξέφερε δὴ καὶ ἄλλας Μηδικὰς στολάς· παμπόλλας γὰρ παρεσκευάσατο, οὐδὲν φειδόμενος, οὔτε πορφυρίδων, οὔτε ὀρφνίνων, οὔτε φοινικίδων, οὔτε καρυκίνων ἱματίων. Another kind of Median robe, called σαραπίς, seems to have been striped alternately white and purple. (Compare Pollux, vii. 13, with Hesychius ad voc. σάραπις.)

of silk,[3] and this statement is confirmed to some extent by Justin, who speaks of their transparency.[4] It may be doubted, however, whether the material was always the same; probably it varied with the season, and also with the wealth of the wearer.

Besides this upper robe, which is the only garment shown in the sculptures, the Medes wore as under garments a sleeved shirt or tunic of a purple colour,[5]

Median head-dress (Persepolis).

and embroidered drawers or trowsers.[6] They covered the head, not only out of doors, but in their houses,[7] wearing either felt caps (πίλοι) like the Persians, or a head-dress of a more elaborate character, which bore the name of *tiara* or *cidaris*.[8] This appears to have been, not a turban, but rather a kind of high-crowned hat, either stiff or flexible, made probably of felt or cloth, and dyed of different hues, according to the fancy of the owner.

---

[3] Procop. *De Bell. Pers.* i. 20, p. 106, C. Silken fabrics were manufactured by the Greeks from the middle of the fourth century B.C. (Aristot. *Hist. An.* v. 19.) They probably imported the raw silk from Asia, where the material was in use from a very early time. The Parthian standards were of silk (Florus, iii. 11); and there can be little doubt that the looms of China, India, and Cashmere produced rich silken fabrics from a remote period, which were exported into the neighbouring countries of Media and Persia.

[4] Justin says of the Parthians: "Vestis olim sui moris; posteaquam accessere opes, ut Medis, perlucida ac fluida." (xli. 2).

[5] See Xen. *Anab.* i. 5, § 8, and compare *Cyrop.* i. 3, § 2.

[6] Ἀναξυρίδας. Xen. *Anab.* l. s. c. Compare Strab. xi. 13, § 9.

[7] Strab. l. s. c.; Herod. iii. 12.

[8] Strictly speaking these words are not synonyms. The name *tiara* was generic, applying to all the tall caps; while *cidaris* or *citaris* was specific, being properly applied to the royal head-dress only. (See Brisson, *De Regn. Pers.* ii. pp. 309-312.)

MEDIAN LOVE OF ORNAMENT.

The Medes took a particular delight in the ornamentation of their persons. According to Xenophon they were acquainted with most of the expedients, by the help of which vanity attempts to conceal the ravages of time, and to create an artificial beauty. They employed cosmetics which they rubbed into the skin, for the sake of improving the complexion. They made use of an abundance of false hair.[10] Like many other Oriental nations, both ancient and modern, they applied dyes to enhance the brilliancy of the eyes,[11] and give them a greater apparent size and softness. They were also fond of wearing golden ornaments. Chains or collars of gold usually adorned their necks, bracelets of the same precious metal encircled their wrists,[12] and ear-rings were inserted into their ears.[13] Gold was also used in the caparisons of their horses, the bit and other parts of the harness being often of this valuable material.[14]

A Mede or Persian wearing a collar and ear-rings (Persepolis).

We are told that the Medes were very luxurious at their banquets. Besides plain meat and game of different kinds, with the ordinary accompaniments

---

[9] Χρώμασιν ἱστράψις. (Xen. Cyrop. i. 3, § 2.)

[10] Κόμαι πρόσθεται. (Ibid.)

[11] Ὀφθαλμοὺς ὑπογραφή. (Ibid.) This practice is ascribed to Sardanapalus (Nic. Dam. Fr. 8; Athen. Deips. xii. 7, p. 529, A; Diod. Sic. ii. 23); and again to Nanarus the Babylonian (Nic. Dam. Fr. 10). It seems to have been adopted from the Medes by the Persians. (Xen. Cyrop. viii. 8, § 20.)

[12] Strab. l. s. c.; Xen. Cyrop. l. 3, § 2.

[13] Ear-rings commonly accompany the Median dress on the Persepolitan sculptures. They are mere plain rings without any pendant. See the above woodcut. Nicolas of Damascus assigns ear-rings (ἐλλόβια) to Nanarus, a satrap under the Medes. (Fr. 10.)

[14] Xen. Cyrop. l. 3, § 3.

of wine and bread, they were accustomed to place before their guests a vast number of side-dishes, together with a great variety of sauces.[14] They ate with the hand, as is still the fashion in the East, and were sufficiently refined to make use of napkins.[15] Each guest had his own dishes, and it was a mark of special honour to augment their number.[17] Wine was drunk both at the meal and afterwards, often in an undue quantity; and the close of the feast was apt to be a scene of general turmoil and confusion.[18] At the Court it was customary for the king to receive his wine at the hands of a cupbearer, who first tasted the draught, that the king might be sure it was not poisoned, and then presented it with much pomp and ceremony.[19]

The whole ceremonial of the Court seems to have been imposing. Under ordinary circumstances the monarch kept himself secluded, and no one could obtain admission to him unless he formally requested an audience, and was introduced into the royal presence by the proper officer.[1] On his admission he prostrated himself upon the ground, with the same signs of adoration which were made on entering a temple.[2] The king, surrounded by his attendants, eunuchs and others, maintained a haughty reserve, and the stranger only beheld him from a distance. Business was transacted in a great measure by writing. The monarch rarely quitted his palace, contenting himself with such reports of the state of his Empire

---

[14] Xen. *Cyrop.* § 4.
[15] Χειρόμακτρα. (Ibid. § 5.)
[17] Ibid. § 6.
[18] See the description in Xenophon. (*Cyrop.* i. 3, § 10.) Compare the Persian practice. (Herod. i. 133.)
[19] *Cyrop.* L. 3, § 8.
[1] Herod. I. 90. Compare Nic. Dam. Fr. 66. (*Fr. Hist. Gr.* vol. iii. p. 402.)
[2] Strab. l. s. c. Σεβασμὸς θεοπρεπὴς εἰς τοὺς Πέρσας παρὰ Μήδων ἀφίκται.

as were transmitted to him from time to time by his officers.[2]

The chief amusement of the Court, in which however the king rarely partook,[3] was hunting. Media always abounded in beasts of chase;[4] and lions, bears, leopards, wild boars, stags, gazelles, wild sheep, and wild asses, are mentioned among the animals hunted by the Median nobles.[5] Of these the first four were reckoned dangerous, the others harmless.[6] It was customary to pursue these animals on horseback, and to aim at them with the bow or the javelin. We may gather a lively idea of some of these hunts from the sculptures of the Parthians, who some centuries later inhabited the same regions. We see in these the rush of great troops of boars through marshes dense with water-plants, the bands of beaters urging them on, the sportsmen aiming at them with their bows, and the game falling transfixed with two or three well-aimed shafts.[7] Again we see herds of deer driven within enclosures, and there slain by archers who shoot from horseback, the monarch under his parasol looking on the while, pleased with the dexterity of his servants.[8] It is thus exactly that Xenophon portrays Astyages as contemplating the sport of his

---

[2] This, at least, is the account of Herodotus (i. 100). But it may be doubted whether he does not somewhat over-state the degree of seclusion affected by the Median kings. Certainly neither Xenophon in his *Cyropædia*, nor Ctesias in the fragments which remain of his writings, appears to hold such extreme views on the subject as "the Father of History."

[3] Herodotus's account would necessarily imply this. Xenophon furnishes no contradiction; for he does not make the king hunt in person.

[4] See above, p. 68.

[5] Xen. *Cyrop.* l. 4, § 7. Nicolas of Damascus mentions the wild boar, the stags, and the wild asses. (Fr. 10.)

[6] Xen. *Cyrop.* l. s. c.

[7] See the engraving in Ker Porter's *Travels*, vol. ii. opp. p. 175, or the more carefully drawn representation in Flandin's *Voyage en Perse*, tom. i. pl. 10.

[8] Ker Porter, vol. ii. opp. p. 177; Flandin, tom. i. pl. 12.

courtiers, complacently viewing their enjoyment, but taking no active part in the work himself."

Like other Oriental sovereigns, the Median monarch maintained a seraglio of wives and concubines;" and polygamy was commonly practised among the more wealthy classes. Strabo speaks of a strange law as obtaining with some of the Median tribes—a law which required that no man should be content with fewer wives than five.¹² It is very unlikely that such a burthen was really made obligatory on any: most probably five legitimate wives, and no more, were allowed by the law referred to, just as four wives, and no more, are lawful for Mahometans. Polygamy, as usual, brought in its train the cruel practice of castration; and the Court swarmed with eunuchs, chiefly foreigners purchased in their infancy.¹³ Towards the close of the Empire this despicable class appears to have been all-powerful with the monarch.¹⁴

Thus the tide of corruption gradually advanced; and there is reason to believe that both Court and people had in a great measure laid aside the hardy and simple customs of their forefathers, and become enervated through luxury, when the revolt of the Persians came to test the quality of their courage, and their ability to maintain their Empire. It would be improper in this place to anticipate the account of this struggle, which must be reserved for the historical chapter; but the well-known result—the speedy and complete success of the Persians—must

---

¹⁰ Xen. *Cyrop.* L 4, § 15. Ἐθέατο τοὺς ἁμιλλωμένους ἐπὶ τὰ θηρία, καὶ φιλοτιμοῦντας, καὶ διώκοντας, καὶ ἀκοντίζοντας.
¹¹ Strab. xi. 13, § 11. Compare Nicolas of Damascus, Fr. 66 (*Fr. Hist. Gr.* vol. iii. p. 403).
¹² Strab. l. s. c.
¹³ Clearch. Sol. ap. Athen. *Deipn.* xii. 2; p. 514, D.
¹⁴ Nic. Dam. Fr. 66 (*Fr. Hist. Gr.* vol. iii. pp. 398 and 402).

be adduced among the proofs of a rapid deterioration in the Median character between the accession of Cyaxares and the death—less than a century later—of Astyages.

We have but little information with respect to the state of the arts among the Medes. A barbaric magnificence characterized, as has been already observed, their architecture, which differed from the Assyrian in being dependent for its effect on groups of pillars rather than on painting or sculpture. Still sculpture was, it is probable, practised to some extent by the Medes, who, it is almost certain, conveyed on to the Persians those modifications of Assyrian forms which meet us everywhere in the remains of the Achæmenian monarchs. The carving of winged genii, of massive forms of bulls and lions, of various grotesque monsters, and of certain clumsy representations of actual life, imitated from the bas-reliefs of the Assyrians, may be safely ascribed to the Medes; since, had they not carried on the traditions of their predecessors, Persian art could not have borne the resemblance that it does to Assyrian. But these first mimetic efforts of the Arian race have almost wholly perished, and there scarcely seems to remain more than a single fragment which can be assigned on even plausible grounds to the Median period. A portion of a colossal lion, greatly injured by time, is still to be seen at Hamadan, the site of the great Median capital, which the best judges regard as anterior to the Persian period, and as therefore most probably Median.[1] It consists of the head and body

---

[1] Flandin, *Voyage en Perse*, p. 17. Sir H. Rawlinson is of the same opinion.

of the animal, from which the four legs and the tail have been broken off, and measures between eleven and twelve feet from the crown of the head to the point from which the tail sprang. By the position of the head and of what remains of the shoulders and thighs, it is evident that the animal was represented in a sitting posture, with the fore legs straight and

Colossal lion (Ecbatana).

the hind legs gathered up under it. To judge of the feeling and general character of the sculpture is difficult, owing to the worn and mutilated condition of the work; but we seem to trace in it the same air of calm and serene majesty that characterises the colossal bulls and lions of Assyria, together with somewhat more of expression and of softness than are seen in the productions of that people. Its posture, which is unlike that of any Assyrian specimen, indicates a certain amount of originality as belonging to the Median artists, while its colossal size seems to shew that the effect on the spectator was still to be produced, not so much by expression, finish, or truth to nature, as by mere grandeur of dimension.

CHAPTER IV.

RELIGION.

Ἀριστοτέλης φησὶ δύο κατ' αὐτοὺς εἶναι ἀρχάς, ἀγαθὸν δαίμονα καὶ κακὸν δαίμονα· καὶ τῷ μὲν ὄνομα εἶναι Ζεὺς καὶ Ὠρομάσδης, τῷ δὲ Ἄδης καὶ Ἀρειμάνιος.—Diog. Laert. *Procem.* p. 2.

THE earliest form of the Median religion is to be found in those sections of the Zendavesta[1] which

---

[1] The Zend-Avesta, or sacred volume of the Parsees, which has now been printed both by Westergaard (1852-1854) and Spiegel (1851-1858), and translated into German by the latter, is a compilation for liturgical purposes from various older works which have been lost. It is composed of eight pieces or books, entitled Yaçna, Visperatu or Visparad, Vendidad, Yashts, Nyâyish, Afrigâns, Gâhs, Sirozah. It is written in the old form of Arian speech called the Zend, a language closely cognate to the Sanscrit of the Vedas and to Achaemenian Persian, or the Persian of the Cuneiform inscriptions. A Pehlevi translation of the more important books, made probably under the Sassanidae (A.D. 235-640), is extant, and a Sanscrit translation of the Yaçna, made about the end of the fifteenth century by a certain Nariosengh. The celebrated Frenchman, Anquetil du Perron, first acquainted the learned of Europe with this curious and valuable compilation. His translation, confused in its order, and often very incorrect, is now antiquated; and students unacquainted with Zend will do well to have recourse to Spiegel, who, however, is far from a perfect translator. The best Zend scholars have as yet attempted versions of some portions of the Zendavesta only—as Burnouf of the first and ninth chapters of the Yaçna (*Commentaire sur le Yaçna*, Paris, 1833; and the *Journal Asiatique* for 1844-1846), and Martin Haug of the Gâthâs (2 vols., Leipsic, 1858-1860), and other fragments (*Essays on the Sacred Language, Writings, and Religion of the Parsees*, Bombay, 1862). Professor Westergaard of Copenhagen is understood to be engaged upon a complete translation of the whole work into English. When this version appears it will probably leave little to be desired.

The word "Zend-Avesta," introduced into the languages of Europe by Du Perron, is incorrect. The proper form is "Avesta-Zend," which is the order always used in the Pehlevi books. This word, "Avesta-Zend," is a contraction of *Avesta u Zend*, "Avesta and Zend," *i. e.* Text and Comment. Avesta (*avo-stâd*) means "text, scripture;" its Pehlevi form is *apistak*, and it is cognate with the late Sanscrit and Mahratta *pustak*, "book." Zend (*zend*) is "explanation, comment." (See Haug's *Essays*, pp. 120-122; and compare Bunsen's *Egypt*, vol. iii. p. 474, note.)

have been pronounced on internal evidence to be the most ancient portions[2] of that venerable compilation; as, for instance, the first Fargard of the Vendidad, and the Gâthâs, or 'Songs,'[3] which occur here and there in the Yaçna, or Book on Sacrifice.[4] In the Gâthâs, which belong to a very remote era indeed,[5] we seem to have the first beginnings of the Religion. We may indeed go back by their aid to a time anterior to themselves—a time when the Arian race was not yet separated into two branches, and the Easterns and Westerns, the Indians and Iranians, had not yet adopted the conflicting creeds of Zoroastrianism and Brahminism. At that remote period we seem to see prevailing a polytheistic nature-worship—a recognition of various divine beings, called indifferently *Asuras* (*Ahuras*),[6] or *Devas*,[7]

---

[1] Haug, *Essays*, pp. 50-116; Bunsen, *Egypt*, vol. iii. p. 470.

[2] It was doubted for some time whether the Gâthâs were really "songs." Brockhaus said in 1850, "Jusqu'ici je n'ai pu découvrir la moindre trace de mésure dans les morceaux que l'on peut regarder comme des Gâthâs." (*Vendidad-Sadé*, p. 357, ad voc. *gâtha*.) But Haug has shown distinctly, not only that they are metrical, but that the metres are of the same nature as those which are found in the Vedic hymns. (*Essays*, pp. 136-138.) And Westergaard has shown by his mode of printing that he regards them as metrical.

[3] Yaçna in Zend is equivalent to *yajna* in Sanscrit, and means "sacrifice." The Yaçna consists chiefly of prayers, hymns, &c., relating to sacrificial rites, and intended to be used during the performance of sacrifice.

[4] Traditionally several of the Gâthâs are ascribed to Zoroaster, whose date was anterior to B.C. 2234 according to Berosus, and whom other writers place still earlier. (See Aristot. ap. Diog. Laert. Pref. 0; Plin. *N. H.* xxx. 1; Hermipp. Fr. 79; Xanth. Lyd. Fr. 20, &c.) Their style shows them to be considerably anterior to the first Fargard of the Vendidad, which must have been composed before the great migration of the Medes southwards from the Caspian region. Haug is inclined to date the Zoroastrian Gâthâs as early as the time of Moses. (*Essays*, p. 255.)

[5] The Sanscrit *s* is replaced most commonly by *h* in Zend. *Asura* or *ahura* is properly an adjective meaning "living." But it is ordinarily used as a substantive, and means "divine or celestial being."

[6] The word *deva* is clearly cognate to the Latin *Deus*, *Divus*, Lithuanian *diewas*, Greek Ζεύς or Δεύς, &c. In modern Persian it has become *div*.

each independent of the rest, and all seemingly nature-powers rather than persons, whereof the chief are Indra, Storm or Thunder; Mithra, Sunlight; Aramati (Armaiti),* Earth; Vayu, Wind; Agni, Fire; and Soma (Homa), Intoxication. Worship is conducted by priests, who are called *kavi*, "seers;" *karapan*, "sacrificers," or *riçikhs*, "wise men."* It consists of hymns in honour of the Gods; sacrifices, bloody and unbloody, some portion of which is burnt upon an altar; and a peculiar ceremony, called that of Soma, in which an intoxicating liquor is offered to the gods, and then consumed by the priests, who drink till they are drunken.

Such, in outline, is the earliest phase of Arian religion, and it is common to both branches of the stock, and anterior to the rise of the Iranic, Median, or Persian system. That system is a revolt from this sensuous and superficial nature-worship. It begins with a distinct recognition of spiritual intelligences— real persons—with whom alone, and not with powers, religion is concerned. It divides these intelligences into good and bad, pure and impure, benignant and malevolent. To the former it applies the term *Asuras* (*Ahuras*), "living" or "spiritual beings," in a good sense; to the latter, the term *Devas*, in a bad one. It regards the "powers" hitherto worshipped as chiefly Devas; but it excepts from this unfavourable view a certain number, and, recognising them as Asuras, places them among the Izeds, or "angels." Thus far it has made two advances, each of great importance, the substitution of real "persons" for "powers," as objects of the religious faculty, and the

---

* *Aramati* is the Sanscrit, *Armaiti* the Zend form.
* Haug, *Essays*, pp. 243-247.

separation of the persons into good and bad, pure and impure, righteous and wicked. But it does not stop here. It proceeds to assert, in a certain sense, monotheism against polytheism. It boldly declares that, at the head of the good intelligences, is a single Great Intelligence, Ahurô-Mazdâo,[16] the highest object of adoration, the true Creator, Preserver, and Governor of the universe. This is its great glory. It sets before the soul a single Being as the source of all good and the proper object of the highest worship. Ahurô-Mazdâo is "the creator of life, the earthly and the spiritual;" "he has made "the celestial bodies,"[1] "earth, water, and trees,"[2] "all good creatures,"[3] and "all good, true things."[4] He is "good,"[5] "holy,"[6] "pure,"[7] "true,"[8] "the Holy God,"[9] "the Holiest,"[10] "the essence of truth,"[11] "the father of all truth,"[12] "the best being of all,"[13] "the master of purity."[14] He is supremely "happy,"[15] possessing every blessing, "health, wealth, virtue, wisdom, immortality."[16] From him comes all good to man; on the pious and the righteous he bestows not only earthly advantages, but precious spiritual gifts, truth, devotion, "the good mind," and everlasting happiness;[17] and, as he rewards

---

[16] Great difference of opinion exists as to the meaning of this name. It has been translated "the great givor of life" (Sir H. Rawlinson's *Persian Vocabulary*, ad voc. *Auramazda*); "the living wise" (Haug, *Essays*, p. 33); "the living Creator of all" (ibid. pp. 256, 257); "the divine much-knowing" (Bruckhaus, *Vendidad-Sadé*, pp. 347 and 385); and "the divine much-giving" (ibid.). Both elements of the name were used commonly to express the idea of "a god."
[17] Haug, *Essays*, p. 257.
[1] *Yaçna*, xxxi. 7.

[8] *Yaçna*, li. 7.
[2] Ibid. xxxi. 7.
[4] Ibid. xliii. 2.
[5] Ibid. xli. 1.
[6] Ibid. xliii. 4, 5.
[7] Ibid. xxxv. 1.
[8] Ibid. xlvi. 2.
[9] Ibid. xliii. 5.
[10] Ibid. xlv. 5.
[11] Ibid. xxxi. 8.
[12] Ibid. xlvii. 1.
[13] Ibid. xliii. 2.
[14] Ibid. xxxv. 1.
[15] Ibid. xxxv. 3.
[16] Haug, *Essays*, p. 257.
[17] *Yaçna*, xxxiv. 1; xlvii. 1, 2, &c.

the good, so he punishes the bad, though this is an aspect in which he is but seldom represented."

It has been said[19] that this conception of Ahura-mazda as the Supreme Being is "*perfectly identical with the notion of Elohim, or Jehovah, which we find in the books of the Old Testament.*" This is, no doubt, an over-statement. Ahura-mazda is less spiritual and less awful than Jehovah. He is less remote from the nature of man. The very ascription to him of health (*haurvatât*) is an indication that he is conceived of as possessing a sort of physical nature.[20] Lucidity and brilliancy are assigned to him, not (as it would seem) in a mere metaphorical sense.[21] Again, he is so predominantly the author of good things, the source of blessing and prosperity, that he could scarcely inspire his votaries with any feeling of fear. Still, considering the general failure of unassisted reason to mount up to the true notion of a spiritual God, this doctrine of the early Arians is very remarkable; and its approximation to the truth sufficiently explains, at once the favourable light in which its professors are viewed by the Jewish Prophets,[22] and the favourable opinion which they form of the Jewish system.[23] Evidently, the Jews and Arians, when they became known to one another,

---

[18] *Yaçna*, xliii. 4, 5.
[19] Haug, *Essays*, l. s. c.
[20] *Haurvatât* (*Khordâd* in later Persian) is translated indifferently "health," "wholesomeness," "completeness," "prosperity." It is explained to be "the good condition in which every being of the good creation has been created by Ahura-mazda." (Haug, *Essays*, p. 177.)
[21] Ahura-mazda is "true, lucid, shining, the originator of all the best things, of the spirit in nature, and of the growth in nature, of the luminaries, and of the self-shining brightness which is in the luminaries." (*Yaçna*, xii. 1, Haug's *Translation*.) He is regarded as the source of light, which most resembles him, and he is called *qâthrô*, "having his own light." (Haug, *Essays*, p. 143, note.) [22] Isaiah xliv. 28; xlv. 1-4.
[23] 2 Chron. xxxvi. 22, 23; Ezra i. 1-4; vi. 10, 12.

recognised mutually the fact that they were worshippers of the same great Being.[24] Hence the favour of the Persians towards the Jews, and the fidelity of the Jews towards the Persians. The Lord God of the Jews being recognised as identical with Ormazd, a sympathetic feeling united the peoples. The Jews, so impatient generally of a foreign yoke, never revolted from the Persians; and the Persians, so intolerant, for the most part, of religions other than their own,[25] respected and protected Judaism.

The sympathy was increased by the fact that the religion of Ormazd was anti-idolatrous. In the early nature-worship, idolatry had been allowed; but the Iranic system pronounced against it from the first.[26] No images of Ahura-mazda, or of the Izeds, profaned the severe simplicity of an Iranic temple. It was only after a long lapse of ages, that, in connexion with a foreign worship, idolatry crept in.[27] The old Zoroastrianism was in this respect as pure as the religion of the Jews, and thus a double bond of religious sympathy united the Hebrews and the Arians.

Under the supreme God, Ahura-mazda or Ormazd, the ancient Iranic system placed (as has been already observed) a number of angels.[28] Some of these,

---

[24] This is clear from such passages as the following:—"*The Lord God of heaven hath given me* (i. e. Cyrus) *all the kingdoms of the earth, and he hath charged me to build him a house at Jerusalem, which is in Judah. Who is there among you of all his people? His God be with him, and let him go up to Jerusalem, and build the house of the Lord God of Israel—he is the God—which is in Jerusalem.*" (Ezra i. 2, 3.)

[25] See the Chapter on the Persian Religion in the "Fifth Monarchy," infra, vol. iv.

[26] *Yaçna,* xxxii. 1, 2; xlv. 11; xlvi. 11; &c.

[27] *Journal of the Asiatic Society,* vol. xv. p. 159; Loftus, *Chaldæa and Susiana,* p. 378. On the first erection of statues in honour of Anaitis, see the Chapter on the Persian Religion in the fourth volume of this work.

[28] *Yazatas* or *izeds.*

as *Vohu-manô*, "the Good Mind;" *Mazda*, "the Wise" (?); and *Asha*, "the True," are scarcely distinguishable from attributes of the Divinity. Armaiti, however, the genius of the Earth, and Sraosha or Serosh, an angel, are very clearly and distinctly personified.[29] Sraosha is Ormazd's messenger. He delivers revelations,[30] shows men the paths of happiness,[31] and brings them the blessings which Ormazd has assigned to their share.[32] Another of his functions is to protect the true faith.[33] He is called in a very special sense, "the friend of Ormazd,"[34] and is employed by Ormazd not only to distribute his gifts, but also to conduct to him the souls of the faithful, when this life is over, and they enter on the celestial scene.[35]

Armaiti is at once the genius of the Earth, and the goddess of piety. The early Ormazd worshippers were agriculturists, and viewed the cultivation of the soil as a religious duty enjoined upon them by God.[1] Hence they connected the notion of piety with earth culture; and it was but a step from this to make a single goddess preside over the two. It is as the angel of Earth that Armaiti has most distinctly a personal character. She is regarded as wandering from spot to spot, and labouring to convert deserts and wildernesses into fruitful fields and gardens.[2] She has the agriculturist under her im-

---

[29] "While the Amesha Spentas," says Haug, "represent nothing but the qualities and gifts of Ahuramazda, Sraosha seems to have been considered as a personality." (*Essays*, p. 201.) Haug even regards Armaiti as not really a person (ibid.).
[30] *Yaçna*, lxiii. 12, 14; xliv. 1.
[31] Ibid. xliii. 3.
[32] Ibid. xliii. 11 and 16.
[33] Ibid. xliv. 9.
[34] Ibid. xliv. 1 and 9.
[35] Ibid. xliii. 8.
[1] *Yaçna*, xxix. passim, xxxi. 9–10.
[2] So Haug expounds the somewhat ambiguous words of *Yaçna*, xxxi. 9. (*Essays*, p. 144, note.)

mediate protection,¹ while she endeavours to persuade the shepherd, who persists in the nomadic life, to give up his old habits and commence the cultivation of the soil. She is of course the giver of fertility, and rewards her votaries by bestowing upon them abundant harvests.⁴ She alone causes all growth.⁵ In a certain sense she pervades the whole material creation, mankind included, in whom she is even sometimes said to "reside."⁶

Armaiti, further, "tells men the everlasting laws, which no one may abolish"⁷—laws, which she has learnt from converse with Ahura-mazda himself. She is thus naturally the second object of worship to the old Zoroastrian; and converts to the religion were required to profess their faith in her in direct succession to Ahura-mazda.⁸

From Armaiti must be carefully distinguished the *gêus urvâ*, or "soul of the earth"⁹—a being who nearly resembles the "anima mundi" of the Greek and Roman philosophers. This spirit dwells in the earth itself, animating it as a man's soul animates his body. In old times, when man first began to plough the soil, *gêus urvâ* cried aloud, thinking that his life was threatened, and implored the assistance of the archangels. They however were deaf to his entreaties (since Ormazd had decreed that there should be cultivation) and left him to bear his pains as he best

---

³ Yaçna, xxxi. 10.
⁴ Ibid. xxxv. 4.
⁵ Ibid. xliii. 16, ad fin.
⁶ Ibid. l. s. c.   ⁷ Ibid. xliii. 6.
⁸ See the formula by which the ancient Iranians received men into their religious community, given in the 12th chapter of the Yaçna, § 1 to § 9.

⁹ Literally "soul of the cow." In the poetical language of the old Iranians, the earth, which sustains all, was compared to a cow, the earliest sustainer of the family among them. (See Oxford Essays for 1856, p. 17.) Perhaps the Greek γῆ (Dor. γᾶ) is connected etymologically with *go* or *gu*, "cattle."

could.[10] It is to be hoped that in course of time he became callous to them, and made the discovery that mere scratches, though they may be painful, are not dangerous.

It is uncertain whether in the most ancient form of the Iranic worship the cult of Mithra was included or no. On the one hand, the fact that Mithra is common to both forms of the Arian creed—the Indian and Iranic—would induce the belief that his worship was adopted from the first by the Zoroastrians; on the other the entire absence of all mention of Mithra from the Gâthâs would lead us to the conclusion that in the time when they were composed his cult had not yet begun. Perhaps we may distinguish between two forms of early Iranic worship, one that of the more intelligent and spiritual—the leaders of the secession—in whose creed Mithra had no place; the other that of the great mass of followers, a coarser and more material system, in which many points of the old religion were retained, and among them the worship of the Sun-god. This lower and more materialistic school of thought probably conveyed on into the Iranic system other points also common to the Zendavesta with the Vedas, as the recognition of Airyaman (Aryaman) as a genius presiding over marriages,[11] of Vitrahâ as a very high angel,[12] and the like.

Vayu, "the Wind," seems to have been regarded as a god from the first. He appears, not only in the later portions of the Zendavesta, like Mithra and

---

[10] *Yaçna*, xxix. [11] Ibid. liv.
[12] See Haug's *Essays*, p. 193 and p. 232. In the Vedas *Vitrahâ* is one of the most frequent epithets of Indra, who would thus seem to have retained some votaries among the Iranians. It meant "killer of Vâra," who was a demon.

Aryaman, but in the Gâthâs themselves." His name is clearly identical with that of the Vedic Wind-god, Vâyu," and is apparently a sister form to the *ventus*, or *wind* of the more western Arians. The root is probably *vi*, "to go," which may be traced in *vis*, *ria*, *vado*, *venio*, &c.

The ancient Iranians did not adopt into their system either Agni, "Fire" (Lat. *ignis*) or Soma (Homa) "Intoxication." Fire was indeed retained for sacrifice;¹³ but it was regarded as a mere material agent, and not as a mysterious Power, the proper object of prayer and worship. The Soma worship,¹⁶

---

¹³ See *Yaçna*, liii. 6.
¹⁴ *Rig-Veda Sanhita*, vol. i. pp. 5, 6, 34, 35, &c.
¹⁵ *Yaçna*, xliii. 9; xlvi. 8; &c.
¹⁶ "The Soma ceremony is one of the most striking features of the old Hindoo religion. Wilson (H. H.) speaks of it as "a singular part of their ritual" (Introduction to *Rig-Veda Sanhita*, vol. i. p. xxxvi.), and describes it as follows:—"The expressed and fermented juice of the Soma plant was presented in ladles to the deities invoked, in what manner does not exactly appear, although it seems to have been sometimes sprinkled on the fire, sometimes on the ground, or rather on the *Kusa*, or sacred grass, strewed on the floor" (and forming the supposed seat of the deities); "and in all cases the residue was drunk by the assistants" (p. xxiii.). "The only explanation," he adds, "of which it is susceptible, is the delight, as well as astonishment, which the discovery of the exhilarating, if not inebriating, properties of the fermented juice of the plant must have excited in simple minds on first becoming acquainted with its effects" (p. xxxvii.). Haug says, "The early Indian tribes, as described in the ancient songs of the Vedas, never engaged themselves in their frequent predatory excursions for robbing cows, horses, sheep, &c., without having previously secured the assistance of Indra by preparing for him a solemn Soma feast. The Karpanî" (priests) "dressed it in the due manner, and the Kavis" (another order of priests) "composed or applied those verses, which were best calculated to induce Indra to accept the invitation. The Kavis were believed to recognise by certain marks the arrival of the god. After he had enjoyed the sweet beverage, the delicious honey, and was supposed to be totally inebriated, then the Kavis promised victory. The inroads were undertaken headed by those Kavis *who had previously intoxicated themselves*, and they appear to have been in most cases successful." (*Essays*, pp. 247, 248.) These orgies may therefore be compared with those which the Greeks celebrated in honour of Bacchus, and may throw light on the supposed Indian origin of that deity.

The Soma plant is said to be the acid *Asclepias* or *Sarcostema viminalis* (Wilson in *Rig-Veda Sanhita*, vol. i. p. 6, note ᵇ.) The important

which formed a main element of the old religion, and which was retained in Brahminism, was at the first altogether discarded by the Zoroastrians; indeed, it seems to have been one of the main causes of that disgust which split the Arian body in two, and gave rise to the new religion." A ceremony in which it was implied that the intoxication of their worshippers was pleasing to the gods, and not obscurely hinted that they themselves indulged in similar excesses was revolting to the religious temper of those who made the Zoroastrian reformation; and it is plain from the Gâthâs that the new system was intended at first to be entirely free from the pollution of so disgusting a practice. But the zeal of religious reformers outgoes in most cases the strength and patience of their people, whose spirit is too gross and earthly to keep pace with the more lofty flights of the purer and higher intelligences. The Iranian section of the Arians could not be weaned wholly from their beloved Soma feasts; and the leaders of the movement were obliged to be content ultimately with so far reforming and refining the ancient ceremony as to render it comparatively innocuous. The portion of the rite which implied that the gods themselves indulged in intoxication was omitted;[1] and for the intoxication of the priests was substituted a moderate use of the liquor, which, instead of giving a religious sanction to drunkenness,

---

part which it holds in the Vedas will be seen by reference to Mr. Wilson's translation of the Rig-Veda, vol. i. pp. 6, 11, 14, 21, 25, &c., and still more by reference to Mr. Stevenson's translation of the Sâma-Veda, which is devoted almost entirely to its praises.

[n] See Yaçna, xxxii. 3, and xlvii. 10.

[1] Instead of pouring the liquor on the fire or on the sacred grass, where the gods were supposed to sit, the Iranian priests simply showed it to the fire and then drank it. (Haug, Essays, p. 230.)

merely implied that the Soma juice was a good gift of God, one of the many blessings for which men had to be thankful.[1]

With respect to the evil spirits or intelligences, which, in the Zoroastrian system, stood over against the good ones, the teaching of the early reformers seems to have been less clear. The old divinities, except where adopted into the new creed, were in a general way called *Devas*, "fiends" or "devils,"[2] in contrast with the *Ahuras*, or "gods." These devas were represented as many in number, as artful, malicious, deceivers and injurers of mankind, more especially of the Zoroastrians or Ormazd-worshippers,[3] as inventors of spells[4] and lovers of the intoxicating Soma draught.[5] Their leading characteristics were "destroying" and "lying." They were seldom, or never, called by distinct names. No account was given of their creation, nor of the origin of their wickedness. No single superior intelligence, no great

---

[1] The restoration of a modified Soma (Homa) ceremony to the Iranian ritual is indicated in "the younger Yaçna" (chs. ix. to xi.), more especially in the so-called *Homa Yasht*, a translation of which by Burnouf is appended to the *Vendidad-Sadé* of Brockhaus.

[2] There is, of course, no etymological connection between *deva* and "devil." *Deva* and the cognate *div* are originally "the sky," "the air" — a meaning which *div* often has in the Vedas. (Compare Lat. *divus*.) From this meaning, while *deva* passed into a general name for god, the form *div* was appropriated to a particular god. (Compare our use of the word "Heaven" in such expressions as "Heaven forbid," "Heaven bless you!") The particular god, the god of the air, appears in Greek as Ζεύς or Ζάν, in Latin as Jupiter, in old German as *Tius*, whence our Tuesday. *Deva* became Lat. *deus*, *divus*, Gr. θεός, Lith. *diewas*, &c. Thus far the word had invariably a good sense. When, however, the Western Arians broke off from their brethren, and rejected the worship of their gods, whom they regarded as evil spirits, the word *deva*, which they specially applied to them, came to have an evil meaning, equivalent to our "fiend" or "devil." "Devil" is of course a mere corruption of διάβολος, Lat. *diabolus*, Ital. *diavolo*, French *diable*, Negro *debbel*.

[3] *Yaçna*, xii. 4; xxx. 6; xxxii. 5; xliv. 16, &c.

[4] Ibid. xxxii. 4. [5] Ibid. xxxii. 3.

Principle of Evil, was placed at their head. Ahriman (Angrô-mainyus) does not occur in the Gâthâs as a proper name. Far less is there any graduated hierarchy of evil, surrounding a Prince of Darkness with a sort of court, antagonistic to the angelic host of Ormazd, as in the later portions of the Zendavesta and in the modern Parsee system.

Thus Dualism proper, or a belief in two uncreated and independent principles, one a principle of good and the other a principle of evil, was no part of the original Zoroastrianism. At the same time we find, even in the Gâthâs, the earliest portions of the Zendavesta, the germ out of which Dualism sprang. The contrast between good and evil is strongly and sharply marked in the Gâthâs; the writers continually harp upon it; their minds are evidently struck with this sad antithesis, which colours the whole moral world to them; they see everywhere a struggle between right and wrong, truth and falsehood, purity and impurity; apparently they are blind to the evidences of harmony and agreement in the universe, discerning nothing anywhere but strife, conflict, antagonism. Nor is this all. They go a step further, and personify the two parties to the struggle. One is a "white," or holy "Spirit" (*çpentô mainyus*), and the other a "dark spirit" (*angrô mainyus*).[1] But this personification is merely poetical or metaphorical, not real. The "white spirit" is not Ahura-mazda, and the "dark spirit" is not a hostile intelligence. Both resolve themselves on examination into mere figures of speech—phantoms of poetic imagery—abstract notions, clothed

---

[1] See especially *Yaçna*, xlv. 2, and compare xxx. 3-6.

by language with an apparent, not a real, personality.

It was natural that, as time went on, Dualism should develop itself out of the primitive Zoroastrianism. Language exercises a tyranny over thought, and abstractions in the ancient world were ever becoming persons.[*] The Iranian mind, moreover, had been struck when it first turned to contemplate the world, with a certain antagonism; and, having once entered on this track, it would be compelled to go on, and seek to discover the origin of the antagonism, the cause (or causes) to which it was to be ascribed. Evil seemed most easily accounted for by the supposition of an evil Person; and the continuance of an equal struggle, without advantage to either side, which was what the Iranians thought they beheld in the world that lay around them, appeared to them to imply the equality of that evil Person with the Being whom they rightly regarded as the author of all good. Thus Dualism had its birth. The Iranians came to believe in the existence of two co-eternal and co-equal Persons, one good and the other evil, between whom there had been from all eternity a perpetual and never-ceasing conflict, and between whom the same conflict would continue to rage through all coming time.

It is impossible to say how soon this development took place.[*] We have evidence, however, that at a period considerably anterior to the commencement of the Median Empire, Dualism, not perhaps in its ulti-

---

[*] See Professor Max Müller's Essay in the *Oxford Essays* for 1856, pp. 34-47.

[*] The date of the separation between the Eastern and Western Arians is ante-historic, and can only be vaguely guessed at.

mate extravagant form, but certainly in a very decided and positive shape, had already been thought out and become the recognized creed of the Iranians. In the first Fargard or chapter, of the Vendidad—the historical chapter in which are traced the early movements of the Iranic peoples, and which from the geographical point whereat it stops must belong to a time when the Arians had not yet reached Media Magna[1]—the Dualistic belief clearly shows itself. The term Angrô-mainyus has now become a proper name, and designates the great spirit of evil as definitely and determinately as Ahuramazda designates the good spirit. The antagonism between Ahura-mazda and Angrô-mainyus is depicted in the strongest colours; it is direct, constant, and successful. Whatever good work Ahura-mazda in his benevolence creates, Angrô-mainyus steps forward to mar and blast it. If Ahura-mazda forms a "delicious spot" in a world previously desert and uninhabitable, to become the first home of his favourites, the Arians, Angrô-mainyus ruins it by sending into it a poisonous serpent,[2] and at the same

---

[1] The Iranian settlements enumerated in the document extend westward no further than Rhages, or at the utmost to Media Atropatênê, which may be indicated by the Varena of § 18. (See Appendix, A.) Thus the Arians, when the document was written, had not yet spread into Media Magna, much less into Persia Proper. It must consequently be anterior to the time of the first Shalmaneser (B.C. 850-824), who found Medes and Persians beyond the Zagros range. (See above, vol. ii. p. 359.)

Dr. Haug thinks that the Fargard is anterior to B.C. 1200, because Bactria occurs in it accompanied by the epithet *erêdhwó-drafsha*, "with the tall banner"—an expression indicating that it was the centre of an empire, which Bactria, he thinks, could not be after the rise of Assyria (B.C. 1200, according to him). See Bunsen's *Egypt*, vol. iii. p. 477, 478, E. T. But the Assyrian records render it absolutely certain that Bactria was an independent country, even at the height of the Assyrian power.

[2] The mention of a serpent as the first creation of Angrô-mainyus is curious. Is it a paradisiacal reminiscence?

time rendering the climate one of the bitterest severity. If Ahura-mazda provides, instead of this blasted region, another charming habitation, "the second best of regions and countries,"[3] Angrô-mainyus sends there the curse of murrain, fatal to all cattle. To every land which Ahura-mazda creates for his worshippers, Angrô-mainyus immediately assigns some plague or other. War, ravages, sickness, fever, poverty, hail, earthquakes, buzzing insects, poisonous plants, unbelief, witchcraft, and other inexpiable sins, are introduced by him into the various happy regions created without any such drawbacks by the good spirit; and a world, which should have been "very good," is by these means converted into a scene of trial and suffering.

The Dualistic principle being thus fully adopted, and the world looked on as the battle-ground between two independent and equal powers engaged in perpetual strife, it was natural that the imagination should complete the picture by ascribing to these superhuman rivals the circumstantials that accompany a great struggle between human adversaries. The two kings required, in the first place, to have their councils, which were accordingly assigned them, and were respectively composed of six councillors. The councillors of Ahura-mazda — called *Amesha Spentas*, or "Immortal Saints," afterwards corrupted into Amshashpands'[4]—were Vohu-manô (Bahman), Asha-vahista (Ardibehesht), Khshathra-vairya (Shahravar), Çpenta-Armaiti (Isfandarmat), Hourvatât (Khordâd), and Ameretat (Amerdât). Those of Angrô-mainyus were Ako-mano, Indra, Çaurva,

---

[3] *Vendidad*, Farg. i. § 5.   [4] Haug's *Essays*, p. 260.

Naonhaitya, and two others whose names are interpreted as "Darkness" and "Poison."[4]

Vohu-manô (Bahman) means "the Good mind." Originally a mere attribute of Ahura-mazda,[5] Vohumanô came to be considered, first, as one of the high angels attendant on him, and then formally as one of his six councillors. He had a distinct sphere or province assigned to him in Ahura-mazda's kingdom, which was the maintenance of life in animals and of goodness in man.

Asha-vahista (Ardibchesht) means "the Highest Truth"—" Veritas optima," or rather perhaps "Veritas lucidissima."[7] He was the "Light" of the universe, subtle, all-pervading, omnipresent. His special business was to maintain the splendour of the various luminaries, and thereby to preserve all those things whose existence and growth depends on light.

Khshathra-vairya (Shahravar), whose name means simply "possessions," "wealth," was regarded as presiding over metals and as the dispenser of riches.

Çpenta-Armaiti (Isfand-armat)—the "white" or "holy Armaiti," represented the Earth. She had from the first, as we have already seen, a distinct position in the system of the Zoroastrians, where she was at once the Earth-goddess and the genius of piety.[8]

Haurvatât (Khordâd) means "health"—"sani-

---

[4] Haug's *Essays*, p. 263. Compare Windischmann's *Zoroastrische Studien*, p. 59, where the original names are given as Tarîc and Zarîc.
[5] See above, p. 90.
[7] " *Vahista* means originally 'most splendid, beautiful,' but was afterwards used in the general sense of 'best.'" (Haug, *Essays*, p. 261.)
[8] See above, p. 99.

tas"⁹—and was originally one of the great and precious gifts which Ahura-mazda possessed himself and kindly bestowed on his creatures.¹⁰ When personification, and the needs of the theology, had made Haurvatât an archangel, he, together with Ameretât (Amerdât), "Immortality," took the presidency of the vegetable world, which it was the business of the pair to keep in good condition.

In the council of Angrô-mainyus, Ako-manô stands in direct antithesis to Vohu-manô, as "the bad mind," or, more literally, "the naught mind"¹¹—for the Zoroastrians, like Plato, regarded good and evil as identical with reality and unreality—τὸ ὄν, and τὸ μὴ ὄν. Ako-manô's special sphere is the mind of man, where he suggests evil thoughts and prompts to bad words and wicked deeds. He holds the first place in the infernal council, as Vohu-manô does in the heavenly one.

Indra, who holds the second place in the infernal council, is evidently the Vedic god, whom the Zoroastrians regarded as a powerful demon, and therefore made one of Angrô-mainyus's chief councillors. He probably retained his character as the god of the storm and of war, the destroyer of crops and cities, the inspirer of armies and the wielder of the thunderbolt. The Zoroastrians, however, ascribed to him only destructive actions; while the more logical Hindoos, observing that the same storm which hurt the crops and struck down trees and buildings, was also the means of fertilizing the lands and purifying

---

⁹ The most exact representative of Haurvatât which the classical languages furnish would seem to be the Greek εὐεξία. It is "the good condition in which every being of the good creation has been created by Ahura-mazda." (Haug, p. 177.)
¹⁰ Yaçna, xxxiv. 1; xlvii. 1; &c.
¹¹ Haug, pp. 142 and 268.

the air, viewed him under a double aspect, as at once terrible in his wrath and the bestower of numerous blessings."

Çaurva, who stands next to Indra, is thought to be the Hindoo Shiva,¹ who has the epithet çarva in one of the Vedas.² But the late appearance of Shiva in the Hindoo system³ makes this highly uncertain.

Naonhaitya, the fourth member of the infernal council, corresponds apparently to the Vedic Nāsatyas, a collective name given to the two Aswins, the Dioscuri of Indian mythology. These were favourite gods of the early Hindoos,⁴ to whose protection they very mainly ascribed their prosperity. It was natural that the Iranians, in their aversion to their Indian brethren, should give the Aswins a seat at Angrô-mainyus's council-table; but it is curious that they should represent the twin deities by only a single councillor.

Taric and Zaric, "Darkness" and "Poison," the occupants of the fifth and sixth places, are evidently personifications made for the occasion, to complete the infernal council to its full complement of six members.

As the two Principles of Good and Evil have their respective councils, so have they likewise their armies. The Good Spirit has created thousands of angelic beings, who everywhere perform his will and

---

¹² For the character of Indra in the Hindoo mythology see Wilson, *Rig-Veda Sanhita*, Introduction, pp. xxx.-xxxii.

¹ Haug, *Essays*, p. 270.

² *Yajur-Veda*, xvi. 28.

³ The name of Shiva does not occur in the Rig-Veda, from which the famous *Trimurtti*, or Trinity of Brahma, Vishnu, and Shiva is wholly absent. (Wilson in Introduction to *Rig-Veda Sanhita*, vol. I. p. xxvi.; Max Müller, *Ancient Sanskrit Literature*, p. 55.)

⁴ On the large share which the Aswins occupied in the early Hindoo worship see Wilson, *Rig-Veda Sanhita*, Introduction, p. xxxv., and compare *Rig-Veda*, vol. I. pp. 8, 50, 94-97, 125-127, 306-325, &c.

fight on his side against the Evil One; and the Evil One has equally on his part called into being thousands of malignant spirits, who are his emissaries in the world, doing his work continually, and fighting his battles. These are the Devas or Divs, so famous in Persian fairy mythology. They are "wicked, bad, false, untrue, the originators of mischief, most baneful, destructive, the basest of all beings." * The whole universe is full of them. They aim primarily at destroying all the good creations of Ahura-mazda; but if unable to destroy they content themselves with perverting and corrupting. They dog the steps of men, tempting them to sin; and, as soon as they sin, obtaining a fearful power over them.

At the head of Ahura-mazda's army is the angel Sraosha (Serosh). Serosh is "the sincere, the beautiful, the victorious, the true, the master of truth." He protects the territories of the Iranians, wounds, and sometimes even slays the demons, and is engaged in a perpetual struggle against them, never slumbering night nor day, but guarding the world with his drawn sword, more particularly after sunset, when the demons have the greatest power.

Angrô-mainyus appears not to possess any such general-in-chief. Besides the six councillors above mentioned, there are indeed various demons of importance, as Drukhs, "destruction;" Aêshemô, "ra-

---

* Yaçna, xii. 4.
* Ibid. xxx. 6.
† See the Serosh Yasht, or hymn in praise of Serosh (Yaçna, lvii. 2). The following particulars concerning Serosh are also contained in the hymn. He was the inventor of the baresom, and first taught its use to mankind. He made the music for the five earliest Gâthâs, which were called the Gâthâs of Zoroaster. He had an earthly dwelling-place — a palace with 1000 pillars erected on the highest summit of Elburz (the peak of Demawend?), which was lighted within by its own light, and without was ornamented with stars. One of his employments was to walk round the world, teaching the true religion.

pinç;" Daivis, "deceit;" Driwis, "poverty," &c.; but no one of these seems to occupy a parallel place in the evil world to that which is assigned to Serosh in the good. Perhaps we have here a recognition of the anarchic character of evil, whose attacks are like those of a huge undisciplined host—casual, fitful, irregular—destitute wholly of that principle of law and order, which gives to the resisting power of good a great portion of its efficacy.

To the belief in a spiritual world composed of all these various intelligences—one half of whom were good, and the other half evil—the early Zoroastrians added notions with respect to human duties and human prospects far more enlightened than those which have usually prevailed among heathen nations. In their system truth, purity, piety, and industry, were the virtues chiefly valued and inculcated. Evil was traced up to its root in the heart of man; and it was distinctly taught that no virtue deserved the name, but such as was co-extensive with the whole sphere of human activity, including the thought as well as the word and the deed." The purity required was inward as well as outward, mental as well as bodily. The industry was to be of a peculiar character. Man was placed upon the earth to preserve the good creation; and this could only be done by careful tilling of the soil, eradication of thorns and weeds, and reclamation of the tracts over which Angrô-mainyus had spread the curse of barrenness. [1] To cultivate the soil was thus a religious duty; the whole community was required to be agricultural; and either as proprietor, as farmer,

---

[a] On the trial of thought, word, and act, see Yaçna, xii. 8; xxxii. 5; xxxiii. 2; xxxv. 1; xlvii. 1 | xlix. 4; &c.; and compare below, p. 114, note ^m.

or as labouring man, each Zoroastrian must "further the works of life" by advancing tillage.* Piety consisted in the acknowledgment of the One True God, Ahura-mazda, and of his holy angels, the Amesha Spentas or Amshashpands, in the frequent offering of prayers, praises, and thanksgivings, in the recitation of hymns, the performance of the reformed Soma ceremony, and the occasional sacrifice of animals. Of the hymns we have abundant examples in the Gâthâs of the Zendavesta, and in the *Yaçna haptanhaiti*, or "Yaçna of seven chapters," which belongs to the second period of the religion. A specimen from the latter source is subjoined below.⁹ The Soma or Homa ceremony consisted in the extraction of the juice of the Homa plant by the priests during the recitation of prayers, the formal presentation of the liquid extracted to the sacrificial fire, the consumption of a small portion of it by one of the officiating priests, and the division of the remainder among the worshippers. As the juice was drunk immediately after extraction and before fermentation had set in, it was not intoxicating. The ceremony seems to have been regarded, in part, as having a mystic

---

* See *Yaçna*, xxxiii. 3.
⁹ "We worship Ahura-mazda, the pure, the master of purity. We worship the Amesha spentas, the possessors of good, the givers of good. We worship the whole creation of the true spirit, both the spiritual and terrestrial, all that supports the welfare of the good creation and the spread of the good mazda-yaçna religion.

"We praise all good thoughts, all good words, all good deeds, which are or shall be; and we likewise keep clean and pure all that is good.

"O Ahura-mazda, thou true, happy being! We strive to think, to speak, and to do only such actions as may be best fitted to promote the two lives" (*i. e.* the life of the body and the life of the soul).

"We beseech the spirit of earth, for the sake of these our best works" (*i. e.* our labours in agriculture), "to grant us beautiful and fertile fields, to the believer as well as to the unbeliever, to him who has riches as well as to him who has no possession." (*Yaçna*, xxxv. 1-4. See Haug's *Essays*, pp. 162, 163.)

force, securing the favour of heaven,[1] in part, as exerting a beneficial effect upon the body of the worshipper through the curative power inherent in the Homa plant.

The sacrifices of the Zoroastrians were never human. The ordinary victim was the horse;[2] and we hear of occasions on which a single individual sacrificed as many as ten of these animals.[3] Mares seem to have been regarded as the most pleasing offerings, probably on account of their superior value; and if it was desired to draw down the special favour of the Deity, those mares were selected which were already heavy in foal. Oxen, sheep, and goats were probably also used as victims. A priest always performed the sacrifice, slaying the animal, and showing the flesh to the sacred fire by way of consecration, after which it was eaten at a solemn feast by the priest and worshippers.

The Zoroastrians were devout believers in the immortality of the soul and a conscious future existence. They taught that immediately after death the souls of men, both good and bad, proceeded together along an appointed path to "the bridge of the gatherer" (*chinvat peretu*).[4] This was a narrow road conducting

---

[1] See the Homa Yasht (*Yaçna*, chs. ix, and x.). It has sometimes been supposed that the personal Homa addressed in his Yasht, and appearing elsewhere as an object of worship to the Zoroastrians, represents the Moon-God (*Journal of Asiatic Society*, vol. xv. p. 254); and the author was formerly of this opinion (*Herodotus*, vol. i., p. 340, 2nd ed.). But further consideration has convinced him that the Zendic Homa answers to one character only of the Vedic Soma, and not to both. Soma is at once the Moon-God and the Genius of Intoxication. (*Rig-Veda Sanhita*, vol. i. p. 118; vol. ii. p 311; &c.) Homa is the latter only.

[2] This practice remained among the Persian Fire-worshippers to a late date. It is mentioned as characteristic of the Persians by Xenophon (*Cyrop.* viii. 3, § 24) and Ovid (*Fasti*, I. 385). [3] *Yaçna*, xliv. 18.

[4] This is evidently the original of Mahomet's famous "way, extended over the middle of Hell, which is sharper than a sword and finer than a hair, over which all must pass." (*Pocock, Spec. Hist. Arab.* p. 278.)

to heaven or paradise, over which the souls of the pious alone could pass, while the wicked fell from it into the gulf below, where they found themselves in the place of punishment. The good soul was assisted across the bridge by the angel Serosh—"the happy, well-formed, swift, tall Serosh"[5]—who met the weary wayfarer and sustained his steps as he effected the difficult passage. The prayers of his friends in this world were of much avail to the deceased and greatly helped him on his journey.[6] As he entered, the archangel Vohu-manô or Bahman rose from his throne and greeted him with the words—"How happy art thou who hast come here to us from the mortality to the immortality!" Then the pious soul went joyfully onward to Ahura-mazda, to the immortal saints, to the golden throne, to Paradise.[7] As for the wicked, when they fell into the gulf, they found themselves in outer darkness, in the kingdom of Angrô-mainyus, where they were forced to remain and to feed upon poisoned banquets.

It is believed by some that the doctrine of the resurrection of the body was also part of the Zoroastrian creed.[8] Theopompus assigned this doctrine to the Magi,[9] and there is no reason to doubt that it was held by the priestly caste of the Arian nations in his day. We find it plainly stated in portions of the Zendavesta, which, if not among the earliest, are at any rate of very considerable antiquity, as in the eighteenth chapter of the Vendidad.[10] It is argued that even in the Gâthâs there is an expression used which shows the doctrine to have been already held when they were composed; but the phrase adduced is so obscure, that its true meaning must be pronounced in the highest degree uncertain." The absence of any plain allusion to the resurrection from the earlier portions of the sacred volume is a strong argument against its having formed any part of the original Arian creed—an argument which is far from outweighed by the occurrence of a mere possible reference to it in a single ambiguous passage.

Around and about this nucleus of religious belief there grew up in course of time a number of legends, some of which possess considerable interest. Like other thoughtful races, the Iranians speculated upon the early condition of mankind, and conceived a golden age, and a king then reigning over a perfectly happy people, whom they called King Yima— Yima-khshaêta[12]—the modern Persian Jemshid. Yima, according to the legend, had dwelt originally in *Aryanem vaêjo*—the primitive seat of the Arians—and had there reigned gloriously and peacefully for awhile; but, the evils of winter having come upon

---

[11] Haug, *Essays*, pp. 143 and 260. The expression relied on is *frashem kerenaon ahîm*, which occurs in the Gâtha ahunavaiti (Yaçna, xxx. 9), and is translated, "they perpetuate the life"—literally "they make the life lasting." Hence, it is said, was formed the substantive *frashô-kereti*, which in the later Zend books becomes a *verbum usitatum*, designating the entire period of resurrection and palingenesis at the end of time. But this only shows that the later Zoroastrians applied a phrase taken from the older books to their doctrine. It does not prove that the phrase had originally the meaning which they put upon it. In its literal sense the expression clearly does not go beyond the general notion of a future existence.

[12] With *khshaeta*, the *epitheton usitatum* of Yima, which undoubtedly means "king"—corresponding to the *rájâ*, which is the epithet of Yama in the Vedas—may be compared the Achæmenian *khshayathiya*, which is the commonest term for "king" in the Persian cuneiform inscriptions.

his country, he had removed from it with his subjects, and had retired to a secluded spot, where he and his people enjoyed uninterrupted happiness."[13] In this place was "neither overbearing nor mean-spiritedness, neither stupidity nor violence, neither poverty nor deceit, neither puniness nor deformity, neither huge teeth nor bodies beyond the usual measure."[14] The inhabitants suffered no defilement from the evil spirit. They dwelt amid odoriferous trees and golden pillars; their cattle were the largest, best, and most beautiful on the earth; they were themselves a tall and beautiful race; their food was ambrosial and never failed them. No wonder that time sped fast with them, and that they, not noting its flight, thought often that what was really a year had been no more than a single day.[15] Yima was the great hero of the early Iranians. His titles, besides "the king" (*khshaêta*), are "the brilliant," "the happy," "the greatly wealthy," "the leader of the peoples," "the renowned in Aryanem vaêjo." He is most probably identical with the Yama of the Vedas,[16] who was originally the first man, the progenitor of mankind and the ruler of the blessed in Paradise, but who was afterwards transformed into "the god of death, the inexorable judge of men's doings and the punisher of the wicked."[17]

Next in importance to Yima among the heroes is Thraêtona—the modern Persian Feridun. He was

---

[13] *Vendidad*, Farg. ii. § 4 to § 41.
[14] Ibid. § 20.   [15] Ibid. § 41.
[16] This identification was first made, I believe, by Burnouf. It rests on the following resemblances. Yama has habitually the title *rajâ* affixed to his name; Yima has the corresponding title *khshaêta*. Yama is the son of *Vivasvat*; Yima, of *Vivanghwat*. Yama is the first Vedic man; Yima is the first Iranic king. Yama reigns over a heavenly, Yima over an earthly paradise.
[17] Haug, *Essays*, p. 234.

born in Varena¹—which is perhaps Atropatênê, or Azerbijan²—and was the son of a distinguished father, Athwyô. His chief exploit was the destruction of Ajis-dahaka (Zohak), who is sometimes represented as a cruel tyrant, the bitter enemy of the Iranian race,³ sometimes as a monstrous dragon, with three mouths, three tails, six eyes, and a thousand scaly rings, who threatened to ruin the whole of the good creation.⁴ The traditional scene of the destruction was the mountain of Demavend, the highest peak of the Elburz range south of the Caspian. Thraêtona, like Yima, appears to be also a Vedic hero. He may be recognized in Traitana,⁵ who is said in the Rig-Veda to have slain a mighty giant by severing his head from his shoulders.

A third heroic personage known in the early times⁶ was Keresaspa, of the noble Sâma family. He was the son of Thrita—a distinct personage from Thraêtona—and brother of Urvakhshaya the Just,⁷ and was bred up in the arid country of Vehkerot (Khorassan). The "glory" which had rested upon Yima

---

¹ *Yashts*, xv. 23; xvii. 33; *Vendidad*, Farg. i. § 18.
² The capital of Atropatênê was sometimes called Vera or Baris, whence perhaps Varena. Or Varena may possibly be Ghilan, since "the initial *s* of the old Iranian usually becomes *g* in modern Persian." (Haug in Bunsen's *Egypt*, vol. iii. p. 487.)
³ *Yashts*, xv. 8; and so in the Shahnameh (Atkinson's *Abridgment*, pp. 12-49).
⁴ *Yaçna*, ix. 8. Burnouf thus translates the passage:—"Thraetona ... qui a tué le serpent homicide aux trois gueules, aux trois têtes, aux six yeux, aux mille forces, cette divinité cruelle qui détruit la pureté, ce pecheur qui ravage les mondes,

et qu'Ahriman a créé le plus ennemi de la pureté dans le monde, existant pour l'anéantissement de la pureté des mondes."
⁵ So Haug (*Essays*, p. 235), Roth (*Zeitschrift der D. morgenlandischen Gesellschaft*, vol. ii. p. 216), and Lassen (*Indische Alterthumskunde*, additions). Professor H. H. Wilson, on the other hand, rejects the proposed identification. (*Rig-Veda Sanhita*, vol. i. p. 143, note.)
⁶ Keresaspa is mentioned in the first Fargard of the Vendidad (§ 10); which has been already shown to be older than the first occupation by the Arians of Media Magna. (See above, p. 107, note ¹.)
⁷ Yaçna, ix. 7.

so many years became his in his day.[8] He was the mightiest among the mighty, and was guarded from all danger by the fairy (*pairika*) Knathaiti,[9] who followed him whithersoever he went. He slew Çravara, the green and venomous serpent, who swallowed up men and horses.[10] He killed Gandarewa with the golden heel, and also Çnâvidhaka, who had boasted that, when he grew up, he would make the earth his wheel and heaven his chariot, that he would carry off Ahura-mazda from heaven and Angrô-mainyus from hell, and yoke them both as horses to his car. Keresaspa appears as Gershasp in the modern Persian legends,[11] where, however, but little is said of his exploits. In the Hindoo books[12] he appears as Kriçâçva, the son of Samyama, and is called king of Vâiçâli, or Bengal!

From these specimens the general character of the early Iranic legends appears sufficiently. Without affording any very close resemblances in particular cases, they present certain general features which are common to the legendary lore of all the Western Arians. They are romantic tales, not allegories;

---

[8] A special "glory" or "lustre" (*çarenô*), the reflex of Ahura-mazda's inborn brilliancy (*qâthrô*), attaches to certain eminent heroes, more especially to Yima and Keresaspa. (*Yashts*, xix. 38.)

[9] The fairy Knathaiti, though originally a creation of Angrô-mainyus (*Vendidad*, Farg. I. 10; xix. 5), "became the protecting genius of heroes, who were indebted to her for their supernatural strength." (Haug in Bunsen's *Egypt*, vol. iii. p. 462.)

[10] *Yashts*, xix. 38-44. Compare Yaçna, ix. 8, which is thus translated by Burnouf—"C'est lui (Keresaçpa) qui tua le serpent açôle qui dévorait les chevaux et les hommes, ce serpent vénimeux et vert, sur le corps duquel ruisselait un vert poison de l'épaisseur du pouce. Keresaçpa fit chauffer au-dessus de lui de l'eau dans un vase d'airain, jusqu'à midi; et le monstre homicide sentait la chaleur, et il siffla. Le vase d'airain, tombant en avant, repandit l'eau faite pour s'écouler. Le serpent, effrayé, s'enfuit; Keresaçpa, au cœur d'homme, recula."

[11] *Shah-nameh*, pp. 117-122 (Atkinson's *Abridgment*).

[12] See the *Bhagavat Purana*, and compare Burnouf in the *Journal Asiatique*, Avril-Mai, 1845, p. 255.

they relate with exaggerations the deeds of men, not the processes of nature.[13] Combining some beauty with a good deal that is *bizarre* and grotesque, they are lively and graphic, but somewhat childish, having in no case any deep meaning and rarely teaching a moral lesson. In their earliest shape they appear, so far as we can judge,[14] to have been brief, disconnected, and fragmentary. They owe the full and closely interconnected form which they assume in the Shahnameh and other modern Persian writings,[15] partly to a gradual accretion during the course of centuries, partly to the inventive genius of Firdausi, who wove the various and often isolated legends into a pseudo-history, and amplified them at his own pleasure. How much of the substance of Firdausi's poem belongs to really primitive myth is uncertain. We find in the Zend texts the names of Gayo-marathan, who corresponds to Kaiomars; of Haoshyanha, or Hosheng; of Yima-shaēta, or Jemshid; of Ajis-dahaka or Zohak; of Athwya or Abtin; of Thraētona or Feridun; of Keresaspa or Gershasp; of Kava Uç or Kai Kavus; of Kava Huçrava or Kai Khosroo; and of Kava Vistaspa, or Gushtasp. But we have no mention of Tahomars, of Gava (or Gau) the blacksmith, of Feridun's sons, Selm, Tur, and Irij, of Zal or Mino'chihr or Rustem, of Afrasiab or

---

[13] It is not intended to deny that there are some portions of the Greek and Roman, and again of the German and Scandinavian mythology which are allegorical, and which are best explained as originally expressive of processes in nature; but only to assert, that the physical element in those mythologies is so overlaid by the historical or quasi-historical as to disappear from sight and be lost, like a drop in the ocean.

[14] It must be remembered that we do not possess the ancient Zendic writings in a complete shape, as we do the Vedas, but only in a curtailed and fragmentary form. (See Haug, *Essays*, p. 219.)

[15] As the *Dabistān* of Mohammed Mohsin Fani, and the *Rauzat-us-Sufu* of Mirkhond.

Kai Kobad, of Sohrab or Isfendiar. And of the heroic names which actually occur in the Zendavesta, several, as Gayo-marathan, Haosbyanha, Kava Uç, and Kava Huçrava, are met with only in the later portions, which belong probably to about the fourth century before our era.[16] The only legends which we know to be primitive are those above related, which are found in portions of the Zendavesta, whereto the best critics ascribe a high antiquity. The negative argument is not, however, conclusive; and it is quite possible that a very large proportion of Firdausi's tale may consist of ancient legends dressed up in a garb comparatively modern.

Two phases of the early Iranic religion have been now briefly described, the first a simple and highly spiritual creed, remarkable for its distinct assertion of monotheism, its hatred of idolatry, and the strongly marked antithesis which it maintained between good and evil; the second, a natural corruption of the first, Dualistic, complicated, by the importance which it ascribed to angelic beings verging upon polytheism. It remains to give an account of a third phase into which the religion passed in consequence of an influence exercised upon it from without by an alien system.

When the Iranic nations, cramped for space in the countries east and south of the Caspian, began to push themselves further to the west, and then to the south, they were brought into contact with various Scythic tribes[17] inhabiting the mountain regions of

---

[16] These names occur, I believe, only in the Yashts, which Hang assigns, on good grounds, to about B.C. 450-350. (*Essays*, p. 224.)

[17] The cuneiform Inscriptions of Armenia, Azerbijan, and Elymais are in Scythic or Turanian dialects. The third column of the trilingual inscriptions of the Zagros range is also Scythic. On the various grounds

Armenia, Azerbijan, Kurdistan, and Luristan, whose religion appears to have been Magism. It was here, in these elevated tracts, where the mountains almost seem to reach the skies, that the most venerated and ancient of the fire-temples (πυραιθεῖα) were established, some

Fire-temples near Nakhsh-i-Rustem.

of which remain, seemingly in their primitive condition, at the present day.[1] Here tradition placed the original seat of the fire-worship;[2] and from hence many taught that Zoroaster, whom they regarded as

---

for regarding the ante-Arian inhabitants of those parts as Scyths, see *Journal of the Asiatic Society*, vol. xv. pp. 235, 230.

[1] See Ker Porter's *Travels*, vol. i. p. 566.

[2] Proofs of this are collected in Sir H. Rawlinson's Article "On the Atropatenian Ecbatana" in the *Journal of the Geographical Society*, vol. x. pp. 79-83.

the founder of Magism, had sprung. Magism was, essentially, the worship of the elements, the recognition of fire, air, earth, and water as the only proper objects of human reverence. The Magi held no personal gods, and therefore naturally rejected temples, shrines, and images, as tending to encourage the notion that gods existed of a like nature with man, i. e. possessing personality—living and intelligent beings. Theirs was a nature worship, but a nature worship of a very peculiar kind. They did not place gods over the different parts of nature, like the Greeks; they did not even personify the powers of nature, like the Hindoos; they paid their devotion to the actual material things themselves. Fire, as the most subtle and ethereal principle, and again as the most powerful agent, attracted their highest regards; and on their fire-altars the sacred flame, generally said to have been kindled from heaven, was kept burning uninterruptedly from year to year and from age to age by bands of priests, whose special duty it was to see that the sacred spark was never extinguished. To defile the altar by blowing the flame with one's breath was a capital offence;

Ctesias called Zoroaster an Armenian (Arnobius, *Adv. Nationes*, i. 52). Moses of Chorene regarded him as a Mede (*Hist. Armen.* i. 16). So Clemens of Alexandria in one place (*Strom.* l. p. 300).

We sometimes find it said that the Magi worshipped fire and water only (Dino, Fr. 9); sometimes that their gods were fire, water, and earth. (Diog. Laert. *Proœm.* § 6.) But there seems to be no real doubt that their worship was actually paid to all the four elements. (Herod. i. 132; Strab. xv. 3, § 13; Theodoret, *Hist. Eccles.* v. 38; &c.)

See this reason assigned in Herod. i. 132.

Hence the name Πύραιθοι borne by the Magi in Cappadocia (Strab. xv. 3, § 15). Compare the *Athrava* of the Zendavesta, derived from *âtar*, "fire." See also Strab. xv. 3, § 14; Lucian, *Jov. Trag.* § 42; Clem. Alex. *Protrept.* v. p 56.

Dio. Chrysost. *Orat. Borysth.* p. 449, A.; Amm. Marc. xxiii. 6; Clem. *Recognit.* iv. 29; Agathias, ii. 25.

Πῦρ ἄσβεστον φυλάττουσιν οἱ Μάγοι. (Strab. xv. 3, p. 15.)

Ibid. § 14. Ὑφάπτουσιν .. οὐ φυσῶντες ἀλλὰ ῥιπίζοντες. τοὺς δὲ φυσήσαντας ... θανατοῦσι.

and to burn a corpse was regarded as an act equally odious.[10] When victims were offered to fire, nothing but a small portion of the fat was consumed in the flame.[11] Next to fire, water was reverenced. Sacrifice was offered to rivers, lakes, and fountains, the victim being brought near to them and then slain, while great care was taken that no drop of their blood should touch the water and pollute it.[12] No refuse was allowed to be cast into a river, nor was it even lawful to wash one's hands in one.[13] Reverence for earth was shown by sacrifice [14] and by abstention from the usual mode of burying the dead.[15]

The Magian religion was of a highly sacerdotal type. No worshipper could perform any religious act except by the intervention of a priest, or Magus, who stood between him and the divinity as a Mediator.[16] The Magus prepared the victim and slew it, chanted the mystic strain which gave the sacrifice all its force, poured on the ground the propitiatory libation of oil, milk, and honey, held the bundle of thin tamarisk twigs—the Zendic barsom (*bareçma*)—the employment of which was essential to every sacrificial ceremony.[17] The Magi were a priest-caste, apparently, holding their office by hereditary succes-

---

[10] Herod. III. 16; Strab. l. s. c.; Nic. Dam. Fr. 68, p. 409.
[11] Some said that no part of the victim was burnt. (Strab. l. s. c. Eustath. *Comment. ad Hom. Il.* l.) But Strabo's statement, that a small portion was consumed in the fire, seems trustworthy. Xenophon's "whole burnt offerings" are a pure fiction. (*Cyrop.* viii. 3, § 24.)
[12] Strab. l. s. c.
[13] Herod. I. 138; Strab. xv. 3, § 10; Agathias, ii. 24, ad fin.
[14] Xen. *Cyrop.* l. s. c.
[15] See below, p. 120, note *.
[16] Herod. I. 132. "Ἄνευ γὰρ δὴ Μάγου οὔ σφι νόμος ἐστὶ θυσίας ποιέεσθαι. Amm. Marc. xxiii. 6. "Erat piaculum aras adire vel hostiam contrectare antequam Magus conceptis precationibus libamenta diffunderet praecursoria." Strabo implies the same without distinctly stating it. (Strab. xv. 3, § 13.)
[17] Strab. xv. 3, § 14 and 15. Compare Herod. I. 132.

sion.[18] They claimed to possess, not only a sacred and mediatorial character, but also supernatural prophetic powers. They explained omens,[19] expounded dreams,[20] and by means of a certain mysterious manipulation of the barsom, or bundle of twigs, arrived at a knowledge of future events, which they communicated to the pious inquirer.[21]

With such pretensions it was natural that the caste should assume a lofty air, a stately dress, and an *entourage* of ceremonial magnificence. Clad in white robes,[22] and bearing upon their heads tall felt caps, with long lappets at the sides, which concealed the jaw and even the lips, each with his barsom in his hand, they marched in procession to their *pyrætheia*, or fire-altars, and standing around them performed for an hour at a time their magical incantations.[23] The credulous multitude, impressed by sights of this kind, and imposed on by the claims to supernatural power which the Magi advanced, paid them a willing homage; the kings and chiefs consulted them; and when the Arian tribes, pressing westward, came into contact with the races professing the Magian religion, they found a sacerdotal caste all powerful in most of the Scythic nations.

The original spirit of Zoroastrianism was fierce and exclusive. The early Iranians looked with con-

---

[18] This is implied in the statement of Herodotus (i. 101), that they were a tribe (φῦλον). It is expressly declared by Ammianus Marcellinus (xxiii. 6), Sozomen (*Hist. Eccl.* ii. 8), and others.

[19] Herod. vii. 37; Cic. *de Div.* i. 41; Val. Max. i. 6.

[20] Herod. i. 107, 108; vii. 10; Cic. *de Div.* i. 23.

[21] Dino, Fr. 6; Schol. Nicandr. Ther. 613.

[22] Diog. Laert. Proem. ἐσθῆς μὲν λευκή.

[23] See the picture which Strabo gives of the Magian priests in Cappadocia (xv. 3, § 15)—a picture drawn from his own experience (ταῦτα μὲν οὖν ἡμεῖς ἑωράκαμεν).

tempt and hatred on the creed of their Indian
brethren; they abhorred idolatry; and were disinclined to tolerate any religion except that which
they had themselves worked out. But with the
lapse of ages this spirit became softened. Polytheistic creeds are far less jealous than monotheism;
and the development of Zoroastrianism had been in a
polytheistic direction. By the time that the Zoroastrians were brought into contact with Magism, the
first fervour of their religious zeal had abated, and
they were in that intermediate condition of religious
faith which at once impresses and is impressed, acts
upon other systems and allows itself to be acted upon
in return. The result which supervened upon contact with Magism seems to have been a fusion—an
absorption into Zoroastrianism of all the chief points
of the Magian belief, and all the more remarkable
of the Magian religious usages. This absorption
appears to have taken place in Media. It was there
that the Arian tribes first associated with themselves,
and formally adopted into their body the priest-caste of
the Magi,[14] which thenceforth was recognised as one
of the six Median tribes.[15] It is there that Magi are

---

[14] Haug imagines that the term Magus is Zoroastrian, that it was used from very ancient times among the Arians to designate the followers of the true religion (*Essays*, pp. 160, 247), and that by degrees it came to be applied especially to the priests. For my own part I doubt the iden-tity of the *maga* or *maghava*, which occurs twice, and twice only, in the whole of the Zendavesta (Wester-gaard, *Introduction to Zendavesta*, p. 17), with the *magush* of the cunei-form inscriptions and the Mάγοι of the Greeks.

[15] Herod. i. 101. The first real proof that we have of any close con-nexion of the Magi with an Arian race, is furnished by the Median his-tory of Herodotus, where we find them a part, but not apparently an original part, of the Median nation. Their position (*fifth*) in the list of tribes, *last of all* except the Budii, who were probably also Scyths, is only to be accounted for, when we consider their high rank and im-portance, by their having been added on to the nation after the four Arian tribes were constituted.

first found acting in the capacity of Arian priests.[m] According to all the accounts which have come down to us, they acquired a predominating influence at the Median court—an influence which they no doubt used to impress their own religious doctrines more and more upon the nation at large, and to thrust into the back-ground, so far as they dared, the peculiar features of the old Arian belief. It is not necessary to suppose that the Medes ever apostatized altogether from the worship of Ormazd, or formally surrendered their Dualistic faith.[1] But, practically, the Magian doctrines and the Magian usages — elemental worship, divination with the sacred rods, dream-expounding, incantations at the fire-altars, sacrifices whereat a Magus officiated— seem to have prevailed; the new predominated over the old; backed by the power of an organised hierarchy, Magism overlaid the primitive Arian creed, and, as time went on, tended more and more to become the real religion of the nation.

Among the religious customs introduced by the Magi into Media, there are one or two which seem to require especial notice. The attribution of a sacred character to the four so-called elements— earth, air, fire, and water—renders it extremely difficult to know what is to be done with the dead. They cannot be burnt, for that is a pollution of fire; or buried, for that is a pollution of earth; or thrown into a river, for that is a defilement of water. If they are deposited in sarcophagi, or exposed, they

---

[m] Herod. L 107, 108.
[1] It is in Media (at Behistun) that the sculptor of a Scythic Inscription—probably himself a Median Scyth—informs his readers that Ormazd was "the god of the Arians." Remark that he says "Arians"—not "Persians"—thus including the Arian Medes.

really pollute the air; but in this case the guilt of the pollution, it may be argued, does not rest on man, since the dead body is merely left in the element in which nature placed it. The only mode of disposal which completely avoids the defilement of every element is consumption of the dead by living beings; and the worship of the elements leads on naturally to this treatment of corpses. At present the Guebres, or Fire-Worshippers, the descendants of the ancient Persians, expose all their dead, with the intention that they shall be devoured by birds of prey.[2] In ancient times, it appears certain that the Magi adopted this practice with respect to their own dead;[3] but, apparently, they did not insist upon having their example followed universally by the laity.[4] Probably a natural instinct made the Arians averse to this coarse and revolting custom; and their spiritual guides, compassionating their weakness, or fearful of losing their own influence over them if they were too stiff in enforcing compliance, winked at the employment by the people of an entirely different

---

[2] See the author's *Herodotus*, vol. i. p. 223, note [4], 2nd ed. Round towers of considerable height, without either door or window, are constructed by the Guebres, having at the top a number of iron bars, which slope inwards. The towers are mounted by means of ladders; and the bodies are placed crossways upon the bars. The vultures and crows which hover about the towers soon strip the flesh from the bones, and these latter then fall through to the bottom.
  The Zendavesta contains particular directions for the construction of such towers, which are called *dakhmas*, or "Towers of Silence." (*Vendidad*, Farg. v. to Farg. viii.)

[3] Strab. xv. 3, § 20. Τοὺς δὲ Μάγους οὐ θάπτουσιν ἀλλ' οἰωνόβρωτους ἐῶσι. Compare Herod. (i. 140), who, however, seems to think that the bodies were buried after dogs or birds had partially devoured them. In this he was probably mistaken.

[4] This appears from the statements made by Herodotus and Strabo as to the actual practice in the passages quoted in the last note. On the other hand, if we refer the composition of the middle portion of the Vendidad (from the fifth to the eighteenth Fargard) to the times of early Magian ascendancy, we must suppose that they wished to put a stop to all burial.

practice. The dead bodies were first covered completely with a coating of wax, and were then deposited in the ground.⁵ It was held, probably, that the coating of wax prevented the pollution, which would have necessarily resulted, had the earth come into direct contact with the corpse.

The custom of divining by means of a number of rods appears to have been purely Magian. There is no trace of it in the Gâthâs, in the *Yaçna haptanhaiti*, or in the older portions of the Vendidad. It was a Scythic practice;⁶ and probably the best extant account of it is that which Herodotus gives of the mode wherein it was managed by the Scyths of Europe. "Scythia," he says, "has an abundance of soothsayers, who foretell the future by means of a number of willow wands. A large bundle of these rods is brought and laid on the ground. The soothsayer unties the bundle, and places each wand by itself, at the same time uttering his prophecy: then, while he is still speaking, he gathers the rods together again, and makes them up once more into a bundle."⁷ A divine power seems to have been regarded as resting in the wands; and they were supposed to be "consulted"⁸ on the matter in hand, both severally and collectively. The bundle of wands thus imbued with supernatural wisdom, be-

---

⁵ Herod. l. s. c. Κατασηρώσαντες τὸν νέκυν Πέρσαι γῇ κρύπτουσι. Simb. l. s. c. Θάπτουσι κηρῷ συγκηλώσαντες τὰ σώματα.

⁶ Schol. Nic. Ther. 613: Μάγοι δὲ καὶ Σκύθαι μυρσίνῃ μαντεύονται ξύλῳ· καὶ γὰρ ἐν πολλοῖς τόποις ῥάβδοις μαντεύονται. Δείνων δὲ . . καὶ τοὺς μάντεις φησὶ Μήδους ῥάβδους μαντεύεσθαι.

⁷ Herod. iv. 67. The only difference seems to be that the European Scyths used willow wands, the Magi twigs of the tamarisk.

⁸ The prophet Hosea evidently refers to this custom when he says (iv. 12)—"My people ask counsel at their stocks; and their staff declareth unto them." It must therefore have been practised in Western Asia at least as early as B. C. 700. See also Ezek. viii. 17. "And, lo, they put the branch to their nose."

came naturally part of the regular priestly costume,[9] and was carried by the Magi on all occasions of ceremony. The wands were of different lengths; and the number of wands in the bundle varied. Sometimes there were three, sometimes five; sometimes as many as seven or nine; but in every case, as it would seem, an odd number.[10]

Another implement which the priests commonly bore must be regarded, not as Magian, but as Zoroastrian. This is the *khrafçthraghna*, or instrument for killing bad animals,[11] frogs, toads, snakes, mice, lizards, flies, &c., which belonged to the bad creation, or that which derived its origin from Angrô-mainyus. These it was the general duty of all men, and the more especial duty of the Zoroastrian priests, to put to death, whenever they had the opportunity. The Magi, it appears, adopted this Arian usage, added the *khrafçthraghna* to the *barsom*, and were so zealous in their performance of the cruel work expected from them as to excite the attention, and even draw upon themselves the rebuke, of foreigners.[12]

A practice is assigned to the Magi by many classical and ecclesiastical writers,[13] which, if it were truly charged on them, would leave a very dark stain on the character of their ethical system. It is

---

[9] *Vendidad*, Farg. xviii. 1-6; Strab. xv. 3, § 14 and § 15.
[10] *Yaçna*, lvii. 6.
[11] *Vendidad*, l. s. c.
[12] Herodotus had evidently seen Magi pursuing their pious pastime, "killing ants and snakes, and seeming to take a delight in the employment" (i. 140). Though speaking in his usual guarded way of a religious custom, he does not fail to indicate that he was shocked as well as astonished.
[13] Xanthus ap. Clem. Alex. *Strom.* iii. p. 515; Ctesias ap. Tertull. *Apolog.* p. 10, C.; Antisthenes ap. Athen. *Deipn.* v. 63, p. 220, C.; Diog. Laert. *Procem.* § 7; Strab. xv. 3, § 20; Catull. *Carm.* xc. 3; Lucian. *De Sacrific.* § 5; Philo Judæus, *De decalog.* p. 778; Tertull. *Ad. Nat.* i. 16; Orig. *Cont. Cels.* v. p. 248; Clem. Alex. *Pæd.* i. 7, p. 131; Minucius, *Octav.* 31, p. 155; Agathias, ii. 24.

said that they allowed and even practised incest of the most horrible kind—such incest as we are accustomed to associate with the names of Lot, Œdipus, and Herod Agrippa. The charge seems to have been first made either by Xanthus the Lydian, or by Ctesias. It was accepted, probably without much inquiry, by the Greeks generally, and then by the Romans, was repeated by writer after writer as a certain fact, and became finally a stock topic with the early Christian apologists. Whether it had any real foundation in fact is very uncertain. Herodotus, who collects with so much pains the strange and unusual customs of the various nations whom he visits, is evidently quite ignorant of any such monstrous practice. He regards the Magian religion as established in Persia, yet he holds the incestuous marriage of Cambyses with his sister to have been contrary to existing Persian laws.[14] At the still worse forms of incest, of which the Magi and those under their influence are accused, Herodotus does not even glance. No doubt, if Xanthus Lydus really made the statement which Clemens of Alexandria assigns to him, it is an important piece of evidence, though scarcely sufficient to prove the Magi guilty. Xanthus was a man of little judgment, apt to relate extravagant tales;[1] and, as a Lydian, he may have been not disinclined to cast an aspersion on the religion of his country's oppressors. The passage in question, however, probably did not come from Xanthus Lydus, but from a much later writer who assumed his name, as has been well shown by a

---

[14] Herod. iii. 31. [1] See his fragments in C. Müller's *Fragm. Hist. Gr.* vol. i. pp. 36-44; and especially Frs. 11, 12, and 19.

living critic.² The true original author of the accusation against the Magi and their co-religionists seems to have been Ctesias,³ whose authority is far too weak to establish a charge intrinsically so improbable. Its only historical foundation seems to have been the fact that incestuous marriages were occasionally contracted by the Persian kings; not, however, in consequence of any law, or religious usage, but because in the plenitude of their power they could set all law at defiance, and trample upon the most sacred principles of morality and religion.⁴

A minor charge preferred against the Magian morality by Xanthus, or rather by the pseudo-Xanthus, has possibly a more solid foundation. "The Magi," this writer said, "hold their wives in common: at least they often marry the wives of others with the free consent of their husbands." This is really to say that among the Magians divorce was over facile; that wives were often put away, merely with a view to their forming a fresh marriage, by husbands who understood and approved of the transaction. Judging by the existing practice of the Persians,⁵ we must admit that such laxity is in

---

² See Müller's Introduction to vol. i. of the *Fragm. Hist. Gr.* pp. xxi. and xxii.

³ If the Antisthenes quoted by Athenæus is the philosopher, as he was contemporary with Ctesias, he may have been the first to make the charge. But there were at least four Greek writers who bore the name of Antisthenes. (See Diog. Laert. vi. 19.)

⁴ Herod. iii. 31. Οἱ βασιλήιοι δικασταί ... ὑπεκρίναντο ... ἐξευρηκέναι νόμον, τῷ βασιλεύοντι Περσέων ἐξεῖναι ποιέειν τὸ ἂν βούληται.

⁵ Ker Porter says—"The lower ranks [of Persians], seldom being able to support more than the privileged number of wives, are often ready to change them on any plea, when time, or any other cause, has a little sullied their freshness.... When matrimonial differences arise, of sufficient magnitude to occasion a wish to separate, the grievances are stated by both parties before the judge; and if duly substantiated, and the complainants persist in demanding a divorce, he furnishes both with the necessary certificates." (*Travels*, vol. i. p. 342.)

accordance with Iranic notions on the subject of marriage—notions far less strict than those which have commonly prevailed among civilized nations. There is, however, no other evidence, besides this, that divorce was very common where the Magian system prevailed; and the mere assertion of the writer who personated Xanthus Lydus will scarcely justify us in affixing even this stigma on the religion.

Upon the whole, Magism, though less elevated and less pure than the old Zoroastrian creed, must be pronounced to have possessed a certain loftiness and picturesqueness which suited it to become the religion of a great and splendid monarchy. The mysterious fire-altars on the mountain tops, with their prestige of a remote antiquity—the ever-burning flame believed to have been kindled from on high—the worship in the open air under the blue canopy of heaven—the long troops of Magians in their white robes, with their strange caps, and their mystic wands—the frequent prayers—the abundant sacrifices[4]—the long incantations—the supposed prophetic powers of the priest-caste—all this together constituted 'an imposing whole at once to the eye and to the mind, and was calculated to give additional grandeur to the civil system that should be allied with it. Pure Zoroastrianism was too spiritual to coalesce readily with Oriental luxury and magnificence, or to lend strength to a government based on the ordinary principles of Asiatic despotism. Magism furnished a hierarchy to support the throne, and add splendour and dignity to the court, while

---

[4] Xen. Cyrop. viii. 3, § 11 and § 24; Herod. vii. 43.

CHAP. IV.   CAUSES OF THE TRIUMPH OF MAGISM.   135

they over-awed the subject-class by their supposed possession of supernatural powers, and of the right of mediating between heaven and man. It supplied a picturesque worship, which at once gratified the senses and excited the fancy. It gave scope to man's passion for the marvellous by its incantations, its divining rods, its omen-reading, and its dream-expounding. It gratified the religious scrupulosity which finds a pleasure in making to itself difficulties, by the disallowance of a thousand natural acts, and the imposition of numberless rules for external purity.[1] At the same time it gave no offence to the anti-idolatrous spirit in which the Arians had hitherto gloried, but rather encouraged the iconoclasm which they always upheld and practised. It thus blended easily with the previous creed of the people, awaking no prejudices, clashing with no interests; winning its way by an apparent meekness and unpresumingness, while it was quite prepared, when the fitting time came, to be as fierce and exclusive as if it had never worn the mask of humility and moderation.[2]

---

[1] See the minute directions for escaping or removing impurity contained in the *Vendidad*, Farg. 8, 9, 10, 11, 16, and 17. All these chapters seem Magian rather than Zoroastrian.

[2] I cannot conclude this chapter without expressing my obligations to Dr. Martin Haug, from whose works I have mainly derived my acquaintance with the real contents of the Zendavesta. I have rarely ventured to differ from him in the inferences which he draws from those contents. In one important respect only do I find my views seriously at variance with his. I regard Magism as in its origin completely distinct from Zoroastrianism, and as the chief cause of its corruption, and of the remarkable difference between the earlier and the later of the Zendic books. In this view I am happy to find myself supported by Westergaard, who writes as follows in his "Preface" to the *Zendavesta* (p. 17):—"The faith ascribed by Herodotus to the Persians is not the lore of Zoroaster; nor were the Magi in the time of Darius the priests of Ormazd. Their name, Magu, occurs only twice in all the extant Zend texts, and here in a general sense, while Darius opposes his creed to

that of the Magi, whom he treated most unmercifully. Though Darius was the mightiest king of Persia, yet his memory and that of his predecessors on the thrones of Persia and Media has long since utterly vanished from the recollections of the people. It was supplanted by the foreign North-Iranian mythology, which terminates with Vishtâspa and his sons; and with these persons the later Persian tradition has connected the Achæmenian Artaxerxes, the Long-Handed, as if he especially had contributed to the propagation and establishment in Western Iran of the Zoroastrian belief. But *this latter would appear early to have undergone some modification, perhaps even from the influence of Magism itself;* and it may have been in this period that the Magi, turning to the faith of their sovereigns" (or rather, turning their sovereigns to their faith), "became the priests of Ormazd."

Chapter V.

LANGUAGE AND WRITING.

Ὁμόγλωττοι παρὰ μικρὸν οἱ Πέρσαι καὶ οἱ Μῆδοι.—Strab. xv. 2, § 8.

On the language of the ancient Medes a very few observations will be here made. It has been noticed already[1] that the Median form of speech was closely allied to that of the Persians. The remark of Strabo quoted above, and another remark which he cites from Nearchus,[2] imply at once this fact, and also the further fact of a dialectic difference between the two tongues. Did we possess, as some imagine that we do, materials for tracing out this diversity, it would be proper in the present place to enter fully on the subject, and instead of contenting ourselves with asserting, or even proving, the substantial oneness of the languages, it would be our duty to proceed to the far more difficult and more complicated task of comparing together the sister dialects and noting their various differences. The supposition that there exist means for such a comparison is based upon a theory that in the language of the Zendavesta we have the true speech of the ancient people of Media, while in the cuneiform inscriptions of the Achæmenian kings it is beyond controversy that we possess the ancient

---

[1] See above, ch. iii. p. 73.
[2] Νέαρχος δὲ τὰ πλεῖστα ἔθη καὶ τὴν διάλεκτον τῶν Καρμανιτῶν Περ- σικά τε καὶ Μηδικὰ εἴρηκε. Strab. xv. 2, § 14.

language of Persia. It becomes necessary therefore to examine this theory in order to justify our abstention from an enquiry on which, if the theory were sound, we should be now called upon to enter.

The notion that the Zend language was the idiom of ancient Media originated with Anquetil du Perron. He looked on Zoroaster as a native of Azerbijan, contemporary with Darius Hystaspis. His opinion was embraced by Kleuker, Herder, and Rask;[1] and again, with certain modifications, by Tychsen[2] and Heeren.[3] These latter writers even gave a more completely Median character to the Zendavesta by regarding it as composed in Media Magna, during the reign of the great Cyaxares. The main foundation of these views was the identification of Zoroastrianism with the Magian fire-worship, which was really ancient in Azerbijan and flourished in Media under the great Median monarch. But we have seen that Magianism and Zoroastrianism were originally entirely distinct, and that the Zendavesta in all its earlier portions belongs wholly to the latter system. Nothing therefore is proved concerning the Zend dialect by establishing a connexion between the Medes and Magism, which was a corrupting influence thrown in upon Zoroastrianism long after the composition of the great bulk of the sacred writings.

These writings themselves sufficiently indicate the place of their composition. It was not Media, but Bactria, or at any rate the north-eastern Iranic country, between the Bolor range and the Caspian.

---

[1] See his work "On the Antiquity and Genuineness of the Zendavesta." pp. 112 et seq.
[2] *Asiatic Nations*, vol. i. p. 322, E. T.
[3] *Comment. Soc. Götting.* vol. xi.

This conclusion, which follows from a consideration of the various geographical notices contained in the Zend books, has been accepted of late years by all the more profound Zend scholars. Originated by Rhode,[1] it has also in its favour the names of Burnouf, Lassen, Westergaard, and Haug.[2] If then the Zend is to be regarded as really a local dialect, the idiom of a particular branch of the Iranic people, there is far more reason for considering it to be the ancient speech of Bactria than of any other Arian country. Possibly the view is correct which recognises two nearly-allied dialects as existing side by side in Iran during its flourishing period—one prevailing towards the west, the other towards the east—one Medo-Persic, the other Sogdo-Bactrian—the former represented to us by the cuneiform inscriptions, the latter by the Zend texts.[3] Or it may be closer to the truth to recognise in the Zendic and Achæmenian forms of speech not so much two contemporary idioms as two stages of one and the same language, which seems to be at present the opinion of the best comparative philologists.[4] In either case Media can claim no special interest in Zend, which, if local, is Sogdo-Bactrian, and, if not local, is no more closely connected with Media than with Persia.

---

[1] See his work *Die Heilige Sage und das gesammte Religions-system der alten Baktrer, Meder, und Perser, oder des Zendvolks,* Frankfort, 1820.

[2] Burnouf, *Commentaire sur le Yaçna,* note, p. xciii.; Westergaard, Preface to *Zendavesta,* p. 16; Haug, *Essays,* p. 42. Dr. Donaldson appears to have adopted the Median theory after it was generally discarded on the continent. See the second edition of his *New Cratylus*

(published in 1850), where he speaks of the Zend language as "exhibiting some strongly-marked features of the Median dialect" (pp. 126-127).

[3] This view has been maintained by Burnouf, and Lassen. It seems to be also held by Haug (*Essays,* pp. 42, 43), and Westergaard (Preface to *Zendavesta,* p. 16).

[4] Max Müller, *Languages of the Seat of War,* p. 32; Bunsen, *Philosophy of History,* vol. iii. pp. 110-115.

It appears then that we do not at present possess any means of distinguishing the shades of difference which separated the Median from the Persian speech.[10] We have in fact no specimens of the former beyond a certain number of words, and those chiefly proper names, whereas we know the latter tolerably completely from the inscriptions. It is proposed under the head of the "Fifth Monarchy" to consider at some length the general character of the Persian language as exhibited to us in these documents. From the discussion then to be raised may be gathered the general character of the speech of the Medes. In the present place all that will be attempted is to show how far the remnants left us of Median speech bear out the statement that, substantially, one and the same tongue was spoken by both peoples.

Many Median names are absolutely identical with Persian; *e.g.* Ariobarzanes,[11] Artabazus,[12] Artæus,[13] Artembares,[14] Harpagus, Arbaces, Tiridates, &c.[15] Others, which are not absolutely identical, approach to the Persian form so closely as to be plainly mere

---

[10] If any difference can be pointed out, it is the greater fondness of the Medes for the termination -*ak*, which is perhaps Scythic. (Compare the terminal guttural so common in the primitive Chaldæan, and the Basque -*c* at the end of names, which is said to be a suffixed article.) We have this ending in Deioces (Dahak), Astyages (Aj-dahak), Arbac-es or Harpag-us, Mandauc-es, Illambac-as, Spitac-es, &c. And we have it again in *spak*, "dog."

[11] A Median Ariobarzanes is mentioned by Tacitus (*Ann.* ii. 4).

[12] Artabazus is given as a Median name by Xenophon (*Cyrop.* i. 4, § 27).

[13] Artæus appears as a Median king in Ctesias (ap. Diod. Sic. ii. 32, § 6), as a Persian in Herod. (vii. 66).

[14] Herodotus has both a Persian (ix. 122) and a Median Artembares (i. 114): both a Persian (vi. 28) and a Median Harpagus (i. 108). Arbaces is probably the same name. According to Ctesias (ap. Diod. Sic. ii. 32, § 5) it was borne by a Median king; according to Xenophon (*Anab.* vii. 8, § 25) by a Persian satrap.

[15] Tiridates appears as the name of a Mede in Nicolas of Damascus (Fr. 66, p. 402); in Q. Curtius (v. 5, § 2) and Ælian (*Hist. Var.* xii. 1) it is the name of a Persian.

variants, like Theodorus and Theodosius, Adelbert and Ethelbert, Miriam, Mariam, and Mariamnë. Of this kind are Intaphres,[14] another form of Intaphernes, Artynes, another form of Artanes,[15] Parmises, another form of Parmys,[16] and the like. A third class, neither identical with any known Persian names, nor so nearly approaching to them as to be properly considered mere variants, are made up of known Persian roots, and may be explained on exactly the same principles as Persian names. Such are Ophernes, Sitraphernes, Mitraphernes, Megabernes, Aspadas, Mazares, Tachmaspates, Xathrites, Spitaces, Spitamas, Rhambacas, and others. In O-phernes, Sitra-phernes, Mitra-phernes, and Mega-bernes, the second element is manifestly the *pharna* or *frana* which is found in Artaphernes and Inta-phernes (*Vida-frana*),[19] an active participial form from *pri*, "to protect." The initial element in O-phernes represents the Zend *hu*, Sans. *su*, Greek εὐ, as the same letter does in O-manes, O-martes, &c.[1] The *Sitra* of Sitraphernes has been explained as probably *khshatra*, "the crown,"[2] which is similarly represented in the *Satro*-pates of Curtius, a name standing to Sitra-phernes, exactly as Arta-patas to Arta-phernes.[3] In Mega-bernes the first element is the well-known *baga*,

---

[14] See *Behistun Inscription*, Col. iv. Par. 14, § 3. For the name of Intaphernes, see Herod. iii. 70.
[15] Artynes is one of Ctesias's Royal Median names (Diod. Sic. ii. 34, § 1); Artanes was a brother of Darius Hystaspis (Herod. vii. 224).
[16] According to Ctesias (*Pers. Exc.* § 3) Parmises was a son of Astyages. Parmys, according to Herodotus, was a daughter of Smerdis, the son of Cyrus (iii. 88).

[19] *Behist. Inscr.* Col. iv. Par. 18, § 4.
[1] See the author's *Herodotus*, vol. iii. p. 451, 2nd edition.
[2] Ibid. p. 453.
[3] Artapatas, a name mentioned by Xenophon (Anab. i, 6, § 11), means probably "protected by fire." Artaphernes (Herod. v. 30) means "protecting the fire." So Satropates means "protected by the crown"— Sitrophernes "protecting the crown."

"God," under the form commonly preferred by the Greeks; and the name is exactly equivalent to Curtius's *Bago*-phanes, which only differs from it by taking the participle of *pa*, "to protect," instead of the participle of *pri*, which has the same meaning. In Aspa-das it is easy to recognise *apa*, "horse" (a common root in Persian names, e. g. *Aspa*-thines, *Aspa*-mitras, Prex-*aspes*, and the like), followed by the same element which terminates the name of Oromaz-*des*, and which means either "knowing" or "giving." Ma-zares presents us with the root *meh*, "much" or "great," which is found in the name of the *M*-aspii, or "Big Horses," a Persian tribe, followed by *zara*, "gold," which appears in Ctesias's Arto-*zares*, and perhaps also in *Zoro*-aster. In Tach-mas-pates, the first element is *takhma*, "strong," a root found in the Persian names Ar-*tochmes* and Tri-

---

See the Inscriptions *passim*. The later ones almost all begin with the formula, *Baga vazarka Auramazdh*, "Deus magnus [est] Oromasdes." *Bagu* has been well compared with the Slavonic *bog*.

The Greeks having really no *b*, since their β had the sound of *v*, were always inclined to express a real *b* by the nearest labial, *m*. Thus they said Mardus, Merdis, or Smerdis for Bardius, Magrus for Bagrus, Marmaridæ for Berbers, and the like. On their frequent representation of the Persian *Baga* by *Mega*—see the author's *Herodotus*, vol. iii. pp. 450, 451, 2nd ed. *Baga*, however, retains its place sometimes. (See Herod. vii. 75; Ctes. Pers. Exc. § 9; Q. Curt. *Vit. Alex.* v. 1).

Q. Curt. *Vit. Alex.* l. s. c.

Compare the frequent occurrence of ἱππος, both as an initial and as a terminal element, in the names of the Greeks.

Dâ in old Arian has this double meaning, corresponding both to δάω and to δίω (δίδωμι) in Greek.

Herod. l. 125. On the animal character of many ethnic names, see the author's *Herodotus*, vol. iii. p. 450.

Ctes. Pers. ap. Phot. *Bibliothec.* lxxii. p. 127.

Various explanations have been given of the name Zoroaster. Some writers regard it as Semitic, and make it equal Zirra-Ishtar, "the seed of Ishtar" (*Journal of Asiatic Society*, vol. xv. p. 248). But most take it to be Arian. Burnouf suggests "having yellow camels," from *zarath*, and *ustra*; Brockhaus makes it "golden star," from *zara* and *thustra*. Windischmann inclines to this last explanation (*Zoroastrische Studien*, pp. 46, 47), but still views it as very doubtful indeed (höchst problematisch).

Behist. Inscr. Col. ii. Par. 14. § 6.

tan-*tachmes*,¹³ while the second is the frequently used *pati*, "lord," which occurs as the initial element in *Pati*-zeithes,¹⁴ *Pati*-ramphes, &c.,¹⁵ and as the terminal in Pharna-*pates*,¹⁶ Ario-*peithes*, and the like. In Xathrites ¹⁷ we have clearly *kshatra* (Zend *khshathra*), "crown" or "king," with a participial suffix -*ita*, corresponding to the Sanscrit participle in -*it*. Spitaces ¹⁸ and Spita-mas ¹⁹ contain the root *spita*, equivalent to *spenta*, "holy,"²⁰ which is found in *Spitho*bates, *Spita*-menes, *Spita*-des, &c. This, in Spita-ces, is followed by a guttural ending, which is either a diminutive corresponding to the modern Persian -*ek*, or perhaps a suffixed article.²¹ In Spit-amas, the suffix -*mas* is the common form of the superlative, and may be compared with the Latin -*mus* in opti*mus*, inti*mus*, supre*mus*, and the like. Rhambacas²² contains the root *rafno*, "joy, pleasure," which we find in Patiramphes, followed by the guttural suffix.

There remains, finally, a class of Median names, containing roots not found in any known names of Persians, but easily explicable from Zend, Sanscrit, or other cognate tongues, and therefore not antagonistic to the view that Median and Persian were two closely connected dialects. Such for instance are the royal names mentioned by Herodotus, Deïoces, Phraortes, Astyages, and Cyaxares; and such also are the following, which come to us from various

---

¹³ Herod. I. 192; vii. 73.
¹⁴ Ibid. iii. 61.
¹⁵ Ibid. vii. 40.
¹⁶ For Ragapates, see Ctes. *Pers. Exc.* § 9; for Pharnapates, see Dio Cass. xlviii. 41.
¹⁷ *Behist. Inscr.* Col. ii. Par. 5, § 1.
¹⁸ Ctes. *Pers. Exc.* § 2.
¹⁹ Ibid.

²⁰ The Iranians disliked the combination of the usual with the dental, and said *Hidush* for *Hendu* (Hindu-stan), *Haetumat* for *Etymandrus*, *pata* for *cratum*, &c. So we have frequently, though not always, *spita* for *spenta*.
²¹ See above, page 140, note ᵖ.
²² Xen. *Cyrop.* v. iii. § 42.

sources:—Amytis, Astibaras, Armamithres or Harmamithres, Mandauces, Parsondas, Ramates, Susiscanes, Tithæus, and Zanasanes.

In Deïoces, or (as the Latins write it) Dejoces, there can be little doubt that we have the name given as Djohak or Zohak in the Shahnameh and other modern Persian writings; which is itself an abbreviation of the Aji-dahaka of the Zendavesta.[22] *Dahaka* means in Zend "biting," or "the biter," and is etymologically connected with the Greek δάκνω, δάκος, ὀδάξ, κ.τ.λ.

Phraortes, which in old Persian was Fravartish,[24] seems to be a mere variant of the word which appears in the Zendavesta as *fravashi*, and designates each man's *tutelary* genius.[25] The derivation is certainly from *fra* (= Gk. προ-), and probably from a root akin to the German *wahren*, French *garder*, English "ward, watch," &c. The meaning is "a protector."

Cyaxares, the Persian form of which was 'Uvakhshatara,[26] seems to be formed from the two elements 'u or *hu* (Gk. εὖ), "well, good," and *akhsha* (Zend *arsna*), "the eye," which is the final element of the name Cyavarsna in the Zendavesta. Cyavarsna is "dark-eyed;"[27] 'Uvakhsha (= Zend *Huraresna*) would be "beautiful-eyed." 'Uvakhshatara appears to be the comparative of this adjective, and would mean "more beautiful-eyed (than others)."

---

[22] See above, ch. iv. p. 119. Mirkhond (*History*, p. 123) derives Zohak from *Deh-ak*, "ten vices"—which is hardly a name that a king would choose to bear.
[24] *Behist. Inser.* Col. ii. Par. 5, § 2.
[25] See Haug, *Essays*, p. 186. The *fravashi* are called *fravardin* in the Pehlevi, and *frohars* in the modern Persian.
[26] *Behist. Inser.* Col. 2, Par. 5, § 4.
[27] Brockhaus, *Vendidad-Sadé*, p. 401.

Astyages, which, according to Moses of Chorênê,[a] meant "a dragon" or "serpent," is almost certainly Ajis-dahaka, the full name whereof Dejoces (or Zohak) is the abbreviation. It means "the biting snake," from *aji* or *azi*, "a snake" or "serpent,", and *dahaka* "biting."

Amytis is probably *ama*, "active, great," with the ordinary feminine suffix *-iti*, found in Armai*ti*, Khnathai*ti*, and the like.[1] Astibaras is perhaps "great of bone,"[2] from Zend *açta* (Sans. *asthi*), "bone," and *bereza*, "tall, great." Harmamithres,[3] if that is the true reading, would be "mountain-lover" (*monticolus*), from *harâm*, acc. of *hara*, "a mountain," and *mithra* or *mitra* (= Gr. φίλος)), "fond of." If however the name should be read as Armamithres, the probable derivation will be from *râma*, acc. of *râman*, "pleasure," which is also the root of *Rama*-tes.[4] Armamithres may then be compared with Rheomithres, Siromitras, and Sysimithres,[5] which are respectively "fond of splendour," "fond of beauty," and "fond of light." Mandauces[6] is perhaps "biting spirit—*esprit mordant*," from *manô*, "cœur, esprit," and *dahaka*, "biting."[7] Parsondas

---

[a] *Hist. Armen.* l. 29. A recent writer maintains that Astyages is a Greek translation of the Median name, of which Astibaras is "another slightly different rendering." He would derive the former from δεινὸ and ὄφις, the latter from δεινὸ and βάρος. (Galloway on *Isaiah*, pp. 343, 384.)

[1] See above, pp. 99 and 120.

[2] Herodotus remarks that the Persian names were often significative of some physical excellence (i. 139).

[3] Herod. vii. 88. Several MSS. give the aspirate. See Gaisford, ad loc.

[4] See above, vol. ii. p. 473, note [6].

[5] Rheomithres is given as a Persian name by Arrian (*Exp. Al.* ii. 11), Sirmitras by Herodotus (vii. 79), and Sysimithres by Q. Curtius (*Vit. Alex.* viii. 4).

[6] Mandauces is one of Ctesias's Median kings. (See below, p. 173, note [1].)

[7] Or *dahaka* may be considered to have passed from an epithet into a name, and the proper translation may be "serpent-minded."

can scarcely be the original form, from the occurrence in it of the nasal before the dental.⁹ In the original it must have been Parsodas, which would mean "liberal, much-giving," from *pourus*, "much," and *da* (= Gk. δίδωμι), "to give." Ramates, as already observed, is from *rama*, "pleasure." It is an adjectival form, like Datis,⁹ and means probably "pleasant, agreeable." Susiscanes¹⁰ may be explained as "splendidus juvenis," from *çuc*, "splendere," pres. part. *çao-cut*, and *kainin*, "adolescens, juvenis." Tithæus¹¹ is probably for Tathæus, which would be readily formed from *tatha*, "one who makes." ¹² Finally, Zanasanes¹³ may be referred to the root *zan* or *jan*, "to kill," which is perhaps simply followed by the common appellative suffix *-ana* (Gk. -άνης).

From these names of persons we may pass to those of places in Media, which equally admit of explanation from roots known to have existed either in Zend or in old Persian. Of these Ecbatana, Bagistana, and Aspadana may be taken as convenient specimens. Ecbatana (or Agbatana, according to the orthography of the older Greeks¹⁴) was in the native dialect Hagmatana, as appears from the Behistun inscription.¹⁵ This form, Hagmatana, is in all probability derived from the three words *ham* "with" (Sans. *sam*, Gk. σύν, Latin *cum*), *gam*, "to

---

⁹ See above, p. 143, note ᵐ. The name Parsondas comes to us through Nicolas of Damascus (Fr. 10).
⁹ See the author's *Herodotus* (vol. iii. p. 448), where Datis is explained as "liberal."
¹⁰ Æschyl. Pers. 939. The foreign names in Æschylus are not always to be depended on. (See Blomfield's Note on the *Persæ*, l. 22.) But still many of them are real names.
¹¹ Herod. vii. 88.
¹² For the termination in *-æus*, compare Bagæus, Magæus, Mazæus, &c., well-known names of Persians.
¹³ Supra, vol. ii. p. 173, note ⁴.
¹⁴ So Æschylus (*Pers.* 16), Herodotus (i. 98), and Aristophanes (*Acharn.* 64).
¹⁵ Col. ii. Par. 13, § 7.

go" (Zend *gâ*, Sans. *gam*), and *çtana* (Mod. Pers. -*stan*) "a place." The initial *ham* has dropped the *m* and become *ha*, just as σύν becomes συ- in Greek, and *cum* becomes *co-* in Latin; *gam* has become *gma* by metathesis; and *çtan* has passed into -*tan* by phonetic corruption. Ha-gma-tana would be "the place for assembly," or for "coming together" (Lat. *comitium*); the place, i. e., where the tribes met, and where, consequently, the capital grew up.

Bagistan, which was "a hill sacred to Jupiter" according to Diodorus,[16] is clearly a name corresponding to the Beth-el of the Hebrews and the Allahabad of the Mahometans. It is simply "the house, or place of God"—from *baga*, "God," and *çtana*, "place, abode," the common modern Persian terminal (compare Farsi-*stan*, Khuzi-*stan*, Affghani-*stan*, Belochi-*stan*, Hindu-*stan*, &c.), which has here not suffered any corruption.

Aspadana contains certainly as its first element the root, *açpa*, "horse."[17] The suffix *dan* may perhaps be a corruption of *çtana*, analogous to that which has produced Hama-*dan* from Hagma-çtan; or it may be a contracted form of *danhu*, or *dainhu*, "a province," Aspadana having been originally the name of a district where horses were bred, and having thence become the name of its chief town.

The Median words known to us, other than names of persons or places, are confined to some three or four. Herodotus tells us that the Median word for

---

[16] Diod. Sic. II. 13, § 2. Ὄρος Ιερὸν Διός.

[17] *Açpa* is a common root in Median local names, as will be seen by reference to the list in Ptolemy (*Geograph.* vi. 2). Besides Aspadana, which Ptolemy places in Persia, we find among his Median towns, Pharaspa, Phanaspa, and Vesaspa. The whole country was famous for its breed of horses.

either the mother or the elder sister of the ancient Persian.

That the Medes were acquainted with the art of writing, and practised it—at least from the time that they succeeded to the dominion of the Assyrians—scarcely admits of a doubt. An illiterate nation, which conquers one in possession of a literature, however it may despise learning and look down upon the mere literary life, is almost sure to adopt writing to some extent on account of its practical utility. It is true the Medes have left us no written monuments; and we may fairly conclude from that fact that they used writing sparingly; but besides the antecedent probability, there is respectable evidence that letters were known to them, and that, at any rate, their upper classes could both read and write their native tongue. The story of the letter sent by Harpagus the Mede to Cyrus in the belly of a hare,[1] though probably apocryphal, is important as showing the belief of Herodotus on the subject. The still more doubtful story of a dispatch written on parchment by a Median king Artæus, and sent to Nanarus, a provincial governor, related by Nicolas of Damascus,[2] has a value, as indicating that writer's conviction, that the Median monarchs habitually conveyed their commands to their subordinates in a written form. With these statements of profane writers agree certain notices which we find in Scripture. Darius the Mede, shortly after the destruction of the Median empire, "signs" a decree, which his chief nobles have presented to him in writing.[3] He also himself "writes"

---

[1] Herod. i. 123.
[2] Nic. Dam. Fr. 10.
[3] Dan. vi. 9. "Wherefore King Darius signed the writing and the decree."

another decree addressed to his subjects generally.[4] In later times we find that there existed at the Persian court a "book of the chronicles of the kings of Media and Persia,"[5] which was probably a work begun under the Median and continued under the Persian sovereigns.

If then writing was practised by the Medes, it becomes interesting to consider whence they obtained their knowledge of it, and what was the system which they employed. Did they bring an alphabet with them from the far East, or did they derive their first knowledge of letters from the nations with whom they came into contact after their great migration? In the latter case, did they adopt, with or without modifications, a foreign system, or did they merely borrow the idea of written symbols from their new neighbours, and set to work to invent for themselves an alphabet suited to the genius of their own tongue? These are some of the questions which present themselves to the mind as deserving of attention, when this subject is brought before it. Unfortunately we possess but very scanty data for determining, and can do little more than conjecture, the proper answers to be given to them.

The early composition of certain portions of the Zendavesta, which has been asserted in this work,[6] may seem at first sight to imply the use of a written character in Bactria and the adjacent countries at a very remote era. But such a conclusion is not necessary. Nations have often had an oral literature, existing only in the memories of men, and have

---

[4] Dan. vi. 25. "Then King Darius wrote unto all people, nations, and languages," &c.
[5] Esther, x. 2.
[6] Supra, ch. iv. p. 107.

handed down such a literature from generation to generation, through a long succession of ages.¹ The sacred lore of Zoroaster may have been brought by the Medes from the East-Caspian country in an unwritten shape, and may not have been reduced to writing till many centuries later. On the whole it is perhaps most probable that the Medes were unacquainted with letters when they made their great migration, and that they acquired their first knowledge of them from the races with whom they came into collision when they settled along the Zagros chain. In these regions they were brought into contact with at least two forms of written speech, one that of the old Armenians,² a Turanian dialect, the other that of the Assyrians, a language of the Semitic type. These two nations used the same alphabetic system, though their languages were utterly unlike; and it would apparently have been the easiest plan for the new comers to have adopted the established forms, and to have applied them, so far as was possible, to the representation of their own speech. But the extreme complication of a system which employed between three and four hundred written signs, and composed signs sometimes of fourteen or fifteen wedges,

---

¹ It is generally allowed that the Homeric poems were for a long time handed down in this way. (Wolf, *Prolegomena de op. Homer.*; Payne Knight, *Prolegomena*, pp. 38-100; Matthiæ, *Greek and Roman Literature*, pp. 12-14; Grote, *Hist. of Greece*, vol. I. pp. 524-529, 2nd edition; &c.). The best Orientalists believe the same of the Vedas. The Druidical poems of the ancient Gauls (Cæs. *Bell. Gall.* vi. 13, 14), the Icelandic Skalds, the Basque tales, the Ossianic poems, the songs of the Calmucks, the modern Greeks, and the modern Persians, are all instances of an oral literature completely independent of writing. It is quite possible that the Zendavesta was orally transmitted till the time of Darius Hystaspis—if not even to a later date.

² The Armenians may perhaps not have been acquainted with writing when the Medes first reached Zagros. But they became a literary people at least as early as the 8th century B.C., while the Medes were still insignificant.

seems to have shocked the simplicity of the Medes, who recognised the fact that the varieties of their articulations fell far short of this excessive luxuriance. The Arian races, so far as appears, declined to follow the example set them by the Turanians of Armenia, who had adopted the Assyrian alphabet, and preferred to invent a new system for themselves, which they determined to make far more simple. It is possible that they found an example already set them. In Achæmenian times we observe two alphabets used through Media and Persia, both of which are simpler than the Assyrian: one is employed to express the Turanian dialect of the people whom the Arians conquered and dispossessed;[9] the other, to express the tongue of the conquerors. It is possible—though we have no direct evidence of the fact—that the Turanians of Zagros and the neighbourhood had already formed for themselves the alphabet which is found in the second columns of the Achæmenian tablets, when the Arian invaders conquered them. This alphabet, which in respect of complexity holds an intermediate position between the luxuriance of the Assyrian and the simplicity of the Medo-Persic system, would seem in all probability to have intervened in order of time between the two. It consists of no more than about a hundred characters,[10] and these are for the most part far less complicated than those of Assyria. If the Medes found this form of writing already existing in Zagros when they arrived, it may have assisted to

---

[9] Before this language had been analysed, it was conjectured to be Median. But Mr. E. Norris has plainly shown its Scythic or Turanian character (*Journal of the Asiatic Society*, vol. xv.); and it is now generally regarded as the speech of the subject population in Media and Persia.

[10] Sir H. Rawlinson in the *Journal of the Asiatic Society*, vol. x. p. 33.

give them the idea of making for themselves an alphabet so far on the old model that the wedge should be the sole element used in the formation of letters, but otherwise wholly new, and much more simple than those previously in use.

Discarding then the Assyrian notion of a syllabarium, with the enormous complication which it involves,[11] the Medes[12] strove to reduce sounds to their ultimate elements, and to represent these last alone by symbols. Contenting themselves with the three main vowel sounds, *a*, *i*, and *u*,[13] and with one breathing, a simple *h*, they recognised twenty consonants, which were the following, *b, d, f, g, j, k, kh, m, n, ñ* (sound doubtful), *p, r, s, sh, t, v, y, z, ch* (as in *much*) and *tr*, an unnecessary compound. Had they stopped here, their characters should have been but twenty-four, the number which is found in Greek. To their ears, however, it would seem, each consonant appeared to carry with it a short *a*, and as this, occurring before *i* and *u*, produced the diphthongs *ai* and *au*, sounded nearly as *é* and *ô*,[14] it seemed necessary, where a consonant was to be directly followed by the sounds *i* or *u*, to have special forms to which the sound of *a* should not attach. This system, carried out completely, would have raised the forms of consonants to sixty, a multiplication that was feared

---

[11] See above, vol. i. pp. 338, 339.
[12] It is here assumed that the Medes were the originators of the system which was afterwards employed by the Persians. There is no positive proof of this. But all the evidence which we possess favours the notion that the early Persian civilisation—and the writing belongs to the time of Cyrus—came to them from the Medes, their predecessors in the Empire. (See Herod. i. 134, 135; Xen. *Cyrop.* i. 3, § 2; viii. 3, § 1; Strab. xi. 13, § 9.)
[13] These were of course sounded broad, as in Italian—the *a* like *a* in "vast;" the *i* like *ee* in "feed;" the *u* like *oo* in "food."
[14] That is, as the Italian *e* and *o aperto*, or as the diphthongs themselves in French, e. g. *fail, faux*, &c.

as inconvenient. In order to keep down the number, it seems to have been resolved, (1.) that one form should suffice for the aspirated letters and the sibilants (viz. *h, kh, ch, ph* or *f, s, sh*, and *z*), and also for *b, y,* and *tr*; (2.) that two forms should suffice for the *tenues, k, p, t,* for the liquids *n* and *r* and for *v*; and consequently (3.) that the full number of three forms should be limited to some three or four letters, as *d, m, j,* and perhaps *g*. The result is that the known alphabet of the Persians, which is assumed here to have been the invention of the Medes, consists of some 36 or 37 forms, which are really representative of no more than 23 distinct sounds.[14]

It appears then, that compared with the phonetic systems in vogue among their neighbours, the alphabet of the Medes and Persians was marked by a great simplicity. The forms of the letters were also very much simplified. Instead of conglomerations of fifteen or sixteen wedges in a single character, we have in the Medo-Persic letters a *maximum* of five wedges. The most ordinary number is four, which is sometimes reduced to three or even two. The direction of the wedges is uniformly either perpendicular or horizontal, except of course in the case of the double wedge or arrow-head, ⟨, where the component elements are placed obliquely. The arrow-head has but one position, the perpendicular, with the angle facing towards the left hand. The only diagonal sign used is a simple wedge, placed obliquely with the point towards the right, ⟍, which is a mere mark of separation between the words.

The direction of the writing was, as with the Arian

---

[14] See Sir H. Rawlinson's analysis of the Persian Alphabet in the *Journal of the Asiatic Society*, vol. x. pp. 35-186.

nations generally, from left to right. Words were frequently divided, and part carried on to the next line. The characters were inscribed between straight lines drawn from end to end of the tablet on which they were written. Like the Hebrew, they often closely resembled one another, and a slight defect in the stone will cause one to be mistaken for another. The resemblance is not between letters of the same class or kind; on the contrary, it is often between those which are most remote from one another. Thus *g* nearly resembles *u*; *ch* is like *d*; *tr* like *p*; and so on: while *k* and *kh*, *s* and *sh*, *p* and *ph* (or *f*) are forms quite dissimilar.

It is supposed that a cuneiform alphabet can never have been employed for ordinary writing purposes,[1] but must have been confined to documents of some importance, which it was desirable to preserve, and which were therefore either inscribed on stone, or impressed on moist clay afterwards baked. A cursive character, it is therefore imagined, must always have been in use, parallel with a cuneiform one;[2] and, as the Babylonians and Assyrians are known to have used a character of this kind from a very high antiquity, synchronously with their lapidary cuneiform, so it is supposed that the Arian races must have possessed, besides the method which has been described, a cursive system of writing. Of this however there is at present no direct evidence. No cursive writing of the Arian nations at this time, either Median or

---

[1] The cuneiform is a very convenient character for impression upon clay, or inscription upon stone. In the former case, a single touch of the instrument makes each wedge; in the latter, three taps of the chisel with the hammer cause the wedge to fall out. But characters composed of wedges are very awkward to write.

[2] *Journal of the Asiatic Society*, vol. x. pp. 31 and 42.

Persian, has been found; and it is therefore uncertain what form of character they employed on common occasions.

The material used for ordinary purposes, according to Nicolas of Damascus[3] and Ctesias,[4] was parchment. On this the kings wrote the dispatches which conveyed their orders to the officers who administered the government of provinces; and on this were inscribed the memorials which each monarch was careful to have composed giving an account of the chief events of his reign. The cost of land carriage probably prevented papyrus from superseding this material in Western Asia, as it did in Greece at a tolerably early date.[5] Clay, so much used for writing on both in Babylonia and Assyria,[6] appears never to have approved itself as a convenient substance to the Iranians. For public documents the chisel and the rock, for private the pen and the prepared skin, seem to have been preferred by them; and in the earlier times, at any rate, they employed no other materials.

---

[3] Frag. 10. See above, p. 149, note [a].
[4] Ap. Diod. Sic. ii. 32, § 4. [5] Herod. v. 58.
[6] Supra, vol. i. p. 84, and p. 334.

CHAPTER VI.

CHRONOLOGY AND HISTORY.

Media .... quam ante regnum Cyri superioris et incrementa Persidis legebant Asiæ reginam totius.—AMM. MARC. xxiii, 6.

THE origin of the Median nation is wrapt in a profound obscurity. Following the traces which the Zendavesta offers, taking into consideration its minute account of the earlier Arian migrations,[1] its entire omission of any mention of the Medes, and the undoubted fact that it was nevertheless by the Medes and Persians that the document itself was preserved and transmitted to us, we should be naturally led to suppose that the race was one which in the earlier times of Arian development was weak and insignificant, and that it first pushed itself into notice after the ethnological portions of the Zendavesta were composed, which is thought to have been about B.C. 1000.[2] Quite in accordance with this view is the further fact, that in the native Assyrian annals, so far as they have been recovered, the Medes do not make their appearance till the middle of the ninth century B.C., and when they appear are weak and

---

[1] See the translation of the first Fargard of the Vendidad in the Appendix to this "Monarchy." The only other geographic notice of any considerable length which the Zendavesta contains, is in the Mithra Yasht, where the countries mentioned are Aiskata (Sagartia, Asagarta of cuneiform Inscriptions?), Pourata (Parthia), Moura (Meru, Merj, Margiana), Haröyû (Aria or Herat), Gau Sughdha (Sogdiana), and Qâirizem (Chorasmia or Kharezm). Here again there is no mention of Media.

[2] Haug, *Essays*, p. 224. In Bunsen's *Egypt* the date suggested is B.C. 1200 (vol. iii. p. 478).

unimportant, only capable of opposing a very slight resistance to the attacks of the Ninevite kings.² The natural conclusion from these data would appear to be, that until about B.C. 850 the Median name was unknown in the world, and that previously, if Medes existed at all, it was either as a sub-tribe of some other Arian race, or at any rate as a tribe too petty and insignificant to obtain mention either on the part of native or of foreign historians. Such early insignificance and late development of what ultimately becomes the dominant tribe of a race is no strange or unprecedented phenomenon to the historical inquirer; on the contrary, it is among the facts with which he is most familiar, and would admit of ample illustration, were the point worth pursuing, alike from the history of the ancient and the modern world.⁴

But, against the conclusion to which we could not fail to be led by the Arian and Assyrian records, which agree together so remarkably, two startling notices in works of great authority but of a widely different character have to be set. In the Toldoth Beni Noah, or "Book of the Generation of the Sons of Noah," which forms the tenth chapter of Genesis, and which, if the work of Moses, was probably composed at least as early as B.C. 1500,⁵ we find the word MADAI—a word elsewhere always signifying "the Medes"—in the genealogy of the sons of Japhet.⁶

---

² See above, vol. II. pp. 359 and 375.

⁴ The Hellenes were an insignificant Greek race until the Dorian conquests. (Herod. i. 56; Thuc. i. 3.) The Latins had originally no pre-eminence among the Italic peoples. The Turks for many ages were on a par with other Tatars. The race which is now forming Italy into a kingdom has only recently shown itself superior to Lombards, Tuscans, and Neapolitans.

⁵ The Exodus is indeed placed by Bunsen as late as B.C. 1320, and by Lepsius as late as B.C. 1314. But the balance of authority favours a date from 200 to 300 years earlier.

⁶ Gen. x. 2.

The word is there conjoined with several other important ethnic titles, as Gomer, Magog, Javan, Tubal, and Meshech; and there can be no reasonable doubt that it is intended to designate the Median people.[7] If so, the people must have had already a separate and independent existence in the fifteenth century, B.C., and not only so, but they must have by that time attained so much distinction as to be thought worthy of mention by a writer who was only bent on affiliating the more important of the nations known to him.

The other notice is furnished by Berosus. That remarkable historian, in his account of the early dynasties of his native Chaldæa, declared, that, at a date anterior to B.C. 2000, the Medes had conquered Babylon by a sudden inroad, had established a monarchy there, and had held possession of the city and neighbouring territory for a period of 224 years.[8] Eight kings of their race had during that interval occupied the Babylonian throne. It has been already observed that this narrative must represent a fact.[9] Berosus would not have gratuitously invented a foreign conquest of his native land; nor would the earlier Babylonians, from whom he derived his materials, have forged a tale which was so little flattering to their national vanity. *Some* foreign conquest of Babylon must

---

[7] Kalisch says in his comment on the passage—"Madai—these are unquestionably the Medes or inhabitants of Media." (*Commentary on the Old Testament*, vol. i. p. 166.) Note that Gomer, Magog, Javan, Tubal, Meshech, Ashkenaz, Togarmah, Elishah, Tarshish, and Kittim (or Chittim) are all elsewhere through Scripture undoubtedly names of nations or countries. Note, moreover, the plural form of Kittim and Dodanim (or Rodanim).

[8] Beros. Fr. 11. "Post hos, qui successione incoucussâ regnum obtinuerunt, derepente Medos collectis copiis Babylonem arpisse ait, Ibique de suis tyrannos constituisse. Hinc nomina quoque tyrannorum Medorum ediserit octo, annosque eorum viginti quatuor supra ducentos."

[9] Supra, vol. i. p. 104.

have taken place about the period named; and it is certainly a most important fact that Berosus should call the conquerors, Medes. He may no doubt have been mistaken about an event so ancient; he may have misread his authorities, or he may have described as Medes a people of which he really knew nothing except that they had issued from the tract which in his own time bore the name of Media. But, while these are mere possibilities, hypotheses to which the mind resorts in order to escape a difficulty, the hard fact remains that he has used the word; and this fact coupled with the mention of the Medes in the Book of Genesis, does certainly raise a presumption of no inconsiderable strength against the view which it would be natural to take, if the Zendavesta and the Assyrian annals were our sole authorities on the subject. It lends a substantial basis to the theories of those who regard the Medes as one of the principal primeval races;[10] who believe that they were well known to the Semitic inhabitants of the Mesopotamian valley as early as the twenty-third century before Christ—long ere Abraham left Ur for Harran—and that they actually formed the dominant power in Western Asia for more than two centuries, prior to the establishment of the first Chaldæan kingdom.

And if there are thus distinct historical grounds for the notion of an early Median development, there are not wanting those obscurer but to many minds more satisfactory proofs, wherewith comparative philology and ethnology are wont to illustrate and confirm the darker passages of ancient history. Recent linguistic research has clearly traced among the *Arba*

---

[10] As Bunsen. See his *Egypt*, vol. iii. p. 583-597.

CHAP. VI. ARIAN ELEMENT IN PRIMITIVE CHALDÆA. 161

Lisun, or "Four Tongues" of ancient Chaldæa, which are so often mentioned on the ancient monuments,[1] an Arian formation, such as would naturally have been left in the country, if it had been occupied for some considerable period by a dominant Arian power. The early Chaldæan ideographs have often several distinct values; and, when this is the case, one of the powers is almost always an Arian name of the object represented.[2] Words like *nir*, "man" (compare Greek ἀνήρ), *ar*, "river" (compare the names *Aras*, *Araxes*, *Eridanus*, *Rha*, *Rhodanus*, &c., and the Greek ῥέω, the Slavonic *rika*, "river," &c.), *san* "the sun" (compare German *sonne*, Slavonic *solnce*, English "sun," Dutch *zon*, &c.), are seemingly Arian roots; and the very term "Arian" (*ariya*, "noble") is perhaps contained in the name of a primitive Chaldæan monarch, "Arioch, King of Ellasar."[3] There is nothing perhaps in these scattered traces of Arian influence in lower Mesopotamia at a remote era that points very particularly to the Medes;[4] but at any rate they harmonize with the historical account that has reached us of early Arian power in these parts, and it is important that they should not be ignored when we are engaged in considering the degree of credence that is to be awarded to the account in question.

Again, there are traces of a vast expansion, apparently at a very early date, of the Median race, such as seems to imply that they must have been a great

---

[1] See above, vol. i. p. 77.
[2] As, for instance, the same ideograph—a rude representation of a house—has the three powers of *é*, *bit*, and *mal*—of which *é* is Hamitic, *bit* or *beth* Semitic, and *mal* Arian.
[3] Gen. xiv. 1.
[4] Unless perhaps it be the name Arioch, which is Medo-Persic in form, and almost identical with Ariaces (Ἀριάκης), the name of a Mede or Persian in Arrian. (*Exp. Al.* iii. 8.)

VOL. III. M

nation in Western Asia long previously to the time of the Iranic movements in Bactria and the adjoining regions. In the *Mat*-ieni of Zagrus and Cappadocia,[3] in the Sauro-*matæ* (or Northern Medes) of the country between the Palus Mæotis and the Caspian,[4] in the *Mætæ* or Mæotæ of the tract about the mouth of the Don,[7] and in the *Mædi* of Thrace,[8] we have seemingly remnants of a great migratory host, which, starting from the mountains that overhung Mesopotamia, spread itself into the regions of the north and the north-west at a time which does not admit of being definitely stated, but which is clearly antehistoric. Whether these races generally retained any tradition of their origin, we do not know; but a tribe which in the time of Herodotus dwelt still further to the west than even the Mædi—to wit, the Sigynnæ, who occupied the tract between the Adriatic and the Danube—had a very distinct belief in their Median descent, a belief confirmed by the resemblance which their national dress bore to that of the Medes.[9] Herodotus, who relates these facts concerning them, appends an expression of his astonishment at the circumstance that emigrants from Media should have proceeded to such a distance from their original home—how it had been brought about he could not conceive. "Still," he sagaciously remarks, "nothing is impossible in the long lapse of ages."[10]

A further argument in favour of the early develop-

---

[3] Herod. i. 72; v. 52; Hecat. Fr. 188, 189; Xanth. Fr. 3.
[4] Herod. iv. 21, 110-117; Strab. xi. 2, § 15; Diod. Sic. ii. 43, § 6; Plin. *H. N.* vi. 7.
[7] Herod. iv. 123. In the Greek inscriptions found in Scythia the Mæotæ of Herodotus are commonly called Mætæ (Μαῖται).
[8] Thucyd. ii. 98; Strab. vii. 5, § 7; Polyb. x. 41, § 4.
[9] Herod. v. 9.
[10] Ibid. γένοιτο δ' ἂν πᾶν ἐν τῷ μακρῷ χρόνῳ.

ment of Median power, and the great importance of the nation in Western Asia at a period anterior to the ninth century, is derivable from the ancient legends of the Greeks, which seem to have designated the Medes under the two eponyms of Medea and Andromeda. These legends indeed do not admit of being dated with any accuracy; but as they are of a primitive type, and probably older than Homer,[11] we cannot well assign them to an age later than B.C. 1000. Now they connect the Median name with the two countries of Syria and Colchis, countries remote from each other, and neither of them sufficiently near the true Median territory to be held from it, unless at a time when the Medes were in possession of something like an empire. Thus the Greek myths harmonise with the narrative of Berosus. And, even apart from any inferences to be drawn from the localities which they connect with the Medes, the very fact that the race was known to the Greeks at this early date—long before the movements which brought them into contact with the Assyrians—would seem to shew that there was some remote period—prior to the Assyrian domination—when the fame of the Medes was great in the parts of Asia known to the Hellenes, and that they did not first attract Hellenic notice (as, but for the myths,[12] we

---

[11] The story of the Argonauts seems to have been in its main particulars known to Homer. (See *Il.* vii. 409; *Od.* x. 137-139; xii. 64-72.) To that of Perseus and Andromeda he does not allude; but its character is peculiarly primitive.

[12] The ethnic character of these myths, though (in one instance) vouched for by Strabo (xi. 13, § 10), may perhaps be doubted by some persons. Medea may be derived from μῆδος, "craft," or μήδομαι, "to act craftily"—and Perseus may be, and indeed has been, connected with σε- πάω and wipαε, and regarded as a mere Solar epithet. (Eustath. *Comment. ad Hom. Od.*; Paley, note ad loc.) But then mere accident would have produced an *apparent* combina-

might have imagined) by the conquests of Cyaxares. Thus, on the whole it would appear, that the statement of Berosus with respect to a Median dynasty at Babylon, prior to B.C. 2000, deserves more attention than it has generally been accorded. We must acknowledge two periods of Median prosperity, separated from each other by a lengthy interval, one anterior to the rise of the first (Cushite) kingdom in Lower Babylonia, the other parallel with the decline and subsequent to the fall of Assyria.

Of the first period we have only very scanty notices in the fragments of Berosus, and of his copyist, Polyhistor. Our chronological computations have already shewn that Berosus placed the commencement of the Median dynasty in B.C. 2458, and its termination in B.C. 2234." It lasted, he said, 224 years, and consisted of a series of eight kings, whose reigns must consequently have averaged twenty-eight years each. If we may believe Syncellus,[1] the first king of the dynasty, according to Polyhistor—who on such a point would be almost certain to follow Berosus—was Zoroaster! Now if Berosus really made this statement, we must consider that the true history of the period was altogether lost—that the very names of the Median kings had perished;[2] and that the

---

tion of Medes with Persians in both myths; for not only is Perseus the husband of Andromeda, but Perses or Perseis is the mother of Æetes (Od. x. 139; Hes. Theog. 957). It is a profound remark of Aristotle's—Οὐ γὰρ συνδυάζεται τὰ κατὰ συμβεβηκός. (Eth. Nic. viii. 4, § 5.)

[2] See above, vol. I. pp. 191-195. Mr. Palmer assigns to the dynasty the years between B.C. 2209 and B.C. 1985. (Egyptian Chronicles, pp. 957, 958.)

[1] Syncell. Chronographia, p. 147.

[2] Mr. Palmer supposes (Egyptian Chronicles, pp. 957, 958) that Syncellus has preserved the names of all but two of the eight Median kings as they were given by Berosus. But, as Syncellus masses together Berosus's dynasties, it is (to say the least) extremely doubtful whether he has preserved any of the Median names besides Zoroaster. The names to which Mr. Palmer refers—Porus, Nechubes, Nabius, Oniballus, and

Chaldæan historian had to trust to his imagination to supply the deficiency. The true Zoroaster seems to have lived nearly a thousand years later;[2] he was a native of Bactria,[4] and was probably never within a thousand miles of Babylon. If we may judge the general character of Berosus's early Median history from this specimen, we need not greatly deplore its loss. The Median kings had probably left neither monuments nor records. All that was really known of them, was the tradition—perhaps not very trustworthy—that their number had been eight, and that they had reigned for 224 years.

At the close of this period of two centuries and a quarter, the Median power suffered a sudden collapse. Cushite emigrants, it is probable, poured into Chaldæa; and the Arians had to yield to their superior skill or numbers, to retire to the mountains, and to commence that series of migratory movements, which took them on the one hand to the vicinity of the Adriatic, on the other to the Caspian and perhaps the Oxus. We have no means at all of tracing these wanderings. From B.C. 2234 to B.C. 835 Median history is a blank. We can only say, negatively, that the early Assyrian kings do not find them in Zagros, and that the Zendic writers do not notice them in Eastern Iran. They may have dwelt, during this obscure period in the tract between Zagros and the desert, or again in the more northern Azerbijan,

---

Zinzerus—are not joined by Syncellus with Zoroaster, but with Evechius and Chomasbolus, the Chaldæans. And the names themselves are Semitic, not Arian.

[3] See above, p. 94, note [4].

[4] The Zendavesta is conclusive on this point. Its statement is confirmed by Hermippus (ap. Arnob. adv. Gentes, i. 52), Justin (i. 1), Ammianus Marcellinus (xxiii. 6), and Moses of Chorené (Hist. Armen. i. 5).

thus inhabiting a portion of the territory which was known as Media in later times. Or they may, while sending out certain offshoots to the north and west,[*] have occupied with their main body the upper Oxus country—the *Aryanem vaejo* of the Zendavesta—either finding it vacant, or becoming joint occupants of the tract with other kindred tribes, who were previously settled in the region. It is conceivable that under the circumstances they laid aside their old appellation of Medes, and knew themselves merely as *Ariya*, "the *noble* race;"[*] and that thus the Zendavesta does not make any mention of their primitive title. When however they once more became a conquering power, and retracing their steps to the westward, proceeded to establish themselves along the mountain-chain which overhung Mesopotamia—the scene of their former glories—they resumed their true ethnic name, and while their neighbours still for the most part knew them as Ariana,[*] called themselves once more *Mada* or "Medes."

The first evidence that we possess of their reappearance towards the west is contained in the annals of Shalmaneser II.—probably the "Shalman" of Hosea[*]—who reigned from B.C. 859 to B.C. 824. This monarch relates that in his 24th year (B.C. 835), after having reduced to subjection the Zimri, who held the Zagros mountain-range immediately to the

---

[*] The Sauromatæ, Matæ, Medi, &c. (See above, p. 162.)

[*] See Professor Max Müller's *Languages of the Seat of War*, p. 29, note; and compare Brockhaus, *Vendidad*, p. 338.

[*] Herod. vii. 62. Οἱ Μῆδοι . . ἐκαλέοντο πάλαι πρὸς πάντων Ἄριοι.

[*] Hosea, x. 14. "Thy fortresses shall be spoiled, as Shalman spoiled Beth-Arbel in the day of battle." Beth-Arbel is probably Arbela, which was among the cities that joined in the revolt at the end of Shalmaneser's reign (supra, vol. ii. p. 371), and which may therefore very probably have been sacked when the rebellion was put down.

cast of Assyria, and received tribute from the Persians, he led an expedition into Media and Arazias, where he took and destroyed a number of the towns, slaying the men, and carrying off the spoil.* He does not mention any pitched battle; and indeed it would seem that he met with no serious resistance. The Medes whom he attacks are evidently a weak and insignificant people, whom he holds in small esteem, and regards as only deserving of a hurried mention. They seem to occupy the tract now known as Ardelan—a varied region containing several lofty ridges, with broad plains lying between them.

It is remarkable that the time of this first contact of Media with Assyria—a contact taking place when Assyria was in her prime and Media was only just emerging from a long period of weakness and obscurity—is almost exactly that which Ctesias selects as the date of the great revolution whereby the Empire of the East passed from the hands of the Shemites into those of the Arians.[10] The long residence of Ctesias among the Persians gave him a bias towards that people, which even extended to their close kin, the Medes. Bent on glorifying these two Arian races, he determined to throw back the commencement of their Empire to a period long anterior to the true date; and, feeling specially anxious to cover up their early humiliation, he assigned their most glorious conquests to the very century, and almost to the very

---

* See above, vol. ii. p. 359; and compare the Black Obelisk Inscription (*Dublin Univ. Mag.* Oct. 1853, p. 424).

[10] Ctesias gave to his eight Median kings anterior to Aspadas or Astyages a period of 282 years. Assuming his date for Astyages' accession to have been the same, or nearly the same, with that of Herodotus (B.C. 593), we have B.C. 875 for the destruction of the Assyrian Empire and rise of the Median under Arbaces.

time, when they were in fact suffering reverses at the hands of the people over whom he represented them as triumphant. There was a boldness in the notion of thus inverting history which almost deserved, and to a considerable extent obtained, success. The "long chronology" of Ctesias kept its ground until recently, not indeed meeting with universal acceptance,[11] but on the whole predominating over the "short chronology" of Herodotus; and it may be doubted whether anything less than the discovery that the native records of Assyria entirely contradicted Ctesias would have sufficed to drive from the field his figment of early Median dominion.[12]

The second occasion upon which we hear of the Medes in the Assyrian annals is in the reign of Shalmaneser's son and successor, Shamas-Iva. Here again, as on the former occasion, the Assyrians were the aggressors. Shamas-Iva invaded Media and Amzins in his third year, and committed ravages similar to those of his father, wasting the country with fire and sword, but not (it would seem) reducing the Medes to subjection or even attempting to occupy their territory. Again, the attack is a mere raid, which produces no permanent impression.[13]

---

[11] The "long chronology" of Ctesias was adopted, among the ancients, by Cephalion, Castor, Polybius, Æmilius Sura, Trogus Pompeius, Nicolaus Damascenus, Diodorus Siculus, Strabo, Velleius Paterculus, and others; among the ecclesiastical writers, by Clement of Alexandria, Eusebius, Augustine, Sulpicius Severus, Agathias, Eustathius, and Syncellus; among the moderns, by Prideaux, Freret, and the French Academicians generally. Scaliger was, I believe, the first to discredit it. He was followed in the last century by the Abbé Sevin and Volney. In the present century the "long chronology" has had few advocates.

[12] Long after the superiority of the scheme of Herodotus was recognised, attempts continued to be made to reconcile Ctesias with him by supposing the list of the latter to be an *eastern* Median dynasty (Heeren's *Manual*, p. 27, E. T.), or to contain a certain number of viceroys (Clinton, *F. H.* vol. i. p. 261).

[13] Compare above, vol. ii. p. 376.

It is in the reign of the son and successor of Shamas-Iva that the Medes appear for the first time to have made their submission and accepted the position of Assyrian tributaries. A people which was unable to offer effectual resistance when the Assyrian levies invaded their country, and which had no means of retaliating upon their foe or making him suffer the evils that he inflicted, was naturally tempted to save itself from molestation by the payment of an annual tribute, so purchasing quiet at the expense of honour and independence. Towards the close of the ninth century B.C., the Medes seem to have followed the example set them very much earlier by their kindred and neighbours, the Persians,[1] and to have made arrangements for an annual payment which should exempt their territory from ravage.[2] It is doubtful whether the arrangement was made by the whole people. The Median tribes at this time hung so loosely together that a policy adopted by one portion of them might be entirely repudiated by another. Most probably the tribute was paid by those tribes only which bordered on Zagros, and not by those further to the east or to the north, into whose territories the Assyrian arms had not yet penetrated.

No further change in the condition of the Medes is known to have occurred[3] until about a hundred

---

[1] The Persians paid tribute to Shalmaneser II. (*Black Obelisk Inscription*, p. 424), and again to Shamas-Iva. They seem to have been at this time dwelling in the immediate vicinity of the Medes, probably somewhere within the limits of Media Magna.

[2] See the Inscription of this king in the *Journal of the Asiatic Society*, vol. xix. p. 185.

[3] There are grounds, however, for suspecting that during the obscure period of Assyrian history which divides Iva-lush IV. from Tiglath-Pileser II. (B.C. 781-744), Media became once more independent, and that she was again made tributary by the last-named monarch. That monarch even sent an officer to exercise authority in the country. (Sir H. Rawlinson in the *Athenæum*, No. 1869, p. 246.)

years later, when the Assyrians ceased to be content with the semi-independent position which had been hitherto allowed them, and determined on their more complete subjugation. The great Sargon, the assailant of Egypt and conqueror of Babylon, towards the middle of his reign, invaded Media with a large army, and having rapidly overrun the country, seized several of the towns, and "annexed them to Assyria," while at the same time he also established in new situations a number of fortified posts.[1] The object was evidently to incorporate Media into the empire; and the posts were stations in which a standing army was placed, to over-awe the natives and prevent them from offering an effectual resistance. With the same view deportation of the people on a large scale seems to have been practised;[2] and the gaps thus made in the population were filled up—wholly or in part—by the settlement in the Median cities of Samaritan captives.[3] On the country thus re-organised and re-arranged a tribute of a new character was laid. In lieu of the money payment hitherto exacted, the Medes were required to furnish annually to the royal stud a number of horses.[4] It is probable that Media was already famous for the remarkable breed which is so celebrated in later times;[5] and that the horses now required of her by the Assyrians were to be of the large and highly valued kind known as "Nisæan."

---

[1] Oppert, *Inscriptions des Sargonides*, p. 25. Compare above, vol. ii. p. 422.
[2] This is not stated in express terms; but Sargon says in one place that he peopled Ashdod with captives from the extreme East (*Inscriptions*, &c., p. 27), while in another he reckons Media the most eastern portion of his dominions.
[3] 2 Kings xvii. 6; xviii. 11.
[4] Oppert, *Inscriptions*, &c., p. 25.
[5] See above, p. 67.

The date of this subjugation is about B.C. 710. And here, if we compare the Greek accounts of Median history with those far more authentic ones which have reached us through the Assyrian contemporary records, we are struck by a repetition of the same device which came under our notice more than a century earlier—the device of covering up the nation's disgraces at a particular period by assigning to that very date certain great and striking successes. As Ctesias's revolt of the Medes under Arbaces and conquest of Nineveh synchronises nearly with the first known ravages of Assyria within the territories of the Medes, so Herodotus's revolt of the same people and commencement of their monarchy under Deioces falls almost exactly at the date when they entirely lost their independence.⁹ As there is no reason to suspect Herodotus either of partiality towards the Medes or of any wilful departure from the truth, we must regard him as imposed upon by his informants, who were probably either Medes or Persians.¹⁰ These mendacious patriots found little difficulty in palming their false tale upon the simple Halicarnassian, thereby at once extending the antiquity of their empire and concealing its shame behind a halo of fictitious glory.

After their subjugation by Sargon, the Medes of Media Magna appear to have remained the faithful subjects of Assyria for sixty or seventy years. During

---

⁹ As Herodotus gives to his four Median kings a period of exactly 150 years, and places the accession of Cyrus 78 years before the battle of Marathon, he really assigns the commencement of the Median monarchy to B.C. 708 (since 480 + 78 + 150 =708).

¹⁰ Herodotus speaks in one place only, (vii. 62) of deriving information from the Medes. He quotes the Persians as his authorities frequently (i. 1-5; 95; iii. 68, &c.).

this period we find no notices of the great mass of the nation in the Assyrian records: only here and there indications occur that Assyria is stretching out her arms towards the more distant and outlying tribes, especially those of Azerbijan, and compelling them to acknowledge her as mistress. Sennacherib boasts that early in his reign, about B.C. 701, he received an embassy from the remoter parts of Media—" parts of which the kings his fathers had not even heard"[11]—which brought him presents in sign of submission and patiently accepted his yoke. His son, Esar-haddon, relates that, about his tenth year (B.C. 670) he invaded Bikni or Bikan,[12] a distant province of Media, "whereof the kings his fathers had never heard the name," and attacking the cities of the region one after another forced them to acknowledge his authority.[13] The country was held by a number of independent chiefs, each bearing sway in his own city and adjacent territory. These chiefs have unmistakeably Arian names, as Sitriparna, or Sitra-phernes, Eparna or Ophernes, Zanasana or Zanasanes, and Ramatiya or Ramates.[14] Esar-haddon says that, having entered the country with his army, he seized two of the chiefs and carried them off to Assyria, together with a vast spoil and

[11] Fox Talbot, *Journal of the Asiatic Society*, vol. xix. p. 143.
[12] Probably Azer-bijan. See above, p. 15, note [4].
[13] Fox Talbot, *Assyrian Texts*, pp. 15, 16; Oppert, *Inscriptions des Sargonides*, p. 67.
[14] The termination *parna* may be compared with the Old Persian *farna*, which is found in Vidafrana (Intaphernes). The initial *Sitir* is perhaps *kshatra*, "crown," or possibly *chitra*, "stock." In Zanasana we have the common Medo-Persic termination *-ana* (= Gk. *-ǎnēs*) suffixed to a root which is probably connected with *san*, "to slay." Ramatiya has for its first element undoubtedly *râmas* (acc. *râma*), "pleasant, agreeable." The remainder of the word is perhaps a mere personal suffix. Or the whole word may be a contraction of *râmô-dâitya*, "given to be agreeable." (Brockhaus, *Vendidad-Sadé*, p. 390.)

FICTITIOUS MEDIAN KINGS.

numerous other captures. Hereupon the remaining chiefs, alarmed for their safety, made their submission, consenting to pay an annual tribute, and admitting Assyrian officers into their territories, who watched, if they did not even control, the government.

We are now approaching the time when Media seems to have been first consolidated into a monarchy by the genius of an individual. Sober history is forced to discard the shadowy forms of kings with which Greek writers of more fancy than judgment have peopled the darkness that rests upon the "origines" of the Medes. Arbaces, Maudaces,[1] Sosarmus, Artycas, Arbianes,[2] Artæus, Deioces—Median monarchs, according to Ctesias or Herodotus, during the space of time comprised within the years B.C. 875 and B.C. 655—have to be dismissed by the modern writer without a word, since there is reason to believe that they are mere creatures of the imagination, inventions of unscrupulous romancers, not men who once walked the earth. The list of Median kings in Ctesias, so far as it differs from the list in Herodotus, seems to be a pure forgery—an extension of the period of the monarchy by the conscious use of a system of duplication. Each king, or period, in Herodotus occurs in the list of Ctesias twice[3]—a

---

[1] So Diodorus (ii. 32) and Eusebius (*Chron. Can.* i. 15). But Syncellus gives the name as Mandauces (*Chronograph,* p. 372), and so does Moses of Chorené (*Hist. Armen.* i. 21).

[2] Moses of Chorené substitutes for Arbianes the entirely different name Cardiceas. (*Hist. Armen.* l. s. c.) Eusebius and Syncellus take only four kings from Ctesias, and then change to the list of Herodotus.

[3] This is manifest from the number of the years which Ctesias assigns to his kings. See the subjoined table.

CTESIAS.		HERODOTUS.	
Kings.	Yrs.	Kings, &c.	Yrs.
Arbaces	28	Interregnum .	—
Maudaces	50	Deioces	53
Sosarmus	30	Interregnum .	—
Artycas	50	Phraortes	22
Arbianes	22	Cyaxares	40
Artæus	40	Phraortes	22
Artynes	22	Cyaxares	40
Astibaras	40		

transparent device, clumsily cloaked by the cheap expedient of a liberal invention of names.⁴ Even the list of Herodotus requires curtailment. His Deioces, whose whole history reads more like romance than truth⁵—the organiser of a powerful monarchy in Media just at the time when Sargon was building his fortified posts in the country and peopling with his Israelite captives the old "cities of the Medes"—the prince who reigned for above half a century in perfect peace with his neighbours,⁶ and who, although contemporary with Sargon, Sennacherib, Esar-haddon, and Asshur-bani-pal—all kings more or less connected with Media—is never heard of in any of their annals, must be relegated to the historical limbo in which repose so many "shades of mighty names;" and the Herodotean list of Median kings must, at any rate, be thus far reduced. Nothing is more evident than that during the flourishing period of Assyria under the great Sargonidæ above-named, there was no grand Median kingdom

---

The first critic who noted this curious method of duplication, so far as I know, was Volney. (See his *Recherches sur l'Histoire Ancienne*, tom. i. pp. 144 et seqq.) Heeren glanced at it in the Appendix to his Manual (p. 476, E. T.). I myself noted it before I found it in Volney. The only weak point in the case is with respect to the interregnum. I presume that Ctesias supposed Herodotus to reckon the interregnum at a generation—30 years, in round numbers—and introduced the change in the case of Arbaces, from 30 to 28, in order to make the principle of alternations, which pervades his list, and furnishes the key to it, less glaring and palpable.

⁴ Ctesias shows no great talent or skill in his invention of names. He has not half the fertility of Æschylus. (See the *Persæ*, passim.) In his Median list, Ariyœa, Artæus, Artynes, are but variants of one and the same name—modifications of the root *artas*, "great." (Hesych. Ἄρτις, μέγας καὶ λαμπρός.) In his Assyrian list he mixes Greek and Persian with Semitic names, and in one part flies off to geography for assistance. In his famous story of the joint conspiracy of Arbaces and Belesis he simply took the actual names of the satraps of Media and Assyria during the time of his own residence in Persia. (See Xen. *Anab.* vii. 8, § 25.) This last fact has, I believe, never been noticed.

⁵ See Mr. Grote's *History of Greece*, vol. iii. pp. 307, 308.

⁶ Herod. i. 102.

upon the eastern flank of the empire. Such a kingdom had certainly not been formed up to B.C. 670, when Esar-haddon reduced the *more distant* Medes, finding them still under the government of a number of petty chiefs.⁷ It is not likely to have been formed during the reign of the fifth Sargonid, Asshur-banipal, who was even more enterprising and powerful than any of his predecessors.⁸ The earliest time at which we can imagine the consolidation to have taken place, consistently with what we know of Assyria, is B.C. 647, the year of the accession of the last Assyrian monarch, the weak and unwarlike Saracus.

The cause of the sudden growth of Media in power about this period, and of the consolidation which followed rapidly upon that growth, is to be sought, apparently, in fresh migratory movements from the Arian head-quarters, the countries east and south-east of the Caspian. The Cyaxares who about the year B.C. 632 led an invading host of Medes against Nineveh, was so well known to the Arian tribes of the north-east, that, when in the reign of Darius Hystaspis a Sagartian raised the standard of revolt in that region, he stated the ground of his claim to the Sagartian throne to be descent from Cyaxares.⁹ This great chief, it is probable, either alone, or in conjunction with his father (whom Herodotus calls Phraortes),¹⁰ led a fresh emigration of Arians from

---

⁷ See above, p. 172.
⁸ See vol. ii. pp. 403, 404.
⁹ See the *Behistun Inscription* (printed in the author's *Herodotus*, vol. ii. ad fin.), Col. ii. Par. 14, § 4.
¹⁰ The name Phraortes in this connection is suspicious. It was borne by a Mede who raised the standard of revolt in the time of Darius Hystaspis; who, however, laid it aside, and assumed the name of Xathrites (*Beh. Inscr.* Col. ii. Par. 5, § 4). If Phraortes had been a royal name previously, it would scarcely have been made to give way to one

the Bactrian and Sagartian country to the regions directly east of the Zagros mountain chain; and having thus vastly increased the strength of the Arian race in that quarter, set himself to consolidate a mountain kingdom capable of resisting the great monarchy of the plain. Accepted, it would seem, as chief by the former Arian inhabitants of the tract, he proceeded to reduce the scattered Scythic tribes which had hitherto held possession of the high mountain region. The Zimri, Minni, Hupuska, &c., who divided among them the country lying between Media Proper and Assyria, were attacked and subdued without any great difficulty;" and the conqueror, finding himself thus at the head of a considerable kingdom and no longer in any danger of subjugation at the hands of Assyria, began to contemplate the audacious enterprise of himself attacking the Great Power, which had been for so many hundred years the terror of Western Asia. The supineness of Saracus, the Assyrian king, encouraged his aspirations; and about B.C. 634, when that monarch had held the throne for thirteen years, suddenly, without warning, the Median troops debouched from the passes of Zagros, and spread themselves over the

---

which had no great associations attached to it.

On the whole it is very doubtful if the Phraortes of Herodotus ought not to be absolutely retrenched, like his Deioces. The testimony of Æschylus, who makes Cyaxares found the Medo-Persian empire (*Pers.* 761), and the evidence of the Behistun Inscription that the Medes traced their royal race to him, and not any higher, seem to show that he was really the founder of Median independence. Still, it has not been thought right wholly to discard the authority of Herodotus, where he is not absolutely contradicted by the monuments.

" Κατεστρίφατο τὴν Ἀσίην (ὁ Φραόρτης), ἀπ' ἄλλου ἐπ' ἄλλο ἰὼν ἔθνος. (Herod. i. 102.) These wars may have been in other directions also, but they must have been in Zagros for Media to have come at the end of them into contact with Assyria. (See the continuation of the passage, ἐς ὁ στρατευσάμενος ἐπὶ τοὺς Ἀσσυρίους κ.τ.λ.)

CHAP. VI. FIRST EXPEDITION AGAINST NINEVEH.   177

rich country at its base. Alarmed by the nearness
and greatness of the peril, the Assyrian king shook
off his lethargy, and putting himself at the head of
his troops, marched out to confront the invader. A
great battle was fought, probably somewhere in Adiabênê, in which the Medes were completely defeated:
their whole army was cut to pieces; and the father
of Cyaxares was among the slain.[13]

Such was the result of the first Median expedition
against Nineveh. The assailants had miscalculated
their strength. In their own mountain country, and
so long as they should be called upon to act only
on the defensive, they might be right in regarding
themselves as a match for the Assyrians; but when
they descended into the plain, and allowed their
enemy the opportunity of manœuvring and of using
his war-chariots,[13] their inferiority was marked. Cyaxares, now, if not previously, actual king, withdrew
awhile from the war, and, convinced that all the
valour of his Medes would be unavailing without
discipline, set himself to organise the army on a new
system, taking a pattern from the enemy, who had
long possessed some knowledge of tactics.[1] Hitherto,
it would seem, each Median chief had brought into
the field his band of followers, some mounted, some
on foot, foot and horse alike armed variously as their
means allowed them, some with bows and arrows,
some with spears, some perhaps with slings or darts;[2]

---

[13] Ὁ Φραόρτης αὐτός τε διεφθάρη, καὶ ὁ στρατὸς αὐτοῦ ὁ πολλός. (Herod. L. a. c.)
[14] Compare the case of the Israel-ites and the old nations of Canaan (Judg. i. 19).
[1] Supra, vol. II. pp. 68, 69.
[2] Herod. i. 103. Herodotus does not mention slingers, but only spear-men and archers. Still, as we find slingers among the Assyrians (supra, vol. ii. p. 43), and among the Egyp-tians (Wilkinson's *Ancient Egyp-tians*, vol. i. p. 316), and as the sling is the natural weapon of moun-taineers, we may conclude that the

and the army had been composed of a number of such bodies, each chief keeping his band close about him. Cyaxares broke up these bands, and formed the soldiers who composed them into distinct corps, according as they were horsemen or footmen, archers, slingers, or lancers. He then, having completed his arrangements at his ease, without disturbance (so far as appears) from Saracus, felt himself strong enough to renew the war with a good prospect of success. Collecting as large an army as he could, both from his Arian and his Scythic subjects, he marched into Assyria, met the troops of Saracus in the field, defeated them signally, and forced them to take refuge behind the strong works which defended their capital. He even ventured to follow up the flying foe and commence the siege of the capital itself; but at this point he was suddenly checked in his career of victory, and forced to assume a defensive attitude, by a danger of a novel kind, which recalled him from Nineveh to his own country.

The vast tracts, chiefly consisting of grassy plains, which lie north of the Black Sea, the Caucasus, the Caspian, and the Jaxartes or Syhun river, were inhabited in ancient times by a race or races known to the Asiatics as *Saka*,[3] to the Greeks as Σκύθαι, "Scythians." These people appear to have been allied ethnically with many of the more southern races, as with the Parthians, the Iberians, the Alarodians, the tribes of the Zagros chain, the Susianians, and

---

Medes were not without them. That the Persians used slings is well established. (Xen. *Anab.* iii. 3, § 18.)

[3] This was especially the *Persian* name (Herod. vii. 64). It is found throughout the Achæmenian inscriptions, but not in the Assyrian or Babylonian, where the term which replaces it is *Gimiri* or *Kimiri* (apparently "Cimmerians"). In the Zendavesta *Turiya* (Turanian) is the appellative of the Scythic races.

others.¹ It is just possible that they may have taken an interest in the welfare of their southern brethren, and that, when Cyaxares brought the tribes of Zagros under his yoke, the Scyths of the North may have felt resentment or compassion. If this view seem too improbable, considering the distance, the physical obstacles, and the little communication that there was between nations in those early times, we must suppose that by a mere coincidence it happened that the subjugation of the southern Scyths by Cyaxares was followed within a few years by a great irruption of Scyths from the trans-Caucasian region. In that case we shall have to regard the invasion as a mere example of that ever recurring law, by which the poor and hardy races of Upper Asia or Europe are from time to time directed upon the effete kingdoms of the south, to shake, ravage, or overturn them as the case may be, and prevent them from stagnating into corruption.

The character of the Scythians, and the general nature of their ravages, have been described in a former volume.² If they entered Southern Asia, as seems probable,³ by the Daghestan route, they would then have been able to pass on without much difficulty,⁴ through Georgia into Azerbijan, and from Azerbijan into Media Magna, where the Medes had now established their southern capital. Four roads lead from Azerbijan to Hamadan or the Greater

---

¹ See the author's *Herodotus*, vol. iv. pp. 163, 169, 188, 204, &c.
² See vol. ii. pp. 510-514.
³ Herodotus says of the Scythians that they marched from Scythia into Media by a roundabout route, ἐν δέξιῃ ἔχοντες τὸ Καυκάσιον ὄρος (i. 104). This description is exactly applicable to the route along the western shores of the Caspian, by Derbend and Bakou.
⁴ The Bakou route conducts into the flat Moghan district at the mouth of the combined Kur and Aras, whence it is easy to march to Tabriz and the Urumiyeh country.

Ecbatana, one through Menjil and Kasvin, and across the Karaghan Hills; a second through Miana, Zenjan, and the province of Khamsch; a third by the valley of the Jaghetu, through Chukli and Tikan-Teppeh; and a fourth through Sefer-Khaneh and Sennah. We cannot say which of the four the invaders selected; but, as they were pressing southwards they met the army of Cyaxares, which had quitted Nineveh on the first news of their invasion, and had marched in hot haste to meet and engage them.[8] The two enemies were not ill-matched. Both were hardy and warlike, both active and full of energy; with both the cavalry was the chief arm, and the bow the weapon on which they depended mainly for victory. The Medes were no doubt the better disciplined; they had a greater variety of weapons and of soldiers; and individually they were probably more powerful men than the Scythians:[9] but these last had the advantage of numbers, of reckless daring, and of tactics that it was difficult to encounter. Moreover, the necessity of their situation in the midst of an enemy's country made it imperative on them to succeed, while their adversaries might be defeated without any very grievous consequences. The Scyths had not come into Asia to conquer so much as to ravage; defeat at their hands involved damage rather than destruction; and the Medes must have felt that, if they lost the battle, they might still hope to maintain a stout defence behind the strong walls of some of their towns.[10] The result was such as might have been expected under these circumstances. Madyes,[11]

---

[8] Herod. L 104.
[9] On the Scythian physique see above, vol. II. p. 510.
[10] As the Northern Ecbatana (supra, p. 24) and perhaps Rhagae.
[11] So Herodotus (i. 103). Strabo gives the name as Madys (i. 3, § 21).

the Scythian leader, obtained the victory; Cyaxares was defeated, and compelled to make terms with the invader. Retaining his royal name, and the actual government of his country, he admitted the suzerainty of the Scyths, and agreed to pay them an annual tribute. Whether Media suffered very seriously from their ravages, we cannot say. Neither its wealth nor its fertility was such as to tempt marauders to remain in it very long. The main complaint made against the Scythian conquerors is, that, not content with the fixed tribute which they had agreed to receive and which was paid them regularly, they levied contributions at their pleasure on the various states under their sway, which were oppressed by repeated exactions.[a] The injuries suffered from their marauding habits form only a subordinate charge against them, as though it had not been practically felt to be so great a grievance. We can well imagine that the bulk of the invaders would prefer the warmer and richer lands of Assyria, Mesopotamia, and Syria,[1] and that, pouring into them, they would leave the colder and less wealthy Media comparatively free from ravage.

The condition of Media and the adjacent countries under the Scythians must have nearly resembled that of almost the same regions under the Seljukian Turks during the early times of their domination.[2] The conquerors made no fixed settlements, but pitched their tents in any portion of the territory that they chose. Their horses and cattle were free to pasture

---

[a] This seems to be the meaning of the somewhat obscure passage, χωρὶς μὲν γὰρ τῶν φόρων ἑπρήσσοντο παρ' ἑκάστων τὸ ἑκάστοισι ἐπιβαλλον. (Herod. i. 106.)

[1] See above, vol. ii. p. 515.
[2] See Gibbon's *Decline and Fall of the Roman Empire*, ch. lvii. (vol. v. pp. 655, 656, 4to edition).

on all lands equally. They were recognized as the dominant race, were feared and shunned, but did not greatly interfere with the bulk of their subjects. It was impossible that they should occupy at any given time more than a comparatively few spots in the wide tract which they had overrun and subjugated; and consequently, there was not much contact between them and the peoples whom they had conquered. Such contact as there was must no doubt have been galling and oppressive. The right of free pasture in the lands of others is always irksome to those who have to endure it,[2] and even where it is exercised with strict fairness, naturally leads to quarrels. The barbarous Scythians are not likely to have cared very much about fairness. They would press heavily upon the more fertile tracts, paying overfrequent visits to such spots, and remaining at them till the region was exhausted. The chiefs would not be able to restrain their followers from acts of pillage; redress would be obtained with difficulty; and sometimes even the chiefs themselves may have been sharers in the injuries committed. The insolence, moreover, of a dominant race so coarse and rude as the Scyths must have been very hard to bear; and we can well understand that the various nations which had to endure the yoke must have looked anxiously for an opportunity of shaking it off, and recovering their independence.

Among these various nations there was probably none that fretted and winced under its subjection

---

[2] The Samnites seem to have had a right of this kind in Campania, which, probably, as much as anything, caused the revolt of the Campanians and their submission to Rome in B.C. 340. (See Arnold, *History of Rome*, vol. ii, pp. 108, 109.) Powerful Arab tribes have sometimes such a right over lands usually in the occupation of inferior tribes.

more than the Medes. Naturally brave and high-spirited, with the love of independence inherent in mountaineers, and with a well-grounded pride in their recent great successes, they must have chafed daily and hourly at the ignominy of their position, the postponement of their hopes, and the wrongs which they continually suffered. At first it seemed necessary to endure. They had tried the chances of a battle, and had been defeated in fair fight—what reason was there to hope that, if they drew the sword again, they would be more successful? Accordingly, they remained quiet: but, as time went on and the Scythians dispersed themselves continually over a wider and a wider space, invading Assyria, Mesopotamia, Syria, Palestine,⁴ and again Armenia and Cappadocia,⁵ everywhere plundering and marauding, conducting sieges, fighting battles, losing men from the sword, from sickness, from excesses,⁶ becoming weaker instead of stronger, as each year went by, owing to the drain of constant wars—the Medes by degrees took heart. Not trusting however entirely to the strength of their right arms, a trust which had failed them once, they resolved to prepare the way for an outbreak by a stratagem which they regarded as justifiable. Cyaxares and his Court invited a number of the Scythian chiefs to a grand banquet, and, having induced them to drink till they were completely drunk, set upon them when they were in this helpless condition and remorselessly slew them all.⁷

---

⁴ Herod. I. 105.
⁵ Strab. xi. 8, § 4. Σάκαι ... τὴν Ἀρμενίαν κατέστησαν τὴν ἀρίστην γῆν ... καὶ μέχρι Καππαδόκων, καὶ μάλιστα τῶν πρὸς Εὐξείνῳ, οὓς Πον- τικοὺς νῦν καλοῦσι, προῆλθον.
⁶ Herod. l. s. c.
⁷ Ibid. I. 106. Herodotus says, absurdly, in this place, that "most of the Scythians" were destroyed

This deed was the signal for a general revolt of the nation. The Medes everywhere took arms, and turning upon their conquerors, assailed them with a fury the more terrible because it had been for years repressed. A war followed, the duration and circumstances of which are unknown;[8] for the stories with which Ctesias enlivened this portion of his history can scarcely be accepted as having any foundation in fact. According to him, the Parthians made common cause with the Scythians on the occasion, and the war lasted many years; numerous battles were fought with great loss to both sides; and peace was finally concluded without either party having gained the upper hand.[9] The Scyths were commanded by a queen, Zariua or Zarinæa,[10] a woman of rare beauty, and as brave as she was fair; who won the hearts, when she could not resist the swords, of her adversaries. A strangely romantic love-tale is told of this beauteous Amazon.[11] It is not at all

---

by this stratagem. But he admits afterwards (iv. 1) that the great bulk of the invaders returned into Scythia.

It is not clear whether Strabo's notice of the origin of the Σάκαια refers to this occasion or so. After relating the extent of the Scythian ravages (see above, note ¹), he says, "the Persian generals of the time set upon them by night as they were feasting off their spoils, and completely exterminated them."

[9] The whole struggle is summed up by Herodotus in three words— Ἐξελάσαντες ὑπὸ Μήδων οἱ Σκύθαι κ.τ.λ.

[*] Dio. Sic. II. 34, § 2.

[10] Zarinæa is the form used by Nicolas of Damascus (Fr. 12); Zarina, by Diodorus (ii. 34, § 3).

[11] Zarina was the wife of Marmareus, the Scythian king, and accompanied him to the war, taking part in all his battles. On one occasion she was wounded and might have been captured by Stryangæus, son-in-law of the King of the Medes; but she begged so earnestly to be allowed to escape, that Stryangæus let her go. Shortly afterwards Stryangæus himself was made prisoner by Marmareus, who was about to put him to death, when Zarina interposed on his behalf, and begged his life in return for her own. Her prayer being refused, in order to save her preserver, she murdered her husband. The pair were by this time in love with one another, and peace having been made between the Saccae and the Medes, Stryangæus went to visit Zarina at her court. There he was most hospitably received; but when, after a while, he revealed the secret of his love, Zarina

clear what region Ctesias supposes her to govern. It has a capital city, called Roxanacé (a name entirely unknown to any other historian or geographer), and it contains many other towns, of which Zarina was the foundress. Its chief architectural monument was the tomb of Zarina, a triangular pyramid, six hundred feet high, and more than a mile round the base, crowned by a colossal figure of the queen made of solid gold.[12] But—to leave these fables and return to fact—we can only say with certainty that the result of the war was the complete defeat of the Scythians, who not only lost their position of pre-eminence in Media and the adjacent countries, but were driven across the Caucasus into their own proper territory.[1] Their expulsion was so complete that they scarcely left a trace of their power or their presence in the geography or ethnography of the country. One Palestinian city only, as already observed,[2] and one Armenian province[3] retained in their names a lingering memory of the great inroad, which but for them would have passed away without making any more permanent mark on the region than a hurricane or a snow-storm.

How long the dominion of the Scyths endured is a matter of great uncertainty. It was no doubt the

---

repulsed him, reminding him of his wife, Rhætæa, whom fame reported much more beautiful than herself, and exhorting him to show his manhood by battling bravely with an unseemly passion. Hereupon Stryangæus retired to his chamber and killed himself, having first written to reproach Zarina with causing his death. (See Nic. Dam. Fr. 12; and compare Demetrius, *De Elocut.* § 219; Tzetz. *Chiliad.* xii. 894; and Anon. *De claris mulieribus*, § 2.)

[12] Diod. Sic. ii. 34, § 5.
[1] Herod. iv. 1 and 4.
[2] Scythopolis. (See above, vol. II. p. 516.) Polyhistor considered that Scythopolis was a town of importance in the time of Nebuchadnezzar. (Polyhist. ap. Euseb. *Præp. Ev.* ix. 39.)
[3] Sacasené, which Strabo says took its name from them. (xi. 8, § 4).

belief of Herodotus that from their defeat of Cyaxares to his treacherous murder of their chiefs was a period of exactly twenty-eight years.[1] During the whole of this space he regarded them as the undisputed lords of Asia. It was not till the twenty-eight years were over that the Medes were able, according to him, to renew their attacks on the Assyrians and once more to besiege Nineveh. But this chronology is very open to objections. There is strong reason for believing that Nineveh fell about B.C. 625;[2] but according to the numbers of Herodotus the fall would, at the earliest, have taken place in B.C. 602.[3] There is great unlikelihood that the Scyths, if they had maintained their rule for a generation, should not have attracted some notice from the Jewish writers. Again, if twenty-eight out of the forty

---

[1] Herod. I. 106. Compare iv. 1.
[2] This belief rests primarily on the statements of Abydenus and Polyhistor, which connect the fall of Nineveh with the accession of Nabopolassar (Ahyd. ap. Euseb. Chr. Can. I. 9; Polyhist. ap. Syncell. Chronograph. p. 396)—an event fixed by the Canon of Ptolemy to B.C. 625. The value of these writers depends of course wholly on their representing to us, where they agree, the statements of Berosus. A second ground for believing that the capture was not much later than this is contained in the Lydian war of Cyaxares, which must have been subsequent to it, yet which seems to be best dated as between B.C. 615 and B.C. 610. It is perhaps worth noticing that Eusebius places the capture in B.C. 618, which is (according to him) the twelfth year of Cyaxares. (Chron. Can. II. p. 328.)
[3] Herodotus represents Cyaxares as ascending the throne 153 years before the battle of Marathon, i.e. in B.C. 633. He first introduces a new system of discipline, which must take at least one year. He then attacks Nineveh, and is recalled by the arming of the Scyths—say in B.C. 632. The massacre is 28 years afterwards, or B.C. 604. Suppose Nineveh attacked for the second time in the very next year, which is unlikely enough, but just possible; it can scarcely have fallen till the year following, or B.C. 602. This is the shortest computation that is at all reasonable. It would be quite fair to claim that two or three years must have been occupied by the organization of the army on a new system; that about the same time would probably elapse between the rejection of the Scythic yoke and the recovery of sufficient strength to attack so great a town as Nineveh; and that the siege may well have occupied two full years, as Diodorus, following Ctesias, makes it. We should then have (633 – 3 – 28 – 2 – 2 =) B.C. 598 as the Herodotean date of the capture.

years assigned to Cyaxares are to be regarded as years of inaction, all his great exploits, his two sieges of Nineveh, his capture of that capital, his conquest of the countries north and west of Media as far as the Halys;' his six years' war in Asia Minor beyond that river, and his joint expedition with Nebuchadnezzar into Syria, will have to be crowded most improbably into the space of twelve years, two or three preceding and ten or nine following the Scythian domination.* These and other reasons lead to the conclusion, which has the support of Eusebius,* that the Scythian domination was of much shorter duration than Herodotus imagined. It may have been twenty-eight years from the original attack on Media to the final expulsion of the last of the invaders from Asia—and this may have been what the informants of Herodotus really intended—but it cannot have been very long after the first attack before the Medes began to recover themselves, to shake off the fear which had possessed them, and to clear their territories of the invaders. If the invasion really took place in the reign of Cyaxares, and not in the lifetime of his father, where Eusebius places it,¹⁰ we must suppose that within eight years of its occurrence Cyaxares found himself sufficiently strong, and his hands sufficiently free, to resume his old projects, and for the second time to march an army into Assyria.

---

⁷ See below, p. 196.
* It is *possible* to tabulate the reign of Cyaxares so as to bring these events within the 12 years above indicated; but their all happening within so brief a space is most improbable.
⁹ Eusebius places the fall of Nineveh in the 12th year of Cyaxares (B.C. 618, according to him). This would imply that the expulsion of the Scyths was at least as early as B.C. 620. He brings the Scyths into Asia in B.C. 631, thus assigning to their domination about eleven years.
¹⁰ Eusebius makes Phraortes reign till B.C. 629, and Cyaxares succeed him in that year. (*Chron. Can.* ii. p. 327.)

The weakness of Assyria was such as to offer strong temptations to an invader. As the famous inroad of the Gauls into Italy in the year of Rome 365, paved the way for the Roman conquests in the peninsula by breaking the power of the Etruscans, the Umbrians, and various other races, so the Scythic incursion may have really benefitted, rather than injured, Media, by weakening the great power to whose Empire she aspired to succeed. The exhaustion of Assyria's resources at the time is remarkably illustrated by the poverty and meanness of the palace, which the last king built for himself at Calah.[11] She lay, apparently, at the mercy of the first bold assailant, her prestige lost, her army dispirited or disorganised, her defences injured, her high spirit broken and subdued.

Cyaxares, ere proceeding to the attack, sent, it is probable, to make an alliance with the Susianians and Chaldæans.[12] Susiana was the last country which Assyria had conquered, and could remember the pleasures of independence. Chaldæa, though it had been now for above half a century an Assyrian fief, and had borne the yoke with scarcely a murmur during that period, could never wholly forget its old glories or the long resistance which it had made before submitting to its northern neighbour. The overtures of the Median monarch seem to have been favourably received; and it was agreed that an army from the south should march up the Tigris and threaten Assyria from that quarter, while Cyaxares

---

[11] See vol. II. pp. 517, 518.
[12] The "turmæ vulgi collecticiæ, quæ à mari adversus Naracum adventabant" (Abyd. ap. Euseb. Chron. Can.

l. 9) must, I think, have been these two nations. The opportuneness of their attack makes it probable that they acted in concert with Cyaxares.

led his Medes from the east, through the passes of Zagros against the capital. Rumour soon conveyed the tidings of his enemies' intentions to the Assyrian monarch, who immediately made such a disposition of the forces at his command as seemed best calculated to meet the double danger which threatened him. Selecting from among his generals the one in whom he placed most confidence—a man named Nabopolassar, most probably an Assyrian—he put him at the head of a portion of his troops and sent him to Babylon to resist the enemy who was advancing from the sea.[13] The command of his main army he reserved for himself, intending to undertake in person the defence of his territory against the Medes. This plan of campaign was not badly conceived; but it was frustrated by an unexpected calamity. Nabopolassar, seeing his sovereign's danger, and calculating astutely that he might gain more by an opportune defection from a falling cause than he could look to receive as the reward of fidelity, resolved to turn traitor and join the enemies of Assyria. Accordingly he sent an embassy to Cyaxares, with proposals for a close alliance to be cemented by a marriage. If the Median monarch would give his daughter Amuhia (or Amyitis) to be the wife of his son Nebuchadnezzar, the forces under his command should march against Nineveh[14] and assist Cyaxares to capture it. Such a proposition arriving at such a time was not likely to meet with a refusal. Cyaxares gladly came into the terms; the marriage

---

[13] Abyd. l. s. c.; Polyhist. ap. Syncell. *Chronograph.* p. 396.
[14] "Copias auxiliares misit [Nabopolassarus], videlicet ut filio suo Nabuchodrossoro desponderet Amu-hiam e filiabus Asdahagis unam." (Polyhist. ap. Euseb. *Chron. Can.* i. 5.) "Ut" seems to mean here ἐφ' ᾧ, "on condition that."

took place; and Nabopolassar, who had now practically assumed the sovereignty of Babylon,¹⁴ either led or sent¹⁵ a Babylonian contingent to the aid of the Medes.

The siege of Nineveh by the combined Medes and Babylonians was narrated by Ctesias¹ at some length. He called the Assyrian king Sardanapalus, the Median commander Arbaces, the Babylonian Belesis. Though he thus disguised the real names, and threw back the event to a period a century and a half earlier than its true date, there can be no doubt that he intended to relate the last siege of the city, that which immediately preceded its complete destruction.² He told how the combined army, consisting of Persians and Arabs as well as of Medes and Babylonians and amounting to four hundred thousand men, was twice defeated with great loss by the Assyrian monarch, and compelled to take refuge in the Zagros chain—how after losing a third battle it retreated to Babylonia—how it was there joined by strong reinforcements from Bactria, surprised the Assyrian camp by night, and drove the whole host in confusion to Nineveh—how, then, after two more victories, it advanced and invested the city, which was well provisioned for a siege and strongly fortified. The siege, Ctesias said, had lasted two full years, and the third year had commenced—success seemed still far off—when an unusually rainy season so swelled the

---

¹⁴ This is implied in his proceedings. Only a king could undertake to treat with a king, and to propose such a marriage as that above spoken of.

¹⁵ "Misit." Polyhist. ap. Euseb. l. s. c. "Contra Ninivem impetum faciebat." Abyden. ap. eund. (l. 8.)

¹ See Diod. Sic. ii. 25–28.

² After this capture Arbaces, according to Ctesias, destroyed Nineveh to its foundations (τὴν πόλιν εἰς ἔδαφος κατέσκαψεν).

waters of the Tigris, that they burst into the city, sweeping away more than two miles (!) of the wall. This vast breach it was impossible to repair; and the Assyrian monarch, seeing that further resistance was vain, brought the struggle to an end by burning himself, with his concubines and eunuchs and all his chief wealth, in his palace.

Such, in outline, was the story of Ctesias. If we except the extent of the breach which the river is declared to have made, it contains no glaring improbabilities.³ On the contrary, it is a narrative that hangs well together and that suits both the relations of the parties⁴ and the localities. Moreover, it is confirmed in one or two points by authorities of the highest order. Still, as Ctesias is a writer who delights in fiction, and as it seems very unlikely that he would find a detailed account of the siege, such as he has given us, in the Persian archives, from whence he professed to derive his history,⁵ no confidence can

---

³ The danger which the cities on the Tigris run from the spring floods may be illustrated from the recent history of Baghdad. In the year 1840 Mr. Loftus, arriving at that place on May 5, found the whole population "in a state of the utmost alarm and apprehension.... The rise in the Tigris had attained the unprecedented height of 22½ feet... Nejib Pasha had, a few days previously, summoned the population *en masse* to provide against the general danger by raising a strong high mound completely round the walls. Mats of reed were placed outside to bind the earth compactly together. The water was thus restrained from devastating the city— not so effectually, however, but that it filtered through the fine alluvial soil, and stood in the serdabs, or cellars, several feet in depth. It had reached within two feet of the top of the bank! On the river side the houses alone, many of which were very old and frail, prevented the ingress of the flood. It was a critical juncture. Men were stationed night and day to watch the barriers. If the dam or any of the foundations had failed, Baghdad must have been bodily washed away. Fortunately the pressure was withstood, and the inundation gradually subsided." (Loftus, *Chaldæa and Susiana*, p. 7.)

⁴ There is nothing improbable in the Medes inducing the Persians to help them, or in the Babylonians getting the assistance of some Arab tribes. (See above, vol. ii. p. 492.) The Bactrian contingent might be a fresh body of emigrant Medes arrived from those regions.

⁵ See Diod. Sic. ii. 32, § 4.

be placed in those points of his narrative which have not any further sanction. All that we *know* on the subject of the last siege of Nineveh is, that it was conducted by a combined army of Medes and Babylonians,[1] the former commanded by Cyaxares, the latter by Nabopolassar or Nebuchadnezzar,[2] and that it was terminated, when all hope was lost, by the suicide of the Assyrian monarch. The self-immolation of Saracus is related by Abydenus,[3] who almost certainly follows Berosus in this part of his history. We may therefore accept it as a fact about which there ought to be no question. Actuated by a feeling which has more than once caused a vanquished monarch to die rather than fall into the power of his enemies, Saracus made a funeral pyre of his ancestral palace, and lighted it with his own hand.[4]

One further point in the narrative of Ctesias we may *suspect* to contain a true representation. Ctesias declared the cause of the capture to have been the destruction of the city wall by an unexpected rise of the river. Now, the Prophet Nahum in his announcement of the fate coming on Nineveh, has a very remarkable expression, which seems most naturally to point to some destruction of a portion of the fortifications by means of water. After relating the steps that would be taken for the defence of the place,

---

[1] See, besides Abydenus and Polyhistor, Tobit xiv. 15, and Josephus (*Ant. Jud.*, x 5., § 1).
[2] The book of Tobit makes Nebuchadnezzar the actual commander.
[3] See the passage quoted at length in vol. ii. p. 505, note [1].
[4] The closest parallel to the conduct of Saracus is the self-destruction of Zimri. (1 K. xvi. 18.) The unheroic spirit of the later Persians not being able to conceive of such an act of self-immolation, ascribed the fire to a thunderbolt. (See the distorted story of the fall of Nineveh in Xenophon, *Anab.* lii. 4, § 11, 12; where the Assyrians are called Medes and the Medes Persians, and where the effeminate Sardanapalus becomes an actual woman—Μηδία γυνὴ βασιλίσσα.)

he turns to remark on their fruitlessness and says:—
"The *gates of the rivers are opened*, and the palace is *dissolved*; and Huzzab is led away captive; she is led up, with her maidens, sighing as with the voice of doves, smiting upon their breasts."[10] Now, we have already seen that at the north-west angle of Nineveh there was a sluice or floodgate,[11] intended mainly to keep the water of the Khosr-su, which ordinarily filled the city moat, from flowing off too rapidly into the Tigris, but probably intended also to keep back the water of the Tigris, when that stream rose above its common level. A sudden and great rise of the Tigris would necessarily endanger this gate, and if it gave way beneath the pressure, a vast torrent of water would rush up the moat along and against the northern wall, which may have been undermined by its force, and have fallen in. The stream would then pour into the city; and it may perhaps have reached the palace platform, which being made of sun-dried bricks and probably not cased with stone *inside* the city, would begin to be "dissolved."[12] Such seems the simplest and best interpretation of this passage, which, though it is not historical but only prophetical, must be regarded as giving an importance, that it would not otherwise have possessed, to the statement of Ctesias with

---

[10] Nahum ii. 6, 7. The authorized version is followed mainly in this translation; but a few improvements are adopted from Mr. Vance Smith's *Prophecies concerning Nineveh*, pp. 242, 243.

[11] See above, vol. i. p. 324.

[12] Mr. Vance Smith argues against this translation of the word נמוג here, though he allows that נמוג is ordinarily "to melt, dissolve," because (he says) "the raised terraces or platforms were very solid and faced with stone." (*Prophecies*, p. 243, note 4.) But we do not know that they were ever so faced except when they formed part of the external defences of a town.

regard to the part played by the Tigris in the destruction of Nineveh.

The fall of the city was followed by a division of the spoil between the two principal conquerors. While Cyaxares took to his own share the land of the conquered people, Assyria Proper, and the countries dependant on Assyria towards the north and the north-west, Nabopolassar was allowed, not merely Babylonia, Chaldæa, and Susiana,[1] but the valley of the Euphrates and the countries to which that valley conducted. Thus two considerable empires arose at the same time out of the ashes of Assyria—the Babylonian towards the south and the south-west, stretching from Luristan to the borders of Egypt, the Median towards the north, reaching from the salt desert of Iran to Amanus and the Upper Euphrates. These empires were established by mutual consent; they were connected together, not merely by treaties, but by the ties of affinity which united their rulers; and, instead of cherishing, as might have been expected, a mutual suspicion and distrust, they seem to have really entertained the most friendly feelings towards one another, and to have been ready on all emergencies to lend each other important assistance.[2] For once in the history of the world, two powerful monarchies were seen to stand side by side, not only without collision, but without jealousy or rancour. Babylonia and Media were content to share between them the Empire of Western Asia—the world was, they thought, wide

---

[1] The dependance of Susiana on Babylon during the Median period is shown by the Book of Daniel, where the prophet goes on the king's business to "Shushan the palace in the province of Elam," during the reign of Belshazzar. (Dan. viii. 2 and 27.)

[2] See below, pp. 209 and 215.

enough for both—and so, though they could not but have had in some respects conflicting interests, they remained close friends and allies for more than half a century.

To the Median monarch the conquest of Assyria did not bring a time of repose. Wandering bands of Scythians were still, it is probable, committing ravages in many parts of Western Asia. The subjects of Assyria, set free by her downfall, were likely to use the occasion for the assertion of their independence, if they were not immediately shown that a power of at least equal strength had taken her place and was prepared to claim her inheritance. War begets war; and the successes of Cyaxares up to the present point in his career did but whet his appetite for power and stimulate him to attempt further conquests. In brief but pregnant words Herodotus informs us, that Cyaxares "subdued to himself all Asia above the Halys."[3] How much he may include in this expression, it is impossible to determine; but, *primâ facie*, it would seem at least to imply that he engaged in a series of wars with the various tribes and nations which intervened between Media and Assyria on the one side and the river Halys on the other, and that he succeeded in bringing them under his dominion. The most important countries in this direction were Armenia and Cappadocia. Armenia, strong in its lofty mountains, its deep gorges, and its numerous rapid rivers—the head streams of the Tigris, Euphrates, Kur, and Aras—had for centuries resisted with unconquered spirit the perpetual efforts of the Assyrian kings to

---

[3] Herod. i. 103. Οὗτός [Κυαξάρης] ἐστιν ... ὁ τὴν Ἄλυος ποταμοῦ ἄνω Ἀσίην πᾶσαν συστήσας ἑωυτῷ.

bring it under their yoke, and had only at last consented under the latest king but one to a mere nominal allegiance.[1] Cappadocia had not even been brought to this degree of dependance. It had lain beyond the furthest limit whereto the Assyrian arms had ever reached, and had not as yet come into collision with any of the great powers of Asia. Other minor tribes in this region, neighbours of the Armenians and Cappadocians, but more remote from Media, were the Iberians,[2] the Colchians, the Moschi, the Tibareni, the Mares, the Macrones, and the Mosynœci.[3] Herodotus appears to have been of opinion that all these tribes, or at any rate all but the Colchians, were at this time brought under by Cyaxares,[4] who thus extended his dominions to the Caucasus and the Black Sea upon the north, and upon the east to the Kizil Irmak or Halys.

It is possible that the reduction of these countries under the Median yoke was not so much a conquest, as a voluntary submission of the inhabitants to the power which alone seemed strong enough to save them from the hated domination of the Scyths. According to Strabo, Armenia and Cappadocia were the regions where the Scythic ravages had been most severely felt.[5] Cappadocia had been devastated from the mountains down to the coast; and in Armenia the most fertile portion of the whole territory had

---

[1] We can scarcely suppose that the submission of Belat-Duri (supra, vol. ii. p. 498, note ⁹) was more than this.
[2] The "Sapeirians" of Herodotus (i. 104; iii. 95; vii. 79).
[3] Herod. iii. 94; vii. 78, 79.
[4] His expression "all Asia above the Halys" (supra, note ¹) is ample enough to cover the whole of this district. That he regards it as part of the Median Empire, and as devolving upon Persia by her conquest of Media, seems to follow from his making no allusion to the conquest of any part of it by Cyrus or his successors.
[5] Strab. xi. 8, § 4.

been seized and occupied by the invaders, from whom it thenceforth took the name of Sacassené. The Armenians and Cappadocians may have found the yoke of the Scyths so intolerable as to have gladly exchanged it for dependance on a comparatively civilized people. In the neighbouring territory of Asia Minor a similar cause had recently exercised a unifying influence, the necessity of combining to resist Cimmerian immigrants having tended to establish a hegemony of Lydia over the various tribes which divided among them the tracts west of the Halys.[9] It is evidently not improbable that the sufferings endured at the hands of the Scyths may have disposed the nations east of the river to adopt the same remedy, and that, so soon as Media had proved her strength, first by shaking herself free of the Scythic invaders, and then by conquering Assyria, the tribes of these parts accepted her as at once their mistress and their deliverer.[10]

Another quite distinct cause may also have helped to bring about the result above indicated. Parallel with the great Median migration from the East under Cyaxares, or Phraortes (?) his father, an Arian influx had taken place into the countries between the Caspian and the Halys. In Armenia and Cappadocia, during the flourishing period of Assyria, Turanian tribes had been predominant.[11] Between the middle and

---

[9] See below, p. 205.
[10] It was observed above, that *primâ facie* the words of Herodotus seem to imply a series of wars. We notice, however, when we look more narrowly at the passage, that the expression used, *ἐχειρώσατο ἑωυτῷ*, is unusual and ambiguous. It might apply to a violent subjugation, but it does not necessarily imply violence. It would be a suitable expression to use if the nations of this part of Asia came under the power of Cyaxares by *arrangement*, and not on compulsion.

[11] This is especially indicated by the Turanian character of the names of those who bear rule in these regions during the whole period covered by the Assyrian historical inscrip-

the end of the seventh century B.C. these tribes appear to have yielded the supremacy to Arians. In Armenia, the present language, which is predominantly Arian, ousted the former Turanian tongue, which appears in the cuneiform inscriptions of Van and the adjacent regions. In Cappadocia, the Moschi and Tibareni had to yield their seats to a new race—the Katapatuka, who were not only Arian but distinctly Medo-Persic, as is plain from their proper names,[1] and from the close connection of their royal house with that of the kings of Persia.[2] This spread of the Arians into the countries lying between the Caspian and the Halys must have done much to pave the way for Median supremacy over those regions. The weaker Arian tribes of the north would have been proud of their southern brethren, to whose arms the queen of Western Asia had been forced to yield, and would have felt comparatively little repugnance in surrendering their independence into the hands of a friendly and kindred people.

Thus Cyaxares, in his triumphant progress to the north and the north-west, made war, it is probable, chiefly upon the Scyths, or upon them and the old Turanian inhabitants of the countries, while by the Arians he was welcomed as a champion come to deliver them from a grievous oppression. Ranging themselves under his standard, they probably helped

---

tions (ab. B.C. 1230-650). It is further proved by the Turanian character of the language in the cuneiform inscriptions of Armenia. (See Sir H. Rawlinson in the author's *Herodotus*, vol. i. p. 537; vol. iv. p. 206.)

[1] Among Cappadocian names are Pharnaces, Smerdis, Artamnes, Ariarathes, Ariaramnes, Orophernes, Ariobarzanes, &c.

[2] According to Diodorus (ap. Phot. *Bibliothec.* p. 1158), Pharnaces, king of Cappadocia (ab. B.C. 650), married Atossa, sister of Cambyses, an ancestor of Cyrus the Great.

him to expel from Asia the barbarian hordes which
had now for many years tyrannized over them; and
when the expulsion was completed, gratitude or habit
made them willing to continue in the subject position
which they had assumed in order to effect it. Cyaxares within less than ten years³ from his capture of
Nineveh, had added to his empire the fertile and
valuable tracts of Armenia and Cappadocia—never
really subject to Assyria—and may perhaps have
further mastered the entire region between Armenia
and the Caucasus and Euxine.

The advance of their western frontier to the river
Halys, which was involved in the absorption of Cappadocia into the Empire, brought the Medes into
contact with a new power—a power, which, like
Media, had been recently increasing in greatness,
and which was not likely to submit to a foreign yoke
without a struggle. The LYDIAN kingdom was one
of great antiquity in this part of Asia. According
to traditions current among its people, it had been
established more than seven hundred years⁴ at the
time when Cyaxares pushed his conquests to its
borders. Three dynasties of native kings—Atyadæ,
Heraclidæ, and Mermnadæ—had successively held
the throne during that period.⁵ The Lydians could
repeat the names of at least thirty monarchs⁶ who

---

³ The fall of Nineveh has been placed in B.C. 625 or a little later. If the eclipse of Thales is considered to be that of B.C. 610, the commencement of the Lydian war will be B.C. 615. This war could not take place till the frontier had been extended to the Halys.

⁴ Three Mermnad kings had reigned 99 years, according to Herodotus, 89 according to Eusebius.

The Heraclidæ had reigned 505 years according to the former. The Atyadæ, who had furnished several kings (Atys, Lydus, Meles, Moxus, &c.), must be assigned more than a century.

⁵ Herod. l. 7-14.

⁶ At least four Atyadæ (see above, note ⁴), 22 Heraclidæ (Herod. i. 7), and four Mermnadæ, Gyges, Ardys, Sadyattes, and Alyattes.

had borne away in Sardis, their capital city, since its foundation. They had never been conquered. In the old times indeed Lydus, the son of Atys, had changed the name of the people inhabiting the country from Mæonians to Lydians'—a change which to the keen sense of an historical critic implies a conquest of one race by another. But to the people themselves this tradition conveyed no such meaning; or, if it did to any, their self-complacency was not disturbed thereby, since they would hug the notion that *they* belonged not to the conquered race but to the conquerors. If a Rameses or a Sesostris had ever penetrated to their country, he had met with a brave resistance, and had left monuments indicating his respect for their courage.⁸ Neither Babylon nor Assyria had ever given a king to the Lydians—on the contrary, the Lydian tradition was, that they had themselves sent forth Belus and Ninus from their own country to found dynasties and cities in Mesopotamia.⁹ In a still more remote age they had seen their colonists embark upon the western waters,¹⁰ and start for the distant Hesperia, where they had arrived in safety, and had founded the great Etruscan nation. On another occasion they had carried their arms beyond the limits of Asia Minor, and had marched southward to the very extremity of Syria, where their general, Ascalus, had founded a great city and called it after his name.¹¹

---

⁷ Herod. I. 7; vii. 74.
⁸ Ibid. ii. 106. Compare ch. 102.
⁹ This is the only possible explanation of the mythic genealogy in Herod. I. 7. (See the author's *Herodotus*, vol. i. p. 292, 2nd edition.)
¹⁰ Ἐπὶ Ἄρυος τοῦ Μάνεω βασιλῆος. Herod. i. 94.

¹¹ Xanth. Lyd. Fr. 23; Nic. Dam. Fr. 20. It is perhaps scarcely necessary to observe that very little confidence can be placed in any of these traditions. They are adduced here merely as helping us to understand the spirit and temper of the people.

Such were the Lydian traditions with respect to the more remote times. Of their real history they seem to have known but little, and that little did not extend further back than about two hundred years before Cyaxares.[12] Within this space it was certain that they had had a change of dynasty, a change preceded by a long feud between their two greatest houses,[13] which were perhaps really two branches of the royal family.[14] The Heraclidæ had grown jealous of the Mermnadæ, and had treated them with injustice: the Mermnadæ had at first sought their safety in flight, and afterwards when they felt themselves strong enough, had returned, murdered the Heraclide monarch, and placed their chief, Gyges, upon the throne. With Gyges, who had commenced his reign about B.C. 700,[15] the prosperity of the Lydians had greatly increased, and they had begun to assume an aggressive attitude towards their neighbours. Gyges' revenue was so great that his wealth became proverbial,[16] and he could afford to spread his

---

[12] The Mermnavæ had, I conceive, been on the throne nearly a century (85 years) when Cyaxares made his attack upon Lydia. The *history* of the Heraclidæ seems to have commenced with Ardys, the fifth ancestor of Candaules (Nic. Dam. Fr. 49), whom Eusebius makes the first king. (Chron. Can. i. 15; ii. p. 318, ed. Mai.) These five Heraclide reigns would cover a space of about 115 years, at the (very probable) rate of reckoning indicated by Herodotus (i. 7, sub fin.).

[13] See Nic. Dam. Fr. 26. An abstract of the passage has been given by the author in his *Herodotus* (vol. i. p. 205, note ¹).

[14] The same names occur in both houses, as Ardys, Sadyattes, and Alyattes (if that is equivalent to Adyattes). Ardys is common to both Mermnads and Heraclides before the usurpation of Gyges. (Nic. Dam. l. s. c.)

[15] The date of Herodotus, B.C. 724, is upset by the discovery that Gyges was contemporary with Asshur-bani-pal. (See above, vol. ii. p. 487, note ⁴.) The date of Eusebius is B.C. 698. (Chron. Can., ii. p. 323, ed. Mai.)

[16] Gyges was known in his lifetime as ὁ πολύχρυσος. (Archiloch. ap. Arist. Rhet. iii. 17.) The epithet attached to him and to his city for ages afterwards. (See Æschyl. Pers. 45; Alpheus in *Anthology*. i. 12; Eurip. *Iph. in Aul.* 786; Nicolaus ap. Stob. xiv. p. 87; &c.)

fame by sending from his superfluity to the distant temple of Delphi presents of such magnificence that they were the admiration of later ages."[17] The relations of his predecessors with the Greeks of the Asiatic coast had been friendly. Gyges changed this policy, and, desirous of enlarging his seaboard, made war upon the Greek maritime towns, attacking Miletus and Smyrna without result, but succeeding in capturing the Ionic city of Colophon.[18] He also picked a quarrel with the inland town of Magnesia, and after many invasions of its territory compelled it to submission.[19] According to some, he made himself master of the whole territory of the Troad, and the Milesians had to obtain his permission before they could establish their colony of Abydos upon the Hellespont.[20] At any rate he was a rich and puissant monarch in the eyes of the Greeks of Asia and the islands, who were never tired of celebrating his wealth, his wars, and his romantic history.[1]

The shadow of calamity had, however, fallen upon Lydia towards the close of Gyges' long reign. About thirty years[2] before the Scythians from the Steppe country crossed the Caucasus and fell upon Media, the same barrier was passed by another great horde of nomads. The Cimmerians, probably a Celtic people,[3]

---

[17] Herod. i. 14.   [18] Ibid.
[19] Xanth. Lyd. Fr. 10; Nic. Dam. p. 50, ed. Orelli. Herodotus does not seem to have been aware of the reduction of this town, which must therefore be regarded as uncertain.
[20] Strab. xiii. 1, § 22.
[1] Archilochus celebrated the wealth of Gyges in the well-known line—
οὐ μοι τὰ Γύγεω τοῦ πολυχρύσου
μέλει (Ar. Rhet. iii. 17). Mimnermus described the war between Gyges and the people of Smyrna (Pausan. iv. 21, § 5). The myth of Gyges which we find in Plato (Republ. ii. 3) was probably derived from an early Greek poet.
[2] The inscriptions of Asshur-bani-pal show us that the Cimmerian invasion of Asia Minor had commenced before the death of Gyges, whose last year is by no writer placed later than B.C. 662. The Scythic invasion has been already assigned to B.C. 632 or 631. (Supra, pp. 186, 187.)
[3] On this subject see the author's Herodotus, vol. iii. pp. 150-156, 2nd edition.

who had dwelt hitherto in the Tauric Chersonese and the country adjoining upon it, pressed on by Scythic invaders from the East, had sought a vent in this direction. Passing the great mountain barrier either by the route of Mozdok¹—the Pylæ Caucasiæ—or by some still more difficult track towards the Euxine, they had entered Asia Minor by way of Cappadocia and had spread terror and devastation in every direction. After a while they had reached Lydia—not perhaps in great force; and Gyges, who was still on the throne, had given them battle and defeated them, capturing several of their chiefs.² But this success did not blind him to the true character of the coming danger. It must have been a presentiment of evil which caused him to open communications with Asshur-bani-pal, king of Assyria, and to court his favour by presents and by sending him his Cimmerian captives. There can be little doubt that he sought protection under the guise of friendship; and though he may not have meant altogether to forfeit his independence, he was ready to accept a semi-dependent position if he could thereby secure Assyria's aid in case of need.³ But the Ninevite monarch, apparently, was indisposed to incur the risks of so remote a war, and Lydia was left to fight her own battles when, in the reign of Ardys, Gyges' son and successor, the expected crisis came. Carrying all before them, the fierce Cymric hordes swarmed in

---

¹ Herodotus makes them march along the coast, the whole way; but this route is impracticable. Probably they proceeded along the foot of the Caucasus, till they reached the Terek, which they then followed up to its source, where they would come upon the famous Pylæ.

² See above, vol. ii. p. 487.

³ The surrender of the captives appears to me a real acknowledgment of suzerainty. Asshur-bani-pal himself viewed the presents as "tribute."

full force into the more western districts of Asia Minor; Paphlagonia, Phrygia, Bithynia, Lydia, and Ionia were overrun;' the frightened inhabitants shut themselves up in their walled towns, and hoped that the tide of invasion might sweep by them quickly and roll elsewhere; but the Cimmerians, impatient and undisciplined as they might be, could sometimes bring themselves to endure the weary work of a siege, and they saw in the Lydian capital a prize well worth an effort. The hordes besieged Sardis, and took it, except the citadel, which was commandingly placed and defied all their attempts. A terrible scene of carnage must have followed. How Lydia withstood the blow, and rapidly recovered from it, is hard to understand; but it seems certain that within a generation she was so far restored to vigour as to venture on resuming her attacks upon the Greeks of the coast, which had been suspended during her period of prostration. Sadyattes, the son of Ardys, following the example of his father and grandfather, made war upon Miletus;[8] and Alyattes, his son and successor, pursued the same policy of aggression. Besides pressing Miletus, he besieged and took Smyrna,[9] and ravaged the territory of Clazomenæ.[10]

But the great work of Alyattes' reign, and the one which seems to have had the most important consequences for Lydia, was the war which he undertook for the purpose of expelling the Cimmerians from

---

[7] On the Cimmerian ravages see Callinus, Fr. 2; Herod. i. 15; iv. 12; Strab. l. 3, § 21; xiv. 1, § 40; Callimach. *Hymn. ad Dian.* 248-260; Eustath. *Comment. ad Hom. Od.* xi. 14; Steph. Byz. ad voc. Ἀππασδρος; and Hesych. ad voc. Λύγδαμις. Compare the author's Herodotus, vol. i. pp. 209-301, 2nd edition, and Mr. Grote's *History of Greece*, vol. ii. pp. 431-434, 2nd edition.

[8] Herod. i. 15, and 18.

[9] Ibid. i. 16; Nic. Dam. p. 52, ed Orelli.

[10] Herod. l. s. c.

Asia Minor. The hordes had been greatly weakened by time, by their losses in war, and probably by their excesses; they had long ceased to be formidable; but they were still strong enough to be an annoyance. Alyattes is said to have "driven them *out of Asia*,"[11] by which we can scarcely understand less than that he expelled them from his own dominions and those of his neighbours—or, in other words, from the countries which had been the scenes of their chief ravages—Paphlagonia, Bithynia, Lydia, Phrygia, and Cilicia.[12] But, to do this, he must have entered into a league with his neighbours, who must have consented to act under him for the purposes of the war, if they did not even admit the permanent hegemony of his country. Alyattes' success appears to have been complete, or nearly so;[13] he cleared Asia Minor of the Cimmerians; and, having thus conferred a benefit on all the nations of the region and exhibited before their eyes his great military capacity, if he had not actually constructed an Empire, he had at any rate done much to pave the way for one.

Such was the political position in the regions west and south of the Halys, when Cyaxares completed his absorption of Cappadocia, and looking across the river that divided the Cappadocians from the Phrygians, saw stretched before him a region of great fertile plains, which seemed to invite an invader. A pretext for an attack was all that he wanted, and this was soon forthcoming. A body of the nomad

---

[11] Κιμμερίους ἐκ τῆς Ἀσίης ἐξήλασε. Herod. l. s. c.
[12] On the Cimmerian invasion of Cilicia, see Strab. l. 3 § 21.
[13] According to Herodotus the Cimmerians made a permanent settlement at Sinope (iv 12); and according to Aristotle (Fr. 190) they maintained themselves for a century at Antandros in the Troad. Otherwise they disappear from Asia.

Scyths—probably belonging to the great invasion, though Herodotus thought otherwise[14]—had taken service under Cyaxares, and for some time served him faithfully, being employed chiefly as hunters. A cause of quarrel, however, arose after a while; and the Scyths, disliking their position or distrusting the intentions of their lords towards them, quitted the Median territory, and marching through great part of Asia Minor, sought and found a refuge with Alyattes, the Lydian king. Cyaxares, upon learning their flight, sent an embassy to the court of Sardis to demand the surrender of the fugitives; but the Lydian monarch met the demand with a refusal, and, fully understanding the probable consequences, immediately prepared for war.

Though Lydia, compared to Media, was but a small state, yet her resources were by no means inconsiderable. In fertility she surpassed almost every other country of Asia Minor,[15] which is altogether one of the richest regions in the world. At this time she was producing large quantities of gold, which was found in

No. 1.   Lydian Coins.   No. 2.

great abundance in the Pactolus, and probably in the other small streams that flowed down on all sides

---

[14] Herod. i. 73. Herodotus seems to have imagined that these Scythians were political refugees from his European Scythia.
[15] On the richness and fertility of this part of Asia, see Virg. Æn. x. 141; Strabo, xiii. 4, § 5; and compare Sir C. Fellows's *Asia Minor*, pp. 16-42.

from the Tmolus mountain-chain.[1] Her people were at once warlike and ingenious. They had invented the art of coining money,[2] and showed considerable taste in their devices.[3] They claimed also to have been the inventors of a number of games, which were common to them with the Greeks.[4] According to Herodotus, they were the first who made a livelihood by shop-keeping.[5] They were skilful in the use of musical instruments,[6] and had their own peculiar musical mode or style, which was in much favour among the Greeks, though condemned as effeminate by some of the philosophers.[7] At the same time the Lydians were not wanting in courage or manliness.[8] They fought chiefly on horseback and were excellent riders, carrying long spears, which they managed with great skill.[9] Nicolas of Damascus tells us that, even under

---

[1] See Herod. i. 93; Soph. *Philoct.* 393; Plin. *H. N.* v. 29, 30; &c. Crœsus had also mines, which he worked, near Pergamus. (See Aristot. *Mirab. Auscult.* 52.)

[2] Xenoph. Coloph. ap. Polluc. ix. 6, § 83; Herod. i. 94; Eustath. *ad Dionys. Perieg.* 840. The claim of the Lydians to be regarded as the inventors of coining has been disputed by some, among others by the late Col. Leake. (*Num. Hellen.* Appendix: *Journal of Classical and Sacred Philology,* vol. iv. pp. 243, 244.) I have discussed the subject in my *Herodotus,* (vol. i. pp. 685, 686, 2nd edition).

[3] Most Lydian coins bear the device of a crowned figure about to shoot an arrow from a bow—which seems to be the pattern from which the Persians copied the emblem on their Darics. A few have the head of a lion, or the fore-parts of a lion and a bull (as that figured above, No. 1, which is supposed to have been struck by Crœsus). Both the animal forms are in this case rendered with much spirit.

[4] Dice, huckle-bones, ball, &c. (Herod. i. 94).

[5] Πρῶτοι κάπηλοι ἐγένοντο. (Herod. l. s. c.)

[6] Pindar related that the *magadis* or *pectis*, a harp with sometimes as many as twenty strings, had been adopted by the Greeks from the Lydians, who used it at their banquets. (Ap. Athen. *Deipn.* xiv. p. 635). Herodotus speaks of the Lydians using both this instrument, and also the *syrinx* (Pan's pipe), and the double flute, in their military expeditions (i. 17).

[7] Plato, *Repub.* iii. 10. Aristotle seems to have entertained an opposite opinion. (*Pol.* viii. 7, ad fin.)

[8] Herodotus, speaking of the Lydians, so late as the time of Cyrus, says, 'Ἦν δὲ τούτου τοῦ χρόνου ἔθνος οὐδὲν ἐν τῇ Ἀσίῃ οὔτε ἀνδρηιότερον οὔτε ἀλκιμώτερον τοῦ Λυδίου (i. 79). They did not change their character till after the Persian conquest.

[9] Herod. l. s. c.

the Heracleid kings, they could muster for service cavalry to the number of thirty thousand.[14] In peace they pursued with ardour the sports of the field,[14] and found in the chase of the wild-boar a pastime which called forth and exercised every manly quality. Thus Lydia, even by herself, was no contemptible enemy; though it can hardly be supposed that, without help from others, she would have proved a match for the great Median Empire.

But such help as she needed was not wanting to her. The rapid strides with which Media had advanced towards the west had no doubt alarmed the numerous princes of Asia Minor, who must have felt that they had a power to deal with as full of schemes of conquest as Assyria, and more capable of carrying her designs into execution. It has been already observed that the long course of Assyrian aggressions developed gradually among the Asiatic tribes a tendency to unite in leagues for purposes of resistance.[15] The circumstances of the time called now imperatively for such a league to be formed, unless the princes of Asia Minor were content to have their several territories absorbed one after another into the growing Median Empire. These princes appear to have seen their danger. Cyaxares may perhaps have declared war specially against the Lydians, and have crossed the Halys professedly in order to chastise them; but he could only reach Lydia through the territories of other nations, which he was evidently intending to conquer on his way; and it was thus apparent that he was actuated, not by anger

---

[10] Nic. Dam. Fr. 49 (*Fragm. Hist. Gr.* vol. iii. p. 382).
[11] Herod. L. 36-43; Nic. Dam. Fr. 49, p. 384.
[12] See above, vol. II. pp. 421, 422.

against a particular power, but by a general design of extending his dominions in this direction. A league seems therefore to have been determined on. We have not indeed any positive evidence of its existence till the close of the war;[13] but the probabilities are wholly in favour of its having taken effect from the first. Prudence would have dictated such a course; and it seems almost implied in the fact, that a successful resistance was made to the Median attack from the very commencement. We may conclude therefore that the princes of Asia Minor, having either met in conclave or communicated by embassies, resolved to make common cause, if the Medes crossed the Halys; and that, having already acted under Lydia in the expulsion of the Cimmerians from their territories, they naturally placed her at their head when they coalesced for the second time.

Cyaxares, on his part, was not content to bring against the confederates merely the power of Media. He requested and obtained a contingent from the Babylonian monarch, Nabopolassar, and may not improbably have had the assistance of other allies also. With a vast army drawn from various parts of inner Asia, he invaded the territory of the Western Powers, and began his attempt at subjugation. We have no detailed account of the war; but we learn from the general expressions of Hero-

---

[13] The evidence of a league is found in the presence of Syennesis, king of Cilicia, at the great battle terminated by the eclipse. (See below, p. 211.) He is manifestly there as an ally of Lydia, just as Labynetus is present as an ally of Media. But if the distant and powerful Cilician monarch joined Alyattes, and fought under him, much more may we be sure that the princes of the nearer and weaker states, Caria, Phrygia, Lycia, Paphlagonia, &c., placed themselves under his protection.

dotus that the Median monarch met with a most stubborn resistance; numerous engagements were fought with varied results; sometimes the Medes succeeded in defeating their adversaries in pitched battles; but sometimes, and apparently as often, the Lydians and their allies gained decided victories over the Medes." It is noted that one of the engagements took place by night, a rare occurrence in ancient (as in modern) times. The war had continued six years, and the Medes had evidently made no serious impression,¹⁵ when a remarkable circumstance brought it suddenly to a termination.

The two armies had once more met and were engaged in conflict, when, in the midst of the struggle, an ominous darkness fell upon the combatants and filled them with superstitious awe. The sun was eclipsed, either totally or at any rate considerably,¹⁶ so that the attention of the two armies was attracted to it; and, discontinuing the fight, they stood to gaze at the phenomenon. In most parts of the East such an occurrence is even now seen with dread—the ignorant mass believe that the orb of day is actually being devoured or destroyed, and that the end of all things is at hand—even the chiefs, who may have some notion that the phenomenon is a

---

¹⁴ Herod. L 74.
¹⁵ Διαφέροντι δέ σφι ἐπ' ἴσης τοῦ πολέμου is the expression of Herodotus (l. s. c.).
¹⁶ It has been customary to assume that the eclipse must have been a total one; and the enquiries of astronomers have been directed to the resolution of the question— What total eclipses were there in Asia Minor in the 50 years from B.C. 630 to B.C. 580? But, though a total eclipse would seem to be required by the descriptive language of Herodotus, no such phenomenon is requisite for the facts of his tale, which alone can be regarded as historical. If the eclipse was *sufficient to be noticed*, it would produce naturally all the superstitious awe, and so all the other results, which Herodotus relates. It is not the darkness, but the portent, that alarms and paralyses the ignorant Asiatic in such cases.

recurrent one, do not understand its cause, and participate in the alarm of their followers. On the present occasion it is said that, amid the general fear, a desire for reconciliation seized both armies.[17] Of this spontaneous movement two chiefs, the foremost of the allies on either side, took advantage. Syennesis, king of Cilicia, the first known monarch of his name,[18] on the part of Lydia, and a prince whom Herodotus calls "Labynetus of Babylon," — probably either Nabopolassar[1] or Nebuchadnezzar—on the part of Media, came forward to propose an immediate armistice; and, when the proposal was accepted on either side, proceeded to the more difficult task of arranging terms of peace between the contending parties. Since nothing is said of the Scythians, who had been put forward as the ostensible grounds of quarrel, we may presume that Alyattes retained them. It is further clear that both he and his allies preserved undiminished both their territories and their independence. The territorial basis of the treaty was thus what in modern diplomatic language is called the *status quo*; matters, in other words, returned to the position in which they had stood before the war broke out. The only difference was that Cyaxares gained a friend and an ally where he had previously had a jealous enemy; since it was agreed that the two kings of Media and Lydia should swear a friendship, and

---

[17] Herod. i. 74. Τῆς μάχης τε ἐπισχόντο καὶ μᾶλλόν τι ἔσπευσαν καὶ ἀμφότεροι εἰρήνην ἑωυτοῖσι γενέσθαι.

[18] The name occurs repeatedly in later Cilician history (Æschyl. *Pers.* 326; Herod. vii. 98; Xen. *Anab.* I. 2, § 23). Apparently it is either a royal title like Pharaoh, or a name which each king assumes when he mounts the throne.

[1] If the true date of the eclipse is B.C. 610, it would fall into the reign of Nabopolassar, which covered the space between B.C. 625 and B.C. 604. If it was the eclipse of B.C. 603, of B.C. 597, of B.C. 585, or of B.C. 583, Nabopolassar would be dead, and Nebuchadnezzar would be king of Babylon.

that, to cement the alliance, Alyattes should give his daughter Aryênis in marriage to Astyages, the son of Cyaxares. The marriage thus arranged took place soon afterwards, while the oath of friendship was sworn at once: According to the barbarous usages of the time and place, the two monarchs having met and repeated the words of the formula, punctured their own arms, and then sealed their contract by each sucking from the wound a portion of the other's blood.[1]

By this peace the three great monarchies of the time—the Median, the Lydian, and the Babylonian—were placed on terms, not only of amity, but of intimacy and (if the word may be used) of blood-relationship. The Crown Princes of the three kingdoms had become brothers.[2] From the shores of the Egean to those of the Persian Gulf, Western Asia was now ruled by interconnected dynasties, bound by treaties to respect each other's rights, and perhaps to lend each other aid in important conjunctures, and animated, it would seem, by a real spirit of mutual friendliness and attachment. After more than five centuries of almost constant war and ravage, after fifty years of fearful strife and convulsion, during which the old monarchy of Assyria had gone down and a new Empire—the Median—had risen up in its

---

[1] Herod. i. 74, ad fin. A practice nearly similar is ascribed to the European Scyths by Herodotus (iv. 70), and to the Armenians and Iberians by Tacitus (*Ann.* xii. 47). One not very different is still found in S. Africa (Livingstone, *Travels*, p. 488). The *rationale* of the custom seems to be, as Dr. Livingstone explains, the notion that by drinking each other's blood the two parties become perpetual friends and relations.

[2] The subjoined table will illustrate this statement—

Nebuchadnezzar and Crœsus were both brothers-in-law of Astyages.

place, this part of Asia entered upon a period of repose which stands out in strong contrast with the long term of struggle. From the date of the peace between Alyattes and Cyaxares (probably B.C. 610),[1] for nearly half a century, the three kingdoms of Media, Lydia, and Babylonia remained fast friends, pursuing their separate courses without quarrel or collision, and thus giving to the nations within their borders a rest and a refreshment which they must have greatly needed and desired.

In one quarter only was this rest for a short time disturbed. During the troublous period the neighbouring country of Egypt, which had recovered its freedom,[2] and witnessed a revival of its ancient prosperity, under the Psammatik family, began once more to aspire to the possession of those provinces which, being divided off from the rest of the Asiatic continent by the impassable Syrian desert, seem politically to belong to Africa almost more than to Asia. Psamatik the First, the Psammetichus of Herodotus,

---

[1] I am still unconvinced by the arguments of Mr. Bosanquet, who regards the eclipse as positively fixed to the year B.C. 585. The grounds of our difference are two-fold. 1. I do not think the eclipse must necessarily have been total. (See above, p. 210, note 16.) And 2. I do not regard astronomical science as capable of pronouncing on the exact line taken by eclipses which happened more than 2000 years ago. The motions of the earth and of the moon are not uniform, and no astronomer can say that all the irregularities which may exist are known to him and have been taken into account with exactness in his back calculations. Fresh irregularities are continually discovered; and hence the calculations of astronomers as to the lines of past eclipses are continually changing. (See the long note in Mr. Grote's *History of Greece*, vol. ii. p. 418, Edition of 1862.)

If, however, Mr. Bosanquet should be right, and the eclipse was really that of B.C. 585, there will be no need of deranging our entire scheme of Oriental chronology. The simple result will be that the battle must be transferred to the reign of *Astyages*, to which Cicero (*De Div.* i. 49), Pliny (*H. N.* ii. 12), and Eusebius (*Chron. Can.* li. p. 331) assign it.

[2] Psammetichus probably became an independent king about B.C. 647, on the death of Asshur-bani-pal. He was previously governor under Assyria. (See above, vol. ii. p. 485.)

had commenced an aggressive war in this quarter, probably about the time that Assyria was suffering from the Median and then from the Scythian inroads. He had besieged for several years the strong Philistine town of Ashdod,[1] which commands the coast-route from Egypt to Palestine, and was at this time a most important city. Despite a resistance which would have wearied out any less pertinacious assailant, he had persevered in his attempt, and had finally succeeded in taking the place. He had thus obtained a firm footing in Syria; and his successor was able, starting from this vantage-ground, to overrun and conquer the whole territory. About the year B.C. 608, Neco, son of Psamatik I., having recently ascended the throne, invaded Palestine with a large army, met and defeated Josiah,[2] king of Judah, near Megiddo in the great plain of Esdraelon, and, pressing forward through Syria to the Euphrates, attacked and took Carchemish, the strong city which guarded the ordinary passage of the river. Idumea, Palestine, Phœnicia, and Syria submitted to him, and for three years he remained in undisturbed possession of his conquests.[3] Then, however, the Babylonians, who had received these provinces at the division of the Assyrian Empire, began to bestir themselves. Nebuchadnezzar marched to Carchemish, defeated the army of Neco, recovered all the territory to the border of Egypt, and even ravaged a portion of that country.[4] It is probable that in

---

[1] Herodotus, who is the authority for this siege, says that it lasted 29 years (ii. 157), which is most improbable. Such a story, however, would not have arisen unless the siege had been one of unusual length.

[2] 2 Kings xxiii. 29; 2 Chr. xxxv. 20-23. Compare Herod. ii. 159.
[3] 2 Kings xxiv. 7; Berosus ap. Joseph. Ant. Jud., x. 11.
[4] Jerem. xlvi. 2-20.

this expedition he was assisted by the Medes. At any rate, seven or eight years afterwards, when the intrigues of Egypt had again created disturbances in this quarter, and Jehoiakim, the Jewish king, broke into open insurrection, the Median monarch sent a contingent,[10] which accompanied Nebuchadnezzar into Judæa, and assisted him to establish his power firmly in South-Western Asia.

This is the last act that we can ascribe to the great Median king. He can scarcely have been much less than seventy years old at this time; and his life was prolonged at the utmost three years longer.[11] According to Herodotus, he died B.C. 593, after a reign of exactly forty years,[12] leaving his crown to his son Astyages, whose marriage with a Lydian princess was above related.

We have no sufficient materials from which to draw out a complete character of Cyaxares. He appears to have possessed great ambition, considerable military ability, and a rare tenacity of purpose, which gained him his chief successes. At the same time he was not wanting in good sense, and could bring himself to withdraw from an enterprise, when he had misjudged the fitting time for it, or greatly miscalculated its difficulties. He was faithful to his friends, but thought treachery allowable towards his enemies. He knew how to conquer, but not how to

---

[10] So Polyhistor related (Fr. 24). Like Ctesias, he called the Median monarch Astibaras.

[11] We cannot suppose Cyaxares to have been much less than thirty years old at his accession—especially if he had previously led into Media a band of emigrants from the Ilsotrian country. (See above, p. 175.)

If he ascended the throne B.C. 633, which is the date of Herodotus, he would consequently be about 67 in B.C. 597, the date of Jehoiakim's captivity.

[12] Herod. I. 100. This number is confirmed by Ctesias (ap. Diod. Sic. ii. 34, § 1.)

organise, an empire; and, if we except his establishment of Magism as the religion of the state, we may say that he did nothing to give permanency to the monarchy which he founded. He was a conqueror altogether after the Asiatic model, able to wield the sword, but not to guide the pen, to subdue his contemporaries to his will by his personal ascendancy over them, but not to influence posterity by the establishment of a kingdom, or of institutions, on deep and stable foundations. The Empire, which owed to him its foundation, was the most shortlived of all the great Oriental monarchies, having begun and ended within the narrow space of three score and ten years[2]—the natural lifetime of an individual.

Astyages, who succeeded to the Median throne about B.C. 593,[1] had neither his father's enterprise nor his ability. Born to an Empire, and bred up in all the luxury of an Oriental Court, he seems to have been quite content with the lot which fortune appeared to have assigned him, and to have coveted no grander position. Tradition says that he was remarkably handsome,[2] cautious,[3] and of an easy and generous temper.[4] Although the anecdotes related of his mode of life at Ecbatana by Herodotus, Xenophon, and Nicolas of Damascus, seem to be for the most part apocryphal, and at any rate come to us upon authority too weak to entitle them to a place in

---

[2] The real "Empire" must date, not from the accession of Cyaxares, but from his conquest of Nineveh, which was B.C. 625 at the earliest. From this to B.C. 558—the first year of Cyrus—is 67 years.

[1] Eusebius makes Astyages ascend the throne B.C. 597; but he obtains this date by assigning to Cyrus one more year, and to Astyages three more years, than Herodotus gives them. On the former point certainly, on the latter probably, he followed the suspicious authority of Ctesias.

[2] Xen. Cyrop. i. 3, § 2.
[3] Æschyl. Pers. 763. φρενὶ γὰρ αὐτοῦ θυμὸν ἀκεσσστροφεῖεν.
[4] Περσαύατος. Nic. Dam. Fr. 66, p. 398.

history, we may perhaps gather from the concurrent descriptions of these three writers something of the general character of the Court over which he presided. Its leading features do not seem to have differed greatly from those of the Court of Assyria. The monarch lived secluded, and could only be seen by those who asked and obtained an audience.[5] He was surrounded by guards and eunuchs, the latter of whom held most of the offices near the royal person.[6] The Court was magnificent in its apparel, in its banquets, and in the number and organization of its attendants. The courtiers wore long flowing robes of many different colours, amongst which red and purple predominated,[7] and adorned their necks with chains or collars of gold, and their wrists with bracelets of the same precious metal.[8] Even the horses on which they rode had sometimes golden bits to their bridles.[9] One officer of the Court was especially called "the King's Eye;"[10] another had the privilege of introducing strangers to him;[11] a third was his cup-bearer;[12] a fourth his messenger.[13] Guards, torch-bearers, serving-men, ushers, and sweepers, were among the orders into which the lower sort of attendants were divided;[14] while among the courtiers of the highest rank was a privileged class known as

---

[5] Herod. i. 99; Xen. *Cyrop.* i. 3, § 8.

[6] Nic. Dam. Fr. 66, pp. 398 and 402.

[7] Xen. *Cyrop.* viii. 3, § 3.

[8] Ibid. i. 3, § 2; ii. 4, § 6, &c.

[9] Ibid. i. 3, § 8.

[10] Ὀφθαλμὸς βασιλέως. Herod. i. 114.

[11] Xen. *Cyrop.* i. 3, § 8. Ὁ . . . τιμὴν ἔχων προσάγειν τοὺς δεομένους Ἀστυάγους, καὶ ἀποκωλύων οὓς μὴ καιρὸς αὐτῷ δοκοίη εἶναι προσάγειν. Compare Nic. Dam. p. 402. Δι' εὐνούχου ἐράμενος τὴν εἴσοδον.

[12] Οἰνοχόος. Nic. Dam. p. 398; Xen. *Cyrop.* l. s. c.

[13] Herod. i. 114.

[14] Δορυφόροι, λαμπαδηφόροι, θεράποντες, ῥαβδοφόροι, and καλλύνοντες —the last divided into cleaners of the Palace, and cleaners of the courts outside the Palace. Nic. Dam. l. s. c.; Dino, Fr. 7.

"the King's table-companions" (ὁμοτράπεζοι). The chief pastime in which the Court indulged was hunting. Generally this took place in a park or "paradise" near the capital;[14] but sometimes the King and Court went out on a grand hunt into the open country, where lions, leopards, bears, wild boars, wild asses, antelopes, stags, and wild sheep abounded, and, when the beasts had been driven by beaters into a confined space, despatched them with arrows and javelins.[15]

Prominent at the Court, according to Herodotus,[17] was the priestly caste of the Magi. Held in the highest honour by both King and people, they were in constant attendance, ready to expound omens or dreams, and to give their advice on all matters of state policy. The religious ceremonial was, as a matter of course, under their charge; and it is probable that high state offices were often conferred upon them. Of all classes of the people they were the only one that could feel they had a real influence over the monarch, and might claim to share in his sovereignty.[18]

The long reign of Astyages seems to have been almost undisturbed, until just before its close, by wars or rebellions. Eusebius indeed relates that he, and not Cyaxares, carried on the great Lydian contest;[19] and Moses of Chorênê declares that he was engaged in a long struggle with Tigranes, an Armenian king.[20] But little credit can be attached to these

---

[14] Xen. *Cyrop.* l. 4, § 5 and § 11.
[15] Ibid. i. 4, § 7.
[17] Herod. L 107, 108, and 120.
[18] Herodotus makes the Magi say to Astyages—Σὸι ἐπιστάται βασιλῆος, καὶ ἄρχομεν τὸ μέρος, καὶ πρὸς πρὸς σέο μεγάλας ἔχομεν. (I. 120.)

[19] *Chron. Can.* ii. p. 331, ed. Mai. This ascription of the war to Astyages is evidently connected with a belief that the Eclipse of Thales was that of B.C. 583.
[20] Mos. Chor. *Hist. Armen.* i. 23-28.

statements, the former of which contradicts Herodotus, while the latter is wholly unsupported by any other writer. The character which Cyaxares bore among the Greeks was evidently that of an unwarlike king.[21] If he had really carried his arms into the heart of Asia Minor, and threatened the whole of that extensive region with subjugation, we can scarcely suppose that he would have been considered so peaceful a ruler. Neither is it easy to imagine that in that case no classical writer—not even Ctesias—would have taxed Herodotus with an error which must have been so flagrant. With respect to the war with Tigranes, it is just possible that it may have a basis of truth;—there may have been a revolt of Armenia from Astyages under a certain Tigranes, followed by an attempt at subjugation. But the slender authority of Moses is insufficient to establish the truth of his story, which is internally improbable, and quite incompatible with the narrative of Herodotus.[22]

There are some grounds for believing[23] that in one direction Astyages succeeded in slightly extending the limits of his Empire. But he owed his success to prudent management, and not to courage or military skill. On his north-eastern frontier, occupying

---

[21] This is implied in the picture drawn by Herodotus (i. 107-128), and in the brief character given by Æschylus (see above, p. 216, note⁴). It is expressly stated by Aristotle, who says—Κῦρος Ἀστυάγη ἐπιτίθεται καὶ τοῦ βίου καταφρονῶν, καὶ τῆς δυνάμεως. διὰ τὸ τὴν μὲν δύναμιν ἐξηργηκέναι, αὐτὸν δὲ τρυφᾶν. (Pol. v. 8, § 15.)

[22] Moses makes Cyrus an independent prince during the reign of Astyages. He and Tigranes are in close alliance. Tigranes, and not Cyrus, attacks and defeats Astyages, and kills him. After this Cyrus assists Tigranes to conquer Media and Persia, which become part of the Armenian king's dominions. Cyrus sinks into insignificance in the narrative of Moses.

[23] The Caduslan story is told by Nicolas of Damascus (Frr. 399, 400), who (it may be suspected) followed Dino, the father of Clitarchus, a writer of fair authority.

the low country now known as Talish and Ghilan, was a powerful tribe called Cadusians, probably of Arian origin,[] which had hitherto maintained its independence. This would not be surprising, if we could accept the statement of Diodorus that they were able to bring into the field 200,000 men.[] But this account, which probably came from Ctesias, and is wholly without corroboration from other writers, has the air of a gross exaggeration; and we may conclude from the general tenor of ancient history that the Cadusians were more indebted to the strength of their country, than to either their numbers or their prowess, for the freedom and independence which they were still enjoying. It seems that they were at this time under the government of a certain king, or chief, named Aphernes or Onaphernes.[] This ruler was, it appears, doubtful of his position, and, thinking it could not be long maintained, made overtures of surrender to Astyages, which were gladly entertained by that monarch. A secret treaty was concluded to the satisfaction of both parties; and the Cadusians, it would seem, passed under the Medes by this arrangement, without any hostile struggle, though armed resistance on the part of the people, who were ignorant of the intentions of their chieftain, was for some time apprehended.

The domestic relations of Astyages seem to have been unhappy. His "mariage de convenance" with the Lydian princess Aryênis, if not wholly unfruitful, at any rate brought him no son;[1] and, as he grew

---

[] The name, Aphernes or Onaphernes, is sufficient evidence of this.
[] Diod. Sic. ii. 33, § 3.
[] The Escurial MS. from which this fragment of Nicolas has been recovered, gives both these forms. Each of them occurs once.
[1] Herodotus declares this in the

CHAP. VI.   DOMESTIC RELATIONS OF ASTYAGES.   221

to old age, the absence of such a support to the throne must have been felt very sensibly, and have caused great uneasiness. The want of an heir perhaps led him to contract those other marriages of which we hear in the Armenian History of Moses— one with a certain Anusia, of whom nothing more is known; and another with an Armenian princess, the loveliest of her sex, Tigrania, sister of the Armenian king, Tigranes.[2] The blessing of male offspring was still, however, denied him; and it is even doubtful whether he was really the father of any daughter or daughters. Herodotus[3] and Xenophon[4] indeed give him a daughter, Mandané, whom they make the mother of Cyrus; and Ctesias, who denied in the most positive terms the truth of this statement,[5] gave him a daughter, Amytis, whom he made the wife, first of Spitaces the Mede,[6] and afterwards of Cyrus the Persian. But these stories, which seem intended to gratify the vanity of the Persians by tracing the descent of their kings to the great Median conqueror, while at the same time they flattered the Medes by showing them that the issue of their old monarchs was still seated on the Arian throne, are entitled to little more credit

---

most express terms. Astyages, he says, was ἄπαις ἔρσενος γόνου (i. 109); so also Justin (i. 1); Ctesias, on the contrary, gives Astyages a son, Parmises (*Pers. Exc.* § 3), and Xenophon (*Cyrop.* l. 5, § 2) a son, Cyaxares. Moses of Chorené is still more liberal, and makes him have several sons by his wife Annsia, who all settle in Armenia. (*Hist. Arm.* l. 29.) Here, as in so many other instances, the monuments confirm Herodotus. For when a pretender to the Median throne starts up in the reign of Darius, who wishes to rest his claim on descent from the Median royal house, he does not venture to put himself forward as the son, or even as the descendant, of Astyages, but goes back a generation, and says that he is "of the race of Cyaxares." (*Beh. Inscr.* col. ii. par. 5, § 4.)

[2] Mos. Chor. *Hist. Armen.* l. 27 and 29.
[3] Herod. i. 107.
[4] Xen. *Cyrop.* i. 2, § 1.
[5] Ctes. *Pers. Exc.* § 2.
[6] Ibid. Compare Nic. Dam. Fr. 66, p. 399.

then the narrative of the Shah-nameh, which declares that Iskander (Alexander) was the son of Darab (Darius) and of a daughter of Failakus (Philip of Macedon).¹ When an Oriental crown passes from one dynasty to another, however foreign and unconnected, the natives are wont to invent a relationship between the two houses,² which both parties are commonly quite ready to accept; as it suits the rising house to be provided with a royal ancestry, and it pleases the fallen one and its partisans to see in the occupants of the throne a branch of the ancient stock—a continuation of the legitimate family. Tales therefore of the above-mentioned kind are, historically speaking, valueless; and it must remain uncertain whether the second Median monarch had any child at all, either male or female.

Old age was now creeping upon the sonless king. If he was sixteen or seventeen years old at the time of his contract of marriage with Aryênis, he must have been nearly seventy in B.C. 558, when the revolt occurred which terminated both his reign and his kingdom. It appears that the Persian branch of the Arian race, which had made itself a home in the country lying south and south-east of Media, between the 32nd parallel and the Persian Gulf, had acknowledged some subjection to the Median kings during the time of their greatness. Dwelling in their rugged mountains and high upland plains, they had however maintained the simplicity of their primitive manners, and had mixed but little with the Medes,

---

¹ See Atkinson's *Shahnameh*, pp. 493, 494.
² See the attempts made to prove that Cambyses was the son of an Egyptian princess (Herod. iii. 2), and other still more wonderful attempts to show that Alexander the Great was the son of Nectanebus. (Mos. Chor. *Hist. Armen.* ii. 13; Syncell. *Chronograph.* p. 487, D.)

being governed by their own native princes of the Achæmenian house, the descendants real or supposed of a certain Achæmenes.⁹ These princes were connected by marriage with the Cappadocian kings;¹⁰ and their house was regarded as one of the noblest in Western Asia. What the exact terms were upon which they stood with the Median monarch is uncertain. Herodotus regards Persia as absorbed into Media at this time, and the Achæmenidæ as merely a good Persian family;¹¹ Nicolas of Damascus makes Persia a Median satrapy, of which Atradates, the father of Cyrus, is satrap;¹² Xenophon, on the contrary, not only gives the Achæmenidæ their royal rank,¹³ but seems to consider Persia as completely independent of Media;¹⁴ Moses of Choréné takes the same view, regarding Cyrus as a great and powerful sovereign during the reign of Astyages.¹⁵ The native records lean towards the view of Xenophon and Moses. Darius declares that eight of his race had been kings before himself, and makes no difference between his own royalty and theirs.¹⁶ Cyrus calls himself in one inscription "the son of Cambyses, *the powerful king*."¹⁷ It is certain therefore that Persia continued to be ruled by her own native monarchs during the whole of the Median period, and that Cyrus led the attack upon Astyages as hereditary Persian king. The Persian records seem rather to

---

⁹ Herod. III. 75, vii. 11; Behist. Inscr. Col. 1. Par. 2, § 6.
¹⁰ Diod. Sic. ap. Phot. Bibliothec. p. 1158.
¹¹ Herod. I. 107. Οἰκίη ἀγαθή.
¹² Nic. Dam. Fr. 66, p. 399.
¹³ Xen. Cyrop. L 2, § 1.
¹⁴ Ibid. L. 5, § 3-5.
¹⁵ Mos. Chor. Hist. Arm. L. 24, 25.

¹⁶ See the *Behistun Inscription*, Col. 1. Par. 4, § 2. "There are eight of my race who have been kings before me. I am the ninth."
¹⁷ This inscription has been found on a brick brought from Senkereh. See the author's *Herodotus*, vol. I. p. 300, note ⁹ (2nd Edition).

imply actual independence of Media; but, as national vanity would prompt to dissimulation in such a case, we may perhaps accord so much weight to the statement of Herodotus, and to the general tradition on the subject,[18] as to believe that there was some kind of acknowledgment of Median supremacy on the part of the Persian kings anterior to Cyrus, though the acknowledgment may have been not much more than a formality, and have imposed no onerous obligations. The residence of Cyrus at the Median Court, which is asserted in almost every narrative of his life before he became king, inexplicable if Persia was independent,[19] becomes thoroughly intelligible on the supposition that she was a great Median feudatory. In such cases the residence of the Crown Prince at the capital of the suzerain is constantly desired, or even required, by the superior Power,[20] which sees in the presence of the son and heir the best security against disaffection or rebellion on the part of the father.

It appears that Cyrus, while at the Median Court, observing the unwarlike temper of the existing generation of Medes, who had not seen any actual service, and despising the personal character of the monarch,[21] who led a luxurious life, chiefly at Ecbatana, amid eunuchs, concubines, and dancing-girls,[1] resolved on raising the standard of rebellion, and seeking at any rate to free his own country. It may be suspected that the Persian prince was not actuated solely by political motives. To earnest Zoroastrians, such as

---

[18] Dino, Fr. 7; Nic. Dam. Fr. 66; Justin, l. 4-6; &c.
[19] Xenophon's notion of a voluntary visit is quite contrary to all experience, in the East or elsewhere.
[20] Compare the policy of Rome as shown with respect to the Parthian and Armenian princes (Tacit. Ann. ii. 1-3), and to the Herods (Joseph. Ant. Jud. xvi. 1, § 2; &c.).
[21] Arist. Pol. v. 8, § 15.
[1] 'Οργηστρίδας. Nic. Dam. p. 403.

the Achæmenians are shown to have been by their inscriptions, the yoke of a Power which had so greatly corrupted, if it had not wholly laid aside, the worship of Ormazd,[2] must have been extremely distasteful; and Cyrus may have wished by his rebellion as much to vindicate the honour of his religion[3] as to obtain a loftier position for his nation. If the Magi occupied really the position at the Median Court which Herodotus assigns to them, if they "were held in high honour by the king, and shared in his sovereignty"[4]— if the priest-ridden monarch was perpetually dreaming and perpetually referring his dreams to the Magian seers for exposition, and then guiding his actions by the advice they tendered him,[5] the religious zeal of the young Zoroastrian may very naturally have been aroused, and the contest into which he plunged may have been in his eyes, not so much a national struggle as a crusade against the infidels. It will be found hereafter that religious fervour animated the Persians in most of those wars by which they spread their dominion. We may suspect, therefore, though it must be admitted we cannot prove, that a religious motive was among those which led them to make their first efforts after independence.

According to the account of the struggle[6] which

---

[2] See above, pp. 127, 128.
[3] The religious ground is just touched in one or two places by Nicolas. He makes Cyrus assign as a reason for his request to leave Ecbatana a desire to offer sacrifice for the king, which apparently he cannot do anywhere but in his own country (p. 402). And he makes him claim that the gods have stirred him up to undertake his enterprise (p. 404).
[4] Herod. i. 120. See above, p. 218, note [10].
[5] Ibid. i. 107, 108, 121.
[6] The story told by Herodotus is quite undeserving of credit. It is a mere sequel to the romantic tale of Mandane, Cyno, and Harpagus, which he prefers to three other quite different stories concerning the early life of Cyrus (i. 95). The narrative of Nicolas (Fr. 68), which is followed in the text, does not come to us on very high authority; but it is graphic, thoroughly oriental, and in

is most circumstantial, and on the whole most probable, the first difficulty which the would-be rebel had to meet and vanquish was that of quitting the Court. Alleging that his father was in weak health, and required his care, he requested leave of absence for a short time; but his petition was refused on the flattering ground that the Great King was too much attached to him to lose sight of him even for a day.' A second application, however, made through a favourite eunuch after a certain interval of time, was more successful: Cyrus received permission to absent himself from Court for the next five months; whereupon, with a few attendants, he left Ecbatana by night, and took the road leading to his native country.

The next evening Astyages, enjoying himself as usual over his wine, surrounded by a crowd of his concubines, singing-girls, and dancing-girls, called on one of them for a song. The girl took her lyre and sang as follows:—" The lion had the wild-boar in his power, but let him depart to his own lair; in his lair he will wax in strength, and will cause the lion a world of toil; till at length, although the weaker, he will overcome the stronger." The words of the song greatly disquieted the king, who had been already made aware that a Chaldæan prophecy designated Cyrus as future king of the Persians. Re-

---

its main features probable. I suspect that its chief incidents came, not from Ctesias, but from Dino. (Compare Dino, Fr. 7.)

' Compare the behaviour of Darius Hystaspis towards Histiæus (Herod. v. 24).

' Dino (l. s. c.) made the singer of the song a certain Angares, a professional minstrel. The words of the song, according to him, were the following—"A mighty beast, fiercer than any wild-boar, has been let depart to the marshes; who, if he gain the lordship of the country round, will in a little while be a match for many hunters."

penting of the indulgence which he had granted him, Astyages forthwith summoned an officer into his presence, and ordered him to take a body of horsemen, pursue the Persian prince, and bring him back, either alive or dead. The officer obeyed, overtook Cyrus, and announced his errand; upon which Cyrus expressed his perfect willingness to return, but proposed that, as it was late, they should defer their start till the next day. The Medes consenting, Cyrus feasted them, and succeeded in making them all drunk; then, mounting his horse, he rode off at full speed with his attendants, and reached a Persian outpost, where he had arranged with his father that he should find a body of Persian troops. When the Medes had slept off their drunkenness, and found their prisoner gone, they pursued, and again overtaking Cyrus, who was now at the head of an armed force, engaged him. They were, however, defeated with great loss, and forced to retreat, while Cyrus, having beaten them off, made good his escape into Persia.

When Astyages heard what had happened, he was greatly vexed; and, smiting his thigh,[*] he exclaimed, "Ah! fool, thou knewest well that it boots not to heap favours on the vile; yet didst thou suffer thyself to be gulled by smooth words; and so thou hast brought upon thyself this mischief. But even now he shall not get off scot free." And instantly he sent for his generals, and commanded them to collect his host, and proceed to reduce Persia to obedience. Three thousand chariots, two hundred thousand horse,

---

[*] Παίσας τὸν μηρόν. This energetic action marks well the inability of the Oriental monarchs to command their feelings. (Compare Herod. iii. 64; vii. 212.)

and a million footmen (!), were soon brought together;[10] and with these Astyages in person invaded the revolted province, and engaged the army which Cyrus and his father Cambyses[11] had collected for defence. This consisted of a hundred chariots,[12] fifty thousand horsemen, and three hundred thousand light-armed foot,[13] who were drawn up in front of a fortified town near the frontier. The first day's battle was long and bloody, terminating without any decisive advantage to either side; but on the second day Astyages, making skilful use of his superior numbers, gained a great victory. Having detached one hundred thousand men with orders to make a circuit and get into the rear of the town, he renewed the attack; and when the Persians were all intent on the battle in their front, the troops detached fell on the city and took it, almost before its defenders were aware. Cambyses, who commanded in the town, was mortally wounded, and fell into the enemy's hands. The army in the field, finding itself between two fires, broke and fled towards the interior, bent on defending Pasargadæ, the capital. Meanwhile Astyages, having given Cambyses honourable burial, pressed on in pursuit.

The country had now become rugged and difficult. Between Pasargadæ and the place where the two days' battle was fought, lay a barrier of lofty hills,

---

[10] The numbers here are excessive. To bring them within the range of probability, we should strike off a cipher from each.

[11] In the narrative of Nicolas, the father of Cyrus is called Atradates; but, as this is certainly incorrect, the name has been altered in the text.

[12] Scythed chariots (ἅρματα δρεπανηφόρα), according to Nicolas; which is quite possible, as in later times they were certainly used by the Persians. (Xen. Cyrop. vi. 1, § 30; viii. 8, § 24.)

[13] Peltasts, according to Nicolas: that is, troops whose equipment was halfway between the ordinary heavy and light armed.

only penetrated by a single narrow pass. On either side were two smooth surfaces of rock, while the mountain towered above, lofty and precipitous. The pass was guarded by ten thousand Persians. Recognising the impossibility of forcing it, Astyages again detached a body of troops, who marched along the foot of the range till they found a place where it could be ascended, when they climbed it and seized the heights directly over the defile. The Persians upon this had to evacuate their strong position, and to retire to a lower range of hills very near to Pasargadæ. Here again there was a two days' fight. On the first day all the efforts of the Medes to ascend the range (which, though low, was steep, and covered with thickets of wild olive[1]) were fruitless. Their enemy met them, not merely with the ordinary weapons, but with great masses of stone,[2] which they hurled down with crushing force upon their ascending columns. On the second day, however, the resistance was weaker or less effective. Astyages had placed at the foot of the range, below his attacking columns, a body of troops with orders to kill all who refused to ascend, or who, having ascended, attempted to quit the heights and return to the valley.[3] Thus compelled to advance, his men fought with desperation, and drove the Persians before them up the slopes of the hill to its very summit, where the women and children had been placed for the sake of security. There, however, the tide of success turned. The taunts and upbraidings of their mothers and

---

[1] Κοτινοι δι πάστη και βουμωνει ἀγριλαιοι τε συνεχεις ἦσαν. (Nic. Dam. p. 406.)
[2] Χερμάσι. (Ibid.)
[3] Nic. Dam. l. s. c. Compare Justin, i. 6; Plut. De Virt. Mulier., p. 246, A.

wives restored the courage of the Persians; and, turning upon their foe, they made a sudden furious charge. The Medes, astonished and overborne, were driven headlong down the hill, and fell into such confusion that the Persians slew sixty thousand of them.

Still Astyages did not desist from his attack. The authority whom we have been following, here to a great extent fails us, and we have only a few scattered notices[4] from which to re-construct the closing scenes of the war. It would seem from these that Astyages still maintained the offensive, and that there was a fifth battle in the immediate neighbourhood of Pasargadæ, wherein he was completely defeated by Cyrus, who routed the Median army, and pressing upon them in their flight, took their camp. All the insignia of Median royalty fell into his hands; and, amid the acclamations of his army, he assumed them, and was saluted by his soldiers "King of Media and Persia." Meanwhile Astyages had sought for safety in flight; the greater part of his army had dispersed, and he was left with only a few friends; who still adhered to his fortunes.[5] Could he have reached Ecbatana, he might have greatly prolonged the struggle; but his enemy pressed him close; and, being compelled to an engagement, he not only suffered a complete defeat, but was made prisoner by his fortunate adversary.[6]

---

[4] As Strabo, xv. 3, § 8; Diod. Sic. ix. 24, § 2; and Herod. i. 128. There is also a paragraph of Nicolas, after the Ctesias, which is important (p. 406).

[5] If we may credit Diodorus, Astyages laid the blame of his defeat on his generals whom he cruelly punished with death. This ill-judged severity produced great discontent among the troops, who threatened to mutiny in consequence. (Diod. Sic. l. s. c.)

[6] Herodotus, Nicolas, and Justin all agree that Astyages was made prisoner after a battle. Ctesias said

By this capture the Median monarchy was brought abruptly to an end. Astyages had no son to take his place and continue the struggle. Even had it been otherwise, the capture of the monarch would probably have involved his people's submission. In the East the King is so identified with his kingdom that the possession of the royal person is regarded as conveying to the possessor all regal rights. Cyrus, apparently, had no need even to besiege Ecbatana; the whole Median State, together with its dependencies, at once submitted to him, on learning what had happened. This ready submission was no doubt partly owing to the general recognition of a close connection between Media and Persia, which made the transfer of Empire from the one to the other but slightly galling to the subjected power, and a matter of complete indifference to the dependent countries. Except in so far as religion was concerned, the change from one Iranic race to the other would make scarcely a perceptible difference to the subjects of either kingdom. The law of the state would still be "the law of the Medes and Persians."[1] Official employments would be open to the people of both countries.[2] Even the fame and glory of Empire would attach, in the minds of men, almost as much to the one nation as the other.[3] If Media descended from her pre-eminent rank, it was to occupy a station only a little

---

that he was taken in Ecbatana, where he had attempted to conceal himself in the palace (*Persic. Exc.* § 2). Moses makes him fall in battle with Tigranes the Armenian king (*Hist. Armen.* i. 28).

[1] Dan. vi. 8. Compare Esther i. 19.

[2] On the high employments filled by Medes under the Persian Kings, see vol. iv. of this work, and compare Herod. i. 156, 162; vi. 84; vii. 88; Dan. ix. 1; *Beh. Inscr.* Col. ii. Par. 14, § 6; Col. iv. Par. 14, § 8.

[3] "Thy kingdom is divided and given to the *Medes* and Persians." Dan. v. 28. Compare the employment of the words ὁ Μῆδος, τὰ Μηδικά, μηδίζουσι, κ.τ.λ. by the Greek writers, where the reference is really to the Persians.

below the highest, and one which left her a very distinct superiority over all the subject races.

If it be asked how Media, in her hour of peril, came to receive no assistance from the great Powers with which she had made such close alliances—Babylonia and Lydia [19]—the answer would seem to be that Lydia was too remote from the scene of strife to lend her effective aid, while circumstances had occurred in Babylonia to detach that state from her and render it unfriendly. The great king, Nebuchadnezzar, had he been on the throne, would undoubtedly have come to the assistance of his brother-in-law, when the fortune of war changed, and it became evident that his crown was in danger. But Nebuchadnezzar had died in B.C. 561, three years before the Persian revolt broke out. His son, Evil-Merodach, who would probably have maintained his father's alliances, had survived him but two years: he had been murdered in B.C. 559 by a brother-in-law, Nergal-shar-ezer or Neriglissar, who ascended the throne in that year and reigned till B.C. 555. This prince was consequently on the throne at the time of Astyages's need. As he had supplanted the house of Nebuchadnezzar, he would naturally be on bad terms with that monarch's Median connexions; and we may suppose that he saw with pleasure the fall of a power to which pretenders from the Nebuchadnezzar family would have looked for support and countenance.

In conclusion, a few words may be said on the general character of the Median Empire, and the causes of its early extinction.

The Median Empire was in extent and fertility of

---

[19] See above, p. 212.

territory equal if not superior to the Assyrian. It stretched from Rhages and the Carmanian desert on the East[11] to the river Halys upon the West, a distance of above twenty degrees, or about 1300 miles. From North to South it was comparatively narrow, being confined between the Black Sea, the Caucasus, and the Caspian, on the one side, and the Euphrates and Persian Gulf on the other. Its greatest width, which was towards the East, was about nine, and its least, which was towards the West, was about four degrees. Its area was probably not much short of 500,000 square miles. Thus it was as large as Great Britain, France, Spain, and Portugal put together.

In fertility its various parts were very unequal. Portions of both Medias, of Persia, of Armenia, Iberia, and Cappadocia were rich and productive; but in all these countries there was a large quantity of barren mountain, and in Media Magna and Persia there were tracts of desert. If we estimate the resources of Media from the data furnished by Herodotus in his account of the Persian revenue, and compare them with those of the Assyrian Empire, as indicated by the same document,[12] we shall find reason to conclude,

---

[11] Some authorities, as Nicolas, extend the Median Empire much further eastward. According to this writer, not only Hyrcania and Parthia, but Bactria and Sacia (!), were provinces of the Empire governed by satraps, who submitted to the victorious Cyrus. But better authorities tell us that Cyrus had to reduce these countries. (Herod. i. 153; Ctesias, *Persic. Exc.* § 2 and § 3.)

[12] According to Herodotus, Media itself furnished to Persia 450 talents, the Caspians and their neighbours in the Ghilan country 200, the Armenians 400, the Sapeirians or Iberians 200, the Moschi, Tibareni, and other tribes on the Black Sea 300. Babylonia and Assyria furnished 1000 talents between them; we may suppose in about equal shares. Allowing 500 talents to Assyria, this would give as the sum raised by the Persians from Satrapies previously included in Media, 2050 talents. A further sum must be added for Cappadocia (included in Herodotus's third satrapy) — say 200 talents, and finally, something must be allowed for Persia, say 300 talents. We thus reach a total of 2550 talents. The

that, except during the few years when Egypt was a province of Assyria, the resources of the Third exceeded those of the Second Monarchy.[1]

The weakness of the Empire arose chiefly from its want of organisation. Nicolas of Damascus, indeed, in the long passage from which our account of the struggle between Cyrus and Astyages has been taken, represents the Median Empire as divided, like the Persian, into a number of *satrapies*;[2] but there is no real ground for believing that any such organisation was practised in Median times, or to doubt that Darius Hystaspis was the originator of the satrapial system.[3] The Median Empire, like the Assyrian,[4] was a congeries of kingdoms, each ruled by its own native prince, as is evident from the case of Persia, where Cambyses was not satrap, but monarch.[5] Such organisation as was attempted, appears to have been clumsy in the extreme. The Medes (we are told) only claimed direct suzerainty over the nations immediately upon their borders; remoter tribes they placed under these, and looked to them to collect and remit the tribute of the outlying countries.[6] It is

---

[1] The satrapies contained within the Assyrian Empire at its most flourishing period were the 4th (Cilicia), the 5th (Syria), half the 6th (Egypt, Cyrene, &c.), the 8th (Susiana), the 9th (Assyria and Babylonia), and a part (say half) of the 10th (Media). Cilicia gave 500 talents, Syria 350, Cissia 300, Assyria and Babylonia 1000; to which may be added for half Egypt 350, and for half Media 225—total 2725 talents.

[2] If we deduct from the sum total of 2725 talents the 350 allowed for half Egypt, there will remain 2375 talents—175 less than the amount which accrued to Darius from the tribute of the Median provinces.

[3] Fr. 66, pp. 399 and 406.

[4] The "princes" appointed by Darius the Mede in Babylon (Dan. vi. 1) were not satraps, but either governors of petty districts in Babylonia, or perhaps "councillors." (See verse 7.)

[5] See above, vol. ii. p. 524.

[6] If we can trust Moses, Tigranes was also "king" of Armenia.

[7] Such seems to be the meaning of a very obscure passage in Herodotus (i. 134, ad fin.). It may be doubted whether there is much truth in the statement.

doubtful if they called on the subject nations for any contingents of troops. We never hear of their doing so. Probably, like the Assyrians,⁷ they made their conquests with armies composed entirely of native soldiers, or of these combined with such forces as were sent to their aid by princes in alliance with them.

The weakness arising from this lack of organisation was increased by a corruption of manners, which caused the Medes speedily to decline in energy and warlike spirit. The conquest of a great and luxurious Empire by a hardy and simple race is followed, almost of necessity, by a deterioration in the character of the conquerors, who lose the warlike virtues, and too often do not replace them by the less splendid virtues of peace. This tendency, which is fixed in the nature of things, admits of being checked for a while, or rapidly developed, according to the policy and character of the monarchs who happen to occupy the throne. If the original conqueror is succeeded by two or three ambitious and energetic princes, who engage in important wars and labour to extend their dominions at the expense of their neighbours,⁸ it will be some time before the degeneracy becomes marked. If, on the other hand, a prince of a quiet temper, self-indulgent and studious of ease, come to the throne within a short time of the original conquests, the deterioration will be very rapid. In the present instance it happened that the immediate successor of the first conqueror was of a peaceful disposition, unambitious, and luxurious in his habits. During a reign which lasted at least thirty-five years

---

⁷ Compare vol. ii. p. 826, note ¹.
⁸ Compare the case of Persia under Cambyses, Darius, and Xerxes.

he abstained almost wholly from military enterprises; and thus an entire generation of Medes grew up without seeing actual service, which alone makes the soldier. At the same time there was a general softening of manners. The luxury of the Court corrupted the nobles, who from hardy mountain chieftains, simple if not even savage in their dress and mode of life, became polite courtiers, magnificent in their apparel, choice in their diet, and averse to all unnecessary exertion. The example of the upper classes would tell on the lower, though not perhaps to any very large extent. The ordinary Mede, no doubt, lost something of his old daring and savagery; from disuse he became inexpert in the management of arms; and he was thus no longer greatly to be dreaded as a soldier. But he was really not very much less brave, nor less capable of bearing hardships, than before;* and it only required a few years of training to enable him to recover himself and to be once more as good a soldier as any in Asia.

But in the affairs of nations, as in those of men, negligence often proves fatal before it can be repaired. Cyrus saw his opportunity, pressed his advantage, and established the supremacy of his nation, before the unhappy effects of Astyages's peace policy could be removed. He knew that his own Persians possessed the military spirit in its fullest vigour; he felt that he himself had all the qualities of a successful leader; he may have had faith in his cause, which he would view as the cause of Ormazd against Ahriman,¹⁰

---

* On the valour of the Medes after the Persian conquest, see Herod. viii. 113, and Diod. Sic. xi. 6, § 3; and compare above, pp. 77, 78.

ᵇ See Nic. Dam. Fr. 66; pp. 404 and 406. Cyrus is represented as claiming a divine sanction to his attempt; and Astyages is regarded as having been deprived of his kingdom by a god (ὑπὸ θεῶν τοῦ)—query, Ormazd?

of pure religion against a corrupt and debasing nature-worship. His revolt was sudden, unexpected, and well-timed. He waited till Astyages was advanced in years, and so disqualified for command; till the veterans of Cyaxares were almost all in their graves; and till the Babylonian throne was occupied by a king who was not likely to give Astyages any aid. He may not at first have aspired to do more than establish the independence of his own country. But when the opportunity of effecting a transfer of Empire offered itself, he seized it promptly; rapidly repeating his blows, and allowing his enemy no time to recover and renew the struggle. The substitution of Persia for Media as the ruling power in Western Asia was less due to general causes than to the personal character of two men. Had Astyages been a prince of ordinary vigour, the military training of the Medes would have been kept up; and in that case, they might easily have held their own against all comers. Had their training been kept up, or had Cyrus possessed no more than ordinary ambition and ability, either he would not have thought of revolting, or he would have revolted unsuccessfully. The fall of the Median Empire was due immediately to the genius of the Persian Prince; but its ruin was prepared, and its destruction was really caused, by the shortsightedness of the Median Monarch.

APPENDIX.

NOTE A (p. 107).

TRANSLATION OF THE FIRST FARGARD OF THE VENDIDAD.

§ 1. AHURA-MAZDA said to the holy Zoroaster:—"I made, most holy Zoroaster, into a delicious spot what was previously quite uninhabitable. For had not I, most holy Zoroaster, converted into a delicious spot what was previously quite uninhabitable, all earthly life would have been poured forth after Aryanem Vaejo.

[§ 2. "Into a charming region (I converted) one which did not enjoy prosperity, the second (region) into the first: in opposition to it is great destruction of the living cultivation.]

§ 3. "As the first best of regions and countries, I, who am Ahura-mazda, created Aryanem Vaejo of good capability. Thereupon, in opposition to it, Angro-mainyus, the Death-dealing, created a mighty serpent, and snow, the work of the Devas.

§ 4. "Ten months of winter are there—two months of summer—[seven months of summer are there—five months of winter; the latter are cold as to water, cold as to earth, cold as to trees; there is mid-winter, the heart of winter; there all around falls deep snow; there is the direst of plagues.]

§ 5. "As the second best of regions and countries, I, who am Ahura-mazda, created Gâu, in which Sughda is situated. Thereupon, in opposition to it, Angro-mainyus, the Death-dealing, created pestilence, which is fatal to cattle, both small and great.

§ 6. "As the third best of regions and countries, I, I Ahura-mazda, created the strong, the pious Mouru. Thereupon Angro-mainyus, the Death-dealing, created, in opposition to it, war and pillage.

§ 7. "As the fourth best of regions and countries, I, I Ahura-mazda, created the happy Bakhdi with the tall banner. Thereupon Angro-mainyus, the Death-dealing, created, in opposition to it, buzzing insects and poisonous plants.

§ 8. "As the fifth best of regions and countries, I, I Ahura-mazda, created Nisai [between Mouru and Bakhdi]. Thereupon Angro-mainyus created, in opposition to it, the curse of unbelief.

§ 9. " As the sixth best of regions and countries, I, Ahura-mazda, created Haroyu, the dispenser of water. Thereupon Angro-mainyus, the Death-dealing, created, in opposition to it, hail and poverty.

§ 10. "As the seventh best of regions and countries, I, Ahura-mazda, created Vackeret, in which Duzhaka is situated. Thereupon Angro-mainyus, the Death-dealing, created, in opposition to it, the fairy Khnathaiti, who attached herself to Keremspa.

§ 11. "As the eighth best of regions and countries, I, Ahura-mazda, created Urva, abounding in rivers. Thereupon Angro-mainyus created, in opposition to it, the curse of devastation.

§ 12. " As the ninth best of regions and countries, I, Ahura-mazda, created Khnenta, in which Vehrkana is situated. Thereupon Angro-mainyus created, in opposition to it, the evil of inexpiable sins, pæderastism.

§ 13. " As the tenth best of regions and countries, I, Ahura-mazda, created the happy Haraqaiti. Thereupon Angro-mainyus, the Death-dealing, created the evil of inexpiable acts, preserving the dead.

§ 14. "As the eleventh best of regions and countries, I, Ahura-mazda, created Haetumat, the wealthy and brilliant. Thereupon Angro-mainyus, the Death-dealing, created, in opposition to it, the sin of witchcraft.

[§ 15. " And he, Angro-mainyus, is endowed with various powers and various forms. Wherever these come, on being invoked by one who is a wizard, then the most horrible witchcraft sins arise: then spring up those which tend to murder and the deadening of the heart: powerful are they by dint of concealing their hideousness and by their enchanted potions.]

§ 16. "As the twelfth best of regions and countries, I, Ahura-mazda, created Ragha with the three races. Thereupon Angro-mainyus, the Death-dealing, created, in opposition to it, the evil of unbelief in the Supreme.

§ 17. "As the thirteenth best of regions and countries, I, Ahura-mazda, created Kakra the strong, the pious. Thereupon Angro-mainyus, the Death-dealing, created the curse of inexpiable acts, cooking the dead.

§ 18. "As the fourteenth best of regions and countries, I, Ahura-mazda, created Varena with the four corners. There was born Thraetona, the slayer of the destructive serpent. Thereupon Angro-mainyus, the Death-dealing, created, in opposition to it, irregularly recurring evils (i. e. sicknesses) and un-Arian plagues of the country.

§ 19. "As the fifteenth best of regions and countries, I, Ahura-mazda, created Hapta Hindu, from the eastern Hindu to the western. Thereupon Angro-mainyus, the Death-dealing, created, in opposition to it, untimely evils and irregular fevers.

§ 20. "As the sixteenth best of regions and countries, I, Ahura-mazda, created those who dwell without ramparts on the sea-coast. Thereupon Angro-mainyus, the Death-dealing, created, in opposition, snow, the work of the Devas, and earthquakes which make the earth to tremble.

§ 21. "There are also other regions and countries, happy, renowned, high, prosperous, and brilliant."

[N. B.—I have followed, except in a few doubtful phrases, the translation of Dr. Martin Haug, as given in Chevalier Bunsen's *Egypt*, vol. iii. pp. 488-490.]

THE FOURTH MONARCHY.

BABYLONIA.

CHAPTER I.

EXTENT OF THE EMPIRE.

"Behold, a tree in the midst of the earth, and the height thereof was great; the tree grew and was strong; and the height thereof reached unto heaven, and the sight thereof to the end of all the earth."—Dan. iv. 10, 11.

The limits of Babylonia Proper, the tract in which the dominant power of the Fourth Monarchy had its abode, being almost identical with those which have been already described under the head of Chaldæa,[1] will not require in this place to be treated afresh at any length. It needs only to remind the reader that Babylonia Proper is that *alluvial* tract towards the mouth of the two great rivers of Western Asia—the Tigris and the Euphrates—which intervenes between the Arabian Desert on the one side, and the more eastern of the two streams on the other. Across the Tigris the country is no longer Babylonia, but Cissia, or Susiana—a distinct region, known to the Jews as Elam—the *habitat* of a distinct people.[2]

---

[1] See vol. I. pp. 3-19. The only difference between Babylonia Proper under Nebuchadnezzar, and Chaldæa under Nimrod and Urukh, is the greater size of the former, arising in part from the gradual growth of the alluvium seawards (vol. i. pp. 5, 8), in part from the extended use of irrigation by Nebuchadnezzar along the south-western or Arabian frontier.

[2] The Susianians appear by their inscriptions to have been a Cushite race, not distantly connected with

Babylonia lies westward of the Tigris, and consists of two vast plains or flats, one situated between the two rivers, and thus forming the lower portion of the "Mesopotamia" of the Greeks and Romans—the other interposed between the Euphrates and Arabia, a long but narrow strip along the right bank of that abounding river. The former of these two districts is shaped like an ancient *amphora*, the mouth extending from Hit to Samarah, the neck lying between Baghdad and Ctesiphon on the Tigris, Mohammed and Mosaib on the Euphrates, the full expansion of the body occurring between Serut and El Khithr, and the pointed base reaching down to Kornah at the junction of the two streams. This tract, the main region of the ancient Babylonia, is about 320 miles long, and from 20 to 100 broad. It may be estimated to contain about 18,000 square miles. The tract west of the Euphrates is smaller than this. Its length, in the time of the Babylonian Empire, may be regarded as about 350 miles,[3] its average width is from 25 to 30 miles, which would give an area of about 9000 square miles. Thus the Babylonia of Nabopolassar and Nebuchadnezzar may be regarded as covering a space of 27,000 square miles—a space a little exceeding the area of the Low Countries.

The small province included within these limits—smaller than Scotland or Ireland, or Portugal or Bavaria—became suddenly, in the latter half of the seventh century B.C., the mistress of an extensive

---

the dominant race of ancient Chaldæa. But they retained their primitive character, while the Babylonians changed theirs and became Semitized.

[3] From the edge of the alluvium to the present coast of the Persian Gulf is a distance of 430 miles. But 80 miles must be deducted from this distance on account of the growth of the alluvium during 24 centuries. (See vol. i. p. 5.)

empire. On the fall of Assyria, about B.C. 625, or a little later, Media and Babylonia, as already observed,¹ divided between them her extensive territory. It is with the acquisitions thus made that we have now to deal. We have to inquire what portion exactly of the previous dominions of Assyria fell to the lot of the adventurous Nabopolassar, when Nineveh ceased to be—what was the extent of the territory which was ruled from Babylon in the latter portion of the seventh and the earlier portion of the sixth century before our era?

Now the evidence which we possess on this point is threefold. It consists of certain notices in the Hebrew Scriptures, contemporary records of first-rate historical value; of an account which strangely mingles truth with fable in one of the books of the Apocrypha; and of a passage of Berosus preserved by Josephus in his work against Apion. The Scriptural notices are contained in Jeremiah, in Daniel, and in the books of Kings and Chronicles.² From these sources we learn that the Babylonian Empire of this time embraced on the one hand the important country of Susiana³ or Elymais (Elam), while on the other it ran up the Euphrates at least as high as Carchemish,⁴ from thence extending westward to the Mediterranean,⁵ and southward to, or rather perhaps into, Egypt.⁶ The Apocryphal book of Judith enlarges these limits in every direction. That the Nabuchodonosor of that work is a reminiscence of

---

¹ Supra, p. 194.
² Jerem. xxvii. 3-7; xlvi. 2-26; xlix. 28-33; lii. 4-30; Dan. ii. 38; iv. 22; viii. 1-27; 2 K. xxiv. 1-7, 10-17; xxv. 1-21; 2 Chr. xxxvi. 6-20.
³ See especially Dan. viii. 1, 2, 27.
⁴ Jerem. xlvi. 2; 2 Chr. xxxv. 20.
⁵ Jerem. xxvii. 3-0. Compare Ezek. xxix. 17, 18.
⁶ Jerem. xlvi. 13-26; Ezek. xxix. 19, 20.

the real Nebuchadnezzar there can be no doubt.[10] The territories of that monarch are made to extend eastward, beyond Susiana, into Persia;[11] northward to Nineveh;[12] westward to Cilicia in Asia Minor;[13] and southward to the very borders of Ethiopia.[14] Among the countries under his sway are enumerated Elam, Persia, Assyria, Cilicia, Cœle-Syria, Syria of Damascus, Phœnicia, Galilee, Gilead, Bashan, Judæa, Philistia, Goshen, and Egypt generally.[15] The passage of Berosus is of a more partial character. It has no bearing on the general question of the extent of the Babylonian Empire, but, incidentally, it confirms the statements of our other authorities as to the influence of Babylon in the West. It tells us that Cœle-Syria, Phœnicia, and Egypt, were subject to Nabopolassar,[16] and that Nebuchadnezzar ruled, not only over these countries, but also over some portion of Arabia.[17]

From these statements, which, on the whole, are tolerably accordant, we may gather that the great Babylonian Empire of the seventh century B.C. inherited from Assyria all the southern and western portion of her territory, while the more northern

---

[10] The name alone is sufficient proof of this. There never was any other powerful king who bore this remarkable appellation. And Nabochodonosor is the exact rendering of the name which the Hellenistic Jews universally adopted. (See the Septuagint, passim; and compare Josephus, *Ant. Jud.* x. 8, § 1; &c.)

[11] Judith, i. 7.

[12] Ibid. verse 1.

[13] Ibid. verse 7.

[14] Ibid. verse 10.

[15] Except in making Nabuchodonosor rule at Nineveh, and bear sway over Persia and Cilicia, the author of the Book of Judith seems to apprehend correctly the extent of his empire. It is even conceivable that, as succeeding to Assyria in the south and west, Nebuchadnezzar may have claimed an authority over both the Persians and the Cilicians.

[16] Beros. ap. Joseph. c. *Ap.* 19: Ἀκούσας ὁ Ναβολάσσαρος ὅτι ὁ τεταγμένος σατράπης ἔν τε Αἰγύπτῳ καὶ τοῖς περὶ τὴν Συρίαν τὴν Κοίλην καὶ τὴν Φοινίκην ἀποστάτης γέγονεν, κ.τ.λ.

[17] Ibid.: Κρατῆσαι δέ φησι τὸν Βαβυλώνιον (sc. Ναβουχοδονόσορον) Αἰγύπτου, Συρίας, Φοινίκης, Ἀραβίας.

CHAP. I.   ELAM OR SUSIANA.

and eastern provinces fell to the share of Media. Setting aside the statement of the Book of Judith (wholly unconfirmed as it is by any other authority), that Persia was at this time subject to Babylon, we may regard as the most eastern portion of the Empire the district of Susiana, which corresponded nearly with the modern Khuzistan and Luristan. This acquisition advanced the eastern frontier of the Empire from the Tigris to the Bakhtiyari Mountains, a distance of 100 or 120 miles. It gave to Babylon an extensive tract of very productive territory, and an excellent strategic boundary. Khuzistan is one of the most valuable provinces of modern Persia.[1] It consists of a broad tract of fertile alluvium, intervening between the Tigris and the mountains,[2] well watered by numerous large streams, which are capable of giving an abundant irrigation to the whole of the low region. Above this is Luristan, a still more pleasant district, composed of alternate mountain, valley, and upland plain, abounding in beautiful glens, richly wooded, and full of gushing brooks and clear rapid rivers.[3] Much of this region is of course uncultivable mountain, range succeeding range, in six or eight parallel lines,[4] as the traveller advances to the north-east; and most of the ranges exhibiting

---

[1] Kinneir's *Persian Empire*, pp. 85-107; *Journal of Geographical Society*, vol. ix. art. II.; vol. xvi. art. i.; Loftus, *Chaldæa and Susiana*, pp. 287-316.

[2] Towards the east, between the Jerahi and the Tab or Hindyan rivers, and again between the Jerahi and the Kuran, the low country consists now in great part of sandy plains and morasses (Kinneir, pp. 85, 86); but a careful system of irrigation, such as anciently prevailed, would at once drain the marshes and spread water over the sandy tracts. Then the whole region would be productive.

[3] See *Journal of the Geographical Society*, vol. ix. pp. 93-97.

[4] Layard, *Nineveh and Babylon*, p. 373; *Geographical Journal*, vol. xvi. p. 50; Loftus, *Chaldæa und Susiana*, p. 308.

vast tracts of bare and often precipitous rock, in the clefts of which snow rests till midsummer.³ Still the lower flanks of the mountains are in general cultivable, while the valleys teem with orchards and gardens, and the plains furnish excellent pasture. The region closely resembles Zagros, of which it is a continuation. As we follow it, however, towards the south-east into the Bakhtiyari country, where it adjoins upon the ancient Persia, it deteriorates in character; the mountains becoming barer and more arid, and the valleys narrower and less fertile.⁴

All the other acquisitions of Babylonia at this period lay towards the west. They consisted of the Euphrates valley, above Hit; of Mesopotamia Proper, or the country about the two streams of the Bilik and the Khabour; of Syria, Phœnicia, Palestine, Idumæa, Northern Arabia, and part of Egypt. The Euphrates valley from Hit to Balis is a tract of no great value, except as a line of communication. The Mesopotamian Desert presses it closely upon the one side, and the Arabian upon the other. The river flows mostly in a deep bed between cliffs of marl, gypsum, and limestone,⁷ or else, between bare hills producing only a few dry sapless shrubs, and a coarse grass;⁸ and there are but rare places where, except by great efforts,⁹ the water can be raised so as to irrigate, to any extent, the land along either bank. The

---

³ *Geograph. Journ.* vol. ix. p. 95.
⁴ Ibid. pp. 77-82.
⁵ Chesney, *Euphrates Expedition*, vol. i. pp. 48-53; Ainsworth, *Travels in the Track of the Ten Thousand*, pp. 78, 79.
⁶ Compare the description of Xenophon, *Anab.* i. 5, § 1 (quoted in vol. i. p. 241, note ⁶); and see Ainsworth, *Travels*, &c., pp. 76 and 81.

⁹ Numerous remains of aqueducts on both banks of the river above Hit show that in ancient times such efforts were made, and that the life-giving fluid was by these means transported to considerable distances. But the works in question scarcely reach to Babylonian times.

course of the stream is fringed by date-palms as high as Anah,[10] and above is dotted occasionally with willows, poplars, sumacs, and the unfruitful palm-tree. Cultivation is possible in places along both banks, and the undulating country on either side affords patches of good pasture.[11] The land improves as we ascend. Above the junction of the Khabour with the main stream, the left bank is mostly cultivable. Much of the land is flat and well-wooded,[12] while often there are broad stretches of open ground, well adapted for pasturage. A considerable population seems in ancient times to have peopled the valley, which did not depend wholly or even mainly on its own products, but was enriched by the important traffic which was always passing up and down the great river.[13]

Mesopotamia Proper,[14] or the tract extending from the head streams of the Khabour about Mardin and Nisibin to the Euphrates at Bir, and thence southwards to Karkesiyeh or Circesium, is not certainly known to have belonged to the kingdom of Babylon, but may be assigned to it on grounds of probability. Divided by a desert or by high mountains from the valley of the Tigris, and attached by means of its streams to that of the Euphrates, it almost necessarily falls to that power which holds the Euphrates under its dominion. The tract is one of considerable extent and importance. Bounded on the north by the range of hills which Strabo calls Mons Masius,[15] and on the east by the waterless upland which lies directly west

---

[10] Chesney, vol. i. p. 53.
[11] On the difficulty of obtaining any great amount of pasture in this region, see Xen. Anab. i. 5, § 5.
[12] Chesney, vol. i. p. 48.
[13] Herod. L 185, 194 ; Strab. xvi. 2, § 4 ; Q. Curt. x. 1.
[14] See Ptolemy, Geograph. v. 18.
[15] Strab. xvi. 1, § 23.

of the middle Tigris, it comprises within it all the numerous affluents of the Khabour and Bilik, and is thus better supplied with water than almost any country in these regions. The borders of the streams afford the richest pasture,[16] and the whole tract along the flank of Masius is fairly fertile.[17] Towards the west, the tract between the Khabour and the Bilik, which is diversified by the Abd-el-Aziz hills, is a land of fountains. "Such," says Ibn Haukal, "are not to be found elsewhere in all the land of the Moslems, for there are more than three hundred pure running brooks."[18] Irrigation is quite possible in this region; and many remains of ancient watercourses show that large tracts, at some distance from the main streams, were formerly brought under cultivation.[19]

Opposite to Mesopotamia Proper, on the west or right bank of the Euphrates, lay Northern Syria, with its important fortress of Carchemish, which was undoubtedly included in the Empire.[20] This tract is not one of much value. Towards the north it is mountainous, consisting of spurs from Amanus and Taurus, which gradually subside into the desert a little to the south of Aleppo. The bare, round-backed, chalky or rocky ranges, which here continually succeed one another, are divided only by narrow tortuous valleys, which run chiefly towards the Euphrates or the lake of Antioch.[21] This mountain tract is succeeded by a region of extensive plains, separated from

---

[16] See Layard's *Nineveh and Babylon*, pp. 310, 312, &c.
[17] Strab. xvi. 1, § 23.
[18] Chesney, vol. i. p. 40. Compare Layard, *Nin. and Bab.*, p. 312.

[19] Layard, l. s. c.
[20] Jerem. xlvi. 2.
[21] On the character of this region see Ainsworth, *Travels in the Track*, pp. 61-65.

each other by low hills, both equally desolate." The
soil is shallow and stony; the streams are few, and of
little volume; irrigation is thus difficult, and, except
where it can be applied, the crops are scanty. The
pistachio-nut grows wild in places; vines and olives
are cultivated with some success; and some grain is
raised by the inhabitants; but the country has few
natural advantages, and it has always depended more
upon its possession of a carrying trade, than on its
home products, for prosperity.

West and south-west of this region, between it
and the Mediterranean, and extending southwards
from Mount Amanus to the latitude of Tyre, lies
Syria Proper, the Cœle-Syria of many writers,[1] a
long but comparatively narrow tract of great fertility and value. Here two parallel ranges of mountains intervene between the coast and the desert,
prolific parents of a numerous progeny of small
streams. First, along the line of the coast, is the
range known as Libanus in the south, from lat.
33° 20' to lat. 34° 40', and as Bargylus[2] in the north,
from lat. 34° 45' to the Orontes at Antioch, a range
of great beauty, richly wooded in places, and abounding in deep glens, foaming brooks, and precipices of
a fantastic form.[3] More inland is Antilibanus, culmi-
nating towards the south in Hermon, and prolonged
northward in the Jebel Shashabu, Jebel Riha, and
Jebel-el-Ala,[4] which extend from near Hems to the

" Porter, *Handbook of Syria and Palestine*, pp. 609-616.

[1] Cœle-Syria is used in this wide sense by Strabo (xvi. 2, § 21), Polybius (v. 80, § 3), Josephus (*Ant. Jud.* i. 11, § 5), and the Apocryphal
writers (1 Esdr. ii. 17, 24; iv. 48; vi. 29, &c.; 1 Mac. x. 69; 2 Mac.
iii. 5; iv. 8, &c.)

[2] This range is now known as the Jebel Nusairiyeh.

[3] Porter, *Handbook of Syria*, pp. 581-589; Chesney, *Euphrates Expedition*, vol. i. pp. 387, 388.

[4] Chesney, vol. i. p. 388; Porter, p. 616.

latitude of Aleppo. More striking than even Lebanon at its lower extremity, where Hermon lifts a snowy peak into the air during most of the year, it is on the whole inferior in beauty to the coast range, being bleaker, more stony, and less broken up by dells and

View of the Lebanon range.

valleys towards the south, and tamer, barer, and less well supplied with streams in its more northern portion. Between the two parallel ranges lies the "Hollow Syria," a long and broadish valley watered by the two streams of the Orontes and the Litany,[1] which, rising at no great distance from one another, flow in opposite directions, one hurrying northwards nearly to the flanks of Amanus, the other southwards to the hills of Galilee. Few places in the world are more remarkable, or have a more stirring history, than this wonderful vale. Extending for above two hundred miles from north to south, almost in a direct line,[2] and without further break than an occasional screen of low hills,[3] it furnishes the most convenient line of passage between Asia and Africa, alike for the journeys of merchants and for the march of armies. Along this line passed Thothmes and Rameses, Sargon and Sennacherib, Neco and Nebuchadnezzar, Alexander and his warlike successors, Pompey, Antony, Kaled, Godfrey of Bouillon; along this must pass every great army which, starting from the general seats of power in Western Asia, seeks conquests in Africa, or which, proceeding from Africa, aims at the acquisition of an Asiatic dominion. Few richer tracts are to be found even in these most favoured portions of the earth's surface. Toward the south the famous El-Bukaa is a land of cornfields and vineyards, watered by numerous small streams which fall into the Litany.[4] Towards the north El-Ghab is even more splendidly fertile,[5] with a dark rich soil, luxu-

---

[1] This is Coele-Syria proper. See the description of Dionysius (*Perieg.* ll. 899, 900):—

Ἡ Κοίλη ἐντεῦθεν ἑκάτερθεν, οὖσα' ἀπ' ἀκτῆς
Ἰδαίου καὶ χθαμαλῇ ὑπέκει ὅσο ὀρέων
ὕψεσιν.

—Compare Stanley, *Sinai and Palestine*, p. 399.

[2] This statement is, of course, to be taken as a general one. Strictly speaking the valley runs first due south to Apamea (50 miles); then S.S.E. to a little beyond Hamath (25 miles); then again due south nearly to Hems (20 miles); and finally S.S.W. to *Kulat-esh-Shukif* (above 100 miles).

[3] One such screen lies a little north of Baalbek; another a little north of Hems. (See Kiepert's map.)

[4] Stanley, p. 399; Porter, pp. 567, 568; Chesney, vol. i. p. 380.

[5] Mr. Porter says of the lower

riant vegetation, and water in the utmost abundance, though at present it is cultivated only in patches immediately about the towns, from fear of the Nusairiyeh and the Bedouins.[10]

Parallel with the southern part of the Cœle-Syrian valley, to the west and to the east, were two small but important tracts, usually regarded as distinct states. Westward, between the heights of Lebanon and the sea, and extending somewhat beyond Lebanon, both up and down the coast, was Phœnicia, a narrow strip of territory lying along the shore, in length from 150 to 180 miles,[11] and in breadth varying from one mile to twenty.[12] This tract consisted of a mere belt of sandy land along the sea, where the smiling palm-groves grew from which the country derived its name,[13] of a broader upland region along the flank of the hills, which was cultivated in grain,[14] and of the higher slopes of the mountains

---

Orontes valley, or El Ghab, "The valley is beautiful, resembling the Bukâa; but still more fertile, and more abundantly watered." And again, "The soil is rich and vegetation luxuriant. What a noble cotton-field would this valley make! Two hundred square miles of splendid land is waiting to pour inexhausted wealth into the pocket of some western speculator." (*Handbook*, p. 619.)

[10] Porter, p. 620.

[11] Mr. Grote estimates the length of Phœnicia at no more than 120 miles (*Hist. of Greece*, vol. ii. p. 445, 2nd edition), which is little more than the distance, as the crow flies, between Antaradus and Tyre. My own inclination is to extend Phœnicia northwards at least as high as Gabala (*Jebleh*), and southwards at least as low as Carmel. This is a distance, as the crow flies, of full 180 miles. (On the different estimates of the Phœnician coast-line, see the author's *Herodotus*, vol. i. p. 478, note ⁴, 2nd edition.)

[12] Scylax (*Peripl.* p. 99) says of Phœnicia that it was "in places not ten furlongs across." Mr. Grote calls it "never more, and generally much less, than 20 miles in breadth" (*Hist. of Greece*, l. s. c.). Mr. Porter speaks of the "plain of Phœnicia Proper" as having "an average breadth of about a mile" (*Handbook*, p. 396).

[13] So Stanley (*Sinai and Palestine*, p. 263) and Twistleton (*Biblical Dictionary*, vol. ii. p. 860). Others regard the name as descriptive of the colour of the race, and parallel to Edomite, Erythræan, and the like. (Kenrick, *Phœnicia*, p. 35.) On the Phœnician palm-groves see Stanley, L. s. c.

[14] Stanley, p. 262.

which furnished excellent timber.[13] Small harbours, sheltered by rocky projections, were frequent along the coast. Wood cut in Lebanon was readily floated down the many streams to the shore, and then conveyed by sea to the ports. A narrow and scanty land made commerce almost a necessity. Here accordingly the first great maritime nation of antiquity grew up. The Phœnician fleets explored the Mediterranean at a time anterior to Homer, and conveyed to the Greeks and the other inhabitants of Europe, and of Northern and Western Africa, the wares of Assyria, Babylon, and Egypt.[14] Industry and enterprise reaped their usual harvest of success; the Phœnicians grew in wealth, and their towns became great and magnificent cities. In the time when the Babylonian Empire came into being, the narrow tract of Phœnicia—smaller than many an English county—was among the most valuable countries of Asia; and its possession was far more to be coveted than that of many a land whose area was ten or twenty times as great.

Eastward of Antilibanus, in the country between that range and the great Syrian desert, was another very important district—the district which the Jews called "Aram-Damasek," and which now forms the chief part of the Pashalik of Damascus. From the eastern flanks of the Antilibanus two great and numerous smaller streams flow down into the Damascene plain, and, carrying with them that strange fertilising power which water always has in hot climates, convert the arid sterility of the desert into a garden

---

[13] See 1 Kings v. 6; 2 Chr. ii. 8, 16; Ezek. xxvii. 5.
[14] Hom. Il. vi. 289; xxiii. 743; Od. iv. 614; xiii. 285; xv. 425; Herod. i. 1.

of the most wonderful beauty. The Barada and the Awaaj, bursting by narrow gorges from the mountain chain, scatter themselves in numerous channels over the great flat, intermingling their waters, and spreading them out so widely, that for a circle of thirty miles the deep verdure of Oriental vegetation replaces the red hue of the Hauran. Walnuts, planes, poplars, cypresses, apricots, orange-trees, citrons, pomegranates, olives, wave above; corn and grass of the most luxuriant growth, below." In the midst of this great mass of foliage, the city of Damascus " strikes out the white arms of its streets hither and thither"[18] among the trees, now hid among them, now overtopping them with its domes and minarets, the most beautiful of all those beautiful towns which delight the eye of the artist in the East. In the south-west towers the snow-clad peak of Hermon, visible from every part of the Damascene plain. West, north-west, and north, stretches the long Antilibanus range, bare, grey, and flat-topped,[19] except where, about midway in its course, the rounded summit of Jebel Tiniyeh breaks the uniformity of the line.[1] Outside the circle of deep verdure, known to the Orientals as *El Merj* ("the Meadow"), is a setting or framework of partially cultivable land, dotted with clumps of trees and groves, which extend for many miles over the plain.[2] To the Damascus country must also be reckoned those many charming valleys of Hermon and Antilibanus which open out into it, sending their waters to increase its

---

[17] Porter, *Handbook*, pp. 459, 460; Chesney, vol. i. p. 527; Lynch, *Expedition to the Dead Sea*, pp. 319 and 325.
[18] Stanley, *Sinai and Palestine*, p. 402.
[19] Porter, p. 470.
[1] Ibid. p. 465. [2] Ibid. p. 459.

beauty and luxuriance, the most remarkable of which
are the long ravine of the Barada,[5] and the romantic
Wady Halbôn,[6] whose vines produced the famous
beverage which Damascus anciently supplied at once
to the Tyrian merchant-princes[7] and to the volup-
tuous Persian kings.[8]

Below the Cœle-Syrian valley, towards the south,
came PALESTINE, the Land of Lands to the Christian,
the country which even the philosopher must acknowledge to have had a greater influence on the world's
history than any other tract which can be brought
under a single ethnic designation. Palestine—etymologically the country of the Philistines[7]—was
somewhat unfortunately named. Philistine influence
may possibly have extended at a very remote period
over the whole of it; but in historical times that warlike people did but possess a corner of the tract, less
than one-tenth of the whole—the low coast region
from Jamnia to Gaza. Palestine contained, besides
this, the regions of Galilee, Samaria, and Judæa, to
the west of the Jordan, and those of Ituræa, Trachonitis, Bashan, and Gilead, east of that river. It
was a tract 140 miles long, by from 70 to 100 broad,
containing probably about 11,000 square miles. It
was thus about equal in size to Belgium, while it was

---

[5] This ravine is well described by Stanley (*Sinai and Palestine*, pp. 401, 402), and by Porter (*Handbook*, pp. 458, 459).
[6] Porter, pp. 495, 496.
[7] Ezek. xxvii. 18. "Damascus was thy merchant in the multitude of the wares of thy making, for the multitude of all riches: *in the wine of Helbon* and white wool."
[8] Strab. xv. 3, § 22: Οἱ βασιλεῖς (τῶν Περσῶν) κυρίως μὲν ἐξ Ἄσσου τῆς Αἰολίδος μετήσσαν, οἶνον δ' ἐκ Συρίας τὸν Χαλυβώνιον.
[7] The word first occurs in Hero-dotus, who generally uses it as an adjective (ἡ Παλαιστίνη Συρίη—Σύροι οἱ Παλαιστῖνοι καλεόμενοι), and attaches it especially to the coast tract (ii. 104; iii. 5; vii. 89). It repre-sents the Hebrew P'hilistim (פלשתים) letter for letter. Josephus always calls the Philistines Παλαιστίνοι.

less than Holland or Hanover, and not much larger than the principality of Wales, with which it has been compared by a recent writer.[8]

The great natural division of the country is the Jordan valley. This remarkable depression, commencing on the west flank of Hermon, runs with a course which is almost due south from lat. 33° 25' to lat. 31° 47', where it is merged in the Dead Sea, which may be viewed, however, as a continuation of the valley, prolonging it to lat. 31° 6'. This valley is quite unlike any other in the whole world. It is a volcanic rent in the earth's surface, a broad chasm which has gaped and never closed up.[9] Naturally, it should terminate at Merom, where the level of the Mediterranean is nearly reached.[10] By some wonderful convulsion, or at any rate by some unusual freak of Nature, there is a channel (αὐλών) opened out from Merom, which rapidly sinks below the sea level, and allows the stream to flow hastily, down and still down, from Merom to Gennesareth, and from Gennesareth to the Dead Sea, where the depression reaches its lowest point,[11] and the land rising into a ridge, separates the Jordan valley from the upper end of the Gulf of Akabah. The Jordan valley divides

---

[8] Mr. Grove, in Dr. Smith's *Biblical Dictionary*, vol. ii. p. 663. This writer limits the name of Palestine to the tract west of the Jordan; but the present author prefers the wider sense which is more usual among moderns. (Stanley, pp. 111, 112; Robinson, vol. i., Preface, p. ix; &c.)

[9] On the traces of volcanic action in the neighbourhood of the Jordan, see Robinson, vol. iii. p. 313; Stanley, p. 279; Lynch, *Narrative*, pp. 111, 115, &c.

[10] The exact elevation or depression of the several parts of the Jordan valley is perhaps not even yet fully ascertained. According to Van de Velde, the level of Merom is 120 feet above the Mediterranean. According to others it is but 60 feet above that sea. (*Geogr. Journal*, vol. xx. p. 228.)

[11] The surface of the Dead Sea is in an ordinary season about 1300 or 1320 feet below the level of the Mediterranean. Its bed is in places from 1200 to 1300 feet lower.

Palestine, strongly and sharply, into two regions. Its depth, its inaccessibility (for it can only be entered from the highlands on either side down a few steep watercourses), and the difficulty of passing across it (for the Jordan has but few fords), give it a separating power almost equal to that of an arm of the sea." In length above a hundred miles, in width varying from one mile to ten, and averaging some five miles, or perhaps six, it must always have been valuable as a territory, possessing, as it does, a rich soil, abundant water, and in its lower portion a tropical climate.[13]

On either side of the deep Jordan cleft lies a highland of moderate elevation, on the right that of Galilee, Samaria, and Judæa, on the left that of Ituræa, Bashan, and Gilead. The right or western highland consists of a mass of undulating hills, with rounded tops, composed of coarse grey stone, covered, or scarcely covered, with a scanty soil, but capable of cultivation in corn, olives, and figs. This region is most productive towards the north, barer and more arid as we proceed southwards towards the desert. The lowest portion, Judæa, is unpicturesque, ill-watered, and almost treeless;[14] the central, Samaria, has numerous springs, some rich plains, many wooded heights, and in places quite a sylvan appearance;[15]

---

[12] Compare Stanley, p. 317.
[13] Ibid. p. 292.
[14] "Those who describe Palestine as beautiful," says Dean Stanley, "must either have a very inaccurate notion of what constitutes beauty of scenery, or must have viewed the country through a highly coloured medium.... The tangled and featureless hills of the Lowlands of Scotland and North Wales are perhaps the nearest likeness, accessible to Englishmen, of the general landscape of Palestine south of the plain of Esdraelon." (*Sinai and Palestine*, p. 136.) Compare Beaufort, *Egyptian Sepulchres and Syrian Shrines*, vol. ii. p. 97; and Russegger, in Ritter's *Erdkunde*, vol. viii. p. 495.
[15] Robinson, *Researches*, vol. ii. pp. 95, 96; Van de Velde, *Syria and Palestine*, vol. i. p. 388; Grove, in

the highest, Galilee, is a land of water-brooks, abounding in timber, fertile and beautiful.[16] The average height of the whole district is from 1500 to 1800 feet above the Mediterranean. Main elevations within it vary from 2500 to 4000 feet.[17] The axis of the range is towards the East, nearer, that is, to the Jordan valley than to the sea. It is a peculiarity of the highland that there is one important break in it. As the Lowland mountains of Scotland are wholly separated from the mountains of the Highlands by the low tract which stretches across from the Frith of Forth to the Frith of Clyde, or as the ranges of St. Gall and Appenzell are divided off from the rest of the Swiss mountains by the flat which extends from the Rhine at Ragatz to the same river at Waldshut, so the western highland of Palestine is broken in twain by the famous "plain of Esdraelon," which runs from the Bay of Acre to the Jordan valley at Beth-Shean or Scythopolis.

East of the Jordan no such depression occurs, the highland there being continuous. It differs from the western highland chiefly in this—that its surface, instead of being broken up into a confused mass of rounded hills, is a table-land, consisting of a long succession of slightly undulating plains.[18] Except in Trachonitis and southern Ituræa, where the basaltic rock everywhere shows itself,[19] the soil is rich and

---

Dr. Smith's *Biblical Dictionary*, vol. ii. p. 669.

[16] Stanley, p. 353; Van de Velde, vol. L. p. 386; Robinson, vol. iii. pp. 380-883.

[17] Jebel Jurmuk (in Galilee) is estimated at 4000 feet; Hebron at 3029 feet; Safed (in Galilee) at 2775 feet; the Mount of Olives at 2724 feet; Ebal and Gerizim at 2700;

Sinjil at 2085; Neby Samwil at 2650; and Jerusalem at 2610. (*Biblical Dictionary*, vol. ii. p. 665.)

[18] Stanley, *Sinai and Palestine*, p. 314 ("A wide table-land, toward about in wild confusion of undulating downs"); Porter, *Handbook of Syria*, p. 295; &c.

[19] Porter, pp. 465 and 506.

productive, the country in places wooded with fine trees, and the herbage luxuriant. On the west the mountains rise almost precipitously from the Jordan valley, above which they tower to the height of 3000 or 4000 feet. The outline is singularly uniform; and the effect is that of a huge wall guarding Palestine on this side from the wild tribes of the desert. Eastward the table-land slopes gradually, and melts into the sands of Arabia. Here water and wood are scarce; but the soil is still good, and bears the most abundant crops.*

Finally, Palestine contains the tract from which it derives its name, the low country of the Philistines, which the Jews called the *Shephêlah*,¹ together with a continuation of this tract northwards to the roots of Carmel, the district known to the Jews as "Sharon," or "the *smooth* place."² From Carmel to the Wady Sheriah, where the Philistine country ended, is a distance of about one hundred miles, which gives the length of the region in question. Its breadth between the shore and the highland varies from about twenty-five miles in the south between Gaza and the hills of Dan, to three miles, or even less, in the north between Dor and the border of Manasseh. Its area is probably from 1400 to 1500 square miles. This low strip is along its whole course divided into two parallel belts

---

* A recent traveller (Rev. H. B. Tristram) gave strong testimony to this effect at the meeting of the British Association in Bath, September, 1864.

¹ *Ha-Shephêlah*, "the Shephelah" or "depressed plain" (from שָׁפֵל, "to depress"), is the ordinary term applied to this tract in the original. The LXX. generally translate it by τὸ πεδίον or ἡ πεδινή; but sometimes they regard it as a proper name. (See Jerem. xxxii. 44; xxxiii. 14; Obad. 19; 1 Mac. xii. 38.)

² Sharon (like Mishor, the term applied to the trans-Jordanic table-land) is derived from יָשָׁר, "just, straightforward," and thence "level." (See Stanley, *Sinai and Palestine*, p. 479, Appendix.)

or lands—the first a flat sandy track along the shore, the *Ramleh* of the modern Arabs; the second, more undulating, a region of broad rolling plains rich in corn, and anciently clothed in part with thick woods,² watered by reedy streams,³ which flow down from the great highland. A valuable tract is this entire plain, but greatly exposed to ravage. Even the sandy belt will grow fruit-trees; and the towns which stand on it, as Gaza, Jaffa, and Ashdod, are surrounded with huge groves of olives, sycamores, and palms,⁴ or buried in orchards and gardens, bright with pomegranates and orange-trees.⁵ The more inland region is one of marvellous fertility. Its soil is a rich loam, containing scarcely a pebble, which yields year after year prodigious crops of grain⁶—chiefly wheat—without manure or irrigation, or other cultivation than a light ploughing. Philistia was the granary of Syria,⁷ and was important doubly, first, as yielding inexhaustible supplies to its conqueror, and secondly, as affording the readiest passage to the great armies which contended in these regions for the mastery of the Eastern World.⁸

---

² Strab. xvi. 2, § 27. Εἶτα δρυμὸς μέγας τις.

³ The modern Arabs call the upper tract of Sharon by the name of Khasmah, "the Reedy." (Stanley, p. 256.) In old times the reedy character of the streams was marked by the name of Kanah (from קנה, "a cane"), given to one of them. (Josh. xvi. 8; xvii. 9.)

⁴ Kenrick, *Phœnicia*, p. 28; Robinson, *Researches*, vol. ii. pp. 368, 376; Grove, in Smith's *Biblical Dictionary*, vol. ii. p. 672.

⁵ Stanley, p. 253.

⁷ Thomson, *The Land and the Book*, p. 552; Van de Velde, *Travels*, vol. ii. p. 175; Stanley, *Sinai and Palestine*, p. 254.

⁸ "La grenier de la Syrie." (Duc de Raguse, quoted in the *Biblical Dictionary*, vol. ii. p. 673, note.)

⁹ The ordinary route of invaders from the south was along the maritime plain, and either round Carmel (which is easily rounded), or over the shoulder of the hills, into the plain of Esdraelon. Hence the march was either through Galilee to Cœle-Syria, or across the plain to Beth-Shean (Scythopolis), and thence by Aphek (*Fik*) and Nave (*Nawa*) to Damascus. Invaders from the north followed the same line, but in the reverse direction.

South of the region to which we have given the name of Palestine, intervening between it and Egypt, lay a tract to which it is difficult to assign any single political designation. Herodotus regarded it as a portion of Arabia, which he carried across the valley of the Arabah and made abut on the Mediterranean.[10] To the Jews it was "the land of the south"[11]—the special country of the Amalekites. By Strabo's time it had come to be known as Idumæa,[12] or the Edomite country; and under this appellation it will perhaps be most convenient to describe it here. Idumæa, then, was the tract south and southwest of Palestine from about lat. 31° 10′. It reached westward to the borders of Egypt, which were at this time marked by the Wady-el-Arish,[13] southward to the range of Sinai and the Elanitic Gulf, and eastward to the Great Desert. Its chief town was Petra, in the mountains east of the Arabah valley. The character of the tract is for the most part a hard gravelly and rocky desert; but occasionally there is good herbage, and soil that admits of cultivation; brilliant flowers and luxuriantly-growing shrubs bedeck the glens and terraces of the Petra range; and most of the tract produces plants and bushes on which camels, goats, and even sheep will browse, while occasional palm-groves furnish a grateful shade and an important fruit.[14] The tract divides

---

[10] Herod. iii. 5.

[11] Num. xiii. 29; Josh. x. 40; &c.

[12] Strab. xvi. 2, § 34. I think it probable that Scylax placed Idumæans between Syria and Egypt; but his work is unfortunately defective in this place. (*Peripl.* p. 102, ed. of 1700.)

[13] See 2 K. xxiv. 7. That the "river of Egypt" here mentioned is not the Nile, but one of the torrent-courses which run from the plateau to the Mediterranean, is indicated by the word used for "river," which is not נָהָר, but נַחַל. Of all the torrent-courses at present existing, the Wady-el-Arish is the best fitted to form a boundary.

[14] Palm-trees are found at Akabah (Stanley, p. 22); and again at the Wady-Ghurundel (ib. p. 85).

itself into four regions—first, a region of sand, low and flat, along the Mediterranean, the *Shephêlah* without its fertility; next, a region of hard gravelly plain intersected by limestone ridges, and raised considerably above the sea level, the Desert of El-Tih, or of "the Wanderings;" then the long, broad, low valley of the Arabah, which rises gradually from the Dead Sea to an imperceptible water-shed,[13] and then falls gently to the head of the Gulf of Akabah, a region of hard sand thickly dotted with bushes, and intersected by numerous torrent courses; finally, a long narrow region of mountains and hills parallel with the Arabah,[14] constituting Idumæa Proper, or the original Edom, which, though rocky and rugged, is full of fertile glens, ornamented with trees and shrubs, and in places cultivated in terraces." In shape the tract was a rude square or oblong, with its sides nearly facing the four cardinal points, its length from the Mediterranean to the Gulf of Akabah being 130 miles, and its width from the Wady-el-Arish to the eastern side of the Petra mountains 120 miles. The area is thus about 1560 square miles.

Beyond the Wady-el-Arish was Egypt, stretching from the Mediterranean southwards a distance of nearly eight degrees, or more than 550 miles. As this country was not, however, so much a part of the Babylonian Empire as a dependency lying upon its

---

[13] It is scarcely yet known exactly where the water-shed is. Stanley places it about four hours (14 miles) north of the Wady Ghurundel. (*Syria and Palestine*, l. s. c.)

[14] This tract, which is the original Edom or Idumæa Proper, consists of three parallel ranges. On the west, adjoining the Arabah, are low calcareous hills. To these succeeds a range of igneous rocks, chiefly porphyry, overlaid by red sandstone, which reaches the height of 2000 feet. Farther east is a range of limestone, 1000 feet higher, which sinks down gently into the plateau of the Arabian Desert. (*Biblical Dictionary*, vol. i. p. 488.) [15] Stanley, p. 88.

borders, it will not be necessary to describe it in this place.

One region, however, remains still unnoticed which seems to have been an integral portion of the Empire. This is Palmyrênê, or the Syrian Desert—the tract lying between Cœle-Syria on the one hand and the valley of the middle Euphrates on the other, and abutting towards the south on the great Arabian Desert, to which it is sometimes regarded as belonging.[18] It is for the most part a hard sandy, or gravelly plain, intersected by low rocky ranges, and either barren or productive only of some sapless shrubs and of a low thin grass. Occasionally, however, there are oases, where the fertility is considerable. Such an oasis is the region about Palmyra itself, which derived its name from the palm groves in the vicinity;[19] here the soil is good, and a large tract is even now under cultivation. Another oasis is that of Karyatcïn, which is watered by an abundant stream, and is well wooded, and productive of grain.[20] The Palmyrênê, however, as a whole, possesses but little value, except as a passage country. Though large armies can never have traversed the desert even in this upper region, where it is comparatively narrow, trade in ancient times found it expedient to avoid the long *détour* by the Orontes valley, Aleppo, and Bambuk, and to proceed directly from Damascus by way of Palmyra to Thapsacus on the Euphrates. Small bands of light troops also occasionally took the same course; and the great saving of distance thus effected

---

[18] Chesney, *Euphrates Expedition*, vol. i. p. 559.
[19] Such, at least, is the common opinion; and the name Tadmor is thought to have had a similar meaning. But both derivations are doubtful. (See Stanley, p. 8, note.)
[20] Chesney, vol. i. pp. 522 and 580.

made it important to the Babylonians to possess an authority[1] over the region in question.

Such, then, in its geographical extent, was the great Babylonian Empire. Reaching from Luristan on the one side to the borders of Egypt on the other, its direct length from east to west was nearly sixteen degrees, or about 980 miles, while its length for all practical purposes, owing to the interposition of the desert between its western and its eastern provinces, was perhaps not less than 1400 miles. Its width was very disproportionate to this. Between Zagros and the Arabian Desert, where the width was the greatest, it amounted to about 280 miles; between Amanus and Palmyra it was 250; between the Mons Masius and the middle Euphrates it may have been 200; in Syria and Idumæa it cannot have been more than 100 or 160. The entire area of the Empire was probably from 240,000 to 250,000 square miles—which is about the present size of Austria. Its shape may be compared roughly to a gnomon, with one longer and one shorter arm.

It added to the inconvenience of this long straggling form, which made a rapid concentration of the forces of the Empire impossible, that the capital, instead of occupying a central position, was placed somewhat low in the longer of the two arms of the gnomon, and was thus nearly 1000 miles removed from the frontier province of the west. Though in direct distance, as the crow flies, Babylon is not more than 450 miles from Damascus, or more than 520 from Jerusalem, yet the necessary *détour* by Aleppo is so great, that it

---

[1] This authority is proved by the march of Nebuchadnezzar through the region. (Beros. ap. Joseph. *contr.* Ap. i. 20: Αὐτὸς ὁρμήσας ὀλίγοστὸς παρεγίνετο διὰ τῆς ἐρήμου εἰς Βαβυλῶνα.)

lengthens the distance, in the one case by 250, in the other by 360 miles. From so remote a centre it was impossible for the lifeblood to circulate very vigorously to the extremities.

The Empire was on the whole fertile and well-watered. The two great streams of Western Asia—the Tigris and the Euphrates—which afforded an abundant supply of the invaluable fluid to the most important of the provinces, those of the south-east, have been already described at length;[1] as have also the chief streams of the Mesopotamian district, the Belik and the Khabour.[2] But as yet in this work no account has been given of a number of important rivers in the extreme east and the extreme west, on which the fertility, and so the prosperity, of the Empire very greatly depended. It is proposed in the present place to supply this deficiency.

The principal rivers of the extreme east were the Choaspes, or modern Kerkhah, the Pasitigris or Eulæus, now the Kuran, the Hedyphon or Hedypnus, now the Jerahi, and the Oroatis, at present the Tab or Hindyan. Of these, the Oroatis, which is the most eastern, belongs perhaps more to Persia than to Babylon; but its lower course probably fell within the Susianian territory. It rises in the mountains between Shiraz and Persepolis,[4] about lat. 29° 45', long. 52° 35' E.; and flows towards the Persian Gulf with a course which is north-west to Failiyun, then nearly W. to Zehitun, after which it becomes somewhat south of west to Hindyan, and then S.W. by S. to the sea. The length of the stream, without

---

[1] See vol. i. pp. 7-17.
[2] Ibid. pp. 234-236.
[4] Kinneir, *Persian Empire*, p. 57;

Chesney, *Euphrates Expedition*, vol. i. p. 202.

counting lesser windings, is 200 miles; its width at Hindyan, sixteen miles above its mouth, is eighty yards,[1] and to this distance it is navigable for boats of twenty tons burthen.[2] At first its waters are pure and sweet, but they gradually become corrupted, and at Hindyan they are so brackish as not to be fit for use.[3]

The Jerahi rises from several sources in the Kuh Margun,[4] a lofty and precipitous range, forming the continuation of the chain of Zagros, about long. 50° to 51°, and lat. 31° 30′. These head-streams have a general direction from N.E. to S.W. The principal of them is the Kerdistan river, which rises about fifty miles to the north-east of Babahan, and flowing south-west to that point, then bends round to the north, and runs north-west nearly to the fort of Mungusht, where it resumes its original direction, and receiving from the north-east the Abi Zard, or "Yellow River"—a delightful stream of the coldest and purest water possible[5]—becomes known as the Jerahi,[10] and carries a large body of water as far as Fellahiyeh or Dorak. Near Dorak the waters of the Jerahi are drawn off into a number of canals, and the river is thus greatly diminished;[11] but still the stream struggles on, and proceeds by a southerly course towards the Persian Gulf, which it enters near Gadi in long. 48° 52′. The course of the Jerahi, exclusively of the smaller windings, is about equal in length to that of the Tab or

---

[1] Kinneir, l. s. c.
[2] Chesney, l. s. c. The Tab was ascended in 1830 by Lieut. Whitelocke, of the Indian Navy.
[3] Kinneir, l. s. c.
[4] Chesney, p. 200.
[5] Sir H. Rawlinson, in the Journal of the Geographical Society, vol. ix. p. 81.
[10] This name is commonly used in the country. It is unknown, however, to the Arabian geographers.
[11] Chesney, vol. I. p. 201; Kinneir, p. 88.

Hindyan. In volume, before its dispersion, it is considerably greater than that river. It has a breadth of above a hundred yards[12] before it reaches Babahan, and is navigable for boats almost from its junction with the Abi Zard. Its size is, however, greatly reduced in its lower course, and travellers who skirt the coast regard the Tab as the more important river.[13]

The Kuran is a river very much exceeding in size both the Tab and the Jerahi.[14] It is formed by the junction of two large streams—the Dizful river and the Kuran proper, or river of Shuster. Of these the Shuster stream is the more eastern. It rises in the Zarduh Kuh, or "Yellow Mountain,"[15] in lat. 32°, long. 51°, almost opposite to the river of Isfahan. From its source it is a large stream. Its direction is at first to the south-east, but after a while it sweeps round and runs considerably north of west; and this course it pursues through the mountains, receiving tributaries of importance from both sides, till, near Aklili, it turns round to the south, and, cutting at a right angle the outermost of the Zagros ranges, flows down with a course S.W. by S. nearly to Shuster, where, in consequence of a bund or dam[1] thrown across it, it bifurcates, and passes in two streams to the right and to

---

[12] Three hundred and fifty feet. (Chesney, p. 200.)

[13] This was the conclusion of Macdonald Kinneir, who travelled from Hushire to Hindyan, and thence to Dorak. (*Persian Empire*, pp. 56, 57.)

[14] Kinneir, p. 87. This writer goes so far as to say that the Kuran, after its confluence with the Abi Zard, contains "a greater body of water than either the Tigris or the Euphrates separately considered." (Ib. p. 298.)

[15] Chesney, vol. i. p. 107; *Geographical Journal*, vol. xvi. p. 60.

[1] This is the famous "Bund of Shapur," constructed by the conqueror of Valerian. The whole process of construction has been accurately described by Sir H. Rawlinson in the *Geographical Journal*, vol. ix. pp. 73–76.

the left of the town. The right branch, which carries commonly about two-thirds of the water,[1] proceeds by a tortuous course of nearly forty miles, in a direction a very little west of south, to its junction with the Dizful stream, which takes place about two miles north of the little town of Bandi-Kir. Just below that town the left branch, called at present Abi-Gargar,[2] which has made a considerable bend to the east, rejoins the main stream, which thenceforth flows in a single channel. The course of the Kuran from its source to its junction with the Dizful branch, including main windings, is about 210 miles. The Dizful branch rises from two sources, nearly a degree apart,[3] in lat. 33° 50′. These streams run respectively south-east and south-west, a distance of forty miles, to their junction near Bahrein,[4] whence their united waters flow in a tortuous course, with a general direction of south, for above a hundred miles to the outer barrier of Zagros, which they penetrate near the Diz fort, through a succession of chasms and gorges.[5] The course of the stream from this point is south-west through the hills and across the plain, past Dizful, to the point where it receives the Balad-rud from the west, when it changes and becomes first south and then south-east to its junction with the Shuster river near Bandi-Kir.[6] The entire course of the Dizful stream

---

[1] Hence called the Chahar Dangah (four parts) by the historians of Timur, while the left branch is called the Du Dangah (two parts). See l'étis de la Croix, tom. II. p. 183.
[2] *Geographical Journal*, vol. ix. p. 74.
[3] Chesney, *Euphrates Expedition*, vol. I. p. 199; *Geographical Journal*, vol. ix. p. 67.
[4] Bahrein means "the two rivers."

[5] *Geographical Journal*, l. s. c.
[6] Bandi-Kir is erroneously called Bundakeel by Macdonald Kinneir (*Persian Empire*, p. 87), and Henderghil by Mr. Loftus. (*Chaldæa and Susiana*, Map to illustrate journeys.) The word is formed from *kir*, "bitumen," because in the dyke at this place the stones are cemented with that substance. (*Geograph. Journal*, l. s. c.)

to this point is probably not less than 280 miles.[9] Below Bandi-Kir, the Kuran, now become "a noble river, exceeding in size the Tigris and Euphrates,"[10] meanders across the plain in a general direction of S.S.W., past the towns of Uris, Ahwaz, and Ismaili, to Sabla, when it turns more to the west, and passing Mohammerah, empties itself into the Shat-el-Arab,[10] about 22 miles below Busra. The entire course of the Kuran from its most remote source, exclusive of the lesser windings, is not less than 430 miles.

The Kerkhah (anciently the Choaspes[11]) is formed by three streams of almost equal magnitude, all of them rising in the most eastern portion of the Zagros range. The central of the three flows from the southern flank of Mount Elwand (Orontes), the mountain behind Hamadan (Ecbatana), and receives on the right, after a course of about thirty miles, the northern or Singur branch, and ten miles further on the southern or Guran branch, which is known by the name of the Gamas-ab. The river thus formed flows westward to Behistun, after which it bends to the south-west, and then to the south, receiving tributaries on both hands, and winding among the mountains as far as the ruined city of Rudbar. Here it bursts through the outer barrier of the great range,

---

[9] This is the estimate of Col. Chesney. (*Euphrates Expedition*, vol. i. p. 197.)

[9] *Geographical Journal*, vol. xvi. p. 52.

[10] Naturally, the Kuran has a course of its own by which it enters the Persian Gulf. This channel runs south-east from Sablah, nearly parallel to the Bah-a-Mishir, and is about 200 yards broad. (Chesney, p. 199.) But almost all the water now passes by the Hafar canal—an artificial cutting—into the Shat-el-Arab.

[11] On the identity of these streams see the author's *Herodotus*, vol. i. p. 260, 2nd edition; and compare Kinneir's *Persian Empire*, pp. 104, 105; Chesney, *Euphrates Expedition*, vol. i. p. 204; *Geographical Journal*, vol. ix. pp. 87-93; vol. xvi. pp. 91-94; Loftus, *Chaldæa and Susiana*, pp. 425-430.

and, receiving the large stream of the Kirrind from the north-west, flows S.S.E. and S.E. along the foot of the range, between it and the Kebir Kuh, till it meets the stream of the Abi-Zal, when it finally leaves the hills and flows through the plain, pursuing a S.S.E. direction to the ruins of Susa, which lie upon its left bank, and then turning to the S.S.W., and running in that direction to the Shat-el-Arab, which it reaches about five miles below Kurnah. Its length is estimated at above 500 miles; its width, at some distance above its junction with the Abi-Zal, is from eighty to a hundred yards.[12]

The course of the Kerkhah was not always exactly such as is here described. Anciently it appears to have bifurcated at Pai Pul, 18 or 20 miles N.W. of Susa, and to have sent a branch east of the Susa ruins, which absorbed the Shapur, a small tributary of the Dizful stream, and ran into the Kuran a little above Ahwaz.[13] The remains of the old channel are still to be traced;[14] and its existence explains the confusion, observable in ancient times, between the Kerkhah and the Kuran, to each of which streams, in certain parts of their course, we find the name Eulæus applied.[15] The proper Eulæus (Ulai) was the eastern branch of the Kerkhah (Choaspes) from Pai Pul to Ahwaz; but the name was naturally extended both northwards to the Choaspes above Pai Pul,[16] and

---

[12] The course of the Kerkhah was carefully explored by Sir H. Rawlinson in the year 1836, and is accurately laid down in the map accompanying his Memoir. (See Journal of the Geographical Society, vol. ix. pp. 49-93, and map opp. p. 120.)

[13] Loftus, Chaldæa and Susiana, pp. 424-431.

[14] Ibid. pp. 424, 425.

[15] See an article by the author on this subject in Smith's Biblical Dictionary, vol. iii. pp. 1586, 1587, ad voc. ULAI.

[16] Plin. H. N. vi. 31.

CHAP. I.   THE SAJUR — THE KOWEIK.   271

southwards to the Kuran below Ahwaz." The latter
stream was, however, known also, both in its upper
and its lower course, as the Pasitigris.

On the opposite side of the Empire the rivers were
less considerable. Among the most important may
be mentioned the Sajur, a tributary of the Euphrates,
the Koweik, or river of Aleppo, the Orontes, or river
of Antioch, the Litany, or river of Tyre, the Barada,
or river of Damascus, and the Jordan, with its tributaries, the Jabbok and the Hieromax.

The Sajur rises from two principal sources on the
southern flanks of Amanus, which, after running a
short distance, unite a little to the east of Ain-Tab."
The course of the stream from the point of junction is
south-east. In this direction it flows in a somewhat
tortuous channel between two ranges of hills for a
distance of about 30 miles to Tel Khalid, a remarkable conical hill crowned by ruins. Here it receives
an important affluent—the Keraskat—from the west,
and becomes suitable for boat navigation. At the
same time its course changes, and runs eastward for
about 12 miles; after which the stream again inclines
to the south, and keeping an E.S.E. direction for
14 or 15 miles, enters the Euphrates by five mouths
in about lat. 36° 37'. The course of the river measures probably about 65 miles.

The Koweik, or river of Aleppo (the Chalus of
Xenophon"), rises in the hills south of Ain-Tab.
Springing from two sources, one of which is known
as the Baloklu-Su, or "Fish River," it flows at first

---

[17] Arrian, *Exp. Al.* vii. 7.
[18] For a full account of the Sajur, see Chesney, *Euphrates Expedition*, vol. i. p. 419.
[19] *Anab.* i. 4, § 9.
[20] Ainsworth, *Travels in the Track of the Ten Thousand*, p. 63; Chesney, p. 412. Xenophon remarks that the Chalus was "full of large fish" (πλήρης ἰχθύων μεγάλων).

eastward, as if intending to join the Euphrates. On reaching the plain of Aleppo, however, near Sayyadok-Koi, it receives a tributary from the north, which gives its course a southern inclination; and from this point it proceeds in a south and south-westerly direction, winding along the shallow bed which it has scooped in the Aleppo plain, a distance of 60 miles, past Aleppo to Kinnisrin, near the foot of the Jebel-el-Sis." Here its further progress southward is barred, and it is forced to turn to the east along the foot of the mountain, which it skirts for eight or ten miles, finally entering the small lake or marsh of El Melak, in which it loses itself after a course of about 80 miles.

The Orontes, the great river of Syria, rises in the Buka'a—the deep valley known to the ancients as Cœle-Syria Proper—springing from a number of small brooks[1] which flow down from the Antilibanus range between lat. 34° 5′ and lat. 34° 12′. Its most remote source is near Yunin, about seven miles N.N.E. of Baalbek. This stream flows at first N.W. by W. into the plain, on reaching which it turns at a right angle to the north-east, and skirts the foot of the Antilibanus range as far as Lebweh, where, being joined by a larger stream from the south-east,[2] it takes its direction and flows N.W. and then N. across the plain to the foot of Lebanon. Here it receives the waters of a much more abundant fountain, which wells out from the roots of that range,[3] and is regarded

---

 See Chesney, pp. 412, 413, and Porter, *Handbook of Syria*, vol. ii. pp. 610, 611.

[1] See Chesney, *Euphrates Expedition*, vol. i. p. 304, and compare the excellent map in Mr. Porter's *Handbook of Syria*, from which much of the description in the text is taken.

[2] Mr. Porter himself regards this spring as the proper source of the Orontes. (*Handbook*, p. 575.)

[3] *Geographical Journal*, vol. vii.

by the Orientals as the true "head of the stream."[1] Thus increased the river flows northwards for a short space, after which it turns to the north-east, and runs in a deep cleft[2] along the base of Lebanon, pursuing this direction for 15 or 16 miles to a point beyond Ribleh, nearly in lat. 34° 30′. Here the course of the river again changes, becoming slightly west of north to the Lake of Hems (Buheiret-Hems), which is nine or ten miles below Ribleh. Issuing from the Lake of Hems about lat. 34° 43′, the Orontes once more flows to the north-east, and in five or six miles reaches Homs itself, which it leaves on its right bank. It then flows for twenty miles nearly due north, after which, on approaching Hamah (Hamath), it makes a slight bend to the east round the foot of Jebel Erbayn,[3] and then entering the rich pasture country of El-Ghab, runs north-west and north to the "Iron Bridge" (Jisr Hadid), in lat. 36° 11′. Its course thus far has been nearly parallel with the coast of the Mediterranean, and has lain between two ranges of mountains, the more western of which has shut it out from the sea. At Jisr Hadid the western mountains come to an end, and the Orontes, sweeping round their base, runs first west and then south-west down the broad valley of Antioch, in the midst of the most lovely scenery,[4] to the coast, which it reaches a

---

pp. 99, 100; vol. xxvi. p. 53; *Handbook of Syria*, p. 570. Col. Chesney erroneously places this fountain "at the foot of the Anti-Lebanon." (*Euphrates Expedition*, vol. i. l. s. c.)

[3] It is called the *Ain el Asy*, or "Fountain of the El Asy" (Orontes), and is perhaps the same with the *Ain* of Numbers xxxiv. 11.

[3] From 200 to 400 feet in depth. (Porter, *Handbook*, 1. s. c.)

[4] Chesney, p. 395.

[7] Dean Stanley says the scenery here has been compared to that of the Wye (*Sinai and Palestine*, p. 400). Col. Chesney speaks of "richly picturesque slopes;" "striking scenery;" "steep and wooded hills;" "banks adorned with the oleander, the arbutus, and other shrubs." (*Euphrates Expedition*, vol. i. p. 397.) Mr. Porter says, "The bridle-path along the bank

little above the 36th parallel, in long. 35° 55'. The course of the Orontes, exclusive of lesser windings, is about 200 miles. It is a considerable stream almost from its source.⁸ At Hamah, more than a hundred miles from its mouth, it is crossed by a bridge of thirteen arches.⁹ At Antioch it is fifty yards in width,¹⁰ and runs rapidly. The natives now call it the Nahr-el-Asy, or "Rebel River," either from its running in an opposite direction to all the other streams of the country,¹¹ or (more probably) from its violence and impetuosity.¹²

There is one tributary of the Orontes which deserves a cursory mention. This is the Lower Kara Su, or "Black River," which reaches it from the Aga Denghis, or Bahr-el-Abiyad, about five miles below Jisr Hadid and four or five above Antioch. This stream brings into the Orontes the greater part of the water that is drained from the southern side of Amanus. It is formed by a union of two rivers, the Upper Kara Su and the Afrin, which flow into the Aga Denghis (White Sea), or Lake of Antioch, from the north-west, the one entering it at its northern, the other at its eastern extremity. Both are considerable streams, and the Kara Su, on issuing from the lake, carries a greater body of water than the Orontes itself,¹³ and thus adds largely to the volume of that stream in its lower course, from the point of junction to the Mediterranean.

---

of the Orontes winds through luxuriant shrubberies. Tangled thickets of myrtle, oleander, and other flowering shrubs, make a gorgeous border to the stream." (*Handbook*, p. 602.) Only a little south of the Orontes, in this part of its course, was the celebrated Daphne.

⁸ Porter, *Handbook*, p. 576.

⁹ Burckhardt, *Travels in Syria*, p. 143.

¹⁰ Porter, p. 603.

¹¹ This is Mr. Porter's explanation (*Handbook*, p. 576).

¹² So Schwarz, as quoted by Dean Stanley (*Sinai and Palestine*, p. 276).

¹³ Chesney, *Euphrates Expedition*, vol. i. p. 395.

The Litany, or river of Tyre, rises from a source at no great distance from the head springs of the Orontes. The almost imperceptible water-shed of the Buka'a runs between Yunin and Baalbek, a few miles north of the latter;[14] and when it is once passed, the drainage of the water is southwards. The highest permanent fountain of the southern stream seems to be a small lake near Tel Hushben,[15] which lies about six miles to the south-west of the Ba'albek ruins. Springing from this source the Litany flows along the lower Buka'a in a direction which is generally a little west of south, receiving on either side a number of streamlets and rills from Libanus and Antilibanus, and giving out in its turn numerous canals for irrigation, which fertilize the thirsty soil. As the stream descends with numerous windings, but still with the same general course, the valley of the Buka'a contracts more and more, till finally it terminates in a gorge, down which thunders the Litany—a gorge a thousand feet or more in depth, and so narrow, that in one place it is actually bridged over by masses of rock which have fallen from the jagged sides.[16] Narrower and deeper grows the gorge, and the river chafes and foams through it,[17] gradually working itself round to the west, and so clearing a way through the very roots of Lebanon to the low coast tract, across which it meanders slowly,[18] as if wearied with its long struggle, before finally emptying itself into the sea. The course of the Litany may be roughly estimated at from 70 to 75 miles.

---

[14] Porter, *Handbook*, p. 575. The elevation of the water-shed above the sea level is about 3200 feet.
[15] Burckhardt, *Travels in Syria*, p. 10; Chesney, *Euphrates Expedition*, vol. I. p. 398.
[16] Porter, p. 571; Robinson, *Later Researches*, p. 423.
[17] Robinson, *Later Researches*, pp. 386, 387.
[18] Chesney, l. s. c.

The Barada, or river of Damascus, rises in the plain of Zebdany—the very centre of the Antilibanus. It has its real permanent source in a small nameless lake[19] in the lower part of the plain, about lat. 33° 41'; but in winter it is fed by streams flowing from the valley above, especially by one which rises in lat. 33° 46', near the small hamlet of Ain Hawar.[20] The course of the Barada from the small lake is at first towards the east; but it soon sweeps round and flows southward for about four miles to the lower end of the plain, after which it again turns to the east and enters a romantic glen, running between high cliffs,[21] and cutting through the main ridge of the Antilibanus between the Zebdany plain and Suk—the Abila of the ancients.[22] From Suk the river flows through a narrow but lovely valley, in a course which has a general direction of south-east, past Ain Fijeh (where its waters are greatly increased),[23] through a series of gorges and glens, to the point where the roots of the Antilibanus sink down upon the plain, when it bursts forth from the mountains and scatters.[24] Channels are drawn from it on either side, and its waters are spread far and wide over the Merj, which it covers with fine trees and splendid herbage. One branch passes right through the city, cutting it in half. Others irrigate the gardens and orchards both to the north and to the south. Beyond the town the ten-

---

[19] Porter, p. 557. The elevation of the plain of Zebdany is about 3500 feet.

[20] Col. Chesney makes this the proper source of the Barada (*Euphrates Expedition*, vol. i. p. 502). Its true character is pointed out by Mr. Porter (*Handbook*, p. 558). Compare Robinson, *Later Researches*, p. 487.

[21] Porter, p. 557.

[22] On the proofs of this identity see Robinson, *Later Researches*, pp. 480-484.

[23] Porter, p. 555; Robinson, p. 476. The quantity of water given out by this fountain considerably exceeds that carried by the Barada above it.

[24] See the excellent description in Dean Stanley's *Sinai and Palestine*, p. 402.

dency to division still continues. The river, weakened greatly through the irrigation, separates into three main channels, which flow with divergent courses towards the east, and terminate in two large swamps or lakes, the Bahret-esh-Shurkiyeh and the Bahret-el-Kibliyeh,* at a distance of sixteen or seventeen miles from the city. The Barada is a short stream, its entire course from the plain of Zebdany not much exceeding forty miles.¹

The Jordan is commonly regarded as flowing from two sources in the Huleh or plain immediately above Lake Merom, one at Banias (the ancient Paneas), the other at Tel-el-Kady, which marks the site of Laish or Dan.² But the true highest present source of the river is the spring near Hasbeiya, called Neba-es-Hasbany, or Ras-en-Neba.³ This spring rises in the torrent-course known as the Wady-el-Teim, which descends from the north-western flank of Hermon, and runs nearly parallel with the great gorge of the Litany, having a direction from north-east to south-west. The water wells forth in abundance from the foot of a volcanic bluff, called Ras-el-Anjah, lying directly north of Hasbeiya, and is immediately used to turn a mill. The course of the streamlet is very slightly west of south down the Wady to the Huleh plain, where it is joined, and multiplied sevenfold,⁴

---

* Porter, in the *Bibliotheca Sacra*, April, 1854, pp. 820-344; Robinson, *Later Researches*, pp. 450, 451.
¹ Mr. Porter estimates the course of the Barada, from the place where it leaves the mountains to the two lakes, at 20 miles. (*Handbook*, p. 490.) Its course among the mountains seems to be of about the same length.
² These sources have been described by many writers. The best description is perhaps that of Stanley (*Sinai and Palestine*, pp. 880-391); but compare Robinson, *Later Researches*, pp. 390 and 408; and Porter, *Handbook*, pp. 436 and 445.
³ Robinson, p. 378; Porter, pp. 451, 452; Lynch, *Narrative of an Expedition to the Dead Sea*, p. 318.
⁴ Dr. Robinson estimates the volume of the Banias source as double

by the streams from Banias and Tel-el-Kady, becoming at once worthy of the name of river. Hence it runs almost due south to the Merom lake, which it enters in lat. 33° 7', through a reedy and marshy tract which it is difficult to penetrate.[5] Issuing from Merom in lat. 33° 3', the Jordan flows at first sluggishly[6] southward to "Jacob's Bridge," passing which it proceeds in the same direction, with a much swifter current, down the depressed and narrow cleft between Merom and Tiberias, descending at the rate of fifty feet in a mile,[7] and becoming (as has been said) a sort of "continuous waterfall."[8] Before reaching Tiberias, its course bends slightly to the west of south for about two miles, and it pours itself into that "sea" in about lat. 32° 53'. Quitting the sea in lat. 32° 42', it finally enters the tract called the Ghor, the still lower chasm or cleft which intervenes between Tiberias and the upper end of the Dead Sea. Here the descent of the stream becomes comparatively gentle, not much exceeding three feet per mile; for though the direct distance between the two lakes is less than seventy miles, and the entire fall above 600 feet, which would seem to give a de-

---

that of the Hasbeiya stream, and the volume of the Tel-el-Kady fountain as double that of the Banias one. (*Later Researches*, p. 395.)

[5] Robinson, *Researches*, vol. iii. p. 340.

[6] See Col. Wikleubruch's account in the *Journal of the Geographical Society*, vol. xx. p. 228; and compare Lynch, *Narrative*, p. 311; Porter, *Handbook*, p. 427. Col. Chesney exactly inverts the real facts of the case. (*Euphrates Expedition*, vol. i. p. 400.)

[7] The fall between the lakes of Merom and Tiberias appears to be from 600 to 700 feet. The direct distance is little more than 9 miles. As the river does not here meander much, its entire course can scarcely exceed 13 or 14 miles. According to these numbers, the fall would be between 43 and 54 feet per mile.

[8] Col. Wikleubruch, in *Geographical Journal*, vol. xx. p. 228. Compare Porter, *Handbook*, p. 427; Lynch, *Narrative*, p. 311; Petermann, in *Geographical Journal*, vol. xviii. p. 103; &c.

scent of nine or ten feet a mile, yet, as the course of the river throughout this part of its career is tortuous in the extreme,⁹ the fall is really not greater than above indicated. Still it is sufficient to produce as many as twenty-seven rapids,¹⁰ or at the rate of one to every seven miles. In this part of its course the Jordan receives two important tributaries, each of which seems to deserve a few words.

The Jarmuk, or Sheriat-el-Mandhur, anciently the Hieromax, drains the water, not only from Gaulonitis or Jaulan, the country immediately east and south-east of the sea of Tiberias, but also from almost the whole of the Hauran.¹¹ At its mouth it is 130 feet wide,¹² and in the winter it brings down a great body of water into the Jordan. In summer, however, it shrinks up into an inconsiderable brook, having no more remote sources than the perennial springs at Mazarib, Dilly, and one or two other places on the plateau of Jaulan. It runs through a fertile country, and has generally a deep course far below the surface of the plain; ere falling into the Jordan it makes its way through a wild ravine, between rugged cliffs of basalt, which are in places upwards of a hundred feet in height.

The Zurka, or Jabbok, is a stream of the same character with the Hieromax, but of inferior dimensions and importance. It drains a considerable portion of the land of Gilead, but has no very remote sources,

---

⁹ The 70 miles of actual length are increased by these multitudinous windings to 200. (*Geograph. Journal*, vol. xviii. p. 04, note; Stanley, *Sinai and Palestine*, p. 277.) The remark of the English sailors deserves to be remembered—"The Jordan is the crookedest river what is." (*Journal of the Asiatic Society*, vol. xviii. p. 113.) ¹⁰ Stanley, p. 276.
¹¹ Porter, *Handbook*, p. 321.
¹² Ibid., l. & c. Mr. Porter is the authority for this entire notice of the Hieromax. He is far more accurate than Col. Chesney. (*Euphrates Expedition*, vol. i. p. 401.)

and in summer only carries water through a few miles of its lower course.[13] In winter, on the contrary, it is a roaring stream with a strong current, and sometimes cannot be forded. The ravine through which it flows is narrow, deep, and in some places wild. Throughout nearly its whole course it is fringed by thickets of cane and oleander, while above, its banks are clothed with forests of oak.

The Jordan receives the Hieromax about four or five miles below the point where it issues from the sea of Tiberias, and the Jabbok about half-way between that lake and the Dead Sea. Augmented by these streams, and others of less importance from the mountains on either side, it becomes a river of considerable size, being opposite Beth-shan (*Beisan*) 140 feet wide, and three feet deep,[14] and averaging, in its lower course, a width of ninety with a depth of eight or nine feet.[15] Its entire course, from the fountain near Hasbeiya to the Dead Sea, including the passage of the two lakes through which it flows, is, if we exclude meanders, about 130, if we include them, about 260 miles. It is calculated to pour into the Dead Sea 6,090,000 tons of water daily.[16]

Besides these rivers the Babylonian territory comprised a number of important lakes. Of these some of the more eastern have been described in a former volume: as the Bahr-i-Nedjif in Lower Chaldæa,[17] and the Lake of Khatouniyeh in the tract between the Sinjar and the Khabour.[18] It was chiefly, however,

---

[13] Porter, *Handbook*, p. 310; *Biblical Dictionary*, vol. i. p. 909.
[14] Chesney, p. 401; Irby and Mangles, p. 304; Burckhardt, *Travels in Syria*, p. 345.
[15] Petermann, in the *Journal of the Geographical Society*, vol. xviii. p. 95.
[16] Chesney, l. s. c.
[17] See vol. i. p. 18.
[18] Ibid. p. 238.

towards the west that sheets of water abounded: the principal of these were the Sabakhah, the Bahr-el-Melak, and the Lake of Antioch in Upper Syria; the Bahr-el-Kades, or Lake of Hems, in the central region: and the Damascus lakes, the Lake of Merom, the Sea of Galilee or Tiberias, and the Dead Sea, in the regions lying furthest to the south. Of these the greater number were salt, and of little value, except as furnishing the salt of commerce; but four—the Lake of Antioch, the Bahr-el-Kades, the Lake Merom, and the Sea of Galilee—were fresh-water basins lying upon the courses of streams which ran through them; and these not only diversified the scenery by their clear bright aspect, but were of considerable value to the inhabitants, as furnishing them with many excellent sorts of fish.

Of the salt lakes the most eastern was the Sabakhah. This is a basin of long and narrow form, lying on and just below the 36th parallel. It is situated on the southern route from Balis to Aleppo, and is nearly equally distant between the two places. Its length is from twelve to thirteen miles; and its width, where it is broadest, is about five miles. It receives from the north the waters of the Nahr-el-Dhahab, or "Golden River" (which has by some been identified with the Daradax of Xenophon[1]), and from the west two or three insignificant streams, which empty themselves into its western extremity. The lake produces a large quantity of salt, especially after wet seasons, which is collected and sold by the inhabitants of the surrounding country.[2]

---

[1] So Col. Chesney (*Euphrates Expedition*, vol. i. p. 415). Mr. Ainsworth combats the view, and endeavours to show that the Daradax was a branch of the Euphrates. (*Travels in the Track*, pp. 65, 66.)

[2] Chesney, l. s. c.

The Bahr-el-Melak, the lake which absorbs the Koweik, or river of Aleppo, is less than twenty miles distant from Lake Sabakhah, which it very much resembles in its general character. Its ordinary length is about nine miles, and its width three or four; but in winter it is greatly swollen by the rains, and at that time it spreads out so widely that its circumference sometimes exceeds fifty miles.³ Much salt is drawn from its bed in the dry season, and a large part of Syria is hence supplied with the commodity. The lake is covered with small islands, and greatly frequented by aquatic birds—geese, ducks, flamingoes, and the like.

The lakes in the neighbourhood of Damascus are three in number, and are all of a very similar type. They are indeterminate in size and shape, changing with the wetness or dryness of the season; and it is possible that sometimes they may be all united in one.⁴ The most northern, which is called the Bahret-esh-Shurkiyeh, receives about half the surplus water of the Barada, together with some streamlets from the outlying ranges of Antilibanus towards the north.⁵ The central one, called the Bahret-el-Kibliyeh, receives the rest of the Barada water, which enters it by three or four branches on its northern and western sides. The most southern, known as Bahret-Hijaneh, is the receptacle for the stream of the Awaaj, and takes also the water from the northern parts of the Ledjah, or region of Argob. The three lakes are in

---

³ Chesney (*Euphrates Expedition*, vol. i. p. 413).
⁴ Only one lake is recognised by the early travellers and map-makers. Even Col. Chesney, writing in 1850, knows apparently but of one. (*Euphrates Expedition*, vol. i. p. 502.) The three lakes were, I believe, first noticed by Mr. Porter, who gave an account of them in the *Journal of the Geographical Society*, vol. xxvi. pp. 43-46, and in the *Journal of Sacred Literature*, vol. iv. pp. 246-259.
⁵ See Mr. Porter's *Handbook*, p. 497.

the same line—a line which runs from N.N.E. to
S.S.W. They are, or at least were recently, separated by tracts of dry land from two to four miles
broad.⁶ Dense thickets of tall reeds surround them,
and in summer almost cover their surface.⁷ Like the
Bahr-el-Melak, they are a home for water-fowl, which
flock to them in enormous numbers.⁸

By far the largest and most important of the salt
lakes is the Great Lake of the South—the Bahr Lut
("Sea of Lot"), or Dead Sea. This sheet of water,
which has always attracted the special notice and observation of travellers, has of late years been scientifically surveyed by officers of the American navy; and
its shape, its size, and even its depth, are thus known
with accuracy.⁹ The Dead Sea is of an oblong form,
and would be of a very regular contour, were it not for
a remarkable projection from its eastern shore near its
southern extremity. In this place, a long and low
peninsula, shaped like a human foot,[10] projects into
the lake, filling up two-thirds of its width, and thus
dividing the expanse of water into two portions,
which are connected by a long and somewhat narrow
passage.[11] The entire length of the sea, from north

---

⁶ See the map of Syria attached to the *Handbook*, and likewise to Dr. Robinson's *Later Researches*, ad fin.

⁷ Porter, *Handbook*, p. 490.

⁸ Ibid. p. 497.

⁹ Great credit is due to the Americans for the spirit which conceived and carried out Captain Lynch's Expedition. The results of the Expedition have been made public partly by means of the *Official Report* published at Baltimore in 1852, but in more detail by Captain Lynch's private *Narrative*, published at London in 1849. An excellent digest of the information contained in these volumes, as well as of the accounts of others, has been compiled by Mr. George Grove, and published in the third volume of Dr. Smith's *Biblical Dictionary*, pp. 1175-1187.

[10] The natives call the peninsula the *Lisan*, comparing its shape with that of the human "tongue."

[11] The passage is narrowed not only by the projecting "tongue," but also by the fact that directly opposite the tongue there is an extensive beach, composed of chalk, marl, and gypsum, which projects into the natural basin of the lake a distance of two miles, while the

to south, is 40 miles; its greatest width, between its eastern and its western shores, is 10¼ miles. The whole area is estimated at 250 geographical square miles." Of this space 174 square miles belong to the northern portion of the lake (the true "Sea"), 29 to the narrow channel, and 46 to the southern portion, which has been called "the back-water," [13] or "the lagoon." [14] The most remarkable difference between the two portions of the lake is the contrast they present as to depth. While the depth of the northern portion is from 600 feet, at a short distance from the mouth of the Jordan, to 800, 1000, 1200, and even 1300 feet further down, the depth of the lagoon is nowhere more than 12 or 13 feet; and in places it is so shallow that it has been found possible, in some seasons, to ford the whole way across from one side to the other." The peculiarities of the Dead Sea, as compared with other lakes, are its depression below the sea-level, its buoyancy, and its extreme saltness. The degree of the depression is not yet certainly known; but there is reason to believe that it is at least as much as 1300 feet,[16] whereas no other lake is known to be depressed more than 570

---

tongue projects about six. Thus the channel is reduced to two miles, or in dry seasons to one. (See Irby and Mangles, *Travels*, p. 454.)

[12] Grove, in *Biblical Dictionary*, vol. i. p. 1174. All these measurements are, it must be remembered, liable to a certain amount of derangement according to the time of year and the wetness or dryness of the season. Lines of drift-wood have been remarked, showing in places a difference of several miles in the water edge at different seasons. (Robinson, *Researches*, vol. ii. pp. 188 and 672.)

[13] Irby and Mangles, *Travels*, passim.

[14] Grove, in *Biblical Dictionary*, vol. i. p. 1174.

[15] Seetzen, *Works*, vol. i. p. 428; vol. ii. p. 358; Lynch, *Narrative*, p. 199; Robinson, *Researches*, vol. ii. p. 235.

[16] Setting aside a single barometrical observation — that of Von Schubert in 1857 — all the other estimates, however made, give a depression varying between 1200 and 1450 feet (See Mr. Grove's note, *Biblical Dictionary*, vol. i. p. 1175.)

feet." The buoyancy and the saltness are not so wholly unparalleled. The waters of Lake Urumiyeh are probably as salt and as buoyant;[18] those of Lake Elton in the steppe east of the Wolga, and of certain other Russian lakes, appear to be even salter.[19] But with these few exceptions (if they are exceptions), the Dead Sea water must be pronounced to be the heaviest and saltest water known to us. More than one-fourth of its weight is solid matter held in solution. Of this solid matter nearly one-third is common salt, which is more than twice as much as is contained in the waters of the ocean.

Of the fresh-water lakes the largest and most important is the Sea of Tiberias. This sheet of water is of an oval shape, with an axis, like that of the Dead Sea, very nearly due north and south. Its greatest length is about thirteen, and its greatest width about six miles.[20] Its extreme depth, so far as has been yet ascertained, is 27½ fathoms, or 165 feet.[21] The Jordan flows into its upper end turbid and muddy, and issues forth at its southern extremity clear and pellucid. It receives also the waters of a considerable number of small streams and springs, some of which are warm and brackish; yet its own water is always sweet, cool, and transparent, and laving everywhere a shelving pebbly beach, has a bright sparkling appearance.[22] The banks are lofty, and in general destitute of ver-

---

[17] The lake Asul, on the Somauli coast, opposite Aden, is said to be depressed to this extent. (Murchison, in *Geographical Journal*, vol. xiv. p. cxvi.)

[18] Compare *Geograph. Journal*, vol. x. p. 7.

[19] The waters of Lake Elton (*Jel-tonskoé*) contain from 24 to 28 per cent. of solid matter, while those of the "Red Sea" near Perekop contain 37 per cent. The waters of the Dead Sea contain about 26 per cent.

[20] Porter, *Handbook*, p. 418; Stanley, *Sinai and Palestine*, p. 302.

[21] Lynch, *Narrative*, p. 95.

[22] Porter, in *Biblical Dictionary*, vol. i. p. 870.

dure. What exactly is the amount of depression below the level of the Mediterranean remains still, to some extent, uncertain, but it is probably not much less than 700 feet.[2] Now, as formerly, the lake produces an abundance of fish, which are pronounced, by those who have partaken of them, to be "delicious."[1]

Nine miles above the Sea of Tiberias, on the course of the same stream, is the far smaller basin known now as the Bahr-el-Huleh, and anciently (perhaps) as Merom.[2] This is a mountain tarn, varying in size as the season is wet or dry,[3] but never apparently more than about seven miles long, by five or six broad.[4] It is situated at the lower extremity of the plain called the Huleh, and is almost entirely surrounded by flat marshy ground, thickly set with reeds and canes, which make the lake itself almost unapproachable.[5] The depth of the Huleh is not known. It is a favourite resort of aquatic birds, and is said to contain an abundant supply of fish.[6]

---

[2] Schubert estimated the depression of the Sea of Tiberias at 535 Paris feet (*Reise*, vol. iii. p. 231); Berton at 230·3 mètres, or about 700 feet (*Bulletin de la Société de Géogr.* Oct. 1850). Lynch, in his *Narrative* (ed. of 1852), Preface, p. vii., calls it 312 feet; and hence probably Stanley's estimate of 300 (*Sinai and Palestine*, p. 270). Mr. Porter, in 1860, calls it 700 feet (*Biblical Dictionary*, vol. i. p. 676). Mr. Ffoulkes, in the same year, says it is 653 feet (ibid. p. 1130). It is to be hoped that a scientific survey of the whole of Palestine will be made before many years are over, and this, with other similar questions, finally settled.

[1] Lynch, *Narrative*, p. 96.

[2] This has been generally assumed; but there are really very slight grounds for the assumption. Merom is mentioned but in one passage of Scripture (Josh. xi. 5-7); and then not at all distinctly as a lake. Josephus calls the Bahr-el-Huleh the Semechonitis.

[3] See the remarks of Col. Wildenbruch in the *Journal of the Geographical Society*, vol. xx. p. 228.

[4] Dean Stanley gives the dimensions of the lake as 7 miles by 6 (*Sinai and Palestine*, p. 382); Col. Chesney as 7 miles by 3½ (*Euphrates Expedition*, vol. i. p. 399, note); Mr. Porter as 4½ miles by 3½ (*Handbook*, p. 435); Dr. Robinson as from 4 to 5 geographical miles by 4 (*Researches*, vol. iii. p. 430); Mr. Grove as 3 miles in each direction (*Biblical Dictionary*, vol. ii. p. 333).

[5] See above, p. 278, note [4].

[6] Chesney, p. 400.

THE SEA OF ANTIOCH.

The Bahr-el-Kades, or Lake of Hems, lies on the course of the Orontes, about 130 miles N.N.E. of Merom, and nearly the same distance south of the Lake of Antioch. It is a small sheet of water, not more than six or eight miles long, and only two or three wide,[1] running in the same direction with the course of the river, which here turns from north to north-east. According to Abulfeda[8] and some other writers, it is mainly, if not wholly, artificial, owing its origin to a dam or embankment across the stream, which is from four to five hundred yards in length, and about twelve or fourteen feet high.[9] In Abulfeda's time the construction of the embankment was ascribed to Alexander the Great, and the lake consequently was not regarded as having had any existence in Babylonian times; but traditions of this kind are little to be trusted, and it is quite possible that the work above mentioned, constructed apparently with a view to irrigation, may really belong to a very much earlier age.

Finally, in Northern Syria, 115 miles north of the Bahr-el-Kades, and about 60 miles N.W.b.W. of the Bahr-el-Melak, is the Bahr-el-Abyad (White Lake), or Sea of Antioch. This sheet of water is a parallelogram,[10] the angles of which face the cardinal points: in its greater diameter it extends somewhat more than ten miles, while it is about seven miles across.[11]

---

[1] Pococke gives the dimensions of the lake of Hems as 8 miles by 3 (*Description of the East*, vol. i. p. 140); Col. Chesney makes them 6 miles by 2 (*Euphrates Expedition*, vol. i. p. 394). Dr. Robinson says the lake is "two hours in length by one in breadth" (*Later Researches*, p. 549), or about 6 miles by 3.

[8] *Tabulæ Syriæ*, ed. Köhler, p. 157.
[9] Robinson, *Later Researches*, l. c.
[10] Chesney, p. 396.
[11] These dimensions, given by Ikenell (*Illustrations of the Expedition of Cyrus*, p. 66), seem to be approved by Mr. Ainsworth (*Travels in the Track*, p. 82, note), who himself explored the lake.

Its depth on the western side, where it approaches the mountains, is six or eight feet; but elsewhere it is generally more shallow, not exceeding three or four feet." It lies in a marshy plain called El-Umk, and is thickly fringed with reeds round the whole of its circumference. From the silence of antiquity,

The Sea of Antioch, from the East.

some writers have imagined that it did not exist in ancient times;[13] but the observations of scientific travellers are opposed to this theory.[14] The lake abounds with fish of several kinds, and the fishery attracts and employs a considerable number of the natives who dwell near it.[15]

Besides these lakes there were contained within

---

[12] Chesney, *Euphrates Expedition*, vol. i. p. 396.
[13] Rennell, *Illustrations of the Expedition of Cyrus*, p. 65.
[14] Ainsworth, *Researches in Mesopotamia*, p. 299.
[15] Chesney, p. 397.

the limits of the Empire a number of petty tarns, which do not merit particular description. Such were the Bahr-el-Taka,[14] and other small lakes on the right bank of the middle Orontes, the Birket-el-Limun in the Lebanon,[15] and the Birket-er-Ram[16] on the southern flank of Hermon. It is unnecessary, however, to pursue this subject any further. But a few words must be added on the chief cities of the Empire, before this chapter is brought to a conclusion.

The cities of the Empire may be divided into those of the dominant country and those of the provinces. Those of the dominant country were, for the most part, identical with the towns already described as belonging to the ancient Chaldæa. Besides Babylon itself, there flourished in the Babylonian period the cities of Borsippa, Dumba, Sippara or Sepharvaim, Opis, Psittacé, Cutha, Orchoë or Erech, and Diridotis or Teredon. The sites of most of these have been described in a former volume;[17] but it remains to state briefly the positions of some few which were either new creations or comparatively undistinguished in the earlier times.

Opis, a town of sufficient magnitude to attract the attention of Herodotus,[18] was situated on the left or east bank of the Tigris, near the point where the Diyaleh or Gyndes joined the main river. Its position was south of the Gyndes embouchure, and it might be reckoned as lying upon either river.[19] The

---

[14] Famous for its abundant fish. (Chesney, p. 395.)
[15] Robinson, *Later Researches*, p. 548.
[16] *Journal of Asiatic Society*, vol. xvi. p. 8; Lynch, *Official Report*, p. 110. This is probably the ancient Phiale, which was believed to supply the fountain at Banias. (Joseph. *B. J.* iii. 10, § 7.)
[17] See vol. i. pp. 26, 27.
[18] Herod. i. 189. Xenophon calls it "a great city" (πόλις μεγάλη, *Anab.* ii. 4, § 25). Strabo says it had a considerable trade (xvi. 1, § 9).
[19] Herodotus, Strabo, and Arrian

true name of the place—that which it bears in the cuneiform inscriptions—was Hupiya; and its site is probably marked by the ruins at Khafaji, near Baghdad, which place is thought to retain, in a corrupted form, the original appellation.[21] Paittacé or Sitacé,[22] the town which gave name to the province of Sittacéné,[23] was in the near neighbourhood of Opis, lying on the same side of the Tigris, but lower down, at least as low as the modern fort of the Zobeid chief. Its exact site has not been as yet discovered. Teredon, or Diridotis, appears to have been first founded by Nebuchadnezzar.[24] It lay on the coast of the Persian Gulf, a little west of the mouth of the Euphrates, and was protected by a quay, or a breakwater, from the high tides that rolled in from the Indian Ocean. There is great difficulty in identifying its site, owing to the extreme uncertainty as to the exact position of the coast-line, and of the course of the river, in the time of Nebuchadnezzar. Probably it should be sought about Zobair, or a little further inland.

The chief provincial cities were Susa and Badaca in Susiana; Anat, Sirki, and Carchemish, on the Middle Euphrates; Sidikan on the Khabour; Harran on the Bilik; Hamath, Damascus,[25] and Jerusalem,

---

(*Exp. Alex.* vii. 7) place it on the Tigris. Xenophon places it on the Physcus (*Hupuako*) or Diyaleh.

[21] Sir H. Rawlinson in the author's *Herodotus* (vol. i. p. 261, note *, 2nd edition).

[22] Sitacé is the form commonly used by the Greeks (Xen. *Anab.* ii. 4, § 13; Ælian, *Hist. An.* xvi. 42; &c.); but Stephen of Byzantium has Psittacé. In the cuneiform inscriptions the name is read as *Patrita*, without the Scythic guttural ending.

[23] Sittacéné is made a province of Babylonia by Strabo (xv. 3, § 12). In Ptolemy it is a province of Assyria (*Geograph.* vi. 1).

[24] Abydenus ap. Euseb. *Præp. Ev.* ix. 41.

[25] Damascus, though destroyed by Tiglath-Pileser II., probably soon rose from its ruins, and again became an important city.

in Inner Syria; Tyre, Sidon, Ashdod, Ascalon, and Gaza, upon the coast. Of these, Susa was undoubtedly the most important: indeed it deserves to be regarded as the second city of the Empire. Here, between the two arms of the Choaspes, on a noble and well-watered plain, backed at the distance of twenty-five miles by a lofty mountain range, the fresh breezes from which tempered the summer heats, was the ancient palace of the Kissian kings, proudly placed upon a lofty platform or mound, and commanding a wide prospect of the rich pastures at its base, which extended northwards to the roots of the hills, and in every other direction as far as the eye could reach."[27] Clustered at the foot of the palace mound, more especially on its eastern side, lay the ancient town, the foundation of the traditional Memnon,[1] who led an army to the defence of Troy.[2] The pure and sparkling water of the Choaspes[3]—a drink fit for kings[4]—flowed near, while around grew palms, konars, and lemon-trees,[5] the plain beyond waving with green grass and golden corn. It may be suspected that the Babylonian kings, who certainly maintained a palace at this place,[6] and sent high officers of their court to "do their business" there,[7] made it their occasional residence, exchanging,

---

[27] For a good description of the situation of Susa see Loftus, *Chaldæa and Susiana*, p. 347. Compare the *Journal of the Geographical Society*, vol. ix. pp. 68-71.

[1] Herod. v. 53. Strabo ascribes the foundation to Tithonus, Memnon's father (xv. 3, § 2).

[2] Diod. Sic. ii. 22; iv. 75; Pausan. x. 31, § 2.

[3] *Geographical Journal*, vol. ix. p. 89.

[4] Herod. i. 188; Plutarch, *De Exsil.* p. 601, D.; Athen. *Deipnosoph.* ii. 25; p. 171. Milton's statement—

"There flows by Choaspes' amber stream,
The drink of none but kings"—

is an exaggeration; for which, however, there is some classical authority. (Solinus, *Polyhist.* § 41.)

[5] Loftus, *Chaldæa and Susiana*, l. s. c.

[6] Dan. viii. 2.

[7] Ibid. verse 27.

in summer and early autumn, the heats and swamps of Babylon for the comparatively dry and cool region at the base of the Luristan hills. But, however this may have been, at any rate Susa, long the capital of a kingdom little inferior to Babylon itself, must have been the first of the provincial cities, surpassing all the rest at once in size and in magnificence.

Among the other cities, Carchemish on the Upper Euphrates, Tyre upon the Syrian coast, and Ashdod on the borders of Egypt, held the highest place. Carchemish, which has been wrongly identified with Circesium,* lay certainly high up the river,* and most likely occupied some site near the modern Balis, which is in lat. 36° nearly. It was the key of Syria on the east, commanding the ordinary passage of the Euphrates, and being the only great city in this quarter. Tyre, which had by this time surpassed its rival, Sidon,* was the chief of all the maritime towns; and its possession gave the mastery of the Eastern Mediterranean to the power which could acquire and maintain it. Ashdod was the key of Syria upon the south, being a place of great strength,* and commanding the coast route between Palestine and Egypt, which was usually pursued by armies. It is scarcely too much to say that the possession of Ashdod, Tyre, and Carchemish, involved the lordship of

---

* There never was much ground for this identification, since Carchemish, "the fort of Chanush," is clearly quite a distinct name from Cir-cesium. The latter is perhaps a mode of expressing the Assyrian Nirki.
* See above, vol. II. p. 316.
* The importance of Tyre at this time is strongly marked by the prophecies of Ezekiel (xxvi. 3-21; xxvii. 2-36; xxviii. 2-19, &c.), which barely mention Sidon (xxviii. 21-23; xxxii. 30).
* The strength of Ashdod, or Azotus, was signally shown by its long resistance to the arms of Psammetichus (Herod. ii. 157). The name is thought to be connected with the Arabic *shdeed*, "strong."

Syria, which could not be permanently retained except by the occupation of those cities.

The countries by which the Babylonian Empire was bounded were Persia on the east, Media and her dependencies on the north, Arabia on the south, and Egypt at the extreme south-west. Directly to the west she had no neighbour, her territory being on that side washed by the Mediterranean.

Of Persia, which must be described at length in the next volume, since it was the seat of Empire during the Fifth Monarchy, no more need be said here than that it was for the most part a rugged and sterile country, apt to produce a brave and hardy race, but incapable of sustaining a large population. A strong barrier separated it from the great Mesopotamian lowland;[12] and the Babylonians, by occupying a few easily defensible passes, could readily prevent a Persian army from debouching on their fertile plains. On the other hand, the natural strength of the region is so great, that in the hands of brave and active men its defence is easy; and the Babylonians were not likely, if an aggressive spirit led to their pressing eastward, to make any serious impression in this quarter, or ever greatly to advance their frontier.

To Media, the power which bordered her upon the north, Babylonia, on the contrary, lay wholly open. The Medes, possessing Assyria and Armenia, with the Upper Tigris valley, and probably the Mons Masius, could at any time, with the greatest ease, have marched armies into the low country, and resumed the contest in which Assyria was engaged for

---

[12] See above, vol. i. p. 250.

so many hundred years with the great people of the south. On this side nature had set no obstacles; and, if danger threatened, resistance had to be made by means of those artificial works which are specially suited for flat countries. Long lines of wall, broad dykes, huge reservoirs, by means of which large tracts may be laid under water, form the natural resort in such a case; and to such defences as these alone, in addition to her armies, could Babylonia look in case of a quarrel with the Medes. On this side, however, she for many years felt no fear. Political arrangements and family ties connected her with the Median reigning house;[u] and she looked to her northern neighbour as an ally upon whom she might depend for aid, rather than as a rival whose ambitious designs were to be watched and baffled.

Babylonia lay open also on the side of Arabia. Here, however, the nature of the country is such that population must be always sparse; and the habits of the people are opposed to that political union which can alone make a race really formidable to others. Once only in their history, under the excitement of a religious frenzy, have the Arabs issued forth from the great peninsula on an errand of conquest. In general they are content to vex and harass without seriously alarming their neighbours. The vast spaces and arid character of the peninsula are adverse to the collection and the movement of armies; the love of independence cherished by the several tribes indisposes them to union; the affection for the nomadic life, which is strongly felt, disinclines

---

[u] Supra, pp. 189, 194, 195, &c.

them to the occupation of conquests. Arabia, as a conterminous power, is troublesome, but rarely dangerous: one section of the nation may almost always be played off against another: if "their hand is against every man," "every man's hand" is also "against them;"¹⁴ blood-feuds divide and decimate their tribes, which are ever turning their swords against each other; their neighbours generally wish them ill, and will fall upon them, if they can take them at a disadvantage; it is only under very peculiar circumstances, such as can very rarely exist, that they are likely even to attempt anything more serious than a plundering inroad. Babylonia, consequently, though open to attack on the side of the south as well as on that of the north, had little to fear from either quarter. The friendliness of her northern neighbours, and the practical weakness of her southern ones, were equal securities against aggression; and thus on her two largest and most exposed frontiers the Empire dreaded no attack.

But it was otherwise in the far south-west. Here the Empire bordered upon Egypt, a rich and populous country, which at all times covets Syria and is often strong enough to seize and hold it in possession.¹⁵ The natural frontier is moreover weak, no other barrier separating between Africa and Asia than a narrow desert, which has never yet proved a serious obstacle to an army.¹ From the side of Egypt, if

---

¹⁴ Gen. xvi. 12.
¹⁵ Egypt appears to have held Syria during the 18th and 19th dynasties (ab. B.C. 1500-1250), and to have disputed its possession with Assyria from about B.C. 723 to B.C. 670. In later times the Ptolemies, and in still later the Fatimite Caliphs, ruled Syria from Egypt. In our own days the conquest was nearly effected by Ibrahim Pasha.

¹ The Egyptian armies readily crossed it during the 18th and 19th dynasties—the Assyrians under Sar-

from no other quarter, Babylonia might expect to
have trouble. Here she inherited from her prede-
cessor, Assyria, an old hereditary feud, which might
at any time break out into active hostility. Here was
an ancient, powerful, and well-organised kingdom
upon her borders, with claims upon that portion of
her territory which it was most difficult for her to
defend effectively.¹ By sea² and by land equally the
strip of Syrian coast lay open to the arms of Egypt,
who was free to choose her time and pour her hosts
into the country when the attention of Babylon was
directed to some other quarter. The physical and
political circumstances alike pointed to hostile transactions between Babylon and her south-western neighbour. Whether destruction would come from this
quarter, or from some other, it would have been impossible to predict. Perhaps, on the whole, it may
be said that Babylon might have been expected to
contend successfully with Egypt—that she had little
to fear from Arabia—that against Persia Proper it
might have been anticipated that she would be able
to defend herself—but that she lay at the mercy of
Media. The Babylonian Empire was in truth an
Empire upon sufferance. From the time of its establishment with the consent of the Medes, the Medes
might at any time have destroyed it. The dynastic
tie alone prevented this result. When that tie was
snapped, and when moreover, by the victories of Cyrus,

---

gon and his successors—the Persians under Cambyses, Darius, Artaxerxes Longimanus, Artaxerxes Mnemon, and Artaxerxes Ochus—the Greeks under Alexander and his successors—the Arabians under Amrou and Saladin—the French under Napo-

leon. As the real desert does not much exceed a hundred miles in breadth, armies can carry with them sufficient food, forage, and water.

¹ See above, p. 204.

² For the naval power of Egypt at this time see Herod. ii. 161 and 182.

Persian enterprise succeeded to the direction of Median power, the fate of Babylon was sealed. It was impossible for the long struggling Empire of the south, lying chiefly in low, flat, open regions, to resist for any considerable time the great kingdom of the north, of the high plateau, and of the mountain-chains.

Chapter II.

CLIMATE AND PRODUCTIONS.

..... Πεδίον περιέσιον, ἔνθα τε πολλοὶ
'Ακράομοι φοίνικες ἐπηρεφίες πεφύασι·
Καὶ μὴν καὶ χρυσεῖο φέρει χαριέστερον ἄλλο,
Ὑγρὴν βηρύλλου γλαυκὴν λίθον, ἢ περὶ χῶρον
Φύνται, ἐν προβολῆς, ὀφιήτιδος Ἰνδοθι πέτρης.
—Dionys. Perieg. II. 1009-1013.

"Έστι δὲ χωρίων αὕτη ἁπασέων μακρῷ ἀρίστη τῶν ἡμεῖς ἴδμεν Δήμητρος
καρπὸν ἐκφέρειν.—Herod. I. 193.

The Babylonian Empire, lying as it did between the thirtieth and the thirty-seventh parallels of north latitude, and consisting mostly of comparatively low countries, enjoyed a climate which was, upon the whole, considerably warmer than that of Media, and less subject to extreme variations. In its more southern parts — Susiana, Chaldæa (or Babylonia Proper), Philistia, and Edom — the intensity of the summer heat must have been great; but the winters were mild and of short duration. In the middle regions of Central Mesopotamia, the Euphrates valley, the Palmyrénè, Cœle-syria, Judæa, and Phœnicia, while the winters were somewhat colder and longer, the summer warmth was more tolerable. Towards the north, along the flanks of Masius, Taurus, and Amanus, a climate more like that of eastern Media prevailed,[1] the summers being little less hot than those of the middle region,[2] while the winters were of considerable severity. A variety of climate thus

---

[1] Supra, pp. 46-50. [2] See vol. i. p. 209.

existed, but a variety within somewhat narrow limits. The region was altogether hotter and drier than is usual in the same latitude. The close proximity of the great Arabian desert, the small size of the adjoining seas, the want of mountains within the region having any great elevation,[3] and the general absence of timber, combined to produce an amount of heat and dryness scarcely known elsewhere outside the tropics.

Detailed accounts of the temperature, and of the climate generally, in the most important provinces of the Empire, Babylonia and Mesopotamia Proper, have been already given,[4] and on these points the reader is referred to the first volume. With regard to the remaining provinces, it may be noticed, in the first place, that the climate of Susiana differs but very slightly from that of Babylonia, the region to which it is adjacent. The heat in summer is excessive, the thermometer, even in the hill country, at an elevation of 5000 feet, standing often at 107° Fahr. in the shade.[5] The natives construct for themselves *serdaubs*, or subterranean apartments, in which they live during the day,[6] thus somewhat reducing the temperature, but probably never bringing it much below 100 degrees.[7] They sleep at night in the open

---

[3] The average elevation of the Mons Masius is estimated at 1300 feet. (Ainsworth, *Researches in Mesopotamia*, p. 28.) Some of its peaks are of course considerably higher. Amanus is said to obtain an elevation of 5387 feet. (Chesney, *Euphrates Expedition*, vol. i. p. 384.) The greatest height of Lebanon is 10,200 feet (*Nat. History Review*, No. V. p. 11); its average height being from 6000 feet to 8000. Hermon is thought to be not much less than 10,000. (Porter, *Handbook*, p. 455.)

[4] See vol. i. pp. 35-38 and 265-267.

[5] Loftus, *Chaldæa and Susiana*, p. 342. For the great heat of the region in ancient times see Strabo, xv. 3, § 10.

[6] Loftus, pp. 304, 311, &c.; Kinneir, *Persian Empire*, p. 107.

[7] This is the temperature of the *serdaubs* at Baghdad, when the temperature of the open air is about 120°. (See vol. i. p. 35.)

air on the flat roofs of their houses.* So far as there is any difference of climate at this season between Susiana and Babylonia, it is in favour of the former. The heat, though scorching, is rarely oppressive;⁹ and not unfrequently a cool invigorating breeze sets in from the mountains,¹⁰ which refreshes both mind and body. The winters are exceedingly mild, snow being unknown on the plains, and rare on the mountains, except at a considerable elevation.¹¹ At this time, however—from December to the end of March—rain falls in tropical abundance;¹² and occasionally there are violent hail-storms,¹³ which inflict serious injury on the crops. The spring-time in Susiana is delightful. Soft airs fan the cheek, laden with the scent of flowers; a carpet of verdure is spread over the plains; the sky is cloudless, or overspread with a thin gauzy veil; the heat of the sun is not too great; the rivers run with full banks and fill the numerous canals; the crops advance rapidly towards perfection; and on every side a rich luxuriant growth cheers the eye of the traveller.¹⁴

On the opposite side of the Empire, in Syria and Palestine, a moister, and on the whole a cooler climate prevails. In Lebanon and Anti-Lebanon there is a severe winter, which lasts from October to

---

* Kinneir, l. s. c.
⁹ Mr. Loftus says: "The temperature was high, but it was perfectly delightful compared with the furnace we had recently quitted at Mohammerah." (*Chaldæa and Susiana*, p. 307.)
¹⁰ Loftus, pp. 206, 307; Kinneir, p. 106.
¹¹ Kinneir, p. 107.
¹² Loftus, p. 310; Kinneir, l. s. c.
¹³ Kinneir, l. s. c.

¹⁴ "Nowhere," says Mr. Loftus, "have I seen such rich vegetation as that which clothes the verdant plains of Shush" (p. 346). "It was difficult to ride along the Shapur," writes Sir H. Rawlinson, "for the luxuriant grass that clothed its banks; and all around the plain was covered with a carpet of the richest verdure." (*Journal of the Geographical Society*, vol. ix. p. 71.)

April;[14] much snow falls, and the thermometer often marks twenty or thirty degrees of frost. On the flanks of the mountain ranges, and in the highlands of Upper and Cœle-syria, of Damascus, Samaria, and Judæa, the cold is considerably less; but there are intervals of frost, snow falls, though it does not often remain long upon the ground,[15] and prolonged chilling rains make the winter and early spring unpleasant. In the low regions, on the other hand, in the *Shephêlah*, the plain of Sharon, the Phœnician coast tract, the lower valley of the Orontes, and again in the plain of Esdraëlon and the remarkable depression from the Merom lake to the Dead Sea, the winters are exceedingly mild;[16] frost and snow are unknown; the lowest temperature is produced by cold rains[18] and fogs,[19] which do not bring the thermometer much below 40°. During the summer these low regions, especially the Jordan valley or Ghor, are excessively hot, the heat being ordinarily of that moist kind which is intolerably oppressive.[20] The upland plains and mountain flanks experience also a high temperature, but there the heat is of a drier character and is not greatly complained of; the nights even in summer are cold, the dews being often heavy;[21] cool winds blow occasionally, and though the sky is for months without a cloud, the prevailing heat produces no injurious effects on those who are exposed to it.[22] In Lebanon and Anti-Lebanon, the

---

[14] Chesney, *Euphrates Expedition,* vol. i. p. 533.
[15] Ibid. p. 534; Robinson, *Researches,* vol. ii. p. 97; Grove, in Smith's *Biblical Dictionary,* vol. ii. p. 692; Josephus, *B. J.* iv. 8, § 3.
[17] Chesney, l. a. c.; Grove, p. 693.
[16] Seetzen, vol. ii. p. 300; *Correspondence de Napoléon,* No. 3903.
[18] Grove, l. a. c.
[19] Robinson, *Researches,* vol. iii. pp. 221, 282, &c.
[20] Grove, l. a. c.; Robinson, vol. ii. p. 99.
[21] Robinson, l. a. c.

heat is of course still less; refreshing breezes blow almost constantly; and the numerous streams and woods give a sense of coolness beyond the markings of the thermometer.

There is one evil, however, to which almost the whole Empire must have been subject. Alike in the east and in the west, in Syria and Palestine, no less than in Babylonia Proper and Susiana, there are times when a fierce and scorching wind prevails for days together—a wind whose breath withers the herbage and is unspeakably depressing to man. Called in the east the *Sherghis*,[1] and in the west the *Khamsin*,[2] this fiery sirocco comes laden with fine particles of heated sand, which at once raise the temperature and render the air unwholesome to breathe. In Syria these winds occur commonly in the spring, from February to April;[3] but in Susiana and Babylonia the time for them is the height of summer.[4] They blow from various quarters, according to the position, with respect to Arabia, occupied by the different provinces. In Palestine the worst are from the east,[5] the direction in which the desert is nearest; in Lower Babylonia they are from the south;[6] in Susiana from the west or the north-west.[7] During their continuance the air is darkened, a lurid glow is cast over the earth, the animal world pines and droops, vegetation languishes, and, if the traveller cannot obtain shelter, and the wind continues, he may sink and die under its deleterious influence.[8]

---

[1] Layard, *Nineveh and Babylon*, p. 364.
[2] Chesney, *Euphrates Expedition*, vol. i. p. 578.
[3] Wilderbruch, as quoted by Mr. Grove in Smith's *Biblical Dictionary*, vol. ii. p. 692.
[4] Kinneir, *Persian Empire*, p. 80; Loftus, *Chaldæa and Susiana*, p. 241.
[5] Beaufort, vol. ii. p. 223.
[6] Loftus, l. s. c.
[7] Kinneir, l. s. c.
[8] See Niebuhr, *Description de l'Arabie*, pp. 7, 8; Burckhardt,

CHAP. II.   PERMANENCY OF THE CLIMATE.   303

The climate of the entire tract included within the limits of the Empire was probably much the same in ancient times as in our own days. In the low alluvial plains indeed near the Persian Gulf it is probable that vegetation was anciently more abundant, the date-palm being cultivated much more extensively then than at present;[9] and so far, it might appear reasonable to conclude that the climate of that region must have been moister and cooler than it now is. But if we may judge by Strabo's account of Susiana, where the climatic conditions were nearly the same as in Babylonia, no important change can have taken place, for Strabo not only calls the climate of Susiana "fiery and scorching,"[10] but says that in Susa, during the summer, if a lizard or a snake tried to cross the street about noon-day, he was baked to death before he had accomplished half the distance."[11] Similarly on the west, though there is reason to believe that Palestine is now much more denuded of timber than it was formerly,[12] and its climate should therefore be both warmer and drier, yet it has been argued with great force from the identity of the modern with the ancient vegetation, that in reality there can have been no considerable change.[13] If then there has been such permanency of climate in the two regions where the greatest alteration seems to have taken place in

---

Travels, p. 191; Chesney, *Euphrates Expedition*, vol. i. pp. 579, 580.

[9] See the description of Dionysius the geographer at the head of this chapter, and compare Herod. I. 193; Amm. Marc. xxiv. 3; Zosim. iii. pp. 173-179.

[10] "Ἔμπυρον καὶ καυματηρὰν." Strab. xv. 3, § 10.

[11] Ibid. τὰς γοῦν σαύρας καὶ τοὺς ὄφεις, θέρους ἀκμάζοντος τοῦ ἡλίου κατὰ μεσημβρίαν, διαβῆναι μὴ φθάνειν τὰς ὁδοὺς τὰς ἐν τῇ πόλει ἀλλ' ἐν μέσαις περιφλέγεσθαι.

[12] Bevan, in Smith's *Biblical Dictionary*, vol. i. p. 631; Stanley, *Sinai and Palestine*, p. 121.

[13] See an article on "The Climate of Palestine in Modern compared to Ancient Times," in the *Edinburgh New Philosophical Journal*, April, 1862.

the circumstances whereby climate is usually affected, it can scarcely be thought that elsewhere any serious change has been brought about.

The chief vegetable productions of Babylonia Proper in ancient times are thus enumerated by Berosus. "The land of the Babylonians," he says, "produces wheat as an indigenous plant, and has also barley, and lentils, and vetches, and sesame; the banks of the streams and the marshes supply edible roots, called *gongæ*, which have the taste of barley-cakes. Palms, too, grow in the country, and apples, and fruit-trees of various kinds."[14] Wheat, it will be observed, and barley are placed first, since it was especially as a grain country that Babylonia was celebrated. The testimonies of Herodotus, Theophrastus, Strabo, and Pliny as to the enormous returns which the Babylonian farmers obtained from their corn lands have been already cited.[15] No such fertility is known anywhere in modern times; and, unless the accounts are grossly exaggerated, we must ascribe it, in part, to the extraordinary vigour of a virgin soil, a deep and rich alluvium; in part perhaps to a peculiar adaptation of the soil to the wheat plant, which the providence of God made to grow spontaneously in this region, and nowhere else, so far as we know, on the whole face of the earth."[16]

Besides wheat, it appears that barley, millet,[17] and

---

[14] Berosus, Fr. 1, § 2.
[15] See vol. i. pp. 39, 40.
[16] Niebuhr says strikingly on this subject: "Woher also kommt das Getreide? Es ist ein unmittelbare Ausstattung des menschlichen Stammes durch Gott; allen ist etwas gegeben; den Asiaten gab er eigentliches Korn, den Americanern Mais. Dieser Umstand verdient ernstliche Erwägung; er ist eine der handgreiflichen Spuren von der Erziehung des menschlichen Geschlechtes durch Gottes unmittelbare Leitung und Vorsehung." (*Vorträge über alte Geschichte*, vol. i. p. 21.)
[17] Millet, which is omitted by Berosus, is mentioned among Babylonian products by Herodotus (i. 193).

lentils were cultivated for food, while vetches were grown for beasts, and sesame for the sake of the oil which can be expressed from its seed.[18] All grew luxuriantly, and the returns of the barley in particular are stated at a fabulous amount.[19] But the production of first necessity in Babylonia was the date-palm, which flourished in great abundance throughout the region, and probably furnished the chief food of the greater portion of the inhabitants. The various uses to which it was applied have been stated in a former volume,[20] where a representation of its mode of growth has been also given.[21]

In the adjoining country of Susiana, or at any rate in the alluvial portion of it, the principal products of the earth seem to have been nearly the same as in Babylonia, while the fecundity of the soil was but little less. Wheat and barley returned to the sower a hundred or even two hundred fold.[22] The date-palm grew plentifully,[23] more especially in the vicinity of the towns.[24] Other trees also were common,[25] as probably konars, acacias, and poplars, which are still found scattered in tolerable abundance over the plain country.[26] The neighbouring mountains could furnish good timber of various kinds,[27] but it appears

---

[18] Herod. L. s. c.; Strab. xvi. 1, § 14.
[19] Three hundred fold. (Strab. l. s. c.)
[20] See vol. I. p. 44.
[21] Ibid. p. 43.
[22] Strab. xv. 3, § 11.
[23] Ibid. xvi. 1, § 9.
[24] The sculptures of Asshur-bani-pal, representing his wars in Susiana, contain numerous representations of palm-trees—particularly by towns. See especially Pl. 49 in Layard's *Monuments of Nineveh*, Second Series.
[25] The Assyrian sculptures represent at least two, if not three, other kinds of trees as growing in Susiana. (See the *Monuments*, Second Series, Pls. 45, 46, and 49.)
[26] Loftus, *Chaldæa and Susiana*, pp. 270, 346; Ainsworth, *Researches*, p. 132; *Geograph. Journal*, vol. ix. p. 70.
[27] *Geographical Journal*, vol. ix. pp. 57, 94, 96, &c.

that the palm was the tree chiefly used for building."
If we may judge the past by the present, we may
further suppose that Susiana produced fruits in abundance; for modern travellers tell us that there is not
a fruit known in Persia which does not thrive in the
province of Khuzistan.¹

Along the Euphrates valley to a considerable distance—at least as far as Anah (or Hena)—the character of the country resembles that of Babylonia
and Susiana, and the products cannot have been very
different. About Anah the date-palm begins to fail,
and the olive first makes its appearance.² Further
up a chief fruit is the mulberry.³ Still higher, in
northern Mesopotamia, the mulberry is comparatively
rare, but its place is supplied by the walnut, the vine,
and the pistachio nut.⁴ This district produces also
good crops of grain, and grows oranges, pomegranates, and the commoner kinds of fruit abundantly.⁵

Across the Euphrates, in northern Syria, the
country is less suited for grain crops; but trees and
shrubs of all kinds grow luxuriantly, the pasture is
excellent, and much of the land is well adapted for
the growth of cotton.⁶ The Assyrian kings cut
timber frequently in this tract;⁷ and here are found

⁎ Strab. xv. 3, § 10.
¹ Kinneir, *Persian Empire*, p. 107. Among the fruits expressly mentioned are lemons, oranges, grapes, apricots, melons, cucumbers (*Iastus*, pp. 313, 314), and the *Amb khasi*, or "Arab nut" (ib. p. 307).
² Ainsworth, *Researches*, p. 49.
³ Ibid. p. 48.
⁴ Pocock, *Description of the East*, vol. ii. p. 108.
⁵ Chesney, *Euphrates Expedition*,
vol. i. p. 107.
⁶ Mr. Porter, speaking of the lower valley of the Orontes, exclaims—" What a noble cotton-field would this valley make!" (*Handbook*, p. 619). And again he says of the tract about the lake of Antioch: "The ground seems adapted for the cultivation of cotton" (ib. p. 609).
⁷ See above, vol. I. p. 385 ; vol. Ii. p. 344, &c.

at the present day enormous planes,[9] thick forests of oak, pine, and ilex, walnuts, willows, poplars, ash-trees, birches, larches, and the carob or locust tree.[9] Among wild shrubs are the oleander with its ruddy blossoms, the myrtle, the bay, the arbutus, the clematis, the juniper, and the honeysuckle;[10] among cultivated fruit-trees, the orange, the pomegranate, the pistachio-nut, the vine, the mulberry, and the olive.[11] The *adis*, an excellent pea, and the *Lycoperdon*, or wild potatoe, grow in the neighbourhood of Aleppo.[12] The castor-oil plant is cultivated in the plain of Edlib.[13] Melons, cucumbers,[14] and most of the ordinary vegetables are produced in abundance and of good quality everywhere.

In southern Syria and Palestine most of the same forms of vegetation occur, with several others of quite a new character. These are due either to the change of latitude, or to the tropical heat of the Jordan and Dead Sea valley, or finally to the high elevation of Hermon, Lebanon, and Anti-Lebanon. The date-palm fringes the Syrian shore as high as Beyrut,[15] and formerly flourished in the Jordan valley,[16] where, however, it is not now seen, except

---

[9] Mr. Ainsworth speaks of one near Dir as measuring 36 feet in circumference, and of another, in the vicinity of the ancient Daphne, measuring 42 feet. (*Researches*, p. 35.)

[9] See Porter, *Handbook*, pp. 598, 609; Ainsworth, p. 305; Chesney, vol. i. p. 432.

[10] Chesney, vol. i. pp. 408, 428-430; Porter, p. 602.

[11] Chesney, pp. 427, 439; Porter, pp. 610, 617; Ainsworth, p. 292. In ancient times the wine of Laodicea (*Ladikiyeh*) was celebrated, and was exported to Egypt in large quantities. (Strab. xvi. 2, § 9.)

[12] Chesney, p. 442.

[13] Porter, p. 616.

[14] Chesney, p. 439.

[15] Ibid. p. 469; Porter, p. 403.

[16] Jericho was known as "the city of Palms" (Deut. xxxiv. 3; Judg. i. 16, iii. 13), from the extensive palm-groves which surrounded it. (Strab. xvi. 2, § 41; Joseph. *B. J.* iv. 8, § 3.) Engedi was called Hazazon-Tamar, "the felling of Palms" (Gen. xiv. 7). The palms of Jericho were still flourishing in the days of the Crusaders.

in a few dwarfed specimens near the Tiberias lake.[17] The banana accompanies the date along the coast, and even grows as far north as Tripoli.[18] The prickly pear, introduced from America, has completely naturalized itself, and is in general request for hedging.[19] The fig-mulberry (or true sycamore), another southern form, is also common, and grows to a considerable size.[20] Other denizens of warm climes, unknown in northern Syria, are the jujube, the tamarisk, the olœagnus or wild olive, the gum-styrax plant (*Styrax officinalis*), the egg-plant, the Egyptian papyrus, the sugar-cane, the scarlet misletoe, the solanum that produces the "Dead Sea apple" (*Solanum Sodomæum*), the yellow-flowered acacia, and the liquorice plant.[21] Among the forms due to high elevation are the famous Lebanon cedar, several oaks and junipers,[22] the maple, berberry, jessamine, ivy, butcher's broom, a rhododendron, and the gum-tragacanth plant.[23] The fruits additional to those of the north are dates, lemons, almonds, shaddocks, and limes.[24]

The chief mineral products of the Empire seem to have been bitumen, with its concomitants, naphtha and petroleum, salt, sulphur, nitre, copper, iron, perhaps silver, and several sorts of precious stones. Bitumen was furnished in great abundance by the

---

(Stanley, *Sinai and Palestine*, p. 143.)
[17] Robinson, *Researches*, vol. ii. p. 266; Hooker, in Smith's *Biblical Dictionary*, vol. ii. p. 685.
[18] Hooker, in Smith's *Biblical Dictionary*, (vol. ii. p. 685).
[19] Porter, p. 404; Hooker, l. s. c.; Grove, in *Biblical Dictionary*, vol. ii. p. 668.
[20] Hooker, B. D. ii. p. 684; Ches-

ney, vol. i. p. 512.
[21] Hooker, pp. 684-688; Chesney, pp. 535-537.
[22] As the *Quercus Cerris*, the *Q. Ehrenbergii* or *castanæfolia*, the *Q. Tæa*, *Q. Libani*, and *Q. mannifera*; the *Juniperus communis*, *J. fœtidissima*, and others. (Hooker, p. 688.)
[23] Ibid. pp. 683, 689.
[24] Ibid. p. 684; Chesney, pp. 455, 480, &c.

springs at Hit or Is,[20] which were celebrated in the days of Herodotus;[21] it was also procured from Arderieca[22] (Kir-Ab), and probably from Ram Ormuz,[23] in Susiana, and likewise from the Dead Sea.[24] Salt was obtainable from the various lakes which had no outlet, as especially from the Sabakhah,[25] the Bahr-el-Melak,[1] the Dead Sea,[2] and a small lake near Tadmor or Palmyra.[3] The Dead Sea gave also most probably both sulphur and nitre, but the latter only in small quantities.[4] Copper and iron seem to have been yielded by the hills of Palestine.[5] Silver was perhaps a product of the Anti-Lebanon.[6]

It may be doubted whether any gems were really found in Babylonia itself, which, being purely alluvial, possesses no stone of any kind. Most likely the sorts known as Babylonian came from the neighbour-

---

[20] These springs continue productive to the present day. They have been well described by the late Mr. Ilich. (*First Memoir on Babylon*, pp. 63, 64.)

[21] Herod. i. 179. Sir G. Wilkinson believes that he has found a mention of bitumen from Hit as early as the reign of Thothmes III. in Egypt. (See the author's *Herodotus*, vol. i. p. 254, note ⁴, 2nd edition.)

[22] Herod. vi. 119; *Journal of the Geographical Society*, vol. ix. p. 94.

[23] *Geograph. Journal*, l. s. c.

[24] Strab. xvi. 2, § 42; Tacit. *Hist.* v. 6; Plin. *H. N.* v. 16.

[25] Supra, p. 281.

[1] Supra, p. 282.

[2] The ridge of Usdum at the south-western extremity of the Dead Sea is a mountain of rock-salt. (Robinson, *Researches*, vol. ii. p. 482.) A little further to the north is a natural salt-pan, the *Birket el Khulil*, from which the Arabs obtain supplies. The Jews say that the Dead Sea salt was anciently in much request for the Temple service. It was known to Galen under the name of "Sodom salt" (ἅλες Σοδομηνοί, *De Simpl. Med. Facult.* iv. 19). Zephaniah (ab. B.C. 630) mentions "salt-pits" in this neighbourhood (ii. 9).

[3] Chesney, vol. i. p. 526. Salt was procurable also from the bitumen-pits at Hit (Ainsworth, *Researches*, p. 86) and Anderiea (Herod. vi. 119).

[4] Balls of nearly pure sulphur are found on the shores of the Dead Sea not unfrequently. (Anderson, in Lynch's *Official Report*, pp. 178, 180, 187, &c.) Nitre is found according to some travellers (Irby and Mangles, pp. 451, 453); but their report is not universally credited. (See Grove, in Smith's *Biblical Dictionary*, vol. iii. p. 1163 d.)

[5] Deut. viii. 9. Compare Euseb. *H. E.* viii. 13, 17.

[6] Silver has been found in the Anti-Lebanon in modern times. (See Burckhardt, *Travels*, pp. 33, 34.)

ing Susiana, whose unexplored mountains may possess many rich treasures. According to Dionysius,[1] the bed of the Choaspes produced numerous agates, and it may well be that from the same quarter came that "beryl more precious than gold,"[2] and those "highly reputed sards,"[3] which Babylon seems to have exported to other countries. The western provinces may, however, very probably have furnished the gems which are ascribed to them, as amethysts, which are said to have been found in the neighbourhood of Petra,[10] alabaster, which came from near Damascus,[11] and the cyanus, a kind of lapis-lazuli,[12] which was a production of Phœnicia.[13] No doubt the Babylonian love of gems caused the provinces to be carefully searched for stones; and it is not improbable that they yielded, besides the varieties already named, and the other unknown kinds mentioned by Pliny,[14] many, if not most, of the materials which we find to have been used for seals by the ancient people. These are, cornelian, rock-crystal, chalcedony, onyx, jasper, quartz, serpentine, sienite, hæmatite, green felspar, pyrites, loadstone, and amazon-stone.

Stone for building was absent from Babylonia Proper and the alluvial tracts of Susiana, but in the other provinces it abounded. The Euphrates valley could furnish stone at almost any point above Hit; the mountain regions of Susiana could supply it in whatever quantity might be required; and in the

---

[1] Dionys. *Perieg.* ll. 1073-1077.
[2] Ibid. ll. 1011-1013.
[3] Plin. *H. N.* xxxvii. 7. "Sarda laudatissima circa Babylonem."
[10] Ibid. xxxvii. 8.
[11] Ibid. xxxvii. 10 (§ 54).
[12] See King, *Antique Gems*, p. 45.

Some have regarded the Cyanus as the sapphire.
[13] Theophrastus, *De Lapid.* 55 (p. 399, ed. Heins.).
[14] As the *Hexecontalithos* (Plin. *H. N.* xxxvii. 10, § 55), the *Mormorion* (ibid. § 63), and the *Sagda* (§ 67).

western provinces it was only too plentiful. Near to Babylonia the most common kind was limestone;[15] but about Haddisah on the Euphrates there was also a gritty, silicious rock alternating with iron-stone,[16] and in the Arabian Desert were sandstone and granite.[17] Such stone as was used in Babylon itself, and in the other cities of the low country, probably either came down the Euphrates,[18] or was brought by canals from the adjacent parts of Arabia. The quantity, however, thus consumed was small, the Babylonians being content for most uses with the brick, of which their own territory gave them a supply practically inexhaustible.

The principal wild animals known to have inhabited the Empire in ancient times are the following:—the lion, the panther or large leopard, the hunting leopard, the bear, the hyæna, the wild ox, the buffalo (?), the wild ass, the stag, the antelope, the ibex or wild goat, the wild sheep, the wild boar, the wolf, the jackal, the fox, the hare and the rabbit.[19] Of these the lion, leopard, bear, stag, wolf, jackal, and fox seem to have been very widely diffused,[20] while

---

[15] Ainsworth, *Researches*, pp. 90, 91.

[16] Ibid. *Travels in the Track*, p. 82.

[17] See above, vol. I. pp. 32 and 48.

[18] Xen. *Anab.* i. 5, § 5.

[19] Most of these animals are mentioned in the Inscription of Asshur-idanni-pal, which records the results of his hunting in Northern Syria and the adjacent part of Mesopotamia. (See above, vol. II. p. 346.) Those not found in that list are mentioned in Scripture among the animals of Palestine.

[20] Lions are represented in early Babylonian reliefs (Loftus, p. 258). They are found at the present day in Susiana (Loftus, p. 332), in Babylonia (Ib. p. 264), on the middle Euphrates and Khabour (Layard, *Nineveh and its Remains*, vol. II. p. 49; *Nin. and Bab.* p. 295); and in Upper Syria (Chesney, vol. I. p. 442). Anciently they were common in Palestine (Judg. xiv. 5; 1 K. xiii. 24; xx. 36; 2 K. xvii. 25; &c.). Bears were likewise common in Palestine (1 Sam. xvii. 34; 2 K. II. 24; &c.). They are still found in Hermon (Porter, p. 453), and in all the wooded parts of Syria and Meso-

the remainder were rarer and, generally speaking, confined to certain localities. The wild ass was met with only in the dry parts of Mesopotamia and perhaps of Syria,[1] the buffalo and wild boar only in moist regions, along the banks of rivers or among marshes.[2] The wild ox was altogether scarce;[3] the wild sheep, the rabbit, and the hare[4] were probably not common.

To this list may be added as present denizens of the region, and therefore probably belonging to it in ancient times, the lynx, the wild-cat, the ratel, the sable, the genet, the badger, the otter, the beaver, the polecat, the jerboa, the rat, the mouse, the marmot, the porcupine, the squirrel,[5] and perhaps the

---

potamia (Ainsworth, in Chesney's *Euphr. Exp.* vol. i. p. 728). The other animals mentioned are still diffused through the whole region.

[1] Xen. *Anab.* l. 5, § 2. The frequent mention of the wild ass by the Hebrew poets (Job vi. 5; xxiv. 5; xxxix. 5; Is. xxxii. 14; Jerem. ii. 24; Hos. viii. 9; &c.) seems to imply that the animal came under their observation. This would only be if it frequented the Syrian desert.

[2] As in Susiana (Ainsworth, *Researches*, pp. 80, 137), Babylonia (supra, vol. i. p. 51), parts of Mesopotamia (Chesney, vol. i. p. 728),

Syria (Ibid. p. 536), and Palestine (Lynch, *Narrative*, p. 218).

[3] See above, vol. ii. pp. 132 and 435.

[4] The hare is sometimes represented upon Babylonian cylinders. We see it either lying down, or carried in the hand by the two hind legs, much as we carry hares nowadays.

[5] This list is given on the authority of Mr. Ainsworth (*Researches*, pp. 37-42), with the two exceptions of the wild-cat and the badger. These are added on the authority of Sir H. Rawlinson.

Hare sitting, from a Babylonian Cylinder.

Hare carried in the hands, from a Babylonian Cylinder.

alligator.⁶ Of these the commonest at the present day are porcupines, badgers, otters, rats, mice, and jerboas. The ratel, sable, and genet belong only to the north;⁷ the beaver is found nowhere but in the Khabour and middle Euphrates;⁸ the alligator, if a denizen of the region at all, exists only in the Euphrates.

The chief birds of the region are eagles, vultures, falcons, owls, hawks, many kinds of crows, magpies, jackdaws, thrushes, blackbirds, nightingales, larks, sparrows, goldfinches, swallows, doves of fourteen kinds, francolins, rock partridges, grey partridges, black partridges, quails, pheasants, capercailzies, bustards, flamingoes, pelicans, cormorants, storks, herons, cranes, wild-geese, ducks, teal, kingfishers, snipes, woodcocks, the sand-grouse, the hoopoe, the green parrot, the becafico, the locust-bird, the humming-bird, and the bee-eater.⁹ The eagle, pheasant, capercailzie, quail, parrot, locust-bird, becafico, and humming-bird are rare;¹⁰ the remainder are all tolerably common. Besides these, we know that in ancient times ostriches were found within the limits of

---

⁶ The officers of Col. Chesney's expedition are said to have seen several times some kind of crocodile or alligator which lived in the Euphrates. (Chesney, vol. I. p. 540; Ainsworth, *Researches*, p. 46.) But they failed to procure a specimen.
⁷ Ainsworth, in Chesney's *Euphr. Exp.* vol. i. p. 728.
⁸ Chesney, p. 442; Layard's *Nin. and Bab.* p. 298.
⁹ See Mr. Ainsworth's account of the Mesopotamian birds in his *Researches*, pp. 42-45; and compare the list in Col. Chesney's work, Appendix to vol. I. pp. 730, 731.

¹⁰ The capercailzie or cock of the wood, and two kinds of pheasants, frequent the woods of northern Syria, where the green parrot is also found occasionally (Chesney, pp. 443 and 731). Eagles are seen on Hermon (Porter, p. 453), Lebanon, and in Upper Syria (Chesney, p. 731); locust-birds in Upper Syria (Ib. p. 443) and Palestine (Robinson, vol. iii. p. 252); the becafico is only a bird of passage (Chesney, p. 731); the humming-bird was seen by Commander Lynch at the southern end of the Dead Sea (*Narrative*, p. 209).

the Empire," though now they have retreated further south into the Great Desert of Arabia. Perhaps bitterns may also formerly have frequented some of the countries belonging to it,[12] though they are not mentioned among the birds of the region by modern writers.[13]

There is a bird of the heron species, or rather of a species between the heron and the stork, which seems to deserve a few words of special description. It is found chiefly in Northern Syria, in the plain of Aleppo and the districts watered by the Koweik and Sajur rivers. The Arabs call it *Tair-el-Raouf*, or "the magnificent." This bird is of a grayish-white, the breast white, the joints of the wings tipped with scarlet, and the under part of the beak scarlet, the upper part being of a blackish-gray. The beak is nearly five inches long and two-thirds of an inch thick. The circumference of the eye is red; the feet are of a deep yellow; and the bird in its general form strongly resembles the stork; but its colour is darker. It is four feet high, and covers a breadth of nine feet when the wings are spread. The birds of this species are wont to collect in large flocks on the North Syrian rivers, and to arrange themselves in several rows

---

[11] Xen. *Anab.* i. 5, § 2. According to Mr. Tristram, the ostrich is still an occasional visitant of the *Belka*, the rolling pastoral country immediately east of the Dead Sea (see his *Report on the Birds of Palestine*, published in the *Proceedings of the London Zoological Society*, Nov. 8, 1864).

[12] Mr. Houghton believes the bittern to be intended by the *kippôd* of Scripture, which is mentioned in connexion with both Babylon (Is. xxxiv. 11) and Nineveh (Zeph. ii. 14). See Smith's *Biblical Dictionary*, vol. iii. Appendix, p. xxxi.

[13] The bittern was not observed by Col. Chesney or Mr. Ainsworth. Nor is it noticed by either Mr. Loftus or Mr. Layard. Col. H. Smith says he was "informed that it had been seen on the ruins of Ctesiphon" (Kitto, *Biblical Cyclopædia*, ad voc. *Kippôd*); but I find no other mention of it as a habitant in these countries.

across the streams where they are shallowest. Here they squat side by side, as close to one another as possible, and spread out their tails against the current, thus forming a temporary dam. The water drains off below them, and when it has reached its lowest point, at a signal from one of their number who from the bank watches the proceedings, they rise and swoop upon the fish, frogs, &c., which the lowering of the water has exposed to view."

Fish are abundant in the Chaldæan marshes, and

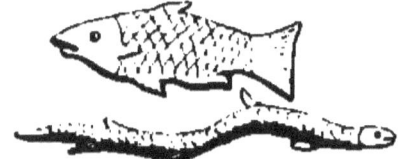

Babylonian fish, from the Sculptures.

in almost all the fresh-water lakes and rivers. The Tigris and Euphrates yield chiefly barbel and carp,[15] but the former stream has also eels, trout, chub, shad-fish, siluruses, and many kinds which have no English names.[16] The Koweik contains the Aleppo eel (*Ophidium masbacambulus*), a very rare variety;[17] and in other streams of Northern Syria are found lampreys, bream, dace, and the black-fish (*Macropteronotus niger*), besides carp, trout, chub, and barbel.[18] Chub, bream, and the silurus are taken in the Sea of Galilee.[19] The black-fish is extremely

---

[14] See Mr. Vincent Germain's description in Col. Chesney's work, vol. I. pp. 781, 732.
[15] Chesney, vol. I. p. 108.
[16] See Mr. Ainsworth's list in Col. Chesney's work, vol. I. p. 739.
[17] Ainsworth, *Researches*, p. 45.
[18] Chesney, p. 444.
[19] Robinson, *Researches*, vol. III. p. 261. Commander Lynch speaks of five kinds of fish—all good—as produced by this lake (*Narrative*, p. 96); but he can only give their Arabic names.

abundant in the Bahr-el-Taka and the Lake of Antioch.[20]

Among reptiles may be noticed, besides snakes, lizards, and frogs, which are numerous, the following less common species—iguanoes, tortoises of two kinds, chamelcons, and monitors.[21] Bats also were common in Babylonia Proper,[22] where they grow to a great size. Of insects the most remarkable are scorpions, tarantulas, and locusts.[23] These last come suddenly in countless myriads with the wind, and, settling on the crops, rapidly destroy all the hopes of the husbandman, after which they strip the shrubs and trees of their leaves, reducing rich districts in an incredibly short space of time to the condition of howling wildernesses. If it were not for the locust-bird, which is constantly keeping down their numbers, these destructive insects would probably increase so as to ruin utterly the various regions exposed to their ravages.

Locusts, from a Cylinder.

The domestic animals employed in the countries which composed the Empire were camels, horses, mules, asses, buffaloes, cows and oxen, goats, sheep and dogs. Mules as well as horses seem to have been anciently used in war by the people of the more southern regions—by the Susianians at any rate,[24] if not also by the Babylonians. Sometimes they were ridden; sometimes they were employed to draw carts

---

[20] Chesney, pp. 305 and 397.
[21] Ainsworth, *Researches*, p. 46.
[22] Strab. xvi. 1, § 7.
[23] Chesney, p. 444.
[24] See the sculptures of Asshur-bani-pal, which represent his campaigns in Susiana, especially those rendered by Mr. Layard in his *Monuments*, Second Series, Pls. 45 and 46.

or chariots. They were spirited and active animals, evidently of a fine breed, such as that for which Khuzistan is famous at the present day.²⁰ The asses from which these mules were produced must also have been of superior quality, like the breed for which Baghdad is even now famous.²¹ The Babylonian horses are not likely to have been nearly so good; for this animal does not flourish in a climate which is at once moist and hot. Still, at any rate under the Persians, Baby-

Sassanian mule (Koyunjik).

Sassanian horses (Koyunjik).

lonia seems to have been a great breeding-place for horses, since the stud of a single satrap consisted of 800 stallions and 16,000 mares.¹ If we may

---

²⁰ Layard, *Nineveh and Babylon*, p. 449, note.
²¹ Ibid. p. 472.
¹ Herod. I. 192. Compare the 800 stallions and 30,000 mares, which Seleucus Nicator kept in the Orontes valley, near Apamea. (Strab. xvi. 2, § 10.)

judge of the character of Babylonian from that of Susianian steeds, we may consider the breed to have been strong and large limbed, but not very handsome, the head being too large and the legs too short for beauty.

The Babylonians were also from very early times famous for their breed of dogs. The tablet engraved in a former volume,[1] which gives a representation of a Babylonian hound, is probably of a high antiquity, not later than the period of the Empire. Dogs are also not unfrequently represented on ancient Babylonian stones and cylinders.[2] It would seem that, as in Assyria, there were two principal breeds, one somewhat clumsy and heavy, of a character not unlike that of our mastiff, the other of a much lighter make, nearly resembling our greyhound.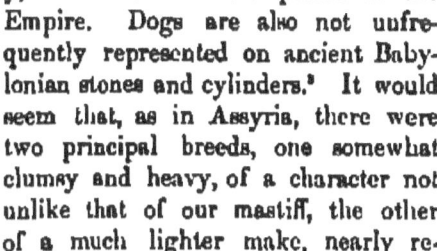

Babylonian dog from a gem.

The former kind is probably the breed known as Indian,[3] which was kept up by continual importations from the country whence it was originally derived.[4]

We have no evidence that camels were employed in the time of the Empire, either by the Babylonians themselves or by their neighbours the Susianians; but in Upper Mesopotamia, in Syria, and in Palestine they had been in use from a very early date. The Amalekites and the Midianites found them serviceable in war;[5] and the latter people employed them also as beasts of burden in their caravan

---

[1] See vol. I. p. 293, No. 11.
[2] Cullimore, *Cylinders*, No. 63; Lajard, *Culte de Mithra*, Pls. xviii. 8; xxxvii. 2; xxxviii. 1; &c.
[3] Herod. I. a. c.
[4] Ctesias, *Indica*, § 5.
[5] Judg. vii. 12; 1 Sam. xxx. 17.

trade.' The Syrians of Upper Mesopotamia rode upon them in their journeys.' It appears that they were also sometimes yoked to chariots,' though from their size and clumsiness they would be but ill fitted for beasts of draught.

Buffaloes were, it is probable, domesticated by the Babylonians at an early date. The animal seems to have been indigenous in the country,[10] and it is far better suited for the marshy regions of Lower Babylonia and Susiana[11] than cattle of the ordinary kind. It is perhaps a buffalo which is represented on an ancient tablet already referred to,[12] where a lion is dis-

Oxen, from Babylonian Cylinders.

turbed in the middle of his feast off a prostrate animal by a man armed with a hatchet. Cows and oxen, however, of the common kind are occasionally represented on the cylinders,[13] where they seem sometimes to represent animals about to be offered to the gods. Goats also appear frequently in this capacity;[14] and they were probably more common than sheep, at any

---

' Gen. xxxvii. 25.
' Ibid. xxiv. 61; xxxi. 17.
' Isaiah xxi. 7.
[10] Among the beasts hunted by the Assyrian kings are thought to be wild buffaloes. (Supra, vol. ii. p. 348.)
[11] On the buffaloes of these districts see Loftus, *Chaldæa and Susiana*, pp. 04, 302; Layard, *Nineveh and Babylon*, p. 566; Ainsworth,

Researches, p. 137.
[12] Supra, p. 311, note ". The tablet is figured by Mr. Loftus, p. 258.
[13] Cullimore, *Cylinders*, Nos. 30, 01, 02, 138; Lajard, *Culte de Mithra*, Pls. xiii. 7; xvi. 1; xviii. 5; &c.
[14] Cullimore, Nos. 26, 20, 49, 52, &c.; Lajard, Pls. xxxvi. 13; xxxvii. 7; xxxviii. 3; &c.

rate in the more southern districts. Of Babylonian sheep we have no representations at all on the monuments; but it is scarcely likely that a country which used wool so largely[18] was content to be without them. At any rate they abounded in the provinces, forming the chief wealth of the more northern nations.[19]

---

[18] See below, p. 414.
[19] See the Assyrian Inscriptions, passim. Compare Gen. xxix. 3; Job I. 3; xlii. 12.

Chapter III.

THE PEOPLE.

"The Chaldæans, that bitter and hasty nation."—Habak. I. 6.

The Babylonians, who under Nabopolassar and Nebuchadnezzar, held the second place among the nations of the East, were emphatically a mixed race. The ancient people, from whom they were in the main descended—the Chaldæans of the First Empire,—possessed this character to a considerable extent, since they united Cushite with Turanian blood, and contained moreover a slight Semitic and probably a slight Arian element.[1] But the Babylonians of later times—the Chaldæans of the Hebrew prophets[2]—must have been very much more a mixed race than their earlier namesakes—partly in consequence of the policy of colonisation pursued systematically by the later Assyrian kings, partly from the direct influence exerted upon them by two races of conquerors. The old Cushite Empire was brought to an end, as we have already seen,[3] by an Arabian invasion about the year B.C. 1518, and an Arab dynasty bore sway in the country from that time till B.C. 1270—a period of nearly two centuries and a half. At the close of this period, the Arabs were succeeded in power by

---

[1] See above, vol. i. pp. 66-70.
[2] The prophets very rarely use the word "Babylonian." I believe it is only found in Ezek. xxiii. 15 and 17. When the term is used it designates the people of the capital; the inhabitants of the land generally are "Chaldæans."
[3] Supra, vol. i. p. 223.

the Assyrians, who established an Assyrian family upon the throne of Nimrod, and held for some time the actual sovereignty of the country.⁴ It was natural that under these two dynasties of Semites, Semitic blood should flow freely into the lower region, Semitic usages and modes of thought become prevalent, and the spoken language of the country pass from a Turanian or Turano-Cushite to a Semitic type. The previous Chaldæan race blended, apparently, with the new comers, and a people was produced in which the three elements—the Semitic, the Turanian, and the Cushite—held about equal shares. The colonisation of the Sargonid kings added other elements in small proportions,⁵ and the result was that among all the nations inhabiting Western Asia, there can have been none so thoroughly deserving the title of a "mingled people"⁶ as the Babylonians of the later Empire.

In mixtures of this kind it is almost always found that some one element practically preponderates, and assumes to itself the right of fashioning and forming the general character of the race. It is not at all necessary that this formative element should be larger than any other; on the contrary, it may be and sometimes is extremely small;⁷ for it does not work

---

⁴ See vol. II. pp. 304-306.
⁵ The settlement of foreigners in Babylonia by the Sargonid kings is not expressly recorded; but may be assumed from their general practice, combined with the fact that they made room for such a population by largely deporting the native inhabitants. (See 2 K. xvii. 24; Ezr. iv. 9; and compare above, vol. ii. pp. 423, 463, &c.)
⁶ Jeremiah speaks of the "mingled people" in the midst of Babylon (l. 37); but the reference is perhaps rather to the crowds of foreigners who were there for pleasure or profit than to the Babylonians themselves.
⁷ Note the case of the Hellenic element in Greece—at any rate according to Herodotus—τὸ Ἑλληνικὸν ... ἐὸν ἀσθενές, ἀπὸ σμικροῦ τεο τὴν ἀρχὴν ὁρμεώμενον, αὔξηται ἐς πλῆθος τῶν ἐθνέων πολλέων, μάλιστα προσκεχωρηκότων αὐτῷ καὶ ἄλλων ἐθνέων βαρβάρων συχνῶν.

by its mass, but by its innate force, and strong vital energy. In Babylonia, the element which showed itself to possess this superior vitality, which practically asserted its pre-eminence and proceeded to mould the national character, was the Semitic. There is abundant evidence that by the time of the later Empire the Babylonians had become thoroughly Semitized; so much so, that ordinary observers scarcely distinguished them from their purely Semitic neighbours, the Assyrians.[*] No doubt there were differences which a Hippocrates or an Aristotle could have detected — differences resulting from mixed descent, as well as differences arising from climate and physical geography; but, speaking broadly, it must be said that the Semitic element, introduced into Babylonia from the west and north, had so prevailed by the time of the establishment of the Empire that the race was no longer one *sui generis*, but was a mere variety of the well known and widely spread Semitic type.

We possess but few notices, and fewer assured representations, from which to form an opinion of the physical characteristics of the Babylonians. Excepting upon the cylinders, there are extant only three or four representations of the human form[*] by Babylonian artists, and in the few cases where this form occurs, we cannot always feel at all certain that the intention is to portray a human being. A few As-

---

[*] Herod. l. 106, 178; iii. 92.
[*] The most important work of this kind is the representation of a Babylonian king (probably Merodach-adan-akhi) on a black stone in the British Museum, which will be found engraved at p. 400. Other instances are—1, the warrior and the priest in the tablet from Sir-Pal-i-Zohab, given at p. 436, which, however, is perhaps rather Cushite than Semitic; 2, the man accompanying the Babylonian hound (Layard, *Nin. and Bab.* p. 527); and 3, the imperfect figures on the frieze represented below, p. 390.

syrian bas-reliefs *probably* represent campaigns in Babylonia;[19] but the Assyrians vary their human type so little, that these tablets must not be regarded as conveying to us very exact information. The cylinders are too rudely executed to be of much service, and they seem to preserve an archaic type which originated with the Proto-Chaldæans. If we might trust the figures upon them as at all nearly representing the truth, we should have to regard the Babylonians as of much slighter and sparer frames than their northern neighbours, of a *physique* in fact approaching to meagreness. The Assyrian sculptures, however, are far from bearing out this idea; from them it would seem that the frames of the Babylonians were as brawny and massive as those of the Assyrians themselves, while in feature there was not much difference between the nations. Foreheads straight but not high, noses well formed but somewhat depressed, full lips, and a well-marked rounded chin constitute the physiognomy of the Babylonians as it appears upon the sculptures of their neighbours.

Babylonian men, from the Assyrian sculptures.

This representation is not contradicted by the few specimens of actual sculpture left by themselves. In these the type approaches nearly to the Assyrian, while there is still such an amount of difference as renders it tolerably easy to distinguish between the productions of the two nations. The eye is larger and

---

[19] Layard, *Monuments of Nineveh*, Second Series, Pls. 25, 27, and 28.

CHAP. III. THE BABYLONIANS LIKE THE ASSYRIANS. 325

not so decidedly almond-shaped; the nose is shorter, and its depression is still more marked; while the general expression of the countenance is altogether more commonplace.

Babylonian woman, from the autor.

These differences may be probably referred to the influence which was exercised upon the physical form of the race by the primitive or Proto-Chaldæan element, an influence which appears to have been considerable. This element, as has been already observed,[n] was predominantly Cushite; and there is reason to believe that the Cushite race was connected not very remotely with the negro. In Susiana, where the Cushite blood was maintained in tolerable purity—

Susianians (Koyunjik).

Elymæans and Kissians existing side by side, instead of blending together[18]—there was, if we may trust the Assyrian remains, a very decided prevalency of a negro type of countenance, as the accompanying specimens, carefully copied from the sculptures, will render evident. The head was

---

[n] Supra, p. 322.
[18] For the separate existence in Susiana of Elymæans and Kissians, see Strab. xvi. 1, § 17, and Ptolemy, vi. 3. That the Elymæans were Semitic seems to follow from Gen. x. 22. In the word "Kissian" we have probably a modification of "Cushite."

covered with short crisp curls; the eye was large, the nose and mouth nearly in the same line, the lips thick. Such a physiognomy as the Babylonian appears to have been would naturally arise from an intermixture of a race like the Assyrian with one resembling that which the later sculptures represent as the main race inhabiting Susiana.[13]

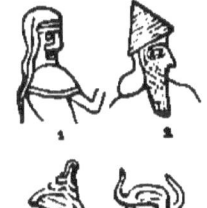

Heads of Babylonians, from the Cylinders.

Head of an Elamitic chief (Koyunjik).

Herodotus remarks that the Babylonians wore their hair long;[14] and this remark is confirmed to some extent by the native remains. These in general represent the hair as forming a single stiff and heavy curl at the back of the head (No. 3). Sometimes, however, they make it take the shape of long flowing locks, which depend over the back (No. 1), or over the back and shoulders (No. 4), reaching nearly to the waist. Occasionally, in lieu of these commoner types, we have one which closely resembles the Assyrian, the hair forming a round mass behind the head (No. 2), on which we can sometimes trace

---

[13] The sculptures of Asshur-bani-pal exhibit two completely opposite types of Susianian physiognomy—one Jewish, the other approaching to the negro. In the former we have probably the Elamitic countenance. It is comparatively rare, the negro type greatly predominating.
[14] Herod. L 195.

indications of a slight wave. The national fashion, that to which Herodotus alludes, seems to be represented by the three commoner modes. Where the round mass is worn, we have probably an Assyrian fashion, which the Babylonians aped during the time of that people's pre-eminence.[15]

Besides their flowing hair, the Babylonians are represented frequently with a large beard. This is generally longer than the Assyrian, descending nearly to the waist. Sometimes it curls crisply upon the face, but below the chin depends over the breast in long, straight locks. At other times it droops perpendicularly from the cheek and the under lip.[16] Frequently, however, the beard is shaven off, and the whole face is smooth and hairless.[1]

The Chaldæan females, as represented by the Assyrians,[2] are tall and large-limbed. Their physiognomy is Assyrian, their hair not very abundant. The Babylonian cylinders, on the other hand, make the hair long and conspicuous, while the forms are quite as spare and meagre as those of the men.

On the whole, it is most probable that the physical type of the later Babylonians was nearly that of their northern neighbours. A somewhat sparer form,

---

[15] It will be observed that the Assyrian sculptures, while they give a peculiar character to the Babylonian hair, do not make it descend below the shoulders. They generally represent it as worn smooth on the top of the head, and depending from the ears to the shoulders in a number of large, smooth, heavy curls. (See the woodcut, p. 324.)

[16] Here again the Assyrian artists tone down the Babylonian peculiarity, generally representing the beard as not much longer than their own.

[1] The priests upon the cylinders are always beardless. We cannot suppose them to have been always, if indeed they were ever, eunuchs. Nanarus, a Babylonian prince, is said by Nicolas of Damascus to have been "right well shaven" (ξυρημένος ὁ μάλα, Fr. 10. p. 360).

[2] Layard, *Monuments of Nineveh*, Second Series, Pls. 25, 27, and 28.

longer and more flowing hair, and features less stern and strong may perhaps have characterized them. They were also, it is probable, of a darker complexion than the Assyrians, being to some extent Ethiopians by descent, and inhabiting a region which lies four degrees nearer to the tropics than Assyria. The Cha'ab Arabs, the present possessors of the more southern parts of Babylonia, are nearly black;[3] and the "black Syrians," of whom Strabo speaks,[4] seem intended to represent the Babylonians.

Among the moral and mental characteristics of the people, the first place is due to their intellectual ability. Inheriting a legacy of scientific knowledge, astronomical and arithmetical, from the Proto-Chaldæans,[5] they seem to have not only maintained but considerably advanced these sciences by their own efforts. Their "wisdom and learning" are celebrated by the Jewish prophets Isaiah, Jeremiah, and Daniel;[6] the Father of History records their valuable inventions;[7] and an Aristotle was not ashamed to be beholden to them for scientific data.[8] They were good observers of astronomical phenomena, careful recorders of such observations,[9] and mathematicians of no small repute.[10] Unfortunately they mixed with their really scientific studies those occult

---

[3] Loftus, *Chaldæa and Susiana*, p. 285.
[4] Strab. xvi. 1, § 2.
[5] See above, vol. i. pp. 120-131.
[6] See Isaiah xlvii. 10: "Thy wisdom and thy knowledge, it hath perverted thee." Jerem. l. 35: "A sword is upon the Chaldeans, saith the Lord, and upon the inhabitants of Babylon, and upon her princes, and upon her wise men." Dan. i. 4: "The learning of the Chaldæans."
[7] Herod. ii. 109. It is uncertain, however, if the Semitized Babylonians, or the early Chaldæans, are the people intended by Herodotus.
[8] See the famous passage of Simplicius (ad Arist. *De Cœlo*, ii. p. 123) quoted at length in the first volume of this work, p. 127, note [1].
[9] Plin. *H. N.* vii. 56; Diod. Sic. ii. 30, § 2.
[10] Strab. xvi. 1, § 6.

pursuits, which, in ages and countries where the limits of true science are not known, are always apt to seduce students from the right path, having attractions against which few men are proof, so long as it is believed they can really accomplish the end that they propose to themselves. The Babylonians were astrologers no less than astronomers;[11] they professed to cast nativities, to expound dreams, and to foretell events by means of the stars; and though there were always a certain number who kept within the legitimate bounds of science and repudiated the astrological pretensions of their brethren,[12] yet on the whole it must be allowed that their astronomy was fatally tinged with a mystic and unscientific element.

In close connection with the intellectual ability of the Babylonians, was the spirit of enterprise which led them to engage in traffic and to adventure themselves upon the ocean in ships. In a future chapter we shall have to consider the extent and probable direction of this commerce.[13] It is sufficient to observe in the present place that the same turn of mind which made the Phœnicians anciently the great carriers between the East and West, and which in modern times has rendered the Jews so successful in various branches of trade, seems to have characterized the Semitized Babylonians, whose land was emphatically "a land of traffic," and their chief city "a city of merchants."[14]

---

[11] Isaiah xlvii. 13; Dan. ii. 2; Diod. Sic. II. 29, § 2; Strab. l. s. c.; Vitruv. ix. 4; &c.
[12] Strabo (l. s. c.), after speaking of the Chaldæan astronomers, says— προστατεύονται δέ τινες καὶ γενεθλια-λογεῖν, οὓς οὐ παραδέχονται οἱ ἕτεροι. But, in reality, astrology was the rule, pure astronomy the rare exception. [13] Infra, ch. vi.
[14] Ezek. xvii. 4. Compare Isaiah xliii. 14.

The trading spirit which was thus strongly developed in the Babylonian people, led naturally to the two somewhat opposite vices of avarice and over-luxuriousness. Not content with fair and honest gains, the Babylonians "coveted an evil covetousness," as we learn both from Habakkuk and Jeremiah.[16] The "shameful custom" mentioned by Herodotus,[16] which required as a religious duty that every Babylonian woman, rich or poor, highborn or humble, should once in her life prostitute herself in the temple of Beltis, was probably based on the desire of attracting strangers to the capital, who would either bring with them valuable commodities or purchase the productions of the country. The public auction of marriageable virgins[17] had most likely a similar intention. If we may believe Curtius,[18] strangers might at any time purchase the gratification of any passion they might feel, from the avarice of parents or husbands.

The luxury of the Babylonians is a constant theme with both sacred and profane writers. The "daughter of the Chaldæans" was "tender and delicate,"[19] "given to pleasures,"[20] apt to "dwell carelessly."[21] Her young men made themselves "as princes to look at—exceeding in dyed attire upon their heads"[22]— painting their faces, wearing earrings, and clothing themselves in robes of soft and rich material.[23] Extensive polygamy prevailed.[24] The pleasures of the

---

[15] Habak. ii. 9; Jerem. li. 13.
[16] Herod. I. 199. See on this custom the remarks of Heeren. (*Asiatic Nations*, vol. ii. p. 199, E. T.)
[17] Herod. I. 196; Nic. Dam. Fr. 131.
[18] Q. Curt. *Hist. Alex.* v. 1 (p. 112, ed. Tauchn.): "Liberos conjugesque cum hospitibus stupro coire, modo pretium flagitii detur, parentes maritique patiuntur."
[19] Isaiah xlvii. 1.
[20] Ibid. ver. 8.
[21] Ibid.
[22] Ezek. xxiii. 15.
[23] Nic. Dam. Fr. 10.
[24] Dan. v. 2; Nic. Dam. Fr. 10, p. 362.

table were carried to excess. Drunkenness was common.[16] Rich unguents were invented.[17] The tables groaned under the weight of gold and silver plate.[21] In every possible way the Babylonians practised luxuriousness of living, and in respect of softness and self-indulgence they certainly did not fall short of any nation of antiquity.

There was, however, a harder and sterner side to the Babylonian character. Despite their love of luxury, they were at all times brave and skilful in war; and, during the period of their greatest strength, they were one of the most formidable of all the nations of the East. Habakkuk describes them, drawing evidently from the life, as "bitter and hasty," and again as "terrible and dreadful—their horses' hoofs swifter than the leopard's, and more fierce than the evening wolves."[18] Hence they "smote the people in wrath with a continual stroke"[19] —they "made the earth to tremble, and did shake kingdoms"[20]—they carried all before them in their great enterprises, seldom allowing themselves to be foiled by resistance, or turned from their course by pity. Exercised for centuries in long and fierce wars with the well-armed and well-disciplined Assyrians, they were no sooner quit of this enemy and able to take an aggressive attitude, than they showed themselves no unworthy successors of that long-dominant nation, so far as energy, valour, and military skill constitute desert. They carried their victorious arms

---

[16] Q. Curt. l. s. c. "Babylonii maxime in vinum, et quæ ebrietatem sequuntur, effusi sunt." Compare Xen. Cyrop. vii. 5, § 15; and Halmk. ii. 5, 16.

[17] The Babylonian unguents were celebrated by Posidonius (Fr. 30). Compare Herod. I. 195: μύροι παν το σώμα.

[18] Nic. Dam. Fr. 10, p. 363.
[19] Habakkuk i. 6-8.
[20] Isaiah xiv. 6.   [21] Ibid. ver. 16.

from the shores of the Persian Gulf to the banks of the Nile; wherever they went, they rapidly established their power, crushing all resistance, and fully meriting the remarkable title which they seem to have received from some of those who felt their attacks, of "the hammer of the whole earth."[1]

The military successes of the Babylonians were accompanied with needless violence, and with outrages not unusual in the East, which the historian must nevertheless regard as at once crimes and follies. The transplantation of conquered races—a part of the policy of Assyria which the Chaldæans adopted—may perhaps have been morally defensible, notwithstanding the sufferings which it involved.[2] But the mutilations of prisoners,[3] the weary imprisonments,[4] the massacre of non-combatants,[5] the refinement of cruelty shown in the execution of children before the eyes of their father[6]—these and similar atrocities, which are recorded of the Babylonians, are wholly without excuse, since they did not so much terrify as exasperate the conquered nations, and thus rather endangered than added strength or security to the Empire. A savage and inhuman temper is betrayed by these harsh punishments,—a temper common in Asiatics, but none the less reprehensible on that account,—one that led its possessors to sacrifice interest to vengeance, and the peace of a kingdom to a tiger-like thirst for blood. Nor was this cruel temper shown only towards the subject nations and

---

[1] Jerem. l. 23. Compare the xxxix. 7; lii. 11; Dan. l. 3.
"Martel" given as a title to Charles the conqueror of the Saracens.
[2] See above, vol. ii. pp. 528, 529.
[3] 2 Kings xx. 18; xxv. 7; Jer. xxv. 7.
[4] Jer. l. a. c.; 2 Kings xxv. 27.
[5] Jer. lii. 27; 2 Kings xxv. 21.
[6] Jer. xxxix. 6; lii. 10; 2 Kings

the captives taken in war. Babylonian nobles trembled for their heads if they incurred by a slight fault the displeasure of the monarch;[7] and even the most powerful class in the kingdom, the learned and venerable "Chaldæans," ran on one occasion the risk of being exterminated, because they could not expound a dream which the King had forgotten.[8] If a monarch displeased his court, and was regarded as having a bad disposition, it was not thought enough simply to make away with him, but he was put to death by torture.[9] Among recognised punishments were cutting to pieces and casting into a heated furnace.[10] The houses of offenders were pulled down and made into dunghills.[11] These practices imply a "violence" and cruelty beyond the ordinary Oriental limit; and we cannot be surprised that when final judgment was denounced against Babylon, it was declared to be sent, in a great measure, "because of men's blood, and for the violence of the land—of the city, and of all that dwelt therein."[12]

It is scarcely necessary to add that the Babylonians were a proud people. Pride is unfortunately the invariable accompaniment of success, in the nation, if not in the individual; and the sudden elevation of Babylon from a subject to a dominant power must have been peculiarly trying, more especially to the Oriental temperament. The spirit which culminated in Nebuchadnezzar, when, walking in the palace of his kingdom, and surveying the magnificent build-

---

[7] Dan. i. 10.
[8] Ibid. ii. 5-13.
[9] Beros. ap. Joseph. c. Apion. i. 20.
[10] Dan. ii. 5; iii. 6, 29.
[11] Ibid.
[12] Habak. ii. 8 and 17. Compare Isaiah xiv. 4-6; Jer. lii. 23, 24.

ings which he had raised on every side from the plunder of the conquered nations and by the labour of their captive bands, he exclaimed—" Is not this great Babylon which I have built by the might of my power and for the honour of my majesty?"[13]— was rife in the people generally, who, naturally enough, believed themselves superior to every other nation upon the earth. "I am, and there is none else beside me," was the thought, if not the speech, of the people,[14] whose arrogancy was perhaps somewhat less offensive than that of the Assyrians, but was quite as intense and as deep-seated.[15]

The Babylonians, notwithstanding their pride, their cruelty, their covetousness, and their love of luxury, must be pronounced to have been, according to their lights, a religious people. The temple in Babylonia is not a mere adjunct of the palace, but has almost the same pre-eminence over other buildings which it claims in Egypt. The vast mass of the Birs-i-Nimrud is sufficient to show that an enormous amount of labour was expended in the erection of sacred edifices; and the costly ornamentation lavished on such buildings is, as we shall hereafter find,[16] even more remarkable than their size. Vast sums were also expended on images of the gods,[17] necessary adjuncts of the religion; and the whole paraphernalia of worship was splendid and magnificent in the extreme.[18] The monarchs were devout worshippers

---

[13] Dan. iv. 30.
[14] Isaiah xlvii. 8: "Thou sayest in thine heart, I am, and none else beside me." Compare ver. 10.
[15] Compare Isaiah xiii. 11; xiv. 13, 14; xlvii. 7; Jer. l. 29, 31, 32; Habak. ii. 5.
[16] See below, ch. v. p. 384.
[17] Dan. iii. 1; Herod. i. 183; Diod. Sic. ii. 9, § 5 and § 6.
[18] Herod. i. 181-183; Diod. Sic. ii. 9, § 7 and § 8.

of the various deities, and gave much of their attention to the building and repair of temples, the erection of images, and the like. They bestowed on their children names indicative of religious feeling,[19] and implying real faith in the power of the gods to protect their votaries. The people generally affected similar names—names containing, in almost every case, a god's name as one of their elements.[20] The seals or signets which formed almost a necessary part of each man's costume,[21] were, except in rare instances, of a religious character. Even in banquets, where we might have expected that thoughts of religion would be laid aside, it seems to have been the practice during the drinking to rehearse the praises of the deities.[22]

We are told by Nicolas of Damascus that the Babylonians cultivated two virtues especially, honesty and calmness.[23] Honesty is the natural—almost the necessary—virtue of traders, who soon find that it is the best policy to be fair and just in their dealings. We may well believe that this intelligent people had the wisdom to see their true interests, and to understand that trade can never prosper unless conducted with integrity and straightforwardness. The very fact that their trade did prosper, that their goods were everywhere in request,[24] is sufficient proof of their

---

[19] As Nabu-kuduri-izzir, which means "Nebo is the protector of landmarks;" Bel-shar-ezir, which is "Bel protects the king," and Evil-Merodach (Ilu - Merodach), which may be "Merodach is a god."

[20] As Belibus, Belesis, Nergal-shar-ezer, Shamgar-nebo, Nebu-zar-adan, Nabonidus, &c. &c.

[21] Herod. I. 195.

[22] Dan. v. 4: "They drank wine, and praised the gods of gold, and of silver, of brass, of iron, of wood, and of stone."

[23] Fr. 131. Ἀσσούριοι δὲ μάλιστα εὐθύτητα καὶ ἀοργησίαν. Nicolas speaks of "Assyrians;" but the context makes it clear that he means "Assyrians of Babylon."

[24] See below, ch. v. p. 414.

commercial honesty, and of their superiority to those tricks which speedily ruin a commerce.

Calmness is not a common Oriental virtue. It is not even in general very highly appreciated, being apt to strike the lively, sensitive, and passionate Eastern as mere dulness and apathy. In China, however, it is a point of honour that the outward demeanour should be calm and placid under any amount of provocation; and indignation, fierceness, even haste are regarded as signs of incomplete civilization which the disciples of Confucius love to note in their would-be rivals of the West. We may conceive that some similar notion was entertained by the proud Babylonians, who no doubt regarded themselves as infinitely superior in manners and culture, no less than in scientific attainments, to the "barbarians" of Persia and Greece. While rage boiled in their hearts, and commands to torture and destroy fell from their tongues, etiquette may have required that the countenance should be unmoved, the eye serene, the voice low and gentle. Such contrasts are not uncommonly seen in the polite Mandarin, whose apparent calmness drives his European antagonist to despair; and it may well be that the Babylonians of the sixth and seventh centuries before our era had attained to an equal power of restraining the expression of feeling. But real gentleness, meekness, and placability were certainly not the attributes of a people who were so fierce in their wars, and so cruel in their punishments.

CHAPTER IV.

THE CAPITAL.

Πόλισμα ὀνομαστότατον καὶ ἰσχυρότατον.—HEROD. i. 178.

BABYLON, the capital of the Fourth Monarchy, was probably the largest and most magnificent city of the ancient world. A dim tradition current in the East gave, it is true, a greater extent, if not a greater splendour, to the metropolis of Assyria; but this tradition first appears in ages long subsequent to the complete destruction of the more northern city;[1] and it is contradicted by the testimony of facts. The walls of Nineveh have been completely traced, and indicate a city three miles in length, by less than a mile and a half in breadth, containing an area of about 1800 English acres.[2] Of this area less than one-tenth is occupied by ruins of any pretension.[3] On the admitted site of Babylon striking masses of ruin cover a space considerably larger than that which at Nineveh constitutes the whole area of the town.[4] Beyond this space in every direction, north, east, south,

---

[1] The tradition is first found in the time of Augustus, in the works of Diodorus and Strabo. Strabo says vaguely that Nineveh was "much larger than Babylon" (πολὺ μείζων τῆς Βαβυλῶνος, xvi. 1, § 3); Diodorus makes it nearly twice as large. (Compare ii. 3, § 2, with ii. 7, § 3.)

[2] See above, vol. i. pp. 316–320.

[3] The two mounds of Koyunjik and Nebbi Yunus cover together an area of 140 acres. (See vol. i. p. 317.)

[4] See below, p. 362.

and west, are detached mounds indicating the former existence of edifices of some size, while the intermediate space between these mounds and the main ruins shows distinct traces of its having been built upon in former days.[1]

Of the actual size of the town modern research gives us no clear and definite notion. One explorer[2] only has come away from the country with an idea that the general position of the detached mounds, by which the plain around Hillah is dotted, enables him to draw the lines of the ancient walls, and mark out the exact position of the city. But the very maps and plans which are put forward in support of this view show that it rests mainly on hypothesis;[3] nor is complete confidence placed in the surveys on which the maps and plans have been constructed. The English surveys, which have been unfortunately lost,[4] are said not to have placed the detached mounds in any such decided lines as M. Oppert believes them to occupy, and the general impression of the British Officers who were employed on the service is that "no vestige of the walls of Babylon has been as yet discovered."[5]

For the size and plan of the city we are thus of necessity thrown back upon the reports of ancient authors. It is not pretended that such reports are in

---

[1] See Rich, *First Memoir on Babylon*, p. 7; Ker Porter, vol. ii. pp. 381, 382; Layard, *Nineveh and Babylon*, pp. 491, 492; Loftus, *Chaldæa and Susiana*, p. 15.

[2] M. Oppert. See his *Expédition Scientifique en Mésopotamie*, tom. i. ch. viii. pp. 220-234.

[3] This is particularly observable with respect to the French savants' "outer wall," which has really no foundation at all in the topography of the country.

[4] A survey of the principal ruins was made and has been published by Captain Selby; but the more elaborate plans of Captain Jones, which included all the neighbouring country, have been mislaid, and are not at present available.

[5] Selby, *Memoir*, p. 3.

this, or in any other case, deserving of implicit credence. The ancient historians, even the more trustworthy of them, are in the habit of exaggerating in

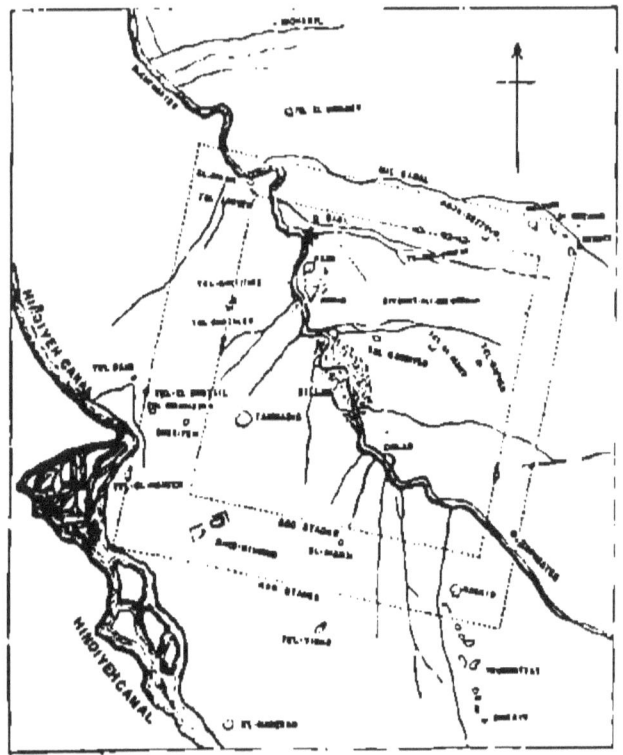

Chart of the Country round Babylon, with the limits of the ancient City, according to Oppert.

their numbers;[19] and, on such subjects as measurements, they were apt to take the declarations of their

---

[19] On the numerical exaggerations of Herodotus, see the author's Essay prefixed to his *Herodotus*, vol. I. pp. 52, 53, note 4, 2nd edition.

native guides, who would be sure to make overstatements. Still, in this instance we have so many distinct authorities—eye-witnesses of the facts—and some of them belonging to times when scientific accuracy had begun to be appreciated, that we must be very incredulous if we do not accept their witness, so far as it is consentient and not intrinsically very improbable.

According to Herodotus,[11] an eye-witness,[12] and the earliest authority on the subject, the *enceinte* of Babylon was a square, 120 stades (about 14 miles) each way—the entire circuit of the walls being thus 56 miles and the area enclosed within them falling little short of 200 square miles. Ctesias,[13] also an eye-witness, and the next writer on the subject, reduced the circuit of the walls to 360 stades, or 41 miles, and made the area consequently little more than 100 square miles. These two estimates are respectively the greatest and the least that have come down to us. The historians of Alexander, while conforming nearly to the statements of Ctesias, a little enlarge his dimensions, making the circuit 365, 368, or 385 stades.[14] The differences here are inconsiderable; and it seems to be established, on a weight of testimony which we rarely possess in such a matter, that the walls of this great town were about forty miles in circumference, and enclosed an area as large as that of the Landgraviat of Hesse Homburg.

---

[11] Herod. i. 178.
[12] I think no discerning reader can peruse the account of Babylon and the adjacent region given by Herodotus (i. 178-185), without feeling that the writer means to represent himself as having seen the city and country. Thus the question of whether he was an eye-witness or not depends on his veracity, which no modern critic has impugned.
[13] Ap. Diod. Sic. ii. 7, § 3.
[14] Clitarchus made the circumference 365 stadia (ap. Diod. Sic. l. s. c.); Q. Curtius, 368 (*Hist. Alex.* v. 1); Strabo, perhaps following Nearchus, made it 385 (Strab. xvi. 1, § 5).

It is difficult to suppose that the real city—the
streets and squares—can at any time have occupied
one-half of this enormous area. A clear space, we
are told, was left for a considerable distance inside
the wall[14]—like the *pomœrium* of the Romans—upon
which no houses were allowed to be built. When
houses began, they were far from being continuous;
gardens, orchards, even fields were interspersed
among the buildings; and it was supposed that the
inhabitants, when besieged, could grow sufficient corn
for their own consumption within the walls.[16] Still
the whole area was laid out with straight streets, or
perhaps one should say with roads (for the houses
cannot have been continuous along them), which cut
one another everywhere at right angles,[17] like the
streets of some German towns.[18] The wall of the
town was pierced with a hundred gates,[19] twenty-five
(we may suppose) in each face, and the roads led
straight to these portals, the whole area being thus
cut up into square blocks. The houses were in
general lofty, being three or even four stories high.[20]
They are said to have had vaulted roofs, which
were not protected externally with any tiling, since
the climate was so dry as to render such a protection
unnecessary.[21] The beams used in the houses were
of palm-wood, all other timber being scarce in the

---

[14] Q. Curt. l. s. c. The perfectly clear space, according to this writer, extended for two stades—nearly a quarter of a mile—from the wall.
[16] Ibid. Herodotus, however, represents Labynetus, the last king, as carefully provisioning the city before its siege by Cyrus (i. 190).
[17] Herod. L 180.
[18] Manheim, for instance. In Greece this mode of laying out a town was called 'Ιπποδάμου νέμησις, from the architect of the Piræus, who laid out the town there, and also the city of Thurii, in this fashion. (See Arist. *Pol*. vii. 10; Hesych. *lex.* ad voc. 'Ιππόδ. νέμ.; Phot. *Lex. Suppy.* p. 111; Diod. Sic. xii. 10.)
[19] Herod. I. 179.
[20] Ibid. i. 180.
[21] Strab. xvi. 1, § 5.

country; and such pillars as the houses could boast were of the same material. The construction of these last was very rude. Around posts of palm-wood were twisted wisps of rushes, which were covered with plaster, and then coloured according to the taste of the owner.[1]

The Euphrates ran through the town, dividing it nearly in half.[2] Its banks were lined throughout with quays of brick laid in bitumen, and were further guarded by two walls of brick, which skirted them along their whole length. In each of these walls were twenty-five gates, corresponding to the number of the streets which gave upon the river; and outside each gate was a sloped landing-place, by which you could descend to the water's edge, if you had occasion to cross the river.[3] Boats were kept ready at these landing-places to convey passengers from side to side; while for those who disliked this method of conveyance a bridge was provided of a somewhat peculiar construction. A number of stone piers were erected in the bed of the stream, firmly clamped together with fastenings of iron and lead; wooden drawbridges connected pier with pier during the day, and on these passengers passed over; but at night they were withdrawn, in order that the bridge might not be used during the dark.[4] Diodorus declares that besides this bridge, to which he assigns a length of five stades (about 1000 yards) and a breadth of 30 feet,[4] the two sides of the river were joined together by a tunnel, which was fifteen feet

---

[1] Strab. l. s. c. Περὶ τοὺς στύ-
λους στρέφοντες ἐκ τῆς καλάμης
σχοινία περιτιθέασιν, εἶτ᾽ ἐπαλεί-
φοντες χρώμασι ἐσταγράφουσι, κ.τ.λ.

[2] Herod. l. 185.
[3] Ibid. i. 180.
[4] Ibid. i. 186.
[5] Diod. Sic. ii. 8, § 2.

wide and twelve high to the spring of its arched roof.[6]

The most remarkable buildings which the city contained were the two palaces, one on either side of the river, and the great temple of Belus. Herodotus describes[7] the great temple as contained within a square enclosure, two stades (nearly a quarter of a mile) both in length and breadth. Its chief feature was the *ziggurat* or tower, a huge solid mass of brickwork, built (like all Babylonian temple-towers) in stages, square being emplaced on square, and a sort of rude pyramid being thus formed,[8] at the top of which was the main shrine of the god. The basement platform of the Belus tower was, Herodotus tells us, a stade, or rather more than 200 yards, each way. The number of stages was eight. The ascent to the highest stage, which contained the shrine of the god, was on the outside, and consisted either of steps, or of an inclined plane, carried round the four sides of the building, and in this way conducting to the top. According to Strabo the tower was a stade (606 feet 9 inches) in height; but this estimate, if it is anything more than a conjecture, must represent rather the length of the winding ascent than the real altitude of the building. The great pyramid itself was only 480 feet high; and it is very questionable whether any Babylonian building ever equalled it. About halfway up the ascent was a resting-place with seats, where persons commonly sat a while on their way to the summit.[9] The shrine which

---

[6] Diod. Sic. II. 9, § 2.
[7] Herod. i. 181. Compare Strab. xvi. 1, § 5, where the temple is called "the tomb of Belus."
[8] Ἦν δὲ πυραμὶς τετράγωνος ἐξ αὐτῆς πλίνθου. (Strab. l. s. c.)
[9] Herod. l. s. c.

crowned the edifice was large and rich. In the time of Herodotus it contained no image; but only a golden table and a large couch, covered with a handsome drapery. This, however, was after the Persian conquest and the plunder of its principal treasures. Previously, if we may believe Diodorus,[10] the shrine was occupied by three colossal images of gold—one of Bel, one of Beltis, and a third of Rhea or Ishtar. Before the image of Beltis were two golden lions, and near them two enormous serpents of silver, each thirty talents in weight. The golden table—forty feet long and fifteen broad—was in front of these statues; and upon it stood two huge drinking-cups, of the same weight as the serpents. The shrine also contained two enormous censers, and three golden bowls, one for each of the three deities.[11]

At the base of the tower was a second shrine or chapel, which in the time of Herodotus contained a sitting image of Bel, made of gold, with a golden table in front of it, and a stand for the image, of the same precious metal.[12] Here too Persian avarice had been busy; for anciently this shrine had possessed a second statue, which was a human figure twelve cubits high, made of solid gold.[13] The shrine was also rich in private offerings. Outside the building, but within the sacred enclosure, were two altars, a smaller one of gold, on which it was customary to offer sucklings, and a larger one, probably of stone, where the worshippers sacrificed full-grown victims.[14]

---

[10] Diod. Sic. ii. 9, § 5.
[11] Ibid. §§ 6–9.
[12] Herod. I. 183. The Chaldæan priests told Herodotus that the gold of the image, table, and stand, weighed altogether 800 talents.
[13] Herod. l. s. c.
[14] The great altar was also that on which a thousand talents' weight of frankincense was offered annually at the festival of the god. (Herod. l. s. c.)

CHAP. IV.   GREAT PALACE—HANGING GARDENS.   345

The great palace was a building of still larger dimensions than the great temple. According to Diodorus, it was situated within a triple enclosure, the innermost wall being twenty stades, the second forty stades, and the outermost sixty stades (nearly seven miles), in circumference.[14] The outer wall was built entirely of plain baked brick. The middle, and inner walls were of the same material fronted with enamelled bricks, representing hunting-scenes. The figures, according to this author, were larger than the life, and consisted chiefly of a great variety of animal forms. There were not wanting, however, a certain number of human forms to enliven the scene; and among these were two— a man thrusting his spear through a lion, and a woman on horseback, aiming at a leopard with her javelin—which the later Greeks believe to represent the mythic Ninus and Semiramis.[15] Of the character of the apartments we hear nothing; but we are told that the palace had three gates, two of which were of brass, and that these had to be opened and shut by a machine.[17]

But the main glory of the palace was its pleasure-ground—the "Hanging Gardens," which the Greeks regarded as one of the seven wonders of the world.[18] This extraordinary construction, which owed its erection to the whim of a woman,[19] was a square, each side of which measured 400 Greek feet.[20] It was sup-

---

[14] Diod. Sic. II. 8, § 4. Quintus Curtius knows, however, of only one enclosure, which corresponds to the innermost wall of Diodorus, having a circuit of twenty stades. According to Curtius, this wall was 80 feet high, and its foundations were laid 30 feet below the surface of the soil. (Exp. Alex. Magn. v. 1.)
[15] Diod. Sic. II. 8, § 6.
[17] Ibid. § 7.
[18] Strab. xvi. 1. § 5.
[19] See below, ch. viii.
[20] Diod. Sic. ii. 10, § 2.

ported upon several tiers of open arches, built one over the other, like the walls of a classic theatre,[3] and sustaining at each stage, or story, a solid platform, from which the piers of the next tier of arches rose. The building towered into the air to the height of at least seventy-five feet, and was covered at top with a great mass of earth, in which there grew not merely flowers and shrubs, but trees also of the largest size.[1] Water was supplied from the Euphrates through pipes, and was raised (it is said) by a screw working on the principle of Archimedes.[2] To prevent the moisture from penetrating into the brickwork and gradually destroying the building, there were interposed between the bricks and the mass of soil, first a layer of reeds mixed with bitumen, then a double layer of burnt brick cemented with gypsum, and thirdly a coating of sheet lead.[3] The ascent to the garden was by steps.[4] On the way up, among the arches which sustained the building, were stately apartments,[5] which must have been pleasant from their coolness. There was also a chamber within the structure containing the machinery by which the water was raised.[6]

---

[3] Ibid. ἔστι τὴν πρόσοψιν εἶναι θεατροειδή.

[1] Diod. Sic. ii. 10, § 5. Quintus Curtius says that the trunks of some of the trees were 12 feet in diameter. (*Exp. Alex. Magn.* v. 1.) Strabo relates that some of the piers were made hollow, and filled with earth, for the trees to strike their roots down them. But few trees have a tap-root.

[2] This is the explanation given of Strabo's κοχλίαι, δι᾿ ὧν τὸ ὕδωρ ἀνήγον εἰς τὸν κῆπον ἀπὸ τοῦ Εὐφράτου, συνεχῶς οἱ πρὸς τοῦτο τεταγμένοι (xvi. 1, § 5; compare Diod. Sic. v. 37, § 3). It is more probable that the water was really raised by means of buckets and pulleys. (See above, vol. i. p. 499.)

[3] Diod. Sic. ii. 10, § 5.

[4] Strab. l. s. c. ἡ δ᾿ ἀνωτάτω στέγη προσβάσεις κλιμακωτὰς ἔχει.

[5] Διαίται βασιλικαί. Diod. Sic. ii. 10, § 6.

[6] Ibid. For representations of Assyrian "hanging gardens," see above, vol. i. p. 388, and vol. ii. p. 221. This garden at Babylon must, however, have been far more complicated and more stately.

Of the smaller palace, which was opposite to the larger one, on the other side the river, but few details have come down to us. Like the large palace, it was guarded by a triple enclosure, the entire circuit of which measured (it is said) thirty stades.¹ It contained a number of bronze statues, which the Greeks believed to represent the god Belus, and the sovereigns Ninus and Semiramis, together with their officers. The walls were covered with battle-scenes, and hunting-scenes,² vividly represented by means of bricks painted and enamelled.

Such was the general character of the town and its chief edifices, if we may believe the descriptions of eye-witnesses. The walls which enclosed and guarded the whole—or which, perhaps one should rather say, guarded the district within which Babylon was placed—have been already mentioned as remarkable for their great extent,³ but cannot be dismissed without a more special and minute description. Like the "Hanging Gardens," they were included among the "world's seven wonders,"⁴ and, according to every account given of them, their magnitude and construction were remarkable.

It has been already noticed that, according to the lowest of the ancient estimates, the entire length of

---

¹ Diod. Sic. II. 8, § 7.
² Διαγραφὰς καὶ συντύπα, Diod. Sic. l. s. c. This statement of the subjects of Babylonian ornamentation is so completely in harmony with the practice of the Assyrians that we cannot doubt its truth. War-scenes and hunting-scenes are decidedly those which predominated on the walls of an Assyrian palace. (See vol. I. p. 429.) It is curious to find the same habits continuing in the same regions as late as the time of the Emperor Julian. See Amm. Marc. xxiv. 6, where we hear of a "diversorium opacum et amoenum, gentiles picturas per omnes aedium partes ostendens, Regis bestias multiplici venatione trucidantis:" to which the author adds the remark, "nec enim apud eos pingitur vel fingitur aliud praeter varias caedes et bella."
³ Supra, p. 340.
⁴ Strab. xvi. 1, § 5.

the walls was 360 stades, or more than forty-one miles. With respect to the width, we have two very different statements,[13] one by Herodotus and the other by Clitarchus and Strabo. Herodotus[14] makes the width 50 royal cubits or about 85 English feet, Strabo and Q. Curtius reduced the estimate to 32 feet.[15] There is still greater discrepancy with respect to the height of the walls. Herodotus says that the height was 200 royal cubits, or 300 royal feet (about 335 feet English); Ctesias made it 50 fathoms, or 300 ordinary Greek feet;[16] Pliny and Solinus[16] substituting feet for the royal cubits of Herodotus, made the altitude 235 feet; Philostratus[16] and Q. Curtius,[17] following perhaps some one of Alexander's historians, gave for the height 150 feet; finally Clitarchus, as reported by Diodorus Siculus,[18] and Strabo,[19] who probably followed him, have left us the very moderate estimate of 75 feet. It is impossible to reconcile these numbers. The supposition that some of them belong properly to the outer, and others to the inner wall,[20] will not explain the discrepancies—for the measurements cannot by any ingenuity be reduced to two sets of dimensions.[1] The only

---

[13] The statement of Pliny (*H. N.* vi. 26), which Solinus copies (*Polyhist.* c. 60), may perhaps not rest on data distinct from those of Herodotus. These writers may merely soften down the cubits of Herodotus into feet.

[14] Herod. I. 178.

[15] Strab. l. s. c.; Q. Curtius, v. 1.

[16] Ap. Diod. Sic. ii. 7, § 3.

[16] See the passages quoted in note 11. Pliny and Solinus make the royal foot exceed the common one by the same amount (3 fingers' breadth) by which Herodotus regards the royal as exceeding the common cubit.

[16] Philostr. *Vit. Alex. Tyan.* l. 25.

[17] Q. Curt. l. s. c.

[18] Diod. Sic. ii. 7, § 4.

[19] Strab. xvi. 1, § 5.

[20] This is M. Oppert's view. (See his *Expédition Scientifique en Mésopotamie*, tom. i. p. 225.) The author of the present work was, he believes, the first to suggest it. (See his article on Babylon in Dr. Smith's *Biblical Dictionary*, vol. i. p. 150.) On the whole, however, the view appears to him not to be tenable.

[1] Without reckoning the late and absurd Orosius, who gave the wall a breadth of 375 feet (*Hist.* ii. 6),

conclusion which it seems possible to draw from the conflicting testimony is, that the numbers were either rough guesses made by very unskilful travellers, or else were (in most cases) intentional exaggerations palmed upon them by the native *ciceroni*. Still the broad facts remain — first, that the walls enclosed an enormous space, which was very partially occupied by buildings;[2] secondly, that they were of great and unusual thickness;[3] and thirdly, that they were of a vast height[4] — seventy or eighty feet at least in the time of Alexander after the wear and tear of centuries and the violence of at least three conquerors.[5]

The general character of the construction is open to but little doubt. The wall was made of bricks, either baked in kilns,[6] or (more probably) dried in the sun, and laid in a cement of bitumen, with

---

or the blundering Scholiast on Juvenal (*Sat.* x. 171), who reversed the numbers of Pliny and Solinus, for the height and breadth, it must be said that there are really four different estimates for the height, and three for the width of the walls. See the subjoined table.

Estimates of Height.		Estimates of Width.	
	Feet.		Feet.
Herodotus (200 royal cubits)	335	(50 royal cubits)	85
Ctesias (50 fathoms)	300	(unknown)	
Pliny (200 royal feet)	225	(50 royal feet)	60
Solinus (ditto)	225	(ditto)	60
Philostratus (3 half plethra)	150	(less than a plethron)	
Q. Curtius (100 cubits)	150	(32 feet)	32
Clitarchus (50 cubits)	75	(unknown)	
Strabo (ditto)	75	(32 feet)	32

[2] See Arist. *Pol.* III. 1. Τοιαύτη δ' ἴσως ἐστὶ καὶ Βαβυλών, καὶ πᾶσα ἥτις περιγραφὴν ἔχει μᾶλλον ἔθνους ἢ πόλεως· ἧς γε φασὶν ἁλωκυίας τρίτην ἡμέραν οὐκ αἰσθέσθαι τι μέρος τῆς πόλεως. Compare Jerem. li. 31.
[3] Jerem. li. 58. [4] Ibid. ver. 53.
[5] Cyrus, Darius, and Xerxes.
[6] So Herodotus (i. 170. ἀλινέαντες δὲ πλίνθους ἱκανάς, ὤπτησαν αὐτὰς ἐν καμίνοισι). But we may be tolerably certain that crude brick formed the main material, and that at the utmost the facings were of burnt brick.

occasional layers of reeds between the courses. Externally it was protected by a wide and deep moat. On the summit were low towers,[1] rising above the wall to the height of some ten or fifteen feet,[2] and probably serving as guard-rooms for the defenders. These towers are said to have been 250 in number;[9] they were least numerous on the western face of the city, where the wall ran along the marshes.[10] They were probably angular, not round; and, instead of extending through the whole thickness of the wall, they were placed along its outer and inner edge, tower facing tower, with a wide space between them—" enough," Herodotus says, " for a four-horse chariot to turn in."[11] The wall did not depend on them for its strength, but on its own height and thickness, which were such as to render scaling and mining equally hopeless.

Such was Babylon, according to the descriptions of the ancients—a great city, built on a very regular plan, surrounded by populous suburbs interspersed among fields and gardens, the whole being included within a large square strongly fortified *enceinte*. When we turn from this picture of the past to contemplate the present condition of the localities, we are at first struck with astonishment at the small traces which remain of so vast and wonderful a metropolis. "The broad walls of Babylon" are "utterly broken" down, and her "high gates burned with fire."[12] "The golden city hath ceased."[13] God has "swept it with the besom of destruction."[14]

---

[1] See the description of Herodotus (l. s. c.).
[2] Q. Curtius says 10 feet (v. 1); Strabo 10 cubits (xvi. 1, § 5).
[9] Diod. Sic. li. 7, § 4.
[10] Ibid. § 5.   [11] Herod. l. s. c.
[12] Jerem. li. 58.   [13] Isaiah xiv. 4.
[14] Ibid. ver. 23.

"The glory of the kingdoms, the beauty of the Chaldees' excellency," is become "as when God overthrew Sodom and Gomorrha."[16] The traveller who passes through the land is at first inclined to say that there are no ruins, no remains, of the mighty city which once lorded it over the earth. By and by, however, he begins to see that though ruins in the common acceptation of the term, scarcely exist—though there are no arches, no pillars, but one or two appearances of masonry even—yet the whole country is covered with traces of exactly that kind which it was prophesied Babylon should leave.[16] Vast "heaps" or mounds, shapeless and unsightly, are scattered at intervals over the entire region where it is certain that Babylon anciently stood, and between the "heaps" the soil is in many places composed of fragments of pottery and bricks, and deeply impregnated with nitre, infallible indications of its having once been covered with buildings. As the traveller descends southward from Baghdad he finds these indications increase, until, on nearing the Euphrates a few miles beyond Mohawil he notes that they have become continuous, and finds himself in a region of mounds, some of which are of enormous size.

These mounds begin about five miles above Hillah,[1] and extend for a distance of above three miles[2] from north to south along the course of the river, lying principally on its left or eastern bank. The ruins on this side consist chiefly of three great

---

[16] Isaiah xiii. 19.
[16] Jerem. li. 37. "And Babylon shall become heaps." Compare l. 26.
[1] Layard, Nineveh and Babylon, p. 502.

[2] Six thousand yards (nearly 3½ miles), according to Capt. Selby. (Memoir on the Ruins of Babylon, p. 4.)

masses of building. The most northern, to which the Arabs at the present day apply the name of BABIL³—the true native appellation of the ancient city⁴—is a vast pile of brickwork of an irregular quadrilateral shape, with precipitous sides furrowed by ravines, and with a flat top. Of the four faces of the ruins the southern seems to be the most perfect.⁵ It extends a distance of about 200 yards,⁶ or almost exactly a stade, and runs nearly in a straight line from west to east. At its eastern extremity it forms a right angle with the east face,⁷ which runs nearly due north for about 180 yards,⁸ also almost in a straight line. The western and northern faces are apparently much worn away. Here are the chief ravines, and here is the greatest seeming deviation from the original lines of the building. The greatest height of the Babil mound is 130 or 140 feet.⁹ It is mainly composed of sun-dried brick, but shows signs of having been faced with fire-burnt brick, carefully cemented with an excellent white mortar.¹⁰ The bricks of this outer

---

³ This is the Mujelibé ("the overturned") of Rich (*Memoirs on Babylon*, passim), and Ker Porter (*Travels*, vol. ii. pp. 339-349). The Arabs now apply the name Mujelibé to the central or Kasr heap. (Layard, *Nin. and Bab.* p. 505).

⁴ The final syllable in Babylon is a Greek nominatival ending. The real name of the city was *Bab-il*, "the Gate of the God Il," or "the Gate of God." The Jews changed the name to Babel (בבל), in derisive reference to the "confusion of tongues."

⁵ Oppert, *Expédition Scientifique*, tom. i. p. 169.

⁶ Rich made the length of the south side of Babil 219 yards (*First Memoir*, p. 28); M. Oppert (l. s. c.) makes it 180 mètres (197 yards).

⁷ Oppert, l. s. c.

⁸ Rich, l. s. c. Compare M. Oppert's plan of the ruin. Ker Porter's 230 feet (*Travels*, vol. ii. p. 340) is an extraordinary misrepresentation.

⁹ Rich estimated the height of the S.E. or highest angle at 141 feet. M. Oppert gives the greatest height of the ruin as 40 mètres, or 131 feet. (*Expédition*, vol. i. p. 168.)

¹⁰ Layard, *Nineveh and Babylon*, p. 505.

CHAP. IV.   THE BABIL MOUND.   353

View of the Babil mound from the Kasr.

facing bear the name and titles of Nebuchadnezzar. A very small portion of the original structure has been laid bare—enough however to show that the lines of the building did not slope like those of a pyramid,[11] but were perpendicular, and that the side walls had, at intervals, the support of buttresses.[12]

This vast building, whatever it was, stood within a square enclosure, two sides of which, the northern

---

[11] M. Oppert regards the Babil mound as the "Tomb of Belus," which he distinguishes from the Temple of Bel. He gives it the shape of a pyramid, inclined at an angle of about 65 degrees. [12] Layard, l. s. c.

VOL. III.   2 A

and eastern, are still very distinctly marked."[13] A long low line of rampart runs for 400 yards parallel to the east face of the building, at a distance of 120 or 130 yards, and a similar but somewhat longer line of mound runs parallel to the north face at rather a greater distance from it. On the west a third line could be traced in the early part of the present century;[14] but it appears now to be obliterated. Here and on the south are the remains of an ancient canal,[15] the construction of which may have caused the disappearance of the southern, and of the lower part of the western line.

Ground-plan of the Babil mound, with its rampart, and traces of an old canal.

Below the Babil mound, which stands isolated from the rest of the ruins, are two principal masses, the more northern known to the Arabs as EL KASR, "the Palace," and the more southern as "the mound of Amran," from the tomb of a reputed prophet, Amrán-ibn-Ali, which crowns its summit.[16] The Kasr mound is an oblong square, about 700 yards long by 600 broad,[17] with the sides facing the cardinal points. Its height[18] above

---

[13] See the plans of Ker Porter (*Travels*, vol. II. pl. 73, opp. p. 349) and Selby. M. Oppert wholly omits this rampart. [14] Ker Porter, p. 345.
[15] See the above plan, which follows the map of Capt. Selby.
[16] Layard, *Nin. and Bab.* p. 508; Loftus, *Chaldæa and Susiana*, p. 17.

[17] "Seven hundred yards both in length and breadth" (Rich, *First Memoir*, p. 22). "Its length is nearly 800 yards, its breadth 600" (Ker Porter, *Travels*, vol. II. p. 355). Capt. Selby and M. Oppert agree in giving the ruin an oblong shape.
[18] Ker Porter, p. 355.

the plain is 70 feet. Its longer direction is from north to south. As far as it has been penetrated, it consists mainly of rubbish—loose bricks, tiles and fragments of stone."[19] In a few places only are there undisturbed remains of building. One such relic is a subterranean passage, seven feet in height, floored and walled with baked brick, and covered in at the top with great blocks of sandstone,[20] which may either have been a secret exit, or more probably an enormous drain. Another is the Kasr, or "palace" proper, whence the mound has its name. This is a fragment of excellent brick masonry in a wonderful state of preservation, consisting of walls, piers, and buttresses, and in places ornamented with pilasters,[1] but of too fragmentary a character to furnish the modern inquirer with any clue to the original plan of the building. The bricks are of a pale yellow colour and of the best possible quality, nearly resembling our fire-bricks.[2] They are stamped, one and all, with the name and titles of Nebuchadnezzar. The mortar in which they are laid is a fine lime cement, which adheres so closely to the bricks that it is difficult to obtain

Ground-plan of the Kasr mound, according to M. Oppert. A. Ruins of Palace. B. Solitary tree. C. Colossal lion.

---

[19] Layard, *Nin. and Bab.* p. 505.
[20] Rich, *First Memoir,* pp. 23, 24; Layard, p. 506.
[1] Layard, pp. 505, 506. Compare Rich, p. 25.
[2] Rich, pp. 22 and 61.

a specimen entire.² In the dust at the foot of the walls are numerous fragments of brick, painted, and covered with a thick enamel or glaze.⁴ Here too have been found a few fragments of sculptured stone,⁵ and slabs containing an account of the erection of a palatial edifice by Nebuchadnezzar.⁶ Near the northern edge of the mound, and about midway in its breadth is a colossal figure of a lion,⁷ rudely carved in black basalt, standing over the prostrate figure of a man with arms outstretched. A single tree grows on the huge ruin, which the Arabs declare to be of a species not known elsewhere, and regard as a remnant of the hanging garden of Bokht-i-nazar. It is a tamarisk of no rare kind, but of very great age, in consequence of which, and of its exposed position, the growth and foliage are somewhat peculiar.⁸

South of the Kasr mound, at the distance of about 600 yards, is the remaining great mass of ruins, the mound of Jumjuma, or of Amran. The general shape of this mound is triangular,⁹ but it is very irregular and ill-defined, so as scarcely to admit of accurate description.¹⁰ Its three sides face respectively a little east of north, a little south

---

³ Layard, p. 506; Rich, p. 25; Ker Porter, vol. II. pp. 365, 366.
⁴ Layard, p. 507; Oppert, tom. I. p. 142.
⁵ As the frieze discovered by Mr. Layard (*Nin. and Bab.* p. 508), of which a representation is given below (p. 390), and one or two fragments recovered by the French.
⁶ See the author's *Herodotus*, vol. ii. p. 480, 2nd edition. Compare Oppert, *Expédition,* tom. i. p. 140.

⁷ Layard, p. 507; Oppert, tom. I. p. 148. According to the latter author, the length of the lion is four mètres, or 13½ feet, and its height three mètres, or 9 feet 10 inches.
⁸ Oppert, pp. 147, 148.
⁹ Ker Porter, vol. II. p. 371. M. Oppert calls it a trapezium (p. 157), but his plan is, roughly speaking, a triangle. Rich says it is shaped like a quadrant (p. 21).
¹⁰ Layard, *Nin. & Bab.* p.509, note.

of east, and a little south of west. The south-western side, which runs nearly parallel with the Euphrates and seems to have been once washed by the river,[11] is longer than either of the others, extending a distance of above a thousand yards,[12] while the south-eastern may be 800 yards, and the north-eastern 700. Innumerable ravines traverse the mound on every side, penetrating it nearly to its centre. The surface is a series of undulations. Neither masonry, nor sculpture is anywhere apparent. All that meets the eye is a mass of débris; and the researches hitherto made have failed to bring to light any distinct traces of building. Occasional bricks are found, generally of poor material, and bearing the names and titles of some of the earlier Babylonian monarchs; but the trenches opened in the pile have in no case laid bare even the smallest fragment of a wall.[13]

Plan of the mound of Amran, according to M. Oppert.

Besides the remains which have been already described, the most remarkable are certain long lines of

---

[11] See the author's article on 'Babylon' in Dr. Smith's *Biblical Dictionary*, vol. i. p. 151. Compare Oppert, *Expédition*, tom. i. p. 157.

[12] Rich says the length is 1100 yards, and the greatest breadth 800 (p. 21). M. Oppert calls the greatest length 500 mètres (547 yards); but his own plan shows a distance of 600 mètres (656 yards). Capt. Selby's map agrees nearly with Rich.

[13] See Layard, *Nin. & Bab.* p. 509.

rampart on both sides of the river, which lie outside the other ruins, enclosing them all, except the mound of Babil. On the left bank of the stream there is to be traced, in the first place, a double line of wall or rampart, having a direction nearly due north and south,[1] which lies east of the Kasr and Amran mounds, at the distance from them of about 1000 yards. Beyond this is a single line of rampart to the north-east, traceable for about two miles, the direction of which is nearly from north-west to south-east, and a double line of rampart to the south-east,[2] traceable for a mile and a half, with a direction from north-east to south-west. The two lines in this last case are from 600 to 700 yards apart, and diverge from one another as they run out to the north-east. The inner of the two meets the north-eastern rampart nearly at a right angle, and is clearly a part of the same work. It is questioned however whether this line of fortification is ancient, and not rather a construction belonging to Parthian times.[3]

A low line of mounds is traceable between the western face of the Amran and Kasr hills, and the present eastern bank of the river, bounding a sort of narrow valley, in which either the main stream of the Euphrates, or at any rate a branch from it, seems anciently to have flowed.

---

[1] See the plans of Rich, Ker Porter, and Selby, which all mark very distinctly the double line in question. Capt. Selby's survey makes the two lines not quite parallel, and gives both of them a slight leaning to the west of north. M. Oppert's plan represents them very meagerly and untruly.

[2] M. Oppert has only a single line here; but a double line is shown by all the other authorities. The true direction of the line was for the first time given by Capt. Selby.

[3] This is the opinion of Sir H. Rawlinson. M. Oppert regards the work as Babylonian.

General Chart of the Ruins of Babylon.

On the right bank of the stream the chief remains are of the same kind. West of the river, a rampart twenty feet high[4] runs for nearly a mile[5] parallel with the general line of the Amran mound, at the distance of about 1000 yards from the old course of the stream. At either extremity the line of the rampart turns at a right angle, running down towards the river, and being traceable towards the north for 400 yards and towards the south for fifty or sixty.[6] It is evident that there was once, before the stream flowed in its present channel, a rectangular enclosure a mile long and 1000 yards broad, opposite to the Amran mound; and there are indications that within this *enceinte* was at least one important building, which was situated near the south-east angle of the enclosure, on the banks of the old course of the river. The bricks found at this point bear the name of Neriglissar.

There are also, besides these ramparts and the great masses of ruin above described, a vast number of scattered and irregular heaps or hillocks on both sides of the river, chiefly however upon the eastern bank. Of these one only seems to deserve distinct mention. This is the mound called El Homeira, "the Red,"—which lies due east of the Kasr, distant from it about 800 yards,—a mound said to be 300 yards long by 100 wide,[7] and to attain an elevation of

---

[4] So Capt. Selby. See his Map, Sheet I.

[5] The line has several gaps, more especially one very wide one in the middle; through which no fewer than five canals have passed at some time or other. But the position of the fragments which remain sufficiently indicates that the work was originally continuous.

[6] See Capt. Selby's plan, which is the only trustworthy authority for the ruins on the right bank.

[7] Ker Porter, *Travels*, vol. ii. p. 363.

60 or 70 feet.[8] It is composed of baked brick of a bright red colour, and must have been a building of a very considerable height resting upon a somewhat confined base. Its bricks are inscribed along their edges, not (as is the usual practice) on their lower face.[9]

The only other ancient work of any importance of which some remains are still to be traced, is a brick embankment on the left bank of the stream between the Kasr and the Babil mounds,[10] extending for a distance of a thousand yards in a line which has a slight curve and a general direction of S.S.W. The bricks of this embankment are of a bright red colour, and of great hardness.[11] They are laid wholly in bitumen. The legend which they bear shows that the quay was constructed by Nabonidus.

Such then are the ruins of Babylon—the whole that can now with certainty be assigned to the "beauty of the Chaldees' excellency"[12]—the "Great Babylon" of Nebuchadnezzar.[13] Within a space little more than three miles long and a mile and three-quarters broad are contained all the undoubted remains[14] of the greatest city of the old world.

---

[8] Ker Porter, l. s. c. Capt. Selby makes the height 65 feet (see his Map, Sheet 1.). M. Oppert calls the mound "very lofty" (très-élevé), but he gives no estimate of its height. (*Expédition*, tom. i. p. 183.)

[9] Ker Porter, vol. ii. p. 354.

[10] This embankment is placed too low in the very imperfect chart of the ruins, which the author drew for the first edition of his *Herodotus* (vol. ii. p. 571). He owes an apology to M. Oppert for having found fault with his emplacement of the work. Capt. Selby's survey shows that in this point M. Oppert was perfectly correct.

[11] Oppert, *Expédition*, tom. i. p. 184.

[12] Isaiah xliii. 19.

[13] Dan. iv. 30.

[14] As we do not *know* what position in the city the Royal quarter occupied (for we must not press the ἐν μέσῳ of Herodotus), we cannot say with absolute certainty that the city contained even such groups as, for instance, those east and north-east of Babil, or again those on the west bank opposite the quay of Na-

These remains, however, do not serve in any way to define the ancient limits of the place. They are surrounded on every side by nitrous soil, and by low heaps which it has not been thought worth while to excavate, but which the best judges assign to the same era as the great mounds, and believe to mark the sites of the temples and other public buildings of the ancient city. Masses of this kind are most frequent to the north and east. Sometimes they are almost continuous for miles; and if we take the Kasr mound as a centre, and mark about it an area extending five miles in each direction (which would give a city of the size described by Ctesias and the historians of Alexander), we shall scarcely find a single square mile of the hundred without some indications of ancient buildings upon its surface. The case is not like that of Nineveh, where outside the walls the country is for a considerable distance singularly bare of ruins.[15] The mass of Babylonian remains extending from Babil to Amran does not correspond to the whole *enceinte* of Nineveh, but to the mound of Koyunjik. It has every appearance of being, not the city, but "the heart of the city"[16]—the "Royal quarter"[17]— outside of which were the streets and squares, and still further off, the vanished walls. It may seem strange that the southern capital should have so

---

Iumidus. It is of course *highly probable* that these and all other neighbouring mounds formed a part of the ancient town.

[15] See above, vol. I. p. 313.

[16] Layard, *Nineveh and Babylon*, p. 491:—"Southward of Babel for the distance of nearly three miles there is almost an uninterrupted line of mounds, the ruins of vast edifices, collected together *as in the heart of a great city*."

[17] M. Oppert (*Expédition Scientifique*, Maps) calls the whole mass of ruins from Babil to Amran the "cité royale de Babylone."

greatly exceeded the dimensions of the northern one. But, if we follow the indications presented by the respective sites, we are obliged to conclude that there was really this remarkable difference.

It has to be considered in conclusion how far we can identify the various ruins above described with the known buildings of the ancient capital, and to what extent it is possible to reconstruct upon the existing remains the true plan of the city. Fancy, if it discards the guidance of fact, may of course with the greatest ease compose plans of a charming completeness. A rigid adherence to existing data will produce, it is to be feared, a somewhat meagre and fragmentary result; but most persons will feel that this is one of the cases where the maxim of Hesiod" applies—πλέον ἥμισυ παντός—"the half is preferable to the whole."

The one identification which may be made upon certain and indeed indisputable evidence is that of the Kasr mound with the palace built by Nebuchadnezzar." The tradition which has attached the name of Kasr or "Palace" to this heap is confirmed by inscriptions upon slabs found on the spot, wherein Nebuchadnezzar declares the building to be his "Grand Palace."' The bricks of that part of the ruin which remains uncovered bear, one and all, the name of this king;' and

---

" Hes. Op. et D. l. 40.
" Dorosus, Fr. 14.
' According to M. Oppert, several pavement slabs found on the Kasr mound bear the following inscription: "Grand palace of Nubuchadnezzar, king of Babylon, son of Nabopolassar, king of Babylon, who walked in the worship of the gods Nebo and Mero-

dach, his lords."
See the *Expédition Scientifique*, tom. i. p. 149.
' Layard, *Nineveh and Babylon*, p. 506. The bricks are all laid with the inscription *downwards*, a sure sign that they have never been disturbed, but remain as Nebuchadnezzar's builders placed them.

it is thus clear that here stood in ancient times the great work of which Berosus speaks as remarkable for its height and splendour.[3] If a confirmation of the fact were needed after evidence of so decisive a character, it would be found in the correspondence between the remains found on the mound and the description left us of the "greater palace" by Diodorus. Diodorus relates that the walls of this edifice were adorned with coloured representations of hunting-scenes;[4] and modern explorers find that the whole soil of the mound, and especially the part on which the fragment of ruin stands, is full of broken pieces of enamelled brick, varied in hue, and evidently containing portions of human and animal forms.[5]

But if the Kasr represents the palace built by Nebuchadnezzar, as is generally allowed by those who have devoted their attention to the subject,[6] it seems to follow almost as a certainty,[7] that the Amran mound is the site of that old palatial edifice to which the erection of Nebuchadnezzar was an addition. Berosus expressly states that Nebuchadnezzar's building "adjoined upon" the former palace,[8] a description which is fairly applicable

---

[3] Berosus, Fr. 14. Βασίλεια ... ἐν τῷ μὲν ἀνάστημα καὶ τὴν ἑτέραν πολυτέλειαν περισσὸν ἴσως ἂν εἴη λέγειν.
[4] Diod. Sic. ii. 8, § 6.
[5] Layard, *Nineveh and Babylon*, p. 507; Oppert, *Expédition Scientifique*, tom. I. pp. 145-145. Portions of a lion, of a horse, and of a human face, have been distinctly recognised.
[6] M. Oppert agrees on this point with Mr. Layard and Sir Henry Rawlinson (*Expédition*, tom. I. pp. 140-150).
[7] M. Oppert (*Expédition*, tom. I. pp. 157-167) argues that the Mound of Amran represents the ancient "hanging gardens." But his own estimate of its area is 15 hectares (37 acres), while the area of the "hanging gardens" was less than four acres according to Strabo (xvi. 1, § 5) and Diodorus (ii. 10, § 2).
[8] Beros. l. a. c. Προσκατασκεύασε τοῖς πατρῴοις βασιλείοις ἕτερα βασι-

to the Amran mound by means of a certain latitude of interpretation, but which is wholly inapplicable to any of the other ruins. This argument would be conclusive, even if it stood alone. It has, however, received an important corroboration in the course of recent researches. From the Amran mound, and from this part of Babylon only, have monuments been recovered of an earlier date than Nebuchadnezzar.⁹ Here and here alone did the early kings leave memorials of their presence in Babylon; and here consequently we may presume stood the ancient royal residence.

If then all the principal ruins on the east bank of the river, with the exception of the Babil mound and the long lines marking walls or embankments, be accepted as representing the "great palace" or "citadel" of the classical writers, we must recognise in the remains west of the ancient course of the river—the oblong square enclosure and the important building at its south-east angle¹⁰—the second or "smaller palace" of Ctesias, which was joined to the larger one, according to that writer, by a bridge and a tunnel.¹¹ This edifice, built or at any rate repaired by Neriglissar,¹² lay directly opposite the more ancient part of the eastern palace, being separated from it by the river, which anciently flowed along the western face of the Kasr and Amran mounds. The

---

ἅμα ἐχόμενα αὐτᾶς. M. Oppert wholly omits to locate the ancient palace.
⁹ See *British Museum Series*, Pl. lii. No. 7; Pl. xlviii. No. 9.
¹⁰ See above, p. 360.

¹¹ Diod. Sic. II. 8. § 3; 9. § 2.
¹² The bricks of this ruin are stamped with Neriglissar's name. Here too was found his cylinder with the inscription given in the *British Museum Series*, Pl. 67.

exact position of the bridge cannot be fixed.[13] With regard to the tunnel, it is extremely unlikely that any such construction was ever made.[14] The "Father of History" is wholly silent on the subject, while he carefully describes the bridge, a work far less extraordinary. The tunnel rests on the authority of two writers only—Diodorus[15] and Philostratus[16]—who both wrote after Babylon was completely ruined. It was probably one of the imaginations of the inventive Ctesias, from whom Diodorus evidently derived all the main points of his description.

Thus far there is no great difficulty in identifying the existing remains with buildings mentioned by ancient authors; but, at the point to which we are now come, the subject grows exceedingly obscure, and it is impossible to offer more than reasonable conjectures upon the true character of the remaining ruins. The descriptions of ancient writers would lead us to expect that we should find among the ruins unmistakable traces of the great temple of Belus, and at least some indication of the position occupied by the Hanging Gardens. These two famous constructions can scarcely, one would think, have wholly perished. More especially, the Belus temple, which was a stade square,[17] and (according to some) a stade in height,[18] must almost

---

[13] M. Oppert regards the bridge of Diodorus (ii. 8, § 2) as a pure invention (*Exp. Scientifique*, tom. I. p. 193). He supposes the real bridge —that of Herodotus and Quintus Curtius—to have been "a little south of Hillah" (ibid.). But this is a mere conjecture.

[14] The tunnel is accepted by M. Oppert (l. a. c.).
[15] Diod. Sic. ii. 9, § 2.
[16] Philostr. *Vit. Apoll. Tyan.* i. 25.
[17] Herod. i. 181; Strab. xvi. 1, § 5.
[18] Strab. l. s. c. Diod. Sic. ii. 9, § 4. Ὑψηλὸν καθ' ὑπερβολήν.

of necessity have a representative among the existing remains. This, indeed, is admitted on all hands; and the controversy is thereby narrowed to the question, which of two great ruins—the only two entitled by their size and situation to attention—has the better right to be regarded as the great and celebrated sanctuary of the ancient Babylon.

That the mound of Babil is the *ziggurat* or tower of a Babylonian temple scarcely admits of a doubt. Its square shape, its solid construction, its isolated grandeur, its careful emplacement with the sides facing the cardinal points,[19] and its close resemblance to other known Babylonian temple-towers, sufficiently mark it for a building of this character, or at any rate raise a presumption which it would require very strong reasons indeed to overcome. Its size moreover corresponds well with the accounts which have come down to us of the dimensions of the Belus temple,[20] and its name and proximity to the other main ruins show that it belonged certainly to the ancient capital. Against its claim to be regarded as the remains of the temple of Belus two objections only can be argued:—these are the absence of any appearance of stages, or even of a pyramidical shape, from the present ruin, and its position on the same side of the Euphrates with the palace. Herodotus expressly declares that the temple of Belus and the royal palace were upon opposite sides of the river,[21] and states moreover that the former was built in stages, which rose one

---

[19] It is more usual in Babylonia for the *angles* of a temple-tower to face the cardinal points. But for the astronomical purposes which the towers subserved (Diod. Sic. l. s. c.) it was indifferent which arrangement was adopted. [20] See above, p. 343. [21] Herod. I. 180, 181.

above the other to the number of eight." Now these two circumstances, which do not belong at present to the Babil mound, attach to a ruin distant from it about eleven or twelve miles—a ruin which is certainly one of the most remarkable in the whole country, and which, if Babylon had really been of the size asserted by Herodotus, might possibly have been included within the walls. The Birs-i-Nimrud had certainly seven, probably eight stages, and it is the only ruin on the present western bank of the Euphrates which is at once sufficiently grand to answer to the descriptions of the Belus temple, and sufficiently near to the other ruins to make its original inclusion within the walls not absolutely impossible. Hence, ever since the attention of scholars was first directed to the subject of Babylonian topography, opinion has been divided on the question before us, and there have not been wanting persons to maintain that the Birs-i-Nimrud is the true temple of Belus,¹ if not also the actual tower of Babel,² whose erection led to the confusion of tongues and general dispersion of the sons of Adam.

With this latter identification we are not in the present place concerned. With respect to the view

---

" Herod. I. 180, 181.
¹ This opinion was first put forward by Mr. Rich. See his *First Memoir on Babylon*, pp. 51-56; *Second Memoir*, pp. 30-31. His views were opposed by Major Rennell in an article published in the *Archaeologia*, London, 1816. They were reasserted and warmly defended by Sir R. Ker Porter in 1822 (*Travels*, vol. ii. pp. 316-327). Heeren adopted them in 1824, in the fourth edition of his *Reflections* (*Asiatic Nations*, vol. ii. pp. 172-175); and about 1826 Niebuhr spoke favourably of them in his lectures (*Vorträge*, vol. i. p. 30). Recently they have been maintained and copiously illustrated by M. Oppert (*Expédition Scientifique*, tom. I. pp. 200-216).

² So Ker Porter, vol. ii. p. 317; Heeren, *As. Nat.* vol. ii. p. 174; Oppert, in Dr. Smith's *Biblical Dictionary*, vol. iii. p. 1554.

that the Birs is the sanctuary of Belus, it may be observed in the first place, that the size of the building is very much smaller than that ascribed to the Belus temple;[3]—secondly, that it was dedicated to Nebo, who cannot be identified with Bel;[4] and thirdly, that it is not really any part of the remains of the ancient capital, but belongs to an entirely distinct town. The cylinders found in the ruin by Sir Henry Rawlinson declare the building to have been "the wonder of Borsippa;"[5] and Borsippa, according to all the ancient authorities, was a town by itself—an entirely distinct place from Babylon.[6] To include Borsippa within the outer wall of Babylon[7] is to run counter to all the authorities on the subject, the inscriptions, the native writer, Berosus,[8] and the classical geographers generally. Nor is the position thus assigned to the Belus temple in harmony with the statement of Herodotus, which alone causes explorers to seek for the temple on the west side of the river. For, though the expression which this writer uses[9] does not

---

[3] Bich, measuring the present ruins, supposed that the dimensions of the Birs would correspond sufficiently with those of the Belus temple (*First Memoir*, p. 49); but Sir H. Rawlinson found, on tunnelling into the mound, that the original base of the Birs tower was a square of only 272 feet. The Belus temple was a square of 606 feet.

[4] To meet this argument, M. Oppert has invented the term Bel-Nebo, for which there is absolutely no foundation.

[5] See the author's *Herodotus*, vol. II. p. 485, 2nd ed.

[6] See Berosus, Fr. 14; Strab. xvi. 1, 7; Arrian, Fr. 20; Justin, xii.

13; Steph. Byz. ad voc., &c.

[7] As M. Oppert does. See the plan, p. 339.

[8] M. Oppert endeavours to reconcile his view with that of the later geographers by saying that though Borsippa was originally within Babylon, i. e. within the outer wall, it afterwards, when the outer wall was destroyed by Darius Hystaspis, came to be outside the town and a distinct place. But it is at the time of Cyrus's siege, when all the defences were in the most perfect condition, that Berosus makes Cyrus "march away" from Babylon to the siege of Borsippa.

[9] Ἐν δὲ φάρσεϊ ἑκατέρῳ τῆς πόλιος ἐτετείχιστο ἐν μέσῳ (Herod. l. 181).

necessarily mean that the temple was in the exact centre of one of the two divisions of the town, it certainly implies that it lay *towards the middle* of one division—well within it—and not upon its outskirts. It is indeed inconceivable that the main sanctuary of the place, where the kings constantly offered their worship, should have been nine or ten miles from the palace! The distance between the Amran mound and Babil, which is about two miles, is quite as great as probability will allow us to believe existed between the old residence of the kings and the sacred shrine to which they were in the habit of resorting.

Still there remain as objections to the identification of the great temple with the Babil mound the two arguments already noticed. The Babil mound has no appearance of stages such as the Birs presents, nor has it even a pyramidical shape. It is a huge platform with a nearly level top, and sinks, rather than rises, in the centre. What has become, it is asked, of the seven upper stages of the great Belus tower, if this ruin represents it? Whither have they vanished? How is it that in crumbling down they have not left something like a heap towards the middle? To this it may be replied, that the destruction of the Belus tower, has not been the mere work of the elements—it was violently broken down either by Xerxes, or by some later king,[19]

Compare the expression of Arrian (*Exp. Alex.* vii. 17):—'Ο γὰρ τοῦ Βήλου νεὼς ἐν μέσῃ τῇ πόλει ἦν τῶν Βαβυλωνίων.

[19] Arrian says by Xerxes (τοῦτον τὸν νεὼν Ξέρξης κατέσκαψεν, l. s. c.). So Strabo (xvi. 1, § 5). But Herodotus seems to have found the building intact; and his visit must have fallen in the reign of Artaxerxes. Xerxes plundered the temple (Herod. i. 183), and may therefore in after times have been thought to have destroyed it, though the destruction was by a later king.

who may have completely removed all the upper stages. Again, it has served as a quarry to the hunters after bricks for more than twenty centuries;[14] so that it is only surprising that it still retains so much of its original shape. Further, when Alexander entered Babylon more than 2000 years ago, 10,000 men were employed for several weeks in clearing away the rubbish and laying bare the foundations of the building.[15] It is quite possible that a conical mass of crumbled brick may have been removed from the top of the mound at this time.

The difficulty remains that the Babil mound is on the same side of the Euphrates with the ruins of the Great Palace, whereas Herodotus makes the two buildings balance each other, one on the right and the other on the left bank of the stream. Now here it is in the first place to be observed that Herodotus is the only writer who does this. No other ancient author tells us anything of the relative situation of the two buildings. We have thus nothing to explain but the bald statement of a single writer—a writer no doubt of great authority, but still one not wholly infallible. We might say, then, that Herodotus probably made a mistake—that his memory failed him in this instance, or that he mistook his notes on the subject.[16] Or we may explain his error by supposing that he confounded a canal from the Euphrates, which

---

[13] Rich, *First Memoir*, p. 31; Layard, *Nineveh and Babylon*, p. 506; Loftus, *Chaldæa and Susiana*, p. 18.
[14] Strab. l. s. c. Compare Arrian, l. s. c.
[15] Herodotus did not always take notes. He appeals sometimes to his recollection of the numbers mentioned to him by his informants. (See ii. 125.)

seems to have anciently passed between the Babil mound and the Kasr" (called *Shebil* by Nebuchadnezzar) with the main stream. Or finally, we may conceive that at the time of his visit the old palace lay in ruins, and that the palace of Neriglissar on the west bank of the stream was that of which he spoke. It is at any rate remarkable, considering how his authority is quoted as fixing the site of the Belus tower to the west bank, that, in the only place where he gives us any intimation of the side of the river on which he would have placed the tower, it is the east and not the west bank to which his words point. He makes those who saw the treachery of Zopyrus at the Belian and Kissian gates, which must have been to the east of the city,[14] at once take refuge in the famous sanctuary,[15] which he implies was in the vicinity.

On the whole, therefore, it seems best to regard the Babil mound as the *ziggurat* of the great temple of Bel (called by some "the tomb of Belus")[16] which the Persians destroyed and which Alexander intended to restore. With regard to the "hanging gardens," as they were an erection of less than half the size of the tower,[18] it is not so necessary

---

[14] See the plan, p. 374.

[15] Town-gates are named in the East from the places to which they lead. (Rich, *First Memoir*, p. 53.) The Kissian gates led to Susiana, which was towards the East. The Belian probably led to Niffer, the "city of Belus." (See above, vol. i. p. 149.) Niffer lies south-east of Babylon. [16] Herod. iii. 158.

[17] As by Strabo (L. s. c.). When M. Oppert identifies the Babil mound with this tomb, he is really admitting that it was the Belus temple-tower. For there is not the shadow of a doubt that the "tomb of Belus" and the "temple of Belus" are one and the same building. (Compare Strab. xvi. 1, § 5, with Arrian, vii. 17, and both with Herod. i. 183, *ad fin.*)

[18] The hanging gardens were a square of 400 (Greek) feet each way; the Belus tower was a square of 600 feet. The area of the one was 160,000 square feet; that of the other 360,000, or considerably more than double.

to suppose that distinct traces must remain of them. Their débris may be confused with those of the Kasr mound, on which one writer places them.¹ Or they may have stood between the Kasr and Amran ruins, where are now some mounds of no great height. Or, possibly, their true site is the modern *El Homeira*, the remarkable red mound which lies east of the Kasr at the distance of about 800 yards, and attains an elevation of sixty-five feet. Though this building is not situated upon the banks of the Euphrates, where Strabo and Diodorus place the gardens,² it abuts upon a long low valley into which the Euphrates water seems formerly to have been introduced, and which may therefore have been given the name of the river. This identification is however, it must be allowed, very doubtful.

The two lines of mounds which enclose the long low valley above mentioned are probably the remains of an embankment which here confined the waters of a great reservoir. Nebuchadnezzar relates that he constructed a large reservoir, which he calls the *Yapur-Shapu*, in Babylon,³ and led water into it by means of an "eastern canal"—the *Shebil*. The *Shebil* canal, it is probable, left the Euphrates at some point between Babil and the Kasr, and ran across with a course nearly from west to east to the top of the *Yapur-Shapu*. This reservoir seems to have been a long and somewhat narrow parallelogram,

---

¹ Q. Curt. *Hist. Alex.* v. 1:— "*Super arce vulgatum Græcorum fabulis miraculum pensiles horti sunt.*" The *arx* of Curtius is the palace.

² Strab. xvi. 1, § 5; Diod. Sic. ii.

³ 10, § 1.

⁴ See the translation of the Standard Inscription of Nebuchadnezzar, which is given in the Appendix, Note A.

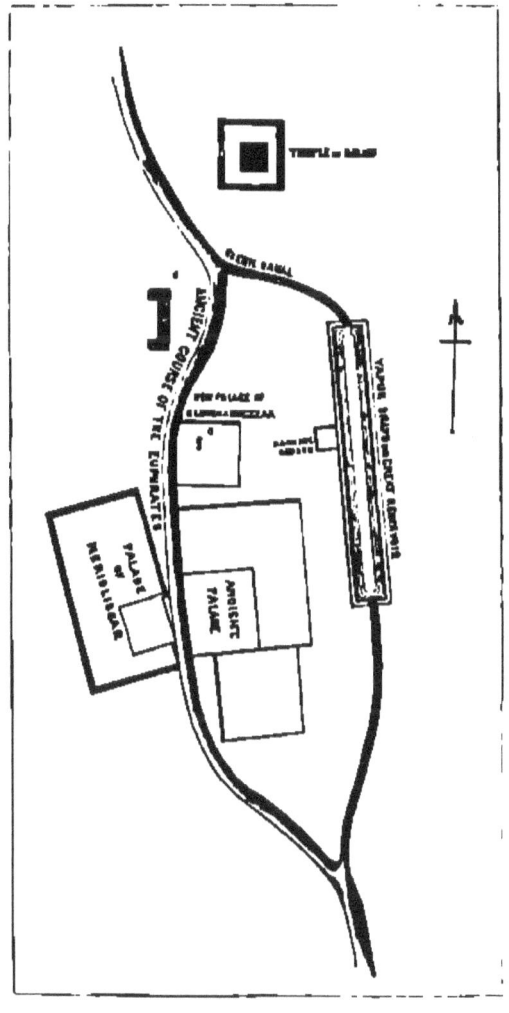

Chart of Ancient Babylon.

running nearly from north to south, which shut in the great palace on the east and protected it like a huge moat. Most likely it communicated with the Euphrates towards the south by a second canal, the exact line of which cannot be determined. Thus the palatial residence of the Babylonian kings looked in both directions upon broad sheets of water, an agreeable prospect in so hot a climate; while, at the same time, by the assignment of a double channel to the Euphrates, its floods were the more readily controlled, and the city was preserved from those terrible inundations, which in modern times have often threatened the existence of Baghdad.[4]

The other lines of mound upon the east side of the river may either be Parthian works,[5] or (possibly) they may be the remains of some of those lofty walls[6] whereby according to Diodorus the greater palace was surrounded and defended.[7] The fragments of them which remain are so placed that if the lines were produced they would include all the principal ruins on the left bank except the Babil tower. They may therefore be the old defences of the eastern palace; though, if so, it is strange that they run in lines which are neither straight nor parallel to those of the buildings enclosed by them. The irregularity of these ramparts is certainly a very strong argument in favour of their having been the work of a people considerably more barbarous and ignorant than the Babylonians.

---

[4] See Loftus, *Chaldæa and Susiana*, p. 7.
[5] This is the opinion of Sir H. Rawlinson.
[6] So M. Oppert (*Expédition Scientifique*, tom. i. p. 195).
[7] Diod. Sic. ii. 8, § 5 and § 6.

CHAPTER V.

ARTS AND SCIENCES.

Τοῦτό γε διαβεβαιώσαιτ' ἄν τις προσηκόντως, ὅτι Χαλδαῖοι μεγίστην ἕξιν ἐν ἀστρολογίᾳ ἁπάντων ἀνθρώπων ἔχουσι, καὶ διότι πλείστην ἐπιμέλειαν ἐποιήσαντο ταύτης τῆς θεωρίας.—Diod. Sic. II. 31.

That the Babylonians were among the most ingenious of all the nations of antiquity, and had made considerable progress in the arts and sciences before their conquest by the Persians, is generally admitted. The classical writers commonly parallel them with the Egyptians;[1] and though, from their habit of confusing Babylon with Assyria, it is not always quite certain that the inhabitants of the more southern country—the real Babylonians—are meant, still there is sufficient reason to believe that, in the estimation of the Greeks and Romans, the people of the lower Euphrates were regarded as at least equally advanced in civilisation with those of the Nile valley and the Delta. The branches of knowledge wherein by general consent the Babylonians principally excelled were architecture and astronomy. Of their architectural works two at least were reckoned among the "Seven Wonders,"[2] while others, not elevated to this exalted rank, were yet considered to be among the most curious and admirable of Oriental constructions.[3] In astronomical science they were thought

---

[1] Herod. I. 93; II. 109; Diod. Sic. II. 29, § 2; &c.
[2] The "walls" and the "hanging gardens." (Strab. xvi. 1, § 5. Compare Q. Curt. *Hist. Alex. Magn.* v. 1, § 32; Hygin. *Fab.* § 223; Cassiodor. *Varior.* vii. 15.)
[3] Q. Curtius says of the bridge

CHAP. V.   BABYLONIAN ARCHITECTURE.   377

to have far excelled all other nations,¹ and the first Greeks who made much progress in the subject confessed themselves the humble disciples of Babylonian teachers.²

In the account, which it is proposed to give in this place, of Babylonian art and science, so far as they are respectively known to us, the priority will be assigned to art, which is an earlier product of the human mind than science; and among the arts the first place will be given to architecture, as at once the most fundamental of all the fine arts, and the one in which the Babylonians attained their greatest excellence. It is as builders that the primitive Chaldæan people, the progenitors of the Babylonians, first appear before us in history;³—it was on his buildings that the great king of the later Empire, Nebuchadnezzar, specially prided himself.⁴ When Herodotus visited Babylon he was struck chiefly by its extraordinary buildings;⁵ and it is the account which the Greek writers gave of these erections that

---

over the Euphrates, "Hic quoque inter mirabilia Orientis opera numeratus est." (*Hist. Alex. Magn.* v. 1, § 29.)

² Diod. Sic. ii. 31. See the heading to this chapter.

³ Hipparchus, who, according to Delambre (*Histoire d'Astronomie Ancienne*, tom. i. p. 184), "laid the foundation of astronomy among the Greeks," spoke of the Babylonians as astronomical observers from a fabulously remote antiquity. (Proclus, *in Tim.* p. 31, C.) Aristotle admitted that the Greeks were greatly indebted for astronomical facts to the Babylonians and Egyptians. (*De Cœlo,* ii. 12, § 3.) Ptolemy made large use of the Babylonian observations of eclipses. Sir Cornewall Lewis allows that "the Greeks were in the habit of attributing the invention and original cultivation of astronomy either to the Babylonians or to the Egyptians, and represented the earliest scientific Greek astronomers as having derived their knowledge from Babylonian or from Egyptian priests." (*Astronomy of the Ancients*, p. 256.) He considers, indeed, that in thus yielding the credit of discovery to others, they departed from the truth; but he does not give any sufficient reasons for this curious belief.

⁴ Gen. xi. 2-5.
⁵ Dan. iv. 30.
⁶ Herod. i. 93; 178-183.

has, more than anything else, procured for the Babylonians the fame that they possess and the position that they hold among the six or seven leading nations of the old world.

The architecture of the Babylonians seems to have culminated in the Temple. While their palaces, their bridges, their walls, even their private houses were remarkable, their grandest works, their most elaborate efforts, were dedicated to the honour and service, not of man, but of God. The Temple takes in Babylonia the same sort of rank which it has in Egypt and in Greece. It is not, as in Assyria,[9] a mere adjunct of the palace. It stands by itself, in proud independence, as the great building of a city, or a part of a city:[10] it is, if not absolutely larger, at any rate loftier and more conspicuous than any other edifice: it often boasts a magnificent adornment: the value of the offerings which are deposited in it is enormous: in every respect it rivals the palace, while in some it has a decided pre-eminence. It draws all eyes by its superior height and sometimes by its costly ornamentation; it inspires awe by the religious associations which belong to it; finally, it is a stronghold as well as a place of worship, and may furnish a refuge to thousands in time of danger.[11]

A Babylonian temple seems to have stood commonly within a walled enclosure. In the case of the great temple of Belus at Babylon, the enclosure is said to have been a square of two stades each way,[12] or in other words to have contained an area of thirty acres. The temple itself ordinarily con-

---

[9] See above, vol. ii. p. 348. [10] Herod. i. 181. [11] Ibid. iii. 158.
[12] Ibid. i. 181. Δύο σταδίων πάντη, ἐὸν τετράγωνον.

sisted of two parts. Its most essential feature was a *ziggurat*, or tower, which was either square, or at any rate rectangular, and built in stages, the smallest number of such stages being two, and the largest known number seven.[12] At the summit of the tower was probably in every case a shrine, or chapel, of greater or less size, containing altars and images. The ascent to this was on the outside of the towers, which were entirely solid; and it generally wound round the different faces of the towers, ascending them either by means of steps or by an inclined plane. Special care was taken with regard to the emplacement of the tower, either its sides or its angles being made exactly to confront the cardinal points. It is said that the temple-towers were used not merely for religious purposes but also as observatories,[14] a use with a view to which this arrangement of their position would have been serviceable.

Besides the shrine at the summit of the temple-tower or *ziggurat*, there was commonly at the base of the tower, or at any rate somewhere within the enclosure, a second shrine or chapel, in which the ordinary worshipper, who wished to spare himself the long ascent, made his offerings. Here again the ornamentation was most costly, lavish use being made of the precious metals for images and other furniture.[15] Altars of different sizes were placed in the open air in the vicinity of this lower shrine, on which were sacrificed different classes of victims, gold being used occasionally as the material of the altar.[1]

---

[12] Where Herodotus speaks of there being eight stages to the tower of the temple of Belus at Babylon, he probably counts the shrine at the top as a stage. Note his words: ἐν δὲ τῇ τελευταίῃ πύργῳ νηὸς ἔπεστι μέγας (l. s. c.).
[14] Diod. Sic. ii. 9, § 4.
[15] Herod. i. 183.
[1] Herod. i. 183.

The general appearance of a Babylonian temple, or at any rate of its chief feature, the tower or *ziggurat*, will be best gathered from a more particular description of a single building of the kind; and the building which it will be most convenient to take for this purpose is that remarkable edifice, which strikes moderns with more admiration than any other now existing in the country,[2] and which has also been more completely and more carefully examined than any other Babylonian ruin[3]—the Birs-i-Nimrud, or ancient temple of Nebo at Borsippa. The plan of this tower has been almost completely made out from data still existing on the spot; and a restoration of the original building may be given with a very near approach to certainty.

Upon a platform of crude brick,[1] raised a few feet above the level of the alluvial plain, was built the first or basement stage of the great edifice, an exact square, 272 feet each way, and probably twenty-six feet in perpendicular height.[5] On this was erected a second stage, of exactly the same height, but a square of only 230 feet; which however was not

---

[2] See Rich, *First Memoir*, pp. 34-37; *Second Memoir*, pp. 30-32; Ker Porter, vol. ii. pp. 306-316; Layard, *Nineveh and Babylon*, p. 495; Loftus, *Chaldæa and Susiana*, p. 27; Oppert, *Expédition Scientifique*, tom. l. p. 200.

[3] See the *Journal of the Asiatic Society*, vol. xviii. art. 1., where a full account is given by Sir H. Rawlinson of the labours by which he discovered the true plan of the building. M. Oppert's speculations in his *Expédition Scientifique* (tom. l. pp. 200-209), which rest upon no original researches, and contradict all the dimensions which Sir H. Rawlinson obtained by laborious tunnelling and careful measurement, are no doubt ingenious; but they can scarcely be regarded as having any scientific value.

[4] M. Oppert believes this "platform" to have been part of a lower stage which would have been found by removing the soil at its base. This is perhaps possible, but at present there is no proof of it.

[5] Sir H. Rawlinson excavated only to the depth of 17 feet. The assignment of 26 feet to this stage rests upon the ascertained fact that both the second and the third stage were exactly of this height. (*Journal of the Asiatic Society*, vol. xviii. p. 19.)

Birs-i-Nimrud, near Babylon.

placed exactly in the middle of the first, but further from its north-eastern than its south-western edge, twelve feet only from the one and thirty feet from the other. The third stage, which was imposed in the same way upon the second, was also twenty-six feet high, and was a square of 188 feet. Thus far the plan had been uniform and without any variety; but at this point an alteration took place. The height of the fourth stage, instead of being twenty-six, was only fifteen feet.* In other respects how-

---

* It will be found hereafter that this fourth stage was that of the Sun, and that it was probably covered with thin plates of gold. This would give a reason for the diminution of height at this point, since thereby would be effected a saving of more than two-fifths of the gold.

ever the old numbers were maintained; the fourth stage was diminished equally with the others, and was consequently a square of 146 feet. It was emplaced upon the stage below it exactly as the former stages had been. The remaining stages probably followed the same rule of diminution⁷—the fifth being a square of 104, the sixth one of 62, and the seventh one of 20 feet. Each of these stages had a height of fifteen feet. Upon the seventh or final stage was erected the shrine or tabernacle, which was probably also fifteen feet high, and about the same length and breadth. Thus the entire height of the building, allowing three feet for the crude-brick platform was 156 feet.⁸

The ornamentation of the edifice was chiefly by means of colour. The seven stages represented the Seven Spheres, in which moved (according to ancient Chaldæan astronomy) the seven planets. To each planet fancy, partly grounding itself upon fact, had from of old assigned a peculiar tint or hue. The Sun was golden, the Moon silver; the distant Saturn, almost beyond the region of light, was black; Jupiter was orange;⁹ the fiery Mars was red; Venus was a pale Naples yellow; Mercury a deep blue. The seven stages of the tower, like the seven walls of Ecbatana,¹⁰ gave a visible embodiment to these

---

⁷ The upper portion of the Birs is in too ruined a condition to allow of the verification of these estimates. They follow as deductions from the ascertained dimensions of the lower stages, and especially from the proved fact, that the alteration in the height of the fourth stage was not accompanied by any change in the rate of diminution of the square.

⁸ Capt. Jones's measurement with the theodolite makes the present height of the building above the alluvial plain 153½ feet. If then the plan of the temple assumed in the text be correct, it has lost less than three feet of its original height.

⁹ Or "sandal-wood colour" (Sandali, Pers.; Σανδαράκινος, Greek). The foundation for this colour, as for that of Mars and Venus, was probably the actual hue of the planet.

¹⁰ Herod. L. 98. See above, p. 25.

CHAP. V.   THE BIRS TEMPLE RESTORED.   363

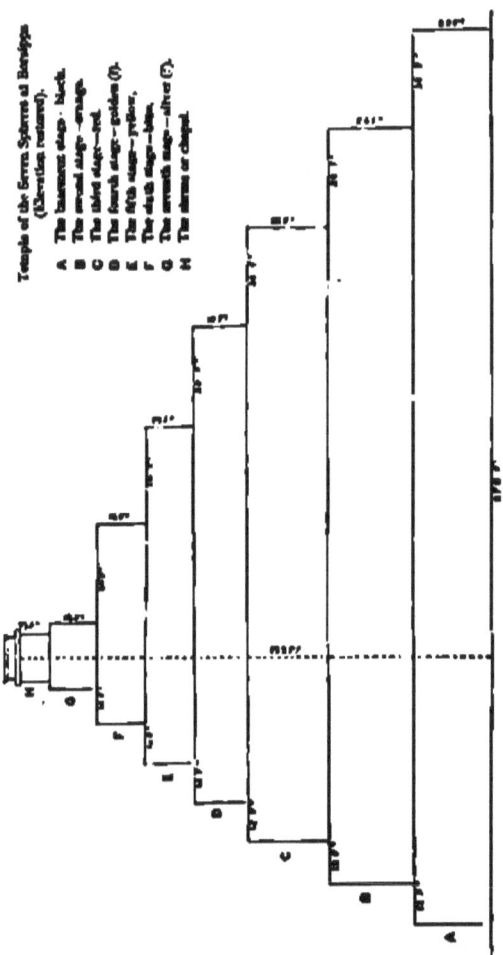

fancies. The basement stage, assigned to Saturn, was blackened by means of a coating of bitumen spread over the face of the masonry;[11] the second stage, assigned to Jupiter, obtained the appropriate orange colour by means of a facing of burnt bricks of that hue;[12] the third stage, that of Mars, was made blood-red, by the use of half-burnt bricks formed of a bright red clay;[13] the fourth stage, assigned to the Sun, appears to have been actually covered with thin plates of gold;[14] the fifth, the stage of Venus, received a pale yellow tint from the employment of bricks of that hue;[15] the sixth, the sphere of Mercury, was given an azure tint by vitrifaction, the whole stage having been subjected to an intense heat after it was erected, whereby the bricks composing it were converted into a mass of blue slag;[16] the seventh stage, that of the Moon, was probably, like the fourth, coated with actual plates of metal.[17] Thus the building rose up in stripes of varied colour, arranged almost as nature's cunning arranges hues in the rainbow, tones of red coming first, succeeded by a broad stripe of yellow, the yellow being followed by blue.

---

[11] *Journal of the Asiatic Society*, vol. xviii. p. 12.
[12] Ibid. p. 19.
[13] Ibid. pp. 9 and 20.
[14] These plates of course do not remain in situ. The evidence of their original employment is to be found, 1. In the mutilated appearance of the present face of this stage, which is "broken as if with blows of the pickaxe" (*As. Soc. Journ.* p. 20); 2. In statements made by Nebuchadnezzar that the walls of his temples were often "clothed with gold;" 3. In the parallel ornamentation of Ecbatana (Herod. i. 98).

[15] *As. Soc. Journ.* pp. 21, 22.
[16] Ibid. pp. 6, 7. This vitrifaction of the upper portions of the tower has given rise to the belief—as old as Benjamin of Tudela—that it had been struck by lightning, and so destroyed, whence he and others argued that it was the true tower of Babel. But the vitrifaction seems really to have been the work of man, and its object was to produce a blue colour.

[17] This is a conjecture, grounded upon the parallel case of Ecbatana (Herod. l. s. c.) and the analogy of the fourth stage. See note [14].

Above this the glowing silvery summit melted into the bright sheen of the sky.

The faces of the various stages were, as a general rule, flat and unbroken, unless it were by a stair or ascent,[18] of which however there has been found no trace. But there were two exceptions to this general plainness. The basement stage was indented with a number of shallow squared recesses, which seem to have been intended for a decoration.[19] The face of the third stage was weak on account of its material, which was brick but half-burnt. Here then the builders, not for ornament's sake, but to strengthen their work, gave to the wall the support of a number of shallow buttresses. They also departed from their usual practice, by substituting for the rigid perpendicular of the other faces a slight slope outwards for some distance from the base.[20] These arrangements, which are apparently part of the original work, and not remedies applied subsequently, imply considerable knowledge of architectural principles on the part of the builders, and no little ingenuity in turning architectural resources to account.

With respect to the shrine which was emplaced upon the topmost, or silver stage, little is definitely known. It appears to have been of brick;[21] and we may perhaps conclude from the analogy of the old Chaldæan shrines at the summits of towers,[22] as well

---

[18] Sir H. Rawlinson believes that staircases occupied most of the north-eastern face or true front of the building. (*As. Soc. Journal*, vol. xviii. p. 10.)

[19] Ibid. p. 13. Similar recesses adorn the great Temple-tower at Nimrud (see vol. i. p. 396), and many buildings of Nebuchadnezzar

[20] (Loftus, *Chaldæa and Susiana*, p. 240, &c.).

[20] *Journal of the Asiatic Society*, vol. xviii. p. 10.

[21] Sir H. Rawlinson thinks that the upper part of the existing ruin belongs to this shrine.

[22] Supra, vol. i. pp. 90, 102, 103, &c.

as from that of the Belus shrine at Babylon,[a] that it was richly ornamented both within and without; but it is impossible to state anything as to the exact character of the ornamentation.

The Tower is to be regarded as fronting to the north-east, the coolest side and that least exposed to the sun's rays from the time that they become oppressive in Babylonia. On this side was the ascent, which consisted probably of a broad staircase extending along the whole front of the building. The side platforms (those towards the south-east and north-west)—at any rate of the first and second stages, probably of all—were occupied by a series of chambers abutting upon the perpendicular wall,[1] as the priests' chambers of Solomon's temple abutted upon the side walls of that building.[2] In these were doubtless lodged the priests and other attendants upon the temple service. The side chambers seem sometimes to have communicated with vaulted apartments within the solid mass of the structure,[3] like those of which we hear in the structure supporting the "hanging gardens."[4] It is possible that there may have been internal staircases, connecting the vaulted apartments of one stage with those of another; but the ruin has not yet been sufficiently explored for us to determine whether or not there was such communication.

The great Tower is thought to have been approached through a vestibule of considerable size.[5]

---

[a] Herod. i. 181.
[1] *Journal of the Asiatic Society*, vol. xviii. p. 19. [2] 1 Kings vi. 5.
[3] *As. Soc. Journal*, p. 11. Compare p. 19.
[4] Diod. Sic. ii. 10, § 6.
[5] Sir H. Rawlinson, in the *Journal of the As. Society*, vol. xviii. p. 16. M. Oppert thinks differently (*Expédition Scientifique*, tom. I. p. 200).

Towards the north-east the existing ruin is prolonged in an irregular manner; and it is imagined that this prolongation marks the site of a vestibule or propylæum, originally distinct from the tower, but now, through the crumbling down of both buildings, confused with its ruins. As no scientific examination has been made of this part of the mound, the above supposition can only be regarded as a conjecture. Possibly the excrescence does not so much mark a vestibule as a second shrine, like that which is said to have existed at the foot of the Belus Tower at Babylon.⁶ Till, however, additional researches have been made, it is in vain to think of restoring the plan or elevation of this part of the temple.⁷

From the temples of the Babylonians we may now pass to their palaces—constructions inferior in height and grandeur, but covering a greater space, involving a larger amount of labour, and admitting of more architectural variety. Unfortunately the palaces have suffered from the ravages of time even more than the temples, and in considering their plan and character we obtain little help from the existing remains. Still, something may be learnt of them from this source, and where it fails we may perhaps be allowed to eke out the scantiness of our materials by drawing from the elaborate descriptions of Diodorus such points as have probability in their favour.

The Babylonian palace, like the Assyrian⁸ and the Susianian,⁹ stood upon a lofty mound or platform.

---

⁶ Herod. I. 183.
⁷ M. Oppert attempts this restoration (see his Plates, *Essai de Restauration de la tour des sept Planètes*), and accomplishes it in a manner which is very unsatisfactory.

⁸ Supra, vol. i. pp. 319-351.
⁹ See the author's *Herodotus*, vol. iii. pp. 207, 208, 2nd edition. Compare Loftus, *Chaldæa and Susiana*, pp. 343-345.

This arrangement provided at once for safety, for enjoyment, and for health. It secured a pure air, freedom from the molestation of insects, and a position only assailable at a few points.[10] The ordinary shape of the palace mound appears to have been square;[11] its elevation was probably not less than 50 or 60 feet.[12] It was composed mainly of sun-dried bricks, which however were almost certainly enclosed externally by a facing of burnt brick, and may have been further strengthened within by walls of the same material, which perhaps traversed the whole mound.[13] The entire mass seems to have been carefully drained, and the collected waters were conveyed through subterranean channels to the level of the plain at the mound's base.[14] The summit of the platform was no doubt paved, either with stone or burnt brick—mainly, it is probable with the latter; since the former material was scarce, and though a certain number of stone pavement slabs have been found,[15] they are too rare and scattered to imply any-

---

[10] As the sides of the platform were perpendicular, the only places at which it could be attacked were its staircases.

[11] The square shape of the Kasr mound is very decided. See the plan, supra, p. 355. Assyrian platforms were in general rectangular (supra, vol. i. p. 351).

[12] It is difficult to reconcile the statements of different writers as to the height of the Babylonian mounds, which have seldom been ascertained scientifically. Rich estimates the Amran mound at 50 or 60 feet (First Memoir, p. 21); M. Oppert at 30 mètres (Expédition, tom. i. p. 158), or nearly 100 feet. The exact height of the Kasr mound I do not find estimated; but Rich says that one of its ravines is "40 or 50 feet deep" (First Memoir, p. 23). I assume it therefore to be higher than the Amran mound; and I imagine that both attain, in places, an elevation of 80 or 90 feet. Of this height I conceive that at any rate not more than 30 feet can be assigned to the débris of the actual palace, and that the remainder must be the height of the mound or platform on which it stood.

[13] Such walls seem to occur wherever the internal structure of the Kasr mound is laid bare. (Rich, First Memoir, p. 24; Ker Porter, Travels, vol. ii. pp. 350, 360; Layard, Nineveh and Babylon, p. 606.)

[14] See above, p. 355.

[15] Oppert, Expédition Scientifique, tom. i. p. 149. These pavement slabs

thing like the general use of stone paving. Upon the platform, most likely towards its centre,[16] rose the actual palace, not built (like the Assyrian palaces) of crude brick faced with a better material, but constructed wholly of the finest and hardest burnt brick laid in a mortar of extreme tenacity,[17] with walls of enormous thickness,[18] parallel to the sides of the mound, and meeting each other at right angles. Neither the ground plan nor the elevation of a Babylonian palace can be given; nor can even a conjectural restoration of such a building be made, since the small fragment of Nebuchadnezzar's palace which remains has defied all attempts to reduce it to system.[19] We can only say that the lines of the building were straight; that the walls rose, at any rate to a considerable height, without windows; and that the flatness of the straight line was broken by numerous buttresses and pilasters.[20] We have also evidence that occasionally there was an ornamentation of the building, either within or without, by means of sculptured stone slabs,[21] on which were represented figures of a small size, carefully wrought. The general ornamentation, however, external as well as internal, we may well believe to have been such as Diodorus states[22]—coloured representations on brick

---

were square, about 20 inches each way.

[16] The existing remains of building are situated towards the centre of the Kasr mound. (See the plan, p. 355.)

[17] Rich, p. 25; Ker Porter, vol. ii. p. 360; Layard, *Nineveh and Babylon*, p. 506.

[18] The existing walls of the Kasr are eight feet thick. (Rich, l. s. c.)

[19] Layard, *Nin. and Bab.* l. s. c. "I sought in vain for some clue to the general plan of the edifice." Even M. Oppert, who is seldom stopped by a difficulty, can only venture to represent the building as a huge square covering not quite one-fourth of the mound.

[20] Rich, p. 25; Layard, p. 506.

[21] Layard, p. 508.

[22] Diod. Sic. ii. 8, § 6.

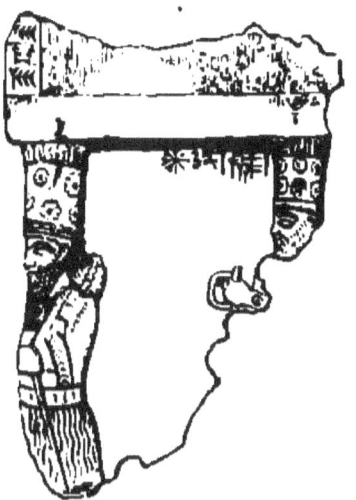

Part of a stone frieze, from the Kasr mound, Babylon.

of war-scenes and hunting-scenes, the counterparts in a certain sense of those magnificent bas-reliefs which everywhere clothed the walls of palaces in Assyria. It has been already noticed that abundant remains of such representations have been found upon the Kasr mound.[13] They seem to have alternated with cuneiform inscriptions, in white on a blue ground, or else with a patterning of rosettes in the same colours.[14]

Of the general arrangement of the royal palaces, of their height, their number of stories, their roofing and their lighting, we know absolutely nothing. The statement made by Herodotus, that many of the private houses in the town had three or four stories,[15]

---

[13] See above, p. 350. [14] Oppert, *Expédition Scientifique*, tom. I. p. 144.
[15] Herod. I. 180.

would naturally lead us to suppose that the palaces were built similarly; but no ancient author tells us that this was so. The fact that the walls which exist, though of considerable height, show no traces of windows, would seem to imply that the lighting, as in Assyria,[m] was from the top of the apartment, either from the ceiling, or from apertures in the part of the walls adjoining the ceiling. Altogether, such evidence as exists favours the notion that the Babylonian palace, in its character and general arrangements, resembled the Assyrian, with only the two differences, that the Babylonian was wholly constructed of burnt brick, while in the Assyrian the sun-dried material was employed to a large extent; and further, that in Babylonia the decoration of the walls was made, not by slabs of alabaster, which did not exist in the country, but mainly—almost entirely"—by coloured representations upon the enamelled brickwork.

Among the adjuncts of the principal palace at Babylon was the remarkable construction known to the Greeks and Romans as "the Hanging Garden." The accounts which Diodorus, Strabo, and Q. Curtius give of this structure[1] are not perhaps altogether trustworthy: still, it is probable that they are in the main at least founded on fact.[2] We may safely believe that a lofty structure was raised at Babylon on several tiers of arches,[3] which supported at the top a mass of

---

[m] See above, vol. I. pp. 382-385.
[n] The frieze above given (p. 300) is the only fragment of stone ornament that has been found.
[1] Diod. Sic. 10, § 2-6; Strab. xvi. 1, § 5; Q. Curt. v. 1.
[2] Strabo and Curtius both clearly describe the "Hanging Garden" (τὸν κρεμαστὸν κῆπον) as still existing in their time. Curtius expressly declares,—"Haec moles inviolata durat."
[3] Ker Porter imagines the Babylonians to have been unacquainted

earth, wherein grew, not merely flowers and shrubs, but trees of a considerable size. The Assyrians had been in the habit of erecting structures of a somewhat similar kind, artificial elevations to support a growth of trees and shrubs; but they were content to place their garden at the summit of a single row of pillars or arches,[4] and thus to give it a very moderate height. At Babylon the object was to produce an artificial imitation of a mountain.[5] For this purpose several tiers of arches were necessary; and these appear to have been constructed in the manner of a Roman amphitheatre, one directly over another, so that the outer wall formed from summit to base a single perpendicular line.[6] Of the height of the structure various accounts are given,[7] while no writer reports the number of the tiers of arches. Hence there are no sufficient data for a reconstruction of the edifice.[8]

Of the walls and bridge of Babylon, and of the ordinary houses of the people, little more is known than has been already reported in the general description of the capital.[9] It does not appear that they pos-

---

with the arch, and therefore suppose, instead of arches, piers roofed in with long blocks of stone (*Travels*, vol. ii. p. 363). But Sir H. Rawlinson found the internal chamber in the Birs covered in with a vaulted roof (*Journal of As. Society*, vol. xviii. p. 11); and arches have been found even in the early Chaldæan buildings. (See above, vol. i. p. 104.)

[4] Supra, vol. i. p. 388; vol. ii. p. 221.

[5] Berosus, Fr. 14; Diod. Sic. l. s. c.; Q. Curt. l. s. c.

[6] This is, I think, the meaning of Diodorus, when he says that the appearance was that of a theatre. ("ἔστι δ' ὁ παράδεισος .... τὰς εἰσόδους ἄλλας ἐξ ἄλλων ἔχων, ὥστε τὴν πρόσοψιν εἶναι θεατροειδῆ.)

[7] Curtius and Diodorus both make the height that of the walls of Babylon, which the former, however, estimates at 150 and the latter at 300 feet. Curtius places the garden on the palace mound (" super arcem"), which would imply for the actual structure of the garden a height of not much more than 90 or 100 feet.

[8] M. Oppert attempts a reconstruction of the ground plan (*Expédition*, maps and plans). He makes the stages nine in number, and each of smaller size than the one below it.

[9] Supra, pp. 342 and 347-350.

sessed any very great architectural merit. Some skill was shown in constructing the piers of the bridge, which presented an angle to the current and then a curved line, along which the water slid gently.[10] The loftiness of the houses, which were of three or four stories,[11] is certainly surprising, since Oriental houses have very rarely more than two stories. Their construction, however, seems to have been rude; and the pillars especially—posts of palm, surrounded with wisps of rushes, and then plastered and painted[12]—indicate a low condition of taste and a poor and coarse style of domestic architecture.

The material used by the Babylonians in their constructions seems to have been almost entirely brick. Like the early Chaldæans,[13] they employed bricks of two kinds, both the ruder sun-dried sort, and the very superior kiln-baked article. The former, however, was only applied to platforms, and to the interior of palace mounds and of very thick walls, and was never made by the latter people the sole material of a building.[14] In every case there was at least a *revêtement* of kiln-dried brick, while the grander buildings were wholly constructed of it.[15] The baked bricks used were of several different qualities, and (within rather narrow limits) of different sizes. The finest quality of brick was yellow, approaching to our Stourbridge or

---

[10] Diod. Sic. ii. 8, § 2.
[11] Herod. i. 180.
[12] Strab. xvi. 1, § 5. See above, p. 342. [13] Supra, vol. i. p. 90.
[14] As it was by the early Chaldæans. (See vol. i. pp. 94, 95.)
[15] The walls of the Kasr, which are eight feet thick (Rich, *First Memoir*, p. 27), are composed of burnt brick throughout their whole breadth.

fire-brick;[16] another very hard kind was blue approaching to black;[17] the commoner and coarser sorts were pink or red, and these were sometimes, though rarely, but half-baked, in which case they were weak and friable.[18] The shape was always square; and the dimensions varied between twelve and fourteen inches for the length and breadth, and between three and four inches for the thickness.[18] At the corners of buildings, half-bricks were used in the alternate rows, since otherwise the joinings must have been all one exactly over another. The bricks were always made

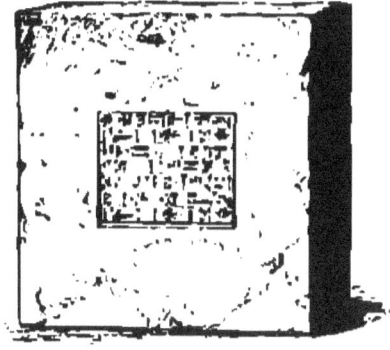

Babylonian brick.

with a mould, and were commonly stamped on one face with an inscription.[20] They were, of course,

---

[16] Rich, p. 61.
[17] Ibid. p. 62. Compare As. Soc. Journal, vol. xviii. p. 6, note *.
[18] As. Soc. Journal, vol. xviii. p. 9.
[19] Compare Rich, First Memoir, p. 61; Sir H. Rawlinson, in the Journal of the Asiatic Society, vol. xviii. p. 8; and M. Oppert, Expédition, tom. i. p. 143.

[20] The stamp on Babylonian bricks is always sunk below the surface. It is of a square or rectangular form, and occurs commonly towards the middle of one of the two larger faces. The letters are indented upon the clay, and must consequently have stood out in relief upon the wooden or metal stamp which impressed them. M.

ordinarily laid horizontally. Sometimes, however, there was a departure from this practice. Rows of bricks were placed vertically, separated from one another by single horizontal layers.¹¹ This arrangement seems to have been regarded as conducing to strength, since it occurs only where there is an evident intention of supporting a weak construction by the use of special architectural expedients.

The Babylonian builders made use of three different kinds of cement.¹² The most indifferent was crude clay, or mud, which was mixed with chopped straw, to give it greater tenacity, and was applied in layers of extraordinary thickness.¹³ This was (it is probable) employed only where it was requisite that the face of the building should have a certain colour. A cement superior to clay, but not of any very high value, unless as a preventive against damp, was bitumen, which was very generally used in basements and in other structures exposed to the action of water. Mortar, however, or lime cement was far more commonly employed than either of the others, and was of very excellent quality, equal indeed to the best Roman material.¹⁴

There can be no doubt that the general effect of the more ambitious efforts of the Babylonian architects was grand and imposing. Even now, in their

---

Oppert observes that the use of such a stamp was the first beginning of printing ("un commencement d'imprimerie," *Expédition*, p. 142). The stamped face of the brick was always placed downwards.

¹¹ This arrangement was found by Sir Henry Rawlinson in one of the stages of the Birs-i-Nimrud. (*Journal of As. Society*, vol. xviii. p. 10.)

¹² Rich, *First Memoir*, p. 62.

¹³ At the Birs, the red clay cement used in the third stage has a depth of two inches. (*As. Soc. Journ.* p. 9.)

¹⁴ On the excellence of the Babylonian mortar, see Rich, p. 25; Layard, *Nineveh and Babylon*, p. 506.

desolation and ruin, their great size renders them impressive; and there are times and states of atmosphere under which they fill the beholder with a sort of admiring awe,[*] akin to the feeling which is called forth by the contemplation of the great works of nature. Rude and inartificial in their idea and general construction, without architectural embellishment, without variety, without any beauty of form; they yet affect men by their mere mass, producing a direct impression of sublimity, and at the same time arousing a sentiment of wonder at the indomitable perseverance which from materials so unpromising could produce such gigantic results. In their original condition, when they were adorned with colour, with a lavish display of the precious metals, with pictured representations of human life, and perhaps with statuary of a rough kind, they must have added to the impression produced by size a sense of richness and barbaric magnificence. The African spirit, which loves gaudy hues and costly ornament, was still strong among the Babylonians, even after they had been Semitized; and by the side of Assyria, her colder and more correct northern sister, Babylonia showed herself a true child of the south—rich, glowing, careless of the laws of taste, bent on provoking admiration by the dazzling brilliancy of her appearance.

---

[*] See Rich, *First Memoir*, pp. 35, 36. Compare M. Oppert (*Expédition*, tom. I. p. 200), who says: "Le Birs-Nimroud apparait bientôt après la sortie de Hillah comme une montagne que l'on croit pouvoir atteindre immédiatement et qui recule toujours. Mais l'effet est bien plus saisissant quand l'atmosphère, et c'est le cas à la pointe du jour et vers le soir, est obscurcie par le brouillard. Alors on ne voit rien pendant une heure et demie; tout-à-coup le brouillard semble se déchirer comme un rideau, et fait entrevoir la masse colossale du Birs-Nimroud, d'autant plus intéressante que son aspect nous frappe de plus près et d'une manière complètement inattendu."

BABYLONIAN MIMETIC ART.

It is difficult to form a decided opinion as to the character of Babylonian mimetic art. The specimens discovered are so few, so fragmentary, and in some instances so worn by time and exposure, that we have scarcely the means of doing justice to the people in respect of this portion of their civilisation. Setting aside the intaglios on seals and gems, which have such a general character of quaintness and grotesqueness, or at any rate of formality, that we can scarcely look upon many of them as the serious efforts of artists doing their best, we possess not half a dozen specimens of the mimetic art of the people in question. We have one sculpture *in the round*, one or two modelled clay figures, a few bas-reliefs, one figure of a king engraved on stone, and a few ancient forms represented on the same material. Nothing more has reached us but fragments of pictorial representations too small for criticism to pronounce upon, and descriptions of ancient writers too incomplete to be of any great value.

The single Babylonian sculpture *in the round* which has come down to our times is the colossal lion standing over the prostrate figure of a man, which is still to be seen on the Kasr mound, as has been already mentioned.[1] The accounts of travellers uniformly state that it is a work of no merit[2]—either barbarously executed, or left unfinished by the sculp-

---

[1] See above, p. 356.
[2] Ker Porter calls the figure one "of very rude workmanship" (*Travels*, vol. II. p. 406). Mr. Layard says it is "either so barbarously executed as to show very little progress in art," or else "left unfinished by the sculptor." (*Nineveh and Babylon*, p. 507.) Mr. Loftus speaks of it as "roughly cut." (*Chaldæa and Susiana*, p. 19.) M. Oppert calls it "très-peu digne de Babylone," and speaks of its "valeur minime comme œuvre d'art." (*Expédition*, tom. i. p. 148.)

tor'—and probably much worn by exposure to the weather. A sketch made by a recent visitor[4] and kindly communicated to the author, seems to show

Lion, standing over a prostrate man (Babylon).

that, while the general form of the animal was tolerably well hit off, the proportions were in some respects misconceived, and the details not only rudely but incorrectly rendered. The extreme shortness of the legs and the extreme thickness of the tail, are the most prominent errors; there is also great awkwardness in the whole representation of the beast's shoulder. The head is so mutilated that it is impossible to do more than conjecture its contour. Still the whole figure is not without a certain air of grandeur and majesty.

The human appears to be inferior to the animal form. The prostrate man is altogether shapeless, and can never, it would seem, have been very much better than it is at the present time.

---

[3] So, besides Mr. Layard (l. s. c.), M. Thomas, who accompanied M. Fresnel (*Journal Asiatique*, Juin, 1853, p. 525), and M. Oppert.

[4] Mr. Claude Clark, now governor of the Military Prison, Southwark.

MODELLED FIGURE IN CLAY.

Modelled figures in clay are of rare occurrence. The best is one figured by Ker Porter,[a] which represents a mother with a child in her arms. The mother is seated in a natural and not ungraceful attitude on a rough square pedestal. She is naked except for a hood, or mantilla, which covers the head, shoulders, and back, and a narrow apron which hangs down in front. She wears ear-rings and a bracelet. The child, which sleeps on her left shoulder, wears a shirt open in front, and a short but full tunic, which is gathered into plaits.

Mother and child (found at Babylon).

Both figures are in simple and natural taste, but the limbs of the infant are somewhat too thin and

---

[a] *Travels*, vol. ii. pl. 80, fig. 3.

delicate. The statuette is about three inches and a half high, and shows signs of having been covered with a tinted glaze.

The single figure of a king, which we possess[a]

Figure of a Babylonian king, probably Merodach-iddin-akhi.

[a] This figure is engraved on a large black stone brought from Babylon, and now in the British Museum. It probably represents the king Merodach-iddin-akhi, who warred with Tiglath-pileser I. about B.C. 1120. (See above, vol. ii. pp. 329, 330.)

(see opposite page), is clumsy and ungraceful. It is chiefly remarkable for the elaborate ornamentation of the head-dress and the robes, which have a finish equal to that of the best Assyrian specimens. The general proportions are not bad; but the form is stiff, and the drawing of the right hand is peculiarly faulty, since it would be scarcely possible to hold arrows in the manner represented.[1]

Figure of a dog (from a black stone of the time of Merodach-iddin-akhi, found at Babylon).

Figure of a bird (from the same stone).

---

[1] The artist has somewhat improved the drawing of this hand in the woodcut. In the original more is seen of the fingers; and the thumb does not touch the arrows.

The engraved animal forms have a certain amount of merit. The figure of a dog sitting, which is common on the "black stones,"[a] is drawn with spirit; and a bird, sometimes regarded as a cock, but more resembling a bustard, is touched with a delicate hand, and may be pronounced superior to any Assyrian representation of the feathered tribe. The

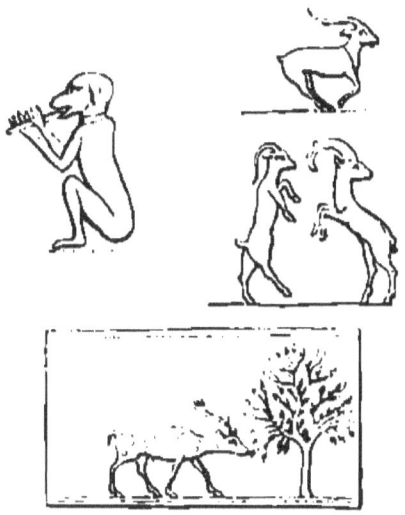

Animal forms (from the cylinders).

hound on a bas-relief, given in the first volume of this work,[b] is also good; and the cylinders exhibit

---

[a] The dog probably represents a constellation or a star—perhaps the Dog-star. The type is a fixed one, and occurs on seals and gems no less than on the "black stones." (See Ker Porter, vol. ii. pl. 80, fig. 2; Lajard, *Culte de Mithra*, pl. xlvi. figs. 23 and 24, pl. liv. B, fig. 15.)

[b] See vol. I. p. 293, No. II. The date of this tablet is uncertain; but Sir H. Rawlinson is on the whole inclined to regard it as Babylonian rather than Proto-Chaldæan.

figures of goats, cows, deer, and even monkeys,[10] which are truthful and meritorious.

It has been observed that the main characteristic of the engravings on gems and cylinders, considered as works of mimetic art, is their quaintness and grotesqueness. A few specimens, taken almost at random from the admirable collection of M. Felix Lajard, will sufficiently illustrate this feature. In

Grotesque figures of men and animals (from a cylinder).

one[11] the central position is occupied by a human figure whose left arm has two elbow-joints, while towards the right two sitting figures threaten one another with their fists, in the upper quarter, and in the lower two nondescript animals do the same with their jaws. The entire drawing of this design seems to be intentionally rude. The faces of the main figures and the right hand of the one towards the left, are evidently intended to be ridiculous; and the heads of the two animals are extravagantly grotesque. On another cylinder[12] three nondescript animals play the principal part. One of them is on the point of taking into his mouth the head of a man who vainly

---

[10] For the goats and cows, see above, p. 319. The exquisite figure of a deer represented above, and the quaint drawing of a monkey playing the pipe, are given by M. Lajard (*Culte de Mithra*, pl. liv. B., No. 8, and pl. xxix. No. 7) from cylinders in the collections of the Duc de Luynes and the Bibliothèque Royale.
[11] Lajard, pl. xxxiii. No. 6.
[12] Ibid. pl. xlii. No. 8.

tries to escape by flight. Another, with the head of a pike, tries to devour the third, which has the head of a bird and the body of a goat. This kind intention seems to be disputed by a naked man with

Men and monsters (from a cylinder).

a long beard, who seizes the fish-headed monster with his right hand, and at the same time administers from behind a severe kick with his right foot. The heads of the three main monsters, the tail and trousers of the principal one, and the whole of the small figure in front of the flying man, are exceedingly quaint, and remind one of the pencil of Fuseli.

Serio-comic drawing (from a cylinder).

The third of the designs [13] approaches nearly to the modern caricature. It is a drawing in two portions. The upper line of figures [14] represents a procession of worshippers who bear in solemn state their offerings

---

[13] Lajard, pl. xxix. No. 1.
[14] The upper line has been omitted, as containing nothing quaint or grotesque.

to a god. In the lower line this occupation is turned to a jest. Nondescript animals bring with a serio-comic air offerings which consist chiefly of game, while a man in a mask seeks to steal away the sacred tree from the temple wherein the scene is enacted.

It is probable that the most elaborate and most artistic of the Babylonian works of art were of a kind which has almost wholly perished. What bas-relief was to the Assyrian, what painting is to moderns, that enamelling upon brick appears to have been to the people of Babylon. The mimetic power, which delights in representing to itself the forms and actions of men, found a vent in this curious byway of the graphic art; and "the images of the Chaldæans, portrayed upon the wall, with vermilion,"[1] and other hues, formed the favourite adornment of palaces and public buildings, at once employing the artist, gratifying the taste of the native connoisseur, and attracting the admiration of the foreigner.

The artistic merit of these works can only be conjectured. The admiration of the Jews,[2] or even that of Diodorus,[3] who must be viewed here as the echo of Ctesias, is no sure test; for the Jews were a people very devoid of true artistic appreciation; and Ctesias was bent on exaggerating the wonders of foreign countries to the Greeks. The fact of the excellence of Assyrian art at a somewhat earlier date, lends however support to the view that the

---

[1] Ezek. xxiii. 14.
[2] Ibid. ver. 16. "As soon as she saw them with her eyes she doted upon them."
[3] Diod. Sic. ii. 8, § 6. Ζῶα παντοδαπὰ φιλοτίχνως τοῖς τε χρώμασι καὶ τοῖς τῶν τύπων ἀπομιμήμασι ἀπεσκευασμένα.

wall-painting of the Babylonians had some real artistic excellence. We can scarcely suppose that there was any very material difference, in respect of taste and æsthetic power, between the two cognate nations, or that the Babylonians under Nebuchadnezzar fell very greatly short of the Assyrians under Asshur-bani-pal. It is evident that the same subjects —war-scenes and hunting-scenes[4]—approved themselves to both people; and it is likely that their treatment was not very different. Even in the matter of colour the contrast was not sharp nor strong; for the Assyrians partially coloured their bas-reliefs.[5]

The tints chiefly employed by the Babylonians in their coloured representations were white, blue, yellow, brown, and black.[6] The blue was of different shades, sometimes bright and deep, sometimes exceedingly pale. The yellow was somewhat dull, resembling our yellow ochre. The brown was this same hue darkened. In comparatively rare instances the Babylonians made use of a red, which they probably obtained with some difficulty. Objects were coloured, as nearly as possible, according to their natural tints—water a light blue, ground yellow, the shafts of spears black, lions a tawny brown, &c.[7] No attempt was made to shade the figures or the landscape, much less to produce any general effect by means of *chiaroscuro*, but the artist trusted for his effect to a careful delineation of forms, and a judicious arrangement of simple hues.

Considerable metallurgic knowledge and skill were

---

[4] Παρατάξεις καὶ κυνήγια. Diod. Sic. ii. 8, § 7.
[5] See above, vol. i. pp. 449-451.
[6] Layard, *Nineveh and Babylon*, p. 507; Oppert, *Expédition*, tom. i. p. 143.
[7] Oppert, p. 144.

shown in the composition of the pigments, and the preparation and application of the glaze wherewith they were covered. The red used was a sub-oxide of copper;[8] the yellow was sometimes oxide of iron,[9] sometimes antimoniate of lead—the Naples yellow of modern artists;[10] the blue was either cobalt or oxide of copper;[11] the white was oxide of tin.[12] Oxide of lead was added in some cases, not as a colouring matter, but as a flux, to facilitate the fusion of the glaze.[13] In other cases the pigment used was covered with a vitreous coat of an alkaline silicate of alumina.[14]

The pigments were not applied to an entirely flat surface. Prior to the reception of the colouring matter and the glaze, each brick was modelled by the hand, the figures being carefully traced out, and a slight elevation given to the more important objects.[15] A very low bas-relief was thus produced, to which the colours were subsequently applied, and the brick was then baked in the furnace.

It is conjectured that the bricks were not modelled singly and separately. A large mass of clay was (it is thought) taken,[16] sufficient to contain a whole subject, or at any rate a considerable portion of a

---

[8] Layard, p. 166, note.
[9] Birch, *Ancient Pottery*, vol. i. p. 148.
[10] Layard, l. s. c.
[11] The French chemists, who analysed bricks from the Birs towards the close of the last century, found the colouring matter of the blue tint to be cobalt. (Birch, l. s. c.) In the Babylonian bricks analysed by Sir H. de la Beche and Dr. Percy the blue glaze was oxide of copper.
[12] Layard, l. s. c.
[13] Birch, p. 149.
[14] Ibid. p. 148.
[15] This statement is made on the authority of M. Oppert. (*Expédition*, tom. l. pp. 144, 145.) No other traveller has remarked an inequality of surface on the enamelled bricks.
[16] M. Thomas, who accompanied M. Oppert as artist, is the author of this theory as to the mode in which these works of art were designed and executed.

subject. On this the modeller made out his design in low relief. The mass of clay was then cut up into bricks, and each brick was taken and painted separately with the proper colours," after which they were all placed in the furnace and baked.[16] When baked they were restored to their original places in the design, a thin layer of the finest mortar serving to keep them in place.

From the mimetic art of the Babylonians, and the branches of knowledge connected with it, we may now pass to the purely mechanical arts,—as the art by which hard stones were cut, and those of agriculture, metallurgy, pottery, weaving, carpet-making, embroidery, and the like.

The stones shaped, bored, and engraved by Babylonian artisans were not merely the softer and more easily-worked kinds, as alabaster, serpentine, and lapis-lazuli, but also the harder sorts,—cornelian, agate, quartz, jasper, sienite, loadstone, and green felspar or amazon-stone.[17] These can certainly not have been cut without emery, and scarcely without such devices as rapidly revolving points, or disks, of the kind used by modern lapidaries. Though the devices are in general rude, the work is sometimes exceedingly delicate, and implies a complete mastery over tools and materials, as well as a good deal of

---

[15] The separate painting and enamelling of the bricks is proved by the fact that the colouring matter and the glaze have often run over from the side painted to all the adjoining surfaces. (Oppert, tom. I. p. 145.)

[16] Mr. Birch believes that they were partially baked before the colour was applied (Ancient Pottery, vol. I. p. 128), and returned to the kiln afterwards.

[17] It is difficult in most instances to decide from the cylinders themselves whether they are Babylonian or Assyrian. We must be chiefly guided by the locality where they were found. It is believed that cylinders have been found in Babylonia of all these materials.

artistic power. As far as the mechanical part of the art goes, the Babylonians may challenge comparison with the most advanced of the nations of antiquity— they decidedly excel the Egyptians,[20] and fall little, if at all, short of the Greeks and Romans.

The extreme minuteness of the work in some of the Babylonian seals and gems, raises a suspicion that they must have been engraved by the help of a powerful magnifying-glass. A lens has been found in Assyria;[21] and there is much reason to believe that the convenience was at least as well known in the lower country.[22] Glass was certainly in use,[23] and was cut into such shapes as were required. It is at any rate exceedingly likely that magnifying-glasses, which were undoubtedly known to the Greeks in the time of Aristophanes,[24] were employed by the artisans of Babylon during the most flourishing period of the empire.

Of Babylonian metal-work we have scarcely any direct means of judging. The accounts of ancient authors imply that the Babylonians dealt freely with the material, using gold and silver for statues, furniture, and utensils, bronze for gates and images, and iron sometimes for the latter.[1] We may assume that they likewise employed bronze and iron for tools and weapons, since those metals were certainly so used by the Assyrians. Lead was made of service in

---

[20] See King's *Antique Gems*, p. 127, note.
[21] Supra, vol. I. p. 484.
[22] We shall find below that, on astronomical grounds, the possession of lenses by the Babylonians is to be suspected.
[23] The Babylonian mounds are covered with fragments of glass. (Layard, *Nin. and Bab.* p. 507.)
[24] Aristoph. *Nub.* 746-748, ed. Botha.
[1] See Daniel iii. 1; v. 4; Herod. I. 181-183; Diod. Sic. II. 8, § 7; 9, § 6.

building;² where iron was also employed, if great strength was needed.³ The golden images are said to have been sometimes solid,⁴ in which case we must suppose them to have been cast in a mould; but undoubtedly in most cases the gold was a mere external covering, and was applied in plates, which were hammered into shape⁵ upon some cheaper substance below. Silver was no doubt used also in plates, more especially when applied externally to walls,⁶ or internally to the woodwork of palaces;⁷ but the silver images, ornamental figures, and utensils of which we hear, were most probably solid. The bronzeworks must have been remarkable. We are told that both the town and the palace gates were of this material,⁸ and it is implied that the latter were too heavy to be opened in the ordinary manner.⁹ Castings on an enormous scale would be requisite for such purposes; and the Babylonians must thus have possessed the art of running into a single mould vast masses of metal. Probably the gates here mentioned were solid:¹⁰ but occasionally, it would seem, the Babylonians had gates of a different kind, composed of a number of perpendicular bars, united by horizontal ones above and below, as

Gate and gateway (from a cylinder).

---

² Herod. i. 186; Diod. Sic. ii. 10, § 5.
³ As in the piers of the great bridge. (Herod. l. s. c.)
⁴ Herod. l. 183.
⁵ Σφυρήλατα. Diod. Sic. ii. 9, § 5.
⁶ Supra, p. 384.
⁷ Nebuchadnezzar states frequently that the walls of his buildings are "clothed with silver."
⁸ Herod. i. 179; Diod. Sic. ii. 8, § 7.
⁹ They are said to have been opened by a machine. (Diod. Sic. l. s. c.)
¹⁰ Like those made by Herod the Great for the Temple (Joseph. Bell. Jud. v. 5, § 3), which required 20 men to close them (ibid. vi. 5, § 3). We have no certain representations of Babylonian town-gates; but those drawn by the Assyrians are always solid.

CHAP. V.   BRONZE FIGURES—POTTERY.   411

in the accompanying woodcut.[11] They had also, it would appear, metal gateways of a similar character.

The metal-work of personal ornaments, such as bracelets and armlets, and again that of dagger-handles, seems to have resembled the work of the Assyrians.[12]

Small figures in bronze were occasionally cast by the Babylonians, which were sometimes probably used as amulets, while perhaps more generally they were mere ornaments of houses, furniture, and the like. Among these may be noticed figures of dogs in a sitting posture,[13] much resembling the dog represented among the constellations,[14] figures of men grotesque in character, and figures of monsters. An interesting specimen which combines a man and a monster, was found by Sir R. Ker Porter at Babylon.[15]

Bronze ornament (found at Babylon).

The pottery of the Babylonians was of excellent quality, and is scarcely to be distinguished from the Assyrian, which it resembles

---

[11] This gate and gateway are represented upon a cylinder figured by Lajard. (*Culte de Mithra*, pl. xli. fig. 5.)
[12] See the figure of a king (supra, p. 400). The bracelets have the almost invariable rosette of the Assyrians (supra, vol. ii. p. 104). The dagger-handles are like those figured vol. ii. p. 66, first woodcut.
[13] Ker Porter, *Travels*, vol. II. p. 425.
[14] See above, p. 401; and infra, p. 410.
[15] See the *Travels*, vol. ii. pl. 80, fig. 4.

alike in form and in material.[16] The bricks of the best period were on the whole better than any used in the sister country, and may compare for hardness and fineness with the best Roman. The earthenware is of a fine terracotta, generally of a light red colour, and slightly baked, but occasionally of a yellow hue, with a tinge of green. It consists of cups, jars, vases, and other vessels. They appear to have been made

Vases and jug (from the cylinders).

upon the wheel,[17] and are in general unornamented. From representations upon the cylinders[18] it appears that the shapes were often elegant. Long and narrow vases with thin necks seem to have been used for water vessels; these had rounded or pointed bases, and required therefore the support of a stand. Thin jugs were also in use, with slight elegant handles.

Vases in a stand (from a cylinder).

It is conjectured that sometimes modelled figures may have been introduced at the sides as handles to the vases;[19] but neither the cylinders nor the extant remains confirm this supposition. The only ornamentation hitherto observed consists in a double band which seems to have been carried round some of the vases in an incomplete spiral.[20] The vases sometimes have two handles; but they are plain and

---

[16] Birch, *Ancient Pottery*, vol. i. p. 144. Compare the specimens of Assyrian pottery represented in the first volume of the present work (pp. 479–482).
[17] Birch, l. s. c.
[18] See Lajard, pls. xxxiii. fig. 1; xxxv. fig. 3; and liv. A, fig. 9.
[19] Birch, *Ancient Pottery*, vol. i. p. 148.
[20] See above, woodcut, No. 2, where both vases are thus ornamented.

small, adding nothing to the beauty of the vessels. Occasionally the whole vessel is glazed with a rich blue colour.

The Babylonians certainly employed glass for vessels of a small size.[21] They appear not to have been very skilful blowers, since their bottles are not unfrequently misshapen. They generally stained their glass with some colouring matter, and occasionally ornamented it with a ribbing. Whether they

Vase with handles (found in Babylonia).

were able to form masses of glass of any considerable size, whether they used it, like the Egyptians,[22] for

Babylonian glass bottles.

beads and bugles, or for mosaics, is uncertain. If we suppose a foundation in fact for Pliny's story of the great emerald (?) presented by a king of Babylon to an Egyptian Pharaoh,[23] we must conclude that very considerable masses of glass were produced by the Babylonians, at least occasionally; for the said

---

[21] Several small glass bottles were found by Mr. Layard in the mound of Habil. (*Nineveh and Babylon*, p. 503.) Broken glass is abundant in the rubbish of the mounds generally. (Rich, *First Memoir*, p. 20; Ker Porter, *Travels*, vol. ii. p. 392.)
[22] Wilkinson, *Ancient Egyptians*, vol. iii. p. 101.
[23] Plin. *H. N.* xxxvii. 5.

emerald, which can scarcely have been of any other material, was four cubits (or six feet) long and three cubits (or four and a half feet) broad.

Of all the productions of the Babylonians none obtained such high repute in ancient times as their textile fabrics. Their carpets especially were of great celebrity, and were largely exported to foreign countries.[34] They were dyed of various colours, and represented objects similar to those found on the gems, as griffins and such-like monsters.[35] Their position in the ancient world may be compared to that which is now borne by the fabrics of Turkey and Persia, which are deservedly preferred to those of all other countries.

Next to their carpets, the highest character was borne by their muslins. Formed of the finest cotton, and dyed of the most brilliant colours, they seemed to the Oriental the very best possible material for dress. The Persian kings preferred them for their own wear;[36] and they had an early fame in foreign countries at a considerable distance from Babylonia.[37] It is probable that they were sometimes embroidered with delicate patterns, such as those which may be seen on the garments of the early Babylonian king (figured page 400).

Besides woollen and cotton fabrics, the Babylonians also manufactured a good deal of linen cloth; the principal seat of the manufacture being Borsippa.[38] This material was produced, it is probable, chiefly for

---

[34] Athen. Deipn. v. p. 107; Arrian, Exp. Al. vi. 29.
[35] Athen. l. s. c.
[36] Arrian. l. s. c.
[37] The "goodly Babylonish garment" coveted by Achan in Palestine shortly after the Exodus of the Jews (Josh. vii. 21) is indicative of the early celebrity of Babylonian apparel.
[38] Strab. xvi. 1, § 7.

home consumption, long linen robes being generally worn by the people.*

From the arts of the Babylonians we may now pass to their science—an obscure subject, but one which possesses more than common interest. If the classical writers were correct in their belief that Chaldæa was the birthplace of Astronomy, and that their own astronomical science was derived mainly from this quarter,¹ it must be well worth inquiry what the amount of knowledge was which the Babylonians attained on the subject, and what were the means whereby they made their discoveries.

On the broad flat plains of Chaldæa, where the entire celestial hemisphere is continually visible to every eye,² and the clear transparent atmosphere shows night after night the heavens gemmed with countless stars, each shining with a brilliancy unknown in our moist northern climes, the attention of man was naturally turned earlier than elsewhere to these luminous bodies, and attempts were made to grasp, and reduce to scientific form, the army of

---

* Herod. i. 105.
¹ See Plat. *Epinom.* p. 987; Hipparch. ap. Procl. *in Tim.* p. 71, ed. Schneider; Phœnix Coloph. ap. Athen. *Deipn.* xii. p. 530, E; Diod. Sic. ii. 31; Cic. *De Div.* l. 1; Plin. *H. N.* vi. 26; Manil. l. 40-45; &c. The late Sir Cornewall Lewis questioned the truth of this belief, and asserted that "the later Greeks appear to have been wanting in that national spirit which leads modern historians of science to contend for the claims of their own countrymen to inventions and discoveries." But he failed to adduce any sufficient proof of this strange idiosyncrasy of the later Greeks, which in his own mind seems to have rested on a conviction that the lively intelligent Greeks could not have been so indebted as they said they were to "the obtuse, uninventive, and immovable intellect of Orientals." (*Astronomy of the Ancients*, pp. 200, 201.)
² Compare Cic. *De Div.* l. s. c. "Principio Assyrii, ob ab ultimis auctoritatem repetam, *propter planitiem magnitudinemque regionum quas incolebant, cum cælum ab omni parte patens atque apertum intuerentur, trajectiones motusque stellarum observitaverunt.*"

facts which nature presented to the eye in a confused and tangled mass. It required no very long course of observation to acquaint men with a truth, which at first sight none would have suspected—namely, that the luminous points whereof the sky was full were of two kinds, some always maintaining the same position relatively to one another, while others were constantly changing their places, and as it were wandering about the sky. It is certain that the Babylonians at a very early date[2] distinguished from the fixed stars those remarkable five, which, from their wandering propensities, the Greeks called the "planets," and which are the only erratic stars that the naked eye, or that even the telescope, except at a very high power, can discern. With these five they were soon led to class the Moon, which was easily observed to be a wandering luminary, changing her place among the fixed stars with remarkable rapidity. Ultimately, it came to be perceived that the Sun too rose and set at different parts of the year in the neighbourhood of different constellations, and that consequently the great luminary was itself also a wanderer, having a path in the sky which it was possible, by means of careful observation, to mark out.

But to do this, to mark out with accuracy the courses of the Sun and Moon among the fixed stars, it was necessary, or at least convenient, to arrange

---

[2] The cosmogony of the Babylonians, as described by Berosus, has the air of a very high antiquity about it. In this document the "five planets" are distinctly mentioned. (Beros. Fr. 1, § 6.) The planetary character of the five gods, Nin, Merodach, Nergal, Ishtar, and Nebo, belongs even to Proto-Chaldæan times. (See above, vol. I. pp. 165-179.)

the stars themselves into groups. Thus too, and thus only, was it possible to give form and order to the chaotic confusion, in which the stars seem at first sight to lie, owing to the irregularity of their intervals, the difference in their magnitude, and their apparent countlessness. The most uneducated eye, when raised to the starry heavens on a clear night, fixes here and there upon groups of stars: in the north, Cassiopeia, the Great Bear, the Pleiades—below the Equator, the Southern Cross—must at all times have impressed those who beheld them with a certain sense of unity. Thus the idea of a "constellation" is formed; and this once done, the mind naturally progresses in the same direction, and little by little the whole sky' is mapped out into certain portions or districts to which names are given—names taken from some resemblance, real or fancied, between the shapes of the several groups and objects familiar to the early observers. This branch of practical astronomy is termed "uranography" by moderns; its utility is very considerable; thus and thus only can we particularise the individual stars of which we wish to speak;' thus and thus only can we retain in our memory' the general arrangement of the stars and their positions relatively to each other.

There is reason to believe that in the early Baby-

' Excepting certain insignificant portions which intervene between one constellation and another. The stars in these portions are called "unformed stars."

' The letters of the Greek alphabet are assigned to the several stars in each constellation; α to the largest, β to the next largest, and so on. Thus astronomers speak of "β Virginis," "γ Piscium," "δ Lyræ," and thereby indicate to each other distinctly the particular star about which they have something to say. (See Ferguson's *Astronomy*, p. 232.)

' Sir John Herschel observes that a proper system of constellations is valuable "as an artificial memory." (*Outlines of Astronomy*, p. 181, note.)

Ionian astronomy the subject of uranography occupied a prominent place. The Chaldæan astronomers not only seized on and named those natural groups which force themselves upon the eye, but artificially arranged the whole heavens into a certain number of constellations or asterisms. The very system of uranography which maintains itself to the present day on our celestial globes and maps, and which is still acknowledged—albeit under protest[1]—in the nomenclature of scientific astronomers, came in all probability from this source, reaching us from the Arabians, who took it from the Greeks, who derived it from the Babylonians. The Zodiacal constellations, at any rate, or those through which the sun's course lies, would seem to have had this origin; and many of them may be distinctly recognised on Babylonian monuments which are plainly of a stellar character.[2] The accompanying representation, taken from a conical black stone in the British Museum, and belonging to the twelfth century before our era, is not perhaps, strictly speaking, a zodiac, but it is almost certainly an arrangement of constellations according to the forms assigned them in Babylonian uranography. The

Top of conical stone, bearing figures of constellations.

---

[1] Astronomers are said at the present day to "treat lightly or altogether to disregard" the outlines of men and monsters which figure on our celestial globes; and the actual arrangement is said to cause confusion and inconvenience. (Herschel, l. s. c.) But the terminology is still used, and α Leonis, β Scorpii, &c., remain the sole expressions by which the particular stars can be designated.

[2] The stellar character of such monuments as that engraved above is sufficiently indicated by the central group, where the male and female sun and the crescent moon are clearly represented.

CHAP. V.   THE ZODIACAL CONSTELLATIONS.   419

Babylonian Zodiac (?)

Ram, the Bull, the Scorpion, the Serpent, the Dog, the Arrow, the Eagle or Vulture, may all be detected on the stone in question, as may similar forms variously arranged on other similar monuments.

The Babylonians called the Zodiacal constellations the "Houses of the Sun," and distinguished from them another set of asterisms, which they denominated the "Houses of the Moon." As the Sun and Moon both move through the sky in nearly the same plane, the path of the Moon merely crossing and recrossing that of the Sun, but never diverging from it further than a few degrees, it would seem that these "Houses of the Moon," or lunar asterisms,[l] must have been a division of the Zodiacal stars different from that employed with respect to the sun, either in the number of the "Houses," or in the point of separation between "House" and "House."

The Babylonians observed and calculated eclipses; but their power of calculation does not seem to have been based on scientific knowledge, nor to have necessarily implied sound views as to the nature of eclipses or as to the size, distance, and real motions of the heavenly bodies. The knowledge which they possessed was empirical. Their habits of observation led them to discover the period of 223 lunations or 18 years 10 days,[m] after which eclipses—especially those of the moon—recur again in the same order. Their acquaintance with this cycle would enable them to predict lunar eclipses with accuracy for many ages, and solar eclipses without much inaccuracy for the next cycle or two.

That the Babylonians carefully noted and recorded eclipses is witnessed by Ptolemy,[1] who had access to a continuous series of such observations reaching back from his own time to B.C. 747. Five of these—all eclipses of the moon—were described by Hipparchus[2] from Babylonian sources, and are found to answer all the requirements of modern science. They belong to the years B.C. 721, 720, 621, and 523. One of

---

[l] The "Houses of the Moon," or divisions of the lunar Zodiac, are said to have been known also both to the Chinese and the Indians.

[m] Geminus, § 15. The exact period is 18 years, 10 days, 7 hours, and 43 minutes. [1] *Magn. Syntax.* iii. 6.
[2] Ib. iv. 5, 8; v. 14.

them, that of B.C. 721, was total at Babylon. The others were partial, the portion of the moon obscured varying from one digit to seven.

There is no reason to think that the observation of eclipses by the Babylonians commenced with Nabonassar.[3] Ptolemy indeed implies that the series extant in his day went no higher;[4] but this is to be accounted for by the fact, which Berosus mentioned,[5] that Nabonassar destroyed, as far as he was able, the previously existing observations, in order that exact chronology might commence with his own reign.

Other astronomical achievements of the Babylonians were the following:—They accomplished a catalogue of the fixed stars, of which the Greeks made use in compiling their stellar tables.[6] They observed and recorded their observations upon occultations of the planets by the sun and moon.[7] They invented the *gnomon* and the *polos*,[8] two kinds of sun-dial, by means of which they were able to measure time during the day, and to fix the true length of the solar day, with sufficient accuracy.

---

[3] Even if we set aside the testimony of Porphyry, recorded by Simplicius (ad Arist. De Cœlo, p. 503, A), on account of the exaggerated number of the Greek text (Lewis, *Astronomy of the Ancients*, p. 296), we have still important testimony to the antiquity of the Babylonian observations: 1. in the words of Aristotle, οἱ πάλαι τετηρηκότες ἐκ πλείστων ἐτῶν..... Βαβυλώνιοι (*De Cœlo*, ii. 12, § 3); 2. in those of Diodorus quoted at the head of this chapter; 3. in those of the author of the Platonic Epinomis (§ 9, p. 987), of Pliny, Cicero, and others. (See above, p. 415, note 1.)

[4] *Magn. Syntax.* iii. 6. Εἰς τὴν ἀρχὴν τοῦ Ναβονασσάρου βασιλείας ... ἀφ᾽ οὗ χρόνου καὶ τὰς παλαιὰς τηρήσεις ἔχομεν ὡς ἐπίπαν μέχρι δεῦρο διασωζομένας.

[5] Ap. Syncell. *Chronograph.* p. 207, B. Ἀπὸ δὲ Ναβονασάρου τοὺς χρόνους τῆς τῶν ἀστέρων κινήσεως Χαλδαῖοι ἠκρίβωσαν ... ἐπειδὴ ... Ναβονάσσαρος συναγαγὼν τὰς πράξεις τῶν πρὸ αὐτοῦ βασιλέων ἠφάνισεν.

[6] Schollast ad Arat. 752.

[7] Aristot. *De Cœlo*, ii. 12, § 3.

[8] Herod. ii. 109.

They determined correctly within a small fraction the length of the synodic revolution of the moon.[9] They knew that the true length of the solar year was 365 days and a quarter, nearly.[10] They noticed comets, which they believed to be permanent bodies revolving in orbits like those of the planets, only greater.[11] They ascribed eclipses of the sun to the interposition of the moon between the sun and the earth.[12] They had notions not far from the truth with respect to the relative distance from the earth of the sun, moon, and planets. Adopting, as was natural, a geocentric system, they decided that the Moon occupied the position nearest to the earth;[13] that beyond the Moon was Mercury, beyond Mercury Venus, beyond Venus the Sun, beyond the Sun Mars, beyond Mars Jupiter, and beyond Jupiter, in the remotest position of all, Saturn.[14] This arrangement was probably based upon a knowledge, more or less exact, of the periodic times which the several bodies occupy in their (real or apparent) revolutions. From the difference in the times the Babylonians assumed a corresponding difference in the size of the orbits, and consequently a greater or less distance from the common centre.

Thus far the astronomical achievements of the Babylonians rest upon the express testimony of ancient writers, a testimony confirmed in many respects by the monuments already deciphered. It is suspected,

---

[9] See Vince's *Astronomy*, vol. ii. p. 251.

[10] Ibid. The exact length of the Chaldæan year is said to have been 365 days, 6 hours, and 11 minutes, which is an excess of two seconds only over the true (sidereal) year.

[11] Ibid. l. s. c. Vince quotes Diodorus as his authority, but I have not been able to find the passage.

[12] Aristot. *De Cœlo*, l. ii. c.

[13] Diod. Sic. ii. 31, § 5.

[14] The arrangement of the great temple at Borsippa, already described, is a sufficient proof of the statement in the text.

that, when the astronomical tablets which exist by hundreds in the British Museum come to be thoroughly understood, it will be found that the acquaintance of the Chaldaean sages with astronomical phenomena, if not also with astronomical laws, went considerably beyond the point at which we should place it upon the testimony of the Greek and Roman writers.[15] There is said to be distinct evidence that they observed the four satellites of Jupiter, and strong reason to believe that they were acquainted likewise with the seven satellites of Saturn. Moreover, the general laws of the movements of the heavenly bodies seem to have been so far known to them that they could state by anticipation the position of the various planets throughout the year.

In order to attain the astronomical knowledge which they seem to have possessed, the Babylonians must undoubtedly have employed a certain number of instruments. The invention of sun-dials, as already observed,[16] is distinctly assigned to them. Besides these contrivances for measuring time during the day, it is almost certain that they must have possessed means of measuring time during the night. The clepsydra, or water-clock, which was in common use among the Greeks as early as the fifth century before our era,[17] was probably introduced into Greece from the East, and is likely to have been a Babylonian invention. The astrolabe, an instrument for measuring the altitude of stars above the horizon,

---

[15] The astronomical tablets discovered in Mesopotamia have now for some time occupied the attention of Sir H. Rawlinson. It is probable that he will give to the world, before many months are past, the results of his studies. They cannot fail to be highly interesting. [16] Supra, p. 421. [17] See Aristoph. Acharn. 853; l'ap. 93, 827.

which was known to Ptolemy, may also reasonably be assigned to them. It has generally been assumed that they were wholly ignorant of the telescope.[h] But if the satellites of Saturn are really mentioned, as it is thought that they are, upon some of the tablets, it will follow—strange as it may seem to us—that the Babylonians possessed optical instruments of the nature of telescopes, since it is impossible, even in the clear and vapourless sky of Chaldæa, to discern the faint moons of that distant planet without lenses. A lens, it must be remembered, with a fair magnifying power, has been discovered among the Mesopotamian ruins.[o] A people ingenious enough to discover the magnifying glass would be naturally led on to the invention of its opposite. When once lenses of the two contrary kinds existed, the elements of a telescope were in being. We could not assume from these data that the discovery was made; but, if it shall ultimately be substantiated that bodies invisible to the naked eye were observed by the Babylonians, we need feel no difficulty in ascribing to them the possession of some telescopic instrument.

The astronomical zeal of the Babylonians was in general, it must be confessed, no simple and pure love of an abstract science. A school of pure astronomers existed among them;[1] but the bulk of those who engaged in the study undoubtedly pursued it in the belief that the heavenly bodies had a mysterious influence, not only upon the seasons, but

---

[h] Sir G. C. Lewis went so far as to deny to the Babylonians, in general terms, the use of any instruments whatsoever. (*Astronomy of the Ancients*, pp. 277, 278.)
[o] See above, vol. i. p. 485.
[1] Strab. xvi. 1, § 6.

upon the lives and actions of men—an influence which it was possible to discover and to foretell by prolonged and careful observation. The ancient writers, Biblical and other,[2] state this fact in the strongest way; and the extant astronomical remains distinctly confirm it. The great majority of the tablets are of an astrological character, recording the supposed influence of the heavenly bodies, singly, in conjunction, or in opposition, upon all sublunary affairs, from the fate of empires to the washing of hands or the paring of nails. The modern prophetical almanack is the legitimate descendant and the sufficient representative of the ancient Chaldee Ephemeris, which was just as silly, just as pretentious, and just as worthless.

The Chaldee astrology was, primarily and mainly, genethlialogical.[3] It enquired under what aspect of the heavens persons were born, or conceived,[4] and, from the position of the celestial bodies at one or other of these moments, it professed to deduce the whole life and fortunes of the individual. According to Diodorus,[5] it was believed that a particular star or constellation presided over the birth of each person, and thenceforward exercised over his life a special malign or benignant influence. But his lot depended, not on this star alone, but on the entire

---

[2] See Diod. Sic. II. 30, § 2; 31, § 1; Cic. De Div. L 1; ii. 42; Clitarch. ap. Diog. Laert. Proem. § 6; Theophrast. ap. Procl. Comment. in Plat. Tim. p. 285, F.; and compare Isaiah xlvii. 13; Dan. ii. 2; &c.

[3] Strab. l. s. c.; Sext. Empir. Adv. Math. v. 27; Vitruv. ix. 4; Cic. De Div. ii. 42; &c.

[4] Many of the ancient astrologers regarded the moment of conception as the true natal hour, and cast the horoscope in reference to that point of time. (See Letronne, Observations sur un Zodiaque Egyptien, p. 84, note 3.)

[5] Diod. Sic. ii. 31, § 1. Compare Sext. Emp. l. s. c.; Censorin. § 8; Hor. Od. ii. 17, 17-22; Juv. Sat. xiv. 248.

aspect of the heavens at a certain moment. To cast the horoscope was to reproduce this aspect, and then to read by means of it the individual's future.

Chaldee astrology was not, however, limited to genethlialogy. The Chaldæans professed to predict from the stars such things as the changes of the weather, high winds and storms, great heats, the appearance of comets, eclipses, earthquakes, and the like.⁴ They published lists of lucky and unlucky days, and tables showing what aspect of the heavens portended good or evil to particular countries.⁵ Curiously enough, it appears that they regarded their art as locally limited to the regions inhabited by themselves and their kinsmen, so that while they could boldly predict storm, tempest, failing or abundant crops, war, famine, and the like, for Syria, Assyria, Babylonia, and Susiana, they could venture on no prophecies with respect to other neighbouring lands, as Persia, Media, Armenia.

A certain amount of real meteorological knowledge was probably mixed up with the Chaldæan astrology. Their calendars, like modern almanacks, boldly predicted the weather for fixed days in the year.⁶ They must also have been mathematicians to no inconsiderable extent, since their methods appear to have been geometrical. It is said that the Greek mathematicians often quoted with approval the works

---

⁴ Diod. Sic. ii. 30, § 5. Ποτὶ μὲν γὰρ πνευμάτων μεγέθη δηλοῦν αὐτοῖς (i. e. τοὺς ἀστέρας), ποτὶ δὲ ὄμβρων ἢ καυμάτων ὑπερβολάς, ἔστι δὲ ὅτε κομητῶν ἀστέρων ἐπιτολάς, ἔτι δὲ ἡλίου τε καὶ σελήνης ἐκλείψεις, καὶ σεισμοὺς, καὶ τὸ σύνολον πάσας τὰς ἐκ τοῦ περιέχοντος γενομένας περιστάσεις ὠφελίμους τε καὶ βλαβερὰς οὐ μόνον ἔθνεσι καὶ τόποις, ἀλλὰ καὶ βασιλεῦσι καὶ τοῖς τυχοῦσιν ἰδιώταις.

⁵ Lists of these two kinds have been found by Sir H. Rawlinson among the tablets.

⁶ Columella, xi. 1, § 3.

of their Chaldæan predecessors, Cidén, Naburianus, and Sudinus.* Of the nature and extent of their mathematical acquirements no account, however, can be given, since the writers who mention them enter into no details on the subject.

---

* Strab. xvi. 1, § 6.

CHAPTER VI.

MANNERS AND CUSTOMS.

"Girded with girdles upon their loins, exceeding in dyed attire upon their heads, all of them princes to look to, after the manner of the Babylonians of Chaldæa, the land of their nativity."—Ezek. xxiii. 15.

THE manners and customs of the Babylonians, though not admitting of that copious illustration from ancient monuments which was found possible in the case of Assyria, are yet sufficiently known to us, either from the extant remains or from the accounts of ancient writers of authority, to furnish materials for a short chapter. Herodotus, Strabo, Diodorus, and Nicolas of Damascus, present us with many interesting traits of this somewhat singular people; the sacred writers contemporary with the acme of the nation, add numerous touches; while the remains, though scanty, put distinctly and vividly before our eyes a certain number of curious details.

Herodotus describes with some elaboration the costume of the Babylonians in his day. He tells us that they wore a long linen gown reaching down to their feet, a woollen gown or tunic above this, a short cloak or cape of a white colour, and shoes like those of the Bœotians.[1] Their hair they allowed to grow long, but confined it by a head-band, or a turban;[2]

---

[1] Herod. i. 195.
[2] Ibid. The μίτρα of Herodotus is generally regarded as a turban, but the monuments make it almost certain that this view is incorrect. Neither in the Assyrian

and they always carried a walking-stick with a carving of some kind on the handle. This portraiture, it is probable, applies to the richer inhabitants of the capital, and represents the Babylonian gentleman of the fifth century before our era, as he made his appearance in the streets.

The cylinders seem to show that the ordinary Babylonian dress was less complicated. The worshipper who brings an offering to a god is frequently represented with a bare head, and wears apparently but one garment, a tunic generally ornamented with a diagonal fringe, and reaching from the shoulder to a little above the knee. The tunic is confined round the waist by a belt. Richer worshippers, who commonly present a goat, have a fillet or head-band, not a turban, round the head. They wear generally the same sort of tunic as the others; but over it they have a long robe, shaped like a modern dressing-gown, except that it has no sleeves, and does not cover the right shoulder. In a few instances only we see underneath this open gown a long inner dress or robe, such as that described by Herodotus. A cape or

Babylonian of the lower ranks presenting an offering.

Babylonian of the upper class in the ordinary costume.

---

nor in the Babylonian remains is there any representation of a turban. But the head-band or fillet is com- | mon. The ordinary meaning of μίτρα is "a fillet."

tippet of the kind which he describes is worn sometimes by a god, but is never seen, it is believed, in any representation of a mortal.[3]

The short tunic, worn by the poorer worshippers, is seen also in a representation (hereafter to be given)[4]

Babylonian wearing a long under garment.

of hunters attacking a lion. A similar garment is worn by the man—probably a slave—who accompanies the dog, supposed to represent an Indian hound;[5] and also by a warrior, who appears on one of the cylinders conducting six foreign captives.[6] There is consequently much reason to believe that such a tunic formed the ordinary costume of the common people, as it does at present of the common Arab inhabitants of the country. It left the arms and right shoulder bare, covering only the left. Below the belt it was not

Babylonian soldier conducting captives (from a cylinder).

---

[3] Unless the figure represented above (p. 326, No. 1) is that of a mortal, which is somewhat doubtful.
[4] Infra, p. 438.
[5] See Layard, *Nineveh and Babylon*, p. 527; Birch, *Ancient Pottery*, vol. i. p. 147.

[6] This cylinder is represented in full by Mr. Layard (*Nineveh and Babylon*, p. 608). Other examples of the simple tunic will be found, infra, p. 440; Cullimore, Pl. vii. No. 30; Pl. viii. No. 39; Pl. xii. No. 64; Pl. xix. No. 98, &c.

made like a frock, but lapped over in front, being in fact not so much a garment as a piece of cloth wrapped round the body. Occasionally it is represented as patterned;[7] but this is somewhat unusual.

In lieu of the long robe reaching to the feet, which seems to have been the ordinary costume of the higher classes, we observe sometimes a shorter, but still a similar, garment—a sort of coat without sleeves fringed down both sides, and reaching only a little below the knee.[8] The worshippers who wear this robe have in most cases the head adorned with a fillet.

Patterned tunic, from a cylinder.

It is unusual to find any trace of boots or shoes in the representations of Babylonians. A shoe patterned with a sort of check work, was worn by the king;[9] and soldiers seem to have worn a low boot in their expeditions.[10] But with rare exceptions the Babylonians are represented with bare feet on the monuments; and if they commonly wore shoes in the time of Herodotus, we may conjecture that they had adopted the practice from the example of the Medes and Persians.[11] A low boot, laced in front, was worn by the chiefs of the

Babylonian wearing a short open coat.

---

[7] Lajard, Pl. lii. fig. 1. Compare Collimore, Pl. viii. No. 39.
[8] Lajard, Pl. xxxvi. fig. 13; Pl. xl. fig. 1.
[9] See the representation of a king, supra, p. 400.
[10] Such a boot appears to be worn by the soldier represented above, p. 430.
[11] Compare above, p. 85.

Susianians. Perhaps the "peculiar shoe" of the Babylonians[19] was not very different.

The girdle was an essential feature of Babylonian costume,[13] common to high and low, to the king and to the peasant. It was a broad belt, probably of leather, and encircled the waist rather high up. The warrior carried his daggers in it; to the common man it served the purpose of keeping in place the cloth which he wore round his body. According to Herodotus,[14] it was also universal in Babylonia to carry a seal and a walking-stick.

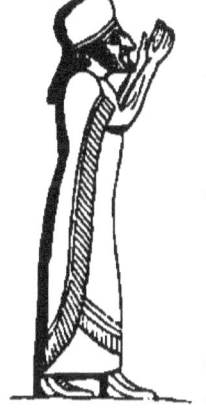

Costume of a Susianian chief (Kouyunjik).

Special costumes, differing considerably from those hitherto described, distinguished the king and the priests. The king wore a long gown, somewhat scantily made, but reaching down to the ankles, elaborately patterned and fringed. Over this, apparently, he had a close-fitting sleeved vest, which came down to the knees, and terminated in a set of heavy tassels. The girdle was worn outside the outer vest, and in war the monarch carried also two cross-belts, which perhaps supported his quiver. The upper vest was,

---

[12] Herod. i. 195. Ὑπόδημα ἐπιχώριον.

[13] See Ezek. xxiii. 15. (Quoted at the beginning of the chapter.) Girdles are worn in almost every representation of a Babylonian upon the monuments.

[14] Herod. l. 195. The seals of the Babylonians have been already described at some length. (Supra, pp. 408, 409.) They were probably worn on a string round the wrist. (Compare vol. i. p. 134.) No clear trace has been found of Babylonian walking-sticks; but it is observable that the court officers at Persepolis are universally represented with sticks in their hands.

like the under one, richly adorned with embroidery. From it, or from the girdle, depended in front, a single heavy tassel attached by a cord, similar to that worn by the early kings of Assyria.[1]

The tiara of the monarch was very remarkable. It was of great height, nearly cylindrical, but with a slight tendency to swell out toward the crown,[2] which was ornamented with a row of feathers round its entire circumference.[3] The space below was patterned with rosettes, sacred trees, and mythological figures. From the centre of the crown there rose above the feathers a projection resembling in some degree the projection which distinguishes the tiara of the Assyrian kings, but rounded, and not squared, at top. This head-dress, which has a heavy appearance, was worn low on the brow, and covered nearly all the back of the head. It can scarcely have been composed of a heavier material than cloth or felt. Probably it was brilliantly coloured.[4]

The monarch wore bracelets, but (apparently) neither necklaces[5] nor ear-rings. These last are assigned by Nicolas of Damascus to a Babylonian governor;[6] and they were so commonly used by the Assyrians, that we can scarcely suppose them unknown to their kindred and neighbours. The Babylonian monuments, however, contain no traces of ear-rings

---

[1] See above, vol. ii. p. 105.
[2] The artist has not represented this tendency sufficiently. It is nearly as marked on the Black Stone as on the frieze represented above, p. 300.
[3] The similarity of this head-dress to that worn by the winged bulls and lions at Khorsabad and Koyunjik, adopted afterwards by the Persians at Persepolis (Flandin, tom. ii. Pls. lxxxi. lxxxii., &c.), is remarkable.
[4] As was the tiara of the Assyrians. (Supra, vol. ii. p. 100.)
[5] A necklace is worn by the king represented on the Sir-i-Zohab tablet (infra, p. 436), but he is thought to be one of the Proto-Chaldæan monarchs.
[6] Fr. 10. See the Fragm. Hist. Gr., vol. iii. p. 360.

as worn by men, and only a few doubtful ones of collars or necklaces;[1] whence we may at any rate conclude that neither were worn at all generally. The bracelets which encircle the royal wrist, resemble the most common bracelet of the Assyrians,[2] consisting of a plain band, probably of metal, with a rosette in the centre.

Fig. 1. Fig. 2.

The dress of the priests was a long robe or gown, flounced and striped, over which they seem to have worn an open jacket of a similar character. A long scarf or ribbon depended from behind down their backs.[3] They carried on their heads an elaborate crown or mitre, which is assigned also to many of the gods.[4] In lieu of this mitre, we find sometimes, though rarely, a horned

Fig. 3.
Costumes of the priests.

Priest wearing a peculiar mitre.

---

[1] A sort of collar or necklace is often worn by a god. Lajard, *Culte de Mithra*, Pl. xxxvii. fig. 1; Pl. xxxviii. figs. 2 and 3, &c. But there are only a very few doubtful cases where the worshipper seems to wear one. (See Lajard, Pl. xxxv. fig. 4; xxxvii. fig. 7, &c.)

[2] See above, vol. ii. p. 104.

[3] This scarf is only an occasional appendage. Instances of it will be found in Lajard, Pl. xii. fig. 16; Pl. xviii. fig. 8; Pl. xxxviii. figs. 3 and 4, &c.

[4] Fig. 3, which follows the representation of Lajard, Pl. lvi. fig. 8, gives probably the most correct representation of the headdress. A similar mitre is represented on the head of the priest in the Sir-i-%obab tablet. (Infra, p. 436.)

cap; and, in one or two instances, a mitre of a different kind.[11] In all sacrificial and ceremonial acts the priests seem to have worn their heads covered.

On the subject of the Babylonian military costume our information is scanty and imperfect. In the time of Herodotus the Chaldæans seem to have had the same armature as the Assyrians[12]—namely bronze helmets, linen breastplates, shields, spears, daggers, and maces or clubs; and, at a considerably earlier date, we find in Scripture much the same arms, offensive and defensive, assigned them.[13] There is, however, one remarkable difference between the Biblical account and that given by Herodotus. The Greek historian says nothing of the use of bows by the Chaldæans; while in Scripture the bow appears as their favourite weapon, that which principally renders them formidable.[14] The monuments are on this point thoroughly in accordance with Scripture. The Babylonian king already represented carries a bow and two arrows.[15] The soldier conducting captives has a bow, an arrow, and a quiver.[16] A monument of an earlier date,[17] which is perhaps rather Proto-Chaldæan than pure Babylonian, yet which has certain Babylonian characteristics, makes

---

[11] See Layard, Pl. xxxvii. fig. 7.
[12] Herod. vii. 63.
[13] The shields and helmets of the Babylonians are mentioned by Ezekiel (xxiii. 24), their breastplates by Jeremiah (li. 3), their spears and swords by the same writer (vi. 23; xlvi. 14, 16), while axes are assigned them by Ezekiel (xxvi. 9).
[14] See Jer. iv. 29, vi. 23, li. 3, &c. And compare Æschyl. Pers. 55, where the Babylonians in the army of Xerxes are characterised as "skilled to draw the bow" (τοξουλκῷ λήματι πιστοὺς).
[15] Supra, p. 400.
[16] Supra, p. 430.
[17] This monument was, I believe, first noticed by Sir H. Rawlinson, who described it in the Journal of the Geographical Society, vol. ix. p. 31. The representation given overleaf is from a sketch made on the spot by that traveller.

the arms of a king a bow and arrow, a club (?), and a dagger. In the marsh fights of the As-

Priest-Vizier presenting captives to a king.

syrians, where their enemies are probably Chaldæans of the low country, the bow is the sole weapon which we see in use.[14]

The Babylonian bow nearly resembles the ordinary curved bow of the Assyrians.[15] It has a knob at either extremity, over which the string passes,

---

[14] See Layard, *Monuments of Nineveh*, 2nd Series, pls. 25 and 27.
[15] Supra, vol. ii. p. 54.

and is thicker towards the middle than at the two ends, the bend is slight, the length when strung less than four feet. The length of the arrow is

Babylonian bow.

about three feet. It is carefully notched and feathered, and has a barbed point. The quiver, as represented in the Assyrian sculptures, has nothing remarkable about it; but the single extant Babylonian representation[20] makes it terminate curiously with a large ornament resembling a spear-head. It is difficult to see the object of this appendage, which must have formed no inconsiderable addition to the weight of the quiver.

Babylonian daggers were short, and shaped like the Assyrian; but their handles were less elegant and less elaborately ornamented.[21] They were worn in the girdle (as they are at the present day in all eastern countries) either in pairs or singly.

Other weapons of the Babylonians, which we may be sure they used in war, though the monuments do not furnish any proof of the fact, were the spear and the bill or axe. These weapons are exhibited in combination upon one of the most curious of the cylinders, where a lion is disturbed in his meal off an ox by two rustics, one

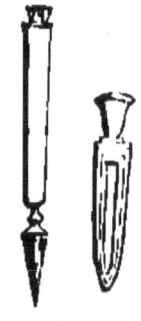

Babylonian quiver and dagger.

---

[20] Compare above, p. 430.   [21] See vol. ii. p. 66.

of whom attacks him in front with a spear, while
the other seizes his tail and assails him in the rear

Lion attacked with spear and axe.

with an axe. With the axe here represented may
be compared another, which is found on a clay
tablet brought from Sinkara, and supposed to belong to the early Chaldæan period.[7] The Sinkara
axe has a simple square blade; the axe upon the
cylinder has a blade with long curved sides and a
curved edge; while, to balance the weight of the
blade, it has on the lower side three sharp spikes.

Axes, Chaldæan and Babylonian.

The difference between the two implements marks the advance of mechanical art in the country between
the time of the first and that of the
fourth monarchy.

Babylonian armies seem to have
been composed, like Assyrian,[1] of
three elements — infantry, cavalry,
and chariots. Of the chariots we appear to have one
or two representations upon the cylinders,[2] but they

---

[7] See Loftus, *Chaldæa and Susiana*, p. 258. The tablet is in the
British Museum.

[1] See vol. ii. pp. 1-43.
[2] Lajard, *Culte de Mithra*, Pl.
xxix. fig. 4, and Pl. xxxiv. fig. 0.

are too rudely carved to be of much value. It is not likely that the chariots differed much either in shape or equipment from the Assyrian, unless they were, like those of Susiana,² ordinarily drawn by mules. A peculiar car, four-wheeled and drawn by four horses, with an elevated platform in front and a seat behind for the driver, which the cylinders occasionally exhibit,⁴ is probably not a war-chariot, but a sacred vehicle, like the *tensa* or *thensa* of the Romans.⁵

The Prophet Habakkuk evidently considered the cavalry of the Babylonians to be their most formidable arm. "They are terrible and dreadful," he said; "from them shall proceed judgment and captivity; their horses also are swifter than the leopards and are more fierce than the evening wolves; and their horsemen shall spread themselves, and their horsemen shall come from far; they shall fly, as the eagle that hasteth to eat."⁶ Similarly Ezekiel spoke of the "desirable young men, captains and rulers, great lords and renowned; *all of them riding upon horses*."⁷ Jeremiah couples the horses with the chariots, as if he doubted whether the chariot force or the cavalry were the more to be dreaded. "Behold, he shall come up

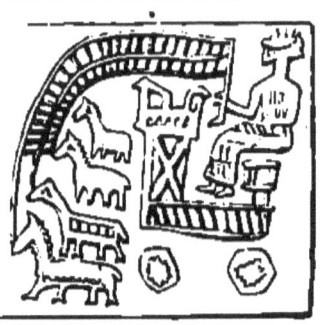

Babylonian four-horse chariot.

---

² See Mr. Layard's *Monuments of Nineveh*, Second Series, Pl. xlv.
⁴ Cullimore, *Cylinders*, Pl. L fig. 6; Lajard, Pl. xli. fig. 3.
⁵ Liv. v. 41, ix. 40; Dio Cass. xlvii. 40; Cic. in Ver. ii. 1, 59.
⁶ Habak. i. 7, 8.
⁷ Ezek. xxiii. 23.

as clouds, and his chariots shall be as a whirlwind; his horses are swifter than eagles. Woe unto us! for we are spoiled."[9] In the army of Xerxes the Babylonians seem to have served only on foot,[8] which would imply that they were not considered in that king's time to furnish such good cavalry as the Persians, Medes, Cissians, Indians, and others, who sent contingents of horse. Darius, however, in the Behistun inscription, speaks of Babylonian horsemen;[10] and the armies which overran Syria, Palestine, and Egypt seem to have consisted mainly of horse.[11]

The Babylonian armies, like the Persian, were vast hosts, poorly disciplined, composed not only of native troops, but of contingents from the subject nations, Cissians, Elamites, Shuhites, Assyrians, and others.[12] They marched with vast noise and tumult,[13] spreading themselves far and wide over the country which they were invading,[14] plundering and destroying on all sides. If their enemy would consent to a pitched battle they were glad to engage with him; but, more usually, their contests resolved themselves into a succession of sieges, the bulk of the population attacked retreating to their strongholds, and offering behind walls a more or less protracted resistance. The weaker towns were assaulted with battering-rams;[15] against the stronger, mounds were raised[16]

---

[9] Jer. iv. 13.
[8] Compare Herod. vii. 63 and 84-87.
[10] Behist. Inscr. col. ii. par. 1, § 2.
[11] See Jer. iv. 29, vi. 23, xlvi. 4, l. 37; Ezek. xxvi. 7, 11, &c.
[12] Compare Is. xxii. 6, with Ezek. xxiii. 23.
[13] Jer. iv. 29. "The whole city shall flee for the noise of the horsemen and the bowmen." Ezek. xxvi.

[10] "Thy walls shall shake at the noise of horsemen, and of the wheels, and of the chariots."
[14] Habak. i. 8.
[15] Ezek. iv. 2, xxi. 22. For the use of battering-rams by the Assyrians, see vol. ii. pp. 78-81.
[16] Habak. i. 10; Jer. vi. 6, xxxii. 24, xxxiii. 4; Ezek. iv. 2, xxi. 22, xxvi. 8.

reaching nearly to the top of the walls, which were then easily scaled or broken down. A determined persistence in sieges seems to have characterised this people, who did not take Jerusalem till the third,[17] nor Tyre till the fourteenth year.[18]

In expeditions it sometimes happened that a question arose as to the people or country next to be attacked. In such cases it appears that recourse was had to divination, and the omens which were obtained decided whither the next effort of the invader should be directed.[19] Priests doubtless accompanied the expeditions to superintend the sacrifices and interpret them on such occasions.

According to Diodorus,[20] the priests in Babylonia were a caste, devoted to the service of the native deities and the pursuits of philosophy, and held in high honour by the people. It was their business to guard the temples and serve at the altars of the gods, to explain dreams and prodigies, to understand omens, to read the warnings of the stars, and to instruct men how to escape the evils threatened in these various ways, by purifications, incantations, and sacrifices. They possessed a traditional knowledge which had come down from father to son, and which none thought of questioning. The laity looked up to them as the sole possessors of a recondite wisdom of the last importance to humanity.

With these statements of the lively but inaccurate Sicilian those of the Book of Daniel are very fairly,

---

[17] 2 K. xxv. 1-3; Jer. lii. 4-6.
[18] Joseph. Ant. Jud. x. 11, § 2.
[19] Ezek. xxi. 21, 22. "For the king of Babylon stood at the parting of the way, at the head of the two ways, to use divination: he made his arrows bright, he consulted with images, he looked in the liver. At his right hand was the divination for Jerusalem, &c."
[20] See Diod. Sic. ii. 29-31.

if not entirely, in accordance. A class of "wise men" is described as existing at Babylon,[?] foremost among whom are the "Chaldæans;"[?] they have a special "learning,"[?] and (as it would seem) a special "tongue;"[?] their business is to expound dreams and prodigies;[?] they are in high favour with the monarch, and are often consulted by him. This body of "wise men" is sub-divided into four classes—"Chaldæans, magicians, astrologers, and soothsayers"—a subdivision which seems to be based upon difference of occupation.[?] It is not distinctly stated that they are priests; nor does it seem that they were a caste; for Jews are enrolled among their number,[?] and Daniel himself is made chief of the entire body.[?] But they form a very distinct order, and constitute a considerable power in the state; they have direct communication with the monarch, and they are believed to possess, not merely human learning, but a supernatural power of predicting future events. High civil office is enjoyed by some of their number.[?]

Notices agreeing with these, but of less importance, are contained in Herodotus and Strabo. Herodotus speaks of the Chaldæans as "priests;"[?] Strabo says that they were "philosophers," who occupied

---

[?] Dan. ii. 12, 14, 24, 27, 48, iv. 6, 18.
[?] The Chaldæans are the spokesmen for the whole body (Dan. ii. 4-11).
[?] Dan. l. 4.   [?] Ibid.
[?] Dan. l. 17, ii. 2-11, iv. 0, 7, v. 7, 8.
[?] Dr. Pusey has successfully shown, against Lengerke, that in Daniel four definite classes of "wise men" are mentioned. (*Lectures on Daniel*, pp. 417-421.) These are the *Casdim* or Chaldæans, the *ashshaphim* or astrologers (compare נֶשֶׁף, "twilight"), the *kharium-mim*, or sacred scribes (from חֶרֶט, "stylus"), and the *me'onahakephim* (Chaldæ, *gazērin*) or "soothsayers."
[?] Dan. l. 4, 20.
[?] Ib. ii. 48, iv. 9. v. 11.
[?] Ib. ii. 49, iii. 30.
[?] Herod. l. 181. Οἱ Χαλδαῖοι ἐόντες ἱρέες τούτου τοῦ θεοῦ (sc. τοῦ Βήλου).

themselves principally in astronomy." The latter writer mentions that they were divided into sects, who differed one from another in their doctrines. He gives the names of several Chaldæans whom the Greek mathematicians were in the habit of quoting. Among them is a Seleucus, who by his name should be a Greek.

From these various authorities we may assume that there was in Babylon, as in Egypt, and in later Persia, a distinct priest class, which enjoyed high consideration. It was not, strictly speaking, a caste. Priests may have generally brought up their sons to the occupation; but other persons, even foreigners, (and if foreigners, then *à fortiori* natives) could be enrolled in the order, and attain its highest privileges.[1] It was at once a sacerdotal and a learned body. It had a literature, written in a peculiar language, which its members were bound to study. This language and this literature was probably a legacy from the old times of the first (Turano-Cushite) kingdom, since even in Assyria it is found that the literature was in the main Turanian, down to the very close of the empire.[2] Astronomy, astrology, and mythology were no doubt the chief subjects which the priests studied; but history, chronology, grammar, law, and natural science most likely occupied some part of their attention.³ Conducting everywhere the worship of the gods, they were of course scattered far and wide through the country; but they had certain special seats of learning, corresponding perhaps in some sort to our universities, the most famous of which were Erech or Orchoë (Warka), and Borsippa,⁴ the town represented by the modern Birs-i-Nimrud. They were diligent students, not wanting in ingenuity, and not content merely to hand down the wisdom of their ancestors. Schools arose among them; and a boldness of speculation developed itself akin to that which we find among the Greeks. Astronomy, in particular, was cultivated with a good deal of success; and stores were accumulated of which the Greeks in later times understood and acknowledged the value.

In social position the priest class stood high. They had access to the monarch;⁵ they were feared and respected by the people; the offerings of the faithful made them wealthy; their position as interpreters of the divine will secured them influence. Being regarded as capable of civil employment, they naturally enough obtained frequently important offices,⁶ which added to their wealth and consideration.

The mass of the people in Babylonia were employed in the two pursuits of commerce and agriculture. The commerce was both foreign and domestic.

---

³ The tablet literature in the early Turanian tongue is believed to embrace all these subjects.
⁴ Rawl. L. s. c. "Ἔστι δὲ καὶ τῶν Χαλδαίων τῶν ἀστρονομικῶν γένη πλεῖω· καὶ γὰρ Ὀρχηνοί τινες προσαγορεύονται καὶ Βορσιππηνοί.
⁵ Dan. i. 20, ii. 2, iv. 7, &c.
⁶ Berosus speaks of the "chief of the Chaldæans" (τὸν βέλτιστον) as keeping the kingdom for Nebuchadnezzar during the interval between his father's death and his own arrival at Babylon. He must have been a sort of Regent of the Empire. Daniel held not only high ecclesiastical but also high civil office (Dan. ii. 48).

Great numbers of the Babylonians were engaged in the manufacture of those textile fabrics, particularly carpets and muslins,⁷ which Babylonia produced not only for her own use, but also for the consumption of foreign countries. Many more must have been employed as lapidaries in the execution of those delicate engravings on hard stone, wherewith the seal, which every Babylonian carried,⁸ was as a matter of course adorned. The ordinary trades and handicrafts practised in the East no doubt flourished in the country. A brisk import and export trade was constantly kept up, and promoted a healthful activity throughout the entire body politic. Babylonia is called "a land of traffic" by Ezekiel, and Babylon "a city of merchants."⁹ Isaiah says that "the cry of the Chaldæans" was "in their ships."¹⁰ The monuments show that from very early times the people of the low country on the borders of the Persian gulf were addicted to maritime pursuits, and navigated the gulf freely, if they did not even venture on the open ocean.¹¹ And Æschylus is a witness that the nautical character still attached to the people after their conquest by the Persians; for he calls the Babylonians in the army of Xerxes "navigators of ships."¹²

The Babylonian import trade, so far as it was carried on by themselves, seems to have been chiefly with Arabia, with the islands in the Persian Gulf, and directly or indirectly with India. From Arabia

---

⁷ Supra, p. 414.
⁸ Herod. I. 195.
⁹ Ezek. xvii. 4.
¹⁰ Is. xliii. 14. This prophet speaks also of the "merchants" of Babylon (xlvii. 15).

¹¹ See above, vol. I. p. 129.
¹² Æschyl. Pers. ll. 52–55. Βαβυλὼν δ' ἡ πολύχρυσος πάμμικτον ὄχλον πέμπει σύρδην, ναῶν τ' ἰσάχουσι, καὶ τοξουλκῷ λήματι πιστούς.

they must have imported the frankincense which they used largely in their religious ceremonies;[13] from the Persian Gulf they appear to have derived pearls, cotton, and wood for walking-sticks;[14] from India they obtained dogs[15] and several kinds of gems.[16] If we may believe Strabo, they had a colony called Gerrha, most favourably situated on the Arabian coast of the gulf, which was a great emporium, and conducted not only the trade between Babylonia and the regions to the south, but also that which passed through Babylonia into the more northern districts.[17] The products of the various countries of Western Asia flowed into Babylonia down the courses of the rivers. From Armenia, or rather Upper Mesopotamia, came wine,[18] gems, emery, and perhaps stone for building;[19] from Phœnicia, by way of Palmyra and Thapsacus, came tin,[20] perhaps copper, probably musical instruments,[21] and other objects of luxury;

---

[13] Herod. i. 183. Compare the report of Nearchus in Arrian's *Indica* (xxxii. 7) with respect to the spice trade between Arabia and Assyria.

[14] It is a reasonable conjecture that the cotton and the "wood for walking-sticks," which were grown in the island of Tylos (Theophrast. *Hist. Plant.* iv. 9, v. 6), supplied the Babylonian market (Heeren, *As. Nat.* vol. ii. pp. 237, 238). The pearl fishery of the Persian Gulf is first mentioned by Nearchus (Arr. *Indica*, xxxviii. 3). It was probably known to the Babylonians from a very early date. (See above, vol. ii. p. 188.)

[15] Herod. i. 192; Ctes. *Indic.* § 5.

[16] Ctes. *Indic.* l. s. c.

[17] Strab. xvi. 3, § 3. Παραπλεύ- σαντι τῆς Ἀραβίας εἰς δισχιλίους καὶ τετρακοσίους σταδίους ἐν βαθεῖ κόλπῳ κεῖται πόλις Γέρρα, Χαλδαίων φυγά- δων ἐκ Βαβυλῶνος .... Πέρμπ-

πορον δ' εἰσὶν οἱ Γερραῖοι τὸ πλέον τῶν Ἀραβίων φορτίων καὶ ἀρωμάτων. Ἀριστόβουλος δὲ τοὐναντίον φησὶ τοὺς Γερραίους τὰ πολλὰ σχεδίαις εἰς τὴν Βαβυλωνίαν ἐμπορεύεσθαι, ἐκεῖ- θεν δὲ τῷ Εὐφράτῃ τὰ φορτία ἀνα- πλεῖν εἰς θάψακον, εἶτα πεζῇ κομί- ζεσθαι πάντη. Compare Strab. xvi. 4, § 18, and Agathemer. *De Mar. Erythr.* § 87.

[18] Herod. I. 194.

[19] Diodorus relates that Semiramis brought a stone obelisk from Armenia down the Euphrates to Babylon (ii. 11, §§ 4, 5).

[20] See above, vol. ii. p. 185.

[21] The Greek names of Babylonian musical instruments (Dan. iii. 5) point to an early commerce between Babylonia and Greece, which would naturally follow this line. (Compare Herod. i. 1.) The instruments imported brought their names with them. (See Pusey's *Daniel*, p. 26.)

from Media and the countries towards the east[20] came fine wool, lapis lazuli, perhaps silk, and probably gold and ivory. But these imports seem to have been brought to Babylonia by foreign merchants rather than imported by the exertions of native traders. The Armenians, the Phœnicians, and perhaps the Greeks,[21] used for the conveyance of their goods the route of the Euphrates. The Assyrians, the Paretaceni and the Medes probably floated theirs down the Tigris and its tributaries.[22]

A large—probably the largest—portion of the people must have been engaged in the occupations of agriculture. Babylonia was, before all things, a grain-producing country—noted for a fertility unexampled elsewhere, and to moderns almost incredible. The soil was a deep and rich alluvium;[23] and was cultivated with the utmost care. It grew chiefly wheat, barley, millet, and sesame,[24] which all flourished with wonderful luxuriance. By a skilful management of the natural water supply, the indispensable fluid was utilised to the utmost, and conveyed to every part of the country.[25] Date-groves spread widely over the land,[26] and produced abundance of an excellent fruit.[27]

For the cultivation of the date nothing was needed but a proper water supply, and a little attention at the time of fructification. The male and female palm are distinct trees, and the female cannot pro-

---

[20] For the existence of this trade see Diod. Sic. ii. 11, § 1. For its probable objects see Heeren's *As. Nat.* vol. ii. pp. 204-213, E. T.
[21] Herod. i. 185.
[22] Diod. Sic. l. s. c.
[23] Strab. xvi. 1, § 9. Βαθεῖα γὰρ ἡ γῆ καὶ μαλακὴ καὶ εὐυδρος.
[24] Herod. i. 193; Strab. xvi. 1, § 14.
[25] Xen. *Anab.* ii. 4, § 13; Herod. L. s. c.
[26] Herod. L. s. c.; Amm. Marc. xxiv. 3; Zosim. iii. pp. 173-179.
[27] On the excellence of one kind of Babylonian date see Theophrast. *Hist. Plant.* ii. 8, p. 35, ed. Heinsius.

duce fruit unless the pollen from the male comes in contact with its blossoms. If the male and the female trees are grown in proper proximity, natural causes will always produce a certain amount of impregnation. But to obtain a good crop, art may be serviceably applied. According to Herodotus, the Babylonians were accustomed to tie the branches of the male to those of the female palm.[1] This was doubtless done at the blossoming time, when it would have the effect he mentions, preventing the fruit of the female, or date-producing palms, from falling off.

The date palm was multiplied in Babylonia by artificial means. It was commonly grown from seed, several stones being planted together for greater security;[2] but occasionally it was raised from suckers or cuttings.[3] It was important to plant the seeds and cuttings in a sandy soil; and, if nature had not sufficiently impregnated the ground with saline particles, salt had to be applied artificially to the soil around as a dressing. The young plants needed a good deal of attention. Plentiful watering was required; and transplantation was desirable at the end of both the first and the second year. The Babylonians are said to have transplanted their young trees in the height of summer; other nations preferred the spring time.[4]

For the cultivation of grain the Babylonians broke up their land with the plough; to draw which they seem to have employed two oxen, placed one before the other, in the mode still common in many parts of

---

[1] Herod. i. 193. That Herodotus misconceives the means whereby the fructification was effected does not invalidate his testimony as to the fact. Theophrastus corrects his error. (*Hist. Plant.* ii. 9, ad fin.)
[2] Theophrast. *Hist. Plant.* ii. 8.
[3] See above, vol. i. p. 15, note " and ".
[4] Theophrast. l. s. c.

England. The plough had two handles, which the ploughman guided with his two hands. It was apparently of somewhat slight construction. The tail rose from the lower part of one of the handles, and was of unusual length.[1]

Men ploughing, from a cylinder.

It is certain that dates formed the main food of the inhabitants. The dried fruit, being to them the staff of life, was regarded by the Greeks as their "bread."[2] It was perhaps pressed into cakes, as is the common practice in the country at the present day.[3] On this and goats' milk, which we know to have been in use,[4] the poorer class, it is probable, almost entirely subsisted. Palm-wine,[5]

Milking the goat, from a cylinder.

---

[1] The plough here represented, which is from a cylinder figured by M. Felix Lajard (*Culte de Mithra*, Pl. xxxiv. fig. 15), may be contrasted with the Assyrian implement, of which a representation has been given above (vol. ii. p. 198). It is of very much lighter structure, but is inferior to the Assyrian in having no apparatus for drilling the seed.

[2] Herod. i. 193; Strab. xvi. 1, § 14.

[3] Rich, *First Memoir in Babylon*, p. 59, note. (See above, vol. i. p. 44, note [1].)

[4] Milking the goat is represented on a cylinder figured by Mr. Lajard, from which the above woodcut is taken. (*Culte de Mithra*, Pl. xli. fig. 5.)

[5] By palm-wine, which is mentioned both by Herodotus and Strabo (ll. s. c.) among the products of Babylonia, is (I think) to be under-

the fermented sap of the tree, was an esteemed, but no doubt only an occasional beverage. It was pleasant to the taste, but apt to leave a headache behind it.[10] Such vegetables as gourds, melons, and cucumbers, must have been cheap, and may have entered into the diet of the common people. They were also probably the consumers of the "pickled bats," which (according to Strabo) were eaten by the Babylonians.[11]

In the marshy regions of the south there were certain tribes whose sole, or at any rate whose chief food, was fish.[12] Fish abound in these districts,[13] and are readily taken either with the hook or in nets. The mode of preparing this food was to dry it in the sun, to pound it fine, strain it through a sieve, and then make it up into cakes, or into a kind of bread.

The diet of the richer classes was no doubt varied and luxurious. Wheaten bread, meats of various kinds, luscious fruits, fish, game, loaded the board; and wine imported from abroad[14] was the usual beverage. The wealthy Babylonians were fond of drinking to excess; their banquets were magnificent, but generally ended in drunkenness;[15] they were not, however, mere scenes of coarse indulgence, but had a certain refinement, which distinguishes them from the riotous drinking-bouts of the less civilised

---

stood the fermented sap of the tree, not the spirit which may be distilled from the fruit. (See above, vol. I. p. 44.)

[10] Xen. *Anab.* ii. 3, § 15.

[11] Strab. xvi. 1, § 7. Τὸ βόρειον ἱερὸν πόλις ἐστὶ . . πληθύουσι δ᾽ ἐν αὐτῇ νυκτερίδες μείζους πολὺ τῶν ἐν ἄλλοις τόποις ἁλίσκονται δ᾽ εἰς βρῶσιν καὶ ταριχεύονται.

[12] Herod. i. 200.

[13] See above, vol. I. p. 51; and compare the woodcut, p. 47.

[14] For the use of wine, see Dan. i. 5, v. 1; Nic. Dam. Fr. 10, p. 360; Q. Curt. v. 1. On its importation from abroad, see Herod. i. 194.

[15] Q. Curt. l. s. c.

Medes." Music was in Babylonia a recognised accompaniment of the feast; and bands of performers, entering with the wine, entertained the guests with concerted pieces." A rich odour of perfumes floated around, for the Babylonians were connoisseurs in unguents." The eye was delighted with a display of gold and silver plate." The splendid dresses of the guests, the exquisite carpets and hangings, the numerous attendants, gave an air of grandeur to the scene, and seemed half to excuse the excess of which too many were guilty.

A love of music appears to have characterised both the Babylonians and their near neighbours and kinsmen, the Susianians. In the sculptured representations of Assyria,²⁰ the Susianians are shown to have possessed numerous instruments, and to have organised large bands of performers. The Prophet Daniel²¹ and the historian Ctesias²² similarly witness to the musical taste of the Babylonians, which had much the same character. Ctesias said that Annarus (or Nannarus), a Babylonian noble, entertained his guests at a banquet with music performed by a company of 150 women. Of these a part sang, while the rest played upon instruments, some using the pipe, others the harp, and a certain number the psaltery.²³ These same instruments²⁴ are assigned to the

---

¹⁵ See above, p. 88.
¹⁷ Nic. Dam. Fr. 10, p. 362.
¹⁸ Herod. I. 195.
¹⁹ Dan. v. 2; Nic. Dam. Fr. 10, p. 363.
²⁰ See above, vol. ii. p. 106; and for the full representation of the entire scene, see Mr. Layard's *Monuments of Nineveh*, 2nd series, Pls. 48 and 49.
²¹ Dan. iii. 5, 7, 10, 15. Compare Ps. cxxxvii. 3; and Is. xiv. 11.

²² Ctes. ap. Athen. *Deipn.* xii. p. 530 B.
²³ Compare Nic. Dam. Fr. 10, p. 362, with the fragment of Ctesias in Athenæus. Nicolas says of the women—αἱ μὲν ἐκιθάριζον, αἱ δ' ηὔλουν, αἱ δὲ ἔψαλλον. Ctesias says—ἔψαλλον δὲ καὶ ᾖδον.
²⁴ Compare the Septuagint version, which translates the Hebrew מַשְׁרוֹקִיתָא by σύριγξ, the קַתְרוֹס by κιθάρα, and the פְּסַנְתֵּרִין by ψαλτήριον

Babylonians by the prophet Daniel, who however adds to them three more—viz. the horn, the *sambuca*, and an instrument called the *sumphonia*, or "symphony." It is uncertain whether the horn intended was straight, like the Assyrian, or curved, like the Roman *cornu* and *lituus*.[z] The pipe was probably the double instrument, played at the end, which was familiar to the Susianians and Assyrians.[a] The harp would

Babylonian harp, from a cylinder.

seem to have resembled the later harp of the Assyrians; but it had fewer strings, if we may judge from a representation upon a cylinder.[b] Like the Assyrian, it was carried under one arm,[c] and was played by both hands, one on either side of the strings.

The character of the remaining instruments is more doubtful. The *sambuca* seems to have been a large harp, which rested on the ground,[d] like the harps of the Egyptians. The psaltery was also a stringed instrument, and, if its legitimate descendant is the modern *santour*,[e] we may presume that it is represented in the

---

μος. Σύριγξ is probably used loosely for αὐλός. It was the technical name for the mouthpiece of the αὐλός. (See Liddell and Scott's *Lexicon*, s. v. αὐλός.)

[z] The Hebrew קרן is generally regarded as the curved horn, in contradistinction to the שופר or straight trumpet. But as the Assyrians seem to have employed the straight horn, and not (so far as we know) the curved one (see vol. ii. p. 162), perhaps the קרן of Daniel may represent the straight instrument. The LXX. render it by σάλπιγξ, which was straight, not curved.

[a] Supra, vol. ii. pp. 150, 157.
[b] Lajard, *Culte de Mithra*, Pl. xxxix., fig. 8.
[c] See above, vol. ii. p. 153.
[d] "Sackbut" is certainly a wrong rendering of *sabka* or *sambuca*, for the sackbut was a wind instrument, whereas the *sambuca* was certainly a kind of harp. (Compare Athen. *Deipn.* iv. p. 175 D; xiv. pp. 633–637; Vitruv. vi. 1; Suidas, ad voc. &c.)
[e] Gesenius regards *santour* as a corruption of *psanterin*, the Chaldee representation of the ψαλτήριον of the Greeks. The resemblance of a

hands of a Susianian musician on the monument which is our chief authority for the Oriental music of the period. The *sumphonia* is thought by some to be the bag-pipe," which is called *sampogna* by the modern Italians: by others it is regarded as a sort of organ.

The Babylonians used music, not merely in their private entertainments, but also in their religious ceremonies. Daniel's account of their instruments occurs casually in his mention of Nebuchadnezzar's dedication of a colossal idol of gold. The worshippers were to prostrate themselves before the idol as soon as they heard the music commence, and were probably to continue in the attitude of worship, until the sound ceased.

The seclusion of women seems scarcely to have been practised in Babylonia with as much strictness as in most Oriental countries. The two peculiar customs on which Herodotus descants at length— the public auction of the marriageable virgins in all the towns of the empire,[1] and the religious prostitution authorised in the worship of Beltis[2] were wholly incompatible with the restraints to which the sex has commonly submitted in the Eastern world. Much modesty can scarcely have belonged to those whose virgin charms were originally offered in the public market to the best bidder, and who were required

---

(Susianian) instrument, represented on the monuments of Assyria, to the modern *santour*, has been already noticed. (See above, vol. II. p. 161; and compare Pusey's *Daniel*, p. 32.)

" (learning, ad voc. סימפניה; Jud Brill, *Comment. in Daniel*, &c.

" Ibn Yahin, *Comment. in Dan.*

iii. 5. Compare Jerome on Luke xv., where the view is mentioned but combated.

" Dan. iii. 5, 7, &c.

[1] Herod. i. 196. Compare Nic. Dam. Fr. 131, and Ælian, *Var. Hist.* iv. 1.

[2] Herod. i. 199. Compare Baruch vi. 43.

by their religion, at least once in their lives, openly to submit to the embraces of a man other than their husband. It would certainly seem that the sex had in Babylonia a freedom—and not only a freedom, but also a consideration—unusual in the ancient world, and especially rare in Asia. The stories of Semiramis and Nitocris may have in them no great amount of truth; but they sufficiently indicate the belief of the Greeks as to the comparative publicity allowed to their women by the Babylonians.[3]

The monuments accord with the views of Babylonian manners thus opened to us. The female form is not eschewed by the Chaldæan artists. Besides images of a goddess (Beltis or Ishtar) suckling a child, which are frequent,[4] we find on the cylinders numerous representations of women, engaged in

Babylonian women making an offering to a goddess.

various employments. Sometimes they are represented in a procession, visiting the shrine of a goddess, to whom they offer their petitions, by the mouth of one of their number,[5] or to whom they bring their

---

[3] See also Dan. v. 10-12, where the queen enters the banqueting-house and gives her advice openly before the lords.
[4] See above, vol. i. p. 176.
[5] Lajard, *Culte de Mithra*, Pl. xxviii. fig. 12.

children for the purpose, probably, of placing them under her protection:[*] sometimes they may be seen amusing themselves among birds and flowers in a garden,[†] plucking the fruit from dwarf palms, and politely handing it one to another. Their attire is in

Babylonian women gathering dates in a garden.

every case nearly the same; they wear a long but scanty robe, reaching to the ankles, ornamented at the bottom with a fringe and apparently opening in front. The upper part of the dress passes over only one shoulder. It is trimmed round the top with a fringe which runs diagonally across the chest, and a similar fringe edges the dress down the front where it opens. A band or fillet is worn round the head, confining the hair, which is turned back behind the head, and tied by a riband, or else held up by the fillet.

Female ornaments are not perceptible on the small figures of the cylinders: but from the modelled image in clay, of which a representation has been already given, we learn that bracelets and ear-rings

---

[*] Ibid. Pl. xl. fig. 8.   [†] Ibid. Pl. xxvii. fig. 7.

of a simple character were worn by Babylonian women,[8] if they were not by the men.[9] On the whole, however, female dress seems to have been plain and wanting in variety, though we may perhaps suspect that the artists do not trouble themselves to represent very accurately such diversities of apparel as actually existed.

From a single representation of a priestess[10] it would seem that women of that class wore nothing but a petticoat, thus exposing not only the arms, but the whole of the body as far as the waist.

The monuments throw little further light on the daily life of the Babylonians. A few of their implements, as saws and hatchets are represented; and from the stools, the chairs, the tables, and the stands for holding water-jars[11] which occur occasionally on the cylinders, we may gather that the fashion of their furniture much resembled that of their northern neighbours, the Assyrians. It is needless to dwell on this subject, which presents no novel features, and has been anticipated by the discussion on Assyrian furniture in the first volume.[12] The only touch that can be added to what was there said is, that in Babylonia the chief — almost the sole — material employed for furniture was the wood of the palm-

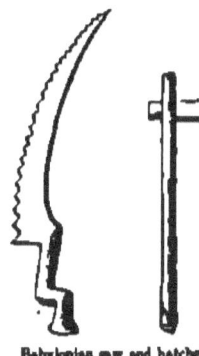
Babylonian saw and hatchet
(from the cylinders).

---

[8] Supra, p. 399.
[9] See above, p. 434.
[10] Lajard, Pl. xl. fig. 6.
[11] Supra, p. 422. Stools will be seen in the illustrations on pp. 404 and 440.
[12] Pp. 486–490.

tree,¹³ a soft and light fabric which could be easily worked, and which had considerable strength, but did not admit of a high finish.¹⁴

---

¹³ Theophrast. *Hist. Plant.* ii. 6. βυλῶσι τάς τε κλίνας καὶ τὰ ἄλλα τῶν φαυλῶν . . . τὸ μὲν κέρσιμον, τὸ δὲ ἄκαρπον ἐξ ὧν οἱ περὶ Βα- | ¹⁴ Ibid. v. 4 and 7.

Chapter VII.

RELIGION.

Ἤνεσαν τοὺς θεοὺς τοὺς χρυσοῦς καὶ ἀργυροῦς καὶ χαλκοῦς καὶ σιδηροῦς καὶ λιθίνους καὶ ξυλίνους.—Dan. v. 4.

The Religion of the later Babylonians differed in so few respects from that of the early Chaldæans, their predecessors in the same country, that it will be unnecessary to detain the reader with many observations on the subject. The same gods were worshipped in the same temples and with the same rites[1]—the same cosmogony[2] was taught and held—the same symbols were objects of religious regard—even the very dress of the priests was maintained unaltered;[3] and, could Urukh or Chedor-laomer have risen from the grave and revisited the shrines wherein they sacrificed fourteen centuries earlier, they would have found but little to distinguish the ceremonies of their own day from those in vogue under the successors of Nabopolassar. Some additional splendour in the buildings, the idols, and perhaps the offerings, some increased use of music as a part of the ceremonial,[4] some advance of corruption with respect to priestly impostures and popular religious customs might probably have been noticed: but otherwise the religion of Nabonidus and Belshazzar was that of

---

[1] Compare vol. i. pp. 138-180.
[2] Ibid. pp. 180-183.
[3] Compare the priest on Urukh's cylinder (supra, vol. i. p. 118) with those represented in the preceding chapter (p. 434).
[4] Supra, p. 453.

Urukh and Ilgi, alike in the objects and the mode of worship, in the theological notions entertained and the ceremonial observances taught and practised.

The identity of the gods worshipped during the entire period is sufficiently proved by the repair and restoration of the ancient temples under Nebuchadnezzar, and their re-dedication (as a general rule) to the same deities. It appears also from the names of the later kings and nobles, which embrace among their elements the old divine appellations. Still, together with this general uniformity, we seem to see a certain amount of fluctuation—a sort of fashion in the religion, whereby particular gods were at different times exalted to a higher rank in the Pantheon, and were sometimes even confounded with other deities commonly regarded as wholly distinct from them. Thus Nebuchadnezzar devoted himself in an especial way to Merodach, and not only assigned him titles of honour which implied his supremacy over all the remaining gods,[5] but even identified him with the great Bel, the ancient tutelary god of the Capital. Nabonidus, on the other hand, seems to have restored Bel to his old position,[6] re-establishing the distinction between him and Merodach, and preferring to devote himself to the former.

A similar confusion occurs between the goddesses Beltis and Nana or Ishtar,[7] though this is not

---

[5] Among the titles given by Nebuchadnezzar to Merodach are the following:—"The great lord," "the first born of the gods," "the most ancient," "the supporter of sovereignty," "the king of the heavens and the earth."

[6] This may be concluded from the fact that in the time of Cyrus the great temple at Babylon was known uniformly as the temple of Belus. It receives some confirmation from the further fact that Nabonidus gave his eldest son a name (Belshazzar) which placed him under Bel's protection.

[7] See above, vol. i. p. 175, and compare the author's *Herodotus*, vol. i. pp. 496, 497, 2nd edition.

peculiar to the later kingdom. It may perhaps be suspected from such instances of connexion and *quasi*-convertibility, that an esoteric doctrine, known to the priests and communicated by them to the kings, taught the real identity of the several gods and goddesses, who may have been understood by the better instructed to represent, not distinct and separate beings, but the several phases of the Divine Nature. Ancient polytheism had, it may be surmised, to a great extent this origin, the various names and titles of the Supreme, which designated His different attributes or the different spheres of His operation, coming by degrees to be misunderstood, and to pass, first with the vulgar, and at last with all but the most enlightened, for the appellations of a number of gods.

The chief objects of Babylonian worship were Bel, Merodach, and Nebo.[8] Nebo, the special deity of Borsippa, seems to have been regarded as a sort of powerful patron-saint, under whose protection it was important to place individuals. During the period of the later kingdom, no divine element is so common in names. Of the seven kings who form the entire list, three certainly,[9] four probably,[10] had appellations composed with it. The usage extended from the royal house to the courtiers; and such names as Nebu-zar-adan, Samgar-Nebo, and Nebu-shazban,[11] show the respect which the upper class of citizens paid to this god. It may even be suspected that

---

[8] This is sufficiently apparent from the native monuments. It is confirmed by the Jewish writers. (See Isaiah xlvi. 1; Jerem. L. 2; li. 44.)

[9] *Nabo*-polassar, *Nebu*-chadnezzar, and *Nabo*-nidus.

[10] *Labo*-rosoarchod, which stands perhaps for *Nabo*-rosoarchod, as *Laby*-netus for *Nabo*-nahid or Nabonidus.

[11] See 2 Kings xxv. 8; Jerem. xxxix. 3 and 13.

when Nebuchadnezzar's Master of the Eunuchs had to give Babylonian names to the young Jewish princes whom he was educating, he designed to secure for one of them this powerful patron, and consequently called him Abed-Nebo ¹³—" the servant of Nebo "—a name which the later Jews, either disdaining ¹⁴ or not understanding, have corrupted into the Abed-nego of the existing text.

Another god held in peculiar honour by the Babylonians was Nergal. Worshipped at Cutha as the tutelary divinity of the town,¹⁴ he was also held in repute by the people generally. No name is more common on the cylinder seals. It is sometimes, though not often, an element in the names of men, as in "Nergal-shar-ezer, the Rab-mag," ¹⁵ and (if he be a different person), in Nerigliasar, the king.

Altogether, there was a strong local element in the religion of the Babylonians. Bel and Merodach were in a peculiar way the gods of Babylon, Nebo of Borsippa, Nergal of Cutha, the Moon of Ur or Hur, Beltis of Niffer, Hea or Hoa of Hit, Ana of Erech, the Sun of Sippara. Without being exclusively honoured at a single site, the deities in question held the foremost place each in his own town. There

---

¹³ Abed-nego is a name which admits of no Semitic derivation. It has indeed been explained as equivalent to Ebed-melech (Arab. Abdalmalik), which means "the servant of the king;" but the only ground for this is the Abyssinian *negus*, "king," which became *naya* in Achæmenian Persian, but of which there is no trace in either Babylonian or Assyrian.

¹³ The Jews seem often to have played with the names of the heathen gods in a spirit of scorn and con-tumely. Thus Zir-banit becomes Succoth-benoth, "tents of daughters" (2 K. xvii. 30); Nebo becomes in one place Nibhaz, "the barker" (ibid. verse 31); Anunit becomes Anammelech, in chime with Adrammelech (ibid.), &c. Similarly Tartak may be suspected to be a derisive corruption of Tir, and Nisroch of Nergal, who was sometimes called simply *Nis* or *Nir*.

¹⁴ Supra, vol. i. p. 172.
¹⁵ Jerem. xxxix. 3.

especially was worship offered to them; there was the most magnificent of their shrines. Out of his own city a god was not greatly respected, unless by those who regarded him as their special personal protector.

The Babylonians worshipped their gods indirectly, through images. Each shrine had at least one idol, which was held in the most pious reverence, and was in the minds of the vulgar identified with the God. It seems to have been believed by some that the actual idol ate and drank the offerings.[1] Others distinguished between the idol and the god, regarding the latter as only occasionally visiting the shrine where he was worshipped.[2] Even these last, however, held gross anthropomorphic views, since they considered the god to descend from heaven in order to hold commerce with the chief priestess. Such notions were encouraged by the priests, who furnished the inner shrine in the temple of Bel with a magnificent couch and a golden table, and made the principal priestess pass the night in the shrine on certain occasions.[3]

The images of the gods were of various materials.[4] Some were of wood, others of stone, others again of metal; and these last were either solid or plated. The metals employed were gold, silver, brass or rather bronze, and iron. Occasionally the metal was laid over a clay model.[5] Sometimes images of one

---

[1] The narrative in the Apocryphal Daniel, which forms the first part of our Book of "Bel and the Dragon," though probably not historical, seems to be written by one well acquainted with Babylonian notions. The king in the narrative evidently regards the idol as the eater of the victuals.

[2] φασὶ δὲ οἱ αὐτοὶ οὗτοι [οἱ Χαλδαῖοι] τὸν θεὸν αὐτὸν φοιτᾷν ἐς τὸν νηὸν, κ.τ.λ. (Herod. L 182.)

[3] Herod. L 181.

[4] See the passage of Daniel quoted at the commencement of this chapter.

[5] This appears to have been the case from the description of the image

metal were overlaid with plates of another, as was the case with one of the great images of Bel, which was originally of silver but was coated with gold by Nebuchadnezzar.⁴

The worship of the Babylonians appears to have been conducted with much pomp and magnificence. A description has been already given of their temples.⁷ Attached to these imposing structures was in every case a body of priests;⁸ to whom the conduct of the ceremonies and the custody of the treasures were entrusted. The priests were married,⁹ and lived with their wives and children, either in the sacred structure itself or in its immediate neighbourhood. They were supported either by lands belonging to the temple,¹⁰ or by the offerings of the faithful. These consisted in general of animals, chiefly oxen and goats;¹¹ but other valuables were no doubt received when tendered. The priest always intervened between the worshipper and the deities, presenting him to them and interceding with uplifted hands on his behalf.¹²

In the temple of Bel at Babylon, and probably in most of the other temples both there and elsewhere throughout the country, a great festival was

---

of Bel in the Apocryphal Daniel. (Οὗτος ἔσωθεν μὲν ἐστὶ πηλὸς, ἔξωθεν δὲ χαλκός. Apoc. Dan. xiv. 6.) Bronze hammered work, laid over a model made of clay mixed with bitumen, has been found in Assyria. (See above, vol. i. p. 465.)

⁶ Sir H. Rawlinson in the author's Herodotus (vol. i. p. 517, 2nd edition).

⁷ Supra, pp. 378-387.

⁸ According to the Apocryphal Daniel seventy priests were attached to the great Temple of Bel at Babylon. (Apoc. Dan. xiv. 9.)

⁹ Ibid. verses 14, 19, and 20. The fact is implied in Diodorus's statement that the priests were a caste. (Diod. Sic. ii. 29, § 4.)

¹⁰ Arrian, Exp. Alex. vii. 16.

¹¹ The goat is the ordinary sacrificial animal on the cylinders; but occasionally we see an ox following the worshipper. (See Cullimore, Pl. xi. No. 60.)

¹² See the figures of priests on page 434.

celebrated once in the course of each year.[13] We know little of the ceremonies with which these festivals were accompanied; but we may presume from the analogy of other nations that there were magnificent processions on these occasions, accompanied probably with music and dancing. The images of the gods were perhaps exhibited either on frames or on sacred vehicles.[14] Numerous victims were sacrificed; and at Babylon it was customary to burn on the great altar in the precinct of Bel a thousand talents' weight of frankincense.[15] The priests no doubt wore their most splendid dresses; the multitude was in holiday costume; the city was given up to merry-making. Everywhere banquets were held. In the palace the king entertained his lords;[16] in private houses there was dancing and revelling.[17] Wine was freely drunk; passion was excited; and the day, it must be feared, too often terminated in wild orgies, wherein the sanctions of religion were claimed for the free indulgence of the worst sensual appetites.

In the temples of one deity excesses of this description, instead of being confined to rare occasions, seem to have been of every day occurrence. Each woman was required once in her life to visit a shrine of Beltis, and there remain till some stranger cast money in her lap and took her away with him. Herodotus, who seems to have witnessed the disgraceful scene, describes it as follows. "Many women of the wealthier sort, who are too proud to mix

---

[13] Herod. i. 183.
[14] See above, page 430. Compare Macrob. Sat. L. 23. "Vehitur enim simulachrum dei Heliopolitani ferculo, uti vehuntur in pompa ludorum Circensium deorum simulachra." The "deus Heliopolitanus" is the Sun-God of Sippara.
[15] Herod. L. s. c.
[16] Dan. v. 1-4.
[17] Herod. l. 101. λέγεται... χορεύειν τε τὸν χρόνον τοῦτον καὶ ἐν συναθροίσει εἶναι.

with the others, drive in covered carriages to the
precinct, followed by a goodly train of attendants,
and there take their station. But the larger number
seat themselves within the holy enclosure with wreaths
of string about their heads,—and *here there is always
a great crowd*, some coming and others going. Lines
of cord mark out paths in all directions among the
women; and the strangers pass along them to make
their choice. A woman who has once taken her seat
is not allowed to return home till one of the strangers
throws a silver coin into her lap, and takes her with
him beyond the holy ground. When he throws the
coin, he says these words—'The goddess Mylitta
(Beltis) prosper thee.' The silver coin may be of
any size; it cannot be refused; for that is forbidden
by the law, since once thrown it is sacred. The
woman goes with the first man who throws her
money, and rejects no one. When she has gone with
him, and so satisfied the goddess, she returns home;
and from that time forth no gift, however great, will
prevail with her. Such of the women as are tall and
beautiful are soon released; but others, who are ugly,
have to stay a long time before they can fulfil the
law. Some have even waited three or four years in
the precinct."[a] The demoralising tendency of this
religious prostitution can scarcely be overrated.[b]

Notions of legal cleanness and uncleanness, akin
to those prevalent among the Jews, are found to some
extent in the religious system of the Babylonians.

---

[a] Herod. i. 199. Compare Baruch vi. 43, and Strabo xvi. 1, § 20.
[b] The statement of Herodotus, that "from that time forth no gift, however great, will prevail with a Babylonian woman," is not repeated by Strabo, and is flatly contradicted by Q. Curtius. (See above, p. 330, note *.)

The consummation of the marriage rite made both the man and the woman impure, as did every subsequent act of the same kind. The impurity was communicated to any vessel that either might touch. To remove it, the pair were required first to sit down before a censer of burning incense, and then to wash themselves thoroughly. Thus only could they re-enter into the state of legal cleanness.[90] A similar impurity attached to those who came into contact with a human corpse.[1]

The Babylonians are remarkable for the extent to which they affected symbolism in religion. In the first place, they attached to each god a special mystic number, which is used as his emblem and may even stand for his name in an inscription. To the gods of the First Triad—Anu, Bel, and Hea or Hoa—were assigned respectively the numbers 60, 50, and 40; to those of the Second Triad—the Moon, the Sun, and the Atmosphere—were given the other integers, 30, 20, and 10 (or perhaps six).[2] To Beltis was attached the number 15,[3] to Nergal 12,[4] to Bar or Nin (apparently) 40, as to Hoa; but this is perhaps a mistake.[5] It is probable that every god, or at any rate all the principal deities, had in a similar way some numerical emblem. Many of these are, however, as yet undiscovered.

Further, each god seems to have had one or more emblematic signs by which he could be pictorially symbolised. The cylinders are full of such forms, which are often crowded into every vacant space

---

[90] Herod. i. 198. [1] Strab. l. s. c.
[2] The Babylonians had a double system of notation, decimal and sexagintal. They wrote in series either 3, 4, 5, 6, or 3, 4, 5, 10. (Sir H. Rawlinson in the author's *Herodotus*, vol. i. p. 600, 2nd edition.)
[3] Ibid. p. 407.   [4] Ibid. p. 621.
[5] Ibid. p. 514.

where room could be found for them.⁵ A certain number can be assigned definitely to particular divinities. Thus a circle, plain or crossed, designates the Sun-god, San or Shamas;⁷ a six-rayed or eight-rayed star the Sun-goddess, Gula or Anunit;⁸ a double or triple thunderbolt the Atmospheric god, Vul;⁹ a serpent probably Hoa;¹⁰ a naked female form Nana or Ishtar;¹¹ a fish Bar or Nin-ip.¹² But besides these assignable symbols, there are a vast number with regard to which we are still wholly in the dark. Among these may be mentioned a sort of double cross ⳩, often repeated three times, a jar or bottle,¹³ an altar, a double lozenge ◇, one or more birds, an animal between a monkey and a jerboa, a dog, a sort of double horn, a sacred tree, an ox, a bee, a spearhead.¹⁴ A study of the inscribed cylinders shews these emblems to have no reference to the god or goddess named in the inscription upon them. Each, apparently, represents a distinct deity; and the object of placing them upon a cylinder is to imply the devotion of the man, whose seal it is, to other deities besides those whose special servant he considers himself. A single cylinder sometimes contains as many as eight or ten such emblems.

⁵ See Cullimore's *Cylinders*, Pl. xviii. Nos. 92 to 95; Pl. xxii. Nos. 113 and 115. Compare Lajard, *Culte de Mithra*, Pls. xxxv. fig. 3; liv. A. fig. 12; liv. B. fig. 15.
⁷ See vol. i. p. 161, where the same usage is assigned to the early Chaldæans.
⁸ Ibid. p. 163.   ⁹ Ibid. p. 164.
¹⁰ Ibid. p. 154.   ¹¹ Ibid. p. 176.
¹² Ibid. p. 168.
¹³ See the engraving of a cylinder on p. 449.
¹⁴ The two last-named emblems are uncommon. For the bee see Cullimore, Pl. xxii. No. 117, and Pl. xxiv. No. 129. For the spearhead, Cullimore, Pl. xxvii. No. 147.

The principal temples of the gods had special sacred appellations. The great temple of Bel at Babylon was known as Bit-Saggath, that of the same god at Niffer as Kharris-Nipra, that of Beltis at Warka (Erech) as Bit-Ana, that of the Sun at Sippara as Bit-Parra, that of Anunit at the same place as Bit-Ulmis, that of Nebo at Borsippa as Bit-Tsida, &c. It is seldom that these names admit of explanation.[15] They had come down apparently from the old Chaldæan times and belonged to the ancient (Turanian) form of speech; which is still almost unintelligible. The Babylonians themselves probably in few cases understood their meaning. They used the words simply as proper names, without regarding them as significative.

[15] Bit-Ana is certainly "the house of the god Anu or Ana," who was worshipped at Erech in conjunction with Beltis. (See above, vol. i. p. 140.) Bit-Parra may be "the house of Ph' Ra," or "the Sun." (Sir H. Rawlinson in the author's *Herodotus*, vol. I. p. 501, note [9], 2nd edition.) The meaning of the other terms has not even (so far as I am aware) been conjectural.

Chapter VIII.

HISTORY AND CHRONOLOGY.

Τῆς δὲ Βαβυλῶνος . . πολλοὶ μέν κου . . ἐγίνοντο βασιλέες . . . οἳ τὰ τείχεά τε ἐπεκόσμησαν καὶ τὰ ἱρά.—HEROD. I. 184.

THE history of the Babylonian Empire commences with Nabopolassar, who appears to have mounted the throne in the year B.C. 625; but to understand the true character of the kingdom which he set up, its traditions and its national spirit, we must begin at a far earlier date. We must examine, in however incomplete and cursory a manner, the middle period of Babylonian history, the time of obscurity and comparative insignificance, when the country was, as a general rule, subject to Assyria, or at any rate played but a secondary part in the affairs of the East. We shall thus prepare the way for our proper subject, while at the same time we shall link on the history of the Fourth to that of the First Monarchy, and obtain a third line of continuous narrative, connecting the brilliant era of Cyaxares and Nebuchadnezzar with the obscure period of the first Cushite kings.

It has been observed that the original Chaldæan monarchy perished through an Arab invasion about B.C. 1500, and that the invaders held possession of the country till B.C. 1273, or B.C. 1270.[1] Their

---

[1] Supra, vol. i. p. 223.

rule was then superseded by that of the Assyrians, who became masters of Babylonia under the first Tiglathi-Nin[2] and governed it for a short time from their own capital. Unable, however, to maintain this unity very long, they appear to have set up in the country an Assyrian dynasty, over which they claimed and sometimes exercised a kind of suzerainty, but which was practically independent and managed both the external and internal affairs of the kingdom at its pleasure. The first king of this dynasty concerning whom we have any information is a Nebuchadnezzar, who was contemporary with the Assyrian monarch Asshur-ris-ilim, and made two attacks upon his territories.[3] The first of these was by the way of the Diyaleh and the out-lying Zagros hills, the line taken by the great Persian military road in later times.[4] The second was directly across the plain. If we are to believe the Assyrian historian who gives an account of the campaigns, both attacks were repulsed, and after his second failure the Babylonian monarch fled away into his own country hastily. We may perhaps suspect that a Babylonian writer would have told a different story. At any rate Asshur-ris-ilim was content to defend his own territories and did not attempt to retaliate upon his assailant. It was not till late in the reign of his son and successor, Tiglath-Pileser I., that any attempt was made to punish the Babylonians for their audacity. Then, however, that monarch invaded the southern kingdom,[5] which had passed into the hands of a king named Merodach-iddin-akhi, probably a son of Nebu-

---

[2] Compare above, vol. ii. p. 304.
[3] An account of these wars has been already given in the History of Assyria. (See vol. ii. pp. 308–310.)
[4] Herod. v. 52.
[5] Compare vol. ii. pp. 329, 330.

chadnezzar. After two years of fighting, in which
he took Kurri-Galazu (Akkerkuf), the two Sip-
paras, Opis, and even Babylon itself, Tiglath-Pileser
retired, satisfied apparently with his victories; but
the Babylonian monarch was neither subdued nor
daunted. Hanging on the rear of the retreating
force, he harassed it by cutting off its baggage, and
in this way he became possessed of certain Assyrian
idols, which he carried away as trophies to Babylon.
War continued between the two countries during the
ensuing reigns of Merodach-shapik-ziri in Babylon
and Asshur-bel-kala in Assyria, but with no important successes, so far as appears, on either side.⁶

The century during which these wars took place
between Assyria and Babylonia, which corresponds
with the period of the later Judges in Israel, is
followed by an obscure interval, during which but
little is known of either country. Assyria seems to
have been at this time in a state of great depression.
Babylonia, it may be suspected, was flourishing; but
as our knowledge of its condition comes to us almost
entirely through the records of the sister country,
which here fail us, we can only obtain a dim and
indistinct vision of the greatness now achieved by
the southern kingdom. A notice of Asshur-idanni-
pal's seems to imply that Babylon, during the period
in question, enlarged her territories at the expense of
Assyria,⁷ and another in Macrobius⁸ makes it probable

---

⁶ Compare vol. ii. p. 332.
⁷ Asshur-idanni-pal tells us that, about the year B.C. 880, he recovered and rebuilt a city on the Diyaleh, which a Babylonian king named Tsibir had destroyed at a remote period. (See above, vol. ii. p. 340.)
⁸ The passage in Macrobius is curious, and seems worth giving at length. "Assyrii quoque," says this writer, "Solem sub nomine Jovis, quem Dis Heliopoliten cognominant, maximis cæremoniis celebrant in civitate quæ Heliopolis nuncupatur.

that she held communications with Egypt. Perhaps these two powers, fearing the growing strength of Assyria, united against her, and so checked for a while that development of her resources which they justly dreaded.

However, after two centuries of comparative depression, Assyria once more started forward, and Babylonia was among the first of her neighbours whom she proceeded to chastise and despoil. About the year B.C. 880, Asshur-idanni-pal led an expedition to the south-east and recovered the territory which had been occupied by the Babylonians during the period of weakness.* Thirty years later, his son, the Black-Obelisk king, made the power of Assyria still more sensibly felt. Taking advantage of the circumstance that a civil war was raging in Babylonia between the legitimate monarch, Merodach-sum-adin, and his younger brother, he marched into the country, took a number of the towns, and having defeated and slain the pretender, was admitted into Babylon itself.[1] From thence he proceeded to overrun Chaldæa, or the district upon the coast, which appears at this time to have been independent of Babylon, and governed by a number of petty kings. The Babylonian monarch probably admitted the suzerainty of the invader but was not put to any tribute. The Chaldæan chiefs, however, had to submit to this

---

Ejus dei simulacrum sumptum est de oppido Ægypti, quod et ipsum Heliopolis appellatur, regnante apud Ægyptios Senemure, seu klem Sonepos nomine fuit, perlatumque est primum in eam per Onjam legatum Deloloris regis Assyriorum sacerdotesque Ægyptios, quorum princeps fuit Partimatis, dignusque habitum apud Assyrios pontus Heliopolin commigravit." (Nat. i. 23.) It is suspected that the Deleboras (or Deboras) here mentioned is identical with the Taibir who took territory from the Assyrians. (See above, vol. ii. p. 331, note 10.)

* Supra, vol. ii. p. 340.
[1] Ibid. p. 361.

indignity. The Assyrian monarch returned to his capital, having "struck terror as far as the sea." Thus Assyrian influence was once more extended over the whole of the southern country, and Babylonia resumed her position of a secondary power, dependent on the great monarchy of the north.

But she was not long allowed to retain even the shadow of an autonomous rule. In or about the year B.C. 821, the son and successor of the Black-Obelisk king, apparently without any pretext, made a fresh invasion of the country.[1] Merodak-belatzu-ikbi, the Babylonian monarch, boldly met him in the field, but was defeated in two pitched battles (in the latter of which he had the assistance of powerful allies[2]), and was forced to submit to his antagonist. Babylon, it is probable, became at once an Assyrian tributary, and in this condition she remained till the troubles which brought the dynasty of Asshur-idanni-pal to an end gave an opportunity for shaking off the hated yoke. Towards the middle of the eighth century B.C. the Babylonians seem once more to have become independent; but the change was accompanied by a disintegration of the country which was more fatal to its recovery of influence than half a dozen defeats. While Nabonassar established himself at the head of affairs in Babylon, a certain Yakin, the father of Merodach-Baladan, became master of the tract upon the coast; and various princes, Nadina, Zakiru, and others, at the same time obtained governments, which they administered in their own name, towards the north. The old Babylonian kingdom was broken up; and the way was prepared for that final sub-

---

[1] Supra, vol. ii. pp. 376, 377.
[2] The Zimri of Mount Zagros, the Aramæans of the middle Euphrates, and the Chaldæans of the south.

jugation, which was ultimately effected by the Sargonids.

Still, the Babylonians seem to have looked with complacency on this period, and they certainly made it an era from which to date their later history. Perhaps, however, they had not much choice in this matter. Nabonassar was a man of energy and determination. Bent probably on obliterating the memory of the preceding period of subjugation, he "destroyed the acts of the kings who had preceded him;"[4] and the result was that the year of his accession became almost necessarily the era from which subsequent events had to be dated.

Nabonassar appears to have lived on friendly terms with Tiglath-Pileser, the contemporary monarch of Assyria, who early in his reign invaded the southern country, reduced several princes of the districts about Babylon to subjection, and forced Merodach-Baladan, who had succeeded his father, Yakin, in the low region, to become his tributary.[5] No war seems to have been waged between Tiglath-Pileser and Nabonassar. The king of Babylon may have seen with satisfaction the humiliation of his immediate neighbours and rivals, and may have felt that their subjugation rather improved than weakened his own position. At any rate it tended to place him before the nation as their only hope and champion—the sole barrier which protected their country from a return of the old servitude.

Nabonassar held the throne of Babylon for fourteen years, from B.C. 747 to B.C. 733.[6] It has generally

---

[4] Berosus, Fr. 11 a. Ναβονάσαρος συναγαγὼν τὰς πράξεις τῶν πρὸ αὐτοῦ βασιλέων ἠφάνισεν.
[5] See vol. ii. pp. 395, 396.
[6] See the "Canon of Ptolemy."

been supposed that this period is the same with that regarded by Herodotus as constituting the reign of Semiramis.[7] As the wife or as the mother of Nabonassar, that lady (according to many) directed the affairs of the Babylonian state on behalf of her husband or her son. The theory is not devoid of a certain plausibility, and it is no doubt possible that it may be true; but at present it is a mere conjecture, wholly unconfirmed by the native records; and we may question whether on the whole it is not more probable that the Semiramis of Herodotus is misplaced. In a former volume it was shown that a Semiramis flourished in Assyria towards the end of the ninth and the beginning of the eighth centuries B.C.[8] — during the period, that is, of Babylonian subjection to Assyria. She may have been a Babylonian princess, and have exercised an authority in the southern capital.[9] It would seem therefore to be more probable that she is the individual whom Herodotus intends, though he has placed her about half a century too late, than that there were two persons of the same name within so short a time, both queens, and both ruling in Mesopotamia.

Nabonassar was succeeded in the year B.C. 733 by a certain Nadius, who is suspected to have been among the independent princes reduced to subjection by Tiglath-Pileser in his Babylonian expedition.[10]

---

[7] Herod. l. 184. Among those who identify the reigns of Semiramis and Nabonassar, and suppose a close tie of relationship to have existed between them, are Larcher (*Hérodote*, tom. i. p. 468), Clinton (*F. H.* vol. i. p. 270, note f), Volney (*Recherches sur l'Histoire Ancienne*, l'art iii. p. 79), Bosanquet (*Journal of Asiatic Society*, vol. xv. p. 280), and Vance Smith (*Prophecies relating to Assyria*, pp. 66, 67).

[8] See above, vol. ii. p. 383.

[9] Ibid. p. 384.

[10] One of these princes bears the name of Nadina, which may have been corrupted into Nadius. (See above, p. 473.)

Nadius reigned only two years—from B.C. 733 to B.C. 731—when he was succeeded by Chinzinus and Porus, two princes whose joint rule lasted from B.C. 731 to B.C. 726. They were followed by an Elulæus, who has been identified[11] with the king of that name called by Menander[12] king of Tyre—the Luliya of the cuneiform inscriptions;[13] but it is in the highest degree improbable that one and the same monarch should have borne sway both in Phœnicia and Chaldæa at a time when Assyria was paramount over the whole of the intervening country. Elulæus therefore must be assigned to the same class of utterly obscure monarchs with his predecessors, Porus, Chinzinus, and Nadius; and it is only with Merodach-Baladan, his successor, that the darkness becomes a little dispelled, and we once more see the Babylonian throne occupied by a prince of some reputation and indeed celebrity.

Merodach-Baladan was the son of a monarch, who in the troublous times that preceded the era of Nabonassar appears to have made himself master of the lower Babylonian territory[13]—the true Chaldæa—and to have there founded a capital city, which he called after his own name, Bit-Yakin. On the death of his father Merodach-Baladan inherited this dominion; and it is here that we first find him, when, during the reign of Nabonassar, the Assyrians under Tiglath-Pileser II. invade the country. Forced to accept the position of Assyrian tributary under this monarch, to whom he probably looked for protection against the Babylonian king, Nabonassar, Merodach-

[11] Bosanquet, *Fall of Nineveh*, p. 40.
[12] Ap. Joseph. *Ant. Jud.* ix. 14.
§ 2.
[13] See above, vol. ii. p. 130.
[14] Supra, page 473.

Baladan patiently bided his time, remaining in comparative obscurity during the two reigns of Tiglath-Pileser and Shalmaneser his successor, and only emerging contemporaneously with the troubles which ushered in the dynasty of the Sargonids. In B.C. 721—the year in which Sargon made himself master of Nineveh[1]—Merodach-Baladan extended his authority over the upper country, and was recognised as king of Babylon. Here he maintained himself for twelve years; and it was probably at some point of time within this space that he sent ambassadors to Hezekiah at Jerusalem,[2] with orders to inquire into the particulars of the curious astronomical marvel,[3] or miracle, which had accompanied the sickness and recovery of that monarch. It is not unlikely that the embassy, whereof this was the pretext, had a further political object. Merodach-Baladan, aware of his inability to withstand singly the forces of Assyria, was probably anxious to form a powerful league against the conquering state, which threatened to absorb the whole of Western Asia into its dominion. Hezekiah received his advances favourably, as appears by the fact that he exhibited to him all his treasures.[4] Egypt, we may presume, was cognizant of the proceedings, and gave them her support.[5] An alliance, defensive if not also offensive, was probably concluded between Egypt and Judæa on the

---

[1] Supra, vol. ii. p. 418, note *.
[2] 2 K. xx. 12; Is. xxxix. 1.
[3] The ingenious explanation which Mr. Bosanquet has given of the going back of the shadow on the dial of Ahaz (*Journal of the Asiatic Society*, vol. xv. pp. 280-295) is probably known to most readers. A way is clearly shown in which the shadow may have gone back without any interference with the course of nature.
[4] Isaiah xxxix. 2, 4.
[5] The dependance of Judæa on Egypt during Hezekiah's reign is indicated by the expressions in 2 K. xviii. 21, 24; Is. xxxvi. 6, 9.

one hand, Babylon, Susiana, and the Aramæan tribes of the middle Euphrates on the other. The league would have been formidable but for one circumstance —Assyria lay midway between the allied states, and could attack either moiety of the confederates separately at her pleasure. And the Assyrian king was not slow to take advantage of his situation. In two successive years Sargon marched his troops against Egypt and against Babylonia, and in both directions carried all before him. In Egypt he forced Sabaco to sue for peace.[6] In Babylonia he gained a great victory over Merodach-Baladan and his allies, the Aramæans and Susianians,[7] took Bit-Yakin, into which the defeated monarch had thrown himself, and gained possession of his treasures and his person. Upon this the whole country submitted; Merodach-Baladan was carried away captive into Assyria; and in the year B.C. 709 an Assyrian viceroy[8]—called by Ptolemy Arceanus ('Αρκέανος)—was placed upon the throne, and Babylonia became once more, after forty years of freedom, an Assyrian dependency.

But this state of things did not continue long. Sargon died in the year B.C. 704, and coincident with his death we find a renewal of troubles in Babylonia.[9] Sargon's viceroy was deposed or slain; various pretenders started up; a son of Sargon and brother of Sennacherib re-established Assyrian influence for a brief space;[10] but fresh revolts followed. A certain

---

[6] Supra, vol. ii. p. 417.
[7] Ibid. p. 419.
[8] Some have suspected that the 'Αρκέανος of Ptolemy is Sargon himself, whose native name was Sargina or Sar-kina. But I know of no other case where the initial s of an Assyrian name is dropped by the Greeks.

[9] An interregnum in the canon (ἐπὶ ἀβασίλευτα) necessarily implies a season of trouble and disorder. It does not show that there was no king, but only that no king reigned a full year.
[10] Polyhist. ap. Euseb. Chron. Can. i. 5, § 1. (See the passage

Hagisa became king of Babylon for a month. Finally, Merodach-Baladan again appeared upon the scene, having escaped from his Assyrian prison, murdered Hagisa, and remounted the throne from which he had been deposed seven years previously.[11] But the brave effort to recover independence failed. Sennacherib in his third year, B.C. 702, descended upon Babylonia, defeated the army which Merodach-Baladan brought against him, drove that monarch himself into exile, after a reign of six months, and reattached his country to the Assyrian crown.[12] From this time to the revolt of Nabopolassar—a period of above three quarters of a century—Babylonia, with few and brief intervals of revolt, continued an Assyrian fief. The Assyrian kings governed her either by means of viceroys, such as Ilelibus, Regibelus, Mesesimordachus, and Saos-duchinus, or directly in their own persons, as was the case during the reign of Esar-haddon,[13] and perhaps during that of Asshur-emit-ilin.[14]

The revolts of Babylon during this period have been described at length in the history of Assyria.[15] Two fall into the reign of Sennacherib, one into that of Asshur-bani-pal, his grandson. In the former, Merodach-Baladan, who had not yet given up his pretensions to the lower country, the region about Bit-Yakin, and a certain Susub, who was acknowledged as king at Babylon, were the leaders. In

---

quoted at length in the second volume of this work, p. 429, note '.)
[12] Ibid.
[13] Supra, vol. ii. p. 450.
[14] Supra, pp. 466 and 478.
[15] Ibid. p. 506. This view depends on a doubtful reading of the name of the monarch in question as *Asshur-irisat-ili-kuin*. As Sarac-us would represent the earlier, so Cinne-ladanus might represent the latter portion of this name.
[16] See above, vol. ii. pp. 449-452, and p. 489.

the latter, Saos-duchinus, the Assyrian viceroy, and brother of Asshur-bani-pal, the Assyrian king, seduced from his allegiance by the hope of making himself independent, headed the insurrection. In each case the struggle was brief, being begun and ended within the year.[16] The power of Assyria at this time so vastly preponderated over that of her ancient rival that a single campaign sufficed on each occasion of revolt to crush the nascent insurrection.[17]

A tabular view of the chronology of this period is appended. (See the opposite page.)

Having thus briefly sketched the history of the kingdom of Babylon from its conquest by the Arabs to the close of the long period of Assyrian predominance in Western Asia, we may proceed to the consideration of the "Empire." And first, as to the circumstances of its foundation.

When the Medes first assumed an aggressive attitude towards Assyria, and threatened the capital with a siege, Babylonia apparently remained unshaken in her allegiance. When the Scythian hordes spread themselves over Upper Mesopotamia and wasted with fire and sword the fairest regions under Assyrian rule, there was still no defection in this quarter.[1] It was not till the Scythic ravages were over, and the Medes for the second time poured

---

[16] As Susub does not appear in Ptolemy's Canon, it is tolerably certain that neither his first nor his second reign lasted a year. The revolt of Saul-mugina (Saos-duchinus) seems to have been put down within a few months. (See vol. ii. p. 489.)

[17] This remark is true of all the known cases of revolt. It might however require some qualification, if the history of the eight years from B.C. 688 to B.C. 680 were recovered. The interregnum of Ptolemy in this place implies either revolt or a rapid succession of viceroys—probably the former.

[1] Supra, vol. ii. p. 617.

CHRONOLOGY OF BABYLON FROM THE ARAB CONQUEST TO NABOPOLASSAR.

B.C.	Kings.	Contemporary kings of Assyria.	Remarkable events.
		Bel-sum-ili-kapi.	
1518 to 1273	Dynasty of Arabs	Bel-nadin. Pad-G. Iva-lush L. Shalmaneser I.	
ab. 1273	Dynasty of Assyrians	Tiglathi-Nin I. Iva-lush II.	Babylon conquered by the Assyrians.
	* * *	Nin-pala-zira. Asshur-dain-il. Mutaggil-Nebo.	
ab. 1150 " 1130 " 1110	Nebuchadnezzar I. Merodach-iddin-akhi. Merodach-shapik-ziri	Asshur-ris-ilim. Tiglath-pileser I. Asshur Bil-kala.	Wars between Assyria and Babylon.
	* * *	* * *	
	Tabhr (Terhures)	Asshur-Mazur	Babylon in alliance with Egypt. Takes territory from Assyria.
	* * *	Asshur-iddin-akhi. Asshur-danin-il I. Iva-lush III. Tiglathi-Nin II.	
ab. 900	*	Asshur-idanni-pal	Assyria recovers her lost territory.
" 894	Merodach-sum-adin	Shalmaneser II.	Civil war in Babylon. Assyria helps the legitimate king.
" 850	Merodach-belatsu-ikbi	Shamas-Iva. Iva-lush IV. Shalmaneser III. Asshur-danil-il II.	Babylon conquered. Peace under Assyria.
747	Nabonassar	Asshur-lush	Babylon re-established but independent.
734 733 731 728 721	* * * Nadius Chinsinus and Porus Khakus Merodach-Baladan	Tiglath-pileser II. Shalmaneser IV. Sargon.	
710 (?)	* * *	* * *	Embassy of Merodach Baladan to Hezekiah.
709 704 702 702 699	Arcennus (viceroy) Interregnum Hagisa Merodach-Baladan Belibus (viceroy) Assaranadius (viceroy)	Sennacherib	Babylon conquered by Sargon. Babylon revolts. Sennacherib conquers Babylon.
693 (?) 694 (?) 693 692	Nunib Regibelus (viceroy) Mesessimordachus (viceroy)		Babylon revolts. Revolts put down. Ditto.
685	Interregnum		Troubles in Babylon. Interregnum of eight years, coinciding with last eight years of Sennacherib.
680	Esarhaddon	Esarhaddon	Babylon recovered by Esarhaddon.
667 647 625	Saos-duchinus (viceroy) Cineladanus Nabopolassar	Asshur-bani-pal Asshur-emit-ilin. * * *	Babylon revolts and again returns to allegiance. Assyrian empire destroyed.

across Zagros into Adiabênê, resuming the enterprise from which they had desisted at the time of the Scythic invasion, that the fidelity of the Southern people wavered. Simultaneously with the advance of the Medes against the Assyrian capital from the east, we hear of a force threatening it from the south,[1] a force which can only have consisted of Susianians, of Babylonians, or of both combined.[2] It is probable that the emissaries of Cyaxares had been busy in this region for some time before his second attack took place, and that by a concerted plan while the Medes debouched from the Zagros passes, the south rose in revolt and sent its hasty levies along the valley of the Tigris.

In this strait the Assyrian king deemed it necessary to divide his forces and to send a portion against the enemy which was advancing from the south, while with the remainder he himself awaited the coming of the Medes. The troops detached for the former service he placed under the command of a certain Nabopolassar[3] (Nabu-pal-uzur), who was probably an Assyrian nobleman of high rank and known capacity.[4] Nabopolassar had orders to proceed to

---

[1] Abyden. ad Euseb. Chron. Can. i. 9. "Saracus . . . certior factus turmarum vulgi collecticiarum quae à muri adversus se adventarent, continuò Busalussorum militiae decem Babylonem mittebat." The sea here mentioned can only be the Persian Gulf.

[2] It has been conjectured that the "turmae vulgi collecticiae" were a remnant of the Scythic hordes which had recently overrun Western Asia. But we cannot well imagine them advancing *from the sea*, or acting in concert with their special enemies, the Medes.

[3] Syncell. Chronograph. p. 210, ll. Οὗτος [ὁ Ναβοπαλάσσαρος] στρατηγὸς ὑπὸ Σαράκου τοῦ Χαλδαίων βασιλέως σταλεὶς, κατὰ τοῦ αὐτοῦ Σαράκου εἰς Νίνον ἐπιστρατεύει. Compare Abyden. ap. Euseb. l. s. c., where Nabopolassar is called Busalussor (leg. Hupalussor) by the same sort of abbreviation by which Nebuchadnezzar has become Bokht-i-nazar among the modern Arabs.

[4] It is unlikely that any one who was not an Assyrian would have received so high an appointment.

Babylon, of which he was probably made viceroy, and to defend the southern capital against the rebels. We may conclude that he obeyed these orders so far as to enter Babylon and install himself in office; but shortly afterwards he seems to have made up his mind to break faith with his sovereign, and aim at obtaining for himself an independent kingdom out of the ruins of the Assyrian power. Having formed this resolve, his first step was to send an embassy to Cyaxares, and to propose terms of alliance, while at the same time he arranged a marriage between his own son, Nebuchadnezzar, and Amuhia, or Amyitis (for the name is written both ways), the daughter of the Median monarch.[6] Cyaxares gladly accepted the terms offered; the young persons were betrothed; and Nabopolassar immediately led, or sent, a contingent of troops to join the Medes, who took an active part in the great siege which resulted in the capture and destruction of the Assyrian capital.[7]

[6] "Sed enim hic, capto rebellandi consilio, Amuhiam Asdahagis Mediorum principis filiam nato suo Nabocolrosoro desponderat." Abyden. 1. s. c. "Is (Sardanapallus) ad Asdahagem, qui erat Medicae gentis princeps et satrapa, copias auxiliares misit, videlicet ut filio suo Nabucolrossoro desponderet Amuhiam e filiabus Asdahagis unam." Alex. Polyhist. ap. Euseb. Chron. Can. 1. 5, § 3. Χαλδαίων ἐβασίλευσεν Ναβοπολάσσαρος ἔτη κά, ὁ πατὴρ τοῦ Ναβουχοδονόσορ. Τοῦτον ὁ πολυίστωρ Ἀλέξανδρος Σαρδανάπαλον καλεῖ, πέμψαντα πρὸς Ἀστυάγην σατράπην Μηδίας, καὶ τὴν θυγατέρα αὐτοῦ Ἀμυίτην λαβόντα νύμφην εἰς τὸν υἱὸν αὐτοῦ Ναβουχοδονόσορ. The marriage of Nebuchadnezzar with a Median princess was attested by Berosus. (Fr. 14.)

[7] That the Medes and Babylonians both took part in the siege is witnessed by Polyhistor (l. s. c.), Josephus (Ant. Jud. x. 5, § 1), and the author of the Book of Tobit (xiv. 15). It was also the view of Ctesias. (Diod. Sic. II. 24-28). Herodotus in his extant work speaks only of the Medes (i. 106), while in our fragments of Abydenus the Babylonians alone are distinctly mentioned.

There is further considerable discrepancy as to the leaders engaged in the siege. Abydenus and Polyhistor make the Median commander Astyages; the author of Tobit calls him Assuerus (Xerxes). This same writer makes the Babylonian commander Nebuchadnezzar. I have followed in the text what seems to me the balance of authority.

A division of the Assyrian Empire between the allied monarchs followed. While Cyaxares claimed for his own share Assyria Proper and the various countries dependant on Assyria towards the north and the north-west, Nabopolassar was rewarded for his timely defection, not merely by independence, but by the transfer to his government of Susiana on the one hand and of the valley of the Euphrates, Syria, and Palestine on the other. The transfer appears to have been effected quietly, the Babylonian yoke being peacefully accepted in lieu of the Assyrian without the necessity arising for any application of force. Probably it appeared to the subjects of Assyria, who had been accustomed to a monarch holding his court alternately at Nineveh and at Babylon, that the new power was merely a continuation of the old, the new monarch a legitimate successor of the old line of Ninevite kings.

Of the reign of Nabopolassar the information which has come down to us is scanty. It appears by the canon of Ptolemy that he dated his accession to the throne from the year B.C. 625, and that his reign lasted twenty-one years, from B.C. 625 to B.C. 604. During the greater portion of this period the history of Babylon is a blank. Apparently the "golden city" enjoyed her new position at the head of an empire too much to endanger it by aggression; and, her peaceful attitude provoking no hostility, she was for a while left unmolested by her neighbours. Media, bound to her by formal treaty as well as by dynastic interests, could be relied upon as a firm

---

Supra, vol. ii. p. 478.
So also Berosus (Fr. 14), and i. 5, § 3).
Polyhistor (ap. Euseb. Chron. Can.
Isaiah xiv. 4.

friend; Persia was too weak, Lydia too remote to be formidable; in Egypt alone was there a combination of hostile feeling with military strength such as might have been expected to lead speedily to a trial of strength; but Egypt was under the rule of an aged and wary prince, one trained in the school of adversity,[11] whose years forbade his engaging in any distant enterprise, and whose prudence led him to think more of defending his own country than of attacking others.[12] Thus, while Psammetichus lived, Babylon had little to fear from any quarter, and could afford to "give herself to pleasures and dwell carelessly."[13]

The only exertion which she seems to have been called upon to make during her first eighteen years of empire, resulted from the close connection which had been established between herself and Media. Cyaxares, as already remarked, proceeded from the capture of Nineveh to a long series of wars and conquests. In some, if not in all, of these he appears to have been assisted by the Babylonians, who were perhaps bound by treaty to furnish a contingent as often as he required it. Either Nabopolassar himself, or his son Nebuchadnezzar, would lead out the troops on such occasions; and thus the military spirit of both prince and people would be pretty constantly exercised.

It was as the leader of such a contingent that Nabopolassar was able on one occasion to play the important part of peace-maker in one of the bloodiest

---

[11] Herod. ii. 151, 152.
[12] The only even apparent exception is the siege and capture of Ashdod (Herod. ii. 157), which may have had a defensive object. Egypt needed for her protection a strong fortress in this quarter.
[13] Isaiah xlvii. 8.

of all Cyaxares' wars.[1] After five years' desperate fighting the Medes and Lydians were once more engaged in conflict when an eclipse of the sun took place. Filled with superstitious dread the two armies ceased to contend, and shewed a disposition for reconciliation, of which the Babylonian monarch was not slow to take advantage. Having consulted with Syennesis of Cilicia, the foremost man of the allies on the other side, and found him well disposed to second his efforts, he proposed that the sword should be returned to its scabbard, and that conferences should be held to arrange terms of peace. This timely interference proved effectual. A peace was concluded between the Lydians and the Medes, which was cemented by a royal intermarriage; and the result was to give to Western Asia, where war and ravage had long been almost perpetual, nearly half a century of tranquillity.[2]

Successful in his mediation, almost beyond his hopes, Nabopolassar returned from Asia Minor to Babylon. He was now advanced in years, and would no doubt gladly have spent the remainder of his days in the enjoyment of that repose, which is so dear to those who feel the infirmities of age creeping upon them. But Providence had ordained otherwise. In B.C. 610—probably the very year of the eclipse—Psammetichus died, and was succeeded by his son Neco, who was in the prime of life and who in disposition was bold and enterprising. This monarch very shortly after his accession cast a covetous eye upon Syria, and in the year B.C. 608,[3] having made

---

[1] See Herod. i. 74, and compare above, pp. 210-212.
[2] Supra, pp. 212, 213.
[3] The last year of Josiah was (I think) B.C. 608—not B.C. 609, as Clinton makes it (F. H. vol. i. p.

NECO INVADES SYRIA.

vast preparations, he crossed his frontier and invaded the territories of Nabopolassar. Marching along the usual route, by the *Shefélah* and the plain of Esdraelon,⁴ he learned, when he neared Megiddo, that a body of troops was drawn up at that place to oppose him. Josiah, the Jewish king, regarding himself as bound to resist the passage through his territories of an army hostile to the monarch of whom he held his crown, had collected his forces, and, having placed them across the line of the invader's march, was calmly awaiting in this position the approach of his master's enemy. Neco, hereupon, sent ambassadors to persuade Josiah to let him pass, representing that he had no quarrel with the Jews, and claiming a divine sanction to his undertaking.⁵ But nothing could shake the Jewish monarch's sense of duty; and Neco was consequently forced to engage with him, and to drive his troops from their position. Josiah, defeated and mortally wounded, returned to Jerusalem, where he died.⁶ Neco pressed forward through Syria to the Euphrates;⁷ and, carrying all before him, established his dominion over the whole tract lying between Egypt on the one hand, and the "Great River" upon the other.⁸ On his return three months later he visited Jerusalem,⁹ deposed Jehoahaz, a younger son of Josiah, whom the people had made king, and gave the crown

---

328), nor B.C. 610, as given in the margin of our Bibles.
⁴ See above. p. 260, note ⁹.
⁵ 2 Chron. xxxv. 21.
⁶ 2 K. xxiii. 29, 30; 2 Chr. xxxv. 23, 24. Compare Herod. ii. 159, where the battle is erroneously placed at Magdolum (Magdala) instead of Megiddo.
⁷ 2 Chr. xxxv. 20; Jer. xlvi. 2.

⁸ This is evident from what is said of the recovery of this tract by the Babylonians (2 K. xxiv. 17), and from the position of Neco's army in B.C. 605, (Jer. l. a. c.) It agrees also with the statements of Herodotus (Fr. 14), except that Neco is there represented as a Babylonian satrap.
⁹ 2 K. xxiii. 33, 34.

to Jehoiakim, his elder brother. It was probably about this time that he besieged and took Gaza,[10] the most important of the Philistine towns next to Ashdod.

The loss of this large and valuable territory did not at once arouse the Babylonian monarch from his inaction or induce him to make any effort for its recovery. Neco enjoyed his conquests in quiet for the space of at least three full years.[11] At length, in the year B.C. 605, Nabopolassar, who felt himself unequal to the fatigues of a campaign,[12] resolved to intrust his forces to Nebuchadnezzar, his son, and to send him to contend with the Egyptians. The key of Syria at this time was Carchemish, a city situated on the left bank of the Euphrates, probably near the site which was afterwards occupied by Hierapolis. Here the forces of Neco were drawn up to protect his conquests, and here Nebuchadnezzar proceeded boldly to attack them. A great battle was fought in the immediate vicinity of the river, which was utterly disastrous to the Egyptians, who "fled away" in confusion,[13] and seem not to have ventured on making a second stand. Nebuchadnezzar rapidly recovered the lost territory, received the submission of Jehoiakim, King of Judah,[14] restored the old frontier line, and probably pressed on into Egypt itself,[15] hoping to cripple or even to crush his pre-

---

[10] Herod. ii. 159; Jer. xlvii. 1.
[11] The great battle of Carchemish, in which Nebuchadnezzar defeated Neco, was in the *fourth* year of Jehoiakim (Jer. xlvi. 2), whom Neco made king after his first successes.
[12] Οὐ δυνάμενος ἔτι κακοπαθεῖν. Beros. Fr. 14.
[13] Jer. xlvi. 5. Compare the narrative of Berosus. Συμμίξας δὲ Ναβουχοδονόσορος τῷ ἀποστάτῃ καὶ παραταξάμενος αὐτοῦ τε ἐκράτησεν καὶ τὴν χώραν ἐκ ταύτης τῆς ἀρχῆς ὑπὸ τὴν αὐτοῦ βασιλείαν ἐποιήσατο. (Fr. 14.)
[14] 2 K. xxiv. 1.
[15] Berosus speaks of Nebuchadnezzar's arranging the affairs of Egypt at this time (l. s. c.).

sumptuous adversary. But at this point he was compelled to pause. News arrived from Babylon that Nabopolassar was dead; and the Babylonian prince, who feared a disputed succession, having first concluded a hasty arrangement with Neco, returned at his best speed to his capital.[16]

Arriving probably before he was expected, he discovered that his fears were groundless. The priests had taken the direction of affairs during his absence, and the throne had been kept vacant for him by the Chief Priest, or Head of the Order."[17] No pretender had started up to dispute his claims. Doubtless his military prestige, and the probability that the soldiers would adopt his cause, had helped to keep back aspirants; but perhaps it was the promptness of his return, as much as anything, that caused the crisis to pass off without difficulty.

Nebuchadnezzar is the great monarch of the Babylonian Empire, which, lasting only 88 years—from B.C. 625 to B.C. 538—was for nearly half the time under his sway. Its military glory is due chiefly to him, while the constructive energy, which constitutes its especial characteristic, belongs to it still more markedly through his character and genius. It is scarcely too much to say that, but for Nebuchadnezzar, the Babylonians would have had no place in history. At any rate, their actual place is owing almost entirely to this prince, who to the military talents of an able general added a grandeur

---

[16] On this occasion Nebuchadnezzar, to save time, traversed the desert with a small body of followers. The troops, the baggage, and the provisions returned by the usual route through Upper Syria. (Beros. l. s. c.)

[17] Berosus, l. s. c. Παραλαβὼν δὲ τὰ πράγματα διοικούμενα ὑπὸ τῶν Χαλδαίων, καὶ διατηρουμένην τὴν βασιλείαν ὑπὸ τοῦ βελτίστου αὐτῶν, κ.τ.λ.

of artistic conception and a skill in construction which place him on a par with the greatest builders of antiquity.

We have no complete, or even general, account of Nebuchadnezzar's wars. Our chief, almost our sole, information concerning them is derived from the Jewish writers.[1] Consequently, those wars only which interested these writers, in other words those whose scene is Palestine or its immediate vicinity, admit of being placed before the reader. If Nebuchadnezzar had quarrels with the Persians, or the Arabians,[2] or the Medes, or the tribes in Mount Zagros, as is not improbable, nothing is now known of their course or issue. Until some historical document belonging to his time shall be discovered, we must be content with a very partial knowledge of the external history of Babylon during his reign. We have a tolerably full account of his campaigns against the Jews, and some information as to the general course of the wars which he carried on with Egypt and Phœnicia; but beyond these narrow limits we know nothing.

It appears to have been only a few years after Nebuchadnezzar's triumphant campaign against Neco, that renewed troubles broke out in Syria. Phœnicia revolted under the leadership of Tyre;[3]

---

[1] As Jeremiah, Ezekiel, the authors of Kings and Chronicles, and Josephus. In the valuable fragment which Josephus has preserved from Berosus (*Contr. Ap.* i. 19), we have an account of only one war—that waged by Nebuchadnezzar in his father's lifetime. (See above, p. 488.)

[2] A phrase in Berosus seems to imply that Nebuchadnezzar not only had a war with the Arabs, but that he conquered a portion of their country. (Κρατήσας δέ φησιν [ό Βηροσσός] τοῦ Βαβυλωνίου Αἰγύπτου, Συρίας, Φοινίκης, Ἀραβίας. Fr. 14.) Is this the conquest of the Moabites and Ammonites of which Josephus speaks? (*Ant. Jud.*, x. 9, § 7.)

[3] Joseph. *Contr. Ap.* i. 21; *Ant. Jud.* x. 11, § 1. Compare Jer. xxvii. 3.

and about the same time Jehoiakim, the Jewish king, having obtained a promise of aid from the Egyptians, renounced his allegiance.⁴ Upon this, in his seventh year (B.C. 598), Nebuchadnezzar proceeded once more into Palestine at the head of a vast army, composed partly of his allies, the Medes, partly of his own subjects.⁵ He first invested Tyre;⁶ but, finding that city too strong to be taken by assault, he left a portion of his army to continue the siege, while he himself pressed forward against Jerusalem.⁷ On his near approach, Jehoiakim, seeing that the Egyptians did not care to come to his aid, made his submission; but Nebuchadnezzar punished his rebellion with death,⁸ and, departing from the common Oriental practice, had his dead body treated with indignity.⁹ At first he placed upon the throne Jehoiachin, the son of the late monarch,¹⁰ a youth of eighteen;¹¹ but three months later, becoming suspicious (probably not without reason) of this prince's fidelity, he de-

---

⁴ 2 K. xxiv. 1. The expectation of help from Egypt, which Josephus expressly asserts (*Ant. Jud.* x. 6, § 2), is implied in 2 K. xxiv. 7. We may suspect that the embassy sent ostensibly to claim Urijah (Jer. xxvi. 22), had really for its object to conclude an arrangement with Neco.

⁵ Alex. Polyhist. Fr. 24. (See above, p. 215.) According to this writer, Nebuchadnezzar's army on this occasion numbered 10,000 chariots, 120,000 horse, and 180,000 foot.

⁶ The grounds for believing that Tyre was invested *before* Jerusalem are given in the author's *Herodotus* (vol. i. p. 422, note ⁴, 2nd edition).

⁷ 2 Chr. xxxvi. 6; Joseph. *Ant. Jud.* x. 6, § 3.

⁸ Josephus (l. s. c.) accuses Nebuchadnezzar of a breach of faith on this occasion; but it is most likely that Jehoiakim surrendered without conditions.

⁹ Joseph. l. s. c. Compare Jerem. xxii. 19, "He shall be buried with the burial of an ass, drawn and cast forth beyond the gates of Jerusalem," and xxxvi. 30, "His dead body shall be cast out in the day to the heat and in the night to the frost."

¹⁰ Jer. xxxvii. 1; Joseph. x. 71, § 1.

¹¹ 2 K. xxiv. 8. The number *eight* in the parallel passage of Chronicles (2 Chron. xxxvi. 9) is evidently corrupt. Nebuchadnezzar would not have placed a boy of eight on the throne. Jehoiachin, moreover, had several wives. (2 K. xxiv. 15.)

posed him and had him brought a captive to Babylon,[12] substituting in his place his uncle, Zedekiah, a brother of Jehoiakim and Jehoahaz. Meanwhile the siege of Tyre was pressed, but with little effect. A blockade is always tedious; and the blockade of an island city, strong in its navy, by an enemy unaccustomed to the sea, and therefore forced to depend mainly upon the assistance of reluctant allies, must have been a task of such extreme difficulty that one is surprised it was not given up in despair. According to the Tyrian historians their city resisted all the power of Nebuchadnezzar for thirteen years.[13] If this statement is to be relied on, Tyre must have been still uncaptured, when the time came for its sister capital to make that last effort for freedom in which it perished.

After receiving his crown from Nebuchadnezzar, Zedekiah continued for eight years to play the part of a faithful vassal. At length, however, in the ninth year,[14] he fancied he saw a way to independence. A young and enterprising monarch, Uaphris—the Apries of Herodotus—had recently mounted the Egyptian throne.[15] If the alliance of this prince could be secured, there was, Zedekiah thought, a reasonable hope that the yoke of Babylon might be shaken off and Hebrew autonomy re-established. The infatuated monarch apparently did not see, that, do what he would, his country had no more than a choice of masters—that by the laws of political

---

[12] 2 K. xxiv. 10-15; 2 Chr. xxxvi. 10.
[13] Joseph. contr. Ap. i. 21. Compare Philostr. ap. Joseph. Ant. Jud. x. 11, § 1.
[14] 2 K. xxv. 1; Jer. xxxix. 1; lii. 4.
[15] The ninth year of Zedekiah was B.C. 588. Uaphris began to reign the same year.

CHAP. VIII. CAMPAIGN AGAINST APRIES AND ZEDEKIAH. 193

attraction Judæa must gravitate to one or other of the two great states between which it had the misfortune of lying. Hoping to free his country, he sent ambassadors to Uaphris, who were to conclude a treaty and demand the assistance of a powerful contingent, composed both of foot and horse.[16] Uaphris received the overture favourably; and Zedekiah at once revolted from Babylon, and made preparations to defend himself with vigour. It was not long before the Babylonians arrived. Determined to crush the daring state, which, weak as it was, had yet ventured to revolt against him now for the fourth time,[17] Nebuchadnezzar came in person, "he and all his host,"[18] against Jerusalem, and after overcoming and pillaging the open country,[19] "built forts" and besieged the city.[20] Uaphris, upon this, learning the danger of his ally, marched out of Egypt to his relief;[21] and the Babylonian army, receiving intelligence of his approach, raised the siege and proceeded in quest of their new enemy. According to Josephus[22] a battle was fought, in which the Egyptians were defeated; but it is perhaps more probable that they avoided an engagement by a precipitate retreat to their own country.[23] At any rate the attempt effectually to relieve Jerusalem

---

[16] Ezek. xvii. 15. "He rebelled against him in sending his ambassadors into Egypt, that they might give him horses and much people." Compare Joseph. *Ant. Jud.* x. 7, § 3.

[17] Jehoiakim seems to have revolted twice—in his 8th and in his 11th year; Jehoiachin either had revolted or was on the point of revolting when he was deposed. Thus Zedekiah's revolt was the fourth within the space of thirteen years (B.C. 601-588).
[18] 2 K. xxv. 1.
[19] Joseph. *Ant. Jud.* x. 7, § 3. Τὴν χώραν κακώσας αὐτοῦ καὶ τὰ φρούρια λαβών. Compare Jer. xxxiv. 7.
[20] 2 K. l. s. c. Jer. lii. 4.
[21] Jer. xxxvii. 5.
[22] *Ant. Jud.* l. s. c. Ἀπαντήσας δὲ τοῖς Αἰγυπτίοις καὶ συμβαλὼν αὐτοῖς τῇ μάχῃ νικᾷ.
[23] See Jer. xxxvii. 7.

failed. After a brief interval the siege was renewed; a complete blockade was established; and in a year and a half from the time of the second investment,[4] the city fell.

Nebuchadnezzar had not waited to witness this success of his arms. The siege of Tyre was still being pressed at the date of the second investment of Jerusalem, and the Chaldæan monarch had perhaps thought that his presence on the borders of Phœnicia was necessary to animate his troops in that quarter. If this was his motive in withdrawing from the Jewish capital, the event would seem to have shewn that he judged wisely. Tyre, if it fell at the end of its thirteen years' siege,[1] must have been taken in the very year which followed the capture of Jerusalem, B.C. 585.[2] We may suppose that Nebuchadnezzar, when he quitted Jerusalem and took up his abode at Riblah in the Cœle-Syrian valley,[3] turned his main attention to the great Phœnician city, and made arrangements which caused its capture in the ensuing year.

The restoration of these two important cities secured to the Babylonian monarch the quiet posses-

---

[4] Joseph. *Ant. Jud.* x. 7, § 4. Προσκαθίσας αὐτῇ μῆνας δεκακαιδέκα ἐπολιόρκει.

[1] It has been questioned whether the real Tyre, the island city, actually fell on this occasion (Heeren, *As. Nat.* vol. ii. p. 11, E. T.; Kenrick, *Phœnicia*, p. 800), chiefly because Ezekiel says, about B.C. 570, that Nebuchadnezzar had "received no wages for the service that he served against it." (Ezek. xxix. 18.) But this passage may be understood to mean that he had had no sufficient wages. Berosus expressly stated that Nebuchadnezzar reduced all Phœnicia—ὅτι καὶ τὴν Συρίαν καὶ τὴν Φοινίκην ἅπασαν ἐκεῖνος κατεστρέψατο. (Ap. Joseph. *Contr. Ap.* i. 20.)

[2] The siege commenced in the 7th year of Nebuchadnezzar and lasted 13 years, terminating consequently in his 20th year, which was B.C. 585. (Joseph. *Contr. Ap.* i. 21.)

[3] 2 K. xxv. 6, 20, 21; Jer. xxxix. 5; lii. 9. Riblah seems to have been an important fortress at this time (2 K. xxiii. 33). Apparently it had taken the place of Hamath.

sion thenceforth of Syria and Palestine. But still he had not as yet inflicted any chastisement upon Egypt; though policy, no less than honour, required that the aggressions of this audacious power should be punished. If we may believe Josephus, however, the day of vengeance was not very long delayed. Within four years of the fall of Tyre, B.C. 581, Nebuchadnezzar, he tells us, invaded Egypt, put Uaphris, the monarch who had succoured Zedekiah, to death, and placed a creature of his own upon the throne.[4] Egyptian history, it is true, forbids our accepting this statement as correct in all its particulars. Uaphris appears certainly to have reigned at least as late as B.C. 569,[5] and according to Herodotus, he was put to death, not by a foreign invader, but by a rebellious subject.[6] Perhaps we may best harmonize the conflicting statements on the subject by supposing that Josephus has confounded two distinct invasions of Egypt, one made by Nebuchadnezzar in his twenty-third year, B.C. 581, which had no very important consequences, and the other made eleven years later, B.C. 570, which terminated in the deposition of Uaphris, and the establishment on the throne of a new king, Amasis, who received a nominal royalty from the Chaldæan monarch.[7]

---

[4] Joseph. Ant. Jud. x. 9, § 7.
[5] Cambyses conquered Egypt B.C. 525. (See the author's Herodotus, vol. ii. p. 1, note 1.) Psammenitus (Psammatik III.) had then been on the throne a few months. Amasis, his father, who succeeded Apries, had reigned 44 years. (Herod. iii. 10. Manetho, as represented by Africanus, and the monuments agree.) This would bring the close of the reign of Apries (Uaphris) to B.C. 569.
[6] Herod. ii. 169.
[7] The prophecies of Jeremiah (xlvi. 13-26) and Ezekiel (xxix. 8-20; xxx. 4-26), especially the latter, are very difficult to reconcile with the historical accounts that have come down to us of the condition of Egypt in the reigns of

Such were the military exploits of this great king. He defeated Neco, recovered Syria, crushed rebellion in Judæa, took Tyre, and humiliated Egypt. According to some writers his successes did not stop here. Megasthenes made him subdue most of Africa, and thence pass over into Spain and conquer the Iberians." He even went further and declared that, on his return from these regions, he settled his Iberian captives on the shores of the Euxine in the country between Armenia and the Caucasus! Thus Nebuchadnezzar was made to reign over an empire extending from the Atlantic to the Caspian, and from the Caucasus to the Great Sahara.

The victories of Nebuchadnezzar were not without an effect on his home administration and on the construction of the vast works with which his name is inseparably associated. It was through them that he obtained that enormous command of naked human strength which enabled him, without undue oppression of his own people, to carry out on the grandest scale his schemes for at once beautifying and benefiting his kingdom. From the time when he first took the field at the head of an army he adopted the Assyrian system° of forcibly removing almost the whole population of a conquered country, and plant-

---

Apries and Amasis. (Herod. ii. 161-182; Diod. Sic. i. 68.) Ezekiel's 40 years' *desolation* of Egypt must (I think) be taken as figurative, marking a time of *degradation*, when independence was lost. Of course such political degradation would be quite consistent with great material prosperity. (See the remarks of Sir G. Wilkinson in the author's *Herodotus*, vol. ii. p. 325, 2nd edition.)

It is never to be forgotten that Berosus distinctly witnessed to the conquest of Egypt by Nebuchadnezzar. (Ap. Joseph. *Contr. Ap.* i. 19. Ἐπαρῆσαι δέ φησὶ τὸν Βαβυλώνιον Αἰγύπτου κ.τ.λ.)

° Abyd. ap. Euseb. *Præp. Ev.* ix. 41. Compare Euseb. *Chron. Can.* i. 10, § 3, and Mos. Chor. *Hist. Armen.* ii. 7.

° See above, vol. ii. pp. 528, 529.

ing it in a distant part of his dominions. Crowds of captives—the produce of his various wars—Jews, Egyptians, Phœnicians, Syrians, Ammonites, Moabites, were settled in various parts of Mesopotamia,[10] more especially about Babylon. From these unfortunates forced labour was as a matter of course required ;[11] and it seems to have been chiefly, if not solely, by their exertions that the magnificent series of great works was accomplished, which formed the special glory of the Fourth Monarchy.

The chief works expressly ascribed to Nebuchadnezzar by the ancient writers are the following. He built the great wall of Babylon,[12] which according to the lowest estimate[13] must have contained more than 500,000,000 square feet of solid masonry, and must have required three or four times that number of bricks.[14] He constructed a new and magnificent palace in the neighbourhood of the ancient residence of the kings.[15] He made the celebrated "Hanging Garden" for the gratification of his wife, Amyitis.[16] He repaired and beautified the great temple of Belus at Babylon.[17] He dug the huge reservoir near Sippara, said to have been 140 miles in circumference, and 180 feet deep, furnishing it with flood-gates,

---

[10] Beros. Fr. 14 ; 2 K. xxiv. 14-16 ; xxv. 11 ; 2 Chr. xxxvi. 20 ; Ezek. L 1 ; Dan. l. 3 ; &c.
[11] Polyhist. Fr. 24.
[12] Abyden. ap. Euseb. Chron. Can. i. 10, § 2 ; ap. eund. Præp. Ev. ix. 41. Nebuchadnezzar, however, in the Standard Inscription, only claims to have repaired the wall.
[13] Taking the height of the wall, that is, at 75 feet, its width at 32 feet, and its circumference at 365 stades. The measurements of Herodotus would raise the cubical contents to more than 5,400,000,000 feet.
[14] Babylonian bricks are about a foot square and from 3 to 4 inches thick. [15] Berosus, Fr. 14.
[16] Ibid. Compare Diod. Sic. II. 10, § 1 ; Q. Curt. i. 5.
[17] Beros. L. s. c. Compare the Standard Inscription. All the inscribed bricks hitherto discovered in the Babil mound bear Nebuchadnezzar's legend.

through which its water could be drawn off for purposes of irrigation.¹⁸ He constructed a number of canals, among them the *Nahr Malcha* or "Royal River," a broad and deep channel which connected the Euphrates with the Tigris.¹⁹ He built quays and breakwaters along the shores of the Persian Gulf, and he at the same time founded the city of Diridotis or Teredon in the vicinity of that sea.²⁰

To these constructions may be added, on the authority either of Nebuchadnezzar's own inscriptions or of the existing remains, the Birs-i-Nimrud, or great Temple of Nebo at Borsippa;²¹ a vast reservoir in Babylon itself, called the *Yapur-Shapu*;²² an extensive embankment along the course of the Tigris, near Baghdad;²³ and almost innumerable temples, walls, and other public buildings at Cutha, Sippara, Borsippa, Babylon, Chilmad, Bit-Digla, &c. The indefatigable monarch seems to have either rebuilt, or at least repaired, almost every city and temple throughout the entire country. There are said to be at least a hundred sites in the tract immediately about Babylon, which give evidence, by inscribed bricks bearing his legend, of the marvellous activity and energy of this king.²⁴

We may suspect that among the constructions of Nebuchadnezzar was another great work, a work

---

¹⁸ Abyden. ap. Euseb. *Præp. Ev.* ix. 41.
¹⁹ Ibid. This is perhaps the *Chebar* of Ezekiel. In Pliny's time it was called the work of a certain *Gobar*, a provincial governor. (*H. N.* vi. 26.)
²⁰ Abyden. l. s. c.
²¹ See the inscription on the Birs-i-Nimrud cylinders. (*Journal of As. Society*, vol. xviii. pp. 27-32.)
²² See above, p. 373; and compare the author's *Herodotus*, vol. ii. p. 486, 2nd edition.
²³ This embankment is entirely composed of bricks which have never been disturbed, and which bear Nebuchadnezzar's name. (Sir H. Rawlinson's *Commentary*, p. 77, note.)
²⁴ Ibid. p. 76.

second in utility to none of those above mentioned, and requiring for its completion an enormous amount of labour. This is the canal called by the Arabs the *Kerek Saideh*, or canal of Saideh, which they ascribe to a wife of Nebuchadnezzar, a cutting 400 miles in length, which commenced at Hit on the Euphrates, and was carried along the extreme western edge of the alluvium close to the Arabian frontier, finally falling into the sea at the head of the Bubian creek, about twenty miles to the west of the Shat-el-Arab. The traces of this canal which still remain[1] indicate a work of such magnitude and difficulty that we can scarcely ascribe it with probability to any monarch who has held the country since Nebuchadnezzar.

The Pallacopas,[2] or canal of Opa (Palga Opa[3]), which left the Euphrates at Sippara (Mosaib) and ran into a great lake in the neighbourhood of Borsippa, whence the lands in the neighbourhood were irrigated, may also have been one of Nebuchadnezzar's constructions. It was an old canal, much out of repair, in the time of Alexander, and was certainly the work, not of the Persian conquerors, but of some native monarch anterior to Cyrus. The Arabs, who call it the Nahr Abba, regard it as the oldest canal in the country.[4]

Some glimpses into the private life and personal character of Nebuchadnezzar are afforded us by certain of the Old Testament writers. We see him in the Book of Daniel at the head of a magnificent Court,

---

[1] Sir H. Rawlinson in the author's *Herodotus*, vol. i. p. 469, note [7], 2nd edition.
[2] Arrian, *Exp. Alex.* vii. 21. Compare Strab. xvi. 1, § 11.
[3] Compare the Hebrew פלג, "rivus." Opa would seem to be a proper name.
[4] Sir H. Rawlinson, l. s. c.

surrounded by "princes, governors, and captains, judges, treasurers, councillors, and sheriffs;" waited on by eunuchs selected with the greatest care, "well-favoured" and carefully educated; attended, whenever he requires it, by a multitude of astrologers and other "wise men," who seek to interpret to him the will of Heaven. He is an absolute monarch, disposing with a word of the lives and properties of his subjects, even the highest. All offices are in his gift. He can raise a foreigner to the second place in the kingdom, and even set him over the entire priestly order. His wealth is enormous, for he makes of pure gold an image, or obelisk, ninety feet high and nine feet broad. He is religious after a sort, but wavers in his faith, sometimes acknowledging the God of the Jews as the only real deity, sometimes relapsing into an idolatrous worship, and forcing all his subjects to follow his example. Even then, however, his polytheism is of a kind which admits of a special devotion to a particular deity, who is called emphatically "his god." In temper he is hasty and violent, but not obstinate; his fierce resolves are taken suddenly and as suddenly repented of; he is moreover capable of bursts of gratitude and devotion, no less than of accesses of fury; like most Orientals, he is vain-glorious; but he can humble himself before the chastening hand of

---

* Dan. iii. 2.   * Ibid. i, 3, 4.
† Ibid. ii. 2; iv. 6, 7.
‡ Ibid. i. 10; ii. 12.
§ Ibid. ii. 48, 49.
¶ Ibid. iii. 1.
‖ Ibid. ii. 47; iii. 20-29; iv. 2, 34, 37.
☐ Ibid. iii. 14; iv. 8.

" Ibid. iii. 4-20.
¹⁴ Ibid. i. 2; iv. 8. Nebuchadnezzar's inscriptions sufficiently show that this favourite god was Bel-Merodach.
¹⁵ Ibid. ii. 12, 46; iii. 20, 26.
¹⁶ Ibid. ii. 46-49; iii. 28-30; iv. 3, 34-37.   ⁷ Ibid. iv. 30.

the Almighty; in his better moods he shows a spirit astonishing in one of his country and time—a spirit of real piety, self-condemnation, and self-abasement, which renders him one of the most remarkable characters in Scripture.[18]

A few touches of a darker hue must be added to this portrait of the great Babylonian king from the statements of another contemporary, the prophet Jeremiah. The execution of Jehoiakim, and the putting out of Zedekiah's eyes, though acts of considerable severity, may perhaps be regarded as justified by the general practice of the age, and therefore as not indicating in Nebuchadnezzar any special ferocity of disposition. But the ill treatment of Jehoiakim's dead body,[19] the barbarity of murdering Zedekiah's sons *before his eyes*,[20] and the prolonged imprisonment both of Zedekiah[21] and of Jehoiachin,[22] though the latter had only contemplated rebellion, cannot be thus excused. They were unusual and unnecessary acts, which tell against the monarch who authorised them, and must be considered to imply a real cruelty of disposition, such as is observable in Sargon and Asshur-bani-pal.[23] Nebuchadnezzar, it is plain, was not content with such a measure of severity as was needed to secure his own interests, but took a plea-

---

[18] See particularly ch. iv. 34, 35, 37. "I blessed the Most High, and I praised and honoured him that liveth for ever, whose dominion is an everlasting dominion, and his kingdom is from generation to generation: and all the inhabitants of the earth are reputed as nothing, and he doeth according to his will in the army of heaven, and among the inhabitants of the earth; and none can stay his hand, or say unto him, What doest thou? Now I, Nebuchadnezzar, praise and extol and honour the king of Heaven, all whose works are truth, and his ways judgment: and those that walk in pride he is able to abase."

[19] Supra, page 491, note [9].
[20] Jer. lii. 10. Compare 2 K. xxv. 7.
[21] Jer. lii. 11. [22] Ibid. lii. 31.
[23] Supra, vol. I. p. 367, note [8]; vol. ii. p. 504.

sure in the wanton infliction of suffering on those who had provoked his resentment.

On the other hand we obtain from the native writer, Berosus, one amiable trait which deserves a cursory mention. Nebuchadnezzar was fondly attached to the Median princess who had been chosen for him as a wife by his father from political motives.[34] Not content with ordinary tokens of affection, he erected, solely for her gratification, the remarkable structure which the Greeks called the "Hanging Garden."[35] A native of a mountainous country, Amyitis disliked the tiresome uniformity of the level alluvium, and pined for the woods and hills of Media. It was to satisfy this longing by the best substitute which circumstances allowed that the celebrated Garden was made. Art strove to emulate nature with a certain measure of success, and the lofty rocks[36] and various[37] trees of this wonderful Paradise, if they were not a very close imitation of Median mountain scenery, were at any rate a pleasant change from the natural monotony of the Babylonian plain, and must have formed a grateful retreat for the fortunate queen, whom they reminded at once of her husband's love and of the beauty of her native country.

The most remarkable circumstance in Nebuchadnezzar's life remains to be noticed. Towards the close of his reign, when his conquests and probably most of his great works were completed,[38] in the

---

[34] See above, p. 483.
[35] Beros. Fr. 14. Κατασκευάσας τὸν καλούμενον κρεμαστὸν παράδεισον, διὰ τὸ τὴν γυναῖκα αὐτοῦ ἐπιθυμεῖν τῆς ὀρείας διαθέσεως, τιθραμ- μένης ἐν τοῖς κατὰ τὴν Μηδίαν τόποις.
[36] Ἀναλήμματα λίθινα ὑψηλά. Beros. l. s. c.
[37] Δένδρα παντοδαπά. Ibid.
[38] Compare Dan. iv. 22 and 30.

midst of complete tranquillity and prosperity, a sudden warning was sent him. He dreamt a strange dream;[20] and when he sought to know its meaning, the Prophet Daniel was inspired to tell him that it portended his removal from the kingly office for the space of seven years, in consequence of a curious and very unusual kind of madness.[20] This malady, which is not unknown to the physicians, has been termed "Lycanthropy."[1] It consists in the belief that one is not a man but a beast, in the disuse of language, the rejection of all ordinary human food, and sometimes in the loss of the erect posture and a preference for walking on all fours. Within a year of the time that he received the warning,[2] Nebuchadnezzar was smitten. The great king became a wretched maniac. Allowed to indulge his distempered fancy, he eschewed human habitations, lived in the open air night and day, fed on herbs, disused clothing, and became covered with a rough coat of hair.[3] His subjects generally, it is probable, were not allowed to know of his condition,[4] though they could not but be aware that he was suffering from some terrible malady. The queen most likely held the reins of power and carried on the government in his name. The dream had been interpreted to mean that the lycanthropy would not be permanent; and even the date of recovery had been announced, only with a certain

---

[20] Compare Dan. iv. verses 10-17.
[20] Ibid. verses 20-28.
[1] See Dr. Pusey's *Lectures on Daniel*, pp. 425-430, and compare the treatise of Weicher entitled *Die Lycanthropie ein Aberglaube und eine Krankheit*, in the 3rd volume of his *Kleine Schriften*, pp. 157 et seq.
[2] Dan. iv. 29.
[3] Ibid. verse 33.
[4] We must not suppose that the afflicted monarch was allowed to range freely through the country. He was no doubt strictly confined to the private gardens attached to the palace.

ambiguity.[4] The Babylonians were thereby encouraged to await events, without taking any steps that would have involved them in difficulties if the malady ceased. And their faith and patience met with a reward. After suffering obscuration for the space of seven years, suddenly the king's intellect returned to him.[5] His recovery was received with joy by his Court. Lords and counsellors gathered about him.[6] He once more took the government into his own hands, issued his proclamations,[7] and performed the other functions of royalty. He was now an old man, and his reign does not seem to have been much prolonged; but "the glory of his kingdom," his "honour and brightness" returned; his last days were as brilliant as his first; his sun set in an unclouded sky, shorn of none of the rays that had given splendour to its noonday. Nebuchadnezzar expired at Babylon[8] in the forty-fourth year of his reign, B.C. 561, after an illness of no long duration.[10] He was probably little short of eighty years old at his death.[11]

The successor of Nebuchadnezzar was his son Evil-

---

[4] Dan. iv. 25. The "seven times" of this passage would probably, but not necessarily, mean seven years.
[5] Ibid. verse 34. It has been thought that there is a reference to Nebuchadnezzar's malady in the Standard Inscription. But this is now doubted. Perhaps we ought scarcely to expect that a king would formally record such an affliction.
[6] Ibid. verse 36. "My counsellors and my lords sought unto me."
[7] Ch. iv. of Daniel is Nebuchadnezzar's proclamation on his recovery. [8] Abyden. Fr. 9.

[9] Berosus, Fr. 14. Ἐμπεσὼν εἰς ἀῤῥωστίαν μετηλλάξατο τὸν βίον. This sober account of the Chaldæan historian contrasts favourably with the marvellous narrative of Abydenus, who makes Nebuchadnezzar first prophesy the destruction of Babylon by the Medes and Persians, and then vanish away out of the sight of men. (Ap. Euseb. Præp. Ev. ix. 41; p. 456, D.)
[11] If we suppose him 15 when he was contracted to the daughter of Cyaxares (B.C. 625), he would have been 36 at his accession and 79 at his death, in B.C. 561.

REIGN OF EVIL-MERODACH.

Merodach,¹² who reigned only two years,¹³ and of whom very little is known. We may suspect that the marvellous events of his father's life, which are recorded in the Book of Daniel, had made a deep impression upon him, and that he was thence inclined to favour the persons, and perhaps the religion, of the Jews. One of his first acts¹⁴ was to release the unfortunate Jehoiachin from the imprisonment in which he had languished for thirty-five years, and to treat him with kindness and respect. He not only recognised his royal rank, but gave him precedence over all the other captive kings resident at Babylon.¹⁵ Josephus says that he even admitted Jehoiachin into the number of his most intimate friends.¹⁶ Perhaps he may have designed him some further advancement, and may in other respects have entertained projects which seemed strange and alarming to his subjects. At any rate he had been but two years upon the throne when a conspiracy was formed against him; he was accused of lawlessness and intemperance;¹⁷ his own brother-in-law, Neriglissar, the husband of a daughter of Nebuchadnezzar, headed the malcontents; and Evil-Merodach lost his life with his crown.

Neriglissar, the successful conspirator, was at once acknowledged king. He is probably identical with the "Nergal-shar-ezer, Rab-Mag" of Jeremiah,¹⁸

---

¹² Beros. Fr. 14; Polyhist. ap. Euseb. Chron. Can. I. 5; Abyden. ap. eund. i. 10.

¹³ So the Astronomical Canon and Berosus (L. s. c.). Polyhistor (L. s. c.) gave him 12 years, and Josephus (Ant. Jud. x. 11, § 2) 18 years.

¹⁴ "In the year that he began to reign." (2 K. xxv. 27. Compare Jer. lii. 31.)

¹⁵ 2 K. xxv. 28; Jer. lii. 32.

¹⁶ Ἐν τοῖς ἀναγκαιοτάτοις φίλοις εἶχε. (Ant. Jud. l. s. c.)

¹⁷ Πρασσὼν τῶν πραγμάτων ἀσέλγῶς καὶ ἀσελγῶς. (Beros. Fr. 14.)

¹⁸ Jer. xxxix. 3 and 13. The real

who occupied a prominent position among the Babylonian nobles left to press the siege of Jerusalem when Nebuchadnezzar retired to Riblah. The title of "Rab-Mag" is one that he bears upon his bricks. It is doubtful what exactly this office was; for we have no reason to believe that there were at this time any Magi at Babylon;[10] but it was certainly an ancient and very high dignity, of which even kings might be proud. It is curious that Neriglissar calls himself the son of a "king of Babylon"—a certain Bel-sum-iskun (or Bel-mu-ingar), whose name does not appear in any of the lists.

During his short reign of four years, or rather three years and a few months,[11] Neriglissar had not time to distinguish himself by many exploits. So far as appears, he was at peace with all his neighbours, and employed his time principally in the construction of the Western Palace at Babylon, which was a large building placed at one corner of a fortified enclosure, directly opposite the ancient royal residence, and abutting on the Euphrates.[12] If the account which Diodorus gives of this palace[13] be not a gross exaggeration of the truth, it must have been a magnificent

---

name of this king, as it appears upon his bricks, was Nergal-sar-uzur, with which the Hebrew Nergal-sharezer is clearly identical. This fact, added to the circumstance that the king bore the office of Rab-Mag, makes it almost certain that he is the person mentioned by Jeremiah.

[10] There is no ground for regarding the Babylonian priests as magi. By none of the old classical writers are they given the name. None of the terms applied to the "wise men" in Daniel resembles it. There is certainly a remarkable resemblance between the *mag* of Rab-Mag and *magus*. But the resemblance is less in the native language, where Rab-Mag is *Rabu-emga*; and the term *emgu* is not used in Babylonian when a Magus is certainly intended. (See Bebist. Ins. Col. I. Par. 13, &c.)

[11] As the nine months of Laborosoarchod are not counted in the Canon, we have to deduct them from the adjoining reigns—those of Neriglissar and Nabonadius.

[12] See above, p. 365.

[13] Diod. Sic. ii. 8, § 7. Compare above, p. 347.

erection, elaborately ornamented with painting and sculpture in the best style of Babylonian art, though in size it may have been inferior to the old residence of the kings on the other side of the river.

Neriglissar reigned from B.C. 559 to B.C. 556, and dying a natural death in the last-named year, left his throne to his son, Laborosoarchod, or Labossoracus.[25] This prince, who was a mere boy,[24] and therefore quite unequal to the task of governing a great empire in critical times, was not allowed to retain the crown many months. Accused by those about him—whether justly or unjustly we cannot say—of giving many indications of a bad disposition,[25] he was deposed and put to death by torture.[26] With him the power passed from the House of Nabopolassar, which had held the throne for just seventy years.[27]

On the death of Laborosoarchod the conspirators selected one of their number, a certain Nabonadius or Nabannidochus,[28] and invested him with the sovereignty. He was in no way related to the late monarch,[1] and his claim to succeed must have been derived mainly from the part which he had played

---

[23] Laborosoarchod is the form which has most authority, since it occurs both in the Canon of Ptolemy and in Berosus (Fr. 14). Labosoracus or Labroracus is the form given in the Armenian Eusebius. Josephus has Laborosdacus in one place (Ant. Jud. x. 11, § 2); Abydenus (ap. Euseb. Præp. Ev. ix. 41) Labassoaracus.

[24] Παῖς ὤν. Berosus, l. s. c.

[25] Διὰ τὸ πολλὰ ἐμφαίνειν κακοήθη. Ibid.

[26] Ἀπετυμπανίσθη. Ibid. The word means literally "was beaten to death."

[27] From the commencement of B.C. 625 to the close of B.C. 556.

[28] The name is read as Nabunahid in Assyrian and Nabu-induk in Hamitic Babylonian. The former is the groundwork of Nabonnedus (Berosus), Nabonadius (Astr. Can.), and Labynetus (Herod.); the latter of Nabannidochus (Abyden.) and Nabrandelus, which should probably be Nabnandochus (Josephus).

[1] Τούτου (sc. Λαβασσοαράσκου) ἀναιρεθέντος βιαίῳ μόρῳ, Ναβαννίδοχον ἀνεδείξασι βασιλέα, προσήκοντα οἱ οὐδέν. (Abyden. Fr. 9.) Compare Berosus, Fr. 14, who calls Nabonadius Βαβυλώνιόν τινα τῶν ἐκ Βαβυλῶνος.

in the conspiracy. But still he was a personage of some rank, for his father had, like Neriglissar, held the important office of Rab-Mag.² It is probable that one of his first steps on ascending the throne was to connect himself by marriage with the royal house which had preceded him in the kingdom.³ Either the mother of the late king Laborosoarchod, and widow of Neriglissar, or possibly some other daughter of Nebuchadnezzar, was found willing to unite her fortunes with those of the new sovereign, and share the dangers and the dignity of his position. Such a union strengthened the hold of the reigning monarch on the allegiance of his subjects, and tended still more to add stability to his dynasty. For as the issue of such a marriage would join in one the claims of both royal houses, he would be sure to receive the support of all parties in the state.

Very shortly after the accession of Nabonadius (B.C. 555) he received an embassy from the far northwest.⁴ An important revolution had occurred on the eastern frontier of Babylonia three years before, in the reign of Neriglissar;⁵ but its effects only now began to make themselves felt among the neighbouring nations. Had Cyrus, on taking the crown, adopted the policy of Astyages, the substitution of

---

² On his bricks and cylinders Nabonidus calls himself the son of Nabu-**-dirba, the Rab-Mag. (See *British Museum Series*, Pl. 68.)

³ This has been at all times the usual practice of usurpers in the East. (See Herod. iii. 68, 88; Josephus, *Ant. Jud.* xiv. 12, § 1; Wilkinson in the author's *Herodotus*, vol. ii. p. 325; &c.) That it was adopted by Nabonadius seems to follow from Belshazzar, his son, being regarded in Daniel as a son (descendant) of Nebuchadnezzar. (Dan. v. 2, 11, 13, 18, 22.)

⁴ Herod. i. 77. The author's reasons for placing the fall of Sardis in B.C. 554, and consequently the embassy sent by Crœsus to Nabonadius to B.C. 555, have been fully given in his *Herodotus*, vol. i. pp. 286, 287, 2nd edition.

⁵ See above, p. 232.

Persia for Media as the ruling Arian nation would have been a matter of small account. But there can be little doubt that he really entered at once on a career of conquest.⁶ Lydia, at any rate, felt herself menaced by the new power, and seeing the danger which threatened the other monarchies of the time, if they allowed the great Arian kingdom to attack them severally with her full force, proposed a league whereby the common enemy might, she thought, be resisted with success. Ambassadors seem to have been sent from Sardis to Babylon in the very year in which Nabonadius became king.⁷ He therefore had at once to decide whether he would embrace the offer made him, and uniting with Lydia and Egypt in a league against Persia, make that power at once his enemy, or refuse the proffered alliance and trust to the gratitude of Cyrus for the future security of his kingdom. It would be easy to imagine the arguments *pro* and *contra* which presented themselves to his mind at this conjuncture; but as they would be destitute of a historical foundation, it is perhaps best to state simply the decision at which he is known to have arrived. This was an acceptance of the Lydian offer. Nabonadius consented to join the proposed league; and a treaty was probably soon afterwards concluded between the three powers whereby they united in an alliance offensive and defensive against the Persians.⁸

Knowing that he had provoked a powerful enemy

---

⁶ Herodotus represents Croesus as the aggressor in his war with Cyrus; but it is probable that he was so formally rather than really. Cyrus's attempt to detach the Greeks from Lydia (Herod. i. 76), and his presence in full force *in Cappadocia* as soon as Croesus invades his territory, are sufficient proof that he was about to attack Croesus. (See the next volume.) ⁷ See above, note.⁴

⁸ Herod. i. 77.

by this bold act, and ignorant how soon he might be called upon to defend his kingdom from the entire force of his foe, which might be suddenly hurled against him almost at any moment, Nabonadius seems to have turned his attention at once to providing means of defence. The works ascribed by Herodotus to a queen, Nitocris, whom he makes the mother of Nabonadius (Labynetus)[9] must be regarded as in reality constructions of that monarch himself,[10] undertaken with the object of protecting Babylon from Cyrus. They consisted in part of defences within the city, designed apparently to secure it against an enemy who should enter by the river, in part of hydraulic works intended to obstruct the advances of an army by the usual route. The river had

---

[9] The Nitocris of Herodotus still remains one of the dark personages of history. She is unknown to the monuments. No other independent author mentions her. Her very name is suspicious, being Egyptian, not Babylonian. Yet still it is hard to imagine her a mere myth. Herodotus heard of her at Babylon, within little more than a century of the time when she was said to have lived. He heard of her in conjunction with another older queen, Semiramis, who is found to be a historical personage, only a little misplaced. (Supra, p. 475.) Again, Nitocris, though not known otherwise as a Babylonian name, was an Egyptian royal name in use at this period. (Wilkinson in the author's Herodotus, vol. II, p. 325, 2nd edition.) Under these circumstances it is perhaps allowable to conjecture, 1. that there was such a person; 2. that she was an Egyptian princess, or at any rate of Egyptian extraction; 3. that she was the wife, or mother, of one of the later Babylonian kings, and was regarded as in some sense reigning conjointly with him. My own impression is that she was a daughter of Nebuchadnezzar, born of an Egyptian mother, and married successively to Neriglissar and Nabonadius, who each ruled partly in her right. I regard her as the mother of Belshazzar, whom Herodotus confounds with his father, Nabonadius; and I suspect that she is the queen who "came into the banqueting-house" at Belshazzar's impious feast, and recommended him to send for Daniel. (Dan. v. 10-12.)

[10] The river walls, which Herodotus ascribes to Nitocris (i. 185), were declared expressly by Berosus to have been the work of this king (ἐπὶ τούτου τὰ περὶ τὸν ποταμὸν τείχη τῆς Βαβυλωνίας ὠπλίσθη ἐξ ὀπτῆς πλίνθου καὶ ἀσφάλτου κατεκοσμήθη. Fr. 14). The bricks of the embankment are found to bear his name.

hitherto flowed in its natural bed through the middle of the town. Nabonadius confined the stream by a brick embankment carried the whole way along both banks, after which he built on the top of the embankment a wall of a considerable height, pierced at intervals by gateways, in which were set gates of bronze.[11] He likewise made certain cuttings, reservoirs, and sluices at some distance from Babylon towards the north, which were to be hindrances to an enemy's march,[12] though in what way is not very apparent. Some have supposed that besides these works there was further built at the same time a great wall which extended entirely across the tract between the two rivers[13]—a huge barrier a hundred feet high and twenty thick[14]—meant, like the Roman walls in Britain and the great wall of China, to be insurmountable by an unskilful foe; but there is ground for suspecting that this belief is ill-founded, having for its sole basis a misconception of Xenophon's.[15]

Nabonadius appears to have been allowed ample time to carry out to the full his system of defences, and to complete all his preparations. The precipitancy of Crœsus, who plunged into a war with Persia single-handed, asking no aid from his allies,[16] and the promptitude of Cyrus who allowed him no oppor-

---

[11] Herod. I. 180. The river walls can scarcely have been built until the embankment was made.
[12] Ibid. I. 185.
[13] Grote, *History of Greece*, vol. iii. p. 180, 2nd edition.
[14] Xen. *Anab.* ii. 4, § 12.
[15] The "Median Wall" rests wholly on Xenophon's authority. It is quite unknown to Herodotus, Strabo, Arrian, and the other historians of Alexander. Excellent reasons have been given for believing that the barrier within which the Ten Thousand penetrated was the old wall of Babylon itself. (See a paper read by Sir H. Rawlinson before the Geographical Society in 1851.)
[16] Herod. i. 71.

tunity of recovering from his first false step," had prevented Nabonadius from coming into actual collision with Persia in the early part of his reign. The defeat of Crœsus in the battle of Pteria, the siege of Sardis, and its capture, followed so rapidly on the first commencement of hostilities, that, whatever his wishes may have been, Nabonadius had it not in his power to give any help to his rash ally. Actual war was thus avoided at this time; and, no collision having occurred, Cyrus could defer an attack on the great kingdom of the south until he had consolidated his power in the north and the north-east,[18] which he rightly regarded as of the last importance. Thus fourteen years intervened between the capture of Sardis by the Persian arms and the commencement of the expedition against Babylon.

When at last it was rumoured that the Persian king had quitted Ecbatana (B.C. 539) and commenced his march to the south-west, Nabonadius received the tidings with indifference. His defences were completed; his city was amply provisioned;[1] if the enemy should defeat him in the open field, he might retire behind his walls, and laugh to scorn all attempts to reduce his capital either by blockade or storm. It does not appear to have occurred to him that it was possible to protect his territory. With a broad, deep, and rapid river directly interposed between him and his foe, with a network of canals spread far and wide over his country, with an almost inexhaustible supply of human labour at his com-

---

[17] Herod. i. 79-86.
[18] Ibid. i. 153 and 177. See the Historical Chapter in the next volume.

[1] Προσισάξαντο σιτία ἐτέων κάρτα πολλῶν. Herod. i. 190. Ἔχοντες τὰ ἐπιτήδεια πλίω ἢ εἴκοσι ἐτῶν. Xen. Cyrop. vii. 5, § 13.

mand for the construction of such dykes, walls, or cuttings as he should deem advisable, Nabonadius might, one would have thought, have aspired to save his land from invasion, or have disputed inch by inch his enemy's advance towards the capital. But such considerations have seldom had much force with Orientals, whose notions of war and strategy are even now of the rudest and most primitive description. To measure one's strength as quickly as possible with that of one's foe, to fight one great pitched battle in order to decide the question of superiority in the field, and then, if defeated, either to surrender or to retire behind walls, has been the ordinary conception of a commander's duties in the east from the time of the Rameside kings to our own day. No special blame therefore attaches to Nabonadius for his neglect. He followed the traditional policy of Oriental monarchs in the course which he took. And his subjects had less reason to complain of his resolution than most others, since the many strongholds in Babylonia must have afforded them a ready refuge, and the great fortified district within which Babylon itself stood[2] must have been capable of accommodating with ease the whole native population of the country.

If we may trust Herodotus, the invader, having made all his preparations and commenced his march, came to a sudden pause midway between Ecbatana and Babylon.[3] One of the sacred white horses, which drew the chariot of Ormazd,[4] had been drowned in crossing a river; and Cyrus had thereupon desisted from his march, and, declaring that he would

---

[2] Supra, p. 340.   [3] Herod. i. 189.   [4] Ibid. vii. 40.

revenge himself on the insolent stream, had set his soldiers to disperse its waters into 360 channels. This work employed him during the whole summer and autumn; nor was it till another spring had come that he resumed his expedition. To the Babylonians such a pause must have appeared like irresolution. They must have suspected that the invader had changed his mind and would not venture across the Tigris. If the particulars of the story reached them, they probably laughed at the monarch who vented his rage on inanimate nature, while he let his enemies escape scot free.

Cyrus, however, had a motive for his proceedings which will appear in the sequel. Having wintered on the banks of the Gyndes in a mild climate, where tents would have been quite a sufficient protection to his army, he put his troops in motion at the commencement of spring,[5] crossed the Tigris apparently unopposed, and soon came in sight of the capital. Here he found the Babylonian army drawn out to meet him under the command of Nabonadius himself,[6] who had resolved to try the chance of a battle. An engagement ensued, of which we possess no details; our informants simply tell us that the Babylonian monarch was completely defeated, and that while most of his army sought safety within the walls of the capital, he himself with a small body of troops threw himself into Borsippa,[7] an important

---

[5] Ὡς .... τὸ δεύτερον ἔαρ ὑπέλαμπε. Herod. i. 180. The two years seem alluded to in Jerem. li. 46.

[6] Berosus, Fr. 14. Αἰσθόμενος Ναβόννηδος τὴν ἔφοδον αὐτοῦ (sc. Κύρου), ἀπαντήσας μετὰ τῆς δυνάμεως καὶ παραταξάμενος, ἡττηθεὶς τῇ μάχῃ,

κ.τ.λ. Compare Polyhistor ap. Euseb. Chron. Can. I. 5, § 3. Herodotus does not say who commanded the army.

[7] Beros. l. s. c. φυγὼν ὀλιγοστός, συνεκλείσθη εἰς τὴν Βορσιππηνῶν πόλιν.

town lying at a short distance from Babylon towards the south-west. It is not easy to see the exact object of this movement. Perhaps Nabonadius thought that the enemy would thereby be obliged to divide his army, which might then more easily be defeated: perhaps he imagined that by remaining without the walls he might be able to collect such a force among his subjects and allies as would compel the beleaguering army to withdraw. Or, possibly, he merely followed an instinct of self-preservation, and, fearing that the soldiers of Cyrus might enter Babylon with his own, if he fled thither, sought refuge in another city.

It might have been supposed that his absence would have produced anarchy and confusion in the capital; but a step which he had recently taken with the object of giving stability to his throne rendered the preservation of order tolerably easy. At the earliest possible moment—probably when he was about fourteen—he had associated with him in the government his son, Belshazzar,* or Bil-shar-uzur, the grandson of the great Nebuchadnezzar. This step, taken most likely with a view to none but internal dangers, was now found exceedingly convenient for the purposes of the war. In his father's absence Belshazzar took the direction of affairs within the city, and met and foiled for a considerable

---

* The proof of this association is contained in the cylinders of Nabo-nadius found at Mugheir, where the protection of the gods is asked for Nabu-nahid and his son Bil-shar-uzur, who are coupled together in a way that implies the co-sovereignty of the latter. (*British Museum Series*, Pl. 68, No. 1.) The date of the association was at the latest B.C. 540, Nabonadius's fifteenth year, since the third year of Belshazzar is mentioned in Daniel (viii. 1). If Belshazzar was (as I have supposed) a son of a daughter of Nebuchadnezzar married to Nabonadius *after he became king*, he could not be more than fourteen in his father's fifteenth year.

time all the assaults of the Persians. He was young and inexperienced, but he had the counsels of the queen-mother to guide and support him,⁹ as well as those of the various lords and officers of the court. So well did he manage the defence that after a while Cyrus despaired,¹⁰ and as a last resource ventured on a stratagem in which it was clear that he must either succeed or perish.

Withdrawing the greater part of his army from the vicinity of the city, and leaving behind him only certain *corps* of observation,¹¹ Cyrus marched away up the course of the Euphrates for a certain distance and there proceeded to make a vigorous use of the spade. His soldiers could now appreciate the value of the experience which they had gained by dispersing the Gyndes, and perceive that the summer and autumn of the preceding year had not been wasted. They dug a channel or channels from the Euphrates¹² by means of which a great portion of its water would be drawn off; and hoped in this way to render the natural course of the river fordable. When all was prepared, Cyrus determined to wait for the arrival of a certain festival,¹³ during which the whole population were wont to engage in drinking and revelling, and then silently in the dead of night to turn the

---

⁹ "The Queen," who "*came into the banqueting-house*," where Belshazzar and his wives were already seated (Dan. v. 2, 10), can only be the wife of Nabonadius and mother of Belshazzar. The tone of her address suits well with this view. (Compare Dr. Pusey's *Lectures on Daniel*, p. 449, which I have read since this note was written.)

¹⁰ Herod. i. 190.   ¹¹ Ibid. i. 191.

¹² According to Herodotus (l. s. c.), Cyrus cut a canal from the Euphrates to the reservoir of Nitocris, which he found nearly empty. According to Xenophon (*Cyrop.* vii. 5, § 10), he cut two canals from a point on the Euphrates above Babylon to another below the town.

¹³ Xen. *Cyrop.* vii. 5, § 15. This is far more probable than the statement of Herodotus that "it happened to be a festival" (τυχεῖν γὰρ σφι ἐοῦσαν ὁρτήν, i. 191, sub fin.).

water of the river and make his attack. All fell out as he hoped and wished. The festival was even held with greater pomp and splendour than usual; for Belshazzar, with the natural insolence of youth, to mark his contempt of the besieging army, abandoned himself wholly to the delights of the season, and himself entertained a thousand lords in his palace.[14] Elsewhere the rest of the population was occupied in feasting and dancing.[15] Drunken riot and mad excitement held possession of the town; the siege was forgotten; ordinary precautions were neglected.[16] Following the example of their king the Babylonians gave themselves up for the night to orgies in which religious frenzy and drunken excess formed a strange and revolting medley.[17]

Meanwhile, outside the city, in silence and darkness,[18] the Persians watched at the two points where the Euphrates entered and left the walls. Anxiously they noted the gradual sinking of the water in the river-bed; still more anxiously they watched to see if those within the walls would observe the suspicious circumstance and sound an alarm through the town. Should such an alarm be given, all their labours would be lost. If, when they entered the river-bed, they found the river-walls manned and the river-gates fast locked, they would be indeed "caught in

---

[14] Dan. v. 1.
[15] Χορεύειν τοῦτον τὸν χρόνον καὶ ἐν εὐπαθείαις εἶναι. Herod. l. s. c. Compare Jer. li. 39.
[16] The non-closing of the river-gates must have been a neglect of this kind. Had the sentries even kept proper watch, the enemy's approach must have been perceived.

[17] Dan. v. 4; Xen. Cyrop. l. s. c. Xenophon appropriately calls these religious revellers κωμασταί.
[18] It is curious that Herodotus does not notice the fact of the attack being by night, which is strongly put by Xenophon (Cyrop. vii. 5, §§ 15-33). Compare Dan. v. 30: "In that night was Belshazzar slain."

a trap."[19] Enfiladed on both sides by an enemy whom they could neither see nor reach, they would be overwhelmed and destroyed by his missiles before they could succeed in making their escape. But, as they watched, no sounds of alarm reached them—only a confused noise of revel and riot, which shewed that the unhappy townsmen were quite unconscious of the approach of danger.

At last shadowy forms began to emerge from the obscurity of the deep river-bed, and on the landing places opposite the river gates scattered clusters of men grew into solid columns—the undefended gateways were seized—a war shout was raised—the alarm was taken and spread—and swift runners started off to "shew the King of Babylon that his city was taken at one end."[1] In the darkness and confusion of the night a terrible massacre ensued.[2] The drunken revellers could make no resistance. The king, paralyzed with fear[3] at the awful handwriting upon the wall which too late had warned him of his peril,[4] could do nothing even to check the progress of the assailants, who carried all before them everywhere. Bursting into the palace, a band of Persians made their way to the presence of the monarch, and slew him on the scene of his impious revelry.[5] Other bands carried fire[6] and sword through the town. When morning came, Cyrus found himself undisputed master of the city, which, if it had not despised his efforts, might with the greatest ease have baffled them.

---

[19] De ἐν κύπρῳ. Herod. i. 191.
[1] Jer. li. 31.
  Xen. Cyrop. vii. 5, §§ 26-31;
Jerem. l. 30; li. 4.
[2] Jer. l. 43.

[3] Dan. v. 6-28.
[4] Xen. Cyrop. vii. 5, §§ 27-30. The picture is graphic, and may well be true.
[5] Jer. l. 32; li. 30, 32, 68.

The war, however, was not even yet at an end. Nabonadius still held Borsippa, and, if allowed to remain unmolested, might have gradually gathered strength and become once more a formidable foe. Cyrus therefore, having first issued his orders that the outer fortifications of Babylon should be dismantled,[1] proceeded to complete his conquest by laying siege to the town where he knew that Nabonadius had taken refuge.[2] That monarch however, perceiving that resistance would be vain, did not wait till Borsippa was invested, but on the approach of his enemy surrendered himself.[3] Cyrus rewarded his submission by kind and liberal treatment. Not only did he spare his life, but (if we may trust Abydenus) he conferred on him the government of the important province of Carmania.[4]

Thus perished the Babylonian empire. If we seek the causes of its fall, we shall find them partly in its essential military inferiority to the kingdom that had recently grown up upon its borders, partly in the accidental circumstance that its ruler at the time of the Persian attack was a man of no great capacity. Had Nebuchadnezzar himself, or a prince of his mental calibre, been the contemporary of

---

[1] Berosus, Fr. 14. Κῦρος δὲ Βαβυλῶνα καταλαβόμενος, καὶ συντάξας τὰ ἔξω τῆς πόλεως τείχη κατασκάψαι, κ.τ.λ. Compare Jer. l. 15; ll. 44, 58. I have replaced κατασκάψαι by "dismantled," because, whatever the orders of Cyrus may have been, the enormous labour of demolishing the wall was certainly not undertaken. The battlements may have been thrown down, and breaches broken in it; but the wall itself existed till the time of Alexander. (Abyden. Fr. 9.)

[2] Ἀπίζυξεν ἐπὶ Βόρσιππον, ἐκπολιορκήσων τὸν Ναβόννηδον. Beros. l. s. c.

[3] Ibid.

[4] Καρμανίης ἡγεμονίην δωρέεται. Fr. 9. Berosus, as reported by Josephus (Contr. Ap. l. 21), only says that Cyrus assigned Carmania to Nabonadius as his place of abode (δοὺς οἰκητήριον αὐτῷ Καρμανίαν).

Cyrus, the issue of the contest might have been doubtful. Babylonia possessed naturally vast powers of resistance—powers which, had they been made use of to the utmost, might have tired out the patience of the Persians. That lively, active, but not over persevering people would scarcely have maintained a siege with the pertinacity of the Babylonians themselves[11] or of the Egyptians.[12] If the stratagem of Cyrus had failed—and its success depended wholly on the Babylonians exercising no vigilance—the capture of the town would have been almost impossible. Babylon was too large to be blockaded; its walls were too lofty to be scaled, and too massive to be battered down by the means possessed by the ancients. Mining in the soft alluvial soil would have been dangerous work, especially as the town ditch was deep and supplied with abundant water from the Euphrates.[13] Cyrus, had he failed in his night attack, would probably have at once raised the siege; and Babylonian independence might perhaps in that case have been maintained down to the time of Alexander.

Even thus, however, the "Empire" would not have continued. So soon as it became evident that the Babylonians were no match for the Persians in the field, their authority over the subject nations was at an end. The Susianians, the tribes of the middle Euphrates, the Syrians, the Phœnicians, the Jews, the Idumæans, the Ammonites and Moabites, would have gravitated to the stronger power, even if the attack of Cyrus on Babylon itself had been repulsed. For the conquests of Cyrus in Asia Minor, the Oxus

---

[11] See above, p. 494.   [12] Herod. ii. 157.   [13] Ibid. i. 178.

region, and Affghanistan, had completely destroyed the balance of power in Western Asia, and given to Persia a preponderance both in men and in resources[1] against which the cleverest and most energetic of Babylonian princes would have struggled in vain. Persia must in any case have absorbed all the tract between Mount Zagros and the Mediterranean, except Babylonia Proper; and thus the successful defence of Babylon would merely have deprived the Persian Empire of a province.

In its general character the Babylonian Empire was little more than a reproduction of the Assyrian.[2] The same loose organisation of the provinces under native kings rather than satraps almost universally prevailed,[3] with the same duties on the part of suzerain and subjects, and the same results of ever-recurring revolt and re-conquest.[4] Similar means were employed under both empires to check and discourage rebellion—mutilations and executions of chiefs, pillage of the rebellious region, and wholesale deportation of its population. Babylon, equally with Assyria, failed to win the affections of the subject nations, and, as a natural result, received no help

---

[1] Judging by the taxation of Darius, the resources of the Persians at this time were nearly five times as great as those of the Babylonians. The Persian Empire included the 1st, 2nd, 3rd, 7th, half the 9th, the 10th, 11th, 12th, 13th, 14th, 15th, 16th, 17th, 18th, and 19th satrapies; while the Babylonian Empire consisted of the 5th, the 8th, and half the 9th. The joint revenue furnished to Darius by the satrapies of the first list was 6000 talents; that furnished by the second list was 1150.

[2] See the description of the Assyrian Empire in vol. ii. pp. 524-529.

[3] This may be concluded from such expressions as "Thou, O king, art a *king of kings*" (Dan. II. 37). "Thou" (*i. e.* Babylon) "shalt no more be called *The lady of kingdoms*" (Is. xlvii. 5). It is confirmed by the history of the Jews (2 K. xxiv. 1-17), and by the list of Tyrian kings contemporary with the Babylonian Empire preserved in Josephus. (*Contr. Ap.* i. 21.)

[4] See above, pp. 490-495.

from them in her hour of need. Her system was to exhaust and oppress the conquered races for the supposed benefit of the conquerors, and to impoverish the provinces for the adornment and enrichment of the capital. The wisest of her monarchs thought it enough to construct works of public utility in Babylonia Proper,[3] leaving the dependant countries to themselves and doing nothing to develop their resources. This selfish system was, like most selfishness, short-sighted; it alienated those whom it would have been true policy to conciliate and win. When the time of peril came, the subject nations were no source of strength to the menaced empire. On the contrary, it would seem that some even turned against her and made common cause with the assailants.[4]

Babylonian civilization differed in many respects from Assyrian, to which however it approached more nearly than to any other known type. Its advantages over Assyrian were in its greater originality, its superior literary character, and its comparative width and flexibility. Babylonia seems to have been the source from which Assyria drew her learning, such as it was, her architecture, the main ideas of her mimetic art, her religious notions, her legal forms, and a vast number of her customs and usages. But Babylonia herself, so far as we know, drew her stores from no foreign country. Hers was apparently the genius which excogitated an alphabet—worked out the simpler problems of arithmetic—invented imple-

---

[3] Abyden. Fr. 8.
[4] It may be suspected that the Susianians revolted from Babylon before the conclusion of the siege and joined Cyrus. (See Isaiah xxi. 2; xxii. 6.)

ments for measuring the lapse of time—conceived
the idea of raising enormous structures with the
poorest of all materials, clay—discovered the art of
polishing, boring, and engraving gems—reproduced
with truthfulness the outlines of human and animal
forms—attained to high perfection in textile fabrics—
studied with success the motions of the heavenly
bodies—conceived of grammar as a science—elabo-
rated a system of law—saw the value of an exact
chronology—in almost every branch of science made
a beginning, thus rendering it comparatively easy
for other nations to proceed with the superstructure.
To Babylonia, far more than to Egypt, we owe
the art and learning of the Greeks. It was from the
east, not from Egypt, that Greece derived her
architecture, her sculpture, her science, her philosophy, her mathematical knowledge, in a word,
her intellectual life. And Babylon was the source
to which the entire stream of eastern civilization
may be traced. It is scarcely too much to say
that, but for Babylon, real civilization might not
even yet have dawned upon the earth. Mankind
might never have advanced beyond that spurious
and false form of it, which in Egypt, India, China,
Japan, Mexico, and Peru contented the aspirations
of the species.

APPENDIX.

A.

STANDARD INSCRIPTION OF NEBUCHADNEZZAR.

The Inscription begins with the various titles of Nebuchadnezzar. It then contains prayers and invocations to the Gods, Merodach and Nebo. The extent of N.'s power is spoken of—it reaches from one sea to the other.

An account is then given of the wonders of Babylon, viz.:—

1. The great temple of Merodach. (The mound of *Babil* is the tower or *ziggurat* of this.)
2. The Borsippa temple (or *Birs*.)
3. Various other temples in Babylon and Borsippa.

The subjoined description of the city follows:—

"The double enclosure which Nabopolassar my father had made but not completed, I finished. Nabopolassar made its ditch. With two long embankments of brick and mortar he bound its bed. He made the embankment of the *Arakha*. He lined the other side of the Euphrates with brick. He made a bridge (?) over the Euphrates, but did not finish its buttresses (?). From * * * (the name of a place) he made with bricks burnt as hard as stones, by the help of the great Lord Merodach, a way (for) a branch of the *Shimat* to the waters of the *Yapur-Shapu*, the great reservoir of Babylon, opposite to the gate of *Nin*.

"The *Ingur-Bel* and the *Nimiti-Bel*—the great double wall of Babylon—I finished. With two long embankments of brick and mortar I built the sides of its ditch. I joined it on with that which my father had made. I strengthened the city. Across the river to the west I built the wall of Babylon with brick. The *Yapur-Shapu*—the reservoir of Babylon—by the grace of Merodach, I filled completely full

ART. A.   INSCRIPTION OF NEBUCHADNEZZAR.   525

of water. With bricks burnt as hard as stones, and with
bricks in huge masses like mountains (?), the *Yapur-Shapu*,
from the gate of *Mulu* as far as *Nana*, who is the protectress
of her votaries, by the grace of his godship (*i.e.* Merodach),
I strengthened. With that which my father had made I
joined it. I made the way of *Nana*, the protectress of her
votaries. The great gates of the *Ingur-Bel* and the *Nimiti-
Bel*—the reservoir of Babylon, at the time of the flood (lit. of
fulness), inundated them. These gates I raised. Against
the waters their foundations with brick and mortar I built
[Here follows a description of the gates, with various architectural details, and an account of the decorations, hangings,
&c.] For the delight of mankind I filled the reservoir.
Behold! besides the *Ingur-Bel*, the impregnable fortification
of Babylon, I constructed inside Babylon on the eastern side
of the river a fortification such as no king had ever made
before me, viz. a long rampart, 4000 *ammas* square, as an
extra defence. I excavated the ditch: with brick and
mortar I bound its bed; a long rampart at its head (?) I
strongly built. I adorned its gates. The folding-doors and
the pillars I plated with copper. Against presumptuous
enemies, who were hostile to the men of Babylon, great
waters, like the waters of the ocean, I made use of abundantly. Their depths were like the depths of the vast ocean.
I did not allow the waters to overflow, but the fulness of
their floods I caused to flow on, restraining them with a
brick embankment. . . . Thus I completely made strong the
defences of Babylon. May it last for ever!

[Here follows a similar account of works at Borsippa.]

"In Babylon—the city which is the delight of my eyes, and
which I have glorified—when the waters were in flood,
they inundated the foundations of the great palace called
Taprati-nisi, or 'the Wonder of Mankind;' (a palace) with
many chambers and lofty towers; the high-place of Royalty;
(situated) in the land of Babylon, and in the middle of
Babylon; stretching from the *Ingur-Bel* to the bed of the
Shebil, the eastern canal, (and) from the bank of the Sippara
river to the water of the *Yapur-Shapu*; which Nabopolassar

my father built with brick and raised up; when the reservoir of Babylon was full, the gates of this palace were flooded. I raised the mound of brick on which it was built, and made smooth its platform. I cut off the floods of the water, and the foundations (of the palace) I protected against the water with bricks and mortar; and I finished it completely. Long beams I set up to support it: with pillars and beams plated with copper and strengthened with iron I built up its gates. Silver and gold, and precious stones whose names were almost unknown [Here follow several unknown names of objects, treasures of the palace], I stored up inside, and placed there the treasure-house of my kingdom. Four years (?), the seat of my kingdom in the city . . . ., which . . . . . did not rejoice (my) heart. In all my dominions I did not build a high place of power; the precious treasures of my kingdom I did not lay up. In Babylon, buildings for myself and the honour of my kingdom I did not lay out. In the worship of Merodach my lord, the joy of my heart (?), in Babylon, the city of his sovereignty and the seat of my empire, I did not sing his praises (?), and I did not furnish his altars (i. e. with victims), nor did I clear out the canals. [Here follow further negative clauses.]

"As a further defence in war, at the *Ingur-Bel*, the impregnable outer wall, the rampart of the Babylonians—with two strong lines of brick and mortar I made a strong fort, 400 ammas square, inside the *Nimiti-Bel*, the inner defence of the Babylonians. Masonry of brick within them (the lines) I constructed. With the palace of my father I connected it. In a happy month and on an auspicious day its foundations I laid in the earth like * * *. I completely finished its top. In fifteen days I completed it, and made it the high place of my kingdom. [Here follows a description of the ornamentation of the palace.] A strong fort of brick and mortar in strength I constructed. Inside the brick fortification another great fortification of long stones, of the size of great mountains, I made. Like *Shedim* I raised up its head. And this building I raised for a wonder; for the defence of the people I constructed it."

B.

ON THE MEANINGS OF BABYLONIAN NAMES.

The names of the Babylonians, like those of the Assyrians,[1] were significant. Generally, if not always,[2] they were composed of at least two elements. These might be a noun in the nominative case with a verb following it, a noun in the nominative with a participle in apposition, or a word meaning "servant" followed by the name of a god.[3] Under the first class came such names as Bel-ipni[4]—"Bel has made (me)" —from *Bel*, the name of the God, and *bana* (Heb. בָּנָה), "to make;" Nabo-nassar—"Nebo protects (me)"—from Nebo and *nazar* (Heb. נָצַר), "to guard, protect;" and Nebo-sallim[5] —"Nebo makes perfect"—from Nebo and a verb cognate with the Hebrew שָׁלַם, which in the *Piel* has the meaning of "complete, make perfect." Names compounded with a noun and participle are such as Nebo-nahid and Nahid-Merodach. Here *nahid* is the participle active of a verb, *nahad*,[6] cognate with the Arabic نَهَدَ and the Hebrew נחה, meaning "to make prosperous" or "bless." A specimen of a name compounded with a word meaning "servant" and the appellation of a god seems to exist in Abed-nego—more properly Abed-Nebo[7]— from *abed* (Heb. עֶבֶד), "a slave," and Nebo, the well-known and favourite god.

More usually a Babylonian name consists of three elements, a noun in the nominative, a verb or participle, and a noun in the accusative following the verb. To this class belong the following:—Nabopolassar, Nebuchadnezzar, Neriglissar, Belshazzar, Merodach-baladan, Merodach-iddin-akhi, Merodach-

---

[1] See Appendix to vol. i. Note A. pp. 538–543.
[2] Such names as Pul, Pornu, Nadius, Arioch, can scarcely contain more than one element.
[3] Of course there may have been other combinations in use besides these; but no others have been as yet distinctly recognized.
[4] Supra, vol. ii. p. 430. Another name of exactly the same type is Shamas-ipni. (See vol. ii. p. 439, note 4.)
[5] See vol. ii. l. s. c.
[6] Oppert, *Expédition Scientifique*, tom. ii. p. 259.
[7] Supra, p. 461.

sum-adin, Merodach-shapik-ziri, Nebo-bil-sumi, and Nebu-zaradan.

Nabopolassar, or more properly Nabu-pal-uzur, means "Nebo protects (my) son,"[a] being formed from the roots *Nabu*, "Nebo," *pal*, "son," and *nazar*, "to protect." Nebuchadnezzar, or Nebuchadrezzar[b] (in the original, Nabu-kudurri-uzur), means either "Nebo is the protector of landmarks," or "Nebo protects the youth." The first and last elements are the same as in Nabopolassar: the middle element *kudur* is a word of very doubtful meaning. It has been connected by some with the Persian κίδαρις, "crown." M. Oppert explains it from the Arabic كُدُر, which means "a young man."[10] Sir H. Rawlinson regards it as meaning "a landmark."

Neriglissar and Belshazzar are names of exactly the same kind. The former, correctly written, is Nergal-sar-uzur; the latter, Bil-sar-uzur. The one means "Nergal protects the king;" the other, "Bel protects the king." The only new element here is the middle one, *sar*, "king" (Heb. שׂר), which is found in Sargon, and perhaps in Shar-ezer.

In Merodach-bal-adan (or Marduk-bal-iddin) we have *bal*, a variant of *pal*, "a son," and *iddin*, the 3rd person singular of *nadan*, "to give" (comp. Heb. נתן). The name consequently means "Merodach has given a son." Similarly, in Marduk-iddin-akhi we have *iddin* from *nadan*, together with *akhi*, the plural of *akhu*, "a brother;" and the meaning of the name is thus "Merodach has given brothers." The two roots Merodach and *iddin* appear also in Merodach-sum-adan (or Marduk-sum-iddin) in conjunction with a new root, *sum*, "a name" (comp. Heb. שֵׁם); and there results the meaning "Merodach has given a name"—or perhaps "Merodach is the giver of fame;" since the Hebrew שֵׁם has likewise that signification.

---

[a] Or, according to M. Oppert, "Nebo, protect my son." (*Expédition*, tom. ii. p. 258.)
[b] This is decidedly the more correct form, and indeed is probably not far from the Babylonian articulation.
[10] *Expédition*, tom. ii. p. 259.

App. D.   MEANINGS OF BABYLONIAN NAMES.   529

Merodach-shapik-ziri[11] may be translated "Merodach produces offspring," the root *shapik* being connected with שָׁפַךְ, "to pour out," derivatives from which have a genitive sense, as שִׁפְעָה, and *ziri* being the plural of *zir*, a root meaning "seed, race, offspring" (comp. Heb. זֶרַע).

In Nabu-bil-sumi,[12] *bil* is used in its original sense of "lord" (comp. Heb. בַּעַל), while *sumi* is the plural of *sum*, "a name." The meaning is thus "Nebo presides over names," or "Nebo is the lord of names."

Nebu-zar-adan[13] is probably a Hebrew corruption of Nebu-zir-iddin, which means "Nebo has given offspring," from roots already explained.

The bulk of the Babylonian names preserved to us in Ptolemy's Canon do not admit of any certain explanation, from the corrupt shape in which they have come down to us. Occasionally we may recognise with some confidence the name of a god in them, as Merodach in *Mesesimordachus* and Bel in *Bagibelus*; but attempts to give the full actual etymology can only be the merest conjectures,[14] with which it would not be worth while to trouble the reader. A few probable explanations of some Babylonian names preserved by the Hebrews, and probably very little changed, will alone be attempted before bringing these remarks on Babylonian nomenclature to a conclusion.

The Samgar-Nebo[1] of Jeremiah probably signifies "one who is devoted to Nebo," *Samgar* being a *shaphel* form from the root *migir*, which means "honouring" or "obeying."[2] Sarsechim, in the same writer,[3] is perhaps "the king consents," from *sar* and the Chaldee סכם, which becomes in the *aphel* אַסְכִּים, and has that meaning. Belteshazzar, the name given by the prince of the eunuchs to Daniel, would have appeared, from the obvious analogy of Belshazzar, to be a contracted form of Bilta-shar-uzur, and therefore to signify

---

[11] Supra, p. 471.
[12] See vol. ii. p. 491.
[13] 2 K. xxv. 8; Jer. xxxix. 9.
[14] Several such conjectures have been published by M. Oppert. *Expédition Scientifique*, tom. ii. pp. 355–357.

[1] Jerem. xxxix. 3.
[2] Sir H. Rawlinson in the *Journal of the Asiatic Society*, vol. xviii. p. 28, note [4].
[3] Jerem. l. c.

"Beltis protects the king." But it is an objection to this that Nebuchadnezzar connects the name with that of "his god,"[4] who must (it would seem) be Bel, and not Beltis. If then we are obliged to seek another derivation, we may perhaps find it in Bel, the god, *tisha* (Heb. בֵּלְטְשַׁאצַּר), "a secret,"[5] and *uzur*, from *nazar*, "to guard, protect." Belteshazzar would then mean "Bel is the keeper of secrets," an appropriate sense, since "secrets" were what Daniel was considered especially to know.[6]

It will be observed that almost every Babylonian name, the etymology of which is known to us, has a religious character. Among the elements is almost universally to be recognised the name of a god. The gods especially favoured are Nebo and Merodach, after whom comes Bel, and then Nergal and Shamas. In the kind of religious sentiment which they express the names closely resemble those of the Assyrians.[7] First, there are names announcing facts of the mythology; as Nebuchadrezzar, "Nebo protects landmarks," Belteshazzar, "Bel guards secrets." Next, there are those in which a glorification of the deity is made, as Nabu-bil-sumi, "Nebo is the lord of names," Nabu-sallim, "Nebo makes perfect," and the like. Thirdly, a number of names contain the idea of thankfulness to the god who has granted the child in answer to prayer, as Merodach-bal-adan, "Merodach has given a son," Bel-ipni, "Bel has made (him)," Nebu-zar-adan, "Nebo has given the offspring," &c. And, finally, there are those which imply special devotion of the individual to a particular deity, either directly, as Shamgar-Nebo, "the devotee of Nebo," Abed-Nebo, "the slave of Nebo," or indirectly, as Nabo-nassar, "Nebo protects (me)," Nabopolassar, "Nebo protects (my) son," Belshazzar, "Bel protects the king," Nabo-nahid, "Nebo (is) protecting (me)," and the like.

In the comparatively rare case of names which contain no divine element, the honour of the king seems to have been

---

[4] Dan. iv. 8. "At the last Daniel came in before me, whose name was Belteshazzar, *after the name of my god*."
[5] See the *Targum* on Prov. xxi. 14.
[6] Dan. iv. 9.
[7] See above, vol. ii. pp. 542, 543.

sometimes,* but not very often, considered. In Yakin, Nudina, Zakiru, Halazu, Hagisa, Arioch, Susub, names which seem to be of a purely secular character, there is contained no flattery of the monarch. Thus far then the Babylonians would appear to have been of a more independent spirit than the Assyrians, with whom this species of adulation was not infrequent.

* See the explanation above given of Sanechim.

END OF VOL. III.

SBN 61473-4

LONDON: PRINTED BY W. CLOWES AND SONS, STAMFORD STREET,
AND CHARING CROSS.

ALBEMARLE STREET, LONDON,
April, 1867.

MR. MURRAY'S
GENERAL LIST OF WORKS.

ALBERT'S (PRINCE) SPEECHES AND ADDRESSES ON PUBLIC OCCASIONS; with an Introduction giving some Outlines of his Character. Portrait. 8vo. 10s. 6d.; or Popular Edition. Portrait. Fcap. 8vo. 1s.

ABBOTTS (Rev. J.) Philip Musgrave; or, Memoirs of a Church of England Missionary in the North American Colonies. Post 8vo. 2s.

ABERCROMBIE'S (John) Enquiries concerning the Intellectual Powers and the Investigation of Truth. 14th Edition. Fcap. 8vo. 6s. 6d.

——— Philosophy of the Moral Feelings. 13th Edition. Fcap. 8vo. 4s.

ACLAND'S (Rev. CHARLES) Popular Account of the Manners and Customs of India. Post 8vo. 2s.

ÆSOP'S FABLES. A New Translation. With Historical Preface. By Rev. THOMAS JAMES. With 100 Woodcuts, by TENNIEL and WOLF, 55th Thousand. Post 8vo. 2s. 6d.

AGRICULTURAL (THE) JOURNAL. Of the Royal Agricultural Society of England. 8vo. Published half-yearly.

AIDS TO FAITH: a Series of Theological Essays. By various Writers. Edited by WILLIAM THOMSON, D.D., Archbishop of York. 8vo. 9s.

AMBER-WITCH (THE). The most interesting Trial for Witchcraft ever known. Translated from the German by LADY DUFF GORDON. Post 8vo. 2s.

ARCHITECTURE OF AHMEDABAD, with Historical Sketch and Architectural Notes by T. C. HOPE and JAMES FERGUSSON, F.R.S. With 2 Maps, 120 Photographs, and 22 Woodcuts. 4to. 5l. 5s.

——— BEJAPOOR, with Historical Sketch and Architectural Essay by Col. MEADOWS TAYLOR and JAS. FERGUSSON. With 2 Maps, 76 Photographs, and 18 Woodcuts. Folio. 10l. 10s.

——— DHARWAR and MYSORE. With Historical Sketch and Architectural Essay by Col. MEADOWS TAYLOR and JAS. FERGUSSON. With 2 Maps, 100 Photographs, and numerous Woodcuts. Folio. 12l. 12s.

ARMY LIST (THE). Published Monthly by Authority. 18mo. 1s. 6d.

ARTHUR'S (LITTLE) History of England. By LADY CALLCOTT. New Edition, continued to 1862. Woodcuts. Fcap. 8vo. 2s. 6d.

ATKINSON'S (Mrs.) Recollections of Tartar Steppes and their Inhabitants. Illustrations. Post 8vo. 12s.

AUNT IDA'S Walks and Talks; a Story Book for Children. By a LADY. Woodcuts. 16mo. 5s.

B

LIST OF WORKS

AUSTIN'S (JOHN) LECTURES ON JURISPRUDENCE; or, the Philosophy of Positive Law. 3 Vols. 8vo. 39s.

———— (SARAH) Fragments from German Prose Writers. With Biographical Notes. Post 8vo. 10s.

ADMIRALTY PUBLICATIONS; Issued by direction of the Lords Commissioners of the Admiralty:—

A MANUAL OF SCIENTIFIC ENQUIRY, for the Use of Travellers. Edited by Sir JOHN F. HERSCHEL, and Rev. ROBERT MAIN. Third Edition. Woodcuts. Post 8vo. 9s.

AIRY'S ASTRONOMICAL OBSERVATIONS MADE AT GREENWICH. 1836 to 1847. Royal 4to. 50s. each.

———— ASTRONOMICAL RESULTS. 1848 to 1858. 4to. 8s. each.

———— APPENDICES TO THE ASTRONOMICAL OBSERVATIONS.
  1836.—I. Bessel's Refraction Tables.
       II. Tables for converting Errors of R.A. and N.P.D. into Errors of Longitude and Ecliptic P.D. } 8s.
  1837.—I. Logarithms of Sines and Cosines to every Ten Seconds of Time.
       II. Table for converting Sidereal into Mean Solar Time. } 8s.
  1842.—Catalogue of 1439 Stars. 8s.
  1845.—Longitude of Valentia. 8s.
  1847.—Twelve Years' Catalogue of Stars. 14s.
  1851.—Maskelyne's Ledger of Stars. 6s.
  1852.—I. Description of the Transit Circle. 5s.
       II. Regulations of the Royal Observatory. 2s.
  1853.—Bessel's Refraction Tables. 3s.
  1854.—I. Description of the Zenith Tube. 3s.
       II. Six Years' Catalogue of Stars. 10s.
  1856.—Description of the Galvanic Apparatus at Greenwich Observatory. 8s.
  1862.—I. Seven Years' Catalogue of Stars. 10s.
       II. Plan of the Building and Ground of the Royal Observatory, Greenwich.
       III. Longitude of Valentia. } 3s.

———— MAGNETICAL AND METEOROLOGICAL OBSERVATIONS. 1840 to 1847. Royal 4to. 50s. each.

———— ASTRONOMICAL, MAGNETICAL, AND METEOROLOGICAL OBSERVATIONS, 1848 to 1864. Royal 4to. 50s. each.

———— ASTRONOMICAL RESULTS. 1858 to 1864. 4to.

———— MAGNETICAL AND METEOROLOGICAL RESULTS. 1848 to 1864. 4to. 8s. each.

———— REDUCTION OF THE OBSERVATIONS OF PLANETS. 1750 to 1830. Royal 4to. 50s.

———— LUNAR OBSERVATIONS. 1750 to 1830. 2 Vols. Royal 4to. 50s. each.
———— 1831 to 1851. 4to. 20s.

BERNOULLI'S SEXCENTENARY TABLE. London, 1779. 4to.

BESSEL'S AUXILIARY TABLES FOR HIS METHOD OF CLEARING LUNAR DISTANCES. 8vo.

———— FUNDAMENTA ASTRONOMIÆ: Regiomonti, 1818. Folio. 60s.

BIRD'S METHOD OF CONSTRUCTING MURAL QUADRANTS. London, 1768. 4to. 2s. 6d.

———— METHOD OF DIVIDING ASTRONOMICAL INSTRUMENTS. London, 1767. 4to. 2s. 6d.

COOK, KING, AND BAYLY'S ASTRONOMICAL OBSERVATIONS. London, 1782. 4to. 21s.

ADMIRALTY PUBLICATIONS—continued.

ENCKE'S BERLINER JAHRBUCH, for 1830. Berlin, 1828. 8vo. 9s.

GROOMBRIDGE'S CATALOGUE OF CIRCUMPOLAR STARS. 4to. 10s.

HANSEN'S TABLES DE LA LUNE. 4to. 20s.

HARRISON'S PRINCIPLES OF HIS TIME-KEEPER. Plates. 1767. 4to. 5s.

HUTTON'S TABLES OF THE PRODUCTS AND POWERS OF NUMBERS. 1781. Folio. 1s. 6d.

LAX'S TABLES FOR FINDING THE LATITUDE AND LONGITUDE. 1821. 8vo. 10s.

LUNAR OBSERVATIONS at GREENWICH. 1783 to 1819. Compared with the Tables, 1821. 4to. 7s. 6d.

MASKELYNE'S ACCOUNT OF THE GOING OF HARRISON'S WATCH. 1767. 4to. 2s. 6d.

MAYER'S DISTANCES of the MOON'S CENTRE from the PLANETS. 1822, 3s.; 1823, 4s. 6d. 1824 to 1835, 8vo. 4s. each.

—————— THEORIA LUNÆ JUXTA SYSTEMA NEWTONIANUM. 4to. 2s. 6d.

—— —— TABULÆ MOTUUM SOLIS ET LUNÆ. 1770. 4to. 5s.

—— —— ASTRONOMICAL OBSERVATIONS MADE AT GOTTINGEN, from 1756 to 1761. 1826. Folio. 7s. 6d.

NAUTICAL ALMANACS, from 1767 to 1870. 8vo. 2s. 6d. each.

—— —— SELECTIONS FROM THE ADDITIONS up to 1812. 8vo. 5s. 1834-54. 8vo. 5s.

—— —— —— SUPPLEMENTS, 1828 to 1833, 1837 and 1838. 8vo. 2s. each.

—— —— —— TABLE requisite to be used with the N.A. 1781. 8vo. 5s.

POND'S ASTRONOMICAL OBSERVATIONS. 1811 to 1835. 4to. 21s. each.

RAMSDEN'S ENGINE for DIVIDING MATHEMATICAL INSTRUMENTS. 4to. 5s.

—— —— ENGINE for DIVIDING STRAIGHT LINES. 4to. 5s.

SABINE'S PENDULUM EXPERIMENTS to DETERMINE THE FIGURE OF THE EARTH, 1825. 4to. 40s.

SHEPHERD'S TABLES for CORRECTING LUNAR DISTANCES. 1772. Royal 4to. 21s.

—— —— TABLES, GENERAL, of the MOON'S DISTANCE from the SUN, and 10 STARS. 1787. Folio. 5s. 6d.

TAYLOR'S SEXAGESIMAL TABLE. 1780. 4to. 15s.

—— —— TABLES OF LOGARITHMS. 4to. 3l.

TIARK'S ASTRONOMICAL OBSERVATIONS for the LONGITUDE of MADEIRA, 1822. 4to. 5s.

—— —— CHRONOMETRICAL OBSERVATIONS for DIFFERENCES of Longitude between Dover, Portsmouth, and Falmouth. 1823. 4to. 5s.

VENUS and JUPITER: Observations of, compared with the Tables, London, 1822. 4to. 2s.

WALES AND BAYLY'S ASTRONOMICAL OBSERVATIONS. 1777. 4to. 21s.

WALES' REDUCTION OF ASTRONOMICAL OBSERVATIONS MADE IN THE SOUTHERN HEMISPHERE. 1764—1771. 1788. 4to. 10s. 6d.

BARBAULD'S (Mrs.) Hymns in Prose for Children. With 112
Original Designs. Small 4to. 5s. Or Fine Paper, 7s. 6d.

BARROW'S (Sir John) Autobiographical Memoir. From Early
Life to Advanced Age. Portrait. 8vo. 16s.

——— Life, Exploits, and Voyages of Sir Francis Drake.
With numerous Original Letters. Post 8vo. 2s.

BARRY'S (Sir Charles) Life. By his son, Alfred Barry, D.D.
With Portrait and Illustrations. 8vo.

BATES' (H. W.) Records of a Naturalist on the River Amazons
during eleven years of Adventure and Travel. Second Edition. Illustrations. Post 8vo. 12s.

BEES AND FLOWERS. Two Essays. By Rev. Thomas James.
Reprinted from the "Quarterly Review." Fcap. 8vo. 1s. each.

BERTHA'S Journal during a Visit to her Uncle in England.
Containing a Variety of Interesting and Instructive Information. Seventh Edition. Woodcuts. 12mo. 7s. 6d.

BIRCH'S (Samuel) History of Ancient Pottery and Porcelain:
Egyptian, Assyrian, Greek, Roman, and Etruscan. With 200 Illustrations. 2 Vols. Medium 8vo. 42s.

BLUNT'S (Rev. J. J.) Undesigned Coincidences in the Writings of
the Old and New Testament, an Argument of their Veracity: containing the Books of Moses, Historical and Prophetical Scriptures, and the Gospels and Acts. 8th Edition. Post 8vo. 6s.

——— History of the Church in the First Three Centuries.
Third Edition. Post 8vo. 7s. 6d.

——— Parish Priest; His Duties, Acquirements and Obligations. Fourth Edition. Post 8vo. 7s. 6d.

——— Lectures on the Right Use of the Early Fathers.
Second Edition. 8vo. 15s.

——— Plain Sermons Preached to a Country Congregation.
Second Edition, 2 Vols. Post 8vo. 7s. 6d. each.

——— Essays on various subjects. 8vo. 12s.

BISSET'S (Andrew) History of the Commonwealth of England,
from the Death of Charles I. to the Battle of Dunbar, 1648–50. Chiefly from the MSS. in the State Paper Office. 2 vols. 8vo. 15s. each.

BERTRAM'S (Jas. G.) Harvest of the Sea: a Contribution to the
Natural and Economic History of British Food Fishes. With 50 Illustrations. 21s.

BLAKISTON'S (Capt.) Narrative of the Expedition sent to explore the Upper Waters of the Yang-Tszs. Illustrations. 8vo. 18s.

BLOMFIELD'S (Bishop) Memoir, with Selections from his Correspondence. By his Son. 2nd Edition. Portrait, post 8vo. 12s.

BOOK OF COMMON PRAYER. Illustrated with Coloured
Borders, Initial Letters, and Woodcuts. A new edition. 8vo. 16s. cloth; 31s. 6d. calf; 36s. morocco

BORROW'S (George) Bible in Spain; or the Journeys, Adventures, and Imprisonments of an Englishman in an Attempt to circulate the Scriptures in the Peninsula. 3 Vols. Post 8vo. 27s.; or *Popular Edition*, 16mo, 3s. 6d.

—— Zincali, or the Gipsies of Spain; their Manners, Customs, Religion, and Language. 2 Vols. Post 8vo. 18s.; or *Popular Edition*, 16mo, 3s. 6d.

—— Lavengro; The Scholar—The Gipsy—and the Priest. Portrait. 3 Vols. Post 8vo. 30s.

—— Romany Rye; a Sequel to Lavengro. *Second Edition*. 2 Vols. Post 8vo. 21s.

—— Wild Wales: its People, Language, and Scenery. *Popular Edition*. Post 8vo. 6s.

BOSWELL'S (James) Life of Samuel Johnson, LL.D. Including the Tour to the Hebrides. Edited by Mr. Croker. Portraits. Royal 8vo. 10s.

BRACE'S (C. L.) History of the Races of the Old World. Post 8vo. 9s.

BRAY'S (Mrs.) Life of Thomas Stothard, R.A. With Personal Reminiscences. Illustrated with Portrait and 60 Woodcuts of his chief works. 4to.

BREWSTER'S (Sir David) Martyrs of Science; or, Lives of Galileo, Tycho Brahe, and Kepler. *Fourth Edition*. Fcap. 8vo. 4s. 6d.

—— More Worlds than One. The Creed of the Philosopher and the Hope of the Christian. *Eighth Edition*. Post 8vo. 6s.

—— Stereoscope! Its History, Theory, Construction, and Application to the Arts and to Education. Woodcuts. 12mo. 5s. 6d.

—— Kaleidoscope: its History, Theory, and Construction, with its application to the Fine and Useful Arts. *Second Edition*. Woodcuts. Post 8vo. 5s. 6d.

BRITISH ASSOCIATION REPORTS. 8vo.

York and Oxford, 1831-32, 13s. 6d.
Cambridge, 1833, 12s.
Edinburgh, 1834, 15s.
Dublin, 1835, 13s. 6d.
Bristol, 1836, 12s.
Liverpool, 1837, 16s. 6d.
Newcastle, 1838, 15s.
Birmingham, 1839, 13s. 6d.
Glasgow, 1840, 15s.
Plymouth, 1841, 13s. 6d.
Manchester, 1842, 10s. 6d.
Cork, 1843, 12s.
York, 1844, 20s.
Cambridge, 1845, 12s.
Southampton, 1846, 15s.
Oxford, 1847, 18s.
Swansea, 1848, 9s.

Birmingham, 1849, 10s.
Edinburgh, 1850, 15s.
Ipswich, 1851, 16s. 6d.
Belfast, 1852, 15s.
Hull, 1853, 10s. 6d.
Liverpool, 1854, 18s.
Glasgow, 1855, 15s.
Cheltenham, 1856, 18s.
Dublin, 1857, 15s.
Leeds, 1858, 20s.
Aberdeen, 1859, 15s.
Oxford, 1860, 25s.
Manchester, 1861, 15s.
Cambridge, 1862, 20s.
Newcastle, 1863, 25s.
Bath, 1864, 18s.
Birmingham, 1865, 25s.

BROUGHTON'S (Lord) Journey through Albania and other Provinces of Turkey in Europe and Asia, to Constantinople, 1809—10. *Third Edition*. Illustrations. 2 Vols. 8vo. 30s.

—— Visits to Italy, 3rd *Edition*. 2 Vols. Post 8vo. 18s.

LIST OF WORKS

BRITISH (MURRAY) CLASSICS. A Series of Standard English
Authors, printed from the most correct text, and edited with notes.
8vo.

Already Published.

I. GOLDSMITH'S WORKS. Edited by PETER CUNNINGHAM, F.S.A.
Vignettes, 4 Vols. 30s.

II. GIBBON'S DECLINE AND FALL OF THE ROMAN EMPIRE.
Edited by WILLIAM SMITH, LL.D. Portrait and Maps. 8 Vols. 60s.

III. JOHNSON'S LIVES OF THE ENGLISH POETS. Edited by PETER
CUNNINGHAM, F.S.A. 3 Vols. 22s. 6d.

IV. BYRON'S POETICAL WORKS. Edited, with Notes. 6 vols. 45s.

In Preparation.

LIFE AND WORKS OF POPE. Edited by Rev. WHITWELL ELWIN.

HUME'S HISTORY OF ENGLAND. Edited, with Notes.

LIFE AND WORKS OF SWIFT. Edited by JOHN FORSTER.

LIFE AND WORKS OF DRYDEN. Edited, with Notes.

BUBBLES FROM THE BRUNNEN OF NASSAU. By Sir
FRANCIS B. HEAD, Bart. 7th Edition, with Illustrations. Post 8vo.
7s. 6d.

BUNYAN (JOHN) and Oliver Cromwell. Select Biographies. By
ROBERT SOUTHEY. Post 8vo. 2s.

BURGON'S (Rev. J. W.) Memoir of Patrick Fraser Tytler.
Second Edition. Post 8vo. 9s.

—————— Letters from Rome. Illustrations. Post 8vo. 12s.

BURN'S (COL.) Dictionary of Naval and Military Technical
Terms, English and French, and French and English. Fourth Edition.
Crown 8vo. 15s.

BURR'S (G. D.) Instructions in Practical Surveying, Topogra-
phical Plan Drawing, and on sketching ground without instruments.
Fourth Edition. Woodcuts. Post 8vo. 6s.

BUTTMAN'S LEXILOGUS; a Critical Examination of the
Meaning of numerous Greek Words, chiefly in Homer and Hesiod.
Translated by Rev. J. R. FISHLAKE. Fifth Edition. 8vo. 12s.

—————— CATALOGUE OF IRREGULAR GREEK VERBS.
With all the Tenses extant—their Formation, Meaning, and Usage,
accompanied by an Index. Translated, with Notes, by Rev. J. R.
FISHLAKE. Fifth Edition. Revised by Rev. E. VENABLES. Post 8vo. 6s.

BUXTON'S (SIR FOWELL) Memoirs. With Selections from his
Correspondence. By his Son. Portrait. 8vo. 16s. *Abridged Edition.*
Portrait. Fcap. 8vo. 2s. 6d.

—————— (CHARLES, M.P.) IDEAS OF THE DAY ON POLICY.
A New and Enlarged Edition. 8vo.

PUBLISHED BY MR. MURRAY. 7

BYRON'S (Lord) Life, Letters, and Journals. By Thomas Moore. Plates. 6 Vols. Fcap. 8vo. 18s.
——— Life, Letters, and Journals. By Thomas Moore. Portraits. Royal 8vo. 9s.
——— Poetical Works. Portrait. 6 Vols. 8vo. 45s.
——— Poetical Works. Plates. 10 Vols. Fcap. 8vo. 30s.
——— Poetical Works. 8 Vols. 24mo. 20s.
——— Poetical Works. Plates. Royal 8vo. 9s.
——— Poetical Works. (Pearl Edition.) Crown 8vo. 2s. 6d.
——— Childe Harold. With 80 Engravings. Small 4to. 21s.
——— Childe Harold. 16mo. 2s. 6d.
——— Childe Harold. Vignettes. 16mo. 1s.
——— Childe Harold. Portrait. 16mo. 6d.
——— Tales and Poems. 24mo. 2s. 6d.
——— Miscellaneous. 2 Vols. 24mo. 5s.
——— Dramas and Plays. 2 Vols. 24mo. 5s.
——— Don Juan and Beppo. 2 Vols. 24mo. 5s.
——— Beauties. Poetry and Prose. Portrait. Fcap. 8vo. 3s. 6d.

CALLCOTT'S (Lady) Little Arthur's History of England. New Edition, brought down to 1852. With Woodcuts. Fcap. 8vo. 2s. 6d.

CAMPBELL'S (Lord) Lives of the Lord Chancellors and Keepers of the Great Seal of England. From the Earliest Times to the Death of Lord Eldon in 1838. Fourth Edition. 10 Vols. Crown 8vo. 6s. each.
——— Lives of the Chief Justices of England. From the Norman Conquest to the Death of Lord Tenterden. Second Edition. 3 Vols. 8vo. 42s.
——— Shakspeare's Legal Acquirements Considered. 8vo. 5s. 6d.
——— Life of Lord Chancellor Bacon. Fcap. 8vo. 2s. 6d.
——— (George) Modern India. A Sketch of the System of Civil Government. With some Account of the Natives and Native Institutions. Second Edition. 8vo. 16s.
——— India as it may be. An Outline of a proposed Government and Policy. 8vo. 12s.
——— (Thos.) Short Lives of the British Poets. With an Essay on English Poetry. Post 8vo. 3s. 6d.

CARNARVON'S (Lord) Portugal, Gallicia, and the Basque Provinces. From Notes made during a Journey to these Countries. Third Edition. Post 8vo. 3s. 6d.
——— Recollections of the Druses of Lebanon. With Notes on their Religion. Third Edition. Post 8vo. 5s. 6d.

CASTLEREAGH (The) DESPATCHES, from the commencement of the official career of the late Viscount Castlereagh to the close of his life. Edited by the Marquis of Londonderry. 12 Vols. 8vo. 14s. each.

CATHCART'S (Sir George) Commentaries on the War in Russia and Germany, 1812-13. Plans. 8vo. 14s.

CAVALCASELLE and CROWE'S History of Painting in Italy, from the Second to the Sixteenth Century, from recent researches, as well as from personal inspection of the Works of Art in that Country. With 100 Illustrations. Vols. I. to III. 8vo. 63s.

—————— Notices of the Lives and Works of the Early Flemish Painters. Woodcuts. Post 8vo. 12s.

CHILD (G. Chaplin, M.D.) Benedicite; or, Song of the Three Children; being Illustrations of the Power, Wisdom, and Goodness of the Creator. 2 Vols. Fcap. 8vo. 12s.

CHORLEY'S (H. F.) STUDIES OF THE MUSIC OF MANY NATIONS; including the Substance of a Course of Lectures delivered at the Royal Institution. 8vo. (In the Press.)

CHURTON'S (Archdeacon) Gongora. An Historical Essay on the Age of Philip III. and IV. of Spain. With Translations. Portrait. 2 Vols. Small 8vo. 15s.

CICERO: HIS LIFE AND TIMES. With his Character viewed as a Statesman, Orator, and Friend. With a Selection from his Correspondence and Orations. By William Forsyth, Q.C. New Edition. With Illustrations. 8vo. 16s.

CLIVE'S (Lord) Life. By Rev. G. R. Gleig, M.A. Post 8vo. 6s. 6d.

COLCHESTER (Lord). The Diary and Correspondence of Charles Abbot, Lord Colchester, Speaker of the House of Commons, 1802-1817. Edited by his Son. Portrait. 3 Vols. 8vo. 42s.

COLERIDGE (Samuel Taylor). Specimens of his Table-Talk. New Edition. Portrait. Fcap. 8vo. 6s.

COLONIAL LIBRARY. [See Home and Colonial Library.]

COOK'S (Rev. Canon) Sermons Preached at Lincoln's Inn Chapel, and on Special Occasions. 8vo. 9s.

COOKERY (Modern Domestic). Founded on Principles of Economy and Practical Knowledge, and adapted for Private Families. By a Lady. New Edition. Woodcuts. Fcap. 8vo. 6s.

CORNWALLIS (The) Papers and Correspondence during the American War,—Administrations in India,—Union with Ireland, and Peace of Amiens. Edited by Charles Ross. Second Edition. 3 Vols. 8vo. 63s.

COWPER'S (Mary, Countess) Diary while Lady of the Bedchamber to Caroline Princess of Wales, 1714-20. Edited by Hon. Spencer Cowper. Second Edition. Portrait. 8vo. 10s. 6d.

CRABBE'S (Rev. George) Life, Letters, and Journals. By his Son. Portrait. Fcap. 8vo. 3s.

—————— Life and Poetical Works. Plates. 8 Vols. Fcap. 8vo. 24s.

—————— Life and Poetical Works. Plates. Royal 8vo. 7s.

CROKER'S (J. W.) Progressive Geography for Children. *Fifth Edition.* 18mo. 1s. 6d.
——— Stories for Children. Selected from the History of England. *Fifteenth Edition.* Woodcuts. 16mo. 2s. 6d.
——— Boswell's Life of Johnson. Including the Tour to the Hebrides. Portraits. Royal 8vo. 10s.
——— Essays on the Early Period of the French Revolution. 8vo. 15s.
——— Historical Essay on the Guillotine. Fcap. 8vo. 1s.
CROMWELL (Oliver) and John Bunyan. By Robert Southey. Post 8vo. 2s.
CROWE and CAVALCASELLE'S Notices of the Early Flemish Painters; their Lives and Works. Woodcuts. Post 8vo. 12s.
——— History of Painting in Italy, from 2nd to 16th Century. Derived from Historical Researches as well as Inspection of the Works of Art in that Country. With 100 Illustrations. Vols. I. II. and III. 8vo. 21s. each.
CUMMING'S (R. Gordon) Five Years of a Hunter's Life in the Far Interior of South Africa; with Anecdotes of the Chase, and Notices of the Native Tribes. *New Edition.* Woodcuts. Post 8vo. 5s.
CUNNINGHAM'S (Allan) Poems and Songs. Now first collected and arranged, with Biographical Notice. 24mo. 2s. 6d.
CURETON (Rev. W.) Remains of a very Ancient Recension of the Four Gospels in Syriac, hitherto unknown in Europe. Discovered, Edited, and Translated. 4to. 24s.
CURTIUS' (Professor) Student's Greek Grammar, for the use of Colleges and the Upper Forms. Edited by Dr. Wm. Smith. Second and Cheaper Edition. Post 8vo. 6s.
——— Smaller Greek Grammar for the use of the Middle and Lower Forms, abridged from the above. 12mo. 3s. 6d.
——— First Greek Course; containing Delectus, Exercise Book, and Vocabularies. 12mo. 3s. 6d.
CURZON'S (Hon. Robert) Armenia and Erzeroum. A Year on the Frontiers of Russia, Turkey, and Persia. *Third Edition.* Woodcuts. Post 8vo. 7s. 6d.
——— Visits to the Monasteries of the Levant. *Fifth Edition.* Illustrations. Post 8vo. 7s. 6d.
CUST'S (General) Annals of the Wars of the 18th & 19th Centuries. 9 Vols. Fcap. 8vo. 5s. each.
——— Lives and Characters of the Warriors of the 17th Century who have Commanded Fleets and Armies before the Enemy. 4 Vols. Post 8vo. 5s. each.
DARWIN'S (Charles) Journal of Researches into the Natural History of the Countries visited during a Voyage round the World. Post 8vo. 9s.
——— Origin of Species by Means of Natural Selection; or, the Preservation of Favoured Races in the Struggle for Life. *Fourth Edition, revised.* Post 8vo. 14s.
——— Fertilization of Orchids through Insect Agency, and as to the good of Intercrossing. Woodcuts. Post 8vo. 9s.
——— Variations of Animals and Plants under Domestication; or, the Principles of Inheritance, Re-version, Crossing, Inter-breeding, and Selection. With Illustrations. 2 Vols. 8vo. (*Nearly ready.*)

LIST OF WORKS

DAVIES (NATHAN) Visit to the Ruined Cities of Numidia and Carthaginia. Illustrations. 8vo. 18s.

—— (SIR J. F.) Chinese Miscellanies: a Collection of Essays and Notes. Post 8vo. 6s.

DAVY'S (SIR HUMPHRY) Consolations in Travel; or, Last Days of a Philosopher. Fifth Edition. Woodcuts. Fcap. 8vo. 6s.

—— Salmonia; or, Days of Fly Fishing. *Fourth Edition.* Woodcuts. Fcap. 8vo. 6s.

DELEPIERRE'S (OCTAVE) History of Flemish Literature. From the Twelfth Century. 8vo. 9s.

DENNIS' (GEORGE) Cities and Cemeteries of Etruria. Plates. 2 Vols. 8vo. 42s.

DERBY'S (EDWARD, EARL OF) Translation of the Iliad of Homer into English Blank Verse. *Fifth Edition, Revised.* 2 Vols. 8vo. 24s.

DE ROSS (LORD) Memorials of the Tower of London. With Illustrations. Crown 8vo. 10s. 6d.

DIXON'S (W. HEPWORTH) Story of the Life of Lord Bacon. Portrait. Fcap. 8vo. 7s. 6d.

DOG-BREAKING; the Most Expeditious, Certain, and Easy Method, whether great excellence or only mediocrity be required. With a Few Hints for those who love the Dog and the Gun. By LIEUT.-GEN. HUTCHINSON. *Fourth Edition.* With 40 Woodcuts. Crown 8vo. 15s.

DOMESTIC MODERN COOKERY. Founded on Principles of Economy and Practical Knowledge, and adapted for Private Families. *New Edition.* Woodcuts. Fcap. 8vo. 6s.

DOUGLAS'S (GENERAL SIR HOWARD) Life and Adventures; From Notes, Conversations, and Correspondence. By S. W. FULLOM. Portrait. 8vo. 15s.

—— Theory and Practice of Gunnery. *5th Edition.* Plates. 8vo. 21s.

—— Military Bridges, and the Passage of Rivers in Military Operations. *Third Edition.* Plates. 8vo. 21s.

—— Naval Warfare with Steam. *Second Edition.* 8vo. 8s. 6d.

—— Modern Systems of Fortification. Plans. 8vo. 12s.

DRAKE'S (SIR FRANCIS) Life, Voyages, and Exploits, by Sea and Land. By JOHN BARROW. *Third Edition.* Post 8vo. 2s.

DRINKWATER'S (JOHN) History of the Siege of Gibraltar, 1779–1783. With a Description and Account of that Garrison from the Earliest Periods. Post 8vo. 2s.

DU CHAILLU'S (PAUL B.) EQUATORIAL AFRICA, with Accounts of the Gorilla, the Nest-building Ape, Chimpanzee, Crocodile, &c. Illustrations. 8vo. 21s.

—— Journey to Ashango Land; and Further Penetration into Equatorial Africa. Illustrations. 8vo. 21s.

DUFFERIN'S (Lord) Letters from High Latitudes, being some Account of a Yacht Voyage to Iceland, &c., in 1856. Fourth Edition. Woodcuts. Post 8vo. 7s. 6d.

—— Lispings from Low Latitudes, or the Journal of the Hon. Impulsia Gushington. With 24 Plates. 4to. 21s.

DYER'S (Thomas H.) History of Modern Europe, from the taking of Constantinople by the Turks to the close of the War in the Crimea. 4 Vols. 8vo. 60s.

EASTLAKE'S (Sir Charles) Italian Schools of Painting. From the German of Kugler. Edited, with Notes. Third Edition. Illustrated from the Old Masters. 2 Vols. Post 8vo. 30s.

EASTWICK'S (E. B.) Handbook for Bombay and Madras, with Directions for Travellers, Officers, &c. Map, 2 Vols. Post 8vo. 24s.

EDWARDS' (W. H.) Voyage up the River Amazon, including a Visit to Para. Post 8vo. 2s.

ELDON'S (Lord) Public and Private Life, with Selections from his Correspondence and Diaries. By Horace Twiss. Third Edition. Portrait. 2 Vols. Post 8vo. 21s.

ELLIS (Rev. W.) Visits to Madagascar, including a Journey to the Capital, with notices of Natural History, and Present Civilization of the People. Fifth Thousand. Map and Woodcuts. 8vo. 16s.

Madagascar Revisited. Setting forth the Persecutions and Heroic Sufferings of the Native Christians, and the eventual toleration of Christianity. Illustrations. 8vo. 16s.

(Mas.) Education of Character, with Hints on Moral Training. Post 8vo. 7s. 6d.

ELLESMERE'S (Lord) Two Sieges of Vienna by the Turks. Translated from the German. Post 8vo. 2s.

ELPHINSTONE'S (Hon. Mountstuart) History of India—the Hindoo and Mahommedan Periods. Fifth Edition, Revised. Map. 8vo. 18s.

ENGEL'S (Carl) Music of the Most Ancient Nations; particularly of the Assyrians, Egyptians, and Hebrews; with Special Reference to the Discoveries in Western Asia and in Egypt. With 100 Illustrations. 8vo. 16s.

ENGLAND (History of) from the Peace of Utrecht to the Peace of Versailles, 1713–83. By Lord Mahon (Earl Stanhope). Library Edition, 7 Vols. 8vo. 93s.; or Popular Edition, 7 Vols. Post 8vo. 35s.

—— From the First Invasion by the Romans. By Mrs. Markham. New and Cheaper Edition, continued to 1863. Woodcuts. 12mo. 4s.

—— (The Student's Hume). From the Invasion of Julius Cæsar to the Revolution of 1688. By David Hume. Corrected and continued to 1858. Edited by Wm. Smith, LL.D. Woodcuts. Post 8vo. 7s. 6d.

—— A Smaller History of England for Young Persons. By Dr. Wm. Smith. New Edition, continued to 1865. Woodcuts. 16mo. 3s. 6d.

—— Little Arthur's History of England. By Lady Callcott. Woodcuts. 18mo. 2s. 6d.

ENGLISHWOMAN IN AMERICA. Post 8vo. 10s. 6d.

ESKIMAUX and English Vocabulary, for Travellers in the Arctic Regions. 16mo. 3s. 6d.

ESSAYS FROM "THE TIMES." Being a Selection from the LITERARY PAPERS which have appeared in that Journal. *Seventh Thousand.* 2 vols. Fcap. 8vo. 8s.

ETHNOLOGICAL SOCIETY OF LONDON, TRANSACTIONS. New Series. Vols. I. to IV. 8vo. 12s. 6d. each.

EXETER'S (BISHOP OF) Letters to Charles Butler, on his Book of the Roman Catholic Church. *New Edition.* Post 8vo. 6s.

FAMILY RECEIPT-BOOK. A Collection of a Thousand Valuable and Useful Receipts. Fcap. 8vo. 5s. 6d.

FARRAR'S (REV. A. S.) Critical History of Free Thought in reference to the Christian Religion. Being the Hampton Lectures, 1862. 8vo. 16s.

— (F. W.) Origin of Language, based on Modern Researches. Fcap. 8vo. 5s.

FEATHERSTONHAUGH'S (G. W.) Tour through the Slave States of North America, from the River Potomac to Texas and the Frontiers of Mexico. Plates. 2 Vols. 8vo. 26s.

FERGUSSON'S (JAMES) Palaces of Nineveh and Persepolis Restored. Woodcuts. 8vo. 16s.

—— History of Architecture in all Countries; from the Earliest Times to the Present Day. With 1400 Illustrations and an Index. 2 Vols. 8vo. 42s. each.

— — History of Architecture. Vol. III.—The Modern Styles. With 312 Illustrations, and an Index. 8vo. 31s. 6d.

— — Holy Sepulchre and the Temple at Jerusalem; being the Substance of Two Lectures delivered at the Royal Institution, 1862 and '65. Woodcuts. 8vo. 7s. 6d.

FISHER'S (REV. GEORGE) Elements of Geometry, for the Use of Schools. *Fifth Edition.* 18mo. 1s. 6d.

—— First Principles of Algebra, for the Use of Schools. *Fifth Edition.* 18mo. 1s. 6d.

FLOWER GARDEN (THE). By REV. THOS. JAMES. Fcap. 8vo. 1s.

FONNEREAU'S (T. G.) Diary of a Dutiful Son. Fcap. 8vo. 4s. 6d.

FORBES (C. S.) Iceland; its Volcanoes, Geysers, and Glaciers. Illustrations. Post 8vo. 14s.

FORSTER'S (JOHN) Arrest of the Five Members by Charles the First. A Chapter of English History re-written. Post 8vo. 12s.

—— Grand Remonstrance, 1641. With an Essay on English freedom under the Plantagenet and Tudor Sovereigns. *Second Edition.* Post 8vo. 12s.

—— Sir John Eliot: a Biography, 1590—1632. With Portraits. 2 Vols. Crown 8vo. 30s.

—— Biographies of Oliver Cromwell, Daniel De Foe, Sir Richard Steele, Charles Churchill, Samuel Foote. *Third Edition.* Post 8vo. 12s.

FORD'S (RICHARD) Handbook for Spain, Andalusia, Ronda, Valencia, Catalonia, Granada, Gallicia, Arragon, Navarre, &c. *Third Edition*, 2 Vols. Post 8vo. 30s.

—— Gatherings from Spain. Post 8vo. 3s. 6d.

FORSYTH'S (WILLIAM) Life and Times of Cicero. With Selections from his Correspondence and Orations. *New Edition*. Illustrations. 8vo. 16s.

FORTUNE'S (ROBERT) Narrative of Two Visits to the Tea Countries of China, 1843-52. *Third Edition*. Woodcuts. 2 Vols. Post 8vo. 18s.

—— Third Visit to China. 1853-6. Woodcuts. 8vo. 16s.

—— Yedo and Peking. With Notices of the Agriculture and Trade of China, during a Fourth Visit to that Country. Illustrations. 8vo. 16s.

FOSS' (EDWARD) Judges of England. With Sketches of their Lives, and Notices of the Courts at Westminster, from the Conquest to the Present Time. 9 Vols. 8vo. 126s.

FRANCE (HISTORY OF). From the Conquest by the Gauls. By Mrs. MARKHAM. *New and Cheaper Edition*, continued to 1856. Woodcuts. 12mo. 6s.

—— (THE STUDENT'S HISTORY OF). From the Earliest Times to the Establishment of the Second Empire, 1852. By W. H. PEARSON. Edited by WM. SMITH, LL.D. Woodcuts. Post 8vo. 7s. 6d.

FRENCH (THE) in Algiers; The Soldier of the Foreign Legion—and the Prisoners of Abd-el-Kadir. Translated by Lady DUFF GORDON. Post 8vo. 2s.

GALTON'S (FRANCIS) Art of Travel; or, Hints on the Shifts and Contrivances available in Wild Countries. *Third Edition*. Woodcuts. Post 8vo. 7s. 6d.

GEOGRAPHY, ANCIENT (THE STUDENT'S MANUAL OF). By Rev. W. L. BEVAN. Woodcuts. Post 8vo. 7s. 6d.

—— MODERN (THE STUDENT'S MANUAL). By Rev. W. L. BEVAN. Woodcuts. Post 8vo. *In the Press*.

—— Journal of the Royal Geographical Society of London. 8vo.

GERMANY (HISTORY OF). From the Invasion by Marius, to Recent times. By Mrs. MARKHAM. *New and Cheaper Edition*. Woodcuts. 12mo. 6s.

GIBBON'S (EDWARD) History of the Decline and Fall of the Roman Empire. Edited, with Notes, by DEAN MILMAN and M. GUIZOT. *A New Edition*. Preceded by his Autobiography. And Edited, with Notes, by Dr. WM. SMITH. Maps. 8 Vols. 8vo. 60s.

—— (The Student's Gibbon); Being an Epitome of the above work, incorporating the Researches of Recent Commentators. By Dr. WM. SMITH. Woodcuts. Post 8vo. 7s. 6d.

GIFFARD'S (EDWARD) Deeds of Naval Daring; or, Anecdotes of the British Navy. *New Edition*. Fcap. 8vo. 3s. 6d.

GOLDSMITH'S (OLIVER) Works. A New Edition. Printed from the last editions revised by the Author. Edited by PETER CUNNINGHAM. Vignettes. 4 Vols. 8vo. 30s.

GLADSTONE'S (Right Hon. W. E.) Financial Statements of 1853, 60, 63, and 66; with Speeches on Tax-Bills and Charities. Second Edition. 8vo, 12s.
—— Farewell Address at the University of Edinburgh. Fourth Edition. 8vo. 2s. 6d.
—— Speeches on Parliamentary Reform in 1866. 3rd Edition. Post 8vo. 6s.

GLEIG'S (Rev. G. R.) Campaigns of the British Army at Washington and New Orleans. Post 8vo. 2s.
—— Story of the Battle of Waterloo. Post 8vo. 3s. 6d.
—— Narrative of Sale's Brigade in Affghanistan. Post 8vo. 2s.
—— Life of Robert Lord Clive. Post 8vo. 3s. 6d.
—— Life and Letters of Sir Thomas Munro. Post 8vo. 3s. 6d.

GONGORA; An Historical Essay on the Times of Philip III. and IV. of Spain. With Illustrations. By Archdeacon Churton. Portrait. 2 vols. Post 8vo. 15s.

GORDON'S (Sir Alex. Duff) Sketches of German Life, and Scenes from the War of Liberation. From the German. Post 8vo. 3s. 6d.
—— (Lady Duff) Amber-Witch: A Trial for Witchcraft. From the German. Post 8vo. 2s.
—— French in Algiers. 1. The Soldier of the Foreign Legion. 2. The Prisoners of Abd-el-Kadir. From the French. Post 8vo. 2s.

GOUGER'S (Henry) Personal Narrative of Two Years' Imprisonment in Burmah. Second Edition. Woodcuts. Post 8vo. 12s.

GRAMMARS (Latin and Greek). See Curtius; Smith; King Edward VIth., &c. &c.

GREECE (The Student's History of). From the Earliest Times to the Roman Conquest. By Wm. Smith, LL.D. Woodcuts. Post 8vo. 7s. 6d.
—— (A Smaller History of, for Young Persons). By Dr. Wm. Smith. Woodcuts. 16mo. 3s. 6d.

GRENVILLE (The) PAPERS. Being the Public and Private Correspondence of George Grenville, including his Private Diary. Edited by W. J. Smith. 4 Vols. 8vo. 16s. each.

GREY'S (Earl) Correspondence with King William IVth. and Sir Herbert Taylor, from November, 1830, to the Passing of the Reform Act in 1832. 2 Vols. 8vo. 30s.
—— On Parliamentary Government and Reform; with suggestions for the Improvement of our Representative System, and an Examination of the Reform Bills of 1859—61. Second Edition. 8vo. 9s.
—— (Sir George) Polynesian Mythology, and Ancient Traditional History of the New Zealand Race. Woodcuts. Post 8vo. 10s. 6d.

CRUNER'S (Lewis) Brick and Terra-Cotta Buildings of Lombardy, Fourteenth and Fifteenth Centuries. From careful Drawings and Restorations. Engraved and printed in Colours. Illustrations. Small folio.

GROTE'S (George) History of Greece. From the Earliest Times to the close of the generation contemporary with the death of Alexander the Great. *Fourth Edition.* Maps. 8 Vols. 8vo. 112s.
——— Plato, and the other Companions of Socrates. *Second Edition.* 3 Vols. 8vo. 45s.
——— (Mrs.) Memoir of Ary Scheffer. Post 8vo. 8s. 6d.
——— ——— Collected Papers. 8vo. 10s. 6d.
GUIZOT'S (M.) Meditations on the Essence of Christianity, and on the Religious Questions of the Day. Post 8vo. 9s. 6d.
——— Meditations on the Present State of the Christian Religion. Post 8vo. 10s.
HALLAM'S (Henry) Constitutional History of England, from the Accession of Henry the Seventh to the Death of George the Second. *Seventh Edition.* 3 Vols. 8vo. 30s. Or *Popular Edition*, 3 Vols. Post 8vo. 18s.
——— History of Europe during the Middle Ages. *Tenth Edition.* 3 Vols. 8vo. 30s. Or *Popular Edition*, 3 Vols. Post 8vo. 18s.
——— Literary History of Europe, during the 15th, 16th and 17th Centuries. *Fourth Edition.* 3 Vols. 8vo. 36s. Or *Popular Edition*, 4 Vols. Post 8vo. 24s.
——— Historical Works. Containing History of England, — Middle Ages of Europe, — Literary History of Europe. 10 Vols. Post 8vo. 6s. each.
——— (Arthur) Remains; in Verse and Prose. With Preface, Memoir, and Portrait. Fcap. 8vo. 7s. 6d.
HAMILTON'S (James) Wanderings in North Africa. With Illustrations. Post 8vo. 12s.
HART'S ARMY LIST. (*Quarterly and Annually.*) 8vo. 10s. 6d. and 21s. each.
HANNAH'S (Rev. Dr.) Bampton Lectures for 1863; the Divine and Human Elements in Holy Scripture. 8vo. 10s. 6d.
HAY'S (J. H. Drummond) Western Barbary, its Wild Tribes and Savage Animals. Post 8vo. 2s.
HEAD'S (Sir Francis) Horse and his Rider. Woodcuts. Post 8vo. 5s.
——— Rapid Journeys across the Pampas. Post 8vo. 2s.
——— Bubbles from the Brunnen of Nassau. Illustrations. Post 8vo. 7s. 6d.
——— Emigrant. Fcap. 8vo. 2s. 6d.
——— Stokers and Pokers; or, N.-Western Railway. Post 8vo. 2s.
——— (Sir Edmund) Shall and Will; or, Future Auxiliary Verbs. Fcap. 8vo. 4s.
HEBER'S (Bishop) Journey through the Upper Provinces of India, from Calcutta to Bombay, with an Account of a Journey to Madras and the Southern Provinces. *Twelfth Edition.* 2 Vols. Post 8vo. 7s.
——— Poetical Works, including Palestine, Europe, The Red Sea, Hymns, &c. *Sixth Edition.* Portrait. Fcap. 8vo. 6s.
——— Hymns adapted to the Weekly Church Service of the Year. 16mo. 1s. 6d.
HERODOTUS. A New English Version. Edited, with Notes and Essays, historical, ethnographical, and geographical, by Rev. G. Rawlinson, assisted by Sir Henry Rawlinson and Sir J. G. Wilkinson. *Second Edition.* Maps and Woodcuts. 4 Vols. 8vo. 48s.
HAND-BOOK—TRAVEL-TALK. English, French, German, and Italian. 18mo. 3s. 6d.

16   LIST OF WORKS

HAND-BOOK—NORTH GERMANY,—Holland, Belgium, and the Rhine to Switzerland. Map. Post 8vo. 10s.

—— —— KNAPSACK GUIDE—BELGIUM AND THE RHINE. Post 8vo. (In the Press.)

—— SOUTH GERMANY, Bavaria, Austria, Styria, Salzburg, the Austrian and Bavarian Alps, the Tyrol, Hungary, and the Danube, from Ulm to the Black Sea. Map. Post 8vo. 10s.

—— —— KNAPSACK GUIDE—THE TYROL. Post 8vo.

—— PAINTING. German, Flemish, and Dutch Schools. Edited by Dr. Waagen. Woodcuts, 2 Vols. Post 8vo. 24s.

—— LIVES OF THE EARLY FLEMISH PAINTERS, with Notices of their Works. By Crowe and Cavalcaselle. Illustrations. Post 8vo. 12s.

—— SWITZERLAND, Alps of Savoy, and Piedmont. Maps. Post 8vo. 9s.

—— KNAPSACK GUIDE—SWITZERLAND. Post 8vo. 5s.

—— FRANCE, Normandy, Brittany, the French Alps, the Rivers Loire, Seine, Rhone, and Garonne, Dauphiné, Provence, and the Pyrenees. Maps. Post 8vo. 10s.

—— PARIS, and its Environs. Map and Plans. Post 8vo. 3s. 6d.
*** Murray's Handbook Plan of Paris, engraved on a large scale mounted on canvas in a case. Price 3s. 6d.

—— SPAIN, Andalusia, Ronda, Granada, Valencia, Catalonia, Gallicia, Arragon, and Navarre. Maps. 2 Vols. Post 8vo. 20s.

—— —— PORTUGAL, Lisbon, &c. Map. Post 8vo. 9s.

—— NORTH ITALY, Piedmont, Liguria, Venetia, Lombardy, Parma, Modena, and Romagna. Map. Post 8vo. 12s.

—— —— CENTRAL ITALY, Lucca, Tuscany, Florence, The Marches, Umbria, and the Patrimony of St. Peter's. Map. Post 8vo. 10s.

—— ROME and its Environs. Map. Post 8vo. 9s.

—— SOUTH ITALY, Two Sicilies, Naples, Pompeii, Herculaneum, and Vesuvius. Map. Post 8vo. 10s.

—— KNAPSACK GUIDE—ITALY. Post 8vo. 6s.

—— SICILY, Palermo, Messina, Catania, Syracuse, Etna, and the Ruins of the Greek Temples. Map. Post 8vo. 12s.

—— PAINTING. The Italian Schools. From the German of Kugler. Edited by Sir Charles Eastlake, R.A. Woodcuts. 2 Vols. Post 8vo. 30s.

—— LIVES OF THE EARLY ITALIAN PAINTERS, and Progress of Painting in Italy—Cimabue to Bassano. By Mrs. Jameson. A New Edition. With additional Portraits. Post 8vo. In the Press.

—— —— NORWAY. Map. Post 8vo. 5s.

—— —— DENMARK, Sweden, and Norway. Maps. Post 8vo. 15s.

—— GREECE, the Ionian Islands, Albania, Thessaly, and Macedonia. Maps. Post 8vo. 15s.

—— TURKEY, Malta, Asia Minor, Constantinople, Armenia, Mesopotamia, &c. Maps. Post 8vo.

HAND-BOOK—EGYPT, Thebes, the Nile, Alexandria, Cairo, the Pyramids, Mount Sinai, &c. Map. Post 8vo. 15s.
——— SYRIA AND PALESTINE, Peninsula of Sinai, Edom, and Syrian Desert. Maps. 2 Vols. Post 8vo. 24s.
——— BOMBAY AND MADRAS. Map. 2 Vols. Post 8vo. 24s.
——— RUSSIA, POLAND, and FINLAND. Maps. Post 8vo. 12s.
——— MODERN LONDON. A Complete Guide to all the Sights and Objects of Interest in the Metropolis. Map. 16mo. 3s. 6d.
——— WESTMINSTER ABBEY. Woodcuts. 16mo. 1s.
——— KENT AND SUSSEX, Canterbury, Dover, Ramsgate, Sheerness, Rochester, Chatham, Woolwich, Brighton, Chichester, Worthing, Hastings, Lewes, Arundel, &c. Map. Post 8vo. 10s.
——— SURREY AND HANTS, Kingston, Croydon, Reigate, Guildford, Winchester, Southampton, Portsmouth, and Isle of Wight. Maps. Post 8vo. 10s.
——— WILTS, DORSET, AND SOMERSET, Salisbury, Chippenham, Weymouth, Sherborne, Wells, Bath, Bristol, Taunton, &c. Map. Post 8vo. 7s. 6d.
——— DEVON AND CORNWALL, Exeter, Ilfracombe, Linton, Sidmouth, Dawlish, Teignmouth, Plymouth, Devonport, Torquay, Launceston, Truro, Penzance, Falmouth, &c. Maps. Post 8vo. 10s.
——— BERKS, BUCKS, AND OXON, Windsor, Eton, Reading, Aylesbury, Uxbridge, Wycombe, Henley, the City and University of Oxford, and the Descent of the Thames to Maidenhead and Windsor. Map. Post 8vo. 7s. 6d.
——— GLOUCESTER, HEREFORD, AND WORCESTERSHIRE. Map. Post 8vo.
——— NORTH AND SOUTH WALES, Bangor, Carnarvon, Beaumaris, Snowdon, Conway, Menai Straits, Carmarthen, Pembroke, Tenby, Swansea, The Wye, &c. Maps. 2 Vols. Post 8vo. 12s.
——— STAFFORD, DERBY, AND LEICESTERSHIRE. Map. Post 8vo. (Just Ready.)
——— YORKSHIRE. Map. Post 8vo. (Just Ready.)
——— DURHAM AND NORTHUMBERLAND, Newcastle, Darlington, Gateshead, Bishop Auckland, Stockton, Hartlepool, Sunderland, Shields, Berwick-on-Tweed, Morpeth, Tynemouth, Coldstream, Alnwick, &c. Map. Post 8vo. 9s.
——— WESTMORELAND, CUMBERLAND, AND THE LAKES. Map. Post 8vo. 6s.
,*, MURRAY'S HANDBOOK MAP OF THE LAKES, engraved on a large scale, for the use of Pedestrians and Travellers, mounted on canvas in a case. Price 3s. 6d.
——— IRELAND — Dublin, Belfast, Donegal, Galway, Wexford, Cork, Limerick, Waterford, the Lakes of Killarney, Coast of Munster, &c. Maps. Post 8vo. 12s.
——— SOUTHERN CATHEDRALS OF ENGLAND— Winchester, Salisbury, Exeter, Wells, Chichester, Rochester, Canterbury. With 110 Illustrations. 2 Vols. Crown 8vo. 34s.
——— EASTERN CATHEDRALS OF ENGLAND— Oxford, Peterborough, Norwich, Ely, and Lincoln. With 90 Illustrations. Crown 8vo. 18s.
——— WESTERN CATHEDRALS OF ENGLAND— Bristol, Gloucester, Hereford, Worcester, and Lichfield. With 60 Illustrations. Crown 8vo. 16s.
——— THREE CHOIRS, OF GLOUCESTER, HEREFORD AND WORCESTER. Illustrations. Post 8vo. 5s. 6d.

HOME AND COLONIAL LIBRARY. A Series of Works adapted for all circles and classes of Readers, having been selected for their acknowledged interest and ability of the Authors. Post 8vo. Published at 2s. and 3s. 6d. each, and arranged under two distinctive heads as follows:—

CLASS A.
HISTORY, BIOGRAPHY, AND HISTORIC TALES.

1. SIEGE OF GIBRALTAR. By JOHN DRINKWATER. 2s.
2. THE AMBER-WITCH. By LADY DUFF GORDON. 2s.
3. CROMWELL AND BUNYAN. By ROBERT SOUTHEY. 2s.
4. LIFE OF SIR FRANCIS DRAKE. By JOHN BARROW. 2s.
5. CAMPAIGNS AT WASHINGTON. By REV. G. R. GLEIG. 2s.
6. THE FRENCH IN ALGIERS. By LADY DUFF GORDON. 2s.
7. THE FALL OF THE JESUITS. 2s.
8. LIVONIAN TALES. 2s.
9. LIFE OF CONDÉ. By LORD MAHON. 3s. 6d.
10. SALE'S BRIGADE. By REV. G. R. GLEIG. 2s.
11. THE SIEGES OF VIENNA. By LORD ELLESMERE. 2s.
12. THE WAYSIDE CROSS. By CAPT. MILMAN. 2s.
13. SKETCHES OF GERMAN LIFE. By SIR A. GORDON. 3s. 6d.
14. THE BATTLE OF WATERLOO. By REV. G. R. GLEIG. 3s. 6d.
15. AUTOBIOGRAPHY OF STEFFENS. 2s.
16. THE BRITISH POETS. By THOMAS CAMPBELL. 3s. 6d.
17. HISTORICAL ESSAYS. By LORD MAHON. 3s. 6d.
18. LIFE OF LORD CLIVE. By REV. G. R. GLEIG. 3s. 6d.
19. NORTH-WESTERN RAILWAY. By SIR F. B. HEAD. 2s.
20. LIFE OF MUNRO. By REV. G. R. GLEIG. 3s. 6d.

CLASS B.
VOYAGES, TRAVELS, AND ADVENTURES.

1. BIBLE IN SPAIN. By GEORGE BORROW. 3s. 6d.
2. GIPSIES OF SPAIN. By GEORGE BORROW. 3s. 6d.
3 & 4. JOURNALS IN INDIA. By BISHOP HEBER. 2 Vols. 7s.
5. TRAVELS IN THE HOLY LAND. By IRBY and MANGLES. 2s.
6. MOROCCO AND THE MOORS. By J. DRUMMOND HAY. 2s.
7. LETTERS FROM THE BALTIC. By A LADY. 2s.
8. NEW SOUTH WALES. By MRS. MEREDITH. 2s.
9. THE WEST INDIES. By M. G. LEWIS. 2s.
10. SKETCHES OF PERSIA. By SIR JOHN MALCOLM. 3s. 6d.
11. MEMOIRS OF FATHER RIPA. 2s.
12. 13. TYPEE AND OMOO. By HERMANN MELVILLE. 2 Vols. 7s.
14. MISSIONARY LIFE IN CANADA. By REV. J. ABBOTT. 2s.
15. LETTERS FROM MADRAS. By A LADY. 2s.
16. HIGHLAND SPORTS. By CHARLES ST. JOHN. 3s. 6d.
17. PAMPAS JOURNEYS. By SIR F. B. HEAD. 2s.
18. GATHERINGS FROM SPAIN. By RICHARD FORD. 3s. 6d.
19. THE RIVER AMAZON. By W. H. EDWARDS. 2s.
20. MANNERS & CUSTOMS OF INDIA. By REV. C. ACLAND. 2s.
21. ADVENTURES IN MEXICO. By G. F. RUXTON. 3s. 6d.
22. PORTUGAL AND GALLICIA. By LORD CARNARVON. 3s. 6d.
23. BUSH LIFE IN AUSTRALIA. By REV. H. W. HAYGARTH. 2s.
24. THE LIBYAN DESERT. By BAYLE ST. JOHN. 2s.
25. SIERRA LEONE. By A LADY. 3s. 6d.

⁎ Each work may be had separately.

HANDBOOK OF FAMILIAR QUOTATIONS. From English Authors. Third Edition. Fcap. 8vo. 6s.

HESSEY (Rev. Dr.). Sunday—Its Origin, History, and Present Obligations. Being the Bampton Lectures for 1860. Second Edition, 8vo. 16s. Or Third and Popular Edition. Post 8vo. 9s.

HICKMAN'S (Wm.) Treatise on the Law and Practice of Naval Courts-Martial. 8vo. 10s. 6d.

HILLARD'S (G. S.) Six Months in Italy. 2 Vols. Post 8vo. 16s.

HOLLWAY'S (J. G.) Month in Norway. Fcap. 8vo. 2s.

HONEY BEE (The). An Essay. By Rev. Thomas James. Reprinted from the "Quarterly Review." Fcap. 8vo. 1s.

HOOK'S (Dean) Church Dictionary. *Ninth Edition.* 8vo. 16s.

——— (Theodore) Life. By J. G. Lockhart. Reprinted from the "Quarterly Review." Fcap. 8vo. 1s.

HOPE'S (A. J. Beresford) English Cathedral of the Nineteenth Century. With Illustrations. 8vo. 12s.

HORACE (Works of). Edited by Dean Milman. With Woodcuts. Crown 8vo.

——— (Life of). By Dean Milman. Woodcuts, and coloured Borders. 8vo. 9s.

HOUGHTON'S (Lord) Poetical Works. Fcap. 8vo. 6s.

HUME'S (The Student's) History of England, from the Invasion of Julius Cæsar to the Revolution of 1688. Corrected and continued to 1858. Edited by Dr. Wm. Smith. Woodcuts. Post 8vo. 7s. 6d.

HUTCHINSON (Gen.) on the most expeditious, certain, and easy Method of Dog-Breaking. *Fourth Edition.* Enlarged and revised, with 40 Illustrations. Crown 8vo. 15s.

HUTTON'S (H. E.) Principia Græca; an Introduction to the Study of Greek. Comprehending Grammar, Delectus, and Exercise-book, with Vocabularies. *Third Edition.* 12mo. 3s. 6d.

IRBY AND MANGLES' Travels in Egypt, Nubia, Syria, and the Holy Land. Post 8vo. 2s.

JAMES' (Rev. Thomas) Fables of Æsop. A New Translation, with Historical Preface. With 100 Woodcuts by Tenniel and Wolf. Forty-eighth Thousand. Post 8vo. 2s. 6d.

JAMESON'S (Mrs.) Lives of the Early Italian Painters—and the Progress of Painting in Italy—Cimabue to Bassano. New Edition. With Woodcuts. Post 8vo.

JESSE'S (Edward) Gleanings in Natural History. *Eighth Edition.* Fcp. 8vo. 6s.

JOHNS' (Rev. B. G.) Blind People; their Works and Ways. With Sketches of the Lives of some famous blind Men. With Illustrations. Post 8vo.

JOHNSON'S (Dr. Samuel) Life. By James Boswell. Including the Tour to the Hebrides. Edited by Mr. Croker. Portraits. Royal 8vo. 10s.

——— Lives of the most eminent English Poets. Edited by Peter Cunningham. 3 vols. 8vo. 22s. 6d.

KEN'S (Bishop) Life. By a LAYMAN, Author of "Life of the Messiah." Second Edition. Portrait. 2 Vols. 8vo. 18s.

——— Exposition of the Apostles' Creed. Extracted from his "Practice of Divine Love." Fcap. 1s. 6d.

——— Approach to the Holy Altar. Extracted from his "Manual of Prayer" and "Practice of Divine Love." Fcap. 8vo. 1s. 6d.

KENNEDY'S (GENERAL SIR J. SHAW) Notes on the Battle of Waterloo. With a Memoir of his Life and Services, and a Plan for the Defence of Canada. With Map and Plans. 8vo. 7s. 6d.

KING'S (REV. C. W.) Antique Gems; their Origin, Use, and Value, as Interpreters of Ancient History, and as Illustrative of Ancient Art. Second Edition. Illustrations. 8vo. 21s.

KING EDWARD VIth's Latin Grammar; or, an Introduction to the Latin Tongue, for the Use of Schools. Seventeenth Edition. 12mo. 3s. 6d.

——— First Latin Book; or, the Accidence, Syntax, and Prosody, with an English Translation for the Use of Junior Classes. Fifth Edition. 12mo. 2s. 6d.

KIRK'S (J. FOSTER) History of Charles the Bold, Duke of Burgundy. Portrait. 2 Vols. 8vo. 80s.

KERR'S (ROBERT) GENTLEMAN'S HOUSE; OR, HOW TO PLAN ENGLISH RESIDENCES, FROM THE PARSONAGE TO THE PALACE. With Tables of Accommodation and Cost, and a Series of Selected Views and Plans. Second Edition. 8vo. 24s.

——— Ancient Lights; a Book for Architects, Surveyors, Lawyers, and Landlords. 8vo. 5s. 6d.

KING GEORGE THE THIRD'S CORRESPONDENCE WITH LORD NORTH, 1769-82. Edited, with Notes and Introduction, by W. BODHAM DONNE. 2 Vols. 8vo. 32s.

KUGLER'S Italian Schools of Painting. Edited, with Notes, by SIR CHARLES EASTLAKE. Third Edition. Woodcuts. 2 Vols. Post 8vo. 30s.

——— German, Dutch, and Flemish Schools of Painting. Edited, with Notes, by DR. WAAGEN. Second Edition. Woodcuts. 2 Vols. Post 8vo. 24s.

LAYARD'S (A. H.) Nineveh and Its Remains. Being a Narrative of Researches and Discoveries amidst the Ruins of Assyria. With an Account of the Chaldean Christians of Kurdistan; the Yezidis, or Devil-worshippers; and an Enquiry into the Manners and Arts of the Ancient Assyrians. Sixth Edition. Plates and Woodcuts. 2 Vols. 8vo. 36s.

⁎ A POPULAR EDITION of the above Work. With Illustrations. Post 8vo. 7s. 6d.

——— Nineveh and Babylon; being the Narrative of a Second Expedition to Assyria. Plates. 8vo. 21s. Or Fine Paper, 2 Vols. 8vo. 30s.

⁎ A POPULAR EDITION of the above Work. With Illustrations. Post 8vo. 7s. 6d.

LESLIE'S (C. R.) Handbook for Young Painters. With Illustrations. Post 8vo. 10s. 6d.

——— Autobiographical Recollections, with Selections from his Correspondence. Edited by TOM TAYLOR. Portrait. 2 Vols. Post 8vo. 18s.

LESLIE'S (C. R.) Life of Sir Joshua Reynolds. With an Account of his Works, and a Sketch of his Contemporaries. By C. R. Leslie and Tom Taylor. Portraits and Illustrations. 2 Vols. 8vo. 42s.

LETTERS FROM THE BALTIC. By a Lady. Post 8vo. 2s.
——— Madras. By a Lady. Post 8vo. 2s.
——— Sierra Leone. By a Lady. Post 8vo. 3s. 6d.

LEWIS (Sir G. C.) Essay on the Government of Dependencies. 8vo. 12s.
——— Glossary of Provincial Words used in Herefordshire and some of the adjoining Counties. 12mo. 4s. 6d.
——— (M. G.) Journal of a Residence among the Negroes in the West Indies. Post 8vo. 2s.

LIDDELL'S (Dean) History of Rome. From the Earliest Times to the Establishment of the Empire. With the History of Literature and Art. 2 Vols. 8vo. 32s.
——— Student's History of Rome, abridged from the above Work. With Woodcuts. Post 8vo. 7s. 6d.

LINDSAY'S (Lord) Lives of the Lindsays; or, a Memoir of the Houses of Crawford and Balcarras. With Extracts from Official Papers and Personal Narratives. Second Edition. 3 Vols. 8vo. 24s.

LISPINGS from LOW LATITUDES; or, the Journal of the Hon. Impulsia Gushington. Edited by Lord Dufferin. With 24 Plates. 4to. 21s.

LITTLE ARTHUR'S HISTORY OF ENGLAND. By Lady Callcott. New Edition, continued to 1862. With 20 Woodcuts. Fcap. 8vo. 2s. 6d.

LIVINGSTONE'S (Dr.) Popular Account of his Missionary Travels in South Africa. Illustrations. Post 8vo. 6s.
——— Narrative of an Expedition to the Zambesi and its Tributaries; and of the Discovery of Lakes Shirwa and Nyassa, 1858-64. By David and Charles Livingstone. Map and Illustrations. 8vo. 21s.

LIVONIAN TALES. By the Author of "Letters from the Baltic." Post 8vo. 2s.

LOCKHART'S (J. G.) Ancient Spanish Ballads. Historical and Romantic. Translated, with Notes. New Edition. Post 8vo. 2s. 6d.

LONDON (OLD). A series of Essays by Dean Stanley; A. J. Beresford Hope, M.P.; G. Scott, R.A.; E. Wetherscott, R.A.; E. Foss, F.S.A.; G. T. Clark; Joseph Burtt; Rev. J. R. Green; and G. Scharf, F.S.A. 8vo.

LONDON'S (Bishop of) Dangers and Safeguards of Modern Theology. Containing Suggestions to the Theological Student under present difficulties. Second Edition. 8vo. 9s.

LOUDON'S (Mrs.) Instructions in Gardening. With Directions and Calendar of Operations for Every Month. Eighth Edition. Woodcuts. Fcap. 8vo. 5s.

LUCAS' (Samuel) Secularia; or, Surveys on the Main Stream of History. 8vo. 12s.

LUCKNOW: a Lady's Diary of the Siege. Fcap. 8vo. 4s. 6d.

LYELL'S (Sir Charles) Elements of Geology; or, the Ancient Changes of the Earth and its Inhabitants considered as Illustrative of Geology. Sixth Edition. Woodcuts. 8vo. 18s.

—— Principles of Geology; or, the Ancient Changes of the Earth and its Inhabitants considered as Illustrative of Geology. Tenth Edition. With Illustrations. Vol. I. 8vo. 18s. (To be completed in 2 Vols.)

—— Geological Evidences of the Antiquity of Man. Third Edition. Illustrations, 8vo. 14s.

LYTTELTON'S (Lord) Ephemera. Post 8vo. 10s. 6d.

LYTTON'S (Lord) Poems. New Edition. Post 8vo. 10s. 6d.

—— Lost Tales of Miletus. Second Edition. Post 8vo. 7s. 6d.

MACPHERSON'S (Major S. C.) Memorials of Service in India, while Political Agent at Gwalior during the Mutiny, and formerly employed in the Suppression of Human Sacrifice in Orissa. Edited by his Brother. With Portrait and Illustrations. 8vo. 12s.

MAHON'S (Lord) History of England, from the Peace of Utrecht to the Peace of Versailles, 1713—83. Library Edition. 7 Vols. 8vo. 98s. Popular Edition, 7 Vols. Post 8vo. 35s.

—— Life of Condé, surnamed the Great. Post 8vo. 3s. 6d.

—— Life of Belisarius. Second Edition. Post 8vo. 10s. 6d.

—— Life of William Pitt, with Extracts from his MS. Papers. Third and cheaper Edition. Portraits. 4 Vols. Post 8vo. 24s.

—— Miscellanies. Second Edition. Post 8vo. 5s. 6d.

—— "Forty-Five;" a Narrative of the Rebellion in Scotland. Post 8vo. 3s.

—— History of British India from its Origin till the Peace of 1783. Post 8vo. 3s. 6d.

—— Spain under Charles the Second; 1690 to 1700. Second Edition. Post 8vo. 3s. 6d.

—— Historical and Critical Essays. Post 8vo. 3s. 6d.

—— Story of Joan of Arc. Fcap. 8vo. 1s.

M'CLINTOCK'S (Capt. Sir F. L.) Narrative of the Discovery of the Fate of Sir John Franklin and his Companions in the Arctic Seas. Twelfth Thousand. Illustrations. 8vo. 16s.

M'CULLOCH'S (J. R.) Collected Edition of Ricardo's Political Works. With Notes and Memoir. Second Edition. 8vo. 16s.

MacDOUGALL'S (Col.) Modern Warfare as Influenced by Modern Artillery. With Plans. Post 8vo. 12s.

MAINE (H. Sumner) On Ancient Law: its Connection with the Early History of Society, and its Relation to Modern Ideas. Third Edition. 8vo. 12s.

MALCOLM'S (Sir John) Sketches of Persia. Post 8vo. 3s. 6d.

MANSEL (Rev. H. L.) Limits of Religious Thought Examined. Being the Bampton Lectures for 1858. Fifth Edition. Post 8vo.

MANSFIELD (Sir William) On the Introduction of a Gold Currency into India: a Contribution to the Literature of Political Economy. 8vo. 3s. 6d.

MANTELL'S (Gideon A.) Thoughts on Animalcules; or, the Invisible World, as revealed by the Microscope. Second Edition. Plates. 16mo. 6s.

MANUAL OF SCIENTIFIC ENQUIRY, Prepared for the Use of Officers and Travellers. By various Writers. Edited by Sir J. F. Herschel and Rev. R. Main. Third Edition. Maps. Post 8vo. 9s. (Published by order of the Lords of the Admiralty.)

MARKHAM'S (Mrs.) History of England. From the First Invasion by the Romans, down to recent Times. New and Cheaper Edition, continued to 1861. Woodcuts. 12mo. 6s.

——— History of France. From the Conquest by the Gauls, to Recent Times. New and Cheaper Edition, continued to 1856. Woodcuts. 12mo. 6s.

——— History of Germany. From the Invasion by Marius, to recent Times. New and Cheaper Edition. Woodcuts. 12mo. 4s.

——— (Clements, R.) Travels in Peru and India, for the purpose of collecting Cinchona Plants, and introducing Bark into India. Maps and Illustrations. 8vo. 16s.

MARRYATS (Joseph) History of Modern and Medieval Pottery and Porcelain. With a Description of the Manufacture. Second Edition. Plates and Woodcuts. 8vo. 31s. 6d.

——— (Horace) Jutland, the Danish Isles, and Copenhagen. Illustrations. 2 Vols. Post 8vo. 24s.

——— Sweden and Isle of Gothland. Illustrations. 2 Vols. Post 8vo. 28s.

MATTHIÆ'S (Augustus) Greek Grammar for Schools, abridged from the Larger Grammar. By Blomfield. Ninth Edition. Revised by Edwards. 12mo. 3s.

MAUREL'S (Jules) Essay on the Character, Actions, and Writings of the Duke of Wellington. Second Edition. Fcap. 8vo. 1s. 6d.

MAYNE'S (Capt.) Four Years in British Columbia and Vancouver Island. Its Forests, Rivers, Coasts, and Gold Fields, and Resources for Colonisation. Illustrations. 8vo. 16s.

MELVILLE'S (Herman) Typee and Omoo; or, Adventures amongst the Marquesas and South Sea Islands. 2 Vols. Post 8vo. 7s.

MILLS' (Rev. John) Three Months' Residence at Nablus, with an Account of the Modern Samaritans. Illustrations. Post 8vo. 10s. 6d.

MILMAN'S (Dean) Historical Works. 15 Vols. Post 8vo. 6s. each. Containing,
1. HISTORY OF THE JEWS. 3 Vols.
2. HISTORY OF EARLY CHRISTIANITY. 3 Vols.
3. HISTORY OF LATIN CHRISTIANITY. 9 Vols.

——— Character and Conduct of the Apostles considered as an Evidence of Christianity. 8vo. 10s. 6d.

——— Translations from the Agamemnon of Æschylus and Bacchanals of Euripides; with Passages from the Lyric and Latin Poets of Greece. With Illustrations, crown 8vo. 12s.

——— Life and Works of Horace. With 300 Woodcuts. Vols. Crown 8vo. 30s.

——— Poetical Works. Plates. 3 Vols. Fcap. 8vo. 18s.

——— Fall of Jerusalem. Fcap. 8vo. 1s.

——— (Capt. E. A.) Wayside Cross. A Tale of the Carlist War. Post 8vo. 2s.

MEREDITH'S (Mrs. Charles) Notes and Sketches of New South Wales. Post 8vo. 2s.

MESSIAH (THE): A Narrative of the Life, Travels, Death, Resurrection, and Ascension of our Blessed Lord. By a Layman, Author of the "Life of Bishop Ken." Map. 8vo. 18s.

MICHIE'S (Alexander) Siberian Overland Route from Peking to Petersburg, through the Deserts and Steppes of Mongolia, Tartary, &c. Maps and Illustrations. 8vo. 16s.

MODERN DOMESTIC COOKERY. Founded on Principles of Economy and Practical Knowledge and adapted for Private Families. New Edition. Woodcuts. Fcap. 8vo. 5s.

MOORE'S (Thomas) Life and Letters of Lord Byron. Plates. 6 Vols. Fcap. 8vo. 18s.

—— Life and Letters of Lord Byron. Portraits. Royal 8vo. 9s.

MOTLEY'S (J. L.) History of the United Netherlands: from the Death of William the Silent to the Twelve Years' Truce, 1609. Embracing the English-Dutch struggle against Spain; and a detailed Account of the Spanish Armada. Portraits. 2 Vols. 8vo. 30s.
*** Vols. 3 and 4. completing the work, are in the Press.

MOUHOT'S (Henri) Siam, Cambojia, and Lao; a Narrative of Travels and Discoveries. Illustrations. 2 vols. 8vo. 32s.

MOZLEY'S (Rev. J. B.) Treatise on Predestination. 8vo. 14s.

—— Primitive Doctrine of Baptismal Regeneration. 8vo. 7s. 6d.

MUNDY'S (General) Pen and Pencil Sketches in India. Third Edition. Plates. Post 8vo. 7s. 6d.

—— (Admiral) Account of the Italian Revolution, with Notices of Garibaldi, Francis II., and Victor Emmanuel. Post 8vo. 12s.

MUNRO'S (General Sir Thomas) Life and Letters. By the Rev. G. R. Gleig. Post 8vo. 3s. 6d.

MURCHISON'S (Sir Roderick) Russia in Europe and the Ural Mountains. With Coloured Maps, Plates, Sections, &c. 2 Vols. Royal 4to. 5l. 5s.

—— Siluria; or, a History of the Oldest Rocks containing Organic Remains. Fourth Edition. Map and Plates. 8vo.
(In the Press.)

MURRAY'S RAILWAY READING. Containing:—

Wellington. By Lord Ellesmere. 6d.
Nimrod on the Chase. 1s.
Essays from "The Times." 2 Vols. 8s.
Music and Dress. 1s.
Layard's Account of Nineveh. 5s.
Milman's Fall of Jerusalem. 1s.
Mahon's "Forty-Five." 3s.
Life of Theodore Hook. 1s.
Deeds of Naval Daring. 3s. 6d.
The Honey Bee. 1s.
James' Æsop's Fables. 2s. 6d.
Nimrod on the Turf. 1s. 6d.
Art of Dining. 1s. 6d.

Bishop's Literary Essays. 2s.
Mahon's Joan of Arc. 1s.
Head's Emigrant. 2s. 6d.
Nimrod on the Road. 1s.
Croker on the Guillotine. 1s.
Holway's Norway. 2s.
Mahon's Wellington. 1s. 6d.
Campbell's Life of Bacon. 2s. 6d.
The Flower Garden. 1s.
Lockhart's Spanish Ballads. 2s. 6d.
Taylor's Notes from Life. 2s.
Rejected Addresses. 1s.
Penn's Hints on Angling. 1s.

MUSIC AND DRESS. By a Lady. Reprinted from the "Quarterly Review." Fcap. 8vo. 1s.

NAPIER'S (Sir Chas.) Life; chiefly derived from his Journals and Letters. By Sir W. Napier. Second Edition. Portraits. 4 Vols. Post 8vo. 48s.

—— (Sir Wm.) Life and Letters. Edited by H. A. Bruce, M.P. Portraits. 2 Vols. Crown 8vo. 28s.

—— English Battles and Sieges of the Peninsular War. Fourth Edition. Portrait. Post 8vo. 9s.

NAUTICAL ALMANACK. Royal 8vo. 2s. 6d. (By Authority.)

NAVY LIST. (Published Quarterly, by Authority.) 16mo. 2s. 6d.

NEW TESTAMENT (THE) Illustrated by a Plain Explanatory Commentary, and authentic Views of Sacred Places, from Sketches and Photographs. Edited by ARCHDEACON CHURTON, M.A., and Rev. BASIL JONES, M.A. With 110 Illustrations, 2 Vols. Crown 8vo. 30s. cloth; 52s. 6d. calf; 63s. morocco.

NICHOLLS' (SIR GEORGE) History of the English, Irish and Scotch Poor Laws. 4 Vols. 8vo.

—— (Rev. H. G.) Historical Account of the Forest of Dean. Woodcuts, &c. Post 8vo. 10s. 6d.

NICOLAS' (SIR HARRIS) Historic Peerage of England. Exhibiting the Origin, Descent, and Present state of every Title of Peerage which has existed in this Country since the Conquest. By WILLIAM COURTHOPE. 8vo. 30s.

NIMROD On the Chace—The Turf—and The Road. Reprinted from the "Quarterly Review." Woodcuts. Fcap. 8vo. 5s. 6d.

OXENHAM'S (REV. W.) English Notes for Latin Elegiacs; designed for early Proficients in the Art of Latin Versification, with Prefatory Rules of Composition in Elegiac Metre. Fourth Edition. 12mo. 3s. 6d.

OXFORD'S (BISHOP OF) Short Life of William Wilberforce. Condensed and Revised from the larger Biography. 8vo. (In the Press.)

PARIS' (Dr.) Philosophy in Sport made Science in Earnest; or, the First Principles of Natural Philosophy inculcated by aid of the Toys and Sports of Youth. Ninth Edition. Woodcuts. Post 8vo. 7s. 6d.

PEEL'S (SIR ROBERT) Memoirs. Edited by EARL STANHOPE and Right Hon. E. CARDWELL. 2 Vols. Post 8vo. 7s. 6d. each.

PENN'S (RICHARD) Maxims and Hints for an Angler and Chessplayer. New Edition. Woodcuts. Fcap. 8vo. 1s.

PENROSE'S (F. C.) Principles of Athenian Architecture, and the Optical Refinements exhibited in the Construction of the Ancient Buildings at Athens, from a Survey. With 40 Plates. Folio. 5l. 5s.

PERCY'S (JOHN, M.D.) Metallurgy of Iron and Steel; or, the Art of Extracting Metals from their Ores and adapting them to various purposes of Manufacture. Illustrations. 8vo. 42s.

—— Metallurgy of Lead, Silver, Gold, Platinum, Tin, Nickel, Cobalt, Antimony, Bismuth, Arsenic, and other Metals. 8vo. (In the Press.)

PHILLIPP (C. S. M.) On Jurisprudence. 8vo. 12s.

PHILLIPS' (JOHN) Memoirs of William Smith, the Geologist. Portrait. 8vo. 7s. 6d.

—— Geology of Yorkshire, The Coast, and Limestone District. Plates. 4to. Part I., 20s.—Part II., 30s.

—— Rivers, Mountains, and Sea Coast of Yorkshire. With Essays on the Climate, Scenery, and Ancient Inhabitants. Second Edition. Plates. 8vo. 15s.

PHILPOTTS' (BISHOP) Letters to the late Charles Butler, on his "Book of the Roman Catholic Church." New Edition. Post 8vo. 6s.

POPE'S (ALEXANDER) Life and Works. *A New Edition.* Containing nearly 500 unpublished Letters. Edited, with a New Life, Introductions and Notes, by REV. WHITWELL ELWIN. Portraits. 8vo. *(In the Press.)*

PORTER'S (REV. J. L.) Five Years in Damascus. With Travels to Palmyra, Lebanon and other Scripture Sites. Map and Woodcuts. 2 Vols. Post 8vo. 21s.

—— Handbook for Syria and Palestine: including an Account of the Geography, History, Antiquities, and Inhabitants of those Countries, the Peninsula of Sinai, Edom, and the Syrian Desert. Maps. 2 Vols. Post 8vo. 24s.

PRAYER-BOOK (Illustrated), with 1000 Illustrations of Borders, Initials, Vignettes, &c. Edited, with Notes, by REV. THOS. JAMES. Medium 8vo. 18s. cloth; 31s. 6d. calf; 36s. morocco.

PUSS IN BOOTS. With 12 Illustrations. By OTTO SPECKTER. 16mo. 1s. 6d. or Coloured, 2s. 6d.

QUARTERLY REVIEW (THE). 8vo. 6s.

RAMBLES among the Turkomans and Bedaweens of the Syrian Deserts. *Second Edition.* Post 8vo. 10s. 6d.

RANKE'S Ecclesiastical and Political History of the Popes of Rome during the 16th and 17th Centuries. Translated from the German by SARAH AUSTIN. 3 Vols. 8vo. 30s.

RAWLINSON'S (REV. GEORGE) Herodotus. A New English Version. Edited with Notes and Essays. Assisted by SIR HENRY RAWLINSON and SIR J. G. WILKINSON. *Second Edition.* Maps and Woodcuts. 4 Vols. 8vo. 48s.

—— Historical Evidences of the truth of the Scripture Records stated anew. *Second Edition.* 8vo. 14s.

—— Five Great Monarchies of the Ancient World, Chaldæa, Assyria, Media, Babylonia, and Persia. Illustrations. 4 Vols. 8vo. 16s. each.

REJECTED ADDRESSES (THE). By JAMES AND HORACE SMITH. Fcap. 8vo. 1s.

RENNIE'S (D. F.) British Arms in Peking, 1860; Kagosima, 1862. Post 8vo. 12s.

—— Peking and the Pekingese: Being a Narrative of the First Year of the British Embassy in China. Illustrations. 2 Vols. Post 8vo. 24s.

—— Story of Bhotan and the Dooar War; Including Sketches of a Residence in the Himalayas and Visit to Bhotan in 1865. Map and Woodcut. Post 8vo. 18s.

REYNOLDS' (SIR JOSHUA) Life and Times. Commenced by C. R. LESLIE, R.A., continued and concluded by TOM TAYLOR. Portraits and Illustrations. 2 Vols. 8vo. 42s.

—— Descriptive Catalogue of his Works. With Notices of their present owners and localities. By TOM TAYLOR and CHARLES W. FRANKS. With Illustrations. Fcap. 4to. *(In the Press.)*

RICARDO'S (DAVID) Political Works. With a Notice of his Life and Writings. By J. R. M'CULLOCH. *New Edition.* 8vo. 16s.

RIPA'S (FATHER) Memoirs during Thirteen Years' Residence at the Court of Peking. From the Italian. Post 8vo. 2s.

ROBERTSON'S (Canon) History of the Christian Church, from the Apostolic Age to the Death of Boniface VIII, a.d. 1123—1304. 3 Vols. 8vo.

ROBINSON'S (Rev. Dr.) Later Biblical Researches in the Holy Land. Being a Journal of Travels in 1852. Maps. 8vo. 15s.

——— Physical Geography of the Holy Land. Post 8vo. 10s. 6d.

ROME (The Student's History of). From the Earliest Times to the Establishment of the Empire. By Dean Liddell. Woodcuts. Post 8vo. 7s. 6d.

——— (A Smaller History of, for Young Persons). By Wm. Smith, LL.D. Woodcuts. 16mo. 3s. 6d.

ROWLAND'S (David) Manual of the English Constitution; Its Rise, Growth, and Present State. Post 8vo. 10s. 6d.

——— Laws of Nature the Foundation of Morals. Post 8vo. 6s.

RUNDELL'S (Mrs.) Domestic Cookery, adapted for Private Families. New Edition. Woodcuts. Fcap. 8vo. 5s.

RUSSELL'S (J. Rutherford) History of the Heroes of Medicine. Portraits. 8vo. 14s.

RUXTON'S (George F.) Travels in Mexico; with Adventures among the Wild Tribes and Animals of the Prairies and Rocky Mountains. Post 8vo. 3s. 6d.

SALE'S (Sir Robert) Brigade in Affghanistan. With an Account of the Defence of Jellalabad. By Rev. G. R. Gleig. Post 8vo. 2s.

SALLESBURY'S (Edward) The Children of the Lake. A Poem. Fcap. 8vo. 4s. 6d.

SANDWITH'S (Humphry) Siege of Kars. Post 8vo. 3s. 6d.

SCOTT'S (G. Gilbert) Secular and Domestic Architecture, Present and Future. Second Edition. 8vo. 9s.

——— (Rev. Robert, D.D., Master of Balliol) Sermons, preached before the University of Oxford. Post 8vo. 6s. 6d.

SCROPE'S (G. P.) Geology and Extinct Volcanoes of Central France. Second Edition. Illustrations. Medium 8vo. 30s.

SHAW'S (T. B.) Student's Manual of English Literature. Edited, with Notes and Illustrations, by Dr. Wm. Smith. Post 8vo. 7s. 6d.

——— Specimens of English Literature. Selected from the Chief English Writers. Edited by Wm. Smith, LL.D. Post 8vo. 7s. 6d.

SHIRLEY (Evelyn P.) on Deer and Deer Parks, or some Account of English Parks, with Notes on the Management of Deer. Illustrations. 8vo.

SIERRA LEONE; Described in Letters to Friends at Home. By A Lady. Post 8vo. 3s. 6d.

SIMMONS (Capt. T. F.) on the Constitution and Practice of Courts-Martial; with a Summary of the Law of Evidence as connected therewith, and some Notice of the Criminal Law of England, with reference to the Trial of Civil Offences. 5th Edition. 8vo. 14s.

SOUTH'S (John F.) Household Surgery; or, Hints on Emergencies. Seventeenth Thousand. Woodcuts. Fcp. 8vo. 4s. 6d.

SMILES (Samuel) Lives of British Engineers; from the Earliest Period to the Death of Robert Stephenson; with an account of their Principal Works, and a History of Inland Communication in Britain. Portraits and Illustrations. 3 Vols. 8vo. 63s.

—— Lives of Boulton and Watt. Comprising a History of the Invention and Introduction of the Steam Engine. With Portraits and 70 Illustrations, 8vo. 21s. Forming the 4th and concluding volume of "Lives of the Engineers."

—— The Huguenots: their Settlements in England. Illustrations. 8vo.

—— Story of George Stephenson's Life, including a Memoir of Robert Stephenson. With Portraits and 70 Woodcuts. Post 8vo. 6s.

James Brindley and the Early Engineers. With Portrait and 50 Woodcuts. Post 8vo. 6s.

—— Self-Help. With Illustrations of Character and Conduct. Post 8vo. 6s.

—— Translated into French as a Reading-Book for Schools. Post 8vo. 5s.

Industrial Biography: Iron-Workers and Tool Makers. A companion volume to "Self-Help." Post 8vo. 6s.

—— Workmen's Earnings—Savings—and Strikes. Fcap. 8vo. 1s. 6d.

SOMERVILLE'S (Mary) Physical Geography. *Fifth Edition.* Portrait. Post 8vo. 9s.

—— Connexion of the Physical Sciences. *Ninth Edition.* Woodcuts. Post 8vo. 9s.

—— On Molecular and Microscopic Science. Illustrations. 2 Vols. Post 8vo. (*In the Press.*)

STANLEY'S (Dean) Sinai and Palestine, in Connexion with their History. Map. 8vo. 14s.

—— Bible in the Holy Land. Woodcuts. Fcap. 8vo. 2s. 6d.

—— St. Paul's Epistles to the Corinthians. 8vo. 18s.

—— History of the Eastern Church. Plans. 8vo. 12s.

—— Jewish Church. First and Second Series. 8vo. 16s. each.

—— Historical Memorials of Canterbury. Woodcuts. Post 8vo. 7s. 6d.

—— Memorials of Westminster Abbey. 8vo.

—— Sermons in the East, with Notices of the Places Visited. 8vo. 9s.

—— Sermons on Evangelical and Apostolical Teaching. Post 8vo. 7s. 6d.

—— Addresses and Charges of Bishop Stanley. With Memoir. 8vo. 10s. 6d.

SOUTHEY'S (Robert) Book of the Church. *Seventh Edition.* Post 8vo. 7s. 6d.

—— Lives of Bunyan and Cromwell. Post 8vo. 2s.

SPECKTER'S (Otto) Puss in Boots. With 12 Woodcuts. Square 12mo. 1s. 6d. plain, or 2s. 6d. coloured.

SMITH'S (Dr. Wm.) Dictionary of the Bible; its Antiquities, Biography, Geography, and Natural History. Illustrations. 3 Vols. 8vo. 105s.
———— Concise Bible Dictionary, for Families and Students. Illustrations. Medium 8vo. 21s.
———— Smaller Bible Dictionary, for Schools and Young Persons. Illustrations. Post 8vo. 7s. 6d.
———— Dictionary of Christian Antiquities: from the Times of the Apostles to the Age of Charlemagne. Illustrations. Medium. 8vo. (In preparation.)
———— Biblical and Classical Atlas. Small follo. (In preparation.)
———— Dictionary of Greek and Roman Antiquities. Woodcuts. 8vo. 42s.
———— Smaller Dictionary of Greek and Roman Antiquities, compiled from the above Work. Woodcuts. Crown 8vo. 7s. 6d.
———— Dictionary of Greek and Roman Biography and Mythology. Woodcuts. 3 Vols. 8vo. 5l. 15s. 6d.
———— Greek and Roman Geography. Woodcuts. 2 Vols. 8vo. 80s.
———— Classical Dictionary for Schools, compiled from the above works. With 750 Woodcuts. 8vo. 18s.
———— Smaller Classical Dictionary, abridged from the above Work. Woodcuts. Crown 8vo. 7s. 6d.
———— Complete Latin-English Dictionary for Schools. With Tables of the Roman Calendar, Measures, Weights, and Money. 8vo. 21s.
———— Smaller Latin-English Dictionary, abridged from the above Work. 12mo. 7s. 6d.
———— Latin-English Vocabulary; for Phædrus, Cornelius Nepos, and Cæsar. 2nd Edition. 12mo. 3s. 6d.
———— Copious English-Latin Dictionary, compiled from original sources. 8vo. and 12mo. (In the Press.)
———— Smaller Classical Mythology for Schools. With Translations from the Ancient Poets. With Illustrations. 12mo. 3s. 6d.
———— Principia Latina—Part I. A Grammar, Delectus, and Exercise Book, with Vocabularies. 6th Edition. 12mo. 3s. 6d.
———— — Part II. A Reading-book of Mythology, Geography, Roman Antiquities, and History. With Notes and Dictionary. 3rd Edition. 12mo. 3s. 6d.
———— Part III. A Latin Poetry Book. Hexameters and Pentameters; Eclog. Ovidianæ; Latin Prosody, &c. 2nd Edition. 12mo. 3s. 6d.
———— Part IV. Latin Prose Composition. Rules of Syntax, with Examples, Explanations of Synonyms, and Exercises on the Syntax. Second Edition. 12mo. 3s. 6d.
———— Part V. Short Tales and Anecdotes for Translation into Latin. 12mo. 3s.
———— Student's Greek Grammar for the Higher Forms. By Professor Curtius. Post 8vo. 6s.
———— Smaller Greek Grammar, abridged from the above Work. 12mo. 3s. 6d.
———— Student's Latin Grammar for the Higher Forms. Post 8vo. 6s.
———— Smaller Latin Grammar, abridged from the above Work. 12mo. 3s. 6d.

LIST OF WORKS

STANHOPE'S (Earl) History of England, from the Peace of Utrecht to the Peace of Versailles, 1713-83. Library Edition. 7 vols. 8vo. 93s. Or Popular Edition, 7 Vols. Post 8vo. 5s. each.

———— History of British India, from its Origin till the Peace of 1783. Post 8vo. 3s. 6d.

———— "Forty-Five;" a Narrative of the Rebellion in Scotland. Post 8vo. 3s.

———— Spain under Charles the Second. Post 8vo. 6s. 6d.

———— Historical and Critical Essays. Post 8vo. 3s. 6d.

———— Life of William Pitt. With Extracts from his MS. Papers. Third and cheaper Edition. Portraits. 4 Vols. Post 8vo. 24s.

———— Miscellanies. Second Edition. Post 8vo. 5s. 6d.

———— Life of Belisarius. Post 8vo. 10s. 6d.

———— Life of Condé. Post 8vo. 3s. 6d.

STUDENT'S HUME. A History of England from the Invasion of Julius Cæsar to the Revolution of 1688. By David Hume. Corrected and continued to 1858. Woodcuts. Post 8vo. 7s. 6d. (Questions on, 2s.)
** A Smaller History of England. 16mo. 3s. 6d.

———— HISTORY OF FRANCE; from the Earliest Times to the Establishment of the Second Empire, 1852. By W. H. Pearson, M.A. Woodcuts. Post 8vo. 7s. 6d.

———— HISTORY OF GREECE; from the Earliest Times to the Roman Conquest. With the History of Literature and Art. By Wm. Smith, LL.D. Woodcuts. Crown 8vo. 7s. 6d. (Questions on, 2s.)
** A Smaller History of Greece. 16mo. 3s. 6d.

———— HISTORY OF ROME; from the Earliest Times to the Establishment of the Empire. With the History of Literature and Art. By Dean Liddell. Woodcuts. Crown 8vo. 7s. 6d.
** A Smaller History of Rome. 16mo. 3s. 6d.

———— GIBBON; an Epitome of the Decline and Fall of the Roman Empire. Incorporating the Researches of Recent Commentators. Woodcuts. Post 8vo. 7s. 6d.

———— MANUAL OF ANCIENT GEOGRAPHY. By Rev. W. L. Bevan, M.A. Woodcuts. Post 8vo. 7s. 6d.

———— MODERN GEOGRAPHY. By Rev. W. L. Bevan. Woodcuts. Post 8vo. (In the Press.)

———— OLD TESTAMENT HISTORY. Maps and Woodcuts. Post 8vo. 7s. 6d. each.

———— NEW TESTAMENT HISTORY. Maps and Woodcuts. Post 8vo. 7s. 6d.

———— MORAL PHILOSOPHY. By W. Fleming, D.D. Post 8vo. 7s. 6d.

———— ENGLISH LANGUAGE. By Geo. P. Marsh. Post 8vo. 7s. 6d.

———— ENGLISH LITERATURE. By T. B. Shaw, M.A. Post 8vo. 7s. 6d.

———— SPECIMENS OF ENGLISH LITERATURE. Selected from the Chief Writers. By Thomas B. Shaw, M.A. Post 8vo. 7s. 6d.

———— BLACKSTONE: a Systematic Abridgment of the Entire Commentaries. By R. Malcolm Kerr, LL.D. Post 8vo. 7s. 6d.

ST. JOHN'S (CHARLES) Wild Sports and Natural History of the Highlands. Post 8vo. 3s. 6d.
——— (BAYLE) Adventures in the Libyan Desert and the Oasis of Jupiter Ammon. Woodcuts. Post 8vo. 2s.
STEPHENSON (GEORGE and ROBERT). The Story of their Lives. By Samuel Smiles. With Portraits and 70 Illustrations. Medium 8vo. 21s. Or Popular Edition, Post 8vo. 6s.
STOTHARD'S (THOS.) Life. With Personal Reminiscences. By Mrs. Bray. With Portrait and 60 Woodcuts. 4to. 21s.
STREETS (G. E.) Gothic Architecture in Spain. From Personal Observations during several journeys through that country. Illustrations. Medium 8vo. 30s.
——— Brick and Marble Architecture of Italy in the Middle Ages. Plates. 8vo. 21s.
SULLIVAN'S (SIR EDWARD) Princes, Warriors, and Statesmen of India; an Historical Narrative of the most Important Events, from the Invasion of Mahmoud of Ghizni to that of Nadir Shah. 8vo. 12s.
SWIFT'S (JONATHAN) Life, Letters, Journals, and Works. By John Forster, 8vo. (In Preparation.)
SYBEL'S (VON) History of the French Revolution. 1789—1795. Translated from the German. By Walter C. Perry. Vols. 1 & 2. 8vo. (In the Press.)
SYME'S (PROFESSOR) Principles of Surgery. 5/A Edition. 8vo. 12s.
TAIT'S (BISHOP) Dangers and Safeguards of Modern Theology, containing Suggestions to the Theological Student under Present Difficulties. 8vo. 9s.
TAYLOR'S (HENRY) Notes from Life, in Six Essays on Money, Humility and Independence, Wisdom, Choice in Marriage, Children, and Life Poetic. Fcap. 8vo. 2s.
THOMSON'S (ARCHBISHOP) Sermons, Preached in the Chapel of Lincoln's Inn. 8vo. 10s. 6d.
THREE-LEAVED MANUAL OF FAMILY PRAYER; arranged so as to save the trouble of turning the Pages backwards and forwards. Royal 8vo. 2s.
TREMENHEERE'S (H. S.) The Franchise a Privilege and not a Right, proved by the Political Experience of the Ancients. Fcap. 8vo. 2s. 6d.
TRISTRAM'S (H. B.) Great Sahara. Wanderings South of the Atlas Mountains. Map and Illustrations. Post 8vo. 15s.
TWISS' (HORACE) Public and Private Life of Lord Chancellor Eldon, with Selections from his Correspondence. Portrait. Third Edition. 2 Vols. Post 8vo. 21s.
TYLOR'S (E. B.) Researches into the Early History of Mankind, and the Development of Civilisation. Illustrations. 8vo. 12s.
TYNDALL'S (JOHN) Glaciers of the Alps. With an account of Three Years' Observations and Experiments on their General Phenomena. Woodcuts. Post 8vo. 14s.
TYTLER'S (PATRICK FRASER) Memoirs. By Rev. J. W. Burgon. M.A. 8vo. 9s.

32　LIST OF WORKS PUBLISHED BY MR. MURRAY.

VAUGHAN'S (Rev. Dr.) Sermons preached in Harrow School.
8vo. 10s. 6d.

WAAGEN'S (Dr.) Treasures of Art in Great Britain. Being an
Account of the Chief Collections of Paintings, Sculpture, Manuscripts,
Miniatures, &c. &c., in this Country. Obtained from Personal Inspection during Visits to England. 4 Vols. 8vo.

VAMBERY'S (Arminius) Travels in Central Asia, from Teheran
across the Turkoman Desert on the Eastern Shore of the Caspian to
Khiva, Bokhara, and Samarcand in 1863. Map and Illustrations. 8vo. 21s.

WELLINGTON'S (The Duke of) Despatches during his various
Campaigns. Compiled from Official and other Authentic Documents. By
Col. Gurwood, C.B. 8 Vols. 8vo. 21s. each.

—————— Supplementary Despatches, and other Papers.
Edited by his Son. Vols. I. to XII. 8vo. 20s. each.

—————— Selections from his Despatches and General
Orders. By Colonel Gurwood. 8vo. 18s.

—————— Speeches in Parliament. 2 Vols. 8vo. 42s.

WILKINSON'S (Sir J. G.) Popular Account of the Private Life,
Manners, and Customs of the Ancient Egyptians. New Edition.
Revised and Condensed. With 500 Woodcuts. 2 Vols. Post 8vo. 12s.

—————— Handbook for Egypt.—Thebes, the Nile, Alexandria, Cairo, the Pyramids, Mount Sinai, &c. Map. Post 8vo. 15s.

—————— (G. B.) Working Man's Handbook to South Australia; with Advice to the Farmer, and Detailed Information for the several Classes of Labourers and Artisans. Map. 12mo. 1s. 6d.

WILSON'S (Bishop Daniel) Life, with Extracts from his
Letters and Journals. By Rev. Josiah Bateman. Second Edition.
Illustrations. Post 8vo. 9s.

—————— (Genl. Sir Robert) Secret History of the French
Invasion of Russia, and Retreat of the French Army, 1812. Second
Edition. 8vo. 15s.

—————— Private Diary of Travels, Personal Services, and
Public Events, during Missions and Employments in Spain, Sicily,
Turkey, Russia, Poland, Germany, &c. 1812-14. 2 Vols. 8vo. 26s.

—————— Autobiographical Memoirs. Containing an Account of
his Early Life down to the Peace of Tilsit. Portrait. 2 Vols. 8vo.
26s.

WORDSWORTH'S (Canon) Journal of a Tour in Athens and
Attica. Third Edition. Plates. Post 8vo. 8s. 6d.

—————— Pictorial, Descriptive, and Historical Account
of Greece, with a History of Greek Art, by G. Scharf, F.S.A. New
Edition. With 600 Woodcuts. Royal 8vo. 28s.

BRADBURY, EVANS, AND CO., PRINTERS, WHITEFRIARS.

www.ingramcontent.com/pod-product-compliance
Lightning Source LLC
Chambersburg PA
CBHW031937290426
44108CB00011B/596